Touch the Future . . . Teach!
STUDENT ESSAY CONTEST

PRIZES AWARDED!

FIRST PRIZE: $500 for student + $250 for sponsoring instructor
2nd Prize: $300 for student + $150 for sponsoring instructor
3rd Prize: $200 for student + $100 for sponsoring instructor

As the largest publisher in Teacher Education, Allyn & Bacon recognizes the exceptional role teachers play in our culture and our communities. You shape the future! Allyn and Bacon's new book, Touch the Future . . . Teach!, presents aspiring teachers with important information about the challenges and the satisfactions of a career in education. For these reasons, Allyn & Bacon is honored to sponsor the "Touch the Future . . . Teach!" essay contest—an opportunity for you and your students to celebrate teaching and its role in our society.

Visit

www.ablongman.com/essaycontest
for details

Sponsor a Student: Make it an optional extra credit activity for your students. Make it a required class assignment. Or simply let students in your class know about the contest. You can sponsor your entire class if you like! Prizes will be awarded to both the student and sponsoring professor.

Eligibility: Applicant must be enrolled as an education major at a 2-year or 4-year college or university.

Essay Topic: Why do you want to become a teacher? What persons or what goals have inspired you to pursue a teaching career, and what impact do you hope to make on the future of individual students and/or on our nation?

No purchase necessary. All entries become the property of Allyn & Bacon. Official contest rules and regulations posted at www.ablongman.com/essaycontest.

Touch the Future . . . Teach!

Carlos F. Diaz
Florida Atlantic University

Carol Marra Pelletier
Boston College

Eugene F. Provenzo, Jr.
University of Miami

PEARSON

BOSTON   NEW YORK   SAN FRANCISCO

MEXICO CITY   MONTREAL   TORONTO   LONDON   MADRID   MUNICH   PARIS

HONG KONG   SINGAPORE   TOKYO   CAPE TOWN   SYDNEY

Executive Editor and Publisher: Stephen D. Dragin
Senior Development Editor: Mary Kriener
Editorial Assistant: Meaghan Minnick
Marketing Manager: Tara Kelly
Production Editor: Annette Joseph
Editorial Production Service: WordCraft, LLC
Composition Buyer: Linda Cox
Manufacturing Buyer: Andrew Turso
Electronic Composition: Omegatype Typography, Inc.
Interior Design / Electronic Illustration: Debbie Schneck
Photo Researcher: Po Yee Oster
Cover Administrator: Linda Knowles

For related titles and support materials, visit our online catalog at www.ablongman.com.

Between the time website information is gathered and then published, it is not unusual for some sites to have closed. Also, the transcription of URLs can result in typographic errors. The publisher would appreciate notification of where these errors occur so they can be corrected in subsequent editions.

Library of Congress Cataloging-in-Publication Data

Diaz, Carlos F. (Carlos Francisco).
  Touch the Future . . . Teach! / Carlos F. Diaz, Carol Marra Pelletier, Eugene F. Provenzo, Jr.
    p.   cm.
  Includes bibliographical references and index.
  ISBN 0-205-37566-9 (alk. paper)
    1. Teaching—United States. 2. Teaching—Vocational guidance—United States. 3.
Teachers—Professional relationships—United States. I. Pelletier, Carol Marra. II.
Provenzo, Eugene F. III. Title.

  LB1775.2.D536 2006
  371.102—dc22

                                                                                    2005050806

Printed in the United States of America

10 9 8 7 6 5 4 3   WEB 10 09 08

BRIEF CONTENTS

CONTENTS

SECTION I   WHO IS INCLUDED IN THE COMMUNITY OF LEARNERS?

Touch the Future . . . Teach!   3

Becoming a Teacher   29

3

Students in Today's Classrooms   71

4

Parents, Families, and the Community: Partners in Education   105

Teaching and the Foundations of Education   135

The Social Context of Schools   167

The Professional and Ethical Context of Teaching   199

Diversity and the Cultural Context of Teaching   227

SECTION III   WHAT ARE THE KEY ELEMENTS OF PROFESSIONAL PRACTICE?

Curriculum: What to Expect in American Schools   263

Planning, Delivering, and Assessing Instruction   291

11

Classroom and Behavior Management: Creating a Positive Learning Environment   329

12

Technology and Teaching   367

SECTION IV   HOW WILL I EVOLVE AS A TEACHER?

13

Becoming a Teacher: Next Steps   397

14

How Will the Teaching Profession Change?   433

What Is Teaching Likely to Look Like in the Future?   434

Evolving Goals of Education   434

SPECIAL FEATURES

Through the Eyes of
Culturally Sensitive Teachers

Problems to Possibilities

BUILDING ON EDUCATIONAL FOUNDATIONS

EDUCATION MATTERS

PREFACE

Touch the Future . . . Teach! is designed to engage teacher candidates in the exploration of essential questions related to decisions about becoming teachers. It encourages reflective thought about the course, past experiences in schools, career decisions, and the passion needed to be an effective teacher. The book is a personal journey about understanding the learning community and the future of teaching and what we, as authors and experienced educators, can share to facilitate that inquiry. The interactive approach of this text will allow you to review your own ideas and to explore the ideas of others—instructors, classmates, and practicing teachers.

The approach to teaching promoted in *Touch the Future . . . Teach!* does not offer one right answer. Rather, it offers a reflective practitioner approach that recognizes the teacher as the critical person to make good choices for diverse students. To do this well, an effective teacher must know his or her students and the needs of the community. The effective teacher needs to know how to gather information, assess his or her own practices, and use this information to modify instruction to meet the needs of *all* students and promote student learning. The changing demographic of communities and students today and in years to come will impact the instructional approaches taken to teaching and learning. This text recognizes the importance of culture and diversity in America's schools and shares important perspectives that will be useful for beginning teachers.

Our goal in this text is to capture your personal vision, to create opportunities for personal and collective reflection, as well as to facilitate guided observation and data collection from teachers in schools. We encourage you to use the data and your own perspectives to respond to the question, "Am I a teacher?" We applaud your choice of teaching as a professional career because the diverse students in America's schools today need passionate, committed, knowledgeable teachers whose goal is teaching for life. As a teacher, you do so much more than pass along information. You *Touch the Future!*

ORGANIZATION

Touch the Future . . . Teach! is organized around four essential questions that explore the *who, what, where, why,* and *how* of teaching in America's schools today and in the future.

- **Section I: Who Is Included in the Community of Learners?** introduces readers to "who's who" in the community of learners. Chapter 2, Becoming a Teacher, highlights motivations and work of teachers and other adults in a school that supports student learning. Chapter 3, Students in Today's Classrooms, takes a careful look at the changing demographic of America's students and what these changes mean for educators. Chapter 4, Parents, Families, and the Community: Partners in Education, provides the reader with a more complete picture of the role of the family in the community of learners, as well as the neighborhoods where students live, work, and play.

- **Section II: How Are Schools and Teachers Shaped by Society, Culture, and Ethics?** provides a context for understanding how the American education system got to where it is today and why our schools are organized and function as they do. These foundations of education chapters provide an important backdrop for educational discussions, as well as the knowledge base for understanding where teachers have been and the trends that lead the profession to new challenges. Chapter 5, Teaching and the Foundations of Education, offers the historical, legal, and philosophical basis for our schools and the larger educational system. Chapter 6, The Social Context of Schools, explores school governance. Chapter 7, The Professional and Ethical Context of Teaching, explains the ethical perspectives of teaching. Finally, Chapter 8, Diversity and the Cultural Context of Teaching, explores the politics of diversity and their effect on schools.

- **Section III: What Are the Key Elements of Professional Practice?** breaks down the practices of teachers. Chapter 9, Curriculum: What to Expect in American Schools, highlights general and specific questions about *what* curriculum is being taught in schools and *how* it functions. Chapter 10, Planning, Delivering, and Assessing Instruction, explores effective classroom instruction with an overview of assessment issues as they relate to student progress in the classroom. Chapter 11, Classroom and Behavior Management, discusses the importance and challenges of creating a positive learning environment. Chapter 12, Technology and Teaching, closes the section with an overview of the use of technology in schools.

- **Section IV: How Will I Evolve as a Teacher?** focuses us on the future, posing the question "Where do I go from here?" Chapter 13, Becoming a Teacher: Next Steps, helps the reader develop a plan for taking the next steps toward becoming a teacher. Chapter 14, How Will the Teaching Profession Change?, provides a framework for class discussions about the future of American education.

SPECIAL FEATURES

Throughout the book, special features have been provided to focus on issues of recurring importance, as well as to aid with review and understanding of key concepts.

- **Six themes** weave their way throughout the book within the narratives, special features, and in the books recommended at the end of each chapter for further reading.

  Professionalism: The recognition of teachers as critical and effective leaders of not only instruction, but of the social settings in which they work.

  Values and Assumptions: The beliefs beginning teachers bring to their work in the profession: attitudes concerning race, gender, and what makes a good teacher.

  Multiculturalism and Diversity: The diverse populations of learners found in our schools, including students from a vast array of cultures, traditions, and sexual orientations and students with special needs and physical challenges.

  Standards: The professional and ethical standards teachers must demonstrate, as well as the academic standards that schools and students are expected to meet.

  Linking Theory and Practice: Listening to the voices of students and teachers, as well as observing practice in the schools in order to identify the key elements of professional practice.

  Ethics and Social Justice: The ethical and moral decisions teachers must make as part of their work, as well as the obligation and duty they have as members of a democratic culture to promote the creation of a more just and equitable society.

- **Who Am I and What Do I Believe?** This three-part pedagogical element is central to this text. It encourages reflective thought about the needs and conceptions of young learners and the role of teachers in meeting those needs. The feature first appears in the chapter opener, where readers respond to prompts that encourage thinking about the big-picture message of the chapter. Within the chapter, readers continue to link the theme of the chapter with their personal background and assumptions and experiences and then to brainstorm and share ideas with classmates and others. The third piece of this feature answers the question, "Where do I go from here?" Readers are prompted to complete Professional Plans that will help them lay out a plan for their teaching future.

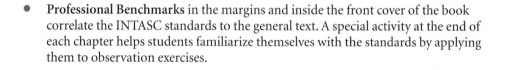

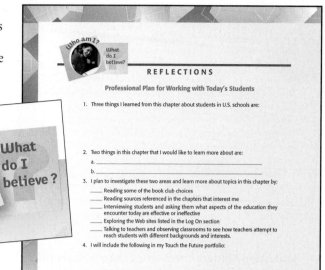

- **Professional Benchmarks** in the margins and inside the front cover of the book correlate the INTASC standards to the general text. A special activity at the end of each chapter helps students familiarize themselves with the standards by applying them to observation exercises.

INTASC

Principle # 1

Instructional Planning Skills: The teacher plans instruction based upon knowledge of subject matter, students, the community, and curriculum goals.

- **Through the Eyes of Culturally Sensitive Teachers** boxes share practicing teachers' perspectives on how culture and student diversity impact instructional professional decisions that teachers must make in all aspects of their careers.

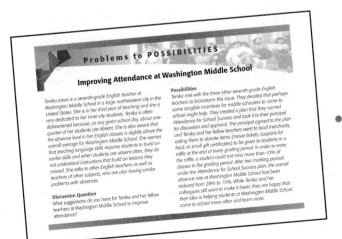

- **Problems to Possibilities** features in every chapter present case studies of common, realistic problems or dilemmas that teachers face in the classroom and help readers explore the ethical considerations as well as possible solutions, including providing a list of helpful resources for finding solutions—or *possibilities*—to the problem.

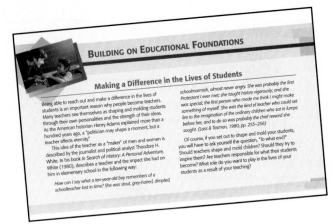

- **Building on Educational Foundations** features explore the legal, historical, and procedural issues in education and identify benchmarks in educational foundations.

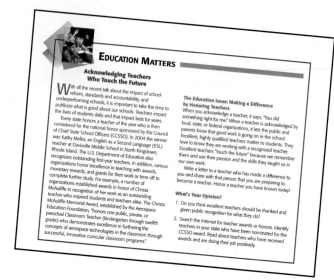

- **Education Matters** boxes take a close look at critical issues in education that affect students, teachers, and communities.

- **Professional Development** pieces at the end of each chapter help prospective teachers link theory to practice. In addition to the *Professional Plans*, special *Linking Theory to Practice* observation and interview exercises will enhance school visits and provide systematic data to review at a later time. Each observation form includes a special *Connecting with INTASC* exercise that helps students begin to understand the standards as they relate to classroom behavior and planning.

- The *Touch the Future Reflective Journal and Portfolio* appendix at the back of the book offers a format for responding to prompts throughout the book and for documenting progress and work. Appendix A, **Conducting Classroom Observations and Interviews,** provides guidelines for school visitations.

Themes of the Times

Expand your knowledge of the concepts discussed in this chapter by reading current and historical articles from the *New York Times* by visiting the "Themes of the Times" section of the Companion Website.

- *Touch the Future . . . Teach!* also includes a special Internet connection that encourages you to go beyond the text to learn all that you can about becoming a teacher. Appearing at the start of each chapter, a **Themes of the Times** icon directs you to the **Companion Website** (www.ablongman.com/diaz) and a direct link to specially selected *New York Times* articles that present differing perspectives on contemporary topics in education.

SUPPLEMENTS AND LEARNING AIDS

FOR STUDENTS

- Prepared by Joseph Fisher from the College of Southern Maryland, this dynamic, interactive **Companion Website** includes an online study guide for students that provides, on a chapter-by-chapter basis, learning objectives, study questions with text page references, "live" links to relevant websites, and additional enrichment material. Other features of the website include an Interactive Timeline that highlights the people and events that have shaped education through history.

- **VideoWorkshop for Foundations of Education** allows you to include video in your course for maximized learning! This total teaching and learning system includes real classroom video footage on an easy-to-use CD-ROM plus a Student Learning Guide and an Instructor's Teaching Guide—both with textbook-specific Correlation Grids. The result? A program that brings textbook concepts to life with ease and helps your students understand, analyze, and apply the objectives of the course. VideoWorkshop is available for your students as a FREE value-pack option with this textbook.

- **Research Navigator™ (with ContentSelect Research Database) (Access Code Required)** (www.researchnavigator.com) is the easiest way for students to start a research assignment or research paper. Complete with extensive help on the research process and three exclusive online databases of credible and reliable source material, including EBSCO's ContentSelect™ Academic Journal Database, New York Times Search by Subject Archive, and "Best of the Web" Link Library, Research Navigator™ helps students quickly and efficiently make the most of their research time. Research Navigator™ is free when packaged with the textbook and requires an Access Code.

- **Research Navigator™ Guide for Education** This free reference guide includes tips, resources, activities, and URLs to help students use the Internet for their research projects. The first part introduces students to the basics of the Internet and the World Wide Web. Part two includes many Net activities that tie into the content of the text. Part three lists hundreds of Internet education resources. Part four outlines how to use the Research Navigator™ resources. The guide also includes information on how to correctly cite research and a guide to building an online glossary. Includes Access Code for Research Navigator™.

- **(mylabschool** *Where the classroom comes to life!* MyLabSchool is a suite of online tools designed to help your students make the transition from student to teacher. Our new **Lesson Builder** makes it easy to create standards-based lesson plans and our videos are organized by both subject and topic, putting the right information at your fingertips. With easily assigned material for class preparation, you save time out of your busy schedule, and our **new Instructor's Manual** makes it easy to integrate MyLabSchool into your course.

  MyLabSchool is perfect for use in any course where video footage of classroom situations, standards integration, portfolio development and PRAXIS preparation are covered. MyLabSchool meets the individual teaching and learning needs of every instructor and every student. It saves you and your students time, and it helps increase success in your course. What's more, it's EASY!

  MyLabSchool is also available in WebCT, Blackboard, and in CourseCompass, Allyn & Bacon's private label course management system.

- The **"What Every Teacher Should Know About" Series** of brief booklets is designed to provide your students with the practical information and essential strategies they need to begin their careers. This series contains a wide variety of innovative teaching ideas, best practices, and teacher-tested tools. Booklet topics include Action Research, Assistive Technology, Classroom Management, Digital Portfolios, Assessment, ELL, IDEA, NCLB, and Multicultural Education. Contact your local rep for packaging details.

FOR THE INSTRUCTOR

- The **Instructor's Resource Manual,** prepared by Janet McNellis of Troy University, includes a wealth of interesting ideas and activities designed to help instructors teach the course. Each chapter includes a Chapter Summary, Chapter Objectives, and a Summary of Key Points and Terms. Also included is an array of classroom activities, from Discussion Starters and Collaborative Exercises to independent Reflective Writing and Presentation topics. The IRM also keys each chapter to appropriate websites with accompanying web-based activities.

- A **Test Bank** of more than 700 questions, including multiple choice items, true/false, short answer, and essay questions. Written by Emilie Johnson of Lindenwood University and Nancy Meryl Cohen of Long Island University, each chapter also includes a case study that presents case descriptions or scenarios involving individuals with special needs, followed by questions that require students to apply, analyze, evaluate, or synthesize concepts from the text.

- **Computerized Test Bank** The printed Test Bank is also available electronically through our computerized testing system: TestGen. Instructors can use TestGen EQ to create exams in only minutes by selecting from the existing database of questions, editing questions, or writing original questions.

- The **Allyn & Bacon Interactive Video: Issues in Education** features news reports from around the country on topics covered in the text. The VHS video contains ten modules of up-to-date news clips exploring current issues and debates in education. Some of the topics include teacher shortages, alternative schools, community-school partnerships, standardized testing, and bilingual classrooms. An accompanying instructor's guide outlines teaching strategies and provides discussion questions to use with the clips.

- **(mylabschool** Where the classroom comes to life! MyLabSchool is a suite of online tools designed to help your students make the transition from student to teacher. Our new **Lesson Builder** makes it easy to create standards-based lesson plans and our videos are organized by both subject and topic, putting the right information at your fingertips. With easily assigned material for class preparation, you save time out of your busy schedule, and our **new Instructor's Manual** makes it easy to integrate MyLabSchool into your course.

  MyLabSchool is perfect for use in any course where video footage of classroom situations, standards integration, portfolio development and PRAXIS preparation are covered. MyLabSchool meets the individual teaching and learning needs of every instructor and every student. It saves you and your students time, and it helps increase success in your course. What's more, it's EASY!

  MyLabSchool is also available in WebCT, Blackboard, and in CourseCompass, Allyn & Bacon's private label course management system.

- **Lecture Questions for Clickers** Assess your students' progress with the Personal Response System (PRS)—a PowerPoint-based classroom response system—prepared by Raymond S. Pastore of Bloomsburg University. PRS enables you to pose questions, record results, and display those results instantly in your classroom, giving you immediate feedback that offers valuable insight into student learning.

- **Allyn & Bacon Transparencies for Foundations of Education/Introduction to Teaching,** a set of one hundred acetate transparencies related to topics in the text.

- **Online Course Management Systems** Powered by Blackboard and hosted nationally, Allyn and Bacon's own course management system, **CourseCompass,** helps you manage all aspects of teaching your course. It features pre-loaded content to support Foundations of Education and Introduction to Teaching courses. For colleges and universities with **Blackboard**™ licenses, special course management packages are available in this format as well. For additional information, please contact your local sales rep.

ACKNOWLEDGMENTS

The authors would like to thank everyone at Allyn & Bacon, in particular Executive Editor and Publisher Steve Dragin, who saw the need for this book and brought the author team together; and Editor-in-Chief Paul Smith, for the many ideas he contributed and for his patience. Also, Mary Kriener, Senior Development Editor, provided patience and valuable insights and organization for this book as it went through each painstaking stage of the development process. Marketing Manager Tara Kelly has been critical in advancing the word about *Touch the Future . . . Teach!* This project is clearly theirs as much as it is ours. We would also like to recognize the work of our production team: Senior Editorial Production Administrator Annette Joseph; Managing Editor for Production Joe Sweeney; and packager Linda Zuk.

The research behind this book was supported by the invaluable assistance of various friends and colleagues at our respective universities and from around the country: Dr. Evelyn Torrey, Mary Davis, and Allison Dobrick at Florida Atlantic University; Arlene Brett, Cory Buxton, Josh Diem, and Jeanne Schumm at the University of Miami; and Alison Garvey, Melita Malley, and Emily Kearns for their assistance in organizing the sources, reading chapters, editing, and suggesting topics to be included. Also, the suggestions of Professor Penny Luken of Broward Community College and Dr. Tunjarnika Coleman-Farrell of Palm Beach Community College were extremely helpful in determining the features of the book. The ongoing feedback and reality checks from each of our students were of incredible assistance.

Finally, we would each like to thank our families:

- My wife, Diane, and my triplet daughters, Elena, Patricia, and Cristina, for their patience and understanding throughout the writing of this book.—Carlos F. Diaz

- Very special thanks go to my wife, Asterie—my best friend and best critic.—Gene F. Provenzo, Jr.

- My husband, David, for his undying patience.—Carol M. Pelletier

The authors would also like to extend special thanks to the many reviewers who provided feedback at various stages of this project. Their insightful comments prompted valuable revisions that strengthened the text. From reviews of the original proposal, to ongoing reviews of various drafts of chapters, to an intense focus group at AERA, the discussions in this book reflect your valuable input and guidance.

Dawn Leigh Anderson
California State University, Fullerton

Ramona M. Bartee
Creighton University

Felicia Blacher-Wilson
ITT Technical Institute

Jackie M. Blount
Iowa State University

Jody S. Britten
Ball State University

David S. Brown
University of Tulsa

Jung-ah (Christine) Choi
Grand Valley State University

Susan H. Christian
Patrick Henry Community College

Marta Y. Cronin
Indian River Community College

Ana Cruz
St. Louis Community College

Omobolade Delano-Oriaran
St. Norbert College

Sally H. Digman
Alderson-Broaddus College

A. Keith Dils
King's College

Ellen Eckman
Marquette University

Robert Farrell
Florida International University

Susan M. Ferguson
University of Dayton

Stephen J. Garger
Marist College

Vickie D. Harry
Clarion University of Pennsylvania

Deborah M. Hill
Southern Utah University

Mary F. Leslie
Louisiana State University at Eunice

Jeffrey L. Lofthus
University of Alaska Southeast

Janet R. McNellis
Troy University

Courtney W. Moffatt
Edgewood College

Jeanne O'Kon
Tallahassee Community College

Yasmeen Qadri
Valencia Community College

Raymond S. Pastore
Bloomsburg University

Iran Pelcyger
Bronx Community College of the City
    University of New York

Mary Louise Poling
The Ohio State University

Sue A. Rieg
Indiana University of Pennsylvania

Anthony M. Roselli
Merrimack College

Gwen Rudney
University of Minnesota, Morris

Barbara Slater Stern
James Madison University

Susan Talburt
Georgia State University

Sharon C. Thomas
Miami-Dade Community College,
    Kendall Campus

Christopher T. Vang
California State University, Stanislaus

Alexander W. Wiseman
University of Tulsa

LaDonna R. Young
Southwest Tennessee Community
    College

The authors wish to extend special dedications to:

- Maria Diaz and Diane Diaz, who personify the competent, caring, and compassionate teacher.

- Gwen Walsh, lover of cats and flowers, dancer, fencer, puppeteer and mime, professor, neighbor, and friend.

- My mother, Marian Mondeau Marra, who always wanted to become a teacher.

Carlos Diaz

Carlos F. Diaz is currently a professor of multicultural education at Florida Atlantic University. Formerly he taught at the secondary and community college levels. He has received five awards in his career for excellence in teaching. Dr. Diaz has been a member of the NCATE board of examiners since 1997. He is coauthor of *Global Perspectives for Educators* and editor and contributing author of *Multicultural Education for the 21st Century,* as well as various articles and chapters in other books. Over the past decade, he has procured grants that have enabled approximately 300 South Florida educators to earn master's degrees with concentrations in multicultural education and ESOL on full scholarships. He and his wife Diane are the proud—but busy—parents of triplet daughters.

Carol Pelletier

Carol Pelletier is currently the Director of Practicum Experiences and Teacher Induction in the Lynch School of Education at Boston College. In that role, she oversees the placement, supervision, and licensing of preservice student teachers for both undergraduate and graduate education. Her new responsibilities, funded by the Carnegie Foundation as part of the Teachers for a New Era project, include supporting teacher education graduates as they enter their first years of teaching. Dr. Pelletier received her Ed.D. from Harvard University in 1996, where she focused her studies on the role of the cooperating teacher with student teachers. She is the author of *Strategies for Successful Student Teaching, Techniques and Strategies for Coaching Student Teachers,* and *Mentoring in Action: A Month-by-Month Curriculum for Mentors and Their New Teachers.* In more than 20 years as a public school teacher, she has received numerous teacher leadership awards, among them the prestigious Christa McAuliffe Fellowship sponsored by the U.S. Department of Education. Dr. Pelletier is actively engaged in preparing prospective teachers through quality field experiences, supporting new teachers though transitional mentoring programs, and creating teacher leadership opportunities for experienced teachers.

Eugene F. Provenzo, Jr.

Eugene F. Provenzo, Jr. is a professor at the University of Miami, where he has worked with prospective teachers since 1976. He completed his bachelor's degree at the University of Rochester in 1972, completed a master's degree in History at Washington University in 1974, and his Ph.D. from the Graduate Institute of Education in the Philosophy and History of Education in 1976. Over his career, he has also taught social studies at the secondary level and has NCATE lifetime certification. Throughout his work, his primary focus has been on education as a social and cultural phenomenon. A particularly important concern of his has been the role of the teacher in American society. Dr. Provenzo has also pursued interests related to the impact of computers on contemporary children, education, and culture. His research on computers and video games has been reviewed in the *New York Times, The Guardian, Mother Jones,* and *The London Economist.* He is married to Asterie B. Provenzo, a professional writer and editor, with whom he collaborates on many projects.

Touch the Future . . . Teach!

1

Touch the Future . . . Teach!

Who am I?

What do I believe?

THINK ABOUT THIS:

Twenty years ago Christa McAuliffe, a teacher from New Hampshire, captured the hearts of all teachers as she prepared for the ultimate field trip—to be the first teacher in space, from where she would teach a science class to students throughout the United States. Although her exploration came to a tragic end on January 28, 1986, when the space shuttle in which she was traveling exploded soon after takeoff, Christa's legacy lives in her inspiring words, "I touch the future, I teach." In taking this course you will be exploring the realities of teaching and your decision to become a teacher. How do you see yourself "touching the future" as a teacher? What do you need to explore and learn more about in order to become an effective teacher?

> I touch the future, I teach.
>
> Christa McAuliffe

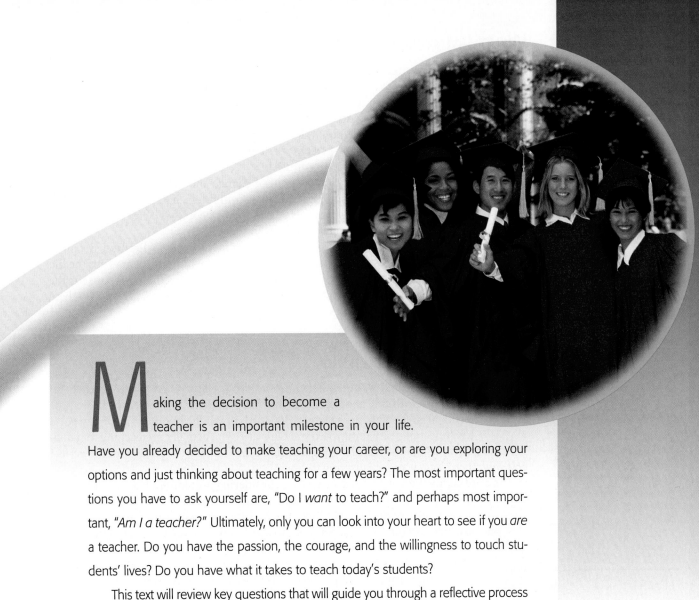

M aking the decision to become a teacher is an important milestone in your life. Have you already decided to make teaching your career, or are you exploring your options and just thinking about teaching for a few years? The most important questions you have to ask yourself are, "Do I *want* to teach?" and perhaps most important, "*Am I a teacher?*" Ultimately, only you can look into your heart to see if you *are* a teacher. Do you have the passion, the courage, and the willingness to touch students' lives? Do you have what it takes to teach today's students?

This text will review key questions that will guide you through a reflective process about becoming a teacher. The honest portrayal of teachers' work as well as a reflective approach to your learning will either validate your decision to teach or at least help you make that decision. This chapter explores the following key questions, which will begin your inquiry into the possibility of teaching:

Key Questions

1. What is involved in the journey into teaching?
2. What does it mean to be a reflective practitioner?
3. What does it mean to teach in today's diverse society?
4. What are factors to consider when preparing for a teaching career?

WHAT IS INVOLVED IN THE JOURNEY INTO TEACHING?

Teaching is more than a job. For many who choose it as a career, it is a way of life—a vocation rather than an occupation. It is service to children, families, and the community. Some say it is a calling for people who are committed to making a difference. The potential of teachers to positively affect the lives of others is almost limitless. Throughout the world, teachers are among the most influential and trusted people in any society. (See Table 1.1.) They shape the future and both help determine and maintain culture.

Schools often are at the forefront of change and innovation. Consider the extent to which new technologies, such as computers, have been introduced to American culture through schools. A great many people who are computer literate first learned about them as students in schools.

Yet even as schools serve as vehicles for the future, the education system in general also serves to maintain the status quo. Providing students with the life skills necessary to function successfully in society helps them prepare for the now while also looking to the future. Along with children's parents, teachers stand at the point of these efforts.

CHOOSING TEACHING

Much is expected from teachers in American society. When master teachers do their work with skill and humanity, they can make teaching look easy. Like a professional golfer who hits a tee shot 300 yards down the middle of a fairway, good teaching looks easy until you try it. Only after you actually try teaching for yourself does it become clear how challenging teaching can be to do well. But as with the perfect golf shot, there are few more satisfying feelings.

You are taking this course because you are considering becoming a teacher. Either you have definitely made up your mind or you have begun the process of checking out the profession. People decide to become teachers for various reasons. What made you consider becoming a teacher? Perhaps you grew up with a teacher in the family. Did you use to play school in your basement or garage? Or maybe you had a favorite teacher in school who inspired you. Perhaps you have just always gotten satisfaction from helping others. Maybe you just always wanted to teach and don't even remember why.

Choosing to teach means making a choice to become part of a profession that contributes to society by serving young people and families. Every teacher who made this choice 30–35 years ago has helped shape the educational and life paths of thousands of students. Your decision to teach is an important one because, like your predecessors, you will shape the profession and impact the lives of thousands of students. You will become part of the next generation of teachers. This is the beginning of your exploration about the teaching profession.

When a teacher candidate decides to become a teacher, the choice is often tied to a content area or grade level. You may find yourself making your career decision based on the fact that you had a good experience with middle school students at a camp; perhaps you have no idea at this point which level or content area you would like to teach but just know that you want to teach. Even if you think you already know you want to teach primary grades, stay open to all your observations in schools. Many teachers change grades during their professional career.

Teacher grade levels for licenses may vary from state to state but basically the broad categories for teachers are as follows:

- Early childhood education, which includes preschool to Grade 2

- Elementary education, which includes Grades 1–6

- Middle school, which could include Grades 5–9, 6–8, or even 7–8 in some states
- High school, which includes Grades 9–12 or 8–12 in some states

If you are not sure what you want to do, you may want to consider teaching in areas where there are teacher shortages across the country, such as special education, sciences, foreign languages, and math. This will guarantee you a teaching position in most states and perhaps offer you some choices between districts.

At this stage of your preparation you should explore the field a bit and interview teachers to find out *what* you would like to teach. Observe them in the classroom and ask them what they like best about their grade level or subject. Ask them to describe a typical day (Perrone, 1991). Develop some questions of your own to find out what teachers do at different grade levels. Understanding a teacher's daily work will inform you in your decision. Don't make this important decision lightly; you may be teaching for many years.

The authors each entered the profession for different reasons; now they work in higher education and in teacher education because they believe in teachers and the value they bring to the future of young people and of the world in general. Next they share with you their reasons for teaching. As you read their thoughts, notice how they have grown and evolved as lifelong learners. How are they similar, and what makes them different? When they entered the profession they didn't know where they would end up. Think about the possibilities for you.

"Your heart is slightly bigger than the average human heart, but that's because you're a teacher."

Courtesy of Aaron Bacall, *The Lighter Side of Teaching*, p. 1. Copyright 2003 by Aaron Bacall. Reprinted by permission of Corwin Press Inc.

Dr. Carol Pelletier

I can't remember when I didn't want to be a teacher. When I think back to my childhood, I can see myself playing school with neighborhood children using discarded papers from school. I loved being the "boss" in the fantasy classroom I had created on my front steps. I am sure my "students" really appreciated being in school all day and then having to "play school" after school and on weekends to be part of my game. I loved mimicking my favorite teachers. It made me feel helpful and important. I loved fantasy teaching!

In high school my guidance counselor discouraged me from teaching and suggested I be a nurse or secretary—two of the few options typically available to women in the 1960s. But teaching was my dream, and I wasn't going to let it go. After attending college in Massachusetts, where I majored in elementary education, I had my very own classroom—fifth grade.

I taught in the Massachusetts public school system for 21 years and got very involved in all aspects of professional development from the very beginning, taking on various leadership roles in my district and at the state level with the state teachers' association. During that time, I also worked with one of the state teacher prep colleges to bring student teachers to our district and received a state teacher fellowship as well as a federal Christa McAuliffe fellowship. Encouraged by these awards and a strong interest to get even more involved in teacher training

Carol Pelletier

and professional development, I decided to leave the classroom to pursue a Ph.D. in education.

My work at Boston College has allowed me to bridge the gap between theory and practice as I promote interaction between higher-education professors and classroom teachers. I love teachers, teaching, and inspiring potential teachers. My next challenge will be to support graduates of our teacher education program who are currently teaching through a program called Project SUCCESS, whose goal is to keep effective beginning teachers in the classroom.

I have never regretted my decision to become part of the teaching profession. I didn't leave the classroom because I was tired of working with students; I chose to work in higher education because my desire to work with student teachers, like you, was the next step for me professionally.

Teaching, talking about teaching with my university colleagues, talking with teachers, listening to teachers, talking with students, and anything to do with student teachers excites me and gives me energy. I feel that I am making a difference.

Eugene F. Provenzo, Jr., Ph.D.

I guess you could say I've always been around education. I was raised in a family of teachers. My father taught social studies and eventually became an administrator in suburban Buffalo, New York, while my mother taught in a private school in Buffalo. After working in the classroom as a second-grade teacher for many years, my mother eventually became headmistress of the school. So it was natural that I would follow my parents' lead and go into education.

I always loved to read when I was younger but didn't really care much for school until the sixth grade, when I transferred to my mother's school. The school and its teachers had a profound effect on me. They encouraged and embraced individual differences and ideas, and that approach really resonated with me. The school helped me develop a strong sense of sharing and to understand the importance of community. At that point I decided that I wanted to teach—but I wanted to be a professor. I don't think I fully understood what that meant, except that you got to spend a lot of time studying things and working with interesting people. Teaching, though, was key to me. I had had several great teachers in high school. I knew they did something special and I wanted to be special in the same way—to make a difference in the lives of students, as my best teachers had made a difference in my life.

In college I majored in history with minors in literature and education. While in school, I spent time tutoring students and found it very satisfying to help people get excited about learning. I loved student teaching and working in classrooms. Upon graduation, I was offered a job teaching high school American history for the following fall. But my goal still was to be a college history teacher, so I turned down the offer and went off to graduate school to study European history. Soon, however, I found that I was not very happy with the direction I'd chosen. While I wanted to be a researcher, I wanted also to work with students and schools. I wanted to create interesting curricula; I wanted to see the excitement of people learning new ideas and to feel that I had somehow helped them learn. So I changed fields and went on to complete a doctorate in the philosophy and history of education, working with beginning teachers during that time.

In my position here at the University of Miami, I help prepare prospective teachers for the world of teaching and help them with their professional development. I love spending time in the schools, whether conducting research or working with practicing and future teachers. I have touched the future by working with thousands of future teachers in my career, as well as influencing the profession through my writing. I believe that what I do makes a difference in people's lives. There is no other job that I would rather have.

Eugene Provenzo

Carlos Diaz, Ed.D.

Unlike my coauthors, I didn't consider teaching as a career until I was in college. I began my studies at a community college in Florida majoring in political science and intent on becoming a lawyer. Toward the end of my sophomore year, my mother—a practicing teacher at the time—suggested that I might want to become certified as a social studies teacher as well, in the event that I did not go to law school immediately after graduation. This seemed a practical suggestion and I took her advice. I spent the last semester of my undergraduate degree student teaching in middle school. My cooperating teacher gave me full control of the classes the second day of my internship! I was a little anxious at first, but forged ahead with the support of this wonderful veteran teacher. The experience was both challenging and wonderful, and I was hooked!

Carlos Diaz

The summer after graduation I decided to take some graduate courses in education. I applied for a master's degree fellowship that focused on preparing faculty to teach low-income and minority community college students. During this time, I also taught Spanish part-time for one year at a local parochial school. After graduation, I taught three years of middle school where I began a bilingual program, working with both native English- and native Spanish speakers. I was amazed by the creativity and insight of my students and my years teaching middle school were very rewarding.

The decision to return to school for my doctorate was a difficult one, as I really loved the honesty and candor of my middle school students, but I also wanted to begin a new challenge of working with older low-income and minority students. I taught at Broward Community College for 12 years, primarily in history and political science as well as an occasional introduction to education course like the one you may be taking now. I also received my doctorate during this time and eventually joined the faculty at Florida Atlantic University.

The single constant throughout my teaching career, whether working with middle school students, freshmen, or graduate students in college, has been my desire to be a catalyst for new ideas. It is immensely rewarding to see that "eureka moment" when students, no matter what age, "get it." Their expressions change visibly, even if they are not aware of it. At that moment, I realize that something I did caused the light to come on and I have, in some way, helped them understand! What a thrill!

My career track has not been typical for an educator, as I am the only person I know who has been tenured as a public schoolteacher, a community college professor, and a university professor. At all three levels, the common element throughout was the opportunity to help students reach their full potential. In looking back on my career, I have chosen the most rewarding profession possible. After all, the teaching profession is the one charged with passing on the collective wisdom to future generations! What greater trust can be placed on any profession?

ROUTES TO TEACHING

As you can see from their stories, each of the authors chose teaching at different points in their lives and for different reasons, and they followed different paths in their careers as professional educators. Today, as a result of a growing need for teachers across the country, we continue to see the pathways into education changing. The National Education Association (NEA) reports that more than 2 million new teachers will be needed in the next 10 to 15 years. Why this growing demand? As student enrollment increases, more than a million

Problems to POSSIBILITIES

Choosing to Be a Teacher

Maria Lopez was always a good student in high school, but like many high school students, she wasn't sure which career path to follow when she went to college. After taking a number of courses in different areas to get a taste of various fields, she took an introduction to education course to learn more about teaching as a career. She had a dynamic professor in Dr. Brady and one of her assignments required her to spend some time observing a classroom at a lab school affiliated with the university and working with a teacher and a small group of students. The experience was wonderful and Maria felt challenged in her class and comfortable working with the teacher and students. At the end of the year, Maria had decided she wanted to become a teacher; when she went home at the end of the year, she went to see her former high school English teacher, Mrs. McGreevey.

"I have decided to become a teacher!" Maria announced with great enthusiasm. "I wanted you to be the first person to know because you were such a great teacher for me!" She told Mrs. McGreevey about her search that year and about her field experience and work with the children. Mrs. McGreevey

responded by saying, "Congratulations! I think you will be a tremendous teacher. You will be a credit to the profession!"

When Maria shared her decision with her family and friends, their reactions were a little more subdued. "Are you really sure that is what you want to do?" asked her father. Her mother remarked, "Maria, have you thought carefully about all other options and majors? You have so much potential. You can do almost anything you set your mind to."

Some of Maria's friends were supportive, but others commented, "Why would you want to go into teaching? You're smart! You could go into a career that will make you a lot more money than teaching!" Another friend made a hurtful remark when she said she was surprised Maria was going to be "just a teacher." After hearing some of these reactions, Maria began to wonder whether she was making the right choice.

Maria went back to speak with Mrs. McGreevey and share some of the positive and negative comments she had received about teaching as her career choice. Mrs. McGreevey advised her that, while money was certainly important, she herself had decided that the ability to control most of her

teachers are nearing retirement. Although teachers have consistently been entering the workforce as these career teachers have aged, the NEA reports that on average 20% of new teachers leave teaching within their first 3 years. The attrition rate is even higher among teachers in urban school districts, where 50% of teachers leave the field within their first 5 years (National Education Association, 2004). In order to meet this new demand, teacher preparation programs constantly explore ways to ease new teachers into the field and provide ongoing support, and states have explored new pathways into teaching that open up opportunities for midcareer professionals who are changing careers, as well as for college students selecting teaching as their first career. Teacher candidates enter the profession by following one of two types of paths: traditional routes and alternative routes.

● **Traditional Routes** The majority of teachers in our schools received their training and education in a traditional program at a 4-year university or college. Some may have started by attending a community college, but eventually they would have transferred to a 4-year school to complete their teacher education program. Although every teacher education program differs to some degree, all require teacher candidates to learn *content knowledge,* which may be evidenced in an arts and sciences degree (history, English, sciences, math, psychology, and so on) or its equivalent; and **pedagogy,** which explores strategies for teaching, often covered in methods courses. They also require participation in prepracticum and full practicum (student teaching) field experiences in school settings. These field experiences provide you with early exposure to students and classroom settings and offer you the opportunity to ease into teaching and to think about what you are doing with students and to reflect on your skills as a teacher.

professional life and looking forward to going to work every day were even more important factors for her. "Although I work within the larger school system, I still feel as though the classroom is under my control. Those students are in my hands, and I love that feeling of independence and responsibility," said Mrs. McGreevey. "Maria, I would suggest that after you have heard everyone's reactions, follow your heart. You will spend many years working at your life's chosen work, and many people work in jobs they dislike just to pay the bills. You need to find what will make you the happiest. You have some time yet to make a final decision. In the meantime, you will get more opportunities to work in schools and investigate your decision further. I still believe you would make a wonderful teacher, but you must be comfortable with the decision."

Discussion Questions

What are the most important considerations in selecting a career? What value do you place on salary, enjoyment of your work, impact of your profession on society, control of your own activities, and other factors?

Possibilities

Mrs. McGreevey touches on an important issue in her advice to Maria. Too often college students feel pressure to make a decision about their career choice and then feel they have to stick with that decision. Maria has time to make sure teaching is the right decision for her. A major reason some new teachers leave after only a few years of teaching is because they feel unprepared for the responsibility they face when they get their own classrooms. Field experiences throughout your teacher preparation program offer a good opportunity to make sure that you are up to the challenges of working with young people. As you complete your field experiences, reflect on what you are learning, the challenges you see in the classrooms, and how you might address those challenges. Speak with your professors, supervising teachers, and other mentors about concerns that arise during your field experiences or in classes. Also, hear what first-year teachers have to say about their experiences. Some great online resources for hearing from first-year teachers, as well as experienced teachers, are as follows:

- Education World (www.educationworld.com)—Offers advice on all facets of teaching. Do a search for "first-year teachers" and read some of the tips and materials that are available.

- U.S. Department of Education, "What to Expect Your First Year of Teaching" (www.ed.gov/pubs/FirstYear/index.html)—This online book offers advice as well as stories from teachers in their own words.

- NEA Today Online (www.nea.org/neatoday)—Check out comments teachers share about real issues that arise in schools today and what teachers do to address the issues.

Many years ago the first classroom experience you might have received as a preservice teacher would have been during your student teaching assignment at the end of your teacher education program. A full-immersion experience such as this would have left you little time to reflect on your career choice or hone your skills before taking charge of a classroom. Today most undergraduate teacher education programs provide preservice teachers with multiple opportunities to work with pre-K–12 students. Prepracticum field experiences are often taken with methods or other courses throughout the program in an effort to bridge the gap between theory and practice. These may include observations of students and teachers in classrooms, interviews with teachers and other professional staff, and limited experiences tutoring individual students or engaging in large-group instruction. These preservice experiences are supervised by university professors or clinical faculty who might observe you teaching a lesson and provide feedback on your teaching. Often a seminar associated with the practicum provides preservice teachers an opportunity to share ideas and challenges of teaching and support each other through their experiences.

A number of colleges and universities across the country take the prepracticum experiences a step further by following the **Professional Development School (PDS)** model. PDS programs involve a close affiliation between local K–12 schools and a college or university teacher education program. In PDS schools, theory and practice are ideally integrated by having experienced classroom teachers work closely with college and university professors to help train future teachers.

- **Alternative Routes**   With the need for more teachers in the coming years, alternative pathways have become necessary in order to meet that demand in the classroom. A

Through the Eyes of
Culturally Sensitive Teachers

A Student Teaching Dilemma

Jodi Schaffler is a high school social studies teacher with 6 years of experience working in an inner-city high school. This semester she has a student teacher working with her. When Rebecca Lysingen first arrived and introduced herself to Jodi, she seemed enthusiastic and eager to get started.

On the third day of Rebecca's student teaching, Jodi was presenting a government lesson about democracy and authority. Students saw contrasts between what was being taught and the way their high school was run. One young woman said, "I nearly dropped out last year and many other kids have dropped out! Teachers degrade you and give you no respect, and it makes you feel like giving up!"

Another student responded, "One teacher wrote me up saying I was prejudiced or something. The teacher changed the story. I don't trust teachers. You are different, Ms. Schaffler, we can talk to you. You accept everything we say."

A third student chimed in, "Nobody wanted to help me out. Teachers just want you to go up to them and beg!"

Jodi glanced over at Rebecca, who looked visibly shaken. While the lesson on authority had gotten students to participate, their comments took on a degree of realism and passion that Jodi had not expected. She certainly had not wanted to scare the new student teacher. After class, Jodi took Rebecca to the teachers' lounge to talk. She told Rebecca that, while the students' comments were blunt, they were making them because they felt safe in airing their views. After all, school was the unit of authority with which students were most familiar and it was natural to relate the lesson to what they knew best. Rebecca confessed that, while students were making unkind remarks about some teachers, she was a little taken aback and wondered how she might handle such a situation. Jodi stated again that the students' honesty was a reflection of their trust in their teacher, which was valuable and would mean that some real learning could take place. She reassured Rebecca that she would ease her into her responsibilities with the class. Rebecca felt much better once they'd spoken and knew that she'd be ready to take over a class when her time came.

Points to Ponder

1. Would it have been better if this discussion with the students had never taken place in front of Rebecca? Why or why not?

2. How might Jodi's handling of the situation help Rebecca become a more effective teacher?

3. As a supervising teacher, how can Jodi help Rebecca come to understand students' perspectives?

development in the last 20 to 30 years has opened the door to professionals outside the teaching field who later in their careers feel that they would like to make a career change to teaching. Most, if not all, states today offer special programs that enable individuals wishing to make midcareer changes to bring their prior experience in business or other fields into the classroom. Often they must complete a set number of core education classes as well as some field experience before being academically certified to teach. Imagine the knowledge and experience a former chemist can bring to a high school chemistry class or that a former accountant can bring to a high school accounting class.

Some programs such as Teach for America provide a fast-track approach over the summer with rigorous instruction in core teacher preparation courses and some limited student teaching during a summer school session. Upon successful completion of the program, candidates are then qualified to enter their own classrooms in the fall after this short but intense orientation into teaching. Check out Teach for America by visiting their Web site at www.teachforamerica.org/flash_movie.html.

How teachers enter the profession is open to considerable debate. Many critics of alternative certification programs argue that becoming an effective teacher requires systematic sustained study and practice; sending beginning teachers into the classroom with minimal coursework and practical experience can be problematic. Broadening the options to enter the field helps fill the teaching void in difficult-to-fill districts, particularly in urban and remote areas. However, the key to the effectiveness of alternative certification programs is that they provide experiences and instruction for future teachers equivalent to those that candidates get in traditional teacher education programs.

BECOMING CERTIFIED

Completing your teacher education program, whether traditional or alternative, however, still does not automatically qualify you for teaching in the public school system. Only state departments of education can issue you a license to teach. In every state, becoming a teacher requires a state license or **certification**. Licenses are issued for age groups and subject areas. **Teaching licenses** are evidence that the person who has been issued or awarded a license has completed the requirements of that state. Most states require some kind of teacher test for entry into the profession. (See Appendix C for the addresses and websites of all the states to inquire about their requirements for licensing and certification.)

Each state offers a variety of pathways or routes to licensing including undergraduate preparation, postgraduate study, master's degrees, and a variety of alternative routes designed for career-changing adults. Teacher education programs in most colleges and universities follow state-approved program guidelines and organize their content based on guidelines or standards established by a national organization, such as those from the **Interstate New Teacher Assessment and Support Consortium (INTASC)**, shown in Figure 1.1. In addition, select universities may also design their teacher education programs following criteria established by national accreditation organizations. The purpose of such organization is to ensure that teacher education programs can adequately prepare future teachers to be competent, caring, and qualified professional educators. Two such organizations are the **National Council for the Accreditation of Teacher Education** (NCATE) and the **Teacher Education Accreditation Council** (TEAC). Because states establish their licensing or certification requirements based on these national guidelines, state requirements are relatively similar. Therefore, a teacher who moves from one state to another does not need to earn a new degree in that state. However, each state often requires new teachers who have not been trained in that state to complete one or two courses in state history or law or to take a state certification test. Some state-approved teacher preparation programs offer graduates **reciprocity** with other states, which means you would not have to complete student teaching or take additional courses in the new state. However, this does not mean you would be exempt from any state licensing tests.

Most states also require teachers to pass a state exam that focuses on pedagogy, learning theory, and knowledge of testing. The **Praxis Series**: Professional Assessments for Beginning Teachers, which was developed by the Educational Testing Service—the same group responsible for the SAT and GRE exams—is a series of tests used by a large number of states to determine teachers' knowledge of subject matter and preparedness. The series consists of tests at three stages:

Praxis I: Academic Skills Assessments—taken in order to enter a teacher training program

Praxis II: Subject Assessments—licensing for entering the profession

Praxis III: Classroom Performance Assessments—taken after the first year of teaching

Upon completion of your teacher education program, for example, you might be required to take the Praxis II exam in order to be licensed to teach in a particular state. Some states, such as Massachusetts, California, Texas, and New York, do not use Praxis and have created their own tests. Because many states require the Praxis exam, taking it allows you to move from state to state with proof of competency. States that do not use the Praxis exam may

INTASC
Principle #9

Professional Commitment and Responsibility: The teacher is a reflective practitioner who continually evaluates the effects of his/her choices and actions on others (students, parents, and other professionals in the learning community) and who actively seeks out opportunities to grow professionally.

FIGURE 1.1

Interstate New Teacher Assessment and Support Consortium (INTASC) Standards for Beginning Teacher Licensing and Development

1. *Knowledge of Subject Matter:* The teacher understands the central concepts, tools of inquiry, and structures of the subject being taught and can create learning experiences that make these aspects of subject matter meaningful for students.

2. *Knowledge of Human Development and Learning:* The teacher understands how children learn and develop, and can provide learning opportunities that support their intellectual, social, and personal development.

3. *Adapting Instruction for Individual Needs:* The teacher understands how students differ in their approaches to learning and creates instructional opportunities that are adapted to diverse learners.

4. *Multiple Instructional Strategies:* The teacher uses various instructional strategies to encourage students' development of critical-thinking, problem-solving, and performance skills.

5. *Classroom Motivation and Management:* The teacher uses an understanding of individual and group motivation and behavior to create a learning environment that encourages positive social interaction, active engagement in learning, and self-motivation.

6. *Communication Skills:* The teacher uses knowledge of effective verbal, nonverbal, and media communication techniques to foster active inquiry, collaboration, and supportive interaction in the classroom.

7. *Instructional Planning Skills:* The teacher plans instruction based on knowledge of subject matter, students, the community, and curriculum goals.

8. *Assessment of Student Learning:* The teacher understands and uses formal and informal assessment strategies to evaluate and ensure the continuous intellectual, social, and physical development of the learner.

9. *Professional Commitment and Responsibility:* The teacher is a reflective practitioner who continually evaluates the effects of his or her choices and actions on others (students, parents, and other professionals in the learning community) and who actively seeks out opportunities to grow professionally.

10. *Partnerships:* The teacher fosters relationships with school colleagues, parents, and agencies in the larger community to support students' learning and well-being.

Source: Council of Chief State School Officers, "Interstate New Teacher Assessment and Support Consortium." Available at http://www.ccsso.org

focus on specific content knowledge such as state history or regional geography. Go to www.ets.org/praxis/index.html to determine whether your state or one where you might teach someday requires the Praxis exam.

Who am I?

What do I believe?

To make this school a better place you should get better teachers.

STUDENT

THINK ABOUT THIS:

Everyone agrees that teacher quality is critical for improving student learning and making a difference in today's classrooms. What it actually means and how it is measured is more complicated. How do you think teacher quality should be measured? How does a teacher's passion for teaching and students relate to teacher quality? Does "capable and highly qualified" mean just passing a test for state licensure?

SHARE
and COMPARE:

Discuss with your classmates the attributes of "highly qualified" teachers. Check the requirements for licensing in your state and compare them with those of one or two other states. Also check to see whether the states have alternative routes to licensing.

INTASC

Principle #9

Professional Commitment and Responsibility: The teacher is a reflective practitioner who continually evaluates the effects of his/her choices and actions on others (students, parents, and other professionals in the learning community) and who actively seeks out opportunities to grow professionally.

WHAT DOES IT MEAN TO BE A REFLECTIVE PRACTITIONER?

A key premise of this book is that to become an effective teacher, you must learn to be a **reflective practitioner,** in which the process of understanding and improving one's teaching begins with reflection on one's own experiences. Furthermore, the process of learning to teach continues throughout a teacher's career. Teaching involves more than just providing students with new information. Good teaching is an act of intellect, knowledge, and social inquiry. It involves actively thinking about instruction and the experience of the learners being taught. It involves thinking about what you have taught, recognizing what elements of what you have taught went well or not so well, and adjusting your teaching in the future to be consistent with what you have experienced. Good teaching is not a static process but is dynamic and requires constant adaptation, imagination, and ultimately reflection.

In his book *The Reflective Practitioner,* Donald Schön (1983) argues against "technical-rationality" as the basis for professional knowledge. He argues instead that professional knowledge should be based in a deeply philosophical process, one that has important implications for teaching.

For Schön, excellence in a profession such as teaching must be based in practice. Reflective practitioners/educators reflect on all that they do. While technical skills are useful, there is no single formula for good teaching. Instead, teachers must allow themselves to be open to surprises, new information, and even, occasionally, confusion. For the reflective practitioner, teaching involves constant experimentation. Ideas about how and what to teach must be tested against the reality of the classroom. This process shapes how you can act and what you can do as a teacher.

Schön also stresses the fact that much of what goes on in good teaching is based on reflective practice and cannot always be easily described. Those who do it very well cannot necessarily explain what it is that they are doing, or even how they do it. Therefore, observing good teachers in the field and reflecting on what they do becomes very important because it provides a means by which to learn what is done in good teaching.

By definition, being a reflective practitioner takes practice. As you begin your teacher training, you may be looking for specific instruction on how to act in a classroom setting. But classrooms (and the students who learn in them) are far too complex to act according to simple textbook models. For the reflective practitioner and teacher, context is critically important. What may work with one class or group of students may not work with another. You will have to start making reflective decisions— personal decisions—from the moment you enter the classroom, whether as an observer or as a teacher.

Part of the purpose of this book is to help you become a reflective practitioner who can adjust to the demands of different

A good teacher demonstrates the ability to adapt to rapidly changing circumstances, a creative imagination and, most importantly, the ability to reflect upon students and the situation to determine what will work best for every student.

educational settings. To do so will require that you do more than simply learn or inquire about teaching. It will require you to think and reflect about who you are as an individual and as a teacher, the background of the people you are working with, and how the community in which you are working shapes and influences what you can or cannot do.

The appendices at the back of this book will help you develop as a reflective practitioner. Throughout this book you will see special features titled Who Am I? What Do I Believe?, as well as Problems to Possibilities, that will prompt you to think about education dilemmas and issues that impact teachers. Appendix B, Creating a Reflective Journal and Portfolio, will help you create and maintain a reflective journal to record your responses to the prompts and establish a portfolio of your work; Appendix A, Conducting Classroom Observations and Interviews, will help you hone your observation and interviewing skills.

Your portfolio can serve as documentation of your work in the course as well as evidence of your developmental thinking, from the beginning prompts to field observation assignments. The portfolio will provide a place for you to store your thought processes and exercises for future reference as you use this text, as well as serving as a resource as you move through your teacher preparation program. As you move through the text, complete each activity thoughtfully and completely before placing it into your portfolio. You will have many more courses and classroom experiences as you begin your teacher education program. Let this course and text serve as the foundation for the journey into teaching. Let your Touch the Future Reflective Thinking Journal and Portfolio be resources you will use and refer to throughout your teacher preparation program.

Who am I? **What do I believe?**

"Education often is just about showing up and watching. You can always learn from good and bad examples."

SECONDARY SOCIAL STUDIES TEACHER

THINK ABOUT THIS:

In traditional cultures people learn by "hanging around" and watching how others behave and how others solve problems or deal with issues as they arise. Donald Schön believes that in emphasizing problem solving, it is critical that the effective teacher not ignore problem setting. According to Schön, problem setting "must be constructed from the materials of problematic situations which are puzzling, troubling, and uncertain." What do you think Schön means by this?

SHARE and **COMPARE:**

What do you feel you will be able to learn by observing teachers and students during your teacher preparation program? How will these opportunities make you a more effective teacher? What do your classmates think?

WHAT DOES IT MEAN TO TEACH IN TODAY'S DIVERSE SOCIETY?

Being a reflective practitioner is particularly important today as the demographic of U.S. classrooms continues to change. (This will be discussed further in Chapter 3.) As reflective practitioners, good teachers not only know their subjects well and have a variety of approaches to teach them, but are also keen observers of human behavior and try to understand their own backgrounds as well as the perspectives of others.

No institution reflects the changing demographic of the U.S. population like schools. Racial, ethnic, and cultural diversity call for teachers to help students and parents navigate the school's culture within the broader social context.

Teachers play complex roles in schools. When some students start school, their home cultures are fairly similar to the expectations of the school culture they must learn to navigate. Other students, however, come from cultural or linguistic backgrounds that are very different from the culture of the schools they will attend. Working in this second context calls for teachers to serve as reflective practitioners who also function using Henry Giroux's model of **border crossers** (Giroux, 1992). Teachers in this role must help students who are unfamiliar with school culture negotiate the expectations and demands of school in ways they can accept. Giroux (1992) reminds us that "culture is not seen as monolithic or unchanging, but a site where multiple and heterogeneous borders, where different histories, experiences, languages and voices intermingle" (p. 169). Teachers who are effective border crossers must understand their own cultural perspectives, those of the school and community in which they teach, and the backgrounds of students they educate. Being a border crosser requires you to be a keen observer and a patient listener.

Students and parents sometimes have to rely on school personnel to help them understand their options. Parents who lack the ability to verify information independently of school authorities may have limited choices if the information they receive is incomplete. As a teacher, you will be in a key position to help unravel the mysteries of school culture for many students and their families. The extent to which you perform this role is very much up to you. As a cultural border crosser, you can play a key role in seeing that information regarding formal school culture is accessible to all students and their parents, by providing copies of materials translated into other languages for limited-English-speaking parents or by actually explaining policies to English-speaking students and parents when they have difficulty understanding formal language.

Helping students and parents understand informal school culture is a bit trickier. Informal school culture could be symbolized by roads or paths that can help you reach your destination, none of which are marked on the map. The only people who know them are those who have lived in an area for a long time and have discovered these unmarked routes by traveling the territory. Perhaps the school has a highly competitive school culture because it prides itself on the number of National Merit Scholars it produces each year. In schools like these, parents asking for additional resources for special education or after-school

INTASC

Principle #3

Adapting Instruction for Individual Needs: The teacher understands how students differ in their approaches to learning and creates instructional opportunities that are adapted to diverse learners.

INTASC

Principle #10

Partnerships: The teacher fosters relationships with school colleagues, parents, and agencies in the larger community to support students' learning and well-being.

BUILDING ON EDUCATIONAL FOUNDATIONS

Teaching in Popular Culture

As a beginning teacher, you will find that many different forces shape how you perceive the teaching profession and what you can or cannot do as a teacher. Compared to a hundred years ago, popular culture in the form of film and television can have significant influences on our image of what it means to teach and to work in classrooms and schools. But are such models always accurate? Do they truthfully convey what teaching is actually like or what teachers need to do to be effective instructors?

Consider, for example, the film *Dangerous Minds* (1995), in which the "heroine" teaches black and Hispanic high school students English literature. The film, based on LouAnne Johnson's book *My Posse Don't Do Homework,* is an account of her teaching experiences in a northern California high school. It portrays Johnson, a former marine, engaging her students in real learning using atypical strategies to motivate them and get their attention.

Dangerous Minds is a classic "feel-good" movie. Beginning teachers often see it as a source of inspiration and a model for their own teaching. Johnson's character, however, is not necessarily a model teacher. She throws out the school's standard English curriculum in favor of studying song lyrics by Bob Dylan—lyrics that clearly have meaning for her, but not necessarily for her students. Johnson takes her students on a field trip to a local amusement park, without permission of the students' parents or the school. In doing so, she puts her students at risk, as well as herself and the school. She allows one of her students—an extremely handsome Hispanic gang leader—to stay alone with her in her apartment overnight when a rival gang leader threatens him.

Other problems are evident in her work as a teacher. When a student wins a prize, Johnson takes the winner out to dinner at a fancy French restaurant. Not knowing what to wear, the winner, a young Hispanic boy, buys an expensive jacket that he cannot afford so that he will be dressed in a way that he thinks his teacher will like.

Dangerous Minds may be enjoyable entertainment, but it is not a good model for beginning teachers to imitate. The movie's messages—finding creative ways to motivate students, connecting with your students, being committed to student learning—are good ones. However, the tactics demonstrated certainly are not typical, and they're not standard. Teachers have to keep student liability in mind at all times and have to maintain a sense of propriety as well. Movies and television shows often embellish on reality for the sake of commercialism. Therefore, it's important to find the greater message in such pop culture.

Think about portrayals of teaching and schooling that you have seen on television or at the movies. Look at the following list of films. Think about the ones you have seen. Do they accurately depict the work and world of teachers? Can they be of use in helping you develop your own skills as a teacher?

Films about Teachers and Teaching

The Miracle Worker (1962). The story of Anne Sullivan and her work as a teacher with the deaf and blind Helen Keller.

To Sir, With Love (1967). A black engineer reluctantly becomes a teacher and finds his calling working with poor students in the London slums.

Up the Down Staircase (1967). Based on Bel Kaufman's hilarious novel about teaching in the New York City schools.

Children of a Lesser God (1986). William Hurt plays a teacher at a school for deaf children.

Stand and Deliver (1988). Jaime Escalante inspires inner-city high school students to excel at mathematics.

Dead Poets Society (1989). Robin Williams plays a prep school teacher who challenges the traditional system.

Lean on Me (1989). A New Jersey principal uses force and intimidation to take back control of an inner-city school.

Mr. Holland's Opus (1996). A dedicated music teacher and composer realizes that his greatest accomplishment is his teaching.

Music of the Heart (1999). True story of an inspired music teacher in East Harlem who teaches children self-discipline and self-esteem by teaching them to play the violin.

The Emperor's Club (2002). Kevin Kline plays a principal who is confronted by a moral dilemma that comes back to haunt him later in his career.

Mona Lisa Smile (2003). A free-thinking art professor teaches conservative 1950s Wellesley College girls to question their traditional societal roles.

tutorial programs may find themselves running into opposition from the school's informal culture. Teachers who are border crossers recognize this need and help children and parents navigate the unwritten expectations of the school.

Meeting these challenges requires current and future teachers who realize that becoming an effective border crosser is a lifelong challenge. There are always new borders to cross. If you relish the challenge of reading the map and helping others cross unfamiliar territory, this is a highly rewarding aspect of the teaching profession. Even more challenging is helping fellow educators, students, and parents navigate roads and paths that are not marked on the map, since these are ever-changing. Some students, parents, or fellow teachers may need little help in navigating the formal and informal cultures of schools, but many do need assistance. The ability to help many decipher the map that historically was familiar to only a few is one of the great rewards of teaching.

WHAT ARE FACTORS TO CONSIDER WHEN PREPARING FOR A TEACHING CAREER?

Your commitment and passion to touching the future will make a difference to the students who will be in your classroom. Figure 1.2 (page 18) identifies the top 10 requirements for good teaching. Many factors will influence your professional life. Some are fairly predictable, while others are not. The following six are particularly important for you to think about as you begin your entry into the teaching profession. Each is important in the overall picture of the world of education today. Although not all-inclusive, they represent major themes that guide teacher preparation today and will affect the professional lives of you and your colleagues in teaching in the foreseeable future.

- *Professionalism:* Professionalism represents the recognition of teachers as critical and effective leaders of not only instruction, but also the social settings in which they work.

- *Values and assumptions:* The attitudes and beliefs you bring to your work in the profession will help determine your transition to the field and your long-term success.

- *Multiculturalism and diversity:* Students in our schools represent a great variety of cultures and traditions as well as a wide range of special needs and individual differences. Understanding the spectrum of needs is a must for today's profession.

- *Standards:* In the past decade, and particularly since the passage of No Child Left Behind, teachers, administrators, and communities face the challenge of strict professional guidelines and the high expectations of academic objectives as in no other time in our nation's academic history.

- *Linking theory and practice:* Through personal reflection and by listening to the voices of students and teachers as well as considering practices in the schools, you explore key elements of professional practice such as classroom management.

- *Ethics and social justice:* The ethical and moral decisions teachers must make as part of their work and the obligation and duty they have as members of a democratic culture promote the creation of a more just and equitable society.

Each of these themes serves as a basis to the overall message of this book, whose purpose is to introduce you to the field of teaching and to get you thinking like a teacher now. When prospective teachers are busy with their courses and field experiences, they often don't take time to think about their professional preparation until they are about to graduate and start thinking about their first teaching position. The best time to develop a professional mindset to be a teacher is now, as you begin your teacher training.

FIGURE 1.2

The Top 10 Requirements for Good Teaching

1. Good teaching is as much about passion as it is about reason. It's about not only motivating students to learn, but teaching them how to learn, and doing so in a manner that is relevant, meaningful, and memorable. It's about caring for your craft, having a passion for it, and conveying that passion to everyone, most importantly to your students.

2. Good teaching is about substance and treating students as consumers of knowledge. It's about doing your best to keep on top of your field, reading sources inside and outside your areas of expertise, and being at the leading edge as often as possible. But knowledge is not confined to scholarly journals. Good teaching is also about bridging the gap between theory and practice. It's about leaving the ivory tower and immersing oneself in the field; talking to, consulting with, and assisting practitioners; and forming liaisons with their communities.

3. Good teaching is about listening, questioning, being responsive, and remembering that each student and class is different. It's about eliciting responses and developing the oral communication skills of the quiet students. It's about pushing students to excel; at the same time, it's about being human, respecting others, and being professional at all times.

4. Good teaching is about not always having a fixed agenda and being rigid, but being flexible and fluid, experimenting, and having the confidence to react and adjust to changing circumstances. It's about getting only 10 percent done of what you wanted to do in a class and still feeling good. It's about easily deviating from the course syllabus or lecture schedule when there is more and better learning elsewhere. Good teaching is about the creative balance between being an authoritarian dictator on one hand and a pushover on the other.

5. Good teaching is about style. Should good teaching be entertaining? You bet! Does this mean that it lacks in substance? Not a chance! Effective teaching is not about being locked with both hands glued to a podium or having your eyes fixated on a slide projector while you drone on. Good teachers work the room and every student in it. They realize that they are the conductors and the class is the orchestra. All students play different instruments and at varying proficiencies.

6. This is very important—good teaching is about humor. It's about being self-deprecating and not taking yourself too seriously. It's often about making innocuous jokes, mostly at your own expense, so that the ice breaks and students learn in a more relaxed atmosphere where you, like them, are human with your own share of faults and shortcomings.

7. Good teaching is about caring, nurturing, and developing minds and talents. It's about devoting time, often invisible, to every student. It's also about the thankless hours of grading, designing or redesigning courses, and preparing materials to still further enhance instruction.

8. Good teaching is supported by strong and visionary leadership and very tangible institutional support—resources, personnel, and funds. Good teaching is continually reinforced by an overarching vision that transcends the entire organization—from full professors to part-time instructors—and is reflected in what is said, but more importantly by what is done.

9. Good teaching is about mentoring between senior and junior faculty, promoting teamwork, and being recognized and promoted by one's peers. Effective teaching should also be rewarded, and poor teaching needs to be remediated through training and development programs.

10. At the end of the day, good teaching is about having fun, and experiencing pleasure and intrinsic rewards—as in locking eyes with a student in the back row and seeing the synapses and neurons connecting, thoughts being formed, the person becoming better, and a smile cracking across a face as learning all of a sudden happens. Good teachers practice their craft not for the money or because they have to, but because they truly enjoy it and because they want to. Good teachers couldn't imagine doing anything else.

Source: R. Leblanc, "Good Teaching: The Top Ten Requirements." *The Teaching Professor, 12* (6) (1998): 1, 7. Reprinted by permission from Magna Publications, Inc., Madison, WI. www.magnapubs.com. Subscriptions and submissions at custserv@magnapubs.com

FOUR ESSENTIAL QUESTIONS FOR BEGINNING TEACHERS

Four essential questions serve as a reflective framework for this text and a road map to guide you on your journey as you explore the question, "Am I a teacher?" Each section of the text will explore one of these essential questions.

● *Who* **Is Included in the Professional Community of Learners?**   School administrators, teachers, students, families, and the community are all part of the professional learning community. Teachers are at the heart of the work with students, and their interaction in classrooms creates the daily work in schools. This work, however, interfaces with other school personnel as well as the students' families.

As a prospective teacher, you need to be aware of all the people who come into contact with students during a school day. This knowledge will help you broaden your perspective of the students' world and understand who they are and what their needs may be. When you visit schools, keep a notebook and jot down notes about the various people (teachers, staff, administrators, and community members) in the school and the different roles they play. Create your own "Who's Who" list and keep track of all the people you learn about in schools or the community.

● *How* **Are Schools and Teachers Shaped by Society, Culture, and Ethics?**   The social context of schools influences how teachers work. Each school develops its own school culture, which is influenced by its location, communities served by the school, and many other factors. School culture is also influenced by national and international trends. Greater emphasis on standardized testing and computer literacy are current examples of how larger trends influence local school practices.

Schools in rural areas of the United States tend to serve more homogeneous student populations than those located in urban or suburban areas. The size of a school affects the personal nature of relationships within that school. In schools with thousands of students, procedures tend to be more formal because it is more difficult for faculty and staff to know everyone personally. Smaller schools tend to be more intimate.

Ethics have become a prominent issue in education today as people look for ways of addressing some of society's ills. Each school teaches students ethical lessons directly and indirectly. Ethics may be part of a class discussion surrounding business or political practices, or students may learn it by watching how administrators, teachers, and students interact in a school. Whether formally or informally, schools teach ethical lessons every day and students take these lessons with them as citizens of the world.

● *What* **Are the Key Elements of Professional Practice?**   Defining the key elements of professional practice is complicated. How teachers teach and how students learn is the focus of much research and there is often disagreement in education as to what really works. What comprises professional practice may mean different things to different people in the learning and larger communities, depending on their roles and responsibilities for student learning.

Curriculum, instruction, and classroom management clearly are important areas. Curriculum includes the content to be taught to students. It may be generated by state or national standards or by teachers themselves. The scope and sequence of the curriculum will depend on the school district and the needs of students. Curriculum is not just the use of textbooks and the instructional materials included in them, but goes beyond this to include concepts and ideas students need to know and activities in which they will participate.

Instruction is what teachers actually do in the classroom. Planning lessons using existing curriculum frameworks to deliver instruction is critical to effective teaching. Assessing how this curriculum is learned is increasingly more important to state and national policymakers.

Classroom management represents an area of prime interest to prospective teachers and practicing teachers alike. Creating and maintaining a classroom environment in which students can be productive is critical to the learning process. Numerous strategies and techniques are being developed every day to ensure success.

INTASC
Principle #10

Partnerships: The teacher fosters relationships with school colleagues, parents, and agencies in the larger community to support students' learning and well-being.

INTASC
Principle #9

Professional Commitment and Responsibility: The teacher is a reflective practitioner who continually evaluates the effects of his/her choices and actions on others (students, parents, and other professionals in the learning community) and who actively seeks out opportunities to grow professionally.

INTASC
Principle #7

Instructional Planning Skills: The teacher plans instruction based upon knowledge of subject matter, students, the community, and curriculum goals.

EDUCATION MATTERS

Acknowledging Teachers Who Touch the Future

With all the recent talk about the impact of school reform, standards and accountability, and underperforming schools, it is important to take the time to publicize what is good about our schools. Teachers impact the lives of students daily and that impact lasts for years.

Every state honors a teacher of the year who is then considered for the national honor sponsored by the Council of Chief State School Officers (CCSSO). In 2004 the winner was Kathy Mellor, an English as a Second Language (ESL) teacher at Davisville Middle School in North Kingstown, Rhode Island. The U.S. Department of Education also recognizes outstanding first-year teachers. In addition, various organizations honor excellence in teaching with awards, monetary rewards, and grants for their work or time off to complete further study. For example, a number of organizations established awards in honor of Christa McAuliffe in recognition of her work as an outstanding teacher who inspired students and teachers alike. The Christa McAuliffe Memorial Award, established by the Aerospace Education Foundation, "honors one public, private, or parochial Classroom Teacher (kindergarten through twelfth grade) who demonstrates excellence in furthering the concepts of aerospace technologies in the classroom through successful, innovative curricular classroom programs."

The Education Issue: Making a Difference by Honoring Teachers

When you acknowledge a teacher, it says, "You did something right for me." When a teacher is acknowledged by local, state, or federal organizations, it lets the public and parents know that good work is going on in the school. Excellent, highly qualified teachers matter to students. They love to know they are working with a recognized teacher. Excellent teachers "touch the future" because we remember them and use their passion and the skills they taught us in our own work.

Write a letter to a teacher who has made a difference to you and share with that person that you are preparing to become a teacher. Honor a teacher you have known today!

What's Your Opinion?

1. Do you think excellent teachers should be thanked and given public recognition for what they do?

2. Search the Internet for teacher awards or honors. Identify teachers in your state who have been nominated for the CCSSO award. Read about teachers who have received awards and are doing their job positively.

● *How* **Will I Evolve as a Teacher?** At this point in your preparation, becoming a first-year teacher may seem like a distant, yet ambitious goal. But what about the rest of your career? How do teachers' professional lives evolve? As you read the personal statements from the three authors of this text at the beginning of this chapter, it should be clear that there is no single pattern or route for career development, but certain things concern most teachers at different stages of their careers.

Beginning teachers are often preoccupied with learning and mastering the essential elements of teaching. Developing lesson plans is of great importance any time, but especially when you have not taught a class or grade level before. Much of what constitutes good teaching takes place in the planning and organization that occurs before a teacher starts the school day. Newer teachers typically have to spend more time planning and developing lessons than their more experienced counterparts. Focusing a great deal of time on the "nuts and bolts" of running a classroom leaves less time for other activities on the part of new teachers.

Once teachers have 4 or 5 years of experience, they typically become more comfortable in the operation of their classes. Many begin to ponder the next phase of their careers. Should they pursue a graduate degree with the intention of remaining in the classroom, going into school administration, or perhaps teaching in higher education? Some teachers choose to take the minimum number of credits or professional workshops to revalidate their teaching licenses, but many opt for graduate degrees. Those who pursue graduate degrees will find that their professional opportunities are much greater than those who do not.

Teachers with 15 to 30 years of experience are mature professionals who long ago mastered classroom routines. One of their challenges is keeping in touch with professional developments and trends that occur on a regular basis. An important professional contribution experienced teachers can make is to serve as cooperating teachers for student interns and mentor new teachers in their schools. The new teacher can benefit from the experienced teacher's background, while the experienced teacher can benefit from new research or trends in education that the new teacher has recently learned. When done effectively, this can be a mutually beneficial relationship.

However, as your career as an educator evolves, one thing is certain: as a future professional, you will be expected to commit yourself to lifelong learning. That is simply what true professionals in all professions do.

ADOPTING A PROFESSIONAL SELF-CONCEPT AS A STUDENT

As a college or university student you have seen how differently fellow students approach their work and their professors. Some come to every class unless an absence is absolutely unavoidable, while others will take every absence the syllabus allows and are often late for the classes they do attend. Similar patterns are also found in preparing and turning in assignments and in taking exams. It is fair to ask, if all of these students manage to become teachers, which one would you want to teach your child? Most parents want teachers that took their teacher preparation programs seriously. By choosing to become a teacher, you will be receiving something from your college or university besides a baccalaureate degree. You will get a recommendation for professional licensing in your state and thus you will join the teaching profession. When is the appropriate time to begin thinking about yourself as a professional? Is it when you are dressed up with your portfolio in hand and are waiting to interview with a principal for your first job? The best time is now, when you are beginning your studies to become a teacher. When you graduate, you will likely approach your former professors for letters of recommendation. Are they required to give you a positive letter or to give you a letter at all? You are asking your former professors to borrow a little of the professional reputations they have spent years building in order to help you get your first job. If you were a serious and dedicated student, your professors will most likely be delighted to recommend you. If you were a student who was always looking to get by with the least amount of work or effort, they could tell you they won't write you a letter, write an honest but uncomplimentary letter, or write a letter that says little or nothing about your abilities.

You should think about yourself as a professional now. You are a professional in training, and you should be seen as particularly well prepared and as a valuable and respected member of the community of learners. Throughout this book you will be asked to reflect on your own thoughts as a prospective educator, and at the end of every chapter you will be asked to complete a professional plan as a way of documenting your immediate professional goals. Keep them as a record of your own development and review them at the end of this course and as you begin your student teaching. Creating a professional plan as a beginning teacher will serve you well, both in the short term and as you enter the career. Professional plans are completed annually in most

Building a sense of professionalism begins with your university career: be a serious and dedicated teacher in training in order to enhance your professional reputation.

school districts and serve to focus teachers on the year ahead and acknowledge what has been completed to date. Starting a professional plan as a beginning education student will serve you well. Be a lifelong learner. Design your plan and "touch the future."

Who am I?   **What do I believe?**

"As you reach into yourself and contemplate what teaching is about remember there are rewards and they will be powerful."

STUDENT TEACHER

THINK ABOUT THIS:

As you read about the teaching profession in this chapter you may feel some apprehension about what it means to be an effective teacher. The journey will empower you to engage in key questions that will inform you about the realities of the profession. The goal of actually being a teacher will not happen for several years, but the preparation for you is now! How will you document your learning? What thoughts about teaching concern you? What do you think the rewards of teaching will be for you?

SHARE and COMPARE:

Talk with your classmates and list the issues that are going through your mind right now about teaching. How can you support each other throughout this course? Share the rewards you are anticipating as teachers. What problems or challenges do you anticipate? What are the common themes in this discussion?

FINAL THOUGHTS

Qualified teachers are the single most important element a society controls that produces high academic achievement in students. The basic goal of the educational system in the United States is to try to educate all students in a meaningful way. Students who fail to achieve this goal have limited occupational choices in the twenty-first century. Teachers serve as the key professionals in this effort.

You have examined different paths to becoming a teacher and hopefully have considered the characteristics of each. Traditional teacher preparation programs have faced some opposition in recent years from those who feel that all you need to be a good teacher is simply to know the content you teach. While subject-area knowledge is important, research has repeatedly shown that when teachers do not have sufficient preparation in pedagogy, foundations of education, testing, and techniques of classroom management, they do not perform as well as teachers with that background and typically do not remain in the teaching profession for the long term. In spite of this, the myth that "anyone can be a good teacher" persists.

As a teacher, you have the potential to take information and make it come alive for young people. You will have the opportunity to open new worlds and possibilities to those you teach. This is what all of us look for in our teaching. It is something we hope we have achieved in our own modest way, and that we believe you can achieve as well. What better way to lead one's life than making a difference in the lives of others? There are few better ways to spend your life than reaching out and "touching the future."

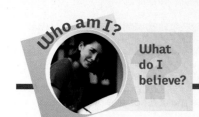

Who am I? **What do I believe?**

REFLECTIONS

My First Professional Plan

Name _____ Date _____

1. Why I am taking this course:

2. My goals for this course:

   a. _____

   b. _____

   c. _____

3. I plan to:

   _____ Teach for life

   _____ Teach for a few years

   _____ Teach for a few years and become an administrator

   _____ Enter a master's program to get a second license

   _____ Enter a master's program for additional content

   _____ Don't know yet

4. One thing I am looking forward to as I enter schools: _____

   _____

5. One thing I am nervous about as I enter schools: _____

   _____

6. Courses (electives) I want to take to prepare me to teach: _____

   _____

7. Two beliefs I have about teaching:

   a. _____

   b. _____

8. Two assumptions I have about becoming a teacher:

   a. _____

   b. _____

9. Why I want to be a teacher:

10. What I need to do to be successful in meeting my professional goals:

23

SUMMARY

What Is Involved in the Journey into Teaching?

- Teachers choose teaching for different reasons, but a common one is to make a positive difference in the lives of others.
- Traditional routes into the teaching profession involve getting a college or university degree with teaching certification.
- Alternative routes into teaching may involve accelerated summer programs with limited practice teaching or going directly into the classroom by passing a test without having had a practice teaching experience.
- University teacher education programs provide training, but only states can issue an actual license to teach. All states requirements differ, but some offer reciprocity.

What Does It Mean to Be a Reflective Practitioner?

- There is no single formula for good teaching, but all good teachers reflect on their teaching and alter their teaching based on their reflections.
- Reflective teachers are closely aware of the context of their teaching and adapt their methods to fit the context.

What Does It Mean to Teach in Today's Diverse Society?

- Today's increasingly diverse classrooms call for teachers who have insights into a variety of students' cultures and are willing to be border crossers.
- Teachers must understand formal and informal school cultures and be able to explain them to parents and students.
- Teachers should help students develop the skills to function well in the mainstream culture while respecting those students' home cultures.

What Are Factors to Consider When Preparing for a Teaching Career?

- Six key themes shape the lives of teachers today: professionalism, values and assumptions, multiculturalism and diversity, standards, linking theory and practice, and ethics and social justice.
- Preservice teachers must explore four essential questions: Who makes up the professional learning community? How do society, culture, and ethics affect schools? What are the key elements of professional practice? How will I evolve as a teacher?
- College and university students preparing to be teachers should view themselves as professionals in training and conduct their student activities as if they were already licensed professionals.

Companion
Website

Visit the **Touch the Future . . . Teach!** Companion Website at
www.ablongman.com/diaz for additional opportunities.

KEY WORDS

CONCEPT REVIEW

1. Explain some of the different motivations that cause people to choose teaching as their profession.

2. Compare your motivations for considering teaching with the factors cited by the three authors of this text explaining why they became educators.

3. Identify key elements of traditional teacher preparation today.

4. Identify key elements of alternative teacher preparation and contrast them with those for traditional teacher preparation.

5. Discuss what it means for teachers to be reflective practitioners.

6. Define and contrast formal and informal school cultures.

7. Explain the concept of a teacher as a border crosser.

8. Discuss key questions all future teachers should pose and answer regarding their teacher preparation programs.

9. Explain the role of ethics, professionalism, and understanding diversity in the preparation of a future teacher.

10. Summarize various stages in a teaching career and explain the elements that are most significant in each stage.

11. Identify how performance as a preservice teacher can affect a candidate's prospects for a permanent teaching position.

12. Describe what is meant by thinking of yourself as a professional while you are still a college or university student.

TOUCH THE FUTURE . . .

Read On

Schoolteacher: a Sociological Study
Dan C. Lortie (Chicago: University of Chicago Press, 1976)
The classic sociological study in the field of teachers and their work.

Schoolteachers and Schooling: Ethoses in Conflict
Eugene F. Provenzo, Jr., and Gary N. McCloskey (Norwood, NJ: Ablex, 1996)
A 20-year follow-up to Lortie's study on teachers.

The Call to Teach
David T. Hansen (New York: Teachers College Press, 1995)
A thoughtful study of why people are drawn to the teaching profession.

Teaching in America: The Slow Revolution
Gerald Grant and Christine E. Murray (Cambridge, MA: Harvard University Press, 1999)
A perceptive analysis of the current state of the teaching profession.

What Keeps Teachers Going?
Sonia Nieto (New York: Teachers College Press, 2003)
One of the country's leading multicultural educators reflects on the work of teachers.

Log On

National Council for the Accreditation of Teacher Education (NCATE)
www.ncate.org
The professional accrediting organization for schools, colleges, and departments of education in the United States; NCATE's website provides extensive information on issues facing teachers working in today's classrooms, as well as requirements for teacher licensing and accreditation.

Teacher Education Accreditation Council (TEAC)
www.teac.org
>A system for accrediting education programs begun in 1997 that has as its purpose improving academic degree programs for professional educators.

New York Times Learning Network
www.nytimes.com/learning
>A news and education resource for teachers from the nation's "newspaper of record"; also found at the website are lesson plans, information on "This Day in History," and other resources useful for beginning and experienced teachers.

Eduhound
www.eduhound.com
>An incredible list of annotated resources available online for teachers and those interested in education.

U.S. Department of Education
www.ed.gov/index.jhtm
>Home page of the U.S. Department of Education—an invaluable resource for your beginning work in education.

Write On

"Teaching gives me a greater sense of my humanity."
>—Camille Banks-Lee, English teacher

In your journal, explain how being a teacher has the potential to "expand our humanity." Is teaching different from other professions in this regard? If yes, why? Write a brief essay outlining your response.

OBSERVATION GUIDE

. . . TEACH: LINKING THEORY TO PRACTICE

Linking Theory to Practice

Part of your informed decision about teaching needs to come from your own desire to see schools firsthand. The following interview and observation guide will help you while completing practical field experiences or during regular visits to schools.

Objective: To interview a teacher who has entered teaching as a professional career choice

Teacher Interviewed: _____   Interviewer: _____
Grade Level and School of Teacher: _____   Date: _____
Subject Taught: _____   Time In: _____   Time Out: _____

Directions: Work with your professor to locate a school where you can feel welcomed to complete an interview. Call the teacher to set up an appointment, then use these questions as a guide or create your own. You may want to audiotape the session (with permission from the teacher) and record your answers on this form at a later time to enhance your own listening at the time of the interview.

Share and compare your interview with other members of the class to identify the common themes related to teachers who choose to teach. After the interview, send a short, personal thank-you by e-mail or regular mail.

1. Why did you choose teaching as a professional career?

2. Did you feel prepared to teach when you first started? What would you do differently if you were to start your preparation now?

3. How long have you been teaching? How long have you known this is what you wanted to do for your life's work?

4. What are the most difficult challenges you are facing right now? How can I avoid them?

5. Do you have a mentor? Are you a mentor? If you are, how is this working out?

6. What types of professional development have you participated in as a teacher? Please describe your involvement in each of the following:
   a. professional organizations
   b. teacher research
   c. team teaching

7. What advice do you have for me as I think about becoming a teacher?

8. Do you have a teaching portfolio? If so, may I see it?

Final Reflection (*To be answered by the interviewer*)
What I learned about teaching from this interview:

Connecting with INTASC

Compare the top 10 requirements for good teaching in Figure 1.2 to the INTASC standards in Figure 1.1. Do you see any correlation between the 10 items in each list? Share each figure with the teacher you interview and ask for the teacher's impression of the two lists.

2

Becoming a Teacher

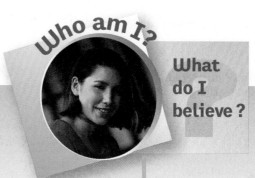

Who am I?

What do I believe?

THINK ABOUT THIS:

As an icon of industry, Lee Iacocca recognizes the value of an educated work force and respects those who educate that workforce. His quote has been used on numerous awards for teachers and in many speeches that highlight the important work of teachers. What does this quote mean to you? How does this quote make you feel? How does a teacher pass along "civilization," and why is this so important to the country?

"In a completely rational society the best of us would aspire to be teachers and the rest of us would have to settle for something less, because passing civilization on from one generation to the next ought to be the highest honor and the highest responsibility anyone could have."

—Lee Iacocca

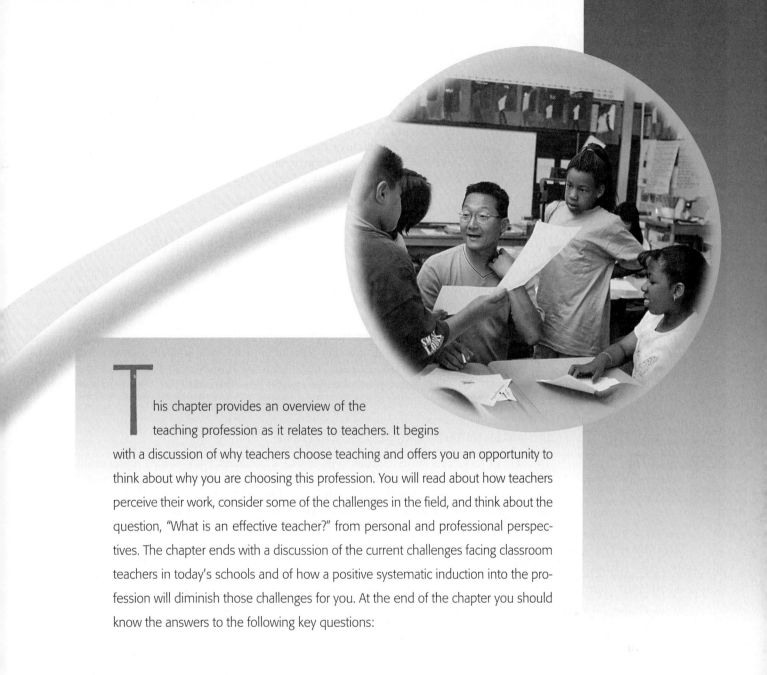

This chapter provides an overview of the teaching profession as it relates to teachers. It begins with a discussion of why teachers choose teaching and offers you an opportunity to think about why you are choosing this profession. You will read about how teachers perceive their work, consider some of the challenges in the field, and think about the question, "What is an effective teacher?" from personal and professional perspectives. The chapter ends with a discussion of the current challenges facing classroom teachers in today's schools and of how a positive systematic induction into the profession will diminish those challenges for you. At the end of the chapter you should know the answers to the following key questions:

Key Questions

1. Who are the teachers in America's schools?
2. What is an effective teacher?
3. What are the challenges for teachers in today's classrooms?

High-quality teachers influence student learning in positive ways. You probably know this from your own experience in school. You remember your favorite teachers and how hard you worked for them and try to forget those you didn't like. You notice those who don't seem to enjoy it, as well as those who seem to be naturals for the profession. You have an opinion about teachers. As you read this chapter, keep an open mind and go beyond your own opinions and possible biases to learn more about teachers and their professional choices.

WHO ARE THE TEACHERS IN AMERICA'S SCHOOLS?

As you can see in Table 2.1, the typical teacher in today's schools is female, white, highly educated, and highly experienced. But these demographics have been changing in recent years and will likely continue to change in the coming years. As a preservice teacher, you should find the experience factor in Table 2.1 particularly interesting. Since 1990, enrollments in public and private elementary and secondary schools have increased by more than 14%, creating an increasingly growing demand for teachers to educate these children (National Center for Education Statistics, 2002). Yet roughly one-third of teachers in our schools today have 20 or more years of experience in the classroom (U.S. Department of Education, 2003), a great many of whom will be retiring in the coming decade.

CHANGES IN THE TEACHER WORKFORCE

The field of K–12 education has long been female dominated, with women representing 65–75% of the teaching positions in both public and private schools. This could change, however, as the teaching population in schools is expected to overturn considerably from 2000 to 2010 as the "baby boomers" of the late 1940s through the early 1960s approach retirement age. They chose teaching as a profession for more than three decades, many of them staying in the same classrooms and schools providing leadership and consistency to the schools and school districts. Polls project that at least 2 million new teachers will be needed to fill the void of these retiring teachers and to meet the demands of a growing school population. A number of states and individual districts around the country report a particular concern as migration and immigration patterns leave some schools bursting at the seams. Florida's Broward County school system, for example, expects to need 13,000 new teachers in the next 10 years to meet the needs of their growing population, currently the fifth-largest district in the country (Goddard, 2005). Unlike 40 years ago, today there are many job options for both men and women, making teaching less of a "fallback" option for women than it was years ago. According to the National Center for Education Statistics, 16% of public schoolteachers and 23% of private schoolteachers in 1999–2000 were beginning teachers, with no detectable difference in the proportions of males and females. Of these beginning teachers, a greater proportion of Black, Asian American, and Hispanic teachers were beginning teachers, although White males and females still represented the greatest *number* of new teachers (U.S. Department of Education, 2003). Look around your classroom at your own demographics for those entering teaching. You and your classmates, whether following a traditional undergraduate career path or making a career change, are the current teacher candidates who will be filling the void left by the retiring teachers. How many are women? How many are men? How many men want to teach at the elementary level? Do you know any older individuals who are entering the profession?

WHY TEACHERS CHOOSE TEACHING

When asked why they chose teaching as a career, prospective teachers often say, "I want to work with young people." Some elementary and early childhood teachers respond by

TABLE **2.1**

Distributions of Full-Time Public and Private Schoolteachers According to Years of Teaching Experience: 1999–2000

TEACHER CHARACTERISTIC	NUMBER OF TEACHERS	AVERAGE EXPERIENCE (IN YEARS)	5 OR FEWER YEARS			MORE THAN 5 YEARS			
			3 OR FEWER YEARS	4–5 YEARS	TOTAL	6–9 YEARS	10–19 YEARS	20 OR MORE YEARS	TOTAL
PUBLIC SCHOOLTEACHERS									
Total	2,742,000	14.8	16.0	9.1	25.0	14.1	25.6	35.3	75.0
Sex									
Male	700,000	15.3	16.7	9.3	26.0	14.0	21.7	38.3	74.0
Female	2,042,000	14.6	15.7	9.0	24.7	14.2	26.9	34.2	75.3
Race/ethnicity[1]									
American Indian	23,000	14.2	17.8	6.1	23.9	13.9	32.2	30.0	76.1
Asian/Pacific Islander	44,000	12.1	21.6	13.9	35.5	16.3	22.9	25.2	64.5
Black	214,000	14.6	18.9	10.3	29.2	12.8	21.9	36.1	70.8
White	2,303,000	15.1	14.9	8.7	23.6	13.9	26.1	36.3	76.4
Hispanic	157,000	11.0	26.0	11.8	37.8	18.2	22.3	21.7	62.2
Have master's degree									
Yes	1,248,000	18.0	6.3	5.5	11.8	12.6	28.4	47.1	88.2
No	1,443,000	12.0	24.2	12.2	36.4	15.4	23.0	25.2	63.6
PRIVATE SCHOOLTEACHERS									
Total	366,000	12.4	22.7	9.7	32.4	15.7	28.1	23.8	67.6
Sex									
Male	86,000	13.1	23.6	9.7	33.3	15.8	23.8	27.1	66.7
Female	280,000	12.2	22.4	9.8	32.1	15.7	29.4	22.8	67.9
Race/ethnicity[1]									
American Indian	2,000	13.7	20.1!	2.8!	22.9!	18.0!	34.4!	24.6!	77.1
Asian/Pacific Islander	6,000	11.5	27.6	9.1!	36.8	18.9	23.2	21.1	63.2
Black	14,000	10.1	32.1	15.9	47.9	9.8!	27.3	14.9	52.1
White	327,000	12.7	21.8	9.4	31.2	15.9	28.0	24.9	68.8
Hispanic	17,000	9.3	30.5	13.2	43.7	15.6	30.8	9.9	56.3
Have master's degree									
Yes	120,000	16.0	11.9	7.5	19.4	13.3	31.4	35.9	80.6
No	219,000	10.9	27.1	10.3	37.5	16.8	27.2	18.6	62.5

[1]American Indian includes Alaska Native, Black includes African American, Pacific Islander includes Native Hawaiian, and Hispanic includes Latino. Race categories exclude Hispanic origin unless specified.
Note: ! Interpret data with caution (estimates are unstable). Detail may not sum to totals because of rounding.
Source: National Center for Educational Statistics, *The Condition of Education 2003* (Table 29.1). (Washington, D.C.: U.S. Department of Education, 2003).

EDUCATION MATTERS

The "Guy" Teacher

"You could be doing more manly things, you could be making more money, gaining glory, for heaven's sake you could be a boss! So why are you going to be a teacher?"

These types of comments made to young men who are thinking about becoming teachers can discourage them from entering the profession. *NEA Today,* the National Education Association members' magazine, describes teaching as an underrated career option for males because these types of comments contribute to the low numbers of male teachers. Just 25% of America's 3 million teachers are men, and most of these men are teaching in middle or high schools. NEA figures indicate that a scant 9% of teachers in elementary schools are men, down from 14% in 1986. Minority male teachers are even fewer in number (*NEA Today,* 2003).

Men can be healthy role models for boys and girls in elementary school and preschool as well as effective authority figures in middle and high school. Men bring a different perspective to a school culture and a worldview that might enhance a child's educational experience. A great deal of anecdotal evidence suggests that a diverse educational experience helps children become more well-rounded and better prepared (*NEA Today,* 2003). So why aren't more men in teaching?

When interviewed, men suggested that money is a factor in choosing other professions. They also indicated that power and prestige don't come with teaching, although it costs a significant amount of money to go to college to prepare to teach.

The Education Issue: Attracting more men into teaching

What's Your Opinion?
Calculate the percentage of students in your class who are male and going into the profession. Compare this to the number of male teachers you had in elementary, middle, and high school. How can education schools recruit and support male teachers? Should school districts make it easier for men to become teachers? Should men be paid higher salaries as an incentive for them to consider teaching?

saying, "I love kids." Their secondary counterparts might say, "I love my content area [history, English, science] and want to pass along that love to students." Many teachers in classrooms explain that "I have always wanted to be a teacher and can't remember when I made the decision." The overwhelming answer is that teachers want to make a difference in the lives of students.

How do these motivations relate to you and your classmates? Are you thinking about teaching as a lifelong career because, like many teachers, you made the decision a long time ago, or are you exploring the possibility of teaching? In *A Sense of Calling: Who Teaches and Why,* Farkas, Johnson, and Foleno (2000) report the feelings of new teachers on a number of issues in education, based on a study of 664 public schoolteachers and 250 private schoolteachers, all having taught for 5 years. The report concludes that "most new teachers are highly motivated professionals who bring a strong sense of commitment and high morale to their work" (p. 36). The participants noted that teachers need to be enthusiastic and share a sense of commitment to do the job. Nearly all the new teachers (96%) stated that teaching is the work they love to do, and four out of five stated that they would choose teaching again if they were starting over. (See Table 2.2.)

Teachers in today's classrooms have chosen to teach for a variety of reasons. Some may have always known they wanted to teach, while others may have thought they would just try it for a few years, and ended up loving the students and stayed to make it their career. Events of the times always influence people's choices. For example, if you ask a veteran female teacher who chose this profession decades ago and is now preparing for retirement why she chose to teach, she might say, "At that time, options for women were limited. Women tended to become a teacher, a secretary, or a nurse. The benefit of teaching was that I would have summers off with my own children." A veteran male teacher, on the other hand, might respond differently, such as, "With the Vietnam War raging, I decided to go to college instead of into the service. I loved history and decided to go into teaching."

Regardless of the social influences of the times that affect people's choices, there have always been a few common reasons people cite for becoming teachers. Can you recognize your reasons for exploring becoming a teacher in this list?

- My parents are teachers and would love me to teach.

- I love math (or any subject you love) and want to get students to love it too.

- I love kids!

- I love being in charge and telling people what to do.

- I eventually want to become a principal or a college professor, and teaching is the first step.

- I don't know what else to do with my major.

- I hated school and want to make it better for students than it was for me.

- I have always wanted to be a teacher, I don't know why.

- I loved my _____-grade teacher and that is why I want to teach.

- I want to make a difference and contribute to society.

Preservice teachers are often asked at some point in their preparation to write brief essays summarizing why they chose teaching. Figure 2.1 provides an example of one

TABLE 2.2

Why Do Teachers in 2000 Teach?

REASON	%
Teaching is the work they love to do	96
They would choose teaching again if they started over	80
Teaching is a lifelong choice	75
They get a lot of satisfaction out of teaching	68
They fell into teaching by chance	12

Source: S. Farkas, J. Johnson & T. Foleno, *A Sense of Calling: Who Teaches and Why.* (New York: The Public Agenda, 2000).

FIGURE 2.1

Why I Chose Teaching

My first memories of becoming a teacher are from my elementary school years. When I was in third grade I loved and admired my teacher. She was my hero and I wanted to be just like her. As I progressed through school I built positive relationships with all of my teachers and confirmed my desire to teach in high school when I decided I loved English. I liked working in groups with my classmates and I understood what the teachers were trying to do as they motivated me to do my best work. I loved school and wanted my students to love it too.

As I entered my teacher education program this past year I knew this profession was for me. Even though I was a bit nervous about entering a classroom to observe experienced teachers in the district near the university, I was convinced this was the profession for me. I am more confident than ever that becoming an English teacher is the best decision I could ever make. I see myself teaching in an urban high school nearby with students from other cultures. I can't remember when I didn't want to be a teacher. I can picture myself with a master's degree and lots of students who want to do well. I know there will be difficult days, but I can't think of anything I would rather do.

BUILDING ON EDUCATIONAL FOUNDATIONS

Making a Difference in the Lives of Students

Being able to reach out and make a difference in the lives of students is an important reason why people become teachers. Many teachers see themselves as shaping and molding students through their own personalities and the strength of their ideas. As the American historian Henry Adams explained more than a hundred years ago, a "politician may shape a moment, but a teacher affects eternity."

This idea of the teacher as a "maker" of men and women is described by the journalist and political analyst Theodore H. White. In his book *In Search of History: A Personal Adventure*, White (1980), describes a teacher and the impact she had on him in elementary school in the following way:

How can I say what a ten-year-old boy remembers of a schoolteacher lost in time? She was stout, grey-haired, dimpled,

schoolmarmish, almost never angry. She was probably the first Protestant I ever met; she taught history vigorously; and she was special, the first person who made me think I might make something of myself. She was the kind of teacher who could set fire to the imagination of the ordinary children who sat in lumps before her, and to do so was probably the chief reward she sought. (Lass & Tasman, 1980, pp. 255–256)

Of course, if you set out to shape and mold your students, you will have to ask yourself the question, "To what end?" Should teachers shape and mold children? Should they try to inspire them? Are teachers responsible for what their students become? What role do you want to play in the lives of your students as a result of your teaching?

---

student's response. What will your essay say? Why do you want to teach? In your Touch the Future journal, write your top three reasons for becoming a teacher from the preceding list. If none of your reasons are included here, add your own.

Teachers' motivations in two professional surveys in 1964 and in 1984 remain surprisingly constant: the desire to reach out to a student or a group of students and know that they had learned (Kottkamp et al., 1986). Intrinsic rewards, such as touching the future through student learning, and extrinsic rewards are two ways in which teachers are rewarded for their work.

● **Intrinsic Rewards**   **Intrinsic rewards,** the internal reasons that keep people in teaching, often are cited by teachers as the most important reasons why they stay in the profession. These may include the smiling face of a student who has just learned how to read; a raised hand of a student who has never before spoken in class; a well-written paper from a student who could become a real leader; a student's poem that touches your heart; or a piece of original music played by a gifted student. These accomplishments make teachers feel that they are making a difference, that they are witnessing something special.

In her book *What Keeps Teachers Going?*, Sonia Nieto (2003) expresses the views of teachers working to make a difference in the lives of students and families by starting out with her own observations:

From that day in 1965 when I first stepped into a fourth grade classroom where I would start my student teaching, I have experienced the exhilaration, anguish, satisfaction, uncertainty, frustration, and sheer joy that typify teaching. Years later, when I began teaching teachers, I fell in love with the profession all over again. Working with teachers who would in turn prepare young people for the future seemed to me a life worth living. (p. 9)

In the book Nieto makes the following observations:

- Teachers who stay are committed to thinking about teaching as an intellectual activity.

- Teaching is about democracy and how to realize its ideals in classrooms.

- Teaching involves love and respect for students and colleagues.

- Autobiography is part of teaching because teachers come with their own history.

Is the light in students' eyes a reflection of the light in our eyes, or is it just the opposite? "So, despite everything in our way, why do some of us end up staying? Is it because our lives continue to be changed forever, for the better, by our students?" (Nieto, 2003, pp. 118–119).

Often, **career-change teachers,** adults who leave other careers to become teachers, seek the intrinsic rewards of teaching. They cite a lack of job satisfaction and the need to feel that they are making a difference as the primary motivation for changing jobs mid-career, regardless of pay.

In his book *Schoolteacher,* Dan Lortie (1975) states that the achievements of former students that brought pride to respondents included admission to prestigious colleges, awards for academic excellence, success in college, high-quality job performance, and attainment of professional status. "Ordinarily, I get the greatest satisfaction from the people who come back after they've gone to college and they say they didn't realize how much the teaching could help them . . . that's the pleasing thing. . . . This year I had the pleasure of seeing two of my students receive awards for outstanding citizenship and academic achievement. . . . Of course you have some who are outstanding in less academic fields and who also come back to you . . . at least they remember you and it gives me satisfaction to know I am remembered . . . since we all have an ego, we like to feel that they are carrying part of our teaching with them, if not in subject matter, perhaps in being a guide to their life" (Lortie, 1975, p. 58).

The comments suggest that students' success indicates the teachers' success! Because teachers do not often get to see how their successful students contribute to society, these small but important interactions with previous students bring great joy to teachers who are still teaching. (Have you written that teacher who made a difference in your life?)

The daily work of teaching and the interaction with other teachers in a cooperative environment also can be its own reward. Teachers get to know each other very well as a result of the collaborative nature of the job. Most teachers who love the profession "talk shop" with each other and enjoy sharing ideas, lesson plans, strategies, and stories. In *Teachers at Work,* educator Susan Moore Johnson (1990) explores the lives of teachers and the challenges they face in classrooms and schools. What *is* the workplace for a teacher? Johnson identifies six broad categories that define the workplace for a teacher:

- The *physical structure* of the school—the space, the windows, the relationship of the classrooms to other teachers' rooms, and the workspace—is important to the daily lives of teachers. Those with their own spacious, well-lit classrooms or with doors that exit directly to the outside of the school often enjoy a sense of autonomy in decision making.

- The *organizational structure* of a teacher's work includes the teaching load (how many classes a teacher teaches), the number of students in each class, and the flexibility of the work day. Teachers often cite these factors first when describing their level of satisfaction with their work. Many schools are creating opportunities for teachers to collaborate and connect during the school day, to cross content areas, and to create innovative ways to work with each other.

- The *sociological relationships* among adults in the school, including administrators and other support personnel as well as interactions with parents, creates a school culture.

- *Political influence* from school boards and state agencies affects decisions for textbooks or supplies, which make a difference in how a teacher's day is carried out.

- *Economic conditions* govern salaries and benefits for teachers, how teachers will be rewarded for their work, and decisions about the allocation of resources that might help teachers complete their jobs effectively.

- *Psychological dimensions* of their work allow teachers to measure their personal success and opportunity for growth.

The workplace for teachers is more than a school building; it is the context of the work itself and how it is valued personally and by others in the school and district. Teachers working in a positive school culture make friends with others who work within the school and create an environment that is nurturing and supportive. Teachers who stay know that teaching is much more than a job—it is a personal connection to others.

● **Extrinsic Rewards**   The most obvious **extrinsic reward** is a teacher's salary. Yet teachers' salaries have long been an issue of contention among educators, community members, and administrators. Historically, teachers' salaries have been low when compared with other professions requiring college degrees, which has affected both recruitment and perception of the profession. Many teachers hold advanced degrees or continue to attend academic workshops in an effort to stay up to date with the field, yet they tend to be seen as public servants, a distinction our society generally doesn't reward well monetarily, no matter its importance. Some people interpret this as a message that the public doesn't value teachers as highly as higher-paying professions, such as lawyers, or doctors, or accountants.

As you see in Table 2.3, salaries for teachers vary across the country. Salaries vary within states as well, based on local contract negotiations and the tax bases of each community. A criticism of economic policy is that education programs in urban areas and poor rural communities are generally underfunded and have difficulty attracting teachers due to less attractive working conditions, fewer resources, and possibly lower salaries. Suburban communities, on the other hand, generally have higher tax bases and therefore can support schools better financially, including offering more attractive salaries. A solution to attracting more qualified teachers to poorer communities would be to pay them higher salaries. However, finding the revenue and deciding where best to allocate the money is a great challenge. For example, many urban public school districts pay fairly well, but the

Watching your students succeed is one of the most satisfying intrinsic rewards. Your students' success is your success as well.

TABLE 2.3

Teacher Salaries

SALARY	BEGINNING TEACHER SALARY	AVERAGE TEACHER SALARY	SALARY	BEGINNING TEACHER SALARY	AVERAGE TEACHER SALARY
Alabama	$29,938	$37,194	Montana	$22,344	$34,379
Alaska	$36,294	$49,418	Nebraska	$26,010	$36,236
Arizona	$27,648	$39,973	Nevada	$28,734	$40,764
Arkansas	$27,565	$36,962	New Hampshire	$25,611	$40,002
California	$34,180	$54,348	New Jersey	$35,311	$53,192
Colorado	$28,001	$40,659	New Mexico	$27,579	$36,440
Connecticut	$34,551	$53,551	New York	$34,577	$52,000
Delaware	$32,868	$48,363	North Carolina	$29,359	$42,680
District of Columbia	$31,982	$47,049	North Dakota	$20,988	$32,253
Florida	$30,096	$39,275	Ohio	$29,953	$44,029
Georgia	$32,283	$44,073	Oklahoma	$27,547	$34,744
Hawaii	$31,340	$42,615	Oregon	$31,026	$46,081
Idaho	$25,316	$39,591	Pennsylvania	$31,866	$50,599
Illinois	$31,761	$49,435	Rhode Island	$30,272	$49,758
Indiana	$28,440	$44,195	South Carolina	$27,268	$39,923
Iowa	$27,553	$38,230	South Dakota	$23,938	$31,295
Kansas	$26,596	$37,093	Tennessee	$28,857	$38,515
Kentucky	$26,813	$37,951	Texas	$30,938	$39,232
Louisiana	$28,229	$36,328	Utah	$26,806	$38,420
Maine	$24,054	$37,300	Vermont	$25,229	$39,158
Maryland	$31,828	$48,251	Virginia	$31,238	$41,731
Massachusetts	$32,746	$50,293	Washington	$28,348	$43,464
Michigan	$32,649	$52,428	West Virginia	$25,633	$36,751
Minnesota	$29,998	$42,194	Wisconsin	$27,397	$42,232
Mississippi	$24,567	$33,295	Wyoming	$26,773	$37,853
Missouri	$27,554	$37,996			

Source: K. Loschert, "J is for Job." *NEA Today 22* (2004, March): 23–29. Retrieved April 20, 2005, from http://www.nea.org/neatoday/0403/cover.html

facilities and resources may be substandard, or the average class size may be large, or the school may be in a rough neighborhood. Potential teachers have to weigh all the factors when deciding whether to take the position.

Does the variation in salaries across school districts mean the work of teachers is perceived differently in different districts or parts of the country? No. The same requirements and expectations apply to all teachers throughout each state, but the local economy plays a significant role in setting salaries. As a result, the varying salary structures can affect teacher attraction and retention. States and districts with lower salary scales often have difficulty attracting or retaining teachers. How do you think teachers in neighboring districts feel when one group is paid more highly than the other? What do you notice about the states or districts that offer higher teacher salaries? Where are the poorly paid teachers working? Why is this so?

Since salaries for yearly teaching contracts vary widely across states and even within states, extrinsic rewards for public schoolteachers often include other forms of benefits, such as excellent health care, professional and financial rewards for taking courses and being lifelong learners, and stable retirement salaries. Early retirement plans may allow them to retire at a younger age and with fewer years in the profession than in other careers. While salaries may increase slowly over the working life of a teacher, the retirement benefits may allow teachers to maintain a similar lifestyle in retirement. Such benefits are highly valued and often not offered in small businesses because of their high cost.

A relatively recent trend is that of awarding **merit pay,** something seen more commonly in the corporate world. Merit pay is a controversial practice of paying teachers bonuses for reaching preset points of excellence. On paper this looks like a really good idea. Why not get paid more for working more hours, trying new curriculum, and bringing fresh ideas to the classroom? The controversy, however, is over how excellence is determined. Will test scores of students drive the decision? What will you do if you have students who need extra help but could lower your merit score? Will the principal's evaluation alone drive the decision? What if the principal doesn't like certain teachers? For these reasons, teacher unions historically have opposed strict merit pay.

One of the most consistent rewards cited by teachers, however, is the schedule. Days start early, and although the work of checking homework and planning lessons certainly continues once students are gone for the day, a teacher's schedule follows that of the school year. When students are out for a holiday, most often the teachers are as well. When school is out for the summer, that time off applies to most teachers as well. For teachers who are also parents, having a schedule that parallels the ebb and flow of their children's schedules is priceless. Critics use the "summers off" concept to highlight what they call the "less demanding" schedule of schools as compared to year-round business schedules. The truth is, however, that many teachers work other jobs in the summer or enroll in graduate professional development classes to improve their skills and stay current with changes in the field. Still the schedule is an extrinsic benefit, and for many teachers, the breaks during the school year and summer schedule offset the reduced pay.

Teachers also realize some degree of job security after a few years in the classroom due to the contracts negotiated with school districts by the local and state teachers' union. Tenure or professional status, as it is called in some states, can provide some security even in the midst of budget crises. As a result of these agreements, when budget crises do affect local or state budgets, a careful process must be followed for reducing the number of teachers in the schools or for identifying who may be let go. Using seniority or other agreed-on rules negotiated between the district and the teachers' union can ensure that a process is followed and no individual teacher will be dismissed without due process. Critics argue that this process only serves to protect ineffective teachers and makes it difficult to keep potentially excellent beginning teachers, but teachers generally appreciate the job protection and security. What do you think would happen to the profession if this were not one of the rewards?

Have you talked with teachers in the field today? Do you have relatives who are teachers? What do they like best about this work? What do they find most challenging? Many factors have influenced your decision to be in this course and you may not actually know why you want to teach at this point. However, by the end of this book and this course, you should have a clearer picture.

THE ROLE OF THE TEACHER IN STUDENT LEARNING

Teachers have an opportunity to improve the quality of their students' lives through education. In their roles as teachers, they have the power to create a community of learners within their own classroom every day. In order to effectively provide optimal learning experiences for all students, teachers must be healthy, active professionals. This means teachers work best in their role of enhancing student learning when they are qualified, satisfied professionals.

Roland Barth (1990) describes the importance of keeping teachers inspired this way:

> It is interesting, in this context, to consider the common instructions given by flight attendants to airline passengers: 'For those of you traveling with small children, in the

event of an oxygen failure, first place the oxygen mask on your face and then—and only then—place the mask on your child's face.' The fact of the matter is, of course, that the adult must be alive and breathing freely in order to help the child. (p. 49)

Teachers need support and encouragement to breathe in new ideas of professional development and be included as part of the community of learners in a school. When a school supports teacher learning and creativity, a learning community emerges for teachers who in turn provide a learning community for their students.

● **Building Relationships to Enhance Student Learning**   How well you, in your role as a teacher, can interact and create positive relationships with other adults in the school will make a difference in how you can influence your own students' learning. When teachers get along with their colleagues, there is usually a harmony in the school that affects students. Teachers who can use other teachers as resources feel less isolated and share more. This can affect the success of students and makes teaching more fun. Good relationships with the parents can also improve success rates, because the information you may gain will give you insights about your students. Think about how well you build trusting relationships and see what may apply here for you as you prepare to become a teacher.

Trusting Colleagues   As you enter a school, as a student teacher or a first-year teacher, you will quickly observe how teachers interact. Some teachers may shut the door and "do their own thing" while others may be outgoing and willing to share ideas with each other. As a beginner you may not feel confident enough to actually share your ideas publicly, but you should not be shy if a teacher asks you to demonstrate something you have learned at the university. Many teachers express the need for new ideas and look forward to interactions with student teachers and new teachers for this very reason.

Trust may mean different things to different teachers, but it is a key quality in gaining respect from each other. Talking in the teachers' lounge about students, their parents, or other teachers is unprofessional and quickly sends a message about who can or cannot be trusted. Confidentiality implies trust, but some teachers also may define trust as being reliable, being open to hearing information, or being a good listener who values what is said (Gimbel, 2003). When you are working with a variety of personalities it will be important for you to discover what trust means in your school. Your relationship to your principal and the principal's relationship to the entire staff will affect the levels of trust.

Bryk and Schneider (2002) identified the four key elements of trust in schools as respect, competence, integrity, and personal regard for others. They concluded that people in a school community are involved in one another's lives, and sometimes they forget about the importance of the way they interrelate with one another and how that makes a difference in the way learning takes place (Bryk & Schneider, 2002; Gerwitz, 2002). Schools where teachers reported a high level of trust between themselves and principals and among the teaching staff also had higher test scores. (See Figure 2.2. on page 40.) Throughout a school year students interact with other teachers from grade to grade or subject to subject, as well as numerous other adults who play important roles in school. (See Table 2.4 on page 41.) As a teacher you will be effective if you can learn how your students interact with other teachers and school personnel. Gather information, talk with other teachers, and use the data to enhance your students' learning. Trusting other adults in the school is an important quality teachers need as they explore many ways to improve the quality of instruction and student learning.

Trusting Parents   Parents are an asset to any teacher. By working closely with parents a teacher can understand the student and in turn provide the best educational strategies possible. Parents may have had difficult experiences in school and may not feel comfortable visiting on open house dates or other public events, but most parents have the best interests of their children in mind.

When you become a teacher it is important to build a trusting relationship with the parents of your students. You may need to think of new ways to connect with them or talk

INTASC

Principle #10

Partnerships: The teacher fosters relationships with school colleagues, parents, and agencies in the larger community to support students' learning and well-being.

FIGURE **2.2**

Trust and Student Achievement

This chart shows that in schools where teachers reported a high level of trust between themselves and principals and among the teaching staff, test scores were higher.

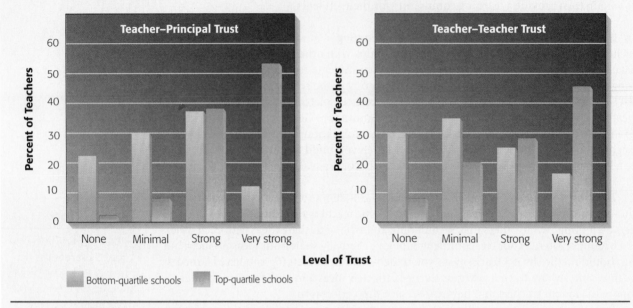

Source: C. Gerwitz, "Trust and Student Achievement," *Education Week.* (2002) Retrieved October 16, 2002, from http://edweek.org/ew/articles/2002/10/16/07trust-sl.h22.html.

with other teachers in the building who have successful parent contacts. Trust is built when the parents know that you have their children's best interest in mind. You will likely have students in your class with cultural backgrounds different from your own. To build trust with your students' parents, it will be important that you make an effort to understand their cultural norms and identify their norms for trust.

● **Teacher Satisfaction and Student Learning**   Teachers are most satisfied with their work and careers when they know their students have learned. Sergiovanni and Starratt (2002) point out that teacher job satisfaction and the conditions that produce it are linked directly to improvements in student achievement. The role of the teacher in a school or district and the way the teacher chose the career sets the tone in a community of learners. Building a professional culture in schools is the work of all teachers and administrators (Lieberman, 1998). If the teachers in a school are supported by an engaged administrator and if they are satisfied with their own teaching and their students' learning, this school will most likely have positive energy and vitality. When interviewing teachers during the course of your training, find out what satisfies them in their work. Remember that there will be positive and negative responses to your questions, but all responses will help you broaden your understanding of the characteristics of the field and of individual environments that make for a productive learning environment.

Teachers who enter the profession and prepare to become teachers progress through a **developmental continuum,** as shown in Figure 2.3 on page 42. In *Life Cycle of a Career Teacher,* Steffy, Wolfe, Pasch, and Enz (2000) divide a teacher's development into three life cycle phases: novice, apprentice, and professional. Beginning teachers learn their craft in

TABLE 2.4

School Personnel

ROLE	BASIC RESPONSIBILITY	EXAMPLES OF WORK
Classroom teachers	Instructional practice for numbers of students. Teachers Pre-K–12 in a school district organize and teach curriculum to classrooms of students.	Teaching a lesson, taking students on field trips, correcting papers, attending meetings, setting up classrooms, designing curriculum, assessing and communicating student progress.
Special-area teachers	Music, art, physical education, technology, and so on. *Note:* Foreign language teachers may be either classroom teachers or special-area teachers, depending on the district.	Teaching students hands-on approaches for all students as an additional part of the day. This teacher "taking over the class" often creates a time slot that is free for the classroom teacher to prepare lessons and correct papers during the school day.
Specialist teachers	Bilingual teachers, occupational therapists, physical therapists, speech pathologists, interpreters for the deaf, vision teachers, and so on.	Working with identified students in a school or district.
Special education teachers	Typically for underachieving students, but in some districts they are also responsible for "gifted and talented" special students. This may include Chapter I or Title I teachers who are funded by the U.S. Dept. of Education.	Working with classroom teachers, parents, and district administrators to create plans for success or to extend achievement with students who have identified learning or behavioral disabilities or gifted skills.
Support personnel	Nurse, school guidance counselor, adjustment counselor.	Counseling students and supporting their health and well-being.
Administrators	Superintendent, principals, assistant principals, headmasters, directors, and so on.	Providing instructional and social leadership for the district and school.
Educational support personnel	Classroom aides, secretaries, custodians, cafeteria workers, paraprofessionals, DARE officers, security police officer, truant officers, school bus drivers, crossing guards.	Supporting the daily operations of the school; getting students to and from school as well as feeding and supporting them as needed.

Source: C. M. Pelletier, *A Handbook of Techniques and Strategies for Coaching Student Teachers,* 2nd ed., p. 118. (Boston: Allyn and Bacon, 2004). Copyright © 2004 by Pearson Education. Reprinted by permission of the publisher.

their beginning years and then have options to advance their learning and enhance their practice through **professional development.** To stay current and energized requires that teachers participate in continuing education efforts such as district workshops and coursework at or sponsored by colleges and universities. Many teachers work toward advanced degrees in the field. These opportunities bring groups of teachers together to learn new skills, share ideas, and reflect on their own practice. Professional conversations and sharing offers teachers an environment for growth and self-discovery.

With the teacher shortage and impending early retirements, there will be a shift in the number of teachers in the later phases of development. For the past decade most teachers were at the professional and expert phases or beyond, with very few novice and apprentice teachers in the school. This demographic will change considerably in the next decade. The impact of this change means that there will be fewer expert teachers to mentor and guide novices.

How will this affect you? As a beginning teacher you may expect to be mentored in a small group as opposed to the one-to-one mentoring that was done in previous years when more veteran teachers were available to mentor. Because you will be with other novice teachers, you will have an opportunity to share ideas, learn together, and collaborate to enhance your skills. Being aware of your new teacher status and understanding that you are not alone will provide you with a source of strength.

INTASC

Principle #9

Professional Commitment and Responsibility: The teacher is a reflective practitioner who continually evaluates the effects of his/her choices and actions on others (students, parents, and other professionals in the learning community) and who actively seeks out opportunities to grow professionally.

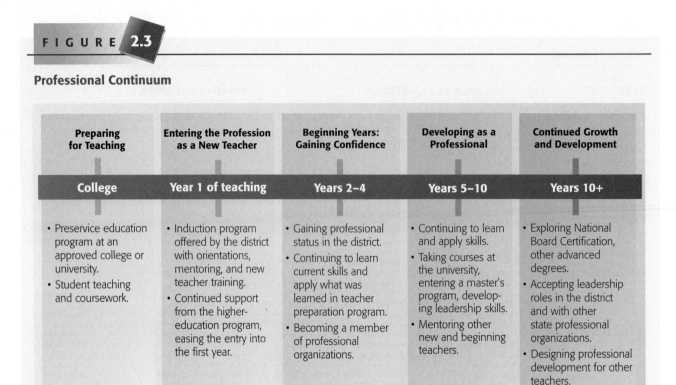

FIGURE 2.3

Professional Continuum

Preparing for Teaching	Entering the Profession as a New Teacher	Beginning Years: Gaining Confidence	Developing as a Professional	Continued Growth and Development
College	**Year 1 of teaching**	**Years 2–4**	**Years 5–10**	**Years 10+**
• Preservice education program at an approved college or university. • Student teaching and coursework.	• Induction program offered by the district with orientations, mentoring, and new teacher training. • Continued support from the higher-education program, easing the entry into the first year.	• Gaining professional status in the district. • Continuing to learn current skills and apply what was learned in teacher preparation program. • Becoming a member of professional organizations.	• Continuing to learn and apply skills. • Taking courses at the university, entering a master's program, developing leadership skills. • Mentoring other new and beginning teachers.	• Exploring National Board Certification, other advanced degrees. • Accepting leadership roles in the district and with other state professional organizations. • Designing professional development for other teachers.

WHAT IS AN EFFECTIVE TEACHER?

Everyone has an opinion about teachers and schools. Often those opinions are shaped by individuals' own experiences. One bad experience with a teacher can sour the rest of a person's school days. On the other hand, students who did well in school and who had good relationships with their teachers may see teachers, and school in general, in a more positive light—perhaps even as friends. Great teachers are defined in many ways. National reports, public opinion, educational researchers, and parents all identify what they think makes a "great" teacher. **Effective teachers,** those who reach students and make a difference in their lives, mean different things to different people. The points of view and experiences of those who assess teacher qualities influence how effective teachers are described. Who determines what an effective teacher is and how do they know? Defining effectiveness is a complicated task, and it depends on whom you ask.

PUBLIC OPINION

Teaching is among the oldest of all professions. There are records of teachers in the ancient Sumerian city of Erech dating back to 3000 B.C. (Kramer, 1989). While technologies and curricular content have changed profoundly over time, the actual art of teaching has remained fairly consistent. Teachers work with groups of students to provide knowledge and to facilitate thinking. As trends in education have changed, so has a teacher's role. There have been times historically when a teacher's role was strictly to recite facts as the students learned by rote, and other times when the students explored on their own and the teacher's role was to help with that exploration. Today teachers incorporate many strategies and theories in order to find the best approaches to learning for each individual. Expectations of what teachers should do at work and how they should do it are shaped by state and national initiatives.

How a teacher's work and worth are defined is based on the status society has chosen to impart on the profession. Consider the status of a dentist, a lawyer, an assembly worker, and a custodian. How would society rate a teacher in this list? Society has expectations of what teachers should be doing for their work. Some teachers often feel that they are expected to "do it all." Be the parent, the psychologist, the academic coach, and the friend to students. The public, and parents in particular, usually regard teachers with high esteem. As noted in Table 1.1, 84% of Americans voted teachers as the most trusted group of people in the country. Public perception is important to the work of teachers because voters on local, state, and national levels control the issues that affect teachers' salaries and the resources that are used to supply schools with teaching supplies, computers, and other materials. Figure 2.4 on page 44 contains a Professional Development IQ Test constructed by the National Staff Development Council (NSDC) from a collection of national surveys and polls. The figure identifies general attitudes of the public, teachers, parents, and students about teachers and education. You can take a closer look at each of these items online at www.nsdc.org/library/publications/tools/tools8-03pdiq.cfm. Can you think of other ways public opinion is important to teachers and their work?

Even though public perception is generally overwhelmingly positive, popular myths affect the perception of teachers and their work. The National Commission Report (Darling-Hammond, 1996) reminds us that it is time to confront these perennial myths so educators can focus on more productive discussions related to the education of students. Unfortunately, the myths live on in spite of all the efforts to provide evidence to the contrary. Some common myths are as follows:

Myth: Anyone can teach.

Response: The old saying, "Those who can, do; those who can't, teach" and the comment, "Teachers are born, not made" reflect an attitude that cannot be ignored. Parents will be the first to tell you the value of the education of their children! Children represent the future of the world, and each day teachers hold that future in their trust. This myth is dangerous in the hands of policymakers. The truth is, teaching is a difficult and challenging career, and those who want to touch the future, *teach!*

Myth: Formal teacher preparation is not much use.

Response: This myth is largely based on many teachers' experiences in their own preparation programs more than 20 years ago. It also implies that teaching is best learned on the job. A large body of evidence exists to contradict both of these ideas, yet they live on. Even with the shortcomings of any teacher preparation program, 30 years of research has shown that fully prepared teachers are more highly rated and more effective.

Myth: Teachers Don't Work Hard Enough

Response: "How hard can it be to work 180 days?" This comment from skeptics and cynics arises often, along with, "Don't most teachers have half the afternoon off too?" and "If teachers' salaries are that much lower, isn't it because they don't work as hard as other professionals?" The truth is that teachers work up to 50–55 hours per week and many days over vacation (National Education Association, 1990–1991). Teachers in overseas schools report that they could not succeed in the conditions under which American teachers work. Because American teachers have little time during the school day to plan lessons, talk with parents, meet individually with students, consult with one another, and assess progress, they often work late into the evening and in the summers.

This last misconception is largely based on the fact that teachers don't work in the summer. When school is in session, however, teachers are involved in their work about 25–30% more than workers in many other fields. Teachers' hours often include between 10 and 15 hours of uncompensated duties such as grading papers, preparing for lessons on their own time, and attending school functions (Waid & McNergeny, 2003). The average number of hours a typical teacher works in a school year works out to about the same

FIGURE 2.4

Professional Development IQ Test

Correct answers are highlighted in bold.

1. According to the public, what is the most important characteristic for teachers to possess?
   a. Ability to communicate with parents
   b. Thoroughly educated in subject area
   c. Understanding how people learn
   d. Well-trained and knowledgeable about how to teach effectively

2. Which strategy does the public believe has the greatest potential for improving schools?
   a. Reducing class size
   b. Recruiting and retaining better teachers
   c. Requiring standardized tests for promotion
   d. Giving greater control to the local level

3. What percentage of the public supports school-financed professional development opportunities as a means of attracting and retaining public school teachers?
   a. 90%   c. 70%
   b. 85%   d. 55%

4. According to research, what school investment yields the greatest increase in student achievement?
   a. Lowering class size
   b. Increasing teacher salaries
   c. Increasing teacher experience
   d. Increasing teacher education

5. According to the National Credibility Index, which of the following people is the most believable when speaking out on public issues?
   a. Member of the Armed Forces
   b. Teacher
   c. Community activist
   d. National expert

6. According to research by Ron Ferguson, which factor constitutes 44% of the impact on student learning?
   a. Class size
   b. Qualifications of teacher
   c. Family involvement and support
   d. Socioeconomic status of family

7. What percentage of the public believes we should increase funding for programs to keep teachers up to date?
   a. 35%   c. 66%
   b. 50%   **d. 70%**

8. What percentage of teachers believe that professional development programs "generally waste their time"?
   a. 10.5%   c. 41.7%
   b. 27.4%   d. 64.7%

9. Which of the following strategies did superintendents and principals identify as the most effective for improving teacher quality?
   a. Reducing class size
   b. Increasing teacher salaries
   c. Increasing professional development opportunities for teachers
   d. Requiring secondary level teachers to major in the subjects they are teaching

10. According to the September 2000 Gallup Poll, what percentage of the public feels that the strategy with the most promise for improving achievement is ensuring that there is a qualified and competent teacher in every classroom?
    a. 10%   c. 39%
    b. 17%   **d. 52%**

11. Of the following, which aspect of teaching is most important to students?
    a. Caring about students
    b. Believing all children can learn
    c. Knowing the subject areas
    d. Maintaining discipline in the classroom

12. According to teachers, what is the number one reason for professional growth?
    a. To improve student achievement
    b. To improve teaching skills
    c. To network
    d. To advance one's career

average number of hours worked in other professions. In some places, the "summers off" argument doesn't even apply as more and more schools hold classes year round.

PERSONAL PERSPECTIVES

● **Beginning Teachers' Points of View**   As you prepare to become a teacher yourself, you will likely model yourself after teachers you admired when you were in school. Of course, you also may have had experiences with teachers who left negative impressions. These experiences, regardless of the tone of their impact, can help your own development as a teacher.

13. What percentage of teachers believe weekly scheduled collaboration with other teachers improves their classroom teaching?
    a. 62%
    c. 82%
    b. 72%
    d. 92%

14. What do principals believe is the most important role of a principal?
    a. Maintaining discipline and safety
    b. Creating a supportive environment for teaching and learning
    c. Supporting parents' involvement in their children's education
    d. Managing the school's budget and obtaining additional funds

15. Which strategy do principals believe is most effective for recruiting and retaining teachers?
    a. Providing financial incentives
    b. Providing mentoring and on-going support for new teachers
    c. Involving teachers in the creation of policies that they will be implementing
    d. Providing career growth opportunities

16. Which professional development activity do most teachers feel improves their teaching?
    a. New methods of teaching
    b. Integration of education technology in their grade or subject
    c. In-depth study in the subject area of their main teaching assignment
    d. Student performance assessment

17. Which of the following professional development activities did the most teachers participate in during the last 12 months?
    a. Regularly scheduled collaboration with other teachers
    b. Networking with teachers outside their school
    c. Individual or collaborative research
    d. Common planning period for team teachers

18. What percentage of public school teachers believe that being mentored formally by another teacher at least once a week improves their classroom teaching moderately or better?
    a. 58%
    c. 78%
    b. 68%
    d. 88%

19. According to the 2001 National Board of Certified Teachers Leadership Survey, what percentage agree that they are satisfied with the quantity and quality of on-going professional development opportunities in their schools?
    a. 70%
    c. 50%
    b. 60%
    d. 40%

20. According to the Educational Testing Service's 2000 Report, *How Teaching Matters,* all of the following increase student outcomes in science except:
    a. Major/minor in science/science education
    b. Professional development in laboratory skills
    c. Professional development in classroom management
    d. Using frequent tests
    e. Hands-on learning

The 2003 August/September issue of *Tools for Schools* offers more information about this test and suggestions for how to use the questions with groups.

As you prepare to become a teacher, you may be interested in reading what some student teachers have said about their favorite teachers and the characteristics that made them their favorites. How do their thoughts compare to your own impressions of teachers?

"He liked me and knew me."

"She taught me something."

Another said, "My fourth-grade teacher talked to me! I was really quiet in class and most of the time teachers just ignored me because I wasn't making trouble. This

INTASC

Principle #2

Knowledge of Human Development and Learning: The teacher understands how children learn and develop, and can provide learning opportunities that support their intellectual, social, and personal development.

teacher actually took the time to know me, to find out what I liked. I liked him for that and will try to do that in my classroom."

Others talked about content knowledge: "My favorite teacher loved her content and got me to love it because she was so enthusiastic!"

One student teacher said, "I hated physics but the teacher was so excited about it that I kept paying attention and eventually I got into it. Now I am becoming a science teacher."

Some responses were similar to this one: "The teacher who taught me the most wasn't my favorite teacher—in fact, when I was in high school I actually hated this teacher. She made me do things I didn't want to do. But now as I prepare to be a teacher I look back and see that this teacher taught me the most. So I guess I am seeing that she is my favorite in that way." We all see how favorite or memorable teachers differ in many ways, depending on the needs they met for us.

Most of us have had teachers who have really made a difference to us. In the book *Mentors, Masters, and Mrs. MacGregor,* Jane Bluestein (1995) compiled stories from various famous people who shared stories of great teachers in their lives. A few stories were from teachers who were inspired to join the profession, but most were testimonials to teachers who had stayed in each adult's life as a personal memory. Some described their teachers in personal ways, such as this description of a first-grade teacher: "The impact came from her personal touch, her personal caring, and her ability to make me feel special."

Another described his physics teacher this way: "He knew how to harness my energy and use it in a positive way."

Another person remembers her seventh-grade teacher as someone who "saw me as a person in need."

A high school Latin teacher was remembered this way: "He told me there was nothing I couldn't do."

Your perspective may match what other student teachers have said or what you have read from successful adults. It is important to note that teachers have a strong personal impact on the lives of their students. To be effective in their role, do teachers have to be remembered?

Who am I? What do I believe?

"It is impossible to teach without the courage to love, without the courage to try a thousand times before giving up."

PAULO FREIRE

THINK ABOUT THIS:
What does Freire mean when he says, "It is impossible to teach without the courage to love"? What does love have to do with teaching? Why would parents want their child's teacher to try a thousand times before giving up?

SHARE and **COMPARE:**
With your classmates, review your answers and answer the preceding question from a parent's point of view. How is it different from your personal teacher's point of view? How does the quote relate to the discussion of effective teaching?

● **Parents' Points of View**   Parents pay taxes that support the schools, and they have expectations for how teachers will interact with their children. Take this opportunity to think like a parent as you read one parent's expectations for her child's teacher. How is this parent defining effectiveness?

> When my daughter starts school, I'm hoping for a teacher who is spontaneous, someone who can follow a curriculum and yet meet the emotional and social needs of the students as well. I hope for someone who has a vivid imagination and knows how to use ordinary objects to teach valuable lessons. I want my daughter to be exposed to as many cultures and ethnic groups as possible, and I want her to be academically motivated and challenged. That will take a teacher who is sensitive to the individual needs of each student. If my daughter is slow, I want a teacher who is immediately looking into that, and if she's surpassing the class, I want her to get what she needs and progress as far as she can. I want a teacher who has conflict resolution skills, who creates discipline, but not from his or her emotions. I want a teacher who uses different methods and different ways of reaching students—who can think in innovative ways and challenge the children while teaching them academically. (Darling-Hammond, 1996, p. 82)

Parents have an investment in their children and, in turn, in the teachers who teach them. Teachers spend the entire school day with their children, and parents want teachers to influence their children's lives in positive ways. Not all parents are as involved with their children, and some may not be involved at all. Research shows that the older the child gets, the less involved the parents are with academics and with school in general. Elementary school parent nights are usually packed with parents; by high school, the only parents who show up are those whose children who are doing well.

● **Students' Points of View**   Students also have a lot to say about what they expect from teachers. Read the following quotes from students and see what they consider to be important qualities in a teacher (Bluestein, 1995). Are these students describing effective teachers? How do you hope to be described by your students?

INTASC

Principle #10

Partnerships: The teacher fosters relationships with school colleagues, parents, and agencies in the larger community to support students' learning and well-being.

Thinking like a parent helps you understand the perspective, expectations, and hopes for the future of that parent's children. Parents can be your most valuable resource in the classroom.

...doesn't give a lot of homework the last week of school. (Laura, 10, Cogan Station, PA)

...listens to everything you have to say...spends time going over things with you... stays after school to talk to you. (Steve, 12, Cherry Hill, NJ)

...can entertain while she's teaching...won't put you down for not knowing stuff. (Graeme, 15, Lethbridge, Alberta, Canada)

...can understand our music and our language...jokes around with us, even when he's teaching...plays basketball with us...can explain things a different way when we don't get it the first time...keeps explaining things until everybody gets it...lets you go ahead once you understand something. (Rasa, 14, Rochester, MI)

...lets us do projects instead of tests to show that we understand things...lets us check our own papers...talks about his family and what he did on the weekend... has discussions about different things when some people agree and some people disagree. (Aimee, 11, Rochester, MI)

...has discussion days where everybody participates so they understand what's going on...gives individualized help before or after school or during lunch so that nobody feels embarrassed about getting special attention in class. (Aaron, 15, Aurora, CO)

...won't be grouchy all the time. (Josh, 9, Anchorage, AK)

...listens to you no matter how boring you might get. (Rebecca, 11, Anchorage, AK)

...will make the students learn the lessons without the students ever knowing they are studying. (Thomas, 14, Surabaya, Indonesia)

...can take a walk in his students' shoes and truly understand how a kid might feel when put in a certain situation. (Kasia, 14, Surabaya, Indonesia)

...makes you laugh so you want to go back and see her every day of the year and you never forget her and you even give her a present for Christmas. (Summer, 13, Boise, ID)

...teaches you not only about school, but about life in general. (Colin, 13, Mishawaka, IN)

INTASC

Principle #5

Classroom Motivation and Management: The teacher uses an understanding of individual and group motivation and behavior to create a learning environment that encourages positive social interaction, active engagement in learning, and self-motivation.

Who am I? **What do I believe?**

"A really great teacher is someone who says hi to me when I come in the room."

HANNAH, 5, CHERRY HILL, NJ

THINK ABOUT THIS:
What does saying hi to a student have to do with being effective? What other behaviors do effective teachers demonstrate? What will you be sure to do with your students when you become a teacher?

SHARE and COMPARE:
List the qualities you brainstormed on the board or overhead. What are the top three for the class? Why do you think the class thinks these are so important? What will all of you do with your students?

PROFESSIONAL PERSPECTIVES

Personal perspectives about the qualities of effective teachers are important because they represent emotional reactions of individuals directly affected by a teacher's behavior and skill. But they are not the only way to determine a teacher's effectiveness, and they represent qualities that are less tangible and more difficult to measure. Professional perspectives, on the other hand, examine clearly defined qualities and skills outlined by a variety of groups that influence the work of teachers. They include professional discipline-specific organizations; national leadership and administrative groups that provide oversight to the direction of education; and professional testing services. Each seeks to define tangible qualities of effectiveness and raise the professional skills of teachers. All these professional groups are influenced by changes in trends and funding by state and federal legislators; therefore, over the years, their definitions of effectiveness adjust to the changing trends and needs of the public.

The most important influence on your teaching perspective will be your university teacher preparation program. This is where you will learn the theory and practical applications of teaching. Your program may be influenced by the mission of your college of education as well as by national standards. It begins with this course as you explore the big picture of the profession and see how you fit.

● **Teacher Education Programs**   The teacher education program in which you are enrolled establishes standards by which to prepare you to become a teacher. These standards relate to various factors deemed necessary to meet the requirements to obtain a state teaching license, including admissions policies, grade point averages for entering teaching courses, teacher tests, and student teaching requirements, to name a few. Whether you are attending a state college or a private college, the teaching license requirements will be the same, but each school may have different ways of meeting those requirements. Some programs are more rigorous because they also may align with national standards established by groups such as the National Council for Accreditation of Teacher Education (NCATE) as well as university and state guidelines.

In a national debate over the definitions of "effective, qualified teachers," former secretary of education Rod Paige's advocacy for experienced content professionals to consider teaching without a need for taking education courses met with strong disapproval by representatives of teacher education programs (Haberman, 2002). In response to Secretary Paige's reference to education courses as "fluff," one teachers' association leader said, "teaching is incredibly complex work and people who think they can walk in off the streets and teach are not fully informed about how complex it is" (Haberman, 2002).

Traditional teacher educators disagree with the movement to create too many alternate routes that create minimum requirements. Susan Moore Johnson, a professor at the Harvard Graduate School of Education, worries that to meet the highly qualified initiatives to address teacher shortages, "There is going to be a rush to stamp as certified programs that may in fact be minimal and inadequate for the expectations of today's classrooms" (Johnson & Kardos, 2002).

Teacher education institutions define effective teachers as those who have both the knowledge of content required and the pedagogy to ensure that they know how to teach America's students. Your participation in a community college or university program is preparing you how to teach beyond knowing just content knowledge in several key ways, including (1) understanding learning theories of instruction and research about human behavior; (2) identifying the attitudes, biases, stereotypes, and perspectives you bring to teaching; (3) practicing effective teaching and learning strategies; and (5) learning approaches to creating classroom climate and maintaining a safe learning environment. Your college or university may also have its own focus on urban education, technology, or working with diverse learners. Whatever the teacher education standards are, they will include more than content knowledge and they will provide you with a framework that will allow you to be an effective teacher. (You will read more about specific aspects of effective teaching in Chapter 10.)

INTASC

Principle #5

Classroom Motivation and Management: The teacher uses an understanding of individual and group motivation and behavior to create a learning environment that encourages positive social interaction, active engagement in learning, and self-motivation.

Practice develops confidence. Prepracticum and full practicum opportunities allow you to become fluent in the strategies you have learned and give you hands-on classroom experience.

The strength of a teacher preparation program is the opportunity to actually practice in classrooms. **Prepracticum** experiences that offer you opportunities to visit classrooms and observe, interview, and practice strategies you are learning give you confidence. Visits may be one day each week, once a month, or perhaps more regularly. The frequency varies with each teacher education program. **Full practicum,** or student teaching, allows you to be in a classroom for a full semester five days a week, or perhaps even for an entire school year. These practical experiences help you ease into teaching and prepare you for your first classroom.

● **Professional Organizations** The field of education has numerous professional organizations you can join that set out to help guide the profession and provide a common language for all educators. Each organization meets different needs of educators, depending on their individual goals and teaching levels. For example, the American Educational Research Association (AERA) appeals to college-level academics and researchers whose focus is more on the overall field of education. Discipline-specific organizations such as the National Council of Teachers of English (NCTE) and the International Reading Association (IRA) focus on each particular discipline and work to develop guidelines, or standards, that improve learning and instruction in their specific fields.

When you visit schools and interview teachers, ask them which professional organizations they have joined and find out about the journals or conferences they offer. What do the teachers enjoy most about being members of these groups? Refer to Appendix C and think about which groups you would like to join. Find out if any have student memberships or reduced fees for journals. Check with your instructor or at your campus library to locate copies of journals that you could read.

● **National Leadership Organizations** In an effort to establish levels of quality control for teachers throughout the country, groups such as the Council of Chief State School Officers (CCSSO) and the National Board for Professional Teaching Standards (NBPTS) have developed qualification standards for the profession. As you read in Chapter 1, the Interstate New Teacher Assessment and Support Consortium (INTASC), part of the CCSSO, has created 10 principles that identify qualities teachers need to strive for in their classrooms.

INTASC

Principle #9

Professional Commitment and Responsibility: The teacher is a reflective practitioner who continually evaluates the effects of his/her choices and actions on others (students, parents, and other professionals in the learning community) and who actively seeks out opportunities to grow professionally.

Through the Eyes of Culturally Sensitive Teachers

A Dilemma with a Teacher Candidate

Rae Shelton was a third-grade teacher at Lincoln Elementary School. She enjoyed working with the culturally and racially diverse students at Lincoln and had become very knowledgeable about the school's community in her 5 years there. She was contacted by the college of education at a local university to see if she would be willing to have an education student complete a field experience in her classroom. Rae agreed and, 2 weeks later when Jennifer Gugliotti arrived, the two sat down and worked out a schedule. Jennifer would visit Tuesday and Thursday mornings and Rae would have her work with students in small groups.

After a month, Rae noticed certain things about Jennifer that concerned her. Jennifer often was late arriving and the students in her small group would get anxious waiting for her. Rae also noticed that Jennifer seemed to be less comfortable working with certain children in the class, specifically those from poor backgrounds or children of color. After waiting for self-correction to occur, Rae decided she needed to step in.

Rae would sit down with Jennifer regularly to give her some feedback and allow Jennifer an opportunity to ask any questions. At one of these meetings, Rae told Jennifer that she was disappointed in her lack of punctuality, noted that professionals are expected to be prompt and punctual, and pointed out that she was letting down the students who were counting on Jennifer for her assistance. She then asked Jennifer how she felt about teaching some of the poorer students and children of color in her small groups. At first Jennifer hesitated to answer, but eventually she told Rae that she wondered whether her efforts in working with these students were going to be fruitful given the circumstances they came from and the obstacles in their lives. Initially Rae was shocked to hear this but realized that she had to respond in a way that would benefit Jennifer. Rae pointed out that "children do not select their home environment" and that a teacher's professional responsibility is not to judge students' backgrounds, but to do everything possible to help all students reach their individual potential. Jennifer nodded and sheepishly stated that one of her professors had mentioned this as well, but she still felt that some of her efforts with "these types of kids" would be wasted. However, she told Rae that she appreciated the feedback and would work on these things.

Indeed, for the rest of the semester, Rae noticed that Jennifer was much more punctual. But she could still sense that Jennifer wasn't totally comfortable working with all of the students. As the semester drew to a close, some of the students in Jennifer's group commented to Rae that Jennifer "doesn't like us." Rae knew that Jennifer was nearly a straight A student at the university, but it was apparent that she needed to work on her interpersonal skills.

When Rae completed the evaluation form on Jennifer that she had to submit to the university education department, she pointed out Jennifer's strengths with the technical skills of teaching but concluded her comments by saying that "Jennifer is a highly capable young woman who did not demonstrate the proper disposition to work with diverse students, whether that is defined socioeconomically or ethnically."

Points to Ponder

1. Why is it important that teachers have welcoming attitudes for *all* students? What are the consequences for students if they don't? What are the consequences for the teachers?

2. If you had been in Rae's position, what would be your greatest concern about Jennifer's interpersonal skills and their impact on young children?

3. Should the fact that Jennifer is a near-straight-A student influence Rae's evaluation of her during this field experience? Why or why not?

4. What do you think the college of education at the university should do with this feedback from Rae? What is their responsibility in this situation?

These principles can serve as a guide as you begin your teaching. As you prepare to observe and interview teachers review the INTASC principles highlighted in Figure 1.1, and try to identify how the teachers you observe incorporate these principles into their instruction. How do these principles relate to effective teaching? You will see one principle at the end of

"Wow! I had no idea aspirin came in such large bottles."

Courtesy of Aaron Bacall, *The Lighter Side of Teaching*, p. 3. Copyright 2003 by Aaron Bacall. Reprinted by permission of Corwin Press Inc.

INTASC

Principle #8

Assessment of Student Learning: The teacher understands and uses formal and informal assessment strategies to evaluate and ensure the continuous intellectual, social, and physical development of the learner.

each chapter in the Observation Guide, which will assist you in applying the words to real-life classroom situations.

The NBPTS, led by Linda Darling-Hammond after the National Commission Report was published in 1996, defines specific standards for teachers who master their skills. The five standards of the NBPTS are:

1. Teachers are committed to students and their learning.

2. Teachers know the subjects they teach and how to teach those subjects to students.

3. Teachers are responsible for managing and monitoring student learning.

4. Teachers think systematically about their practice and learn from experience.

5. Teachers are members of learning communities.

Teachers who apply for a national license complete a rigorous reflection on their own practice that includes a portfolio. These teachers have to demonstrate their classroom practice and reflection while they are teaching to achieve the status of National Board Certified Teachers. They are then recognized in their states and districts as teacher leaders and are often called on to share their expertise with beginning teachers in mentor roles or with colleagues as professional developers.

National Board Certified Teachers have demonstrated that they are effective teachers. They have documented their practice and the learning of their students. They have illustrated in many ways that they understand student learning and can reach their students.

● **State Testing Initiatives** To be a "highly qualified" teacher, according to the current education reform initiative No Child Left Behind, a teacher must complete the state certification/licensing requirements as described by the department of education in the state. Several routes may be taken to meet licenses for teachers; among them are alternatives for midcareer professionals. Most states require a written test of literacy skills as well as a content knowledge test. These tests do not usually include knowledge of how to teach or require an understanding of students because they are based on the premise that "content knowledge" is the basis of a highly qualified teacher. According to the law, new teachers must also have a bachelor's degree.

Some states have created their own tests for licensing, including California, Massachusetts, Texas, Florida, and New York. Many other states use The Praxis Series: Professional Assessments for Beginning Teachers, a set of validated assessments developed by Educational Testing Service (ETS), the developers of a number of major standardized tests including the SAT. The Praxis Series includes three categories of assessments. Praxis I: Academic Skills Assessments measures a teacher candidate's academic skills prior to entering a college or university program. It measures reading, writing, mathematics, and listening skills. Praxis II: Subject Assessments is a licensing test for candidates entering the profession that measures candidates' knowledge of the subjects they will teach, as well as pedagogical skills and knowledge. Praxis III: Classroom Performance Assessments is conducted during the first year of teaching and evaluates a beginning teacher's teaching practices. These assessments are "conducted in the classroom by local assessors who employ nationally validated criteria to observe and evaluate a teacher's performance" (Educational Testing Service, 2004). Did you need to take the Praxis I test to enter your education program?

Many perspectives are part of the current educational debate as to what contributes to creating an effective teacher. You will certainly want to have students describe you as a great teacher. You also want the word *effective* to mean that you were effective in the classroom at teaching all of your students. Think about all the perspectives in this section that contribute to the discussion of the key question, "What is an effective teacher?" and use this information to continue to clarify your beliefs.

"A really great teacher is someone who . . . can understand our music and our language."

RASA, 14, MICHIGAN

THINK ABOUT THIS:

How do good teachers teach English-language learners? Is English your second language? If so, how did teachers help you learn your academic content? If not, how will you teach students who do not speak English? How does knowing a student's culture (such as music) help a teacher connect academically with a student?

SHARE and COMPARE:

How many students in this class are English as a Second Language learners? What did effective teachers do that helped them learn? How many students in your class had teachers who knew them personally?

WHAT ARE THE CHALLENGES FOR TEACHERS IN TODAY'S CLASSROOMS?

Most teachers have chosen the profession because they want to make a difference in the lives of students. They find the intrinsic rewards enticing. It is important, however, to enter the field fully aware of the benefits and the obstacles that can challenge one's work. Seeing the bigger issues beyond the classroom will help you participate fully in discussions that will influence your daily work and help you get started on the right foot. As you read this section, think about how your awareness and knowledge of these challenges can help you become a better teacher.

EDUCATION REFORM

"The standards movement is, first and foremost, a challenge to adults because it is what they do that will determine the quality of the work the kids do."

Anthony Alvarado, 1998

With the implementation of high-stakes testing for both students and teachers, teachers today are becoming more aware of **education reform** and its impact on daily classroom practices. Education reform has existed as long as there have been academicians and politicians. When the perception exists that other nations might be advancing in certain areas faster than the United States, such as in science or commerce, political leaders immediately look for ways we can improve, and the critical eye often focuses on education. For example, when the Soviet Union launched the *Sputnik* satellite ahead of the United States in the 1950s, political leaders cried out that U.S. schools were failing in the sciences, and efforts to improve in the sciences were promoted immediately. The good news about all this "tendency" is that people recognize that change and improvement begins with educating young people. The bad news, however, is that education is always scrutinized closely and rarely escapes the draft of the ever-changing political winds.

The recent current of reform at the federal level began in 1981 when the secretary of education created a National Commission on Excellence in Education. Their report, *A Nation at Risk,* published in 1983, examined the United States' position in the international marketplace, specifically jobs and competition from abroad, and called for widespread and systematic reform. "Better schools mean better jobs," was the cry. The nation's governors continued the call to improve schools and teachers' work by developing a set of six National Education Goals and insisting that they be achieved by 2000. Having the goals identified was the first step in the process of implementing education reform in the schools. Classroom teachers, however, had not been part of the original discussions to change schools, nor were they part of the governors' rationale for improving schools. Needless to say, the goals were not met in 2000, which led to further studies and the publication of yet another report.

What Matters Most: Teaching for America's Future, published by the National Commission on Teaching & America's Future (Darling-Hammond, 1996), continued with the theme of national reform for the improvement of schools. In this report, the commission offered what it believed to be the single most important strategy for achieving America's educational goals: a blueprint for recruiting, preparing, and supporting excellent teachers in all of America's schools. It states that a caring, competent, and qualified teacher for every child is the most important ingredient in education reform. The report is organized around three simple premises:

1. What teachers know and can do is the most important influence on what students learn.

2. Recruiting, preparing, and retaining good teachers is the central strategy for improving our schools.

3. School reform cannot succeed unless it focuses on creating the conditions in which teachers can teach and learn well.

These premises have served as guides to reform initiatives at all national, state, and local levels since the report was published.

The No Child Left Behind (NCLB) Act is the most current legislation related to students and teachers. NCLB declares that a highly qualified teacher will be in every classroom by 2006 and provides specific directions to states for improving student performance. The reform focuses on student achievement as measured by tests, as well as teacher accountability that relates to content knowledge. By introducing standards and implementing high-stakes testing, policymakers have focused on the performance outcomes of students on tests as the measure of success.

With all reform movements, the challenge for classroom teachers is to implement the changes mandated by state and national regulations. Many teachers, especially veterans, balk at reforms, saying, "I have seen this before and will see it again." As with all reforms, teachers are expected to change their practices in order to meet the new requirements. Because reform directs change, some teachers feel it implies that teachers are doing something wrong in their classrooms. Critics of NCLB and the standards movement feel that focusing on performance outcomes has proved to be a simplistic solution to a more complex issue in response to the question, "Are all the students learning?" It has led to many new questions such as, "Who decides what students should learn? Who decides what is included on the tests? Are the tests the sole measure of the growth of a student? How are second-language learners and learning style differences accounted for?" These questions are ongoing as

INTASC

Principle #10

Partnerships: The teacher fosters relationships with school colleagues, parents, and agencies in the larger community to support students' learning and well-being.

reformers move the agenda to more specific practices and measures in schools. In response to many of these and other criticisms, scholars and educators argue that NCLB is flawed and needs reform. Table 2.5 outlines some suggested amendments to the act.

● **How Education Reform Relates to You** You may be wondering what all of this has to do with you. Most teachers just want to teach and prefer to avoid the politics of education reform, as the issues can seem daunting and conflicting at times. One set of standards may place importance on measuring content knowledge using short-answer tests, while another may emphasize the depth of students' understanding and learning. As a beginning teacher it is important that you understand which initiative your school is following. Read the standards, speak with your administrators and other teachers and use the information to plan your lessons, and fully participate in the process of standards reform.

Former Harvard educator and current author and education consultant Roland Barth suggests in his book *Learning by Heart* (2001) that teachers need to become involved in education reform, suggesting that "teachers are reformers at the school level." He indicates that school reform is about much more than just reorganizing classroom instruction or curricula; it's also about changing who you are as a teacher—changing from within by seeking new ideas and techniques from which your students can benefit. Barth encourages teachers to be **lifelong learners,** educators who learn and grow alongside their students, thereby adapting to the ongoing changes in the field. In Figure 2.5 on page 56, Barth offers a series of questions teachers and administrators might use to guide reform discussions in

---

TABLE 2.5

Proposed Changes to NCLB

Assessment	Use the National Assessment of Educational Progress to benchmark student performance in reading and mathematics, while letting states craft standards and tests in other subjects.
Value-added measures	Judge schools using "value-added" measures that look at the growth of individual students over time, particularly for those with disabilities or with limited proficiency in English.
Consequences	Require schools identified for improvement to offer supplemental services the first year and transfers to other schools the second year, rather than the reverse.
Testing	Revamp state testing cycles to identify schools in need of improvement several months before the school year begins or, alternatively, delay penalties for 1 year or base penalties on multiyear averages.
School choice	Pay more attention to expanding the supply of schools to which students can transfer.
Disabilities	Permit states to develop alternate assessments for students with moderate disabilities that are based on the same academic standards as those for other students, but that lead to grade-level performance.
English-language learners	Keep students with limited English proficiency in that subgroup for accountability purposes even after they are designated as "proficient" in the language. Let local authorities decide when individual students are ready to be tested in English, and do not require English-language learners to take tests that have not been normed for such children.

Source: L. Olson, "No Child Left Behind Act Changes Weighed." *Education Week, 24* (2004): 4.

FIGURE 2.5

Questions to Ask about School Reform

1. *Who are the school-based reformers?* Who in your school is creating solutions to school-based problems?

2. *What is the logic behind reforming your school?* What are your goals for reform? What are you trying to change and why?

3. *Do you really believe your school needs a complete overhaul?* Are external forces from state standards and national legislation driving the changes you are making in your school? Does your school "just need an oil change instead of rebuilding the whole engine"?

4. *Teachers and administrators: Are you prepared to acknowledge your contributions to the problems of schools and change your assumptions and practices?* Look in the mirror and ask if there are changes individuals can make to solve the problems. Would these changes make a difference?

5. *How can you build a high-performing school improvement team from a cast of bright, stubborn, willful, idiosyncratic goats—or from a herd of sheep?* Collective effort is required to make serious change in schools. Putting six people at a table from representative groups does not make a team, so how will you do this?

6. *How much reform is enough? Are things working regularly or intermittently?*

7. *What about your school needs to be reformed?* Daily changes take place in the school and standards are added; how do you measure what needs to be changed on a regular basis?

8. *Can school people reform the schools?* With all the work that is already on the public schools' agenda, this is an important question. Yogi Berra said you can't think and hit at the same time. Can schools operate daily and reform at the same time?

Source: R. S. Barth, *Learning by Heart,* pp. 168–181. (San Francisco: Jossey-Bass, 2001).

schools. You can find out more about reform and its impact on schools by using the questions as a guide when interviewing principals and teachers as you visit schools during your early field experiences. You also can use these questions as a way to integrate standards into the day-to-day conversations you will be having as you enter schools. Standards are not actualized until someone implements them, and in many cases implementation may not be clearly recognizable. Stay updated on current standards and how they are incorporated in schools.

● **Standards and Professional Development for Teachers** Many of the current standards and much of the education reform discussion focuses on student learning. (Are students learning? What are they learning? What do teachers need to know and be able to do to provide evidence of student learning?) However, education reform goes beyond student testing. It also includes initiatives that affect teacher learning, preparing teachers for the profession, and professional development. In-service development for teachers in the past included workshops and in-school activities that may or may not have been linked to student learning. Thomas Gusky, a professor of education policy studies and evaluation at the University of Kentucky, encourages districts and schools to evaluate their own professional development programs to make sure students are learning (Stigler, 2002). How teachers use their professional learning to raise student achievement is the education reform question of the day.

Efforts to create systems that look not only at student work in outcomes, but also the teachers' preparation to teach certain skills, are bringing professional development to center stage. Years ago in-service training consisted of teachers sitting and listening to presentations and then going back to their classrooms and incorporating that knowledge into their instruction. The new model of professional development involves the teacher as an active participant in the process.

Professional development of teachers on the job will become increasingly important as emphasis on accountability and standards continues to grow, requiring a greater understanding of the expectations of state and local agencies. Proponents of the standards movement argue that it brings a "common language" to the table and ensures a consistency of curriculum, making sure teachers are not teaching different things in the isolation of their own classrooms. Some schools, however, are not designed to support teachers as continuous learners. The organization and culture of many American schools is, in most respects, the same as they were in the late nineteenth and early twentieth centuries, when teachers acted as solo practitioners operating in isolation to deliver content to groups of students.

Isolation has long been an issue for teachers who find themselves in a classroom all day with students and no time to actually talk with colleagues. Such an environment can stifle creativity and inhibit change. Current professional development efforts focus on identifying ways for teachers to work together on common planning time and professional development. Collaboration is a skill that requires two or more teachers to work together. In many undergraduate programs you may have worked in groups to present projects. You will continue this type of work in schools. Integrated curricula allow teachers at the secondary levels to cross subject areas. Teachers who have participated in collaborative work find it exciting and stimulating.

A school community is shaped by all of the individuals in the school, including teachers, students, administrators, and all other adults. How you, as a beginning teacher, balance the isolation and collaboration of your work with students will be key to how the school community develops. Schools are complex places, and teachers and administrators have the challenge of creating an environment where all students and professionals can learn and grow. Author and lecturer Peter Senge (2000) suggests that school communities must develop the "capacity to learn" and argues that they can do so only if those responsible for implementing change are actively involved in designing it. In other words, teachers and school administrators must work together to identify the change that is best suited for their school. Senge identifies five key themes of "organizational learning" that provide you with different ways to look at your work as a teacher in a school: personal mastery (developing personal goals), shared vision, shared mental models (encouraging awareness of various attitudes), team learning (practicing positive group interaction), and thinking systematically. These ideas are not reforms or programs to be implemented, but rather skills or practices that offer teachers, administrators, and students genuine guidance for dealing with daily life in schools.

In today's climate, even the most severely underperforming schools must meet the same accountability standards as the schools with rich resources and capable students. When all students are measured by a "one size fits all" test, issues of equity and social justice arise. "Prior training and experience has not prepared [educators for] extreme poverty, unprecedented cultural and language diversity and unstable family and community patterns" (Elmore, 2002). New teachers are typically vibrant forces of energy and enthusiasm for other teachers who may be tired or need some renewal. Your role in becoming a member of a school is important because you as a novice bring new ideas, new life, and new perspectives to an existing culture. Recognize your influence and use it to enhance the learning community. You will have a ripple effect when you collaborate and share your enthusiasm.

INTASC

Principle #9

Professional Commitment and Responsibility: The teacher is a reflective practitioner who continually evaluates the effects of his/her choices and actions on others (students, parents, and other professionals in the learning community) and who actively seeks out opportunities to grow professionally.

TEACHER RETENTION

Nationwide studies show that 50% of teachers leave teaching in the first 5 years (Colbert & Wolff, 1992), a statistic of great concern to administrators, parents, and those who prepare teachers. Reasons given for leaving vary and include low salaries, inadequate working conditions, and dissatisfaction with the field, to name a few. Many of those who have left informally also have shared that they were overwhelmed and felt unprepared for all that teaching involved. They may have had the content knowledge, but felt unprepared to deal with the discipline issues or the responsibilities of planning.

It is important to note that some teachers leave teaching early because that is part of their life plan. Some may have gone into teaching knowing they would eventually leave once they started a family. Others may have chosen to teach for several years as a contribution to the students in a district before going back to school in another field. Some may have been involved in a program such as Teach for America, which helps address teacher shortages by preparing individuals to teach in urban schools for a short-term commitment, usually 2 years. Research does not distinguish how many of these "planned leaves" are part of the percentages quoted. What is the possible downside to such turnover?

● **Induction into the Profession**   The greatest challenge for beginning teachers is adjusting to the sharp learning curve in the first 3 years on the job. Most teachers will say that the first year is pure survival. A first-year teacher must focus on getting to know the school, the district, and the students all at once, while also getting a grasp of the district's curriculum requirements and various policies and rules. The second year is much easier, as you will have a better grasp of policies and guidelines and will have learned by trial and error from the first year strategies that were successful and those that weren't. In the second year, you are more familiar with the community and the students and can focus on honing your instructional plans. The third year is most enjoyable because by now you will have established your own instructional style in the classroom. The challenges are worth it, say most beginning teachers, and you will quickly realize that each year becomes less challenging.

Research shows that nationally 30% of new teachers leave before their second year. In some urban areas around the country, the rate can be as high as 50% leaving teaching within their first 3 years (Goddard, 2005). Although their reasons vary some, most indicate a surprise over the rigor and professional expectations. As you can see in Table 2.6, new teachers

Workshops for sharing of professional experience can help new teachers adjust to the requirements of particular schools as well as hone instructional skills. Workshops help introduce experienced teachers to new strategies and techniques that have been proven to work.

TABLE 2.6	
New Teacher Challenges	
Professional development	**Time** to participate in skills- and curriculum-based training so they could teach district curriculum. These workshops and courses were required and new teachers wanted to attend. They just took time away from other anticipated needs in year 1. (All new teachers who responded stated that time was the one thing they wished they had more of in their first year.)
Working with other adults in the room	Most had not worked with another adult where directions had to be given to either an aide or a paraprofessional assigned to a student. It takes **time** to give directions, to follow up, and to check work done.
Duties	Student teachers don't always do the duty schedule, so it comes as a surprise that there are so many duties for first-year teachers and that they take **time** away from teaching. Bus duty, cafeteria duty, and hall duty have to be factored into the day.
Committee work and school meetings	After-school or before-school meetings take **time** away from correcting papers and meeting with students. Curriculum committees, faculty meetings, and school councils include new teachers.
Parent conferences and contact	Taking **time** to write notes, call parents, and meet at formal meetings took more than first-year teachers realized.

Source: Massachusetts Coalition, New Teacher Panel Presentation. (Sturbridge, MA: Author, 2000).

had different surprises, but all agreed that time was the biggest factor of all. They just didn't realize how long it took to prepare and to teach lessons, and how many other things were required of teachers.

As you see in the table, a teacher must attend to many tasks beyond classroom instruction in a school day. It is important to be aware of the reality of the work in order to be fully prepared for the promises of teaching as a professional career. Many new teachers indicate that if they had known what teaching was really like, they would have prepared differently. Theory and content knowledge are required for your teacher preparation, but the best teacher has to know how to relate the content in practice to the students in the classroom while also dealing with parents, administrators, coworkers, and the politics of the system. When you make school visits and eventually student teach, you will have the support of supervisors back on campus and cooperating teachers in the room or nearby. In your first year, however, you will be responsible for your own classroom. In an effort to improve the retention rate of new teachers to the profession, a number of programs have been initiated at various levels in order to ease the shock of induction.

The University's Role In an effort to improve new teacher retention, universities are making greater efforts to follow their graduates into their first years of teaching. Schools that are part of NCATE, for example, are required to provide postgraduate support, which often involves professional development workshops or graduate courses that help new teachers reach their next license level. Some states—including Kentucky, Texas, and Florida—have designed observation models that allow supervisors to visit schools where a cohort of new teachers are hired. Some universities offer e-mentoring to their graduates teaching in rural areas. Early feedback indicates new teachers find this postgraduate support very valuable.

Problems to POSSIBILITIES

How Do Teachers Raise Morale and Celebrate Success Stories?

Janice and Sherrod were just hired to teach at West Middle School. Each had taught the previous year in two other schools in the district, but because of redistricting they were assigned to a new school. They had enjoyed their previous schools and the ways the teachers at those schools included them. This new school "felt different" to them. Even though many of the teachers were younger, the morale in the school was low, and Janice and Sherrod heard a lot of negative talk in the teachers' lounge and in meetings.

At their first two schools, both Janice and Sherrod had felt included, they had mentors, and the staff generally got along well. "Why is this school so different?" they wondered. Why did these teachers see only the negative? Janice and Sherrod didn't know what to do. If they wanted to be included, it looked as if they had to sit and complain too, and they didn't want to do that. They didn't think teaching was going to be like this.

Discussion Questions

What would you do if you were Janice or Sherrod? What possible challenges can you anticipate as a beginning teacher in trying to boost morale in a new school for you?

Possibilities

These two beginning teachers could be at any school in the country. As new teachers soon discover, school culture plays an enormous part in adult interactions and the quality of the school day. The school principal, the department chair, and any formal or informal teacher leaders have the power to establish a positive tone. So what do you do when they don't fulfill their role in doing that? As teachers you can take the lead and do things that will influence the climate and the culture of the school. By becoming involved and seeking out other positive teachers in the school you will begin to create a critical mass of positive people. Less negative talk at meetings and a balance of positive comments will make a difference and shift the energy in the room.

In a special initiative called Teachers for a New Era, funded by the Carnegie Foundation, 11 universities across the United States are piloting models that will provide specific support activities to their graduates for 2 years. For example, Boston College, one of the participating universities, offers its new graduates a 3-day professional conference in August called Summer Start that provides a jump start for new teachers as they set up their first classroom. Teachers for a New Era stresses collaboration between schools of education, university faculty, and school districts, with the primary focus on improving student learning by improving professionalism and the clinical approach to teaching. The first four universities involved in the Teachers for a New Era initiative were California State University–Northridge, Michigan State University, the University of Virginia, and Bank Street College of Education in New York City. A year later seven more universities were added to the initiative: Boston College, Florida A&M University, the University of Connecticut, Stanford University, the University of Texas at El Paso, the University of Washington, and the University of Wisconsin–Milwaukee. Additional universities are expected to become part of the initiative in coming years. Does your university program offer any follow-up support?

The District's Role School districts recognize the consequences of teacher turnover and are taking greater steps to reduce those rates. When a teaching staff works together for several years, they develop a sense of teamwork, just as does a successful athletic team. Teachers learn to know what to expect from each other and how to work with each other, whether in coordinating curricular subjects or handling discipline issues in the hallway.

In this case two new teachers can work together to raise morale, and it could become a lot easier for them. Sometimes it is just one lonely new teacher, who may feel that she can't approach others to be more positive. The opposite could also happen. The two new teachers could isolate themselves from the other teachers in the school and complain about how low the morale is! This would not improve their situation, nor would it make the quality of their lives in school better. New teachers can influence existing staff by bringing their energy and enthusiasm into the school. They just have to work together and bring others on board. Everyone likes to have fun; finding ways to overcome negativity will vary from school to school. You will need to find allies and work together.

There are several ways to influence morale and school climate as a teacher, including the following:

1. Clean the teachers' lounge so it is a pleasant place to be. Everyone feels better when they are in a colorful environment. You can even take turns bringing fresh flowers or plants.

2. Participate in a community service activity with other teachers in the school. This adds a positive purpose to your work and gets you away from the daily complaints to see others who have greater needs.

3. Do something fun together, such as running a road race, skiing, or having dinner out together. Beginning teachers need to socialize. Don't be afraid to take the first step. Having Sherrod and Janice do it together makes it easier to get something going.

4. Reach out professionally. Visit the National Education Association online at www.nea.org, where you can find the latest news on developments in education and share ideas with one of the largest online communities in education. In particular, explore the NEA member magazine *NEA Today* (www.nea.org/neatoday) to read about how today's teachers deal with dilemmas in their schools. Be sure to check the archives of past issues. For example, in a special feature called Dilemma, a teacher from North Dakota shares that her staff brings noisemakers to staff meetings. "Teachers take turns telling others about something that's gone well in class—a creative idea they have tried, or another success story. After each story, the rest of us toot our horns. This starts all the meetings on an upbeat note."

Search the Internet and see what you can find to boost morale as a beginning teacher. It will make a difference in the quality of your day in school.

When teachers leave, for whatever reason, a period of adjustment exists as teachers and students become familiar with each other. As mentioned earlier, first-year teachers, in particular, have a steep learning curve. Most schools will lose one or two teachers in a given year; but when they lose a number of their teachers, the transition can be very disruptive to student learning.

School districts in most states now recognize the challenges facing new teachers, and therefore offer special induction programs designed to help beginning teachers ease into the field and get them started on the right foot. Support includes providing a mentorship program in which a veteran teacher works with a beginning teacher, in-service workshops that provide teachers with new knowledge and assistance with adjustments, and opportunities to meet other teachers and share ideas.

Districts that support their new teachers by assigning them lighter workloads and more time to talk with their colleagues are retaining more of them (Johnson & Kardos, 2002). Because teachers can now enter the profession through various preparation routes, school districts have a variety of ways to fill their openings and these individuals can offer some diverse experiences to the staff. But this can also limit the common language among a district's teachers. Therefore, teachers and administrators alike need to find ways to find a common ground and learn from each other.

Whether or not the school district where you take a job provides a formal program, you will surely be inducted by just showing up each day. The challenge for you will be participating fully and with awareness to discover your needs as you start your first year. Initially you may not even know what you don't know. But your district, your university program, and your own networks will be available to provide you with the support you will need to be an effective teacher.

The Beginning Teacher's Role   What will you do to support yourself? First, you need to be aware of everything that is available to you within the state and the district. (Chapter 12 expands on this further.) The challenge before you will be to actively engage in the discussion. Be aware of what exists, ask for help when you need it, and make time for the programs that will make a difference for you in that crucial first year. Making time to attend free training programs and orientations may be a challenge for your already overloaded schedule, but the time will be well spent. In addition, one of the most important steps you can take to adjust to your first teaching job is to get to know the veteran teachers in the school. If no formal mentoring program exists, do not be afraid to extend yourself to your coworkers and seek their advice and assistance.

As a beginning teacher who has prepared in a school of education, you will have had a number of opportunities to observe and get practical experience in schools prior to starting out, and you may feel prepared and knowledgeable in your content areas and pedagogy, but you will still have challenges. Full participation in programs the district offers will allow you to share what you bring to the district from your teacher preparation, as well as to learn new ways to integrate your ideas and knowledge.

There is a lot of support for you. The sink-or-swim method of entering the profession is a practice of the past, as schools offer formal induction programs. Isolation is not accepted as the norm and real efforts are being made to promote collaboration among teachers. You are entering the profession at a time when the focus is on student achievement and new teacher support.

It is easier to have a positive perspective of the work of teaching when support is available. As a new teacher you will have many support systems as part of an induction program designed to help you enter the profession and the school district. Well-conceived induction programs for new teachers provide orientations, workshops, mentoring, and ongoing support to ensure that you are successful in the classroom. Read more about being inducted into the profession at the end of this chapter. Mentoring by an experienced teacher has been shown to make a difference in retaining beginning teachers and offers support that allows the work to be seen positively (Bemis, 1999). Your mentor may work one-on-one or you may have a small group of new teachers working together. You will feel supported and will be able to discuss your challenges with a teacher who can assist you. Unlike the teachers who were burned out and listed their complaints about standards, you will be able to integrate your creativity with the standards as you work with your mentor. This will ensure that your students have creative hands-on experiences that meet the standards.

● **Promoting Longevity**   Unfortunately there is no guarantee that a teacher who makes it past the first few years will always remain in teaching. As in any career, teachers may experience **burnout.** Gary Dworkin (2002) defines *burnout* as "an extreme form of role-specific alienation characterized by a sense that one's work is meaningless and that one is powerless to effect changes which would make the work more meaningful" (p. 660). It is typically a result of job-related stress based on any of a number of things, including lack of collegial support, lack of public support for the profession, discipline problems, denial of professional autonomy and freedom, or imposition of external pressures in the teacher's personal life unrelated to teaching (Dworkin, 2002).

Education reform has been cited by a number of teachers as a source of external stress that can bring additional pressure to their daily work. With the pressure of high-stakes testing and accountability, the public eye is focused on teachers more and more these days. They say:

"With every year, I was required to teach more curriculum based on testing."

"All my creative talents seemed to go by the wayside due to drill and kill they wanted me to do."

"I don't mind standards, but too much emphasis is placed on testing. It has taken the fun out of it, and you feel like you don't have time for art, PE, music, etc."

"I thought I'd be able to use the many lessons I'd developed, but because of increased accountability, I've had to use state and district mandated materials" (Tye & O'Brien, 2002)

Burnout is real; however, not all burned-out teachers leave teaching. Some stay because they have invested so many years into teaching. As you enter the profession you will meet teachers at different developmental stages with different attitudes. Use your energy and enthusiasm to collaborate and contribute to the school beyond your classroom. Read Problems to Possibilities to see how you as a beginning teacher can change morale as you enter the profession. It is important to be aware of potential burnout issues early so you can keep yourself renewed and supported. Teaching is difficult, and when teachers cannot see the positive or lose the joy, it is difficult to remain in the profession. Sometimes these attitudes affect other colleagues.

Experienced teachers often have professional support in the form of workshops or renewal activities. Both efforts are designed to maintain a positive outlook as well as to provide needed skills. Support systems for experienced teachers in search of renewal also may be found in memberships in professional organizations and programs designed to meet the needs of career professionals. The book *Stories of the Courage to Teach* (Intrator, 2002) shares the experiences of veteran teachers making efforts to reclaim their "hearts" in teaching. They want to be present in the classroom and in the school. The teachers highlight ways to deepen their participation and look beyond the daily practices that may not work. The book also includes a professional development program of personal and professional renewal for experienced teachers or beginning teachers who are losing their idealism. The goal of the program is putting the heart back into teaching so teachers will want to stay in the profession by regaining their original enthusiasm.

Whether you are a beginning teacher participating in an induction program or an experienced teacher renewing your vision, many types of support systems are available. You will want to become aware of the professional organizations that can provide you with innovative ideas as well as a feeling of belonging to a group outside your own school.

INTASC

Principle #10

Partnerships: The teacher fosters relationships with school colleagues, parents, and agencies in the larger community to support students' learning and well-being.

Who am I? **What do I believe?**

"It was really difficult last year. There was no set way of doing things. Everything was kind of up in the air. It was chaos."

GWEN, A FIRST-YEAR TEACHER IN AN URBAN SCHOOL
(JOHNSON & KARDOS, 2002)

THINK ABOUT THIS:
The first year can be chaos for you if you don't reach out to others who can assist you. How can university programs help prospective teachers become better aware of time-related expectations in order to prepare them for their first year of teaching?

SHARE and COMPARE:
Brainstorm with one or two classmates to develop some ideas that university teacher education programs might initiate to help their graduates ease into the teaching profession.

FINAL THOUGHTS

Teachers are a special category of professional workers. They have many characteristics of other professionals such as doctors and lawyers, yet there are some differences too. As public servants, teachers do not select their own students, nor do they have final say over the curriculum they will teach. Their work is governed by public officials and paid by public funds according to teacher contracts.

Teachers are accountable for the work they do and the results they produce that relate to student learning, just as for all professionals. However, in recent years more and more teachers are being evaluated based on the scores their students have received on tests. This controversial system of productivity has raised concerns from teachers' unions and parents. Other professions do not base their success on the abilities of their clients or patients, but rather their own success in performing their duties. Should student success on tests be the only measure of a teacher's success? Compare this scenario to one of a doctor who is responsible for treating a patient's disease, but is not held responsible for the patient's attitude or behavior or for having caught the disease in the first place.

Teachers are required to be licensed as are other professions, yet they do not have a single board of professionals that governs them like the American Bar Association or the American Medical Association. Teachers report to principals, who report to superintendents who oversee the entire district, who report to school boards made up of community members. Some people would say that teaching is not a profession because it does not regulate its own members as do other professions. Yet the public sees teaching as a highly regarded profession, recognizing that teachers use their expert knowledge to influence student learning and personal development.

The challenges of teaching are real. You will become a better teacher by knowing them, analyzing them, and being encouraged to change the context of teaching to improve the quality of education for all students. Your goal as you prepare to become a teacher is to consider all of the issues as you prepare to collaborate with others in schools to take steps that will influence students' learning. Teaching is exciting and powerful work for courageous people.

REFLECTIONS

Professional Plan for Becoming a Teacher

1. Three things I learned from this chapter about teachers are:

2. Two things in this chapter that I would like to learn more about are:

    a. _____

    b. _____

3. I plan to investigate these two areas and learn more about topics in this chapter by:

    _____ Reading some of the selections in the Read On section

    _____ Reading sources referenced in the chapter that interest me

    _____ Interviewing the following teachers about their reasons for going into teaching and challenges they face every day:

    a. _____

    b. _____

    c. _____

    _____ Exploring the websites listed in the Log On section:

    _____ Observing several classrooms and taking notes on the specific strategies teachers use

4. I will include the following in my Touch the Future portfolio: (List various features in this chapter or other materials assigned by your instructor.)

SUMMARY

Who Are the Teachers in America's Schools?

- The demographic of the teacher workforce is changing considerably and will continue changing far into the next decade.
- Teachers choose teaching for a variety of reasons, which may include intrinsic and extrinsic rewards including job security and retirement.

- Teacher salaries vary considerably among states and cities.
- Teaching as a career is a continuum that includes preparation for teaching, the first year, the beginning years, and ongoing professional development, with the possibility of advanced degrees.
- The teacher has an important role in enhancing student learning by building trusting relationships with both colleagues and parents.

What Is an Effective Teacher?

- Teachers' work is defined and perceived differently by public opinion, students, and popular myths.
- Personal and professional perspectives offer a different view of what defines the effective teacher.
- Professional organizations define criteria and standards for effective teachers.

What Are the Challenges for Teachers in Today's Classrooms?

- Education reform directly affects classroom practice. Reforms resulting from the No Child Left Behind Act have placed a major focus on standards and high-stakes testing.
- Professional development and standards work together to meet the challenges in today's schools and will be increasingly more important.
- Teacher retention is a critical issue in education.
- Induction programs provided by districts and universities provide support for new teachers as they enter the profession.
- Teachers leave because they perceive the work as difficult and overwhelming. Some may be burned out and unable to renew themselves.

Visit the **Touch the Future . . . Teach!** Companion Website at www.ablongman.com/diaz for additional opportunities.

KEY WORDS

burnout 62	effective teacher 42	merit pay 38
career-change teacher 35	extrinsic reward 36	prepracticum 50
developmental continuum 40	full practicum 50	professional development 41
education reform 53	intrinsic reward 34	
	lifelong learner 55	

CONCEPT REVIEW

1. Articulate why you want to be a teacher and state two common reasons others have given.

2. State three professional rewards of teaching, using extrinsic and intrinsic examples.

3. Describe the career development stages in a developmental professional continuum of a teacher who stays in the profession.

4. Explain why teachers leave the profession within the first 3 years and what districts can do to prevent this.

5. Summarize the qualities of an effective teacher from several perspectives.

6. List the types of teachers, support personnel, and administrators in a school and the roles they play in supporting student learning and give examples of sharing among school personnel.

7. Summarize the most recent education reform movement and its impact on teachers.

8. Select one myth and articulate why it is a myth.

9. Identify one thing the American education system can do to address potential teacher shortages in the near future.

10. Discuss the importance of professional development.

TOUCH THE FUTURE . . .

Read On

Learning by Heart
Roland Barth (San Francisco: Jossey-Bass, 2001)
Barth's passion and humor highlight ways in which teachers can participate fully in schools.

Teachers at Work: Achieving Success in Our Schools
Susan Moore Johnson (New York: Basic Books, 1990).
An insightful description of teachers' work in schools is vividly captured and clearly defined.

What's Worth Fighting For?
Andy Hargreaves & M. Fullan (Toronto: Ontario Public School Teachers' Federation, 1998)
The authors discuss why schools must value teachers as the foundation for school improvement.

Log On

Council of Chief State School Officers (CCSSO)
www.ccsso.org
> Check the Projects section of the CCSSO website and explore information about accountability and the INTASC standards.

National Education Association (NEA)   American Federation of Teachers (AFT)
www.nea.org   www.aft.org
> The two largest teachers' unions in the United States; explore their websites to learn more about the various advice and assistance they offer teachers.

About.com
www.about.com/education
> About.com provides you with a range of educational topics and subjects ranging from lesson plans to professional development.

Teachers for a New Era
> Each of the first four universities involved in the Teachers for a New Era initiative maintain websites outlining their individual initiatives. Check out the following sites: California State University–Northridge (http://tne.csun.edu), Michigan State University (www.tne.msu.edu), the University of Virginia (www.virginia.edu/provost/tneuva), and Bank Street College of Education in New York City www.bankstreet.edu/TNE).

Write On

"I have seen the teaching profession honored and yet not listened to. I hope I have spread the message that all education that takes place in the classroom and any reform movement must begin with the teachers in the classroom."

—Marianne Moran, Massachusetts Teacher of the Year

Write a short response to this quote in your journal. What does it mean that teachers are honored and yet not listened to? How can teachers be part of education reform?

OBSERVATION GUIDE

TEACH: LINKING THEORY TO PRACTICE

Linking Theory to Practice

Part of your informed decision about teaching needs to come from your own desire to explore all aspects of teaching. The following interview and observation guide will help you while completing practical field experiences or during regular visits to schools.

Objective: To explore a teacher's perspectives on teaching

School (use code name): _____   Observer: _____

Grade Level: _____   Date: _____

Subject(s): _____   Time In: _____   Time Out: _____

Directions: In this observation and interview activity, think about the teacher topics you have read about in this chapter. Ask to speak with the teacher after class to ask a few questions to follow up your observations. Use these questions as a guide and create some of your own, using this chapter to assist you. Write a brief summary of your findings once you have finished your observation and interview. You may choose to complete this observation with a variety of teachers and write a comparison paper.

General Observations

1. As you walk through the building, notice individual classrooms. Notice classroom climate and interactions between teachers and students. What are the indicators of positive learning and student teacher interactions?

2. Visit one classroom for a period. Observe the way it is organized as well as the teacher/student interactions. What is your impression of this classroom?

Interview Questions after the Observation

1. How long have you been teaching and why did you choose this occupation? (Where would you place this person on the developmental continuum on page 42?)

2. What are the primary rewards you get from teaching?

3. What are the biggest challenges you face in a typical day?

4. Can you share a positive example of something that happens in a typical day with me?

5. Are you planning to teach for your career? Why or why not?

6. What is your advice to me as I begin my preparation to become a teacher?

Connecting with INTASC: Principle 10

Partnerships: The teacher fosters relationships with school colleagues, parents, and agencies in the larger community to support students' learning and well-being.

In your interview, find out what the teacher does to meet Principle 10 by asking the following questions:

What efforts are made in the school to encourage collaboration with other teachers and personnel in the school? What does the teacher specifically do to meet this standard and to identify any obstacles that might arise?

3

Students in Today's Classrooms

Who am I?

What do I believe?

THINK ABOUT THIS:

When you become a teacher, you likely will feel fairly comfortable with the students in your class who share all or most of the characteristics you had as a student. But what about the rest of the class? How will you connect with them in order to ensure that all of your students will be motivated to pursue knowledge? Acquiring significant knowledge about your students' backgrounds will allow you to make the types of human connections that will enhance your students' learning. What do you think teachers can do to reach all students in their classes? Why might it be important to understand the cultural, family, and individual backgrounds of students in order to teach effectively?

"What we want is to see the child in pursuit of knowledge, and not knowledge in pursuit of the child."

George Bernard Shaw

This chapter addresses the nature of the population of students in elementary and secondary schools in the United States. It explores the changes in the student population as well as challenges and circumstances faced by students in U.S. schools. Different categories of students will be analyzed and school practices will be examined in terms of how they affect different students. As you read this chapter, you will explore the following key questions about today's students:

Key Questions

1. What social changes are affecting school demographics?
2. Is education equitable to all students?
3. Are student accountability and equity complementary or competing interests?
4. What educational options are best for racial and language minority students?

WHAT SOCIAL CHANGES ARE AFFECTING SCHOOL DEMOGRAPHICS?

Throughout the history of the United States, one thing that has always been constant about the country is that "nothing is constant." As a society, we are in a perpetual state of flux, with people migrating from one part of the country to another, as well as a steady flow of immigrants arriving from throughout the world, all in an effort to seek out better life opportunities. What has changed over the years is where these new immigrants come from and the effect this movement has on the social structure of the country, including the country's educational system.

DEMOGRAPHIC SHIFTS IN THE STUDENT POPULATION

The general population of students in the public schools in the United States is increasing in numbers and diversity. In 1988, 45.4 million students attended U.S. public schools. By 2001, that figure had grown to 53.9 million and by the year 2013, the U.S. student population is expected to be around 56.4 million, an increase of around 5%. While this increase shows healthy growth, it is a much more modest increase than the 19% growth public schools experienced between 1988 and 2001, a growth partly explained by the children of the baby boom generation, sometimes referred to as the "baby boom echo."

High school graduates have increased from 2.8 million (2.5 million public and 0.27 million private) in 1988 to 2.9 million (2.6 million public and 0.28 million private) in 2001 and are expected to climb to 3.2 million in 2013 (2.8 million public and 0.33 million private) (U.S. Department of Education, 2003). It is evident from these figures that the increasing number of students in the United States makes education a growth field for the foreseeable future. It is equally evident that public schools will be responsible for 85–90% of high school graduates.

While the influx of immigrants and the effects of the "baby boom echo" help explain the overall growth in the student population, the numbers become more interesting when we look at another characteristic of contemporary life in the United States—mobility. Approximately 3 million children are born in the United States each year, but in the same period of time, up to 40 million Americans move. Although most migration occurs within the same state, 6 to 8 million people move from one state to another each year (Hodgkinson, 2000/2001).

Student populations are projected to increase in 30 states, with Alaska (17%), Hawaii (16%), and California (16%) expecting the greatest increases; 20 states are projected to lose students, with the greatest decreases expected to occur in West Virginia (6%) and Kentucky (6%) (Gerald & Hussar, 2003).

Regionally, the U.S. Department of Education (2004) estimates that between 2003 and 2013, the greatest increase in public school enrollment in Grades Pre-K–12 will take place in the West. Over this same period, enrollment is expected to decrease in the Northeast, remain relatively stable in the Midwest, and increase slightly in the South. Of course, the specific impact on the schools of a region depends largely on where they are located. For example, schools in Las Vegas, Nevada, and Fort Lauderdale, Florida, have experienced rapid enrollment growth in recent years, a trend likely to continue for a while. Schools in rural Montana or the Dakotas, on the other hand, have seen declining numbers of students. So besides differences in the increase or decrease of the student population in different regions of the nation, there can be significant variations within each region.

● **Racial and Ethnic Changes**   From 2000 to 2010, ethnic groups in the general population are expected to increase across the board: Whites by 5 million, Hispanics by 9 million, African Americans by 3.8 million, Asian Americans by 3.8 million, and Native Americans by

TABLE 3.1

**Percentage Distribution of Public School Students Enrolled in
Grades K–12 Who Were Minorities, October 1972–2000**

| OCTOBER | WHITE | MINORITY ENROLLMENT | | | |
		TOTAL	BLACK	HISPANIC	OTHER
1972	77.8%	22.2%	14.8%	6.0%	1.4%
1973	78.1	21.9	14.7	5.7	1.4
1974	76.8	23.2	15.4	6.3	1.5
1975	76.2	23.8	15.4	6.7	1.7
1976	76.2	23.8	15.5	6.5	1.7
1977	76.1	23.9	15.8	6.2	1.9
1978	75.5	24.5	16.0	6.5	2.1
1979	75.8	24.2	15.7	6.6	1.9
1980	72.8	27.2	16.2	8.6	2.4
1981	72.4	27.6	16.0	8.7	2.9
1982	71.9	28.1	16.0	8.9	3.2
1983	71.3	28.7	16.1	9.2	3.4
1984	71.7	28.3	16.1	8.5	3.6
1985	69.6	30.4	16.8	10.1	3.5
1986	69.1	30.9	16.6	10.8	3.6
1987	68.5	31.5	16.6	10.8	4.0
1988	68.3	31.7	16.5	11.0	4.2
1989	68.0	32.0	16.6	11.4	4.0
1990	67.6	32.4	16.5	11.7	4.2
1991	67.1	32.9	16.8	11.8	4.2
1992	66.8	33.3	16.9	12.1	4.3
1993	67.0	33.0	16.6	12.1	4.3
1994	65.8	34.2	16.7	13.7	3.8
1995	65.5	34.5	16.9	14.1	3.5
1996	63.7	36.3	16.6	14.5	5.3
1997	63.0	37.0	16.9	14.9	5.1
1998	62.4	37.6	17.2	15.4	5.1
1999	61.9	38.1	16.5	16.2	5.5
2000	61.3	38.7	16.6	16.6	5.4

Note: Percentages may not add to 100.0 due to rounding.
Source: U.S. Department of Commerce, Bureau of the Census, *October Current Population Surveys, 1972–2000.*

266,000 (Hodgkinson, 1998). As you can see in Table 3.1, public schools are much more racially and ethnically diverse today than they were three decades ago. In 1972, White students made up almost 78% of the public school student population, while African Americans represented almost 15% and Hispanics 6%. In 2000, Whites represented 61.3% of public school students, African Americans were 16.6 percent, and Hispanics were 16.6 percent (U.S. Department of Education, 2002). A longer-term estimate predicts that the

Schools throughout the United States reflect the changing ethnic demographics of communities. The 2000 census indicated that Hispanic was the fastest growing sector of the population. How do you think this growth will affect decision making in education?

I N T A S C

Principle #3

Adapting Instruction for Individual Needs: The teacher understands how students differ in their approaches to learning and creates instructional opportunities that are adapted to diverse learners.

population of non-Hispanic Whites in U.S. public schools will continue to decline—from 65% in 2000 to 56% in 2020 and less than 50% in 2040 (Spring, 2004). While these are significant changes in the student population, no change is felt equally in all schools in this nation. Teachers in urban schools still are more likely than their rural and suburban counterparts to have a more equitable distribution of students who are White, African American, Hispanic, Asian American, or immigrants. Nonetheless, data from the 2000 U.S. census indicate that student populations in urban, suburban, and even rural areas are generally becoming more diverse.

School districts that receive significant numbers of immigrant children are the ones increasing most in diversity. Historically, 90% of immigrants to the United States came from Europe, adding mainly to the nation's White population. Today, however, only 12% of immigrants come from Europe (Hodgkinson, 1998, p. 5). The great majority come from Latin America and Asia, adding mostly to the ranks of students of color. Regardless of where immigrant students originate, many face significant difficulties adapting to life in the United States and to the American education system. But this challenge can be lessened with knowledgeable and compassionate teachers. More than ever before, teachers need to be aware of their students' backgrounds.

Traditional notions of Black/White diversity in the U.S. population are quickly being replaced with a much more complex mixture of cultures and people, blurring the racial/ethnic backgrounds of students. As the student population changes, however, some of the most rapidly increasing groups of students are not experiencing the same rates of academic success as their peers. For example, Hispanics represent the most numerous ethnic minority group in the United States, yet the high school dropout rate for Hispanics throughout the country (27%) far exceeds that for African American (13%) or White (7%) students. Many Hispanic students fall behind their peers in elementary school and never catch up (Collison, 1999). Table 3.2 identifies the projected dropout rates of select ethnic groups in select states. Teachers in the twenty-first century have to find new ways to reach Hispanic students and English language learners.

TABLE 3.2

High School Dropouts, Selected States

STATE	TOTAL 9TH–12TH GRADERS	NUMBER OF DROPOUTS	RATE (9TH–12TH)	AMERICAN INDIAN/ ALASKA NATIVE	ASIAN/ PACIFIC ISLANDER	HISPANIC	BLACK, NON-HISPANIC	WHITE, NON-HISPANIC
Alaska	38,914	3,177	8.2	12.7	8.6	11.0	11.4	6.3
Arizona	234,367	25,632	10.9	17.0	5.0	16.8	13.9	7.1
Connecticut	155,731	4,649	3.0	3.7	1.8	7.0	5.3	2.0
Florida	674,817	29,965	4.4	3.9	2.4	5.6	5.9	3.5
Iowa	158,050	4,193	2.7	10.4	2.3	9.1	7.3	2.3
Louisiana	196,040	16,361	8.3	9.7	4.8	8.8	10.8	6.5
New Jersey	351,496	9,882	2.8	12.0	1.0	5.6	5.7	1.6
New York	809,036	30,898	3.8	6.5	2.9	7.2	6.3	2.1
North Dakota	346,424	21,773	6.3	10.0	3.2	3.2	3.9	1.5
Texas	1,116,518	46,973	4.2	5.0	2.2	6.1	5.4	2.5
Wisconsin	259,047	6,002	2.3	5.7	2.4	6.5	9.8	1.4
American Samoa	3,773	73	1.9	0.0	1.9	0.0	0.0	0.0
Guam	8,775	1,001	11.4	0.0	6.1	0.0	0.0	0.0
Puerto Rico	166,476	1,737	1.0	0.0	0.0	1.0	0.0	0.0

Source: National Center for Education Statistics, *Projections of Education Statistics to 2013* (NCES 2004013) November 2003. (Washington, DC: U.S. Government Printing Office, November 2003).

The changing face of today's classroom serves as a microcosm of the world in general. By 2010, Whites are projected to account for only 9% of the world's population, compared to 17% in 1997, making them the world's smallest ethnic minority (Hodgkinson, 1998). As a teacher, you will need to prepare your students to understand increasing diversity nationally and internationally.

● **Changes to the Family Environment**   Teachers will continue to teach a significant percentage of students who live in single-parent households, belong to blended families where one or both parents have gone through divorce, or are being raised by grandparents or legal guardians. Teachers must re-examine many of the traditional assumptions about children's homes and the support children are able to get with school work. The student may or may not have two parents at home, or the parents or guardians may or may not have the skills necessary to assist the student. In such cases, the teacher and the school need to be careful not to draw inferences about parents' concern for the child's education.

The socioeconomic position of students and their families also will continue to be an important variable in the classroom (see Figure 3.1 on page 76). Approximately 20% of children in the United States live below the poverty line, exactly the same percentage as 15 years ago (Hodgkinson, 2000/2001). Teachers in the United States will continue to teach the highest proportion of students living in poverty of any major Western industrialized nation. Some teachers, particularly those in inner-city and rural settings, have considerably more than one-fifth of their students living below the poverty line.

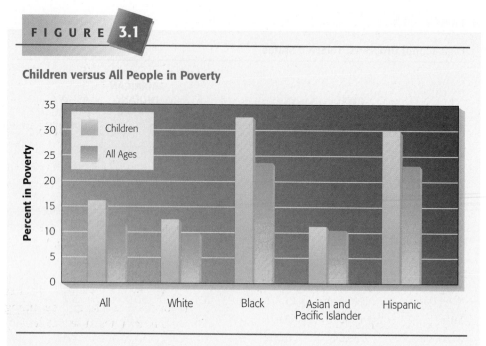

Source: U.S. Bureau of the Census, *Statistical Abstract of the United States* (121st ed., p. 442). (Washington, DC: U.S. Government Printing Office, 2001).

> "When you go out there (to teach) armed with this knowledge and confidence, you ask yourself, what difference have you been able to make for students?"
>
> MIRIAM, ELEMENTARY TEACHER

THINK ABOUT THIS:

Given the evolving nature of students in today's classroom, write down three important things a good teacher can do, in addition to subject-matter instruction, to help students succeed.

SHARE and **COMPARE:**

Ask a classmate to list three answers to the preceding question and compare responses. How many of your answers are the same? Discuss with your classmate why each of you chose your answers.

SOCIAL PROBLEMS AND ACADEMIC ACHIEVEMENT

In spite of the intent to "treat all children equally" and the efforts of No Child Left Behind (NCLB) legislation of 2001 to level the playing field for all students, social problems affecting America's youth can have a significant impact on academic achievement. By requiring schools to report results on annual standardized tests for each segment of the student population, NCLB helps identify poorly performing groups of students and issues that may need to be addressed. But not all schools face the same social problems to the same degree, a factor not reflected in the NCLB legislation. Although performance is partly a function of individual ability, social problems such as substance abuse, truancy, teen pregnancy, violence in the home or society, and poverty are examples of circumstances faced by U.S. students that can inhibit academic achievement. When students are exposed to these factors (even students with high academic ability), low school performance is likely to result. Table 3.3 identifies the prevalence of certain behaviors that place today's students at risk.

In general, the severity of problems decreases from urban to suburban and from suburban to rural schools, with two exceptions—drug and alcohol abuse. Teachers in all three types of schools rated drug and alcohol problems as equally serious. Student use of alcohol actually increased from urban to suburban to rural schools (Shen, 1997).

As noted in Table 3.3, almost 50% of high school students indicate they are sexually active. While there is no direct correlation between sexual activity and academic achievement, some social issues related to sexual activity, such as teen pregnancy, can affect student achievement. Efforts in U.S. schools to curb teenage sexual activity and reduce pregnancy rates among teens have concentrated on abstinence-only programs as well as abstinence-based programs that include information about and access to birth control methods. While the teen pregnancy rate has gone down in recent years, the United States still has the highest rate of any industrialized nation, with nearly 1 million girls becoming pregnant in the United States each year despite reporting similar rates of sexual activity

INTASC

Principle #2

Knowledge of Human Development and Learning: The teacher understands how children learn and develop, and can provide learning opportunities that support their intellectual, social, and personal development.

TABLE 3.3

Youth Risk Behavior Surveillance System

To monitor the priority health-risk behaviors of young people, the Centers for Disease Control developed the Youth Risk Behavior Surveillance System (YRBSS) beginning in 1990. The 2003 survey of high school students reported they had:

Rarely or never worn a seat belt	18.2%
Ridden with a driver who had been drinking alcohol during the 30 days preceding the survey	30.2%
Carried a weapon such as a gun, knife, or club during the 30 days preceding the survey	17.1%
Drunk alcohol during the 30 days preceding the survey	44.9%
Used marijuana during the 30 days preceding the survey	22.4%
Attempted suicide during the 12 months preceding the survey	8.5%
Ever had sexual intercourse	46.7%
Not used a condom at last sexual intercourse if sexually active	37.0%
Ever injected an illegal drug	3.2%
Smoked cigarettes during the 30 days preceding the survey	21.9%
Not eaten five or more servings of fruits and vegetables during the day preceding the survey	78.0%
Not attended physical education class daily	71.6%
Felt too unsafe to go to school	5.4%
Been in a physical fight on school property within the last 12 months	33.0%
Had property stolen or deliberately damaged on school property within the last 12 months	29.8%

Source: Compiled from Centers for Disease Control and Prevention (May 21, 2004). *CDC Surveillance Summaries,* (MMWR), 2004: 53(No.SS-2).

(Henshaw, 2003). (See Figures 3.2 and 3.3.) Unfortunately, far too many young women drop out of school feeling that they cannot continue their education and care for a child. Many of these students may have been struggling already. For pregnant teens doing poorly in school, pregnancy frequently becomes the final reason to drop out. School districts have responded in various ways, such as providing alternative schools for teen mothers to continue their education or special programs within their regular schools that provide additional counseling and support.

For teens who drop out of school, no matter the reason, getting a high school general equivalency diploma (GED) is an option. However, students with GED are far less likely to attend or complete college than those with traditional high school diplomas. There is some evidence that by age 25, GED recipients do not fare any better in wages than high school dropouts (Mittelstadt, 1997).

● **Influencing At-Risk Students**   Teachers of the twenty-first century face challenges as well as exciting possibilities. Very few things are more rewarding than positively influencing an at-risk student and watching that student succeed academically. This requires teachers who have a deep and abiding belief that every student is capable of learning if given the proper encouragement and high-quality instruction. It isn't sufficient to simply "raise the bar" when students are having difficulty meeting expectations at lower levels.

The role of the teacher is constantly evolving. Teachers cannot successfully instruct students who have problems outside the school if they define themselves strictly as subject-matter specialists. **Resiliency** has been defined as the ability to bounce back from adversity and adapt successfully. More than ever before, successful teachers must become **resiliency mentors** (Greenberg, 1999/2000). This requires teachers to understand the home lives of

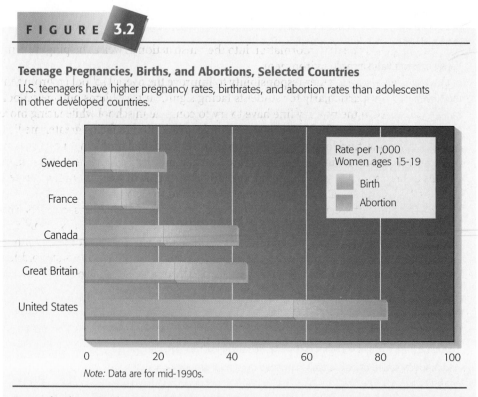

FIGURE 3.2

Teenage Pregnancies, Births, and Abortions, Selected Countries

U.S. teenagers have higher pregnancy rates, birthrates, and abortion rates than adolescents in other developed countries.

Rate per 1,000
Women ages 15-19
■ Birth
■ Abortion

Note: Data are for mid-1990s.

Source: The Alan Guttmacher Institute (AGI), "Teenagers' Sexual and Reproductive Health: Developed Countries." *Facts in Brief.* (New York: AGI, 2002). http://www.guttmacher.org/pubs/fb_teens.pdf, accessed April 20, 2005.

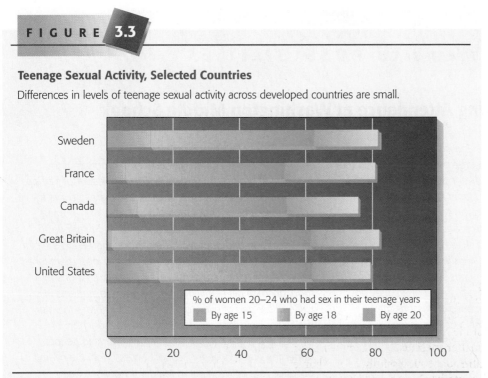

FIGURE 3.3

Teenage Sexual Activity, Selected Countries

Differences in levels of teenage sexual activity across developed countries are small.

Source: The Alan Guttmacher Institute (AGI), "Teenagers' Sexual and Reproductive Health: Developed Countries." *Facts in Brief*. (New York: AGI, 2002). http://www.guttmacher.org/pubs/fb_teens.pdf, accessed April 20, 2005.

students and incorporate that information into their instruction as well as helping students adapt to the overall school environment.

Educators also have a larger responsibility to improve the overall school environment for all students, but particularly for students facing significant problems outside school. Students living below the poverty line have to try to compete in school while facing more burdens than their more affluent peers. For example, in addition to facing greater medical problems, about one-third of poor children have untreated dental problems and 10% have lead levels in their blood high enough to cause learning problems (Lewis, 2001). Teachers who want to help students with problems need to become part of a continuum of professionals in schools and social services helping students and their families.

There is a point of view in education that teachers are subject-matter specialists who understand teaching methods, but they are not social workers or counselors. Some students respond quite well to an impersonal style of teaching while other students do not. However, many students would agree with a middle school student who once told her teacher, "I don't care how much you know, until I know how much you care."

IS EDUCATION EQUITABLE TO ALL STUDENTS?

American public schools have been regarded historically as great engines of socioeconomic mobility. Education is the major factor that individuals can affect that correlates with future economic position in society. Ideally, a democratic society should provide a high-quality public education for all of its citizens, as society benefits from having more of its citizens educated to greater levels.

INTASC

Principle #2

Knowledge of Human Development and Learning: The teacher understands how children learn and develop, and can provide learning opportunities that support their intellectual, social, and personal development.

Problems to POSSIBILITIES

Improving Attendance at Washington Middle School

Tenika Jones is a seventh-grade English teacher at Washington Middle School in a large northeastern city in the United States. She is in her third year of teaching and she is very dedicated to her inner-city students. Tenika is often disheartened because, on any given school day, about one-quarter of her students are absent. She is also aware that the absence level in her English classes is slightly above the overall average for Washington Middle School. She worries that teaching language skills requires students to build on earlier skills and when students are absent often, they do not understand instructions that build on lessons they missed. She talks to other English teachers as well as teachers of other subjects, who are also having similar problems with absences.

Discussion Question

What suggestions do you have for Tenika and her fellow teachers at Washington Middle School to improve attendance?

Possibilities

Tenika met with the three other seventh-grade English teachers to brainstorm this issue. They decided that perhaps some tangible incentives for middle schoolers to come to school might help. They created a plan that they named Attendance for School Success and took it to their principal for discussion and approval. The principal agreed to the plan and Tenika and her fellow teachers went to local merchants, asking them to donate items (movie tickets, coupons for food, or small gift certificates) to be given to students in a raffle at the end of every grading period. In order to enter the raffle, a student could not miss more than 10% of classes in the grading period. After two marking periods under the Attendance for School Success plan, the overall absence rate at Washington Middle School had been reduced from 28% to 15%. While Tenika and her colleagues still want to make it lower, they are happy that their idea is helping students at Washington Middle School come to school more often and learn more.

Educators must be knowledgeable about the legal rights of students. Special education students have a right to be educated in "the least restrictive environment." Students who are provided adapted instruction because they are English-language learners should learn the same academic content as their English-fluent peers. Magnet programs or other high-prestige educational opportunities cannot exclude students on the basis of race or socioeconomic class. Teachers and school staff must be current on requirements and legislation in order to help provide an equitable education for a wide range of students.

EQUAL VERSUS EQUITABLE INSTRUCTION

INTASC

Principle #3

Adapting Instruction for Individual Needs: The teacher understands how students differ in their approaches to learning and creates instructional opportunities that are adapted to diverse learners.

Some important questions to ask at this juncture are, "What constitutes high quality, equitable, educational opportunities?" "How widely available are these opportunities to students across the United States?" "How much inequality can the nation afford in its public schools before the general welfare is significantly affected?"

Equitable treatment can be defined as "providing instruction and support that meet the needs of students." This is a more complicated notion of education than equal treatment because it requires much more of educators than being able to claim sameness of treatment. It refutes the "one size fits all" notion of education. Equitable treatment is decidedly more difficult to achieve than equal treatment, but is a more worthy goal. **Equal treatment** of students can be verified once it is shown that all students are subject to the same process. Equitable treatment forces educators to focus on results and to evaluate teaching methods in light of these results. For example, one teacher may enjoy lecturing while

As new schools are built, policymakers and administrators stress the importance that they include the latest technology and innovations in order to provide students with the best opportunities for learning. Do "excellent facilities" guarantee learning?

another teacher prefers to have students work individually at their desks. Even though these two teachers are comfortable relying heavily on these methods, should they continue this pattern if student performance in their classes is disappointing? Clearly, the proof that a method is effective lies in how much students learn.

When parents say that their sons or daughters attend "excellent schools," what do they generally mean? Is it that their particular child is being served well in that school, or that the school provides excellent instruction for all students, or perhaps both? A highly competitive suburban high school may produce more than its proportional share of National Merit Scholars, have an extensive advanced-placement curriculum, and place a fair number of graduates in selective universities. Schools with these qualities are often seen as "excellent schools." What if this same high school had a dropout rate well above the district's average, had very little diversity in advanced-placement courses (in spite of a fairly diverse student population), and had a disproportionate suspension rate for minority students? Would it still be considered an "excellent school"?

For some, the answer may still be yes, while for others it would be a definite no. The reality may be that this high school may be serving the needs of the top 25–30% of its students very well, but the school's culture may not be accommodating to students in the bottom third of their classes. This hypothetical high school is performing part of its mission superbly while failing to provide a high-quality, equitable educational opportunity for all students.

In the current age of educational accountability, high-stakes testing is often seen as another major indicator of a school's "excellence." Test scores must not only be examined as aggregate totals for a school, but also disaggregated to look at how different populations in a school are faring academically. A school may have acceptable average standardized test scores while segments of that school's population are faring poorly, but are not noticeable in the overall average. No Child Left Behind requires the disaggregation of student test scores.

THE EFFECT OF TEACHERS ON STUDENT LEARNING

The single most important factor that society controls in providing an equitable education is the quality of the teacher. After examining a number of studies on the impact of school resources on academic achievement, Darling-Hammond and Youngs (2002) conclude that "teacher qualifications appear to have the greatest impact on what students learn and that qualified teachers are unequally allocated to students by race, income and location" (p. 17). Teacher qualifications include subject-matter mastery, versatile teaching and evaluation skills, advanced degrees, and teaching experience. This finding is encouraging for students who are planning to become teachers: You are the single most significant element in your students' academic life. Acquiring strong subject-matter mastery and sound pedagogical skills will yield significant results for your future students. The discouraging side of this finding is that teachers with the strongest qualifications are more often found serving academically proficient rather than academically needy students.

All states have some portion of their teachers working on temporary or emergency credentials (see Figure 3.4). These teachers are much more likely to be found in schools serving higher proportions of poor or minority students than in schools serving larger numbers of middle- or upper-middle-class majority students (David & Shields, 2001). An important question to raise is, "If schools are committed to equitable instruction for all students, shouldn't teachers with temporary credentials be fairly equally distributed among all schools?" If not, what factors influence the concentration of these teachers in classrooms and schools that serve mostly academically needy students? The teaching vacancies that are most difficult to fill are not just positions in mathematics and science. Teaching positions in poor rural or inner-city schools generally have more turnover than those in middle-class suburban ones. Good teachers are important for all students, but they are critical for stu-

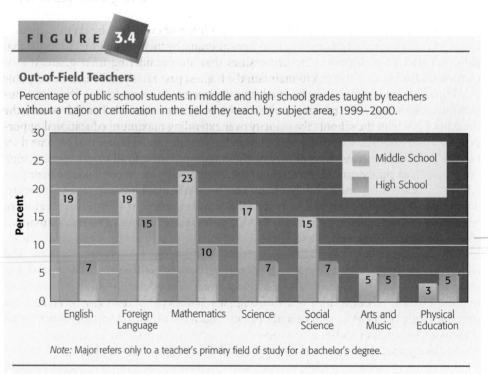

FIGURE 3.4

Out-of-Field Teachers

Percentage of public school students in middle and high school grades taught by teachers without a major or certification in the field they teach, by subject area, 1999–2000.

Note: Major refers only to a teacher's primary field of study for a bachelor's degree.

Source: M. M. Seastrom, K. J. Gruberm, R. R. Henke, D. J. McGrath, & B. A. Cohen. *Qualifications of the Public School Teacher Workforce: Prevalence of Out-of-Field Teaching 1987–1988 to 1999–2000* (NCES 2002-603, Tables B-8 and B-9). (2002) Data from U.S. Department of Education, NCES, Schools and Staffing Survey (SASS), "Public Teacher Questionnaire," 1999–2000 and "Charter Teacher Questionnaire," 1999–2000. Retrieved April 20, 2005, from http://nces.ed.gov/programs/coe/2003/charts/chart28.asp.

dents who face poverty, racism, or significant social problems. Teachers are often one of the major guiding lights for students facing social ills. When these students persevere and succeed academically, it is often because of the dedication, confidence, and support of superior teachers.

Nieto (2002/2003) raises some profound questions about equity in schooling. She is concerned that while the proportion of students of color increased from 22% in 1972 to 37% in 1998, the teaching force is 87% White and is likely to become less diverse in the near future. Nieto also cites two studies (Clewell, Puma, & McKay, 2001; Dee, 2000) that suggest that higher numbers of teachers of color in a school, particularly African American and Hispanic, can promote the achievement of African American and Hispanic students.

As a prospective teacher, what does the trend that Nieto cites suggest for your own teacher preparation? An encouraging note on this issue is that the quality of teachers is much more important than their race or ethnicity in promoting student learning.

PREPARING STUDENTS FOR HIGHER EDUCATION

Another equity issue in education is the preparation of U.S. public school students for admission into highly competitive universities. Traditionally, the most elite and competitive universities, whether public or private, have relied heavily on students' high school grade point averages and standardized test scores. Attewell (2000) notes that "the average freshman entering UCLA has a grade point average of 4.16. The University of California at Berkeley turns away hundreds of applicants with a straight A average." This phenomenon occurs when students take advanced-placement or honors courses where an A counts as 4.5 quality points instead of 4.0 points as in a regular course. Many students attending poor inner-city or rural schools where few or no advanced-placement or honors courses are offered cannot produce averages over 4.0, even if they earned nothing lower than an A in 4 years of high school.

Some public high schools try to cultivate a tradition of excellence by claiming perfect or near-perfect pass rates on advanced-placement exams by their graduates. They trust that these pass rates will impress elite universities that are considering their graduates for admission. However, in the zeal to maintain the highest pass rates possible, some very able students may be counseled away from advanced-placement courses for fear that these students may bring down the pass rate on advanced-placement exams. When this occurs, the interests of a few in the school take priority over extending maximum educational opportunities for all students. Over time, schools develop climates and cultures that become their trademarks. These climates may or may not be equally receptive to all students in a school.

Students in public schools throughout the United States are encouraged by their parents and teachers to do their best in school. This is sound advice because academic performance is a very important variable in college success as well as in affecting gains at work later in life. Students are often unaware that the public schools they attend may or may not give them an education that places them in a competitive posture to attend elite colleges and universities, or to succeed if admitted. Quite naturally, students assume that if they are doing well at their current level, they are prepared to be successful at the next.

The number of high school graduates increased steadily each year during the 1990s and is expected to continue to increase through the first decade of the twenty-first century. This increasing demand for college and university education is occurring when most states have cut the budgets of higher education—in some cases by 25% or more (Attewell, 2000). The resulting imbalance between demand and supply has created high levels of competition for university admission—especially at the most prestigious state universities—as well as increases in the cost of higher education that must be borne by the student or the student's family. In 2003, the board that governs the State University of New York System proposed a 41% increase in tuition which would raise tuition an average of $1,400 for in-state undergraduates ("New York: 41 Percent Increase," 2003). Similar measures have been enacted by legislatures and governing boards in other states.

Once isolated in special education rooms, all children with disabilities experienced limited social interaction. Today, as a result of inclusion efforts, teachers in traditional classrooms and special education centers work together to provide an environment that is both academically and socially inclusive.

Two of the most important equity issues in special education today are the appropriate identification of students in various special education programs and the overall proportion of students from different ethnic groups placed in special education classes.

INTASC

Principle #8

Assessment of Student Learning: The teacher understands and uses formal and informal assessment strategies to evaluate and ensure the continuous intellectual, social, and physical development of the learner.

● **Appropriate Identification** The first step in getting a student into the process that may result in special education placement is referral by a regular classroom teacher. It is critical that classroom teachers be aware of signs of learning disabilities (other special education categories) in order to make referrals based on accurate evidence and not on misinterpretations of cultural differences. Likewise, teacher attitudes toward students with disabilities can play a role in referrals. One study of preservice teachers produced the following result: More than one-third of respondents felt that children in a traditional classroom would be uncomfortable with disabled children and said that disabled children feel sorry for themselves (Maushak, Kelley, & Blodgett, 2001). These attitudes would hamper the judgments of this group of future teachers when they have to make decisions referring students for special education placement.

Another topic involving the proportion of special education students is their growing share of the overall public school student population in most states. Some states have become concerned about the growing numbers of special education students because they increase the budget for public education. Most of this growth has been in categories that do not involve physical disabilities. Blindness, deafness, and severe physical disabilities are relatively rare, occurring in less than 1% of the total school population. On the other hand, learning disabilities have been found in about 5% of children in U.S. public schools (Hehir, 2002). The typical special education student costs 1.9 times as much to educate as a general education student. The assessment process alone may cost around $1,800 per student (Buntin, 2002). Some states have discussed capping the overall number of special education students.

In the past decade, there has been much more emphasis on educating special education students in the least restrictive environment. This has prompted the **inclusion** of many special education students in general education classes. Presently, about 73% of students with mild disabilities are taught in general education classrooms (Maheady, Harper, & Mallette, 2001). Ideally, general classroom teachers co-teach or work with special education teachers to meet the needs of special education students in their classrooms. Special education students in public schools generate greater revenues than general education students in order to allow for smaller class sizes, aides, and other supports necessary to meet their needs. When these students are placed in special education classes, such resources are generally concentrated there. However, under the inclusion model, resources are supposed to follow the special education students that generate them, but they do not always do so. When general education teachers are assigned special education students, but feel that additional resources allocated for these students have been diverted to other parts of the school, frustration may result. Students with mild disabilities who encounter problems in the general education classroom often have difficulty in the following domains:

- Basic academic skills (such as reading, writing, spelling, and mathematics);

- Academic-related behaviors (such as school survival skills and study and organizational skills);

- Behavioral and interpersonal interactions (such as motivation and prosocial behavior) (Maheady, Harper, & Mallette, 2001).

In order to make the inclusion model successful, general education teachers may need additional training to assist special education students, and resources (special education teachers, aides, assistive technology) have to be available in the general education classroom.

In some schools, a division develops between general and special education teachers in which the full responsibility for educating special education students is placed solely on special education teachers. Some schools have developed innovative programs that minimize the labeling of students and have general and special education teachers sharing the responsibility for the success of special education students. Some states, such as New York, have required public schools to include special education students in statewide testing as well as to report these students' results separately. The national No Child Left Behind legislation has similar requirements to those of New York for special education students to be tested, even though alternative assessments may be used. As this law is implemented nationally, other states may look to New York to track the progress of special education students (Buntin, 2002, p. 46).

Some special educators (Salend, Duhaney, & Montgomery, 2002) have suggested that alternative assessments be employed along with more traditional standardized testing. Among these techniques, they suggest the use of performance-based and portfolio assessment, curriculum-based measurement, rubrics, and student journals. These assessments can provide a fuller picture of special education students' abilities, weaknesses, and learning styles.

The combination of increased monitoring of progress, better diagnostic techniques, and cooperation between general and special education teachers should improve the success rate for students with learning disabilities. Traditionally, these students have dropped out of high school at twice the rate of non-learning-disabled students (Hehir, 2002).

One of the equity issues regarding special education that remains to be answered is, "Will the emphasis on high-stakes state-mandated testing help or hurt special education students?" If the additional monitoring results in greater attention to the scores of special education students (because they count for the school's score), and this provides students with better teachers and instruction, it will be a beneficial reform. If it results in special education students having to clear a higher bar with few or no changes, or if special education students and their teachers are resented by other segments of the school for "bringing down the average," it will prove harmful. Time and additional research will show which answer is closer to being correct.

PLACEMENT BASED ON RACE AND ETHNICITY

Disproportional placement of students from racial and ethnic minorities in special education plagues many special education programs across the United States. In general, racial and ethnic minority students are overrepresented in special education categories that involve a learning or behavioral disability, while being underrepresented in the gifted category. One warning sign to educators in this area is that if the number of students in special

INTASC

Principle #3

Adapting Instruction for Individual Needs: The teacher understands how students differ in their approaches to learning and creates instructional opportunities that are adapted to diverse learners.

education are far greater or fewer than their numbers in the general school district population, care should be taken to review for bias in the referral and testing mechanisms.

An example of this was reported in a study that looked at a sample of 200 White and 200 African American students in Grades 1–4. From these 400 students, 28 White students and 54 African American students were referred for special education (Eisenman, 2001). It is very likely that the educators who made these referrals did not perceive any bias in the process, but the overall ratio of students referred suggests that there may be problems with the special education placement process.

When race and ethnicity are examined as predictors of special education placement in various states, they show that states with higher populations of White students served more special education students in general classroom settings. In states with higher proportions of minority students, more special education students were taught in special education classes. More students in states with high minority populations left high school with a certificate of completion rather than the more desirable high school diploma. The reason why disproportionality occurs fairly widely in special education placements is not fully understood, but investigators suggest that it is related to poverty, cultural bias in referral and assessment, unique factors related to ethnicity, and school-based factors (Oswald, Coutinho, & Best, 1999). Agbenyega & Jiggets (1999) suggested that when budget crises reduce preschool and kindergarten services for millions of at-risk students in urban areas, this generates additional referrals to special education classes. They also add that minority parents often do not have advocacy groups to educate them about alternatives to special education, reassessment, and deplacement.

STUDENTS IN GIFTED EDUCATION

African American and Hispanic students are also subject to disproportionate placement in another area of special education: gifted programs. Some districts have hired specialists to address the underrepresentation of African American and Hispanic students in gifted education. Because of the elite status of gifted programs in most school districts, these limited slots are highly desired by many parents. Equity issues arise in the assessment and placement of students in these programs. For instance, most students who show high potential must wait to be recognized and then referred for testing by a general classroom teacher. Once referred, there may be a long wait for the school psychologist to actually test the student.

While entry criteria may vary among districts, an IQ score of 130 or 135 is commonly required. Some students are tested privately by their parents (often more than once), and repeated testing generally improves a student's score because of greater familiarity with the test. The best score is then submitted to the school district for admission into the gifted program.

A key question here is, "What constitutes **giftedness?**" Is it strictly a high score on an IQ test (a more restrictive definition) or does giftedness also include outstanding ability in one field (a more inclusive definition)? Generally, school districts that incorporate both definitions of giftedness will have a more diverse student population in gifted programs than districts that use only the first definition (Soller, 2003).

One justification for teaching gifted students in separate classrooms away from the general population is that because of their outstanding abilities, gifted students would quickly get bored in the general education classroom because they will finish their work too quickly. A gifted classroom, where the work is paced more to gifted students' abilities, should eliminate any potential issues over "slower students holding back the gifted." In general gifted students are self-motivated learners, although some may lack the skills to accomplish their goals. Classrooms that emphasize autonomy and cooperation better accommodate most gifted students (Porath, 1996).

However, another approach to this issue is the inclusion of gifted students in general classrooms with support from gifted specialists. This way, activities are ready when gifted students complete their "regular work." When gifted students in general classrooms are not provided with sufficient challenge, the results are quite predictable. One study of gifted students in general classrooms found that most did not find their social studies and language arts classes challenging. About 75% found a challenge in mathematics and classes designed for gifted students, and most found science classes challenging only if they were involved with hands-on activities (Gallagher, Harradine, & Coleman, 1997).

Another important issue is that parents whose children are in the gifted program may become less concerned about students in the general school population. Some critics of gifted education also question that if lower class sizes, expertly trained teachers, additional field trips, and other supports work to improve the performance of gifted students, wouldn't these factors also improve the performance of students in the general school population? Policymakers must consider this issue of resource allocation. High-status knowledge can be made available to a wide array of students, not just those who are extremely talented, if educators believe they may all profit from it and are willing to explain these concepts in accessible ways to the general student population.

"What the best and wisest parent wants for his own child, that is what the community must want for all of its children."

JOHN DEWEY

THINK ABOUT THIS:
How does Dewey's quote relate to the discussion on equitable education?

SHARE and **COMPARE:**
Contact your state department of education for a breakdown of per-pupil expenditures for each district in your state. Notice the difference in per-pupil expenditures between the lowest- and highest- spending districts. Discuss the gap in per-pupil expenditures with a classmate. Do either of you think that money spent on pupils gives them an advantage or a disadvantage in a competitive educational system? Why or why not?

WHAT EDUCATIONAL OPTIONS ARE BEST FOR RACIAL- AND LANGUAGE-MINORITY STUDENTS?

GROUPING PRACTICES

Parents, educators, and policymakers may agree that a quality education is important for all students in the United States, but they often disagree over how to bring this about. Historically, most students of different social classes, races, and ethnicities were educated separately from one another. There was an implicit assumption that in order to achieve excellence, equity had to be sacrificed. Some people's reasoning behind separating students was pure bias, while others felt that without this separation very capable students wouldn't reach their potential. There are some valid reasons for grouping students for instruction. However, when students are placed in remedial or slow groups, one common problem is that these students are stigmatized or even ridiculed by their peers. When an elementary teacher disguises the levels of reading groups by calling them *bluebirds, cardinals* and *robins,* students immediately know if the robins have the lowest reading proficiency. These early labels can leave a stigma that lasts for life.

INTASC

Principle #5

Classroom Motivation and Management: The teacher uses an understanding of individual and group motivation and behavior to create a learning environment that encourages positive social interaction, active engagement in learning, and self-motivation.

PREPARING STUDENTS FOR WORK AFTER HIGH SCHOOL

Nearly all high schools have programs aimed at students who plan to enter the world of work immediately after high school. They have different labels such as *on-the-job training* (OJT), *diversified cooperative training* (DCT), or *partnerships with business.* Whatever the label, these programs attempt to give the student some practical work experience while still in high school. Some programs allow the student to leave school early to work while others may give credit for after-school work. While there is no single national model, these programs tend to have formal connections between the teacher in charge of the program and the employer. Students are frequently rated on their performance at work as well as at school. Many students who have performed well at work while still in high school are offered permanent positions by employers as a result of these programs.

ARE STUDENT ACCOUNTABILITY AND EQUITY COMPLEMENTARY OR COMPETING INTERESTS?

I N T A S C

Principle #8

Assessment of Student Learning: The teacher understands and uses formal and informal assessment strategies to evaluate and ensure the continuous intellectual, social, and physical development of the learner.

The issue of equity in education has precipitated much controversy over the years. What is meant by *equity*? Is it providing each student the ideal educational environment? Do we mean educating all students to their fullest potential? If so, who determines what that potential is? What resources should be devoted to the education of your child? Is the answer the same when considering the education of other people's children?

These questions have generated much debate over time, but one thing is certain: No debate about equity in education can ignore how society distributes resources for education or how students of different social class backgrounds have access to resources.

Many states have enacted statewide high-stakes testing in which students from all of the state's public schools are measured by the same yardstick. The tests tend to be fairly similar, testing almost entirely verbal and quantitative skills instead of the entire curriculum that students take in school. However, the following characteristics tend to vary widely among public schools: per-pupil expenditures, access to quality and subject-certified teachers, access to honors curricula, and access to high-quality physical facilities. Advocates of statewide **high-stakes testing** argue that similar expectations on standardized tests will raise the bar in low-performing schools. Presumably, teachers and students will try harder to meet the common standards for all schools. Failure to meet these standards frequently has very negative effects for both students and schools. While the penalties vary from state to state, students may not pass to the next grade or may get a certificate of completion instead of a high school diploma if they don't achieve minimum scores on the state's high-stakes test. For schools, penalties may range from being placed on probation or losing funds to possibly losing their students to other schools and being closed.

Opponents of high-stakes testing argue that meeting common state-wide standards is fine as long as schools have similar levels of resources and quality of teachers and the entire school curriculum is emphasized, not just verbal and quantitative skills. Opponents argue that these circumstances are not found very frequently in U.S. public schools and school reform should involve the whole school environment and not just testing. Asking students to meet higher standards without looking at systemic change in schools is like asking a high jumper to jump higher by raising the bar instead of changing the training.

Besides meeting state standards, student test data on the state's high-stakes test is used to determine **adequate yearly progress (AYP)** mandated by No Child Left Behind. The proficiency levels for reading and mathematics at a school must increase over the years until they reach 100% in the 2013–2014 academic year. Time will tell whether this goal is met or whether it will be an optimistic desire of policymakers.

Another key issue in providing equity in education is the role played by factors that schools do not control. One study of North Carolina elementary schools examined reading and mathematics achievement among fourth graders over 3 years. This study found that

BUILDING ON EDUCATIONAL FOUNDATIONS

How Are Educational Resources Distributed?

Any society such as the United States has a finite number of resources. This is certainly true in the case of how much money is spent on education. Whenever a school budget is put together, the question arises: "What should we spend our resources on?" This is an especially difficult question when we consider special and gifted education.

Assume that a school district spends, on average, $7,000 per year on educating each of its students. Do certain groups deserve more funding than others? For example, should a student with a special talent as a violinist be provided lessons to help him develop his talent? Is this more important than giving a student with learning disabilities extra tutoring so that she can do a minimally passable level of academic work?

Some would argue that the school's and society's obligation is to provide all students with the opportunity to become all that they are capable of being. But what if resources are scarce? Is it more important to build a new city hall, or to use the same money to pay for an enrichment program for performing art students in a large school district?

Should schools help children who come from poorer families get reduced or free lunches? Is this actually part of an educational system's responsibility? Should schools provide students with medical assistance such as an annual physical checkup? What about providing contraceptives for sexually active teenagers?

Do you think that a wealthy school district with a large tax base needs to share its resources with poorer districts? This is happening in Kentucky, where school systems in more affluent parts of the state, such as Louisville, are sharing revenues from the local taxes they collect with poorer districts in rural Appalachia.

What do you think? What should be the guidelines for making decisions concerning the use of educational resources in American society in order to meet the needs of all students?

student demographic factors (percentage of students on free/reduced lunch, parents' average level of education) were the best predictors of mathematics and reading achievement (Okpala, 2002). When schools are asked to meet certain minimum standards in skill achievement, some schools cannot fail to achieve these by virtue of the economic advantages many of their pupils enjoy. Other schools, with mostly economically disadvantaged student populations, must show enormous improvements in order to reach the same minimum standard. Schools with many economically disadvantaged students that make greater gains but still miss the minimum standards are often subject to sanctions not given schools in wealthier communities that make lesser gains, but still achieve standardized test scores above the target.

With a public school structure that encompasses 50 state departments of education and thousands of local school boards, the U.S. education system is not designed to produce a common product. This structure is highly sensitive to local needs, but it is very difficult to make wholesale changes in U.S. public schools that will affect each and every student. This same decentralized school governance structure is mirrored in a public school financing structure that creates significant gaps in per-pupil funding not only among states, but within a state as well (see Figure 3.5 on page 90).

The issue of exactly how much money affects the quality of education, when compared to other factors such as teacher effort and student initiative, is a topic that has been widely debated. Students have no choice but to face the financial circumstances present in their schools. However, when it comes to money and the quality of public education, it is difficult to argue with one educator's observation: "I would rather be with it than without it."

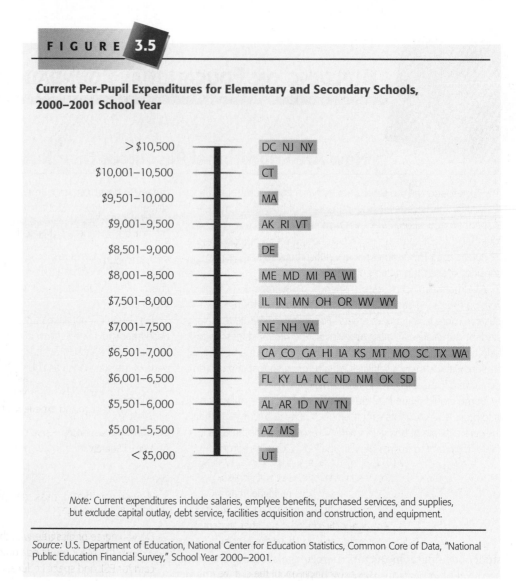

FIGURE 3.5

Current Per-Pupil Expenditures for Elementary and Secondary Schools, 2000–2001 School Year

> $10,500	DC NJ NY
$10,001–10,500	CT
$9,501–10,000	MA
$9,001–9,500	AK RI VT
$8,501–9,000	DE
$8,001–8,500	ME MD MI PA WI
$7,501–8,000	IL IN MN OH OR WV WY
$7,001–7,500	NE NH VA
$6,501–7,000	CA CO GA HI IA KS MT MO SC TX WA
$6,001–6,500	FL KY LA NC ND NM OK SD
$5,501–6,000	AL AR ID NV TN
$5,001–5,500	AZ MS
< $5,000	UT

Note: Current expenditures include salaries, emplyee benefits, purchased services, and supplies, but exclude capital outlay, debt service, facilities acquisition and construction, and equipment.

Source: U.S. Department of Education, National Center for Education Statistics, Common Core of Data, "National Public Education Financial Survey," School Year 2000–2001.

Most educators would concur that significant funding gaps among public schools create a great obstacle to providing equity in public education.

ACCOUNTABILITY AND INCLUSION OF SPECIAL EDUCATION STUDENTS

Education for students with disabilities has undergone significant changes in the past four decades. In 1975, the U.S. Congress passed the Education for All Handicapped Children Act (also known as Public Law 94–142). This act was reauthorized in 1990 as the Individuals with Disabilities Education Act (IDEA). Key features of this legislation were that people between ages 3 and 21 must be provided with a **free and appropriate education** and that education should tale place in the **least restrictive environment.** Additional language mandating individualized instruction for qualifying students resulted in requiring an **individualized education program (IEP)** for each student. These stipulations in the law were included so that students with disabilities would receive the necessary attention that had often eluded them in the past. No longer could these students be relegated to the back of a classroom, labeled as "slow learners," and simply ignored when they did not achieve at the levels expected for other students.

Through the Eyes of Culturally Sensitive Teachers

Fair Grading Standards for All Students

Miguel Suarez is a fourth-grade teacher in a large U.S. school district. He noticed that the box marked M (for modified curriculum), which was used for English-language learners and for special education students, had been removed from the report card. He was very concerned and shared the concerns in the following letter with one of his professors:

Dear Professor,

I am sending you this letter because I feel there is something wrong with the district's new report card. Last year, English-language learners and special education students received grades with M (for modified curriculum) marked in the standards box. This year the M has been removed. Additionally, teachers of English-language learners are being told by administrators that, with rare exceptions, English-language learners are to receive grades no higher than a C. Grades of A or B indicate that these students are not being challenged and need more difficult work. Any other students who have English as a native language have the possibility of achieving A or B grades.

I questioned my assistant principal about the change in report card format as well as the directions ESL teachers were receiving not to award grades of A or B. She was not happy with my questions. She began to lose her temper and told me to "forget about it." She said the decision had been made and there would be no changes. I asked who made the decision and why, but she responded, "It doesn't matter." When I suggested asking someone in the district office about the report card change, she said, "You can't do that" (meaning contacting people in higher positions).

After recovering from this shock, I concluded that something was fishy about this whole thing. I feel very annoyed because the structure of this new report card will paint a very negative picture of our English-language learners and shows a blatant disregard for our ESL student population. Maybe this is nothing new, but it shouldn't go unchallenged.

I think I have done enough venting for now. I would appreciate some of your valuable time to let me know if you think this new report card is fair to our ESL students. I would also like to know what steps you suggest, since you have more knowledge and experience than I do.

Thank you so much,
Miguel Suarez

Points to Ponder

1. Why do you think the assistant principal resists answering Miguel's questions?

2. Do you agree or disagree with the district policy to remove the M for modified curriculum from the report card for ESL and special education students? Give at least one reason for your response.

3. What, if anything, would you advise Miguel to do at this point?

4. What are some of the potential risks and rewards of pursuing this matter or "forgetting about it" for Miguel? For the English-language learners in his school district?

Today all states have certification standards for teachers of students in various categories of special education (see Figure 3.6 on page 92). Some states permit teachers to teach students with a wide range of disabilities with a "varying exceptionalities" certification, while other states require a certification for each specific exceptionality. The varying exceptionalities certification has the advantage of allowing the teacher to be certified with a wide range of special education students and to be more versatile. The single certification for each exceptionality generally provides teachers with greater background about one category of special education students.

FIGURE 3.6

Special Education Teaching Assignments

Learning disabilities	Orthopedic impairment
Mental retardation	Mild disability
Emotional and behavioral disorders	Severe disability
Speech and hearing impairment	Autism
Special education, general	Developmental disability
Deaf and hard of hearing	Early childhood special education
Visual impairment	Other special education

Some schools use **tracking** to place students on different paths for all subjects. In many high schools, students are advised and scheduled into classes for the college- or university-bound, the business or work experience track, or perhaps a vocational/technical curriculum. Advocates of tracking argue that this makes instruction easier for teachers and more effective for students because classes have a narrower range of backgrounds and abilities among students. Opponents of tracking point out that if a student's "direction" is determined at an early age, the child's options may be limited later in the school years. For example, if "high-status knowledge" necessary for college or university success is given only to students in one track, then those in other tracks who later wish to pursue a college education will have a very difficult time. Additional concerns regarding tracking are that often students with great academic potential are immature at the age when tracking begins and mistakes are frequently made with students who have yet to show their full potential.

While tracking is very prevalent in U.S. schools today, studies have shown that the only difference between high and low tracks is that students in lower tracks are consistently taught less complex subject matter than what they would need later if they decide to enter higher education (Oakes, 1995). Tracking serves to lower aspirations of students in the lower tracks. About 64% of African American students expect to finish college, but only 25% enroll in high school college preparatory courses (Mallery & Mallery, 1999, p. 14). Jeannie Oakes, one of the leading scholars of tracking, notes that "schools far more often judge African American and Latino students to have learning deficits and limited potential" (1995, p. 682).

About 80% of U.S. public high schools engage in some form of tracking on a school-wide basis (Mallery & Mallery, 1999). Perceptions by educators of students' abilities are influenced by the track they may have been assigned early in elementary school. Frazier (1997) observes, "Ability grouping eventually leads to tracking. We aren't going to be able to separate the two. Society still carries the baggage of classism and racism and that baggage will flow into the school system" (p. 13). Assuming that this baggage exists in our public schools, what can current and future educators do to minimize it for students?

If schools are going to group students according to abilities, every conceivable precaution should be taken to ensure that low-ability groups have as much opportunity to learn high-status knowledge as their peers. Students in English as a Second Language and special education classes must be regarded as integral parts of a school's community. Teachers in the general program who are organizing special activities should take care to include all students. Adults often assume that students attending the same school are enjoying the same school climate. This cannot be taken for granted because students of differing backgrounds experience different aspects of school culture. They are often sharing the common areas (cafeteria, hallways) of a school, not the classrooms, with students from different tracks.

INTASC

Principle #5

Classroom Motivation and Management: The teacher uses an understanding of individual and group motivation and behavior to create a learning environment that encourages positive social interaction, active engagement in learning, and self-motivation.

EDUCATION MATTERS

Minority Teachers for Minority Students

According to the American Association of Colleges for Teacher Education (1999), ethnic minority teachers represent about 9% of U.S. public schoolteachers, but that number is expected to drop to less than 5% in the coming years. Meanwhile, ethnic minority students constitute 40% of the total student body in the United States, and this proportion is expected to increase significantly. This has always been an issue, but the situation is getting worse because fewer culturally diverse students are entering teaching. Most are now pursuing degrees in business and other fields with greater salaries.

In a school district in Arizona, leaders spoke with ethnic minority staff members and created several strategies for attracting and retaining them. Their plan includes hot topics such as considering paying these teachers more money to attract them and starting support groups that discuss racism with other faculty and students while they are working in the districts. They want districts to take time to talk with them and learn about them. You can read all about this issue in *Educational Leadership (*May 2001), "Supporting a Diverse Teacher Corps."

The Education Issue: The need for more ethnically diverse teachers for diverse students

Students in schools who never see a teacher who looks like them, or is at least different from the mainstream, have no role models as teachers. Students from other countries entering school have a need to belong and feel part of the new school culture. Having teachers in the school building who are bilingual and understand another culture creates a level of tolerance for differences. Students can identify with teachers who understand that differences are strengths to be shared. One concern for schools is that the number of cultural groups far exceeds the ethnic groups for teachers. Even teachers of ethnic groups would be teaching students of other origins. These teachers would also have to reach out to learn other new cultures.

What's Your Opinion?

Do you agree that bonuses are a way to attract and retain diverse teachers? What would other teachers in the district think about that? What would be an important incentive for you? How many diverse teacher candidates are in your teacher education class? How will you provide students with role models for all of the various cultures in your classroom? What did you learn from this Education Matters? How will you use what you learned?

EDUCATING IMMIGRANT STUDENTS

When immigrant students enter school in the United States, they have significant adaptations to make. Many factors affect these adaptations: age at the time of immigration, time spent in the host country, the socioeconomic background of the student, family aspirations, and so on. One of the key elements in effective immigrant education is the ability of educators to clarify their own philosophical approaches (Schoorman, 2001). Clearly, immigrant students need to function in American society. To achieve this goal, teachers need to be sensitive to the cultural and language differences that immigrant students bring with them. Encouragement to "speak only English" may be intended to help immigrant students adapt more quickly to the United States, but students can misconstrue it to imply that their language has no place, or is inferior. Such a message can be devastating to immigrant students, especially when delivered by a teacher.

Because of the growing nature of diversity in today's classrooms, teachers must be careful to avoid sending a message of *American exceptionalism*. While certainly not the norm, this philosophy may be encountered on occasion. This belief goes beyond the general notion that U.S. schools should instill a love of country and patriotism in students. Gutek (2004) defines American exceptionalism as a notion that "the American nation, its

INTASC

Principle #5

Classroom Motivation and Management: The teacher uses an understanding of individual and group motivation and behavior to create a learning environment that encourages positive social interaction, active engagement in learning, and self-motivation.

INTASC

Principle #6

Communication Skills: The teacher uses knowledge of effective verbal, nonverbal, and media communication techniques to foster active inquiry, collaboration, and supportive interaction in the classroom.

Meeting the needs of English language learners in our schools is one of the greatest challenges facing educators today and into the future. What steps are you taking in your preparation to make sure you are able to meet the needs of ESL students?

people and their culture are different from people of other countries: they are extraordinary" or "superior" (p. 164). There is a fine, but important, line between being proud of who you are and being convinced that you are superior to others. The latter view, no matter how well intended, is not likely to be admired by students in U.S. schools who do not come from mainstream U.S. culture and are trying to learn it. Teachers who are border crossers help parents and students who do not come from mainstream U.S. culture understand the virtues and challenges of this nation, while still valuing their own backgrounds.

In communities that receive a significant number of immigrant students, school districts have begun "newcomer programs" to help newly arrived students with the adaptation process. These programs may vary in approach. Some have devoted an entire school solely to newcomers, while others use the "school within a school" model. Some offer English as a Second Language, others have bilingual education, and some offer both. These programs, which are generally one to three semesters long, typically focus on middle and high school students because adaptation to the U.S. curriculum at these levels is more demanding than in elementary school (Short & Boyson, 2000).

Students in English as a Second Language classes in science or history earn the same credits as other students taking these subjects in the general program, but they may not always be taught an equivalent amount of material. At the end of high school these students are tested to assess their skill levels in mathematics and English, typically by a standardized test. In some cases, students who have been studying English for 2 years are asked to meet proficiency standards that researchers say take 5 or more years to attain. When states impose expectations that cannot be met within a given period of time, advocates for immigrant students are likely to challenge these practices in the courts.

Most immigrant students are pleased to be attending schools in the United States and tend to see a public education as an opportunity for a better life than what they may have had in their countries of origin. It is not unusual for an immigrant student just starting to learn English to go through a "silent period." Some may think the student is withdrawing or perhaps is very shy. What is happening is that the student is focusing on listening to English and building vocabulary. Once time passes and a significant number of English words are familiar, the student will begin to speak more English.

American schools have been teaching immigrant students for more than two centuries. The philosophy today is often quite different from the past. Immigrant students today are not usually asked to reject their original culture and language in order to learn English and receive an education in American schools.

PATTERNS OF STUDENT SEGREGATION AND INTEGRATION

Population migration of the past two decades has resulted in a growing trend toward resegregation of the public school system. Desegregation efforts of the 1970s often involved court orders to enforce changes in attendance boundaries that school boards were reluctant to impose because they were politically unpopular. With the passing of time, racial and ethnic characteristics of neighborhoods changed, particularly in cities. As "White flight" to the suburbs increased, the old court orders did not fit the new reality of residential patterns. Courts were sometimes reluctant to extend desegregation orders that were 15 or 20 years old. The net result has been U.S. public schools becoming more segregated than they were in the 1980s.

This movement toward resegregation has led some people to now argue in favor of **neighborhood schools,** the preferable apolitical term that seems to favor more "segregated schools." Nonetheless, when neighborhoods are racially and ethnically segregated, and most are, then a neighborhood school becomes a segregated school. Thus, successful arguments for neighborhood schools result in significant racial/ethnic segregation without appearing to favor segregation.

Unfortunately, as urban schools lose more middle- and upper-class parents (with their significant political influence) to suburban or private schools, the schools become more resource poor, which affects educational opportunities. Berliner and Biddle (1995, p. 55) have suggested a student achievement law that reads, "Regardless of what anyone claims about student and school characteristics, **opportunity to learn** is the single most powerful predictor of student achievement." If these authors are correct, how consistent is the opportunity to learn in the United States? How does the average educational opportunity given to racial, ethnic, and linguistic minority students compare with that given to their mainstream peers?

"Must you keep reminding me by wearing that shirt?"

Courtesy of Aaron Bacall, *The Lighter Side of Teaching,* p. 60. Copyright 2003 by Aaron Bacall. Reprinted by permission of Corwin Press Inc.

OTHER FACTORS AFFECTING STUDENT ACHIEVEMENT

No element of an opportunity to learn is more important than a quality well-prepared teacher. Mora (2000) observes the following about teachers of students with **limited English proficiency (LEP):** "In the early 1990's, only 30% of teachers with LEP students had received any form of LEP instruction training" (p. 722). Clearly, even the best-intentioned teachers cannot be expected to adequately teach a student population they have not been prepared to teach.

- **Bilingual Needs** There is a difference in public support if people are asked whether they support bilingual education or dual-language programs. *Bilingual education* is seen as teaching in English and in the native language only to students who speak a first language other than English. *Dual-language programs* teach in English and a foreign language as well, but in these programs the student population is composed of native English speakers as well as English as a Second Language learners. Generally, public support is stronger for dual-language programs than for bilingual programs. Since both programs teach in English and another language, what would account for the difference? Could it be that dual-language programs involve native English speakers and thus are not perceived to be remedial in any way?

Dual-language programs may also be called **two-way immersion (TWI)** programs. Although relatively rare in U.S. schools, they represent a promising alternative for educating English as a Second Language learners and simultaneously providing second-language competency to native English speakers. Some programs assign "buddies" to students who will mentor them in language acquisition. The buddies are students who are more proficient in the target language (Li & Nes, 2001). This can be done for English as well as the other language in a TWI program. Although research on these relatively new programs is limited, most studies confirm that students in TWI programs perform as well or better on English standardized achievement tests compared to students in monolingual English or transitional bilingual programs. In addition, there is some evidence that TWI programs promote positive cross-cultural relationships among students (Christian, Howard, & Loeb, 2000).

INTASC

Principle #3

Adapting Instruction for Individual Needs: The teacher understands how students differ in their approaches to learning and creates instructional opportunities that are adapted to diverse learners.

I N T A S C

Principle #5

Classroom Motivation and Management: The teacher uses an understanding of individual and group motivation and behavior to create a learning environment that encourages positive social interaction, active engagement in learning, and self-motivation.

● **Classroom Climate**   Teachers and school administrators cannot make assumptions about classroom or school climate. Each should be objectively assessed and, if found lacking, steps should be taken to improve it. Often, students who feel uncomfortable in a school respond with "oppositional behavior" and resist what teachers or administrators are asking them to do. If students feel that we do not value them, they will often resist performing well. From this perspective, doing well in the class of a teacher who doesn't value you is like rewarding the last person you want to reward. While this may not make sense to most adults, some adolescents feel it is justified.

In some schools, students of color have defined high academic achievement as "acting White." These students are clearly alienated from the school's culture and have wrongly defined good grades and excellent performance as belonging to another group besides their own. These students don't recognize that knowledge is not the property of any group and getting good grades is not "acting White." All groups in this nation have had many people that have excelled academically. As one university professor remarked, "Let nothing that is human be alien to you." This message that knowledge belongs to all of us must reach more of our students who feel academically dispossessed.

A number of factors make for the best learning environments for all students:

1. Students have teachers who are subject-matter competent and versatile in their teaching methods.

2. Students' home cultures and languages are valued and respected by school staff.

3. Teachers have high expectations of all students and are willing to provide the necessary assistance or modifications to reach high goals.

4. Schools emphasize the acquisition of broad knowledge as well as verbal and quantitative skills.

5. Parents of all of a school's constituencies have a proportional influence in school policymaking.

6. School staff establishes a personal bond of caring and monitoring student success.

When these characteristics are present in abundance, students of all backgrounds are much more likely to thrive. While administrators play a key role in setting the climate in which the preceding characteristics may thrive, they can't do it without significant support from teachers. In any educational institution, the faculty is mainly responsible for the academic climate as well as creating the atmosphere that allows students to feel comfortable learning.

FINAL THOUGHTS

This chapter has examined changes in the student population and issues that affect the ability of a wide range of students to attain an equitable education. Students are becoming more diverse, requiring teachers to be more multiculturally aware than ever before in order to be effective. Some may view this as an imposition, while others look at it as a professional challenge that will enable them to better meet the needs of an ever-changing student population.

Social problems are always issues that concern educators, particularly because they interfere with students' welfare and academic achievement. While public schools cannot eradicate all social problems, educators can work with other governmental and community agencies to help students overcome many of life's challenges. What could be more rewarding than having a student tell a teacher, "If it weren't for you, I wouldn't be graduating"? For some students facing significant social problems, teachers may be some of the few stable adults in their lives. It is quite natural that teachers serve as mentors for all students, but particularly for students with social problems. When Americans are asked who have been the most important people in their lives outside their family members, a common answer is "teachers." Few occupations have this type of influence.

Schools often struggle with resource issues, and the decentralized nature of American education makes it difficult to make wholesale changes or to generate a similar product. Over the years, students, parents, and educators have worked to achieve equity in education. This notion of "equity in education" is a journey, not a destination. All forces in society are not always aligned behind this goal. The public dialogue does not always reflect this. Resources are always an issue in education, and which students enjoy the limited resources in schools will always generate debate.

Special education is an effort to provide the most appropriate education and teachers with specific training to assist students with special needs. Whether this occurs in a general classroom or in special education classrooms, care should be taken to ensure that students with a special education designation are appropriately placed and that no cultural or other bias plays a part in their placement. When students of a particular racial or ethnic group are disproportionately placed in special education classes, this should be seen as a warning sign to examine placement procedures. Special education designations should also be periodically reviewed to ensure that they are still accurate and do not become lifelong labels.

While the promise of education is held out to all students, a brief look at the outcomes in American education shows that all students are not profiting equally. As this nation moves into the twenty-first century, it will need students of color, immigrant students, and linguistic minorities to be fairly represented among the highly educated segments of American society. Therefore, the appropriate education of racial and linguistic minority students is far more than simply the fair thing to do. Failure to have these students achieve at a level commensurate with their peers will have negative consequences for the nation's future.

Education represents the single most important variable that individuals control for personal and economic betterment. Education represents a journey. It should not be a superhighway for some and a two-lane road filled with potholes for others. One thing that unites educators of all types is students. Their success is the ultimate test of a school's mission.

REFLECTIONS

Professional Plan for Working with Today's Students

1. Three things I learned from this chapter about students in U.S. schools are:

2. Two things in this chapter that I would like to learn more about are:

   a. _____

   b. _____

3. I plan to investigate these two areas and learn more about topics in this chapter by:

   _____ Reading some of the book club choices

   _____ Reading sources referenced in the chapters that interest me

   _____ Interviewing students and asking them what aspects of the education they encounter today are effective or ineffective

   _____ Exploring the Web sites listed in the Log On section

   _____ Talking to teachers and observing classrooms to see how teachers attempt to reach students with different backgrounds and interests.

4. I will include the following in my Touch the Future portfolio:

SUMMARY

What Social Changes Are Affecting School Demographics?

- The overall student population in the United States will increase at about 5% per year until 2013.
- Some areas of the United States will experience increases in the number of students while others will show losses.
- Racial, ethnic, and linguistic diversity is increasing among U.S. students.
- More students are coming from blended families rather than the traditional nuclear family.

- Social problems such as drugs, alcohol, and teenage pregnancy retard academic progress.
- Successful teachers must be resilient and recognize social issues their students face in order to learn.

Is Education Equitable to All Students?

- A school may have an overall rating of "excellent" and fail to reach all types of students that attend it.
- Certified and high-quality teachers are not evenly distributed across all public schools in a district, a state, or the nation.
- While most states have formulas to try to alleviate funding differences in public schools, significant disparities still exist.
- Special education students are guaranteed a "free and appropriate education" in the "least restrictive environment" by Public Law 94–142.
- Disproportional placement of students from some minority groups in special education programs remains a contentious issue.
- The No Child Left Behind law requires schools to report the adequate yearly progress (AYP) for all categories of students, and the targets increase with time.

Are Student Accountability and Equity Complementary or Competing Interests?

- Advocates of high-stakes testing suggest that schools "raise the bar" every year to improve student performance.
- Opponents of high-stakes testing argue that financial resources and teacher quality must be equal if we are to hold all students to similar standards.
- Special education students should be taught in the "least restrictive environment."
- Inclusion is the practice of educating special education students in the regular classroom rather than in separate special education classrooms.
- There is a disproportionate placement of minority students in many special education classrooms.
- Giftedness may be defined as a high IQ score or as outstanding ability in one field.

What Educational Options Are Best for Racial and Language Minority Students?

- Ability grouping of students often results in the lower groups being stigmatized.
- Immigrant students are often expected to complete academic work in English before they have had a full opportunity to master academic English.
- Two-way immersion (bilingual) programs are relatively rare in U.S. schools despite the support for these programs in the research.
- About 80% of U.S. schools engage in some form of tracking students.
- Students who feel alienated by a school's culture often act out with "oppositional behavior" against the school or school authorities.

Companion Website

Visit the **Touch the Future . . . Teach!** Companion Website at www.ablongman.com/diaz for additional opportunities.

KEY WORDS

adequate yearly progress (AYP)   88

equal treatment   80

equitable treatment   80

free and appropriate education   90

giftedness   86

high-stakes testing   88

inclusion   84

individualized education program (IEP)   90

least restrictive environment   90

limited English proficiency (LEP)   95

neighborhood school   95

opportunity to learn   95

resiliency   78

resiliency mentors   78

tracking   92

two-way immersion (TWI)   95

CONCEPT REVIEW

1. Identify the areas of the United States that are experiencing the greatest gains in numbers of public school students.

2. Explain what has happened to the high school dropout rate in the past decades.

3. Compare the current racial and ethnic nature of the public school student population with earlier patterns that existed in U.S. schools.

4. Identify changes in the family structure and socioeconomic backgrounds of U.S. students and analyze how these patterns affect schools.

5. Understand which social problems involving students tend to be more common in which school environments.

6. Define various conceptions of excellence in education.

7. Choose at least three issues involving equity in education and analyze the significance of each.

8. Explain how the decentralized nature of U.S. public schools contributes to differences in funding levels.

9. Identify the rights that special education students have and know why schools cannot legally segregate special education students from the general student population.

10. Summarize the reasons why gifted programs exist and identify some concerns about gifted programs.

11. Explain reasons for and against the grouping and tracking of students.

12. Identify patterns of access to well-qualified teachers in schools serving different socioeconomic populations.

13. Select at least three characteristics of schools with the best learning environments.

14. Understand the potential of the teaching profession in shaping the lives of students.

TOUCH THE FUTURE . . .

Read On

Uncertain Lives: Children of Promise, Teachers of Hope
Robert V. Bullough, Jr. (New York: Teachers College Press, 2001)
A source of heartwarming anecdotes about teachers who have made a difference.

Against the Odds: How "At Risk" Students Exceed Expectations
Janine Bempechat (San Francisco: Jossey-Bass, 1998)
Gives the reader some insight into school success under trying circumstances.

Meeting the Needs of Multiethnic and Multiracial Children in Schools
Francis Wardle and Marta I. Cruz-Janzen (Boston: Allyn & Bacon, 2004)
Excellent guidance for teachers to understand students of multiracial backgrounds. The authors explain racial identity and provide suggestions that show how to avoid miscategorizing people.

Learner-Centered Teaching: Five Key Changes to Practice
Maryellen Weimer (San Francisco: Jossey-Bass, 2002)
Provides some very practical suggestions for moving instruction from a teacher-centered to a learner-centered approach.

Urban Teaching: The Essentials
Lois Weiner (New York: Teachers College Press, 1999)
Keen insights into the urban teaching experience as well as suggestions for teachers working in urban schools.

Log On

Diversity: Issues and Responses
www.cde.ca.gov/iasa/diversity.html
A general site on diversity and the issues it raises for U.S. students and schools, includes detailed information on demographic changes in the United States.

Native American Culture
www.ewetribe.com/NACulture
Provides information about various aspects of Native American culture, including education, social issues, belief systems, and traditions.

Open Dialogue
www.opendialogue.org/english/home.html
A very informative site regarding American Muslims, provides facts, perspectives, and an opportunity for dialogue.

Retanet: Resources for Teaching about the Americas
http://ladb.unm.edu/retanet/plans
Provides lesson plans and information about various Latin American cultures.

Smithsonian Institution: African American History and Culture
www.si.edu/resource/faq/nmah/afroam.htm
The Smithsonian's comprehensive site, with links to information about African American culture, history, children's stories, and much more.

Write On

"I am always willing to learn, but I do not always like being taught."
—Sir Winston Churchill

In your journal, explain what you think Winston Churchill meant by this statement. Write a brief essay explaining whether current students would agree with this statement and what this means for teachers.

OBSERVATION GUIDE

TEACH: LINKING THEORY TO PRACTICE

Part of your informed decision about teaching needs to come from your own desire to explore all aspects of teaching. The following interview and observation guide will help you while completing practical field experiences or during regular visits to schools.

Objective: To explore students' perspectives about effective teaching

School (use code name): _____   Observer: _____
Student: (use code name): _____   Date: _____
Time Interview Began: _____   Time Ended: _____

Directions: Work with your professor to locate a school where you might be welcomed to speak with students, or arrange to speak with young children you know personally. If working with a local school, call the teacher to set up an appointment, then use these questions as a guide or create your own. Interview at least three students and then write a short essay comparing and contrasting student responses to the following questions. Make it clear to the students before beginning your interview that you don't want any references to teachers' names. The important thing to record is the students' perceptions.

Share and compare your interview with other members of the class to identify the common themes related to understanding today's students.

1. Think of the best teacher you ever had. What two things did that teacher do to deserve being regarded as your best teacher?

2. When teachers are presenting a lesson, what two or three things do they do that tend to confuse you?

3. What do teachers do when presenting a lesson that you find most helpful?

4. How useful are the examples teachers use? Please provide an example that helped you understand and one that did not.

5. How important is the way you feel in a class in order to learn properly?

6. What advice would you give future teachers you may have that would result in your being very comfortable in their classes?

Connecting with INTASC: Principle 2

Knowledge of Human Development and Learning: The teacher understands how children learn and develop, and can provide learning opportunities that support their intellectual, social, and personal development.

Speak with a K–12 teacher and find out what the teacher does to meet Principle 2. How does the teacher identify and incorporate children's backgrounds into daily lessons? How does the teacher interact with students in a way that is sensitive to each one's personal needs?

4

Parents, Families, and the Community: Partners in Education

Who am I?

What do I believe?

THINK ABOUT THIS:

The work of a teacher requires you to deal not only with students, but also with those who influence students outside school. Children reflect the values and attitudes of their families and the general communities in which they live. As American society has become more complex over the years, so too have the interactions with your students' families. How will the families of the children you teach affect your work as a teacher? Will the forces that shape them influence your classroom? What will you need to know in order to do your job effectively and meet the needs of your students?

"Family life is full of major and minor crises . . . and all kinds of characters. It is tied to places and events and histories. With all of these felt details, life etches itself into memory and personality. It's difficult to imagine anything more nourishing to the soul."

Thomas Moore

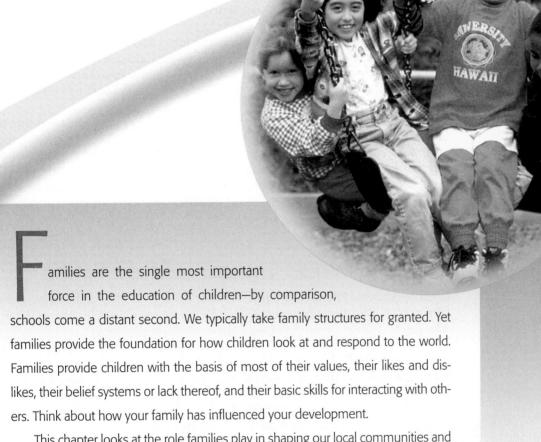

Families are the single most important
force in the education of children—by comparison,
schools come a distant second. We typically take family structures for granted. Yet
families provide the foundation for how children look at and respond to the world.
Families provide children with the basis of most of their values, their likes and dislikes, their belief systems or lack thereof, and their basic skills for interacting with others. Think about how your family has influenced your development.

This chapter looks at the role families play in shaping our local communities and
the schools where you will be working. It argues that families are complex social institutions that are subject to many different cultural and economic forces, and that you
will need a wide-range of skills and insights to work well with different types of families and the larger communities in which they and the schools where you will work
will be located.

The following key questions will guide you through your exploration of families
and communities and their impact on schools and classrooms:

Key Questions

1. How have families changed in recent years?
2. How does a community shape the climate of a school?
3. How are relationships built between schools and parents?
4. What can schools do to reach out to communities?

Society as a whole often takes the social structures of families for granted and also tends to underestimate their importance in the education of children. However, families provide the foundation for how children look at and respond to the world. The home environment provides children with their basic value systems, shapes their likes and dislikes, and teaches them basic skills for interacting with others.

Over the years as larger social and economic forces have evolved, we have seen changes to the structure of the family and how these forces have affected the family. Consider, for example, how the movement of women out of the home and into the American workforce since the late 1960s has affected home life. How might having both parents work change the family experience?

Educational reform that fails to take into account the changing role and structure of the family in American society is simply not realistic. The growth of after-school programs in the last few decades, for example, in which students have their school day extended while parents are at work or doing other activities, requires that school facilities be designed to be more flexible and capable of multiple uses. Likewise, the education teachers need has had to change, as they take more extended and different roles in the education of children.

HOW HAVE FAMILIES CHANGED IN RECENT YEARS?

Psychologist David Elkind (1995) argues that schools are a "mirror of the society and of the family" (p. 8). What occurs in our families and as part of our social systems is crucial to what teachers can or cannot do in the schools.

Many myths exist about families in the United States. Until fairly recently the general public and the media often encouraged an idealized and romantic model of the American family in which the father serves as the principal wage earner who goes off to work every day and "brings home the bacon" while the mother stays home and raises the children.

Such families are small (typically two or three children), with well-defined relationships. Throughout the 1950s and 1960s, this model was reinforced through the media, particularly on television, where programs such as *Ozzie and Harriet, Leave it to Beaver,* and *The Donna Reed Show* created the homogenous and heterogeneous image of a white, highly uniform, middle-class family as being the norm in American society. Such a simple idealized model of the American family probably never existed entirely, and it certainly does not exist today. But the image existed.

The idealized images found in TV Land and reruns of old television shows are hard to find in real life today. Mothers are actively engaged in the workforce along with men, and divorce is much more common in American culture than it used to be. The nontraditional family is becoming more of a norm every year—women and men choosing to become single parents, gay and lesbian couples adopting or having children, and multiracial marriages. Just as with the general population of the United States, diversity increasingly characterizes American families.

So diverse is the American home that the U.S. Census Bureau now distinguishes between families and households. A **household** includes all of the people who live together in one housing unit, which could be two roommates sharing rent. A **family household,** however, is a social unit of two or more people who live together in a household related by birth, marriage, or adoption. Families can include a married couple with children, a married couple without children, an unmarried couple that has lived together for many years and shared expenses and a personal involvement (Casper & Fields, 2000), a gay or lesbian couple with a child, or one or more grandparents raising a child (U.S. Census Bureau, 2003a.)

The majority of households in the United States are families. Currently 69% of all children in the United States live in families with two parents. Another 23% live in single-mother households, 5% in single-father families, and the remaining 4% in households with neither parent present (U.S. Census Bureau, 2000.)

As Figure 4.1 indicates, the demographics of households in the United States have changed considerably in the past 30 years. Some people believe this to be bad for the American family. Others maintain that the American family is simply evolving out of necessity in response to the societal forces around us. What are some of the forces that are shaping the contemporary American family?

NEW MODELS OF THE FAMILY

One commonly cited statistic is the increase in the divorce rate and the growth in the number of single parents in the United States that took place in the second half of the twentieth century. Between 1960 and 1982, the divorce rate tripled. During the same period, the number of children living with a single parent doubled. At the present time, it is estimated that 50% of all first marriages and 60% of all second marriages will end in divorce within 40 years (Coontz, 1992).

FIGURE 4.1

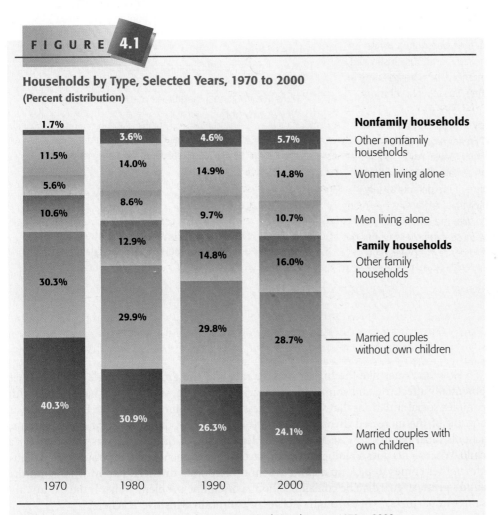

Households by Type, Selected Years, 1970 to 2000
(Percent distribution)

Source: U.S. Census Bureau. *Current Population Survey,* March Supplements: 1970 to 2000.

Through the Eyes of
Culturally Sensitive Teachers

Different Models of Families

Diane Pomeroy was a veteran second-grade teacher who was looking forward to her 26th year in the profession. She had her second-grade classroom at High Road Elementary School well organized and ready for the first open house of the year, where she would be able to meet the parents of most of her 28 students. When the evening of the open house came, students and their parents and guardians started trickling into Diane's classroom. She immediately noticed that two of her students, Freddy and Susan, were drawing stares from their classmates. While most students had parents in their 20s and 30s, Susan had brought her 80-year-old grandmother. Diane heard some kids muttering under their breaths, "Susan, your momma sure is old!"

Freddy came accompanied by two gentlemen in their 30s. One introduced himself as Freddy's dad and then introduced the other as "my partner, Dave." Again, Diane heard one of her second graders remark, "Look, Freddy has two daddies!" Diane noticed some of the parents taking second glances, and she could tell that Freddy was beginning to feel somewhat uncomfortable with the attention.

Diane asked everyone to have a seat in order to address the group. Diane said, "Ladies and gentlemen, welcome to High Road Elementary and to our second-grade classroom. I am delighted to have so many parents, guardians, and grandparents here! At High Road Elementary we realize that our students come from a variety of backgrounds, and we cherish that diversity. There is no one family that cares about its children more than another!" With that, she went on to discuss some of the projects her class was working on and the efforts of their children. With their attention regained, everyone went on to discuss the year's curriculum and activities without any further distraction.

Points to Ponder

1. In your opinion, did Diane do the right thing by calling attention to the fact that Susan's and Freddy's families were less traditional than those of the other students? Why or why not?

2. How do teachers' opinions about nontraditional families affect how they relate to students who are from such households?

3. How did Diane demonstrate responsible leadership? What hidden message does this send to parents and students?

4. What, differences, if any, are there between relating to parents and to grandparents who are the guardians of a student?

INTASC

Principle #10

Partnerships: The teacher fosters relationships with school colleagues, parents, and agencies in the larger community to support students' learning and well-being.

How do issues like the higher divorce rate and the growth of single-parent homes potentially affect you and your work as a teacher? To begin with, you will have to deal with complex social situations that were not necessarily as common in the past. For example, as a result of the increased divorce rate and the increase in the number of single parents, schools must be much more aware of the legal rights of different adults who care for a child. What rights does a biological father have? What happens when the boyfriend of a single mother comes to pick up a child at school? Should a divorced parent who is not the child's primary guardian be consulted about a discipline problem? What if the parents are same-sex partners, as in Through the Eyes of Culturally Sensitive Teachers?

● **Permeable Families** There are no simple answers for the preceding questions. Each case has to be decided on its own. A divorced father may have visitation rights only on the

TABLE 4.1

Modern vs. Postmodern Families

	MODERN ERA	**POSTMODERN ERA**
Paradigm assumptions	*Progress* toward equity and harmony. *Universality:* laws of nature that accommodate generalization. *Regularity:* the world is an orderly place.	Different forms and types of progress; some are better than others. *Particulars:* circumstances differ and approaches can't be generalized. *Irregularity:* the world is illogical and disorderly.
Family sentiments	*Romantic love:* couples select one another based on mutual attraction. *Maternal love:* women have a maternal instinct and an innate need to care for children. *Domesticity:* relationships within the family are more powerful and binding than those outside the family.	*Consensual love:* realistic and practical; based on an agreement between partners. *Shared parenting:* childrearing is shared by mother, father, and professional caregivers. *Reality-based:* children are pushed, or hurried, to grow up fast.
Children	Innocent	Competent
Teenagers	Immature	Sophisticated

weekend. A stepfather or other care provider may be the legal guardian for a child. David Elkind (1995) maintains that the movement from the modern culture of the early to mid-1900s to today's postmodern culture has resulted in a shift from the nuclear family to a **permeable family.**

Elkind (1995) characterizes the traditional nuclear family as consisting of "two parents, with one staying at home to care for the children" (p. 6.) The nuclear family was guided by three basic assumptions of the modern era: progress, universality, and regularity (see Table 4.1) The traditional nuclear family was patriarchal and children were considered innocent, supposedly shielded from the realities of adult life—such as sex, drugs, and financial problems—by the protective shell of the family.

The assumptions of the postmodern era, however, focus on differences, particulars, and irregularity, and the postmodern permeable family reflects these assumptions. Out of necessity of the times, perspectives have evolved. The perspective is now more global and ever-changing and families have had to adjust with those changes. According to Elkind (1995), the permeable family may include single parents, two working parents, or blended remarried and adoptive parents. Children are seen as competent and sophisticated.

● **Working Families**   One the most important characteristics of the permeable family is working parents—either as part of a couple or as single parents, particularly working mothers. This represents a fundamental shift since the early 1960s, when 39% of married women, with children between ages 6 and 17, worked outside the home (U.S. Census Bureau, 1999). In 1970 this number had increased to 49.2%; in 1980, to 61.7%; and to 73.6% in 1990. By 2000 the rate was up to 77.2% (U.S. Census Bureau, 2003b). In 2002, 62% of all children under age 18 had both parents working in the labor force (U.S. Census Bureau, 2003b). Table 4.2 on page 110 identifies a further breakdown of the growth of working mothers in the workforce over the years.

INTASC

Principle #3

Adapting Instruction for Individual Needs: The teacher understands how students differ in their approaches to learning and creates instructional opportunities that are adapted to diverse learners.

TABLE 4.2

Employment Rate of Women with Children, by Marital Status

| YEAR | CHILDREN UNDER 6 | | CHILDREN 6 TO 17 | |
	MARRIED	OTHER*	MARRIED	OTHER*
1960	18.6%	40.5%	39.0%	65.9%
1970	30.3	52.2	49.2	66.9
1980	45.1	60.3	61.7	74.6
1990	58.9	63.6	73.6	79.7
2000	62.8	76.6	77.2	85.0
2003	59.8	74.3	77.0	84.8

* Widowed, divorced, or separated.
Source: U.S. Census Bureau, *Statistical Abstract of the United States: 2004–2005.* (Table 579, p. 377). (Washington, DC: U.S. Government Printing Office, 2004); U.S. Census Bureau, *Statistical Abstract of the United States: 1999.* (p. 417). (Washington, DC: U.S. Government Printing Office, 1999).

Having both parents working can significantly change the home–school interaction, regardless of the affluence of the community. One result of the growth in the number of working parents, for example, is the loss of **social capital** for teachers and students. *Social capital* refers to the social networks and interactions of people within a community that promote involvement, commitment, and trust (Smith, 2001). Working parents have less time to volunteer for school activities, such as chaperoning a field trip, providing supplies for a fund-raising effort, or helping sell tickets to the school play. As a result, it may be more difficult for a teacher to arrange to meet with parents about a student because of the demands of work and the lack of flexible schedules for many people. Having a telephone in your classroom may be increasingly important, since this may be the best means by which to get in contact with busy parents. But is it the most practical? Scheduling meetings before school may be necessary for parents who may not be easily available later in the day.

When there is an emergency, you may find yourself dealing with multiple caregivers. A relative or babysitter may be the primary caregiver to a child after school. A parent may expect a child to go to an after-school program, but consideration must be made for what to do if the child is sick. These are just a few of the challenges that you will have to face that are different from what teachers had to address even only just 20 or 30 years ago.

CHANGES IN THE EXPERIENCES OF CHILDHOOD

As the family has changed, so has the childhood experience, which is profoundly different from what most children experienced only 40 or 50 years ago. Some researchers believe that childhood, as we have traditionally understood it, has disappeared in recent years (Postman, 1982; Winn, 1983; Elkind, 1993). This is not to suggest that children have disappeared, but that many of the social customs and traditions associated with their childhood have fallen by the wayside. Up until 20 or 30 years ago, for example, much more information was kept secret from children than is today. Talk to a grandparent or older person to find out how much they knew as children about sex, and what they were allowed to discuss openly with their families. Until very recently, sexual issues were not openly discussed on television. In situation comedies in the 1950s a husband and wife were not shown in the

INTASC

Principle #2

Knowledge of Human Development and Learning: The teacher understands how children learn and develop, and can provide learning opportunities that support their intellectual, social, and personal development.

same bed on television. There was no discussion of sexual orientation or alternative lifestyles. Now, some of the main characters in popular television comedies are gay.

Thirty or 40 years ago, children were much more protected from the conflicts and problems in their families than they are today. With the increase in the demands placed on families today, children are less isolated from larger social and cultural forces. As a result, children enter the classroom with a different set of experiences and assumptions than they would have had even a generation or two ago. Nothing has played a greater role in redefining the childhood experience like the advances in technology, particularly television and the Internet.

● **Television** Think about how children's lives have changed as a result of cable television. Prior to the 1980s, television was limited to the three major networks—ABC, CBS, and NBC—and small local stations and public broadcasting. Children's programming was limited to the late afternoon and Saturday morning. Today the American public has many more viewing options available: 24-hour programming, of all types, from around the world. As a result, the competition for viewers, young and old, has led producers to push the envelope on creativity, outrageousness, violence, and sex, leaving children open to seeing and hearing whatever their remote control can find.

In particular, children are targeted with special programming and advertising much more than they were even 10 or 15 years ago. Cable television offers entire channels, such as the Disney Channel, dedicated to continuous children's programming. One cannot help wonder whether the crisis in childhood obesity might be, at least in part, a result of the growth in the fast-food industry, which presents a constant stream of advertisements on television for both children and adults to view.

Music television (MTV, VH1), first introduced in the early 1980s and originally intended to promote record albums, has become an artistic and media form in its own right, much as *American Bandstand* was in the 1960s and 1970s. However, in transforming the basic music experience for adolescents by introducing young people to new forms of dancing and new genres of music, MTV and VH1 also have served as vehicles of expressions of attitudes about sex, violence, and lifestyle to which they might not have been exposed otherwise.

Ultimately, television keeps very few secrets from children. Violence is commonplace in contemporary television, as well as references to adult sexual material that only a generation ago was considered appropriate only for adults.

● **The Internet** While television has profoundly changed the knowledge base of children in the last 50 years, it is by no means the only technological and information source redefining the experience of children in American society. In the last 15 years, the Internet has placed virtually unlimited information at children's fingertips, as well as the ability to communicate inexpensively with friends and relatives—and even strangers—across vast distances. Add to this cell phones capable of taking and sending instant photos and very little is private anymore.

As a result, children are increasingly exposed to more information and ideas that may or may not be appropriate for them, and that certainly change the experience of growing up. Just as parents must adjust to their "sophisticated" children, so too must educators. So the question arises, "What should be the role of teachers and schools in shaping children whose needs have changed as part of a postmodern culture?"

INTASC

Principle #3

Adapting Instruction for Individual Needs: The teacher understands how students differ in their approaches to learning and creates instructional opportunities that are adapted to diverse learners.

Through passive observation of television programs, children are exposed indiscriminately to pop culture's attitudes about sex and violence. How do these attitudes affect behaviors in schools?

Whether teaching in a rural community or in a suburban community, you have to be able to understand and adapt to the local culture and the needs of the community. What can you do to become aware of the important values of a community and incorporate those values into your teaching?

INTASC

Principle #10

Partnerships: The teacher fosters relationships with school colleagues, parents, and agencies in the larger community to support students' learning and well-being.

Research on school–community relations within American Indian communities, for example, indicates that these communities want Native American culture to play a central role in schooling. They are sometimes wary of non-Indian educators who simply want to teach, but are not particularly interested in learning Indian ways. "Listen to us, learn our ways" is a frequent comment made by Indian parents to educators (Robinson-Zañartu & Majel-Dixon, 1996, p. 40). Teaching in Native American communities requires teachers to become well acquainted with forms of thinking that are not linear or hierarchical. Holistic teaching (whole to parts) is more in tune with traditional Native American teaching approaches than the linear (parts to whole) teaching style that is most often found in U.S. schools. When schools incorporate, rather than resist, traditional ways of thinking in their instruction, they are going to be more successful. Community traditions may be defined by a number of factors including ethnicity, socioeconomic status, religion, and even geographic location.

INTASC

Principle #9

Professional Commitment and Responsibility: The teacher is a reflective practitioner who continually evaluates the effects of his/her choices and actions on others (students, parents, and other professionals in the learning community) and who actively seeks out opportunities to grow professionally.

● **Rural Communities** Working with students in rural communities requires an appreciation of rural culture as well as the assets and challenges found in many rural schools. Teachers working in rural schools have a number of advantages. Generally, class sizes are small and it is easy for teachers to communicate with parents. Rural communities tend to be close-knit, where most people know each other well. As a result, relationships are given a high priority, and people's words are truly their bonds. This attitude carries over to the school, which often is a focal point of community life, and leads to a high level of community participation in the school. Teachers who are not natives may feel more isolated at first.

A major drawback of teaching in rural areas is that salaries tend to be lower than in urban or suburban communities. The economy of rural areas can vary a great deal, but rural communities tend to have more low-wage, low-benefit jobs and average three-quarters of the median income of urban areas (see Figure 4.2). This may be offset to some degree, however, by the lower cost of living in rural areas. In addition, in small communities the behavior of teachers is often scrutinized more closely than in urban areas (Bauch, 2001). Rural communities tend to be somewhat conservative, preferring to preserve the way things are done. Therefore, it may be a little more difficult to discuss necessary, but controversial, issues in the classroom. But people who teach in rural schools like the tight bond of the community, the active support, and the personable interaction. Knowing the community and providing advance organizers to parents before, not after, controversial

FIGURE 4.2

The Students You Teach: Demographics

- Nearly two-thirds of counties in the United States are rural; less than one-fifth of U.S. children live in rural America.
- Of the 50 poorest counties in America, 48 are rural.
- Sixteen percent of children in the United States live in one of the 50 largest cities in the country.
- The national child poverty rate is 17%; in large cities the rate is 26%.
- Twelve percent of children do not have health insurance.

Neighborhood Characteristics

Children in neighborhoods with:

- a high poverty rate   23%
- a high rate of males not in the labor force   14%
- a high rate of female-headed families   17%
- a high rate of high school dropouts   25%

Economic Conditions of Families

- Median income of families with children: $50,000
- Children in extreme poverty (income below 50% of poverty level)   7%
- Female-headed families receiving child support or alimony   36%
- Children under age 6 in paid child care while parents work   26%

Source: Adapted from Annie E. Casey Foundation, *Kids Count 2003: United States Profile, Background Information.* (Baltimore, MD: Annie E. Casey Foundation, 2003). Available from http://www.aecf.org/kidscount.

issues are taught is particularly important in rural schools. Educators should also realize that when communities are small and culturally, racially, and religiously homogeneous, the local consensus may or may not reflect national trends. Nonetheless, rural educators have to present a curriculum that meets national standards while respecting local sensibilities.

● **Suburban Communities**   While not all suburban school districts are affluent, the most affluent districts in the United States tend to be in suburbs. Educators working in affluent suburban communities are likely to enjoy the highest salaries of any public school-teachers in the nation. Parents and community members are often able to raise additional funds for extra activities not found in other school districts. However, many of these sub-urban school environments can be keenly competitive, and the main standards by which schools are judged are standardized test scores and the percentage of graduates who receive acceptance to highly selective colleges and universities. Teachers working in these schools, while relatively well compensated, may face significant pressures from parents or the com-munity to produce top scholars out of nearly all students. If a student is not achieving at a very high level, it may be perceived strictly as a weakness of the teacher.

Parent involvement in school or class activities may be high because many parents have more disposable time. However, teachers may find this to be a double-edged sword. While most suburban parents are very supportive of teachers' efforts and willing to assist teachers at home in any way they can, teachers also may find that some parents second-guess their teaching techniques or fail to give them the appropriate professional respect. There are challenges to be met even in the most affluent school districts, although they may be dif-ferent from those of schools in other communities.

Urban communities offer unique challenges, including a highly diverse student population, high student–teacher ratios, and unique safety issues. What do you think would be the greatest challenge of teaching in an urban setting?

INTASC

Principle #10

Partnerships: The teacher fosters relationships with school colleagues, parents, and agencies in the larger community to support students' learning and well-being.

● **Urban Communities** Like their counterparts in rural and suburban communities, teachers working in urban communities also face challenges that are unique to their setting. Just as schools in rural and suburban areas reflect the social and economic traits of their communities, so do the urban schools. Although not true in all urban schools, teachers often must deal with overcrowded classrooms, get by with fewer materials and equipment than their counterparts in other communities, and be aware of safety issues. An urban school system must allocate funds to all schools throughout the entire city, and those funds are often spread thin. However, salaries are often higher than the national average in order to attract individuals willing to embrace the challenges of working in an urban environment.

Perhaps the most important variable that distinguishes urban schools from rural and suburban schools is the diversity of their student populations. Educators who serve urban communities must be cognitively flexible and willing to adjust to the complexities and needs of their students. Urban schools are likely to have very diverse student populations from a wide range of socioeconomic, ethnic, and cultural backgrounds. Urban educators have to expect to teach a proportion of English-language learners and immigrant students. They need to embrace professional development that will allow them to do this successfully if it was not part of their initial teacher preparation.

This flexibility must carry over into relationships with parents and the general community. A school administrator learned a valuable lesson about class differences after giving a speech on school reform to parents one evening. Afterward he was approached by the mother of a student who told him, "It took me two days to find a babysitter for tonight. I am working two jobs. So is my husband. I want to be kept informed, but there is no way that I can be involved" (Vollmer, 2001, p. 28). The administrator realized that this woman could not be involved, not because she didn't care, but because nearly all of her and her husband's available time was spent trying to hold their lives together. School reform, while important to this mother, simply had to take a back seat to economic survival. The school administrator in this story was a person of middle-class background who assumed that participation in a child's education was a given. However, middle-class parents generally do not face the same dilemmas as this mother in order to attend a school function in the evening.

An urban teacher also may face the dilemma of having students whose parents are not legal residents of the United States. While teachers may solicit parental participation at school meetings, many parents may be afraid that teachers and other school personnel may be agents of the government who will communicate the parents' identities to immigration authorities. While this is rarely true, the perception that this could happen will keep many such parents from interacting with the school.

RESPECTING FAMILY VALUES

Among the most widely debated issues in schools is the extent to which the schools provide instruction that in the past was provided by the family. Whose values should be shaping our children? What if certain values promoted by the larger society conflict with values of individual families? Is it appropriate, for example, for children in a conservative religious community to learn about HIV prevention and AIDS at school? Thorough instruction about HIV prevention requires discussion of sexual behavior, a discussion some people feel should be strictly limited to the family. Parents may assume that their children will be abstinent sexually, and therefore do not need to know the specifics about how HIV and other sexually transmitted diseases are spread. In addition, some believe that by talking about

BUILDING ON EDUCATIONAL FOUNDATIONS

Family Rights and the Rights of the State

An essential tension needs to be understood about the relationship of families to the public schools. Schools represent an arm of the government or state and therefore claim an interest in the child. In doing so, they take away a significant portion of the control of parents. Is this something they should be able to do?

Several important Supreme Court cases have directly addressed the rights of parents over the government in the education of their children. In *Pierce v. Society of the Sisters,* 268 U.S. 510 (1925) the Court determined whether local governments could compel children to attend public rather than private schools. The Court came to the conclusion that under the Constitution the religious rights of the family superseded those of the state, and families were guaranteed the right to send their children to private schools, provided that adequate instruction was provided to them in secular subjects.

In *West Virginia State Board of Education v. Barnette,* 319 U.S. 624 (1943), the State of West Virginia required students and teachers to salute the flag. Failure to comply with the rule led to dismissal from school. A group of Jehovah's Witnesses refused to salute the flag because they felt it represented a graven image that was not recognized as part of their religious belief. The Supreme Court ruled that the law interfered with the right of the children and their families to practice their religion without interference.

In *Wisconsin v. Yoder,* 406 U.S. 205 (1972), members of the Old Order Amish religion and the Conservative Amish Mennonite Church were convicted of violating Wisconsin's compulsory school-attendance law by refusing to send their children to public or private school after they had graduated from the eighth grade. According to the Wisconsin law, they were required to keep their children in school until they were 16. Evidence presented to the Court showed that the defendants believed that education beyond the eighth grade was contrary to the Amish way of life. The Amish parents feared that the salvation of their children would be endangered by continued school attendance. As in the Barnette decision, the Court determined that enforcement of the law by the State of Wisconsin was a violation of the rights of the Amish parents and their children to follow their religious beliefs.

Considering the preceding court cases, what do you think should be the rights of the government or state in the education of children, and what should be the rights of families?

---

these topics—particularly outside the context of family values—children will be encouraged to be more sexually active.

So whose values should predominate, those of the family or those of the larger culture? There is no simple answer to this question. (See Building on Educational Foundations) Clearly, families have certain rights with regard to their children. But does that mean that parents have the final say about all things all the time? Are children solely the responsibility of their parents? If so, there would have been no need for the development of child welfare services or child labor laws. History has demonstrated that parents must share this responsibility with governmental systems, including schools. But where do we draw the line between each group's level of involvement?

In the 1920s, some states attempted to restrict parental input concerning the education of children in an effort to make sure all children received a well-rounded education. Laws were passed that not only made attendance at school compulsory, but also required that children go to public schools. As a result, in Portland, Oregon, for example, local officials closed down Catholic and other parochial schools. Eventually, the Supreme Court ruled in *Pierce v. Society of the Sisters of the Holy Names of Jesus and Mary* (1925) "the child of man is his parent's and not the state's." This means that unless a child is abused or mistreated, it is not the place of the state (that is, the schools) to interfere with the education

INTASC

Principle #9

Professional Commitment and Responsibility: The teacher is a reflective practitioner who continually evaluates the effects of his/her choices and actions on others (students, parents, and other professionals in the learning community) and who actively seeks out opportunities to grow professionally.

"The students in my contemporary literature class are quoting from deejay Baby Puff Dragon. I have no idea what they're talking about."

Courtesy of Aaron Bacall, *The Lighter Side of Teaching*, p. 68. Copyright 2003 by Aaron Bacall. Reprinted by permission of Corwin Press Inc.

INTASC

Principle #3

Adapting Instruction for Individual Needs: The teacher understands how students differ in their approaches to learning and creates instructional opportunities that are adapted to diverse learners.

INTASC

Principle #10

Partnerships: The teacher fosters relationships with school colleagues, parents, and agencies in the larger community to support students' learning and well-being.

that parents most desire for their children. This does not mean that the state cannot regulate what children learn (by requiring certain courses or mandating curricula and standards) or the physical conditions under which they learn, but it does clearly establish the rights of parents in the education of their own children.

Every community has its hot topics, and teachers and administrators need to become aware of these topics. As a teacher you will have to be sensitive to the backgrounds and values of the parents whose children you teach. There is no magic formula that outlines what you should or should not do. What is perfectly acceptable in one community may not be okay in another setting. For example, for most people Dungeons and Dragons is a harmless fantasy role-playing game. Its references to magic and the occult, however, can make it objectionable to families with more traditional religious beliefs. Even within communities you need to be aware of different cultures and value systems. When most people think of *cultural diversity,* they often think of ethnicity—but diversity within a community can take many different shapes. For example, Mid-Prairie School District in eastern Iowa represents a consolidated district whose students come from a number of small, rural towns throughout an area that is very homogenous racially. What makes the district interesting is the blend of the religious backgrounds in the area, where Catholic and Methodist children attend school alongside Mennonite students from sects of varying degrees of conservatism. In addition, the region contains a fairly large Amish community, a very conservative group with strict beliefs and rules about lifestyles. Anyone working in this community, including teachers, needs to be aware of the dynamics that exist within the community as a result and plan accordingly.

So what should you do as a teacher? You need to review materials carefully before you use them to teach. In doing so, you will have to know your children and be sensitive to them and the values of their families. Religious issues can come up in informal learning situations. If you are teaching biology, be sensitive to the creationism-versus-evolution conflict. If you have students who are Jewish or Seventh-Day Adventists, be sensitive about scheduling a field trip or special event on a Saturday, their religious day of observance.

A good rule is to be patient and listen carefully to people's needs. A single mother may find it very difficult to get off work for an after-school meeting. Can you meet with her before school, or can you talk with her over the phone later in the evening, or when she is off work? While you should not let yourself be taken advantage of, you need to respect the needs of students and their families and be open and flexible in meeting those needs.

HOW ARE RELATIONSHIPS BUILT BETWEEN SCHOOLS AND PARENTS?

Research on family–school relations does not directly address whether or how schools buffer their core functions from the uncertainties that parents may introduce (Ogawa, 1998). In other words, schools may ask for parent and community participation, but is this participation welcomed at the center of school activities or only at the fringes? Just because parents are welcomed to raise funds, provide transportation for field trips, or serve as volunteers in school functions does not mean that their input is necessarily welcome on core educational decisions.

While high levels of contact with parents is desirable, the nature of those contacts must be examined rather than the total number of school–parent interactions (Finn, 1998). As a

EDUCATION MATTERS

Healthy Students and Families

After weighing and measuring students in local school districts as part of a health initiative, parents in Pennsylvania and Florida received letters from the district informing them of their child's body mass index, a measurement endorsed by all major health and fitness agencies as an indicator of healthy weight. Parents were shocked to read that their children might be at risk for heart disease or Type 2 diabetes if they scored high on the index. But as recent studies and news reports indicate, our nation's children are at greater risk for certain diseases simply because they are far less active and more overweight than in the past. Whereas parents used to count on their children receiving ample time for exercise and play at school, this simply is not the case these days.

With a focus on No Child Left Behind agendas of content accountability and testing, schools with low-performing students are finding themselves having to make tough decisions. In an effort to maximize their efforts on core curricular areas, schools all over the United States are reducing the amount of time for recess and cutting physical education classes to save time in the school day. Health officials, however, point to the cutbacks in physical education as one of the factors contributing to the obesity epidemic in our nation, particularly among young people. If physical education is cut back or dropped at school, parents and guardians will have to encourage more exercise at home.

Health agencies throughout the country protest this new trend. The American Heart Association and the National Association for Sports and Physical Education (NASPE) are among the many organizations that recommend daily physical exercise in Grades K–12. Howard Wechsler of the Centers for Disease Control and Prevention argues that society needs to take advantage of the time students are in school to teach them the attitudes and skills necessary to live an active lifestyle. Most agencies cite that children are more alert and perform better academically when they exercise.

Students who sit all day in classrooms and just move between classes get little to no exercise. Physical education classes get students up and moving either playing sports or doing individual exercises. In health classes they learn the benefits of physical care and nutrition, and gain an understanding of behaviors that can place their health at risk. Many professionals and parents argue that the absence of a systematic physical education and health program in the schools can have a far greater long-term effect on young people than spending 10 minutes less time daily studying math or science or English. But because physical education is not seen as part of the core curriculum it is often one of the first programs to be cut, along with other "noncore" subjects such as music, art, and drama—programs that put students in touch with their kinesthetic and aesthetic selves.

The Education Issue: Academics versus health and physical activity

What's Your Opinion?

Did you take physical education in school? Did you feel there was a benefit to taking it? Are schools putting students' health at risk by focusing on academics? Who is more responsible for teaching young people healthy lifestyles, schools or parents? What do you think schools could do to help students become fit?

---

general rule, opportunities for parents to become involved with schools diminish as students get older and become more independent. Also, since parent–teacher contacts tend to increase when students are having difficulties in school, high parental engagement with schools and teachers does not necessarily indicate high academic achievement by students, because schools with fewer problems tend to reach out less to parents to help resolve problems. The National Parent Teacher Association has identified six areas for schools to focus on when developing partnerships with parents and communities and the attitudes that must be taken to help the partnership succeed:

- *Communicating*—Communication between home and school is two-way and meaningful.

- *Parenting*—Parenting skills are promoted and supported.

- *Student Learning*—Parents play an integral role in assisting student learning.

- *Volunteering*—Parents are welcome in the school and support and assistance are sought.

- *School Decision Making and Advocacy*—Parents are full partners in the decisions that affect children and families.

- *Collaborating with Community*—Community resources are used to strengthen schools, families and student learning (White, 1998, p. 8).

Implementing these steps depends on the culture of a school and its relationship with the communities it serves. Not all teachers and administrators subscribe to the assumption that more parent involvement is better (Ogawa, 1998). Schools that have very traditional administrations will be happy to have parents organizing fund-raisers but would be reluctant to involve parental representatives in real decision-making roles. If teachers and administrators take strictly an **educentric perspective,** or "expert view" of education, then it follows that parents and communities will mainly be recipients of information from educational experts and not shapers of school policy. Dunlap and Alva (1999) found that teachers with 13 or more years of experience were more likely to maintain a more educentric perspective, while those with 8 or fewer years of experience were more receptive to family and community involvement in schools.

Even when schools have structures in place that suggest a significant role for parents in decision making, those committees or other structures must be closely analyzed to see whether they are engaging in independent decision making or are simply rubber-stamping decisions already made by the principal. Educators who fail to involve parents in the core functions of schools tend to do so because they fear diminishing their professional status and losing control of classroom teaching or classroom management (Epstein & Sanders, 1998). Once teachers understand that forging true partnerships with parents and communities will make their professional lives easier, they are much more eager to do so.

"Inner-city parents work hard at very hard jobs, and they can't afford to take time off to come to school to talk to you . . . They are not going to do it. They are going to expect you to take care of the problem . . . they just can't spend the time coming in for a day and losing a day's wages because their kid did something dumb."

SENIOR HIGH SCHOOL ENGLISH TEACHER, MIAMI, FL

THINK ABOUT THIS:

Many teachers grow frustrated with mandates requiring greater parental interaction and involvement. Sometimes that frustration grows out of a perception of unexpected demands on their work; sometimes it springs from the inability to obtain the cooperation of parents.

SHARE and **COMPARE:**

To what degree do you think parents should get involved with the decision making of the school?

WHAT CAN SCHOOLS DO TO REACH OUT TO COMMUNITIES?

In all schools, standard communications (field trip, permission slips, report cards, graduation announcements) are sent to parents and the community. However, some schools inform the community of what the school's needs are and expect community members to do their best to satisfy them. Other schools engage in active community outreach and are willing to transform the school's mission to align with the needs of the community, even if these needs go beyond instruction at the elementary or secondary level. The two highest levels of involvement, community outreach and advocacy, indicate a desire to reach out and affect the lives of people beyond their immediate environments (Shepard, Trimberger, & McClintock, 1999, p. 34).

UNDERSTAND COMMUNITY NEEDS

Learning effectively about the community in which they teach requires educators to realize that they need the knowledge parents and community members have about their students just as much as the community needs the expertise that teachers provide. When such a foundation is present, school–parent–community relations can become a partnership. "If parents fail to become involved in their children's elementary education, it is improbable that they will become involved in future years" (p. 115). Therefore schools need to conduct an audit to measure the extent of parent and community involvement and to see whether parents perceive the school to be family-friendly (Buttery & Anderson 1999).

When educators learn about the families and communities they serve, confidence and mutual trust with the public served needs to be developed, and the information gained must be used to benefit students. Educators should also understand that some families or communities may not wish to reveal all aspects of their lives to school representatives. Certain aspects may be revealed in time, when greater trust and confidence have been established.

When teachers are not members of a community in which they teach, learning as much as possible about that community would seem to be a logical approach to better relations with parents and community members. But this may be easier said than done as teachers, like most people, may come to this task with preconceptions. As a teacher, you need to be careful not to judge the communities you serve using standards that do not encompass the realities of those communities. Falling back on the standards of the communities in which you were raised may be comfortable, but you need to be open to the customs and cultures of the community in which you work. For example, in a Southern California middle school, Hispanic parents were brought to school for a variety of classes under the sponsorship of the *Instituto Familiar* (Family Institute). When asked for thoughts on parent involvement, teachers working in the *Instituto Familiar* had the following contrasting reactions:

Positive Reactions

- "On Saturday, the hallway is filled with parents and students at the computers. Parents are enhancing their information and knowledge."
- "The more educated they become, the better we all are. They become better parents and give more support to their children."
- "These parent classes have bridged the gap between home and school."

Negative Reactions

- "These parents don't participate. They just think about today. They don't care."
- "They won't learn the language."
- "These parents are so short sighted. They don't have vision" (Dunlap & Alva, 1999, p. 127).

INTASC

Principle #10

Partnerships: The teacher fosters relationships with school colleagues, parents, and agencies in the larger community to support students' learning and well-being.

As an educator, you have a responsibility to remain open to cultural differences and to acknowledge any changes in demographics, not only within your school, but in society in general.

The irony of these reactions is that they all came from teachers who worked with the same Hispanic parents. Why would these teachers have such different perspectives? Because people sometimes react to other cultures using their own culture as a lens.

When educators immerse themselves in community needs, they must be ready to respond to what they find. They must be prepared for the unexpected. For example, perhaps the goal of a community inquiry is to ascertain how parents and community members could assist elementary and secondary students. During the process of surveys and interviews, the school identifies a need for additional medical services beyond the typical school nurse and beyond school hours. Some schools might respond by saying that this is beyond the scope of what schools have traditionally done. Or a school might respond by approaching the public health department to see whether, by combining the school's and the department's resources, a clinic might become a reality. The difference between these two approaches is a desire by the school to do everything possible to meet the community's needs.

In the Arlington, Virginia, public schools, a survey of the community found that 43% of their students were English-language learners, with Spanish being the first language of 70% of that group. As a result of a request made by parents for Saturday classes, two programs were created called Empowering Families through Literacy and Escuela Bolivia. Along with reinforcing English and mathematics skills for students, these programs also taught them Spanish literacy and the cultural traditions of their parents and grandparents. In addition, schools provided a bilingual teacher to teach illiterate parents Spanish literacy and provide a transition to English literacy within 2 years (Osterling, Violand-Sánchez, & von Vacano, 1999). Parents of English-language learners were delighted with these new opportunities. An argument could be made that these were not services traditionally provided by the Arlington public schools. However, the Arlington schools historically had not had such a large percentage of ESL students nor large numbers of parents that needed both Spanish and English literacy. The schools simply responded to the changing demographics and needs of the communities they served.

TEACHER OUTREACH

Whenever possible, it is advantageous for future teachers to be placed in culturally diverse schools as part of field placement during their teacher preparation programs. Culturally diverse field placements are also a requirement for accreditation in colleges of education accredited by the National Council for the Accreditation of Teacher Education (NCATE). One study of student teachers found that community involvement has greater meaning when the school's community differs from that of the student teacher (Stachowski & Mahan, 1998). No amount of pre-employment field placement will substitute for actually getting to know the communities served by the school where you work, but the experience can be as valuable as the coursework you take.

Teachers who get to know their communities well may be faced with occasional dilemmas. They may encounter language minority parents who speak only English to their children at home. Parents sometimes try to remove their native language from the home, not because they don't want their children to know it, but because they have accepted the conventional wisdom that speaking it will retard their children's English-language acquisition. Teachers who are familiar with the research on second-language acquisition may relay to parents that first-language skills and literacy helps, not hinders, the acquisition of a second language. If parents listen to this and still choose not to use their native language at home, then parental wishes must be respected.

After getting to know the school's various community groups well, you may realize that students from all groups are not served equally by the school. The question is, do you then become an advocate for students from the underserved community? If so, at what level of personal or professional risk? Some communities have very effective advocates for their children that carry significant influence with school boards and other policymakers without major involvement from teachers. Other communities lack such influence with policymakers and need significant advocacy from teachers as well as other groups. Local circumstances dictate the extent and role of teacher advocacy, but as a rule, you need to consider the options available to a community without teacher support. Numerous experts have suggested ways to learn more about school communities and to bring the community into a meaningful partnership with the school (Rich, 1998; Simkins, 1996; Jackson, 1996; Edelmann, 1997; Morris, 2002).

1. Schools must be willing to adjust their activities and programs to reflect the communities they serve.

2. The principal needs to be active in community activities outside the school and be perceived as a community leader.

3. Parent and community involvement in school governance is present when making major decisions and should not be limited to fund raising or functions at the periphery of school life.

4. The entire school staff should regard community members as part of their extended family.

5. Community members should be asked to participate in paid and volunteer positions in schools and be frequently asked to share their wisdom and experiences in classes.

6. Schools need to provide in-service training for teachers and staff to help them work more effectively with parents and the community.

7. Schools must seek partnerships with businesses and other community-based institutions to support individual students with scholarships or to enhance school programs.

> **INTASC**
>
> **Principle #10**
>
> *Partnerships:* The teacher fosters relationships with school colleagues, parents, and agencies in the larger community to support students' learning and well-being.

Learning about the community in which you teach is very important. However, if you do not use that knowledge to change or improve school programs, then learning about communities is purely an academic exercise with few practical consequences.

COMMUNICATE EFFECTIVELY WITH PARENTS FROM DIVERSE BACKGROUNDS

Parents or community members from culturally or linguistically diverse communities represent a wide spectrum of individuals. Teachers working in the Silicon Valley of California, for instance, may encounter a number of foreign-born parents with doctoral degrees who work in the computer industry. Faculty working in university communities may encounter a similar situation if they teach the children of foreign-born professors. These parents are highly educated and are more likely to be familiar with the school system in the United States and be able to effectively advocate for their children.

Other teachers may work in areas with large immigrant populations that came to the United States looking to establish a better life or to escape oppression or that experience a constant flux in their population due to the transience of migrant workers. These teachers may encounter students and parents from culturally and linguistically diverse backgrounds who are not highly educated and are living around the poverty line. These parents, in particular, need understanding teachers or school personnel willing to explain all options available for their children.

Effective communication between school personnel and parents or guardians from diverse backgrounds rests on two assumptions: that parents trust that the schools operate in the best interests of their children, and that school personnel respect and value the backgrounds and perspectives that parents from diverse backgrounds bring to schools. If either of these two assumptions are not met, communication with parents from diverse backgrounds will be filled with fear, suspicion, and mistrust.

● **Obstacles**   Parents from diverse cultural and language backgrounds are particularly disadvantaged by educators with an educentric orientation because these parents are less likely than most to be familiar with the language and contexts that experts use. Because teachers tend to view families and communities through their own cultural prisms (Dunlap & Alva, 1999), they may be perceived as not being able to provide literacy support to their children. Nowhere is this **deficit model,** which focuses on what students and their families lack rather than what they have, more likely to be used than in schools that serve low-income, minority communities (Hulsebosch & Logan, 1998). Some educators express this deficit perspective with statements such as, "If they would speak and read English to their children, we would not have reading problems" (Osterling, Violand-Sánchez, & von Vacano, 1999, p. 64). In communicating with parents from diverse cultural and language backgrounds, you must have a positive and understanding attitude for such relationships to be productive.

Some parents may not have fond memories of their own school experiences, which could generate some skepticism now that they have to relate to schools as parents. While some parents from culturally diverse backgrounds may lack familiarity with the language and culture of schools in this country, this should not be interpreted by school officials as lack of concern for their children's education. Immigrants may come from a culture where parents simply entrust their children to teachers and school authorities without any expectations of parent involvement in their children's education. This formal relationship with schools contrasts with the typical expectations in the United States, in which parents are expected to become involved in their children's education and be active in school activities.

When parents from linguistically or culturally diverse backgrounds approach school staff, they are often more unsure than the average parent. Even those parents who speak relatively fluent English can be confused by educational terminology. There is often deference to those who speak the "language of expertise and power." It is difficult for these parents to question placement or other decisions made by educators for their children. Sometimes they encounter less than full disclosure or consultation from schools. The statistics on which students are most commonly found in various educational tracks are ample testimony to this (Oakes & Lipton, 1992). Some of the discrepancies in the placement of ethnic or racial minority students in gifted or advanced courses are attributable to the fact that the parents of these students may not know how to challenge school decisions as effectively as the parents of mainstream students. Therefore, culturally and linguistically diverse parents are in particular need of educators who will advocate for their children, since the usual bureaucratic or diagnostic procedures allow a disturbingly large number of their children to fall through the cracks.

● **Building Trust**   As a teacher, being able to speak the language of a limited- or non-English-speaking parent is a definite asset. However, teachers who do not speak the non-English language also can be very effective in working with these parents as long as they are working with a competent translator and convey to students and parents genuine care and concern. Figure 4.3 offers some guidelines for developing good relations with all parents, particularly those from culturally diverse backgrounds. A mistake some teachers make when speaking with parents who don't command English is to use the child as a translator. Children do not generally have a bilingual vocabulary that allows them to translate educational issues accurately, and some topics may not be suitable for a child to translate. Instead, always use an adult to translate, preferably a professional with second-language skills. It is often a good ice breaker if the teacher learns a few words or a phrase in the parents' home language. While this is not enough to carry on a conversation, it shows parents that the teacher has taken a little bit of time to meet them on their terms. Parents appreci-

INTASC

Principle #9

Professional Commitment and Responsibility: The teacher is a reflective practitioner who continually evaluates the effects of his/her choices and actions on others (students, parents, and other professionals in the learning community) and who actively seeks out opportunities to grow professionally.

INTASC

Principle #10

Partnerships: The teacher fosters relationships with school colleagues, parents, and agencies in the larger community to support students' learning and well-being.

FIGURE 4.3

Do's and Don'ts for Working with Parents

Do's:

1. Respect the culture and language students and parents have, especially if they differ from the school's culture and language.

2. If you are unfamiliar with a student's or parent's cultural background, ask a fellow teacher or staff member from that background to serve as a "culture broker" until your own background is satisfactory.

3. Give parents specific guidance and activities they may perform at home to support your instruction.

4. Assume that the parents/guardians of culturally or linguistically diverse students care as much about their children's education as other parents.

5. If you are unsure of where a conversation is going, follow the leads or questions parents pose; be an attentive listener.

6. Speak to parents whenever students have done positive things. Too often, they only hear from teachers or schools when something is wrong.

Don'ts:

1. Don't allow the student to be the sole means of communication between you and the parent: establish your own independent channel of communication.

2. Don't characterize a student as "bad" to parents. If the student has engaged in inappropriate behavior, focus very specifically on the behavior.

3. Don't allow students to assume that their homes are places you can't be bothered to go. Make home visits whenever necessary.

4. Don't confine your parent/community outreach activities to the compensated school day. Often, time spent "caring" about students before or after school will result in a much more congenial school year.

5. Don't focus on the skills and resources that students or parents may lack. Concentrate on their abilities.

ate the teacher who is willing to make at least one home visit to discuss the child's educational progress. While this may be inconvenient, teachers who do this impress parents with their level of care and commitment.

Another effective technique is to show parents from culturally or linguistically diverse backgrounds that you have learned about their history, culture, and background and, to the extent possible, legitimize it by incorporating it into the curriculum.

In communicating effectively with parents from diverse backgrounds, teachers need to accurately assess the amount of disposable time parents have to work with their children and support school activities. Sixty-six percent of employed parents with children in school report that they don't have sufficient time for their children (Buttery & Anderson, 1999). For parents struggling to support their families, the proportion is likely to be much higher, so time is a particularly critical factor for lower-income parents from all backgrounds. The fact that parents missed the school's open house should not be interpreted as meaning that they don't care about their children's education, but it is sometimes seen this way. There is no rule that says that all meetings involving school personnel and parents must occur on school grounds. Sometimes attendance may be boosted by bringing educators to community centers or other facilities in minority communities. These meetings can supplement, not replace, parent–teacher meetings at the school site. Teachers working in schools in high-poverty areas often live outside the communities in which they teach. For these teachers, having visibility in the community surrounding the school is an asset that can help in parent and community relations. Many teachers who are culturally different from their students' parents and live outside the school's attendance zone are still excellent communicators with culturally different parents. Regrettably, not all teachers fit this description. The difference between the two is a willingness to recognize what culturally different parents can bring to education and to communicate with parents and communities as equals.

PARTNERING WITH THE COMMUNITY

Traditionally, schools handled education and people went elsewhere to receive other services. Parents went to the local public health clinic for medical services and to the local employment office if they were seeking a job. School guidance counselors counseled students and referred their parents to community agencies for non-educational services. School counselors continue to advise today, but a growing trend in recent decades has been to include a much wider array of services in the schools themselves. In **community schools** you find educational, health, employment, legal and other governmental services for parents and their families (see Figure 4.4).

What is emerging from this concept of "one-stop shopping" on the school campus is the **full-service school,** where parents can access a wide range of social and health services without leaving the school campus (Dryfoos, 1996; Walker & Hackmann, 1999). Figure 4.5 shows the full-service model toward which schools are moving. Establishing a full-service school is a significant undertaking because it requires a great deal of coordination among agencies, but such efforts are popping up across the country:

- In New York City, the Children's Home Society has targeted four schools where 98% of students qualify for free or reduced-cost lunch to bring additional services for students and their parents directly on the schools' campuses. Parent self-help workshops, English as a Second Language classes, and full-service clinics with pediatricians and dentists operate from the schools (Agosto, 1999). At Intermediate School 218 in New York City, the Family Resources Center provides social services, immigration, housing and employment consultations, and services from a health and dental clinic.

- The Marshalltown, Iowa, schools have established the Caring Connection, an organization of mostly nonschool employees that works on school sites to provide services to more than 1,000 families per year. Among the services offered are primary health care, substance abuse counseling, family development, tutoring and dental care (Walker & Hackmann, 1999). The Caring Connection tries to exemplify "the art of the possible" with the support of the Marshalltown schools.

- The Palm Beach County, Florida, schools received services from Project CASAS, a program that focused on Hispanic and Haitian students and provided home visitations to train parents, tutoring sessions for students, translators and

INTASC

Principle #10

Partnerships: The teacher fosters relationships with school colleagues, parents, and agencies in the larger community to support students' learning and well-being.

FIGURE 4.4

Traditional versus Community Schools

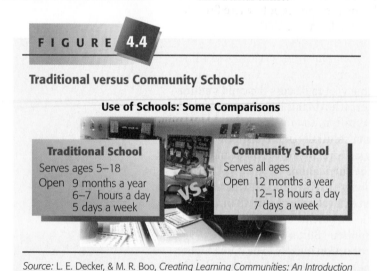

Use of Schools: Some Comparisons

Traditional School
Serves ages 5–18
Open   9 months a year
         6–7 hours a day
         5 days a week

Community School
Serves all ages
Open   12 months a year
         12–18 hours a day
         7 days a week

Source: L. E. Decker, & M. R. Boo, *Creating Learning Communities: An Introduction to Community Education* (p. 11). (Fairfax, VA: National Community Education Association, 1995).

FIGURE 4.5

Full-Service School Model

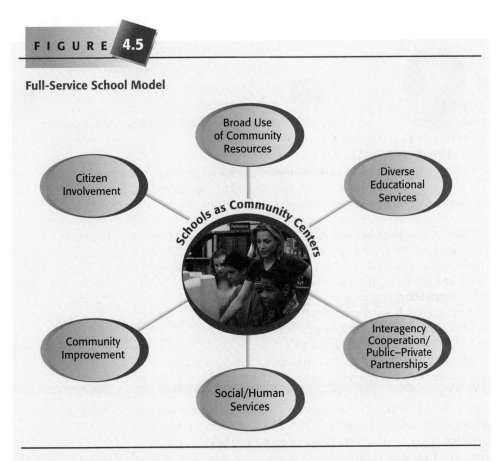

Source: L. E. Decker, & M. R. Boo, *Creating Learning Communities: An Introduction to Community Education* (p. 11). (Fairfax, VA: National Community Education Association, 1995).

transportation for parents at school meetings, and referrals to social service agencies. Since the grant that funded Project CASAS ended, the Palm Beach County school district is going to institutionalize many of the Project CASAS functions by training a cohort of bilingual/bicultural counselors and placing them in schools where Project CASAS had a significant presence (Schoorman & Jean-Jacques, 2003).

The advantages of offering community members a wide array of services on a school campus are undeniable. Efforts such as the Children's Home Society, the Caring Connection, and Project CASAS suggest that the "effective school" today involves more than simply effective instruction. Much of the literature about effective schools has focused on issues such as teacher effectiveness, outcome-based education, and internal school reform (Taylor, 2002; Lewis, 2002; Chrispeels, 2002). While these issues are important in achieving effective schools, students must have their basic needs met first before education can become a priority. To do this, schools need to establish and maintain close relations with social service, health, juvenile, and other agencies in order to assist parents and communities with many of life's necessities. Schools cannot simply say "we teach" and remain unconcerned about other aspects of students' or their families' lives. The academic achievement of students is affected by other factors besides good teaching. Students who lack proper nutrition, effective health care, and appropriate safety cannot learn efficiently or be expected to compete academically with students who have all of these benefits. Effective access to services that can help resolve the major and minor crises in the lives of families and communities has become an integral part of today's effective schools.

Who am I? What do I believe?

"The relationship between the teacher and parent is crucial . . . [but] I have seen [situations] when teachers and parents get too chummy. Let's just say there are some Saturdays when a trip to the supermarket turns into a parent conference."

CAROL, MIDDLE SCHOOL READING SPECIALIST

THINK ABOUT THIS:

Active involvement within a community is important for gaining an understanding of the community and the trust of parents. Reaching out to help students and their families is a natural impulse for teachers; however, at the same time you have to be careful to keep professional and social lives separate. What potential conflicts can arise when teachers become overly involved with families in the community? Is this more likely to occur in rural, suburban, or urban school districts?

SHARE and COMPARE:

Brainstorm with others in your class the types of issues or conflicts that can arise when working closely with parents and community representatives. Identify strategies for reducing the level of conflict.

FINAL THOUGHTS

This chapter has examined seven key questions describing the significance of families and communities in the process of education. Nearly all of the research literature encourages parent and community participation in the schools. It also points out that teachers and other school professionals are often concerned about parental involvement in functions such as curriculum, school policy, and student discipline. Yet parents and communities were the students' first teachers and they possess valuable information that educators need to know. How do teachers forge partnerships with parents and communities that do not threaten teachers' sense of professionalism? When properly established, these partnerships demystify for parents most or all of what occurs in schools. The key element for establishing appropriate partnerships is trust.

Effective teachers and administrators listen to what parents and communities are asking and trust that this input is an effort to help students, not to usurp a teacher's or principal's role as educational professionals. When this trust abounds, schools have the community's permission to change and meet the needs of those both care the most about: the students.

REFLECTIONS

Professional Plan for Understanding the Community

1. Three things I learned from this chapter about families and communities are:

2. Two things in this chapter I would like to learn more about are:

   a. _____

   b. _____

3. I plan to investigate these two areas and learn more about topics in this chapter by:

   _____ Reading some of the books following selections from the Read On section

   _____ Reading sources referenced in the chapter that interest me

   _____ Interviewing parents about their relationships with schools

   _____ Exploring the Web sites listed in the Log On section

   _____ Interviewing members of a parent–teacher–student association, school–business partnership, or other community organizations that support schools to learn about the nature of these partnerships

4. I will include the following in my Touch the Future portfolio:

   _____ Responses to the "Who Am I?" prompts

   _____ A brief essay on the chapter's Problems to Possibilities

   _____ My responses to the Linking Theory to Practice observation exercise

   _____ Other assignments given by my instructor (list)

SUMMARY

How Have Families Changed in Recent Years?

- There have been important cultural and demographic changes in families in recent years.
- The traditional nuclear family is now competing with new models of the family, including the permeable family.
- The lives of children are more closely integrated with those of adults than has been true in the recent past.

How Does a Community Shape the Climate of a School?

- The geographical, socioeconomic, racial, and ethnic nature of the communities served by a school are key elements in shaping school culture.
- All school communities present some promises as well as challenges for teachers in their schools.

- There are potential conflicts between the government and society's right to educate children and the rights of families to do the same.
- Teachers can learn about the communities in which they teach by participating in community activities, conducting survey research of community needs, and developing close associations with parents and other community members.

How Are Relationships Built between Schools and Parents?

- Parents are not always welcome as active participants in the primary activities of the school. Schools often are not interested in parents shaping school policy.
- Parents' involvement diminishes as students progress to higher grade levels.
- Parental interaction with schools often reflects problems and issues with students rather than being positively oriented.
- The National PTA has identified 6 areas for parent school collaboration: communicating, parenting, student learning, volunteering, school decision making and advocacy, and collaborating with community.
- Teachers and administrations are often reluctant to have parents act as collaborators because such collaboration can potentially diminish their power and authority as professionals.

What Can Schools Do to Reach Out to Communities?

- Parents from culturally different backgrounds may be upset if they encounter a condescending or expert view from school personnel.
- Parents look for school personnel who show a caring and congenial attitude toward their children.
- The expansion of services in full-service schools recognizes that students must have a wide range of basic needs met before they can be academically successful.
- Full-service schools provide parents a wide range of services such as health care, adult education and governmental services in addition to providing education, for students.

Visit the **Touch the Future . . . Teach!** Companion Website at www.ablongman.com/diaz for additional opportunities.

KEY WORDS

community schools 126	family household 106	permeable family 109
deficit model 124	full-service school 126	social capital 110
educentric perspective 120	household 106	

CONCEPT REVIEW

1. What is a permeable family? How is it different from a nuclear family?

2. How have families changed in recent years, and how are these changes significant for teachers working in the schools?

3. What important forces have brought about changes in families?

4. How are children and their experience specifically different from what existed in the United States 100 or even 50 years ago?

5. What are the rights of the government or state in the education of families? What are the rights of families in the education of their children?

6. Why do culturally different parents sometimes have a difficult time communicating with school personnel?

7. What are some advantages of teaching in rural, suburban, and urban communities?

8. What are some challenges encountered when teaching in rural, suburban, and urban communities?

9. Why is it easier to involve parents in activities at the periphery of school functions than at the core?

10. What are three things that any teacher could do to improve relations with parents and communities?

11. How can teachers' own cultural or community backgrounds influence the way they relate to communities in which they teach?

12. How have full-service schools changed the way schools are perceived as providers of services to the community?

13. What role does trust play in building effective school–community relations?

TOUCH THE FUTURE . . .

Read On

The Hurried Child: Growing Up Too Fast Too Soon
David Elkind (Cambridge, MA: DaCapo Press, 2001)
One of the best and most accessible books on children and the family in contemporary society.

The Way We Really Are: Coming to Terms with America's Changing Families
Stephanie Coontz (New York: Basic Books, 1997)
Explores the myths of family life in the United States and what families are actually like.

Home, School, and Community Partnerships
Larry Decker and Virginia Decker (Lanham, MD: Scarecrow Press, 2003)
A comprehensive book on establishing school–community partnerships. Also contains numerous references to associations involved in promoting community involvement in schools as well as additional Web sites on this and related topics..

School, Family, and Community Partnerships: Your Handbook for Action (2nd ed.)
Joyce Epstein, Marvin Sanders, Beth Simon, Karen Salinas, Natalie Jansorn, and Frances Van Voorhis (Thousand Oaks, CA: Corwin Press, 2002).
Hands-on realistic strategies for building partnerships with parents and communities, including how to form action teams for partnerships and organize volunteers.

Parents as Partners in Education: Families and Schools Working Together (6th ed.)
Eugenia Berger (Englewood Cliffs, NJ: Prentice Hall, 2003)
Examples of successful school programs in parent–community involvement, with a focus on generating involvement in the early years of a child's education.

Including Every Parent: A Step-by-Step Guide to Engaging and Empowering Parents at Your School
Darren Cunningham, Wynne Freed, Amy Gallunas, Kim Sprague, Danette Adams, Kate Boyd, Maggie Lodge, Cristina Santos, and Sharon Williams (New York: Teachers College Press, 2003)
Written by a team of parents and teachers; chronicles successful school–parent–community partnerships forged at Patrick O'Hearn Elementary School in Boston, Massachusetts.

Log On

National Parent Teachers Association
www.pta.org
> A not-for-profit association of parents, educators, students, and other citizens active in their schools and communities.

Parents for Public Schools
www.parents4publicschools.com
> An organization dedicated to promoting involvement by *all* families in school efforts to make sure *all* children are served.

National Coalition for Parent Involvement in Education
www.ncpie.org
> Advocates for strong school partnerships between parents and communities in every school in the United States; provides resources for parents, teachers, and school administrators.

National Center for Family Literacy
www.famlit.org
> Focuses on promoting educational opportunities for at-risk students and families across the United States.

Write On

> *"The family is the cornerstone of our society. More than any other force, it shapes the attitude, the hopes, the ambitions, and the values of the child. And when the family collapses it is the children that are usually damaged. When it happens on a massive scale the community itself is crippled. So, unless we work to strengthen the family, to create conditions under which most parents will stay together, all the rest— schools, playgrounds, and public assistance, and private concern— will never be enough."*
>
> —President Lyndon Baines Johnson

Write President Johnson's quote in your journal and reflect on how families are either succeeding or failing to meet the needs of contemporary children. Briefly explain whether you agree or disagree with President Johnson and support your decision. How can you as a teacher help to improve family life in the United States?

OBSERVATION GUIDE

TEACH: LINKING THEORY TO PRACTICE

Linking Theory to Practice

Part of your informed decision about teaching needs to come from your own desire to explore all aspects of teaching. The following interview and observation guide will help you while completing practical field experiences or during regular visits to schools.

Objective: To look at communities through the eyes of an anthropologist

School (use code name): _____   Observer: _____
Grade Level: _____   Date: _____
Subject(s): _____   Time In: _____ Time Out: _____

Directions: Look at the attendance boundary map of a local school. Given your knowledge of the local area how many different communities does it serve? (If only one, select another local school that serves a different community so you can have some contrast in this exercise.) Walk or drive around each community and note the following information:

1. What types of businesses are prevalent in each community?

2. What seems to be the predominant type of housing for families?

3. In what language(s) are the signs?

4. Do people congregate in any predictable patterns? If so, what are they?

5. What sounds do you hear in the community?

Connecting with INTASC: Principle 10

Partnerships: The teacher fosters relationships with school colleagues, parents, and agencies in the larger community to support students' learning and well-being.

Speak with local residents in each community and ask them their opinions of the local school. Ask local residents and agencies, if they (or the community at large) could do one thing to improve the local school, what that would be? Write your answers for each question so that responses for each community can be compared on one page. What patterns emerge, if any? Which questions have answers with very little difference? Which questions show the greatest contrast? Do residents agree or disagree in their opinions of the school and suggestions to improve it?

After analyzing the answers, write a short essay summarizing your findings and identify what the school district might be able to do to partner with the community.

5

Teaching and the Foundations of Education

Who am I?

What do I believe?

As you begin your teaching career, think about the work of teachers and the function and purpose of education in American society. Try to understand how your classroom and the school you work in are connected to the larger educational system and to the community in which you teach.

Rousseau alludes to this in his quote. As a teacher, you are preparing the next generation to deal with society, the good and the bad. How do you think your work as a teacher will be shaped by the good and bad forces at work in American society? Which of these forces will have an impact on the lives of your students? How do philosophical issues and belief systems influence your work as a teacher?

"The teacher's art consists in this: To turn the child's attention from trivial details and to guide his thoughts continually towards relations of importance which he will one day need to know, that he may judge rightly of good and evil in society."

Jean-Jacques Rousseau

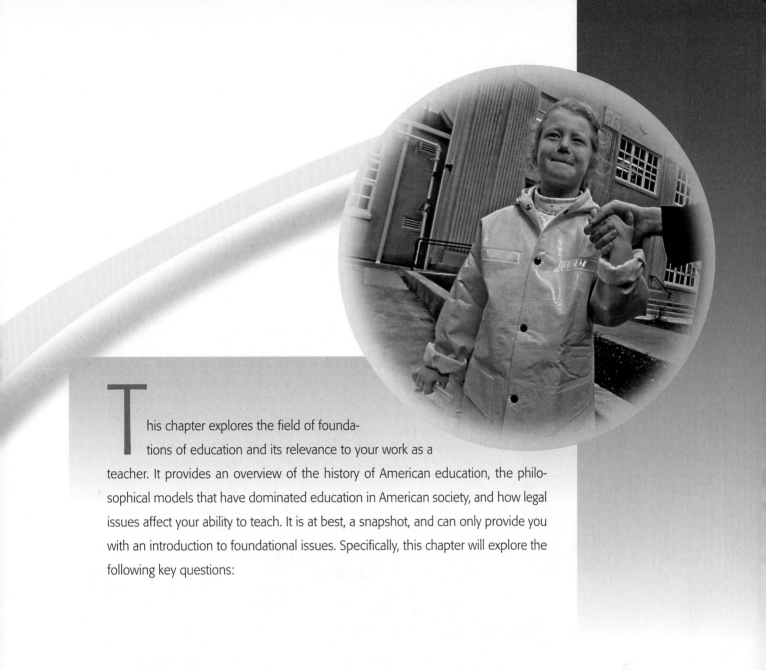

This chapter explores the field of foundations of education and its relevance to your work as a teacher. It provides an overview of the history of American education, the philosophical models that have dominated education in American society, and how legal issues affect your ability to teach. It is at best, a snapshot, and can only provide you with an introduction to foundational issues. Specifically, this chapter will explore the following key questions:

Key Questions

1. What is meant by the foundations of education?
2. How have historical trends affected education today?
3. How have philosophical changes influenced education?
4. How do legal issues affect your ability to teach?
5. How are the foundations of education useful to you as a teacher?

WHAT IS MEANT BY THE FOUNDATIONS OF EDUCATION?

The Council of Learned Societies in Education defines the **foundations of education** as follows:

> Foundations of Education refers to a broadly-conceived field of educational study that derives its character and methods from a number of academic disciplines, combinations of disciplines, and area studies, including: history, philosophy, sociology, anthropology, religion, political science, economics, psychology, cultural studies, gender studies, comparative and international education, educational studies, and educational policy studies. (Council of Learned Societies in Education, 1996)

According to the council, the purpose of foundational studies is to use these disciplinary resources as a means of "developing interpretive, normative, and critical perspectives on education" (1996).

This may all seem a bit overwhelming. The foundations of education, after all, represent the total knowledge that we have across the academic disciplines (history, philosophy, law, sociology, and so on) about the forces that shape schools. This knowledge is complex and is essentially interdisciplinary. It needs to be integrated and synthesized. This is no easy task, even for those with experience in the field.

You might ask, "Why is foundations knowledge important for a beginning teacher?" "How is it relevant?" Or you may say, "I need to worry about discipline and classroom management, or about subject content. I don't have time for this stuff." On the surface this may indeed seem to be the case. Consider, however, an analogy with a car. What's important appears to be on the surface—the tires, the steering wheel, and the body of the car. What runs the car, however, is the engine. While the outside of the car is important, what goes on under the hood is equally important. It is also much more complicated.

The foundations of education deal with what is underneath the hood of the car: the engine that powers our schools and, ultimately, our society. Getting to the engine and seeing how it operates is what the foundations of education are all about. Disciplinary fields such as history and philosophy are some of the tools that let you get under the hood and take apart the engine. Continuing the metaphor, legal issues (that is, the law) are what tune your engine.

HOW HAVE HISTORICAL TRENDS AFFECTED EDUCATION TODAY?

How can you best begin to develop an understanding of the foundations of education? Understanding the broad sweep of the history of American education provides a good starting point. Learning the history of the field will require more advanced courses, but consider the following to be a brief introduction to a complex and fascinating field of study.

EDUCATION DURING THE COLONIAL ERA

Historically, the American people have always placed a great deal of faith in education, with its roots dating back to the colonial period. Soon after establishing the Massachusetts Bay Colony in 1630, for example, Puritan settlers set up churches and schools. In 1635, what was to become the Boston Latin Grammar School was founded—a school that still operates as part of the Boston public school system. The following year, in 1636, Harvard University was founded, making it the oldest institution of higher education in the United States.

● **Education in New England**   Education, and life in general, in the New England colonies was supposed to prepare people for the "life hereafter." The Massachusetts Bay Colony was a religious colony, a fact reflected in the most famous educational law to come out of the colonial period, the Old Deluder Act, also known as the Old Deluder Satan Act. Passed in 1647, the opening paragraph of the law argued that:

> It being one chief project of that old deluder, Satan, to keep men from the knowledge of the Scriptures, as in former times by keeping them in an unknown tongue, so in these latter times by persuading from the use of tongues, that so that at least the true sense and meaning of the original might be clouded and corrupted with false glosses of saint-seeming deceivers; and to the end that learning may not be buried in the grave of our forefathers, in church and commonwealth, the Lord assisting our endeavors.

The act went on to require:

> …that every township in this jurisdiction, after the Lord hath increased them to fifty households shall forthwith appoint one within their town to teach all such children as shall resort to him to write and read, whose wages shall be paid either by the parents or masters of such children, or by the inhabitants in general, …" (*Records of the Governor,* 1853)

In essence, the Old Deluder Act recognized the value in promoting learning as a way of maintaining their religious culture and focusing on the classics. Every town with one hundred or more families was required to operate a more advanced, or higher-level, school to teach Latin grammar.

The emphasis on religion in the early Puritan schools can be seen in the content of the most famous textbook to come out of the colonial period, *The New England Primer.* A rhyming alphabet with frequent religious references and allusions, short prayers, and historical discussions of religious martyrs fill its pages. Often the message was fairly grim, describing not only the frailty of men and women, but also their inevitable death. In the rhyming alphabet, for example, the letter G stands for "As runs the Glass, Our Life doth pass." Despite their religious emphasis, however, early schools in the colonies also had the practical function of making people sufficiently literate so that they could conduct business and take care of their daily affairs.

● **Education in the Middle Colonies**   As in the New England colonies, education in the middle colonies such as Pennsylvania, New York, Maryland, and New Jersey focused on religion. But because there was a greater variety of religious groups in this region, the schools tended to be locally oriented to reflect the regional diversity. German schools, for example, were established in Pennsylvania by Mennonite settlers. Quakers established schools in and around Philadelphia. Opposed to slavery, the Quakers also established schools for blacks. The most famous of these schools was begun in Philadelphia in 1770 by Anthony Benezett (Button & Provenzo, 1989). Schooling was also available largely through church-affiliated schools in New York and New Jersey. Private tutors and mistresses who taught basic reading and numeracy were also common. The most rudimentary free publicly supported schools in the United States were not established in the United States until several decades after the American Revolution (1775–1783).

● **Education in the Southern Colonies**   Education in the South during the colonial era developed somewhat differently than in New England. For one thing, the Church of England was the main religious institution, unlike in New England where Congregationalism dominated. In addition, the greater distances between settlements, as well as the plantation economy in place, meant that formal schools were much less common than in the North. In Virginia, for example, the establishment of schools was more difficult than

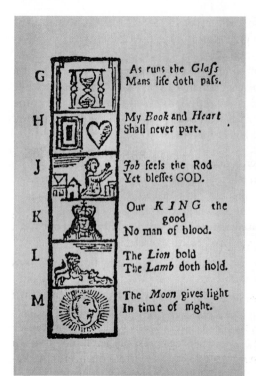

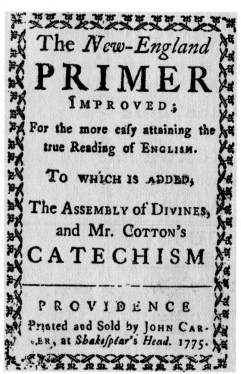

The content of The New England Primer, *the most famous textbook from the colonial period, illustrates the strong emphasis on religion in early Puritan schools.*

in New England because the settlers were much more spread out. Among wealthy planters in Virginia, tutors were often hired to educate children. Philip Vickers Fithian, a graduate of Princeton training to become a Presbyterian minister, was employed in the fall of 1773 by Colonel and Mrs. Robert Carter to educate their two sons, five daughters, and a nephew. In a letter to a friend, Fithian explained that instruction for the older children included Latin, while instruction for the younger ones focused on reading and spelling.

Although schools did exist in the South, they simply were not as common as in the New England colonies. However, the literacy rate in the South during the colonial period was moderately high. In Elizabeth City, Virginia, between 1763 and 1771, for example, 9 out of 10 white men and 2 out of 3 white women could read. Education for blacks, however, was fairly limited, but not totally restricted as it was throughout the South by the beginning of the 1830s (Button & Provenzo, 1989, pp. 41–44).

POSTREVOLUTION AMERICA AND THE RISE OF NATIONALISM

Education during the colonial period was essentially "English" education, transferred to the colonies. After the American Revolution, the new nation was faced with an interesting dilemma: how to educate people to be "American."

Noah Webster

In 1783, just 2 years after the defeat of the British, new "American" textbooks such as Noah Webster's three-volume *Grammatical Institutes of the English Language* (1783) were being published. Consciously American, it emphasized the American use of language (Webster, of course, being the author of *Webster's Dictionary*) rather than British. The most famous of the three volumes was the first, commonly known as the "blue-back speller" because its cover was blue.

Webster's reading books and books such as Jedidiah Morse's 1784 *Geography Made Easy* (which emphasized American rather than English geography) were documents that were consciously concerned with nation building. Both Webster's and Morse's work were highly practical and reflected what were not only ideological and political needs, but also the very practical need of teaching children how to read.

● **Thomas Jefferson's Vision of Schooling**　The most clearly conceived philosophical model of education to emerge from the late eighteenth century was that formulated by Thomas Jefferson (1743–1826). According to Jefferson, a democratic society needed an educational system that would make it possible for its citizens to pursue their personal happiness and needs, as well as conduct their business and fulfill their obligation as citizens.

In 1779, Jefferson put forward a bill in the Virginia House of Burgesses that would create a system of public education in Virginia. This Bill for the More General Diffusion of Knowledge would create a three-tier school system that would provide a free general education for all citizens, as well as instruction at higher levels for the leaders of the culture.

Under Jefferson's system, three years of free public schooling would be provided to all citizens. Basic instruction would be provided in reading, writing, mathematics, and civics. The second phase of his system involved the establishment of Latin grammar schools for men only. Grammar schools were an early type of secondary school that emphasized the teaching of Latin. According to Jefferson's plan, twenty grammar schools would be set up throughout Virginia. Students could pay tuition to attend or, if they were very talented, attend the school on a scholarship. The most talented graduates of the grammar schools would then be given scholarships to continue their education at the College of William and Mary. Those who did not receive scholarships but had the money could also pay their own tuition to the college.

Jefferson's idea was to create a meritocracy—in which merit and ability would be enable people to advance through the educational system regardless of their family's wealth or status. In this context, the educational system would act as the great equalizer in American society.

Jefferson's ideas unfortunately were not adopted. If they had been, something close to a universal system of free education would have been established throughout the United States by the beginning of the nineteenth century.

● **The Northwest Ordinance of 1787**　In 1787 the new American government passed the Northwest Ordinance, which divided federally owned land in the wilderness regions of the country into townships of 36 sections. Each section measured 1 square mile. The 16th section of each township was set aside by Congress for the support of public education. Schools could be built on this property, which was located in the center of the township, and any profits realized from its sale would go into a fund to support the schools.

As will be discussed in more detail in Chapter 8, Diversity and the Cultural Context of Teaching, schools have until very recently been controlled largely at the state and local level. The U.S. Constitution has no mention of education and public schooling. Under the Constitution, duties not assigned to the federal government revert to the states. Such is the case with education.

NINETEENTH-CENTURY EDUCATION AND BEYOND

Different types of public and private schools at the elementary and secondary levels, such as reading schools, academies, and seminaries, were established throughout the United States during the early part of the nineteenth century. A large, wide-scale system, however, did not come into being until the creation of the Common Schools.

● **The Common Schools**　The Common School movement had its origins in industrialized states such as Massachusetts, Connecticut, New York, and Pennsylvania. Its purpose was to provide mass universal public education at the elementary level, "a common schooling," to all people. In many aspects, it embodied (at least at the elementary level) Jefferson's idea of a universal educational system for citizens based on merit.

The Common School movement had a profound impact on the profession of teaching in the United States. Men had dominated teaching throughout the colonial period, as well as in the early years of the new republic. Women were increasingly recruited into teaching starting in the late 1830s, however, since they provided a much less expensive source of labor for the rapidly increasing number of schools. As a result, early in our history, teaching

Horace Mann

became associated with being "women's work." While, to some extent, women were widely exploited in a highly sexist society, it was one of the few professions that granted easy access to women. Thus, teaching provided important opportunities for women in terms of education and employment.

Educational historians such as Michael Katz, Herbert Gintis, and Samuel Bowles have shown that the founding of the Common Schools, while in many respects admirable, also represented an attempt to reproduce existing lines of power, authority, and control in the society. The Common Schools, while promoting literacy among the general population, also had the purpose of reinforcing social, cultural, and political values of those in power.

In his *Twelfth Report* (1848) as the Secretary of the Massachusetts Board of Education, Horace Mann (1796–1859) wrote that "the true business of the school room connects itself, and becomes identical, with the great interests of the society. The former is the infant, immature state of those interests; the latter, their developed, adult state. As 'the child is father to the man,' so may the training of the schoolroom expand into the institutions and fortunes of the state" (Cremin, 1957, p. 80). In 1852, under Mann's supervision, Massachusetts passed the first compulsory education law.

Common School education was not free and universal, however, for all people. During the decades prior to the Civil War, for example, slaves in the South were actually prohibited from learning how to read and write. Native Americans, when provided with schooling throughout the nineteenth century, were given instruction primarily so that they could be subdued and assimilated. During this same period, women were often restricted in terms of their access to schooling—particularly higher education. In general, though, the country had embraced the idea of public education as being a universal good for the great majority of its citizens.

● **The Emergence of "The One Best System"**   Public education continued to expand in the decades following the Civil War, becoming what the educational historian David Tyack has referred to as "the one best system." While schools were technically under the control of local school boards, there developed—particularly in cities—increasingly elaborate systems of bureaucratic control. It was during this period that large city school systems developed the administrative positions that we now take for granted in our educational system, such as superintendents and principals. This was also a time that saw the development of **normal schools** for the training of teachers. By the end of the nineteenth century, normal schools became increasingly associated with college and university education.

Public schooling grew along with the American nation. As the country's population and geographical base expanded, schools became more important. Particularly in urban areas, schools came to be seen as potential vehicles for social reform. In the 1890s, for example, a major liberal progressive reform movement emerged that pushed for the improvement of education as a powerful vehicle of social reform. People such as John Dewey (1859–1952) proposed new philosophical models of schooling and new ways to teach in the classroom.

John Dewey

● **John Dewey and Pragmatics**   During John Dewey's lifetime, the United States changed from a rural and agricultural country to an urban, industrial nation. Dewey was a leader in the philosophical movement known as **pragmatism.** He believed that schools should be places where children learned through experience. The simple transmission of knowledge was insufficient for him. Instead, he felt that children needed to do activities in the classroom that had real interest and meaning for them. As he explained in the very first paragraph of "My Pedagogic Creed" (1897):

> all education proceeds by the participation of the individual in the social consciousness of the race. This process begins unconsciously almost at birth, and is continually shaping the individual's powers, saturating his consciousness, forming his habits, training his ideas, and arousing his feelings and emotions. Through this unconscious education the individual gradually comes to share the intellectual and moral resources which humanity has succeeded in getting together. (pp. 77–80)

EDUCATION MATTERS

The Ideal of the Common Schools

How do public schools contribute to our democracy? This question has fueled considerable debate in recent years. The public schools have been criticized as having an unfair monopoly on schooling—a monopoly that discourages choice and excellence in education. This description of contemporary public education is in sharp contrast to the tradition of the Common Schools that emerged during the 1830s and 1840s.

In following the idea of Thomas Jefferson that a nation could not be ignorant and free at the same time, Horace Mann believed schools were the foundation of the democracy. In 1841, as secretary of the Massachusetts schools, Mann declared, "The common school is the greatest discovery ever made by man" (Cremin, 1957, p. 15). According to Mann, schools prepared children to share a common culture and heritage. Schooling was a responsibility of all citizens:

In a government like ours, each individual must think of the welfare of the state as well as the welfare of his own family; and therefore, of the children of others as well as his own. It becomes then a momentous question, whether the children in our schools are educated in reference to themselves and their private interests only, or with a regard to the great social duties and prerogatives that wait them. (Cremin, 1957, p. 64)

For Mann, public schools were essential to the continuation of the democracy. In recent years, many Americans would question Mann's vision. Since the 1980s there has been a powerful movement to privatize American public education. Efforts at privatization challenge the fundamental role of public education in our culture. Some education researchers maintain that privatizing schools takes the control of schools out of the hands of the public. In doing so, the public loses control of what is "arguably the most important institutions for shaping the future . . . Giving up on public schooling as our accepted norm would mean leaving our nation's children in the hands of unknown baby-sitters with unknown agendas. To want to know who the baby-sitter is and what he or she is up to is not a right versus a left issue" (Meier, 1995, p. 8). Meier believes that the American public has a "legitimate role in setting the agenda for our own individual children; we have an equally important role in setting the agenda for our children at large" (Meier, 1995, pp. 8–9). What goes on in the public schools not only represents a shared responsibility, but also determines the goals we can achieve as a democratic society.

The Education Issue: The role of public schools in creating a common good

What's Your Opinion?

1. What role do public schools play in the creation of a common good?

2. Based on what you know about the beliefs of Horace Mann, what do you think he would think of No Child Left Behind?

Dewey argued, "True education comes through the stimulation of the child's powers by the demands of the social situations in which he finds himself" (1897). Thus, education should be grounded in the real world and the actual experience of the child. As is described in greater detail in Chapter 6, the struggle over the curriculum in American schools throughout the twentieth century, and continuing to the present, is really about the issue of how children learn best. Critics of Dewey feel that he allowed children too much freedom and inadequately directed them in terms of their values and beliefs. Supporters maintain that Dewey understood, in unique ways, how children learn and how the schools could play a role in shaping their democratic consciousness.

● **The Great School Legend** American society has always given lip service to the idea that schools play an important role in the promotion of democratic values. With the development of the universal free public education throughout much of the country by the late nineteenth century, it would seem that a model of free education for all citizens was largely in place. In fact, this was true for only a selected part of the population. While African American children were provided with free public schooling, their schools were not as well

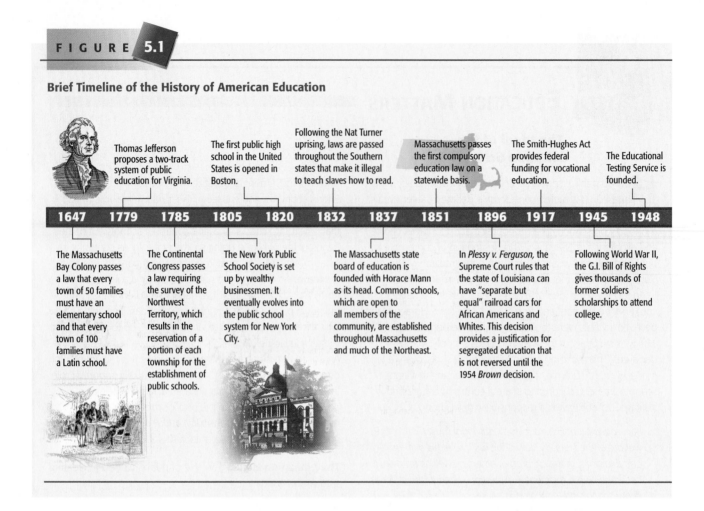

FIGURE 5.1

Brief Timeline of the History of American Education

Thomas Jefferson proposes a two-track system of public education for Virginia.

The first public high school in the United States is opened in Boston.

Following the Nat Turner uprising, laws are passed throughout the Southern states that make it illegal to teach slaves how to read.

Massachusetts passes the first compulsory education law on a statewide basis.

The Smith-Hughes Act provides federal funding for vocational education.

The Educational Testing Service is founded.

| 1647 | 1779 | 1785 | 1805 | 1820 | 1832 | 1837 | 1851 | 1896 | 1917 | 1945 | 1948 |

The Massachusetts Bay Colony passes a law that every town of 50 families must have an elementary school and that every town of 100 families must have a Latin school.

The Continental Congress passes a law requiring the survey of the Northwest Territory, which results in the reservation of a portion of each township for the establishment of public schools.

The New York Public School Society is set up by wealthy businessmen. It eventually evolves into the public school system for New York City.

The Massachusetts state board of education is founded with Horace Mann as its head. Common schools, which are open to all members of the community, are established throughout Massachusetts and much of the Northeast.

In *Plessy v. Ferguson,* the Supreme Court rules that the state of Louisiana can have "separate but equal" railroad cars for African Americans and Whites. This decision provides a justification for segregated education that is not reversed until the 1954 *Brown* decision.

Following World War II, the G.I. Bill of Rights gives thousands of former soldiers scholarships to attend college.

funded as those for White students. Women had far fewer educational opportunities than men. The children of immigrants often had to attend schools in poorer sections of the cities that were not as well supported as those in more established neighborhoods.

Scholars who believe that American public education is essentially equitable refer to this concept as the **Great School Legend.** Colin Greer described the legend in this way: "Once upon a time there was a great nation that became great because of its public schools. . . . The public school system . . . built American democracy. It took the backward poor, the ragged, ill-prepared ethnic minorities who crowded into the cities, educated and Americanized then into the homogenous, productive middle class that is America's strength and pride" (Greer, 1972, pp. 3–4).

How much truth is there in the Great School Legend? Has it been truer for some groups rather than for others? Has it worked better for Whites than for African Americans, Native Americans, and other people of color? Has it served men better than women? To what extent has it lifted groups economically?

The rhetoric of the Great School Legend has typically referred to the idea of education as the great equalizer in American culture. While the public schools have acted as vehicles of social change and reform throughout much of the nineteenth and twentieth centuries, they have done so imperfectly, however, typically serving some groups better than others. No one who has carefully studied the history of American education can ignore the fact that there has been a great struggle to achieve equality in American society, and that the schools have been one of the main arenas in which this struggle for equity has been fought.

Often the schools worked against the interests of minority groups such as Blacks, Native Americans, and Hispanics. In some cases, this was done by means of overt discrim-

A federal court orders the integration of the Little Rock, Arkansas, public schools. President Eisenhower sends federal troops to enforce the court order.

The *Bilingual Education Act* provides federal assistance to students whose primary language is not English.

Title IX requires that women be given the same opportunities as men in educational settings or federal funding will be withheld.

The *Education for All Handicapped Children Act* is passed. It maintains that all students with special needs are entitled to a fair and appropriate education.

The *Individuals with Disabilities Education Act* (IDEA) is passed, requiring that schools plan for the transition of adolescents with disabilities into further education for employment.

The *No Child Left Behind Act* calls for increasing accountability at all levels of K–12 education and greatly expands the federal role in education.

1954   1957   1965   1968   1972   1974   1975   1983   1990   1997   2002

In *Brown v. Board of Education of Topeka,* the Supreme Court unanimously overturns *Plessy v. Ferguson,* arguing that segregated schools are "inherently unequal" and must be eliminated.

The *Elementary and Secondary Education Act* provides federal funding for public schools with the intent of reducing educational inequality.

In *Lau v. Nichols,* the Supreme Court rules that students who do not speak English must be provided with instruction in their native language. The *Equal Educational Opportunities Act* is passed, which states that students may not be denied equal educational opportunity because of their race, color, sex, or national origin.

The National Commission on Excellence in Education releases *A Nation at Risk,* which sets in motion a conservative educational reform program that dominates the 1980s, the 1990s, and the early years of the new century.

The *Individuals with Disabilities Education Act* adds provisions to the original IDEA for greater parental and classroom teacher involvement in the education of students with special needs.

---

ination. In other instances it was achieved by cultural assimilation of minorities—a process that was often inherently discriminatory.

Assimilation of Native Americans Nowhere is the process of assimilation through education more evident than in the case of Native Americans. The Native American population was displaced, both physically and culturally, as a result of the growth and development of the United States. Between 1778 and 1871 a total of 389 treaties were made between the U.S. government and tribal groups. Native American groups ceded more than a billion acres of land to the federal government. In exchange, they were given reservation lands and limited financial remuneration and educational resources.

In 1819 the Office of Indian Affairs was established, and government funds began to be made available for Native American schools. In general, the purpose of Indian education was to "civilize" Native Americans in terms of religion (Christianity) and Western cultural traditions. There was little respect for Native Americans and their languages or religious and cultural traditions. Instead it was believed that they must be blended or assimilated into the mainstream culture. This general attitude was expressed in the slogan "Killing the Indian and Saving the Man."

Nowhere is this more clear than in the reservation and boarding schools, which dominated Native American education well into the twentieth century. Typical was the Carlisle Indian Barracks School in Pennsylvania, which was founded in 1879 by Captain Richard Henry Pratt. The school took children from Western tribes such as the Sioux and brought them East to be "civilized." After being trained to do manual labor (carpentry, farming, and so on), they were eventually sent back to their tribes, where they often had trouble reintegrating themselves. No longer culturally connected to their families and tribe, they were

INTASC

Principle #7

Instructional Planning Skills: The teacher plans instruction based upon knowledge of subject matter, students, the community, and curriculum goals.

The forceful assimilation of Native Americans in the nineteenth century resulted in large numbers of children severed from their cultural traditions. Why did these children often have difficulty integrating themselves in both their tribes and the mainstream culture? What was the government's rationale for this assimilation? Illustrated in this late-nineteenth-century photograph are students at the Carlisle Indian Barracks School in Pennsylvania.

still discriminated against by the mainstream culture because they were Native Americans (Button & Provenzo, 1989, pp. 275–276).

Native Americans were not granted citizenship until after World War I. Schooling and the education of Native Americans remained largely under government control until the early 1970s. As an extension of the civil rights movement, Native Americans gained control of their own schools and the education of their children.

Catholic Education   Assimilation was not limited to groups such as Native Americans. Catholics were also targets for assimilation. When their numbers increased as a result of Irish and German immigration in the late 1840s, increasing efforts were made to use the public schools to "Americanize" them. This typically involved the imposition of Protestant values and traditions. In places such as New York City, Catholics resisted this process, eventually setting up their own private schools. These schools became the foundation of the modern Catholic parochial system of education (Button & Provenzo, 1989, pp. 142–145).

Interestingly, Catholic education, from its earliest beginnings (with the exception of its emphasis on religious instruction), used a curriculum that was remarkably like that of the public schools. Nineteenth-century immigrant Catholics (primarily Irish and Germans) tried to be as mainstream "American" as possible, while holding onto their specific religious traditions. This has certainly been the case with more recently arrived Catholic immigrant groups, such as Poles, Czechs, Italians, and various Hispanic groups, including Mexican Americans.

Hispanic Groups and Assimilation   The education of Hispanic groups in the United States has often focused on issues of cultural conformity and language assimilation. In the southwestern United States of the late nineteenth century, "many schools eliminated the use of Spanish, Mexican history and culture. School officials, in many cases, believed that the native language and culture of Mexican children should not be used in schools because they were incompatible with or inferior to American values and speech patterns" (Kloosterman, 2003, p. 5) Some schools employed "Spanish detention," which students earned if they were overheard speaking Spanish anywhere on the school campus. Hispanics in New Mexico opposed the establishment of English-only school laws during the 1890s.

In 1897 Texas courts declared Mexican Americans to be "non-White" and in 1930 Texas courts upheld the right to segregate Mexican Americans in public schools. In 1930, California's attorney general Ulysses Webb declared Mexican Americans to be Indian and in 1935 California passed a law allowing for public school segregation of Mexican Americans as Indians. This practice was legal until the *Mendez vs. Orange County Schools* decision of 1946 (Spring, 2004). There were conflicting attitudes at this time about educating Mexican American children. Some outside the Mexican American community did not want Mexican Americans in school because it meant they were not available for farm work, while others favored public school attendance because it provided an opportunity for Americanization.

As the largest language minority group in the United States, Hispanics have had to wrestle with the issue of whether their home language, Spanish, should be reflected in their children's education. Historically, non-English-speaking European groups gave up their home languages and received English-only instruction in public schools. This conformed to an expectation that in order to fit into American society, immigrants, or their children, were to follow a pattern of language replacement, not language addition. It also resulted in the children and grandchildren of these immigrants losing the non-English language by the second, or almost certainly by the third, generation. Faced with this historical backdrop, Hispanic parents have had to face the dilemma that if they wanted their children to be bilingual and biliterate (a definite economic and academic asset), they risked the criticism that they weren't following in the path of the "good old immigrants." Some critics of bilingual education have seized on disappointing rates of academic achievement among Hispanic students in the United States as evidence of the failure of bilingual education, without recognizing that only a small percentage of Hispanic students are enrolled in bilingual programs.

According to the U.S. Supreme Court in its 1982 decision of *Plyler v. Doe*, the documented or legal status of a student may not be used to deny admission to public schools in the United States. Some Hispanic students fall into the undocumented category, but the overwhelming majority are U.S.-born or legal residents. Over the past three decades, the high school graduation rate among Hispanic students has been increasing slightly—from 56.7% in 1980 to 59.1% in 1990 and 64.1% in 2000 (President's Advisory Commission, 2003)—but still remains disappointing when compared with other groups of students in the United States. When the growing size of the Hispanic population is taken into account, this represents a significant problem in American schools. It also calls to our attention the importance of having highly qualified teachers who understand Hispanic students and are prepared to meet their needs.

HOW HAVE PHILOSOPHICAL CHANGES INFLUENCED EDUCATION?

Who should control the public schools in a democracy such as the United States? Some people have argued that it should be an elite group of experts who are particularly knowledgeable about issues of how children learn and how schools are best administered. The problem with this notion is that there is no consensus on what is the best way to educate children. Each group of experts holds a particular view on what is the best way to educate children based on their own ideological and political values. While many philosophical ideas have, historically, shaped American education, there are five that have been particularly influential.

FIVE PHILOSOPHICAL MODELS

Historically, five different philosophical models of education have dominated discussions of education in the United States: essentialism, perennialism, progressivism, social reconstructionism, and existentialism. Each model reflects specific ideological and cultural values that often reflect the historical period in which they were conceived.

- **Essentialism**   In the **essentialism** model, the purpose of education is to learn certain basic or "essential" knowledge. The term *essentialism* was first introduced by the American educator William Bagley (1874–1946). The model is based on the belief that specific knowledge is provided by disciplines such as literature, math, science, and history, and that this knowledge is basic to any education.

- **Perennialism**   Closely related to essentialism, **perennialism** is based on the belief that "perennial" wisdom or knowledge has been accumulated over the ages. This wisdom is found in great works of literature and art, as well religious texts such as the Qur'an and the Bible.

- **Progressivism**   Unlike perennialism, **progressivism** does not draw so much on great works, but instead on the idea that the child is the center of the educational process. As formulated in the work of theorists such as John Dewey, progressive education has a strong practical or pragmatic orientation to it. According to Dewey, children learn through the process of doing interesting and useful things that relate to their lives. Schooling is not focused only on learning from traditional texts, but also on the idea of learning through practical hands-on experiences.

- **Social Reconstructionism**   The **social reconstruction** model of education uses schools to create a more just social and political order. This model is most clearly articulated in the work of George Counts (1889–1974), who believed that schools are a place to examine and test ideas critically. Although a student of John Dewey's, Counts was dissatisfied with the progressive education movement's lack of moral, political, and economic emphasis—something he felt schools and teachers needed to focus on if they were to function effectively. In a contemporary context, critical educators such as Henry Giroux and Peter McLaren agree with many of the ideas of George Counts.

- **Existentialism**   Existential models of education reject the idea that there is any type of definitive or authoritative knowledge. An **existentialism** model of schooling maintains that students know from within what is important for them to pursue in terms of their own education. The British educator and founder of the Summerhill School A. S. Neill (1883–1973) is most closely associated with this philosophy of schooling.

EDUCATION AS TRANSMISSION OR SELF-DISCOVERY

There has been a battle in American public education for more than a century over whether schools should be concerned primarily with the basics and transmit predetermined knowledge to their students, or should teach students *how* to think and act creatively on their own. Critics of student-directed learning claim that students do not know enough to know what they need to know, and that all children must learn certain fundamental things if they are to be effective citizens. These ideas must be passed on from one generation to the next.

Critics of this transmission model of learning argue that children cannot simply be "inoculated" with knowledge. Learning must be meaningful to the student and engage them in ways that has meaning for their own lives. The novelist Pat Conroy, for example, recounts his experiences teaching poor African American children on Yamacraw Island off the coast of Georgia in the late 1960s:

> The school library would have been funny if it had not been such a tragic commentary on administrative inefficiency and stupidity. Each day we had a half hour reading period during which the kids could read anything they liked. . . . Cindy Lou chose a book to read called Tommy the Telephone as her personal favorite. Each time Cindy read to me about Tommy, the irony struck me: a girl reading about telephones who has never used a telephone. Other books with negligible relationship to life on the island populated the

INTASC

Principle #2

Knowledge of Human Development and Learning: The teacher understands how children learn and develop, and can provide learning opportunities that support their intellectual, social, and personal development.

Problems to POSSIBILITIES

Watching Shakespeare

Tori Ovington is a ninth-grade English teacher. Her classes have been reading Shakespeare's Romeo and Juliet, *one of her favorite plays. Her first experience with the story was from watching the 1968 movie version of the play directed by Franco Zeffirelli. As a reward to her second-period class, which has struggled with reading the play, she has decided to show a more recent and modernized film version of the play to her class. She chooses the 1996 film version,* Romeo + Juliet, *starring Leonardo DiCaprio and Claire Danes.*

The following week she is called into Principal Rittner's office.

"Who authorized you to show the Romeo and Juliet film in class?" Principal Rittner asked.

"No one," replied Tori, surprised that she would have needed "authorization." "But the kids had worked hard and had struggled with some of the story. I used the movie as a reward for having worked so hard."

"Well, we've gotten a couple of complaints from parents."

"Complaints?"

"Yes, one of your parents objects to the fact that you are teaching a play about people who commit suicide and disobey their parents. They say that it offends their religious beliefs and they don't want their son reading stories like this."

"But it's Shakespeare and the play is part of the approved curriculum," said Tori. "You said there was a second complaint?"

"Yes," said Ms. Rittner. "It came from Melanie Shipp's father, who teaches at the community college. He doesn't like the Leonardo DiCaprio version—says it's too modern—actually called it an MTV version of the play. He said you should have shown the 1968 version of the film that was directed by Franco Zeffirelli."

"Are you serious?" said Tori.

"I'm not only serious," said Ms. Rittner, "but I expect you to call up both parents and speak with them directly. Frankly, Tori," continued Principal Rittner, "I'm a little concerned that you would take valuable instruction time just for the purpose of showing a movie."

Discussion Questions

What external factors do you need to be aware of when planning your curriculum? Did Tori use good judgment in showing the movie in her class? If you were Tori what would you do? How might knowledge from the foundations of education help her deal with the problem?

Possibilities

There really are two issues here. First, it's not unusual to field complaints from parents about choices you make in your classroom, including topics you discuss and strategies you choose for making your points, which is why it's always helpful if the principal or department chair is there to support your efforts. Therefore, it's important that they be aware of your instruction plans. A teacher's degree of autonomy in the classroom varies in every school, which is why it is important that you become aware of such parameters in the school.

The second issue here is Tori's use of pop culture in the classroom. Was it appropriate to show a movie in class? Using pop culture as a learning tool can be very helpful as everyone learns differently, and the use of pop culture may tap into the learning styles of some students better than other strategies. But you have to make sure you use the material wisely. Everyone's tastes differ, and not everyone will agree with the examples you use. These are some ways Tori could have minimized criticism:

- Be sure to review the movie first. Rule number one: Never use something in class unless you're fully aware of its contents.

- Never miss an opportunity to capitalize on a teachable moment. Using the movie as a reward can be maximized by also using it to reinforce concepts discussed in class. Tori could have created her own lesson plan for using the movie, or she could have sought outside suggestions for using movies in class. She might have used Shakespeare Help.com (www.shakespearehelp.com) or Teach With Movies (www.teachwithmovies.org) to create a plan that could reinforce key concepts, particularly if students were struggling to understand some concepts.

At this point, Tori should contact both parents, because her principal has asked her to and because it actually offers a good opportunity to create an open dialogue with parents. She can use the opportunity to explain her rationale for her choice, to discuss how she used the movie in class, and to demonstrate her openness to respecting the difference of opinions. Additionally, speaking with the parents will help her better understand her community and identify potential problems. An important point to remember is that there were only two complaints. Tori needs to hear objections, but she also needs to be careful not to overreact to every complaint.

shelves. There were books on Eskimos, Scandinavians, dairy farms in Wisconsin, and the Japanese pearl divers, but I could find no books or information on the rural blacks in the Yamacraw school library. (Conroy, 1972, p. 49)

How does a teacher deal with the problem of introducing students to new ideas and information that go beyond their experience while maintaining respect for their perspective and the world that they inhabit on a day-to-day basis? This remains a fundamental philosophical question for all educators, and especially anyone interested in reforming or improving American schools.

Being a good teacher requires that you carefully articulate a personal philosophy of teaching and learning. As you work through your teacher preparation program, you will explore, discuss, and debate philosophical approaches to education and to teaching itself. Eventually you will begin to identify your own philosophy. A certain model or philosophy of education may make sense to you right now, but as you near graduation and your first classroom, you may find yourself thinking differently. Chapter 9, The Professional and Ethical Context of Teaching, will help you continue with this process as it explores developing a personal philosophy in more detail.

Who am I? What do I believe?

"What should be the ultimate purposes of education in a democratic society?"

KATHY HYTTEN, EDUCATIONAL THEORIST

THINK ABOUT THIS:

Hytten feels that this metaphysical question and others like it are seldom addressed by those studying education. Instead, the focus tends to be on "engineering questions" that are more goal-oriented: Should students be able to choose their schools? How can we efficiently implement an educational strategy such as cooperative learning? What is the best way to teach biology? But such questions fail to consider the reasons *why* we do something: What is the purpose of schooling?

What do you feel is the purpose of schooling in American society? Are its purposes always positive? Does it always meet the needs of the students whom it serves? Does it serve some students better than others?

SHARE and COMPARE:

Discuss this topic with a classmate or friend and contrast that person's views and opinions with what you believe.

HOW DO LEGAL ISSUES AFFECT YOUR ABILITY TO TEACH?

Teachers, like all citizens, are affected in their personal and professional lives by the law. As a teacher you will be affected primarily by laws that affect policy and reform in the schools. Until 1954, the federal government had almost no involvement in public education other than to collect comparative statistical information about how public schools functioned across different states. State and local control of schools was based largely on the philosophy that communities throughout the country would know what was best for the education of their children. For the most part this system worked very well. Local educators developed curricula that met the needs of their students with regard to regional history, geography, and culture. Local and state control of education, however, did not always mean equal treatment for all people. Understanding issues of equity (or inequity) is an important part of understanding the role of the law in education.

LEGISLATION AND EQUITY

Understanding the law in relation to racial issues is absolutely crucial for those working in the schools. The law represents a forum in our culture where we try to codify our beliefs. In 1896, for example, the Supreme Court decision of *Plessy* v. *Ferguson* established a rationale for separate but equal treatment of the Black and White races in the United States. The law reflected the biases and prejudices of the period. It provided direct evidence of what the values and beliefs of the society were and what types of rights different individuals, including students, had. In education it allowed communities to maintain separate schools for Blacks and Whites.

In 1954 *Brown* v. *Board of Education of Topeka* overturned *Plessy v. Ferguson* by arguing that students at all levels of the educational system must have equal access to the opportunity to learn, and that racial differences cannot be used as a means to classify or discriminate against any group of individuals in the society. The separation was inherently discriminatory.

The decision in *Brown v. Board of Education* later served as the basis for legislation both inside and outside the racial context. For example, a logical extension and interpretation of the *Brown* decision has led to women being provided equal opportunities to participate in sports activities. The 1972 Title IX legislation passed by the U.S. Congress guaranteed women equal access to sports facilities and programs because not to do so was seen as denying them equal opportunity.

The logic of the *Brown* decision also eventually led to laws being passed that gave people with special needs greater access to the educational system. Just as *Brown* established the concept of equal access to the advantages provided by the educational system to African Americans, the same principle had to be applied to students with special physical and learning needs. In the early 1970s, for example, only half of the 8 million children in American schools identified with special needs had access to programs that were appropriate to their needs. When Congress passed the **Vocational Rehabilitation Act of 1973,** section 504 of the act stipulated that "no otherwise qualified handicapped individual in the United States . . . shall, solely by reason of his handicap, be excluded from the participation in, be denied the benefits of, or be subjected to discrimination under any program or activity receiving federal assistance." The act essentially provided a rationale for equitable treatment of people with special needs in all areas involving support from the federal government.

The Vocational Rehabilitation Act was followed a few years later by the passage of **Public Law 94-142.** Signed into law by President Gerald Ford in November 1975, the law argued that students with special needs must be educated in the least restrictive environment possible. This concept of **mainstreaming** students means that whenever possible, students with special needs (both physically and mentally challenged, as well as gifted and talented) should be integrated into "normal" educational settings.

As a nation, we have been concerned constantly with reforming our schools in an effort to create the best possible environment for all children to learn. We have often done this through the passage of new

"Recess is over now, Edward. If you want a longer recess you'll have to get elected to Congress."

Courtesy of Aaron Bacall, *The Lighter Side of Teaching,* p. 74. Copyright 2003 by Aaron Bacall. Reprinted by permission of Corwin Press Inc.

Through the Eyes of Culturally Sensitive Teachers

Foundations Issues Arise in a High School Classroom

Elena Diaz was a second-year high school social studies teacher working in an inner-city high school in Philadelphia. She was teaching a twelfth-grade U.S. government class when she began a discussion of national versus state powers and responsibilities. When she got to the 10th Amendment, which says that any powers not specifically given to the national government are "reserved" to the states and the people, she chose education as an example. "We don't have a national system of education and most decisions affecting public schools are made at the state or local levels," Elena told her seniors.

Takesha Jones was a student who had great critical-thinking skills. She asked Elena why states didn't take similar care of the education of all of their students. She remarked, "I have been to high schools in the suburbs and they have equipment and facilities we can only dream about in this school and campuses that look like small colleges. I don't see how the government can allow such large differences in money for public schools if it really cared equally for all of the people!"

Elena was impressed by Takesha's observation and quickly began to think of an answer for a very deep and perceptive question. She remembered from one of her college education courses the case of *San Antonio School District v. Rodriguez,* in which the issue of equal funding for schools was challenged. However, she also remembered that the challenger, had lost the case because the Supreme Court had ruled that equal funding for public schools was not guaranteed in the U.S. Constitution. Should she share this fact with Takesha and her

classmates, when it would probably cause them to feel less valued by their government?

Elena decided to share the *Rodriguez* decision with the class, and it was met with the expected disappointment and cries that "this decision was not fair. We matter as much as any other students in this state." As time was running out in the period, Elena used the students' frustration with the *Rodriguez* case as motivation to get them interested in registering to vote. She told them if they didn't like the *Rodriguez* case, they should work to elect legislators, governors, and presidents that would support laws barring great gaps in funding for public schools. Elena closed the class by saying, "Perhaps with your efforts, funding for public schools will be more even for your children than it was for you."

Points to Ponder

1. Do you think Elena's response to Takesha and her classmates was too blunt, too weak, or just right? Why?

2. What would you have done if you had been in Elena's situation and had just a few seconds to think of an answer to Takesha's question?

3. Is it ever right for teachers to withhold knowledge they have from a class if they feel that students may be seriously disappointed with the truth? If you answered yes, explain why. If you answered no, explain why not.

4. What is your opinion of Elena's closing suggestion to get involved and work to change the impact of the *Rodriguez* case?

---

laws. Many of the significant laws affecting education came about as a result of court cases in which an individual or group of individuals sought to force equitable changes. Nowhere have the laws concerning education in American society been more shaped and influenced than by the Supreme Court. Figure 5.2 identifies major cases that have had a significant impact on the work teachers do in the schools. State and federal legislatures also enact laws as part of political initiatives intended to address the needs of their constituents. No law in recent years has had as great an impact on education and teaching as the passage by the federal government of the No Child Left Behind legislation.

(text continues on page 154)

FIGURE 5.2

Supreme Court Decisions Affecting Education

Meyer v. State of Nebraska, 262 U.S. 390 (1923)

The case: Robert Meyer, a Catholic schoolteacher in Nebraska, violated a 1919 law requiring English-only instruction in all public and private schools in the state. Charges were brought against him for teaching a 10-year-old child a story from the Bible in German. The Supreme Court struck down his conviction, arguing that he could teach in a foreign language.

Importance: The use of languages other than English is permissible in the regular instruction of children.

Pierce v. Society of the Sisters of the Holy Names of Jesus and Mary, 268 U.S. 510 (1925)

The case: A 1922 Oregon compulsory-education law required parents or guardians to send their children to public schools. The Society of Sisters, a group of Catholic nuns who ran parochial schools, objected. The Supreme Court ruled that the state, in this case Oregon, could not compel students to go only to public schools.

Importance: Individuals have the right to attend private schools, whether religious or nondenominational, instead of public schools.

West Virginia State Board of Education v. Barnette, 319 U.S. 624 (1943)

The case: Jehovah's Witness schoolchildren were suspended from school for refusing to salute the American flag—a violation of their religious beliefs. The Court ruled that the religious rights of the students guaranteed under the First Amendment could not be violated.

Importance: Students may refuse to participate in certain otherwise required school activities based on their religious beliefs.

Everson v. Board of Education of Ewing Township, 330 U.S. 1 (1947)

The case: A New Jersey law allowed the parents of students attending religious private schools to be reimbursed for their bus transportation to school. The Supreme Court ruled that this was permissible, because services such as bussing are not part of the religious function of the school.

Importance: Some types of funding from public sources for private education is permissible.

McCollum v. Board of Education, 333 U.S. 203 (1948)

The case: In 1940 different religious groups in Champaign, Illinois, offered voluntary classes in religion to public school students in schools during the school day. Students not interested in participating in religious instruction were provided alternative classes. The Court ruled that this program was a violation of the separation of church and state and declared it illegal.

Importance: Religious instruction cannot take place in a public school setting.

Sweatt v. Painter, 339 U.S. 629 (1950)

The case: In 1946 a Black man, Marion Sweatt, applied for admission to the University of Texas Law School. Sweatt was denied acceptance based on his race. Sweatt asked the state court to order his admission. The university responded by opening a separate Black law school. The Supreme Court decided that the new law school would not be equal in terms of facilities to the existing law school, and therefore concluded that Sweatt was being discriminated against.

Importance: Equal facilities must be provided to all citizens.

Adler v. Board of Education, 342 U.S. 485 (1952)

The case: A law was passed in New York to protect children from communist influence. Irving Adler was dismissed from his position in the schools because of his affiliation with the Communist Party. The court ruled that his dismissal was permissible, since the organization which he belonged to had advocated the overthrow of the government by force.

Importance: Schools and the local community can limit certain political affiliations on the part of teachers.

Zorach v. Clauson, 343 U.S. 306 (1952)

The case: Public school students wishing to attend religious instruction were released from school with their parents' permission. Objections were raised, but the Court decided that the students were allowed to do so as part of exercising their religious beliefs.

Importance: Students may be excused from school for the purposes of religious instruction.

FIGURE 5.2

Supreme Court Decisions Affecting Education (*continued*)

Brown v. Board of Education, 347 U.S. 483 (1954)

The case: A Black student, Linda Brown, was transported from her primarily White neighborhood and its all-White school to a Black neighborhood's school many blocks away. It was argued that her treatment was discriminatory. The court ruled in her favor, overturning the concept of "separate but equal." This finding was further elaborated on with the a second ruling the following year: *Brown v. Board of Education,* 349 U.S. 294 (1955), which ordered that segregated public schools had to be integrated "with all deliberate speed."

Importance: Students cannot be segregated based on race.

Engel v. Vitale, 370 U.S. 421 (1962)

The case: Under the First Amendment prohibition against the enactment of laws "respecting an establishment of religion," the recitation by students of an official denominationally neutral state prayer at the beginning of each school day cannot be required of students.

Importance: Prayer cannot be a formal activity in the classroom.

Abington School District v. Schempp, 374 U.S. 203 (1963)

The case: According to the establishment clause of the First Amendment of the Constitution, religious choice is guaranteed to all citizens. No state law or school board may require that passages from the Bible or the Lord's Prayer can be recited in school at the beginning of each day—even if individual students are excused from participation in the exercise.

Importance: Prayer cannot be a formal activity in the classroom.

Epperson v. Arkansas, 393 U.S. 97 (1968)

The case: An Arkansas science teacher challenged the constitutionality of a state law that prohibited the teaching of evolution in his classroom. The Court ruled that the teacher had the right to discuss various models of creation in his courses.

Importance: Evolution, as well as other models of creation, can be taught as part of public instruction.

Tinker v. Des Moines School District, 393 U.S. 503 (1969)

The case: John Tinker, a 15-year-old student, and his sister Mary Beth Tinker, age 13, together with 16-year-old Christopher Echardt, protested against the Vietnam War by wearing black armbands to their school. The school expelled them when they refused to remove their armbands. The Supreme Court ruled that the students had the right to display their political feelings, as long as it did not unreasonably interfere with the running of the school.

Importance: Students do not necessarily lose their political and rights to free expression when they enter a school.

Swann v. Board of Education, 402 U.S. 1 (1971)

The case: The Charlotte-Mecklenberg School District in North Carolina had systematically delayed implementing desegregation of its schools following the 1954 *Brown* decision. The Court ruled that it could intervene and compel the school system to become active in a desegregation plan.

Importance: School districts can be forced to desegregate and respond to Court mandates.

Lemon v. Kurtzman, 403 U.S. 602 (1971)

The case: Attempts were made to use public funding to pay for teachers' salaries in private schools in Pennsylvania. The Supreme Court determined that the use of such funds was a violation of the separation of church and state.

Importance: Public funding cannot be used to support private schools.

Wisconsin v. Yoder, 406 U.S. 205 (1972)

The case: Based on their religious belief, which saw education beyond the eighth grade as a distraction from a religious life, three Amish families in Wisconsin objected to the requirement that their children attend school until age 16. The Supreme Court ruled that compulsory-education laws violated the right of the Amish families to freely exercise their religious beliefs.

Importance: Students and their parents do not lose their right to the free exercise of religion when they enter the classroom.

San Antonio School District v. Rodriguez, 411 U.S. 1 (1973)

The case: A case in Texas called for equitable redistribution of funds across the state's school districts. The Supreme

Court ruled that it could not make a decision in the matter, because the Constitution does not specifically make education a right.

Importance: Funding for schools does not necessarily need to be equal across districts in a state.

Lau v. Nichols, 414 U.S. 563 (1974)

The case: The San Francisco school system's failure to provide English-language instruction to its nearly 2,000 Chinese-speaking students, or to provide them with adequate alternative instruction, denies them the opportunity to participate in the public educational program and violates the Civil Rights Act of 1964, which bans discrimination based "on the ground of race, color, or national origin," in "any program or activity receiving Federal financial assistance."

Importance: Students must be provided with comprehensible instruction in the schools that takes into account their specific language needs and background.

Edwards v. Aguillard, 482 U.S. 578 (1987)

The case: A Louisiana law prohibited the teaching of evolution in the public schools unless accompanied by the teaching of a biblically based creation science model. The Supreme Court ruled that the law entangled the interests of church and state and was thus unconstitutional.

Importance: Creation science does not have to be taught along with evolution in public schools.

Hazelwood School District v. Kuhlmeier, 484 U.S. 260 (1988)

The case: Prepublication content of a student-written newspaper for a public school in Hazelwood, Missouri, was considered inappropriate. The school's principal stopped the publication of the newspaper. A case was brought arguing that the student's constitutional rights to free speech were being violated. The Court ruled that the school system had the right to limit the free speech of students, since the newspaper was a school-based activity.

Importance: Students lose some of their free speech rights when they participate in school-based activities.

Westside Community Board of Education v. Mergens, 496 U.S. 226 (1990)

The case: A group of students in Nebraska wanted to form a Christian club in their high school. The local school district

decided that the club could not have a faculty sponsor, since this would represent a violation of the separation of church and state. The Court ruled that the students had the right to start their club, as long as a faculty monitor did not participate and as long as nonstudents did not participate in the club's activities.

Importance: Students can organize religiously oriented clubs and prayer groups as part of after-school activities.

Lamb's Chapel v. Center Moriches School District, 508 U.S. 384 (1993)

The case: An Evangelical group in New York wished to use public school facilities for religious services after school. The Court decided that their use of public facilities was a violation of the separation of church and state.

Importance: Religious use of public school facilities is not allowed.

Board of Education of Kiryas Joel v. Grumet, 512 U.S. 687 (1994)

The case: In 1989, the New York state legislature drew boundaries for a school district around the village of Kiryas Joel, a location heavily populated by Orthodox Jews of the Satmar Hasidim sect. The idea was to provide them with special services consistent with their religious needs. Taxpayers objected, arguing that the Jewish group's isolation as a school district was exclusionary. The Court agreed.

Importance: In order to meet the needs of certain groups in a school district, individuals outside of that group cannot be automatically excluded.

Board of Education of Independent School District No. 92 v. Earls, (2002)

The case: The Tecumseh, Oklahoma, school district required all middle and high school students to consent to urinalysis testing for drugs in order to participate in any extracurricular activity. Parents and students objected, saying that the practice was a violation of the Fourth Amendment. The Court held that the school district's policy was a reasonable means of furthering the school district's efforts to discourage and prevent drug use among its students and does not violate the student's right to privacy.

Importance: The students you teach can be tested for drug use as a requirement to participate in sports programs and other extracurricular activities.

THE NO CHILD LEFT BEHIND ACT (PUBLIC LAW 107-110)

As a nation, the United States is currently involved in a movement that views the improvement of schools and the education of our children as depending on increased standards and measurements of achievement and programs that hold both students and teachers accountable for what is, or is not, learned in the classroom. On January 8, 2002, President George W. Bush signed Public Law 107-110, the **No Child Left Behind Act.** On the surface, the intent of the No Child Left Behind legislation is admirable, explaining that "The purpose of this title is to ensure that all children have a fair, equal and significant opportunity to obtain a high-quality education and reach at a minimum, proficiency on challenging state academic achievement standards and state academic assessments." Specifically, No Child Left Behind is intended to do the following:

1. Improve classroom instruction

2. Improve the skills of teachers

3. Recruit effective school leaders

4. Remove barriers to learning

5. Provide students with a successful start in education

6. Hold schools accountable for student success

While the purposes of the No Child Left Behind Act are generally admirable, some of its means—such as the increased role of the federal government in education and the pressure on teachers to produce good test grades by all students—make the act highly controversial.

It would be hard to disagree with any of these purposes. How to achieve them, however, is an extremely difficult and hotly debated issue. Where people stand on the issue is directly related to what they believe about how children learn and what role they feel that education should play in American society. For example, the No Child Left Behind legislation includes a strong accountability component that requires schools to test children's academic achievement regularly. Schools are being held to specific standards. The idea is that *all* of the children going to our schools will be provided a decent education and that no one will be "left behind" or be disadvantaged because of a lack of adequate instruction.

The effect of the No Child Left Behind Act has been to expand the role of the federal government in education. Many, including teacher educators, school superintendents, and principals, feel that the law is either politically motivated or aimed at undermining the public schools. Teachers are increasingly teaching to tests—making sure that students do well enough on the tests to indicate that their schools are meeting required national standards.

The effect on the schools of the No Child Left Behind legislation is raising a large amount of controversy at the state and local level. It has led to more and more people asking basic questions about the purpose of our public schools; questions that are the heart and soul of the field of the foundations of education.

HOW ARE THE FOUNDATIONS OF EDUCATION USEFUL TO YOU AS A TEACHER?

Educational foundations provide beginning teachers with the means by which to connect what they do in the classroom to issues and forces at work in the larger society. They enable you to try to understand what goes on in the classroom in the context of the larger society and the historical and political forces that shape American society. They also encourage you to develop your own value positions regarding education on the basis of critical study and your own reflections. Magnus O. Bassey argues that foundational studies in education should "awaken" students in teacher education to their consciousness (Bassey, 2003).

EQUITY AS AN ISSUE IN THE FOUNDATIONS OF EDUCATION

If a single issue has dominated change in American education, particularly in the last 50 years, it has been the issue of equity. Should all Americans be provided an equal education? A foundational perspective provides an understanding of whether equity has been evident in American education and how it has been addressed.

Historical data, for example, can provide us with comparisons of how men and women were educated in the nineteenth century. We can learn whether men received preferential treatment. Philosophy, as a discipline, provides the means by which to better understand and reflect on the mainstream culture's belief about the potential and worth of different groups of people. Knowledge of the law informs us of how different people have been discriminated against or protected through our legal system and how our current laws affect what goes on in classrooms, and identifies laws that have been enacted to bring about change.

Other foundational areas, such as psychology, sociology, and anthropology, can also provide insights. Contemporary sociological and anthropological research, for example, can inform us about whether women were given equal attention in traditional classroom settings. Researchers have found that in many American classrooms, girls are taught to be deferential and passive to avoid demonstrating that they are smart. Boys, in contrast, are expected to be more proactive because their intelligence is more appreciated and praised (Sadker & Sadker, 1995).

Imagine for a moment that you are beginning your first year of work as a teacher. Maybe you're an elementary school teacher working in an inner-city classroom with students who are racially and culturally different from you, or perhaps you work in a school and community much like the school you attended and the community in which you grew up. Whatever the setting, consider what you need to understand about your students and the community from a foundations context in order to work effectively as a teacher. An examination of four variables of equity—race, ethnicity, socioeconomic status, and gender—provides an understanding of how foundational considerations can inform your teaching.

- **Race** First you need to understand how **race** works in the context of the classroom in which you are teaching. Race, to a large extent, is a socially constructed phenomenon that in Western culture has often been used as a means to justify economic, social, political, psychological, religious, ideological, and legal systems of inequality. Race can play a role in determining your students' general perspectives. In American society, being White has been the norm. Historically, American society has provided special privileges to those who are of northern European origins and part of the mainstream. If you are White and teaching lower socioeconomic African American students, your perceptions about education may differ from theirs. Why? Because, as a result of racial prejudice and discrimination, the social and economic benefits provided by schools have not been as great for them as for the White population. Therefore, the dialogue in your classroom may be different depending on the race of your students, as well as other variables.

INTASC

Principle #9

Professional Commitment and Responsibility: The teacher is a reflective practitioner who continually evaluates the effects of his/her choices and actions on others (students, parents, and other professionals in the learning community) and who actively seeks out opportunities to grow professionally.

INTASC

Principle #3

Adapting Instruction for Individual Needs: The teacher understands how students differ in their approaches to learning and creates instructional opportunities that are adapted to diverse learners.

It is important to encourage classroom dialogues that reflect an appreciation and understanding of the backgrounds of all students.

● **Ethnicity**   Of course race does not function in a vacuum, nor is it unconnected to other variables. **Ethnicity**—defined by a common national origin, set of customs, and/or language—combines with race to shape and define the cultural and social identity of the students you teach. For example, it may be obvious that you are teaching African American students, but do you know their ethnic background? Are their families originally from the rural South, or do they have a history of always having lived in the North? Are they from the Caribbean? Africa? This may not seem terribly important at first, but the difference can be very significant. Haitian American Blacks are more likely to be Catholic than Protestant. Their cultural experiences, including traditions of family life, food, and work, will be significantly different from a Black Southern Baptist. African Blacks may be Islamic, introducing an entirely different system of mores. But in the United States, since we often define people first by the color of their skin, it is easy to make false and inaccurate assumptions about individuals.

Remember, as discussed in Chapter 1, as a teacher you need to become a border crosser in your classroom. Border crossers function comfortably in cultures other than their own. You cannot do this unless you are acutely aware of who your students are in terms of their social and culture identity.

● **Socioeconomic Status**   A third variable in the discussion on equity in education is **socioeconomic status (SES)**, which uses economic success as a social characteristic or marker. Despite efforts to minimize the existence of class differences in the United States, distinctions among people based on social class and privilege are very much at work in American society. Look no further than the disparities between public schools and private schools throughout much of the country. Private schools in most large urban areas have far greater financial resources to tap into in order to provide the best academic challenges and assistance. Yet people from lower socioeconomic groups have limited access to a private school education because of the high cost of tuition. The trend continues in higher education as well. Not all students get into the college of their choice based solely on merit. Wealthy alumni and donors to colleges and universities often get preferential treatment in the form of "legacies" for their children. This is a reality we don't like to talk about, but it is nonetheless true.

BUILDING ON EDUCATIONAL FOUNDATIONS

Theory as a Means of Understanding the World around You

Often there is a tendency to dismiss theory in education as not being sufficiently rooted in the real world. The foundations of education would argue against this point of view, maintaining that theory provides us the means by which to interpret what we often take for granted every day.

Consider the subject of privilege, which can be defined as circumstances in which one person receives preferential treatment over someone else. Privilege exists in many areas of life, including educational settings. In American higher education, for example, some people are often given preferential consideration on getting admitted to a college over other people. It may be the child of a donor or a prominent figure in the community who gets special treatment. It may be an athlete or the child of an alumnus.

Think about privilege along the dimensions of race, ethnicity, gender, and socioeconomic status. Did people in the high school that you attended receive privileged treatment because of any of these variables? Similarly, did you see people who were discriminated against because of these variables? How could a careful analysis of privilege and how it functions help you be a better teacher?

Can you think of other examples where theory combined with insights from the foundations of education might help you understand more clearly how schools function?

Let's say that you are teaching high school English in a consolidated high school composed of students from several small towns with a wide range of socioeconomic backgrounds. You have a very bright and talented student whom you are encouraging to go on to a highly competitive, academically excellent, upper-level university. If this student comes from a financially well-to-do family, such an aspiration may be possible. If the student comes from a lower-socioeconomic background, the idea may be less realistic. Tuition may, even with the help of scholarships and loans, be beyond what the poorer student can afford. The family may consider higher education a luxury, and believe that their child should enter the workforce as soon as possible. Attending an elite institution of higher education may involve breaking away from home, friends, and the local community—a difficult task for students from lower-socioeconomic backgrounds. A local university or community college may be seen as a more viable option for some students. Entering the workforce as quickly as possible also may be seen as a better option.

Among economic elites, on the other hand, acceptance into a high-status college or university is often more of a priority than for those who come from a lower-socioeconomic background. Such aspirations can seriously affect the character of a school, as high-achieving parents may demand "the best" for their children and consider rigorous academic preparation essential. This situation can become absurd as academic programs and college preparation are driven further down into the grades, even to the point where getting into the "right" kindergarten becomes the first step in getting into the "right" college. These agendas affect the school's climate and decisions made about the school—curriculum, after-school programs, spending initiatives, and tax proposals. You have to be aware of your students' needs and situations in order to offer the best guidance.

● **Gender**   Finally, **gender** will be a variable that may be more subtle or institutionalized. Gender classifies individuals' sex but also often may be used to describe the socially inscribed characteristics of women and men. Historically, men and women, and boys and girls, have been treated differently in American society, and the practice still remains an important issue. As a teacher you will have to factor in how traditional sex roles may or may

What are some common institutional biases that exist in society? What can you, as a teacher, do to help prevent their perpetuation?

not affect the aspirations of your students. Certain career paths—rightly or wrongly—may be considered more appropriate for one sex or the other by the students whom you teach. Nursing, for example, is still usually considered a feminized profession in the United States. That the profession of nursing should be limited largely to women is, of course, absurd, but nonetheless the reality of this bias is evident in our culture. Girls may be discouraged from competing in "unfeminine" sports such as football or wrestling. What do you do if you have a male student who is really interested in nursing, or a female student who really wants to play on the school's football team? What obligation do you have as a teacher to help students consider alternatives to traditional gender roles and orientations?

KEY QUESTIONS THAT INFORM YOUR TEACHING

As a field, foundations of education raise many interesting questions that you will need to think about throughout your career. Following are 10 of the most important issues raised by the field.

1. *What should we teach in the schools? What is worth teaching? Whose knowledge should be most valued in our society?*

Probing this question in detail requires that we consider whether those who determine the curriculum have certain types of power and influence. By asking the question, we quickly realize that knowledge, and in turn learning, is not neutral, but value-laden. This question goes to the core of your work as a teacher. It forces you to reflect on what knowledge it is that you are presenting to your students in your class and why.

2. *Who is to be educated? In a democratic society such as the United States, is equal education for all possible or even desirable? Does a gifted child need the same support and resources as an average child or a child with a disability?*

This question raises the issue of how we should distribute our financial and instructional resources. It forces us to consider our priorities and what things we value over others. It asks teachers to reflect on how we treat students differently, and what resources we as a society are willing to invest in them.

3. *What makes a good school? Does the definition of a good school differ depending on the social and economic background of its students? Can we compare schools with different types of students who have different types of needs?*

This question forces us to consider whether all schools need to be the same, and whether schools with very different types of populations can be compared with one another. Is it fair, for example, to compare what a teacher accomplishes who is working with emotionally challenged students to a "normal" student population? How do we measure and compare what are essentially two very different things? Thinking about this question will help you better understand what is good or bad, as well as appropriate, in the setting in which you are working.

4. *What types of obligations do schools have beyond simply educating students? Should schools address the moral development of students, for example, or provide health services?*

This question asks what role public institutions should play in teaching our children. Should children who are neglected by their parents or whose parents are poor be provided additional resources by the schools? At what level should the schools intervene in what are personal or family matters? This question should help you reflect on what you do in your work that goes beyond simply providing information and instruction. It should also help you think about issues such as whether it is appropriate for you to intervene in the lives of your students and their families.

5. *Should schooling be compulsory? What is considered a sufficient education? Should students be compelled to learn things they or their parents oppose on moral and personal grounds?*

This question addresses the issue of the extent to which the educational system and the state have the right not only to require attendance, but also to compel students to learn certain things. This question should help you think about the obligations of the state to provide at least a minimal level of learning to all students, as well as the fact that many students may consider themselves coerced by the system.

6. *What role should religion play in schooling? Should selected religious practices or sects be allowed in the schools? Should certain religious groups be excluded? What is equitable?*

This question raises the issue of personal freedoms and liberties guaranteed by the Constitution. Reflecting and thinking carefully about this question will help you understand potential sources of conflict with families, and why people who see religion as playing a significant role in their life often feel that schools are "godless" and lacking the spiritual and moral dimensions they want for their children.

7. *What constitutes the necessary and proper means of training teachers? Who should be allowed to teach? To what extent should teachers have the right to act in the classroom according to the dictates of their own values? What constitutes good teaching? Why is it considered good teaching?*

This question should help you think about why and what you are doing in the classroom, and what type of training and background will help you become the most effective teacher possible.

8. *What is the role of business in shaping and influencing the content of education? What type of influence should business have in shaping the curriculum of the schools? Should students be trained for the specific jobs that are being demanded by the business system?*

Reflecting on this question will help you understand the forces that may be at work in your community—what funds are allocated for what types of programs and why. These considerations will also help you understand something of the nature of power and influence in American society.

9. *Should there be national standards and guidelines for the curriculum of the schools? Should the content of curriculum be controlled at the local and state level or by the federal government? Who should determine what gets taught in the schools?*

This question will help you address whether testing and evaluation is a positive force in American education, as well as what standards are appropriate for the children whom you are teaching.

10. *To what extent should schools be used as a means of correcting or compensating for past social injustices? Should the schools be used to desegregate the society and bring about greater equality? Should some people be given special compensatory treatment because of past injustices?*

As a teacher, you will have to confront the issue of the schools being used to help create a more equitable society. You may be in an inner-city school where there is a reduced-cost or free lunch program for many students, or you may be asked to compare two equal students for a special program, one who comes from a historically discriminated group. Should their background play into the decision you make?

These are all important questions. The foundations of education can provide you with a starting point for reflecting on what it means to be a teacher.

"A hundred years from now it will not matter what my bank account was, the sort of house I lived in, or the kind of car I drove . . . but the world may be different because I was important in the life of a child."

KATHY DAVIS

THINK ABOUT THIS:

Rightly or wrongly, children enter your classroom carrying the weight of society's preconceptions—social, philosophical, and political. Teachers often feel as though they get caught in the middle of political battles, when all they really want to do is just teach. But by being aware of the political battles and social challenges of communities, a teacher can help provide fairness and balance in a child's life. Can schools really make a difference in the lives of people? How do people benefit from schooling?

SHARE and COMPARE:

Talk to a classmate or friend about why you think public schools are a source of social capital in American culture. Discuss whether the mission of public schools is different from or the same as that of private education.

FINAL THOUGHTS

The foundations of education is a complex interdisciplinary field. It provides teachers and those who are concerned with the schools the means by which to ask important questions about who and what we are as a people and what we want our educational system to accomplish. In doing so, it also challenges many of our assumptions about American society.

If we look at the history of American education, we are forced to challenge our assumption as stated in the Declaration of Independence that "all men are created equal." The foundations of education show us that this certainly has not always been the case throughout our history—not for women, African Americans, Native Americans, and many others. The foundations of education as a field forces us to better understand the forces that shape and direct us as people and as educators. It compels us to reflect on our work as educators and ultimately how we shape and influence the children we teach. It is essential in the education of all who wish to become teachers.

REFLECTIONS

Professional Plan for Understanding the Foundations of Education

1. Three questions I think are most important from a foundations perspective are:

2. Two questions about schools or education that I wish had been raised in this chapter are:

   a. _____

   b. _____

3. I plan to investigate these two areas and learn more about topics in this chapter by:

   _____ Reading some of the book club choices

   _____ Reading sources referenced in the chapter that interest me.

   _____ Doing further research about key figures in education and looking through local newspapers to investigate educational issues being discussed by state and community leaders

   _____ Exploring the Web sites listed in the Log On section

   _____ Meeting with my instructor to discuss the role of politics in education.

4. Three ways that I can expand my knowledge of schools and how they function outside my coursework are:

   a. _____

   b. _____

   c. _____

5. I will include the following in my Touch the Future portfolio:

SUMMARY

What Is Meant by the Foundations of Education?

- The foundations of education is an interdisciplinary field that contextualizes the work teachers do as it relates to issues in the larger society.
- The foundations of education are concerned with interpreting and reflecting about schools and education.

How Have Historical Trends Affected Education Today?

- The United States has had a strong commitment to public education dating back to the colonial period.
- Schools and their curriculum were used to create a sense of national identity during the period following the American Revolution.
- The Northwest Ordinance of 1787 was the federal government's first significant involvement in education.
- The Common School movement had as its purpose providing a system of free public elementary education to the majority of the population.
- Compulsory-education laws were first introduced into American schools in the middle of the nineteenth century.
- Theorists such as John Dewey proposed that education should be grounded in the experience of the child.
- The Great School Legend argues that schools have been engines of social advancement and progress.

How Have Philosophical Changes Influenced Education?

- Various philosophical movements have shaped American education.
- American education has warred throughout much of its history as to whether it should primarily be about the transmission of specific cultural knowledge, or the creation of independent and critical thinkers.

How Do Legal Issues Affect Your Ability to Teach?

- Legal decisions affect what you can or cannot do in the classroom.
- The 1954 *Brown v. Board of Education* decision ushered in a new period of federal involvement in the schools.
- The No Child Left Behind legislation of 2002 is an attempt to improve schools by improving standards.

How Are the Foundations of Education Useful to You as a Teacher?

- American education has often been preoccupied with the idea of reforming its schools.
- Race, ethnicity, socioeconomic status, and gender are key variables in the issue of equity and understanding how it is addressed from a foundational perspective.
- The foundations of education encompass a series of critical questions about the nature of schools and American culture.

Companion
Website

Visit the **Touch the Future . . . Teach!** Companion Website at
www.ablongman.com/diaz for additional opportunities.

KEY WORDS

Brown v. Board of Education of Topeka   149

Common Schools   139

essentialism   146

ethnicity   156

existentialism   146

foundations of education   136

gender   157

Great School Legend   142

mainstreaming   149

No Child Left Behind Act   154

normal schools   140

perennialism   146

Plessy v. Ferguson   149

pragmatism   140

progressivism   146

Public Law 94-142   149

race   155

social reconstruction   146

socioeconomic status (SES)   156

Vocational Rehabilitation Act of 1973   149

CONCEPT REVIEW

1. Define the foundations of education.

2. Explain why the foundations of education are relevant to teachers and their work.

3. Identify the disciplinary fields that provide the knowledge base for the foundations of education.

4. Explain how the content of textbooks and what is taught in the schools might reflect social, political, and cultural values.

5. Describe the role education played in establishing the United States' identity after the American Revolution.

6. Explain the basic principles of the Common School movement of the middle of the nineteenth century.

7. Describe the essential argument underlying John Dewey's approach to education.

8. Explore how reform has shaped American education in recent years.

9. Describe how race, ethnicity, socioeconomic status, and gender intersect in American culture and education.

TOUCH THE FUTURE . . .

Read On

American Education: The Colonial Experience, 1607–1783
American Education: The National Experience, 1783–1876
American Education: The Metropolitan Experience, 1876–1980
Lawrence Cremin (New York: Harper & Row, 1970, 1980, and 1988)
Cremin's three-volume history of American education, which won the Pulitzer Prize and the Bancroft Award for its excellence; the definitive history in the field.

Challenges of Educational Change
Daniel Duke (Boston: Allyn & Bacon, 2004)
A comprehensive and recent examination of research and practice related to educational change, addressing how to lead, evaluate, and explain educational change; a nice blend of practical advice on bringing about change.

Left Back: A Century of Failed School Reforms
Dianne Ravitch (New York: Simon & Schuster, 2000)
A critical exploration of how American schools developed in the last hundred years and the history of school reform and its failure in the twentieth century.

The Aims of Education
Roger Marples, ed. (London, New York: Routledge, 1999)
International philosophers of education examine the aims and purposes of education by exploring issues such as social justice, national identity, curriculum, critical thinking, and social practices.

Tinkering toward Utopia: A Century of Public School Reform
David Tyack and Larry Cuban (Cambridge, MA: Harvard University Press, 1995)
A study of the role of reform in American education.

Log On

History of Education Society
http://academics.sru.edu/history_of_ed_quarterly/heshome.htm
Home page of the History of Education Society, which publishes the primary historical journal on the history of education and sponsors an annual conference.

Philosophy of Education Society
http://cuip.net/pes
  Home page of the Philosophy of Education Society, which includes many useful links to publications by the organization.

History of American Education Web Project
www.nd.edu/~rbarger/www7
  Recognized as an Internet Site of the Day by *The Chronicle of Higher Education;* began as an undergraduate project at Notre Dame and evolved into a thorough chronology of education in America.

Blackwell History of Education Museum
www.cedu.niu.edu/blackwell
  Located at Northern Illinois University in DeKalb, Illinois, the Blackwell Museum offers an extensive collection of artifacts from American education. Online you can access artifacts including lesson plans from various periods of history.

The Homeroom
www.mala.bc.ca/homeroom
  Once you've investigated artifacts from the history of American education, visit The Homeroom to investigate the history of Canadian education. Compare your findings of the progression of education in the two countries.

Write On

"They say that we are better educated than our parents' generation. What they mean is that we go to school longer. They are not the same thing."

—Douglas Yates

Consider the preceding quote and write a brief essay in your journal about what you think Yates is saying. What do you believe is an adequate education for most Americans? What should it include and how long should it last?

OBSERVATION GUIDE

TEACH: LINKING THEORY TO PRACTICE

Linking Theory to Practice

Objective: To observe how education is reported in newspapers
Newspaper: _____   Observer: _____
Dates Reviewed: _____

Directions: In this observation activity you will look at a week's worth of local newspapers and review their reporting on educational issues. If at all possible, look at newspapers from your local community; otherwise, consult a national newspaper online such as *The New York Times* or *The Washington Post.* Use the following questions to help you collect information necessary to write a two to three page double-spaced essay to be submitted to your instructor that discusses the newspaper's perspective on education and what it considers important issues in your schools.

1. What types of things does your newspaper report?

2. Is there a clear point of view in the reporting of your local paper?

3. Is your paper more concerned with local than national issues in education? Can you see any important differences in how it reports either one?

4. Do you think that the reporting provided by your local newspaper is useful? Accurate?

5. What might you want to see reported about schools and education that is not currently included? Why?

Connecting with INTASC: Principle 1

Knowledge of Subject Matter: The teacher understands the central concepts, tools of inquiry, and structures of the subject being taught and can create learning experiences that make these aspects of subject matter meaningful for students.

Based on your analyses of coverage of education in local or national newspapers, identify any philosophies or approaches that appear important to the local community. If you were to teach in the community where you go to school, how might the community perspective affect how you would approach teaching your subject matter? What subjects might be more sensitive to the community philosophy and perspectives?

6

The Social Context of Schools

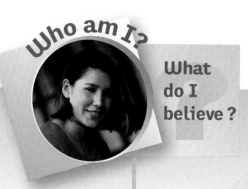

Who am I?

What do I believe?

THINK ABOUT THIS:

Schools often reflect the social mores of their surrounding communities. Therefore, just as examining the community informs us about the school, examining the school informs us about the community. Reflect for a few minutes about your own experience with the good and bad aspects of your own schooling. What contributed to the positive forces or experiences in your schooling? What were the causes of the negative things? Could the negative aspects of your experience have been eliminated?

"It is at the level of public school education that the most basic schemata of the culture are systematically presented and reinforced."

C. A. Bowers

How do you think that you, as a teacher, can create a learning environment that is as positive as possible? How do you think that you can address the institutional limitations put on schools by the government and by society in general?

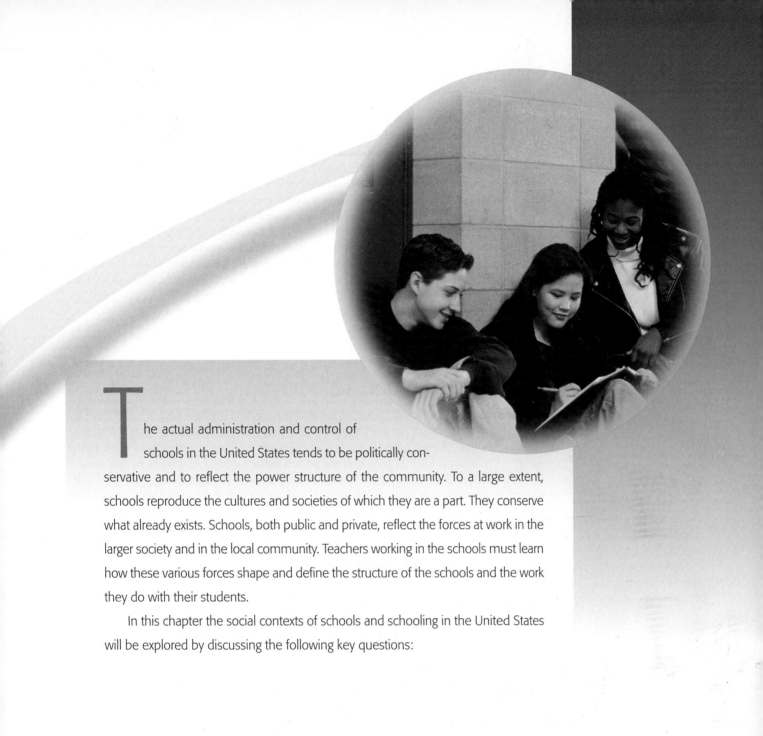

The actual administration and control of schools in the United States tends to be politically conservative and to reflect the power structure of the community. To a large extent, schools reproduce the cultures and societies of which they are a part. They conserve what already exists. Schools, both public and private, reflect the forces at work in the larger society and in the local community. Teachers working in the schools must learn how these various forces shape and define the structure of the schools and the work they do with their students.

In this chapter the social contexts of schools and schooling in the United States will be explored by discussing the following key questions:

Key Questions

1. What makes a good school?
2. How does school culture affect a learning community?
3. Who controls the schools?
4. How are schools financed in the United States?

Schooling and education are not necessarily the same thing. The origin of the word *school* is found in the ancient Greek language. A *schole* was a place of learning. It could also be a place of leisure. The *Oxford English Dictionary* (1989) defines a school as "an establishment in which boys or girls, or both, receive instruction"; *schooling* is "the action of teaching, or the state or fact of being taught, in a school"; *education* is the process of "nourishing or rearing a child or young person." Thus, a parent can educate a child, as can a friend or a member of the community, including a teacher. Parents, however, are not typically involved in schooling, with the exception of home schooling. Schools and schooling imply the idea of institutional, or governmental, involvement. Often schools and schooling are compulsory— required by law. Schooling serves the needs of the state in ways that are different from education, which is more closely associated with the individual and does not have the same institutional associations. In the United States, schools include both public and private institutions.

INTASC

Principle #9

Professional Commitment and Responsibility: The teacher is a reflective practitioner who continually evaluates the effects of his/her choices and actions on others (students, parents, and other professionals in the learning community) and who actively seeks out opportunities to grow professionally.

WHAT MAKES A GOOD SCHOOL?

Educational researcher Larry Cuban argues that throughout the twentieth century there has been considerable debate in the United States about what constitutes a "good" school or "good schooling." He asks, "Are schools that effectively prepare students for the workforce 'good'? Are schools with high standardized test scores 'good'? Are schools that seek to develop the mind, body, and emotions of each child 'good'?" (Cuban & Shipps, 2000, p. 148). Cuban argues that in a pluralistic and diverse culture such as the United States, there can be many different schools that are "good." What might be good for one group of children or type of student is not necessarily good for all children or students (Cuban & Shipps, 2000).

CHARACTERISTICS OF GOOD SCHOOLS

Comparing two types of schools raises an interesting set of questions. School A, for example, is quiet and orderly, with students showing respect for the administration and teachers. There are high academic expectations at the school and a great deal of competition to achieve. Drill and practice are emphasized, along with "standards." The curriculum is very carefully defined. School B is much more informal. Children are encouraged to discover the world around them and are trusted to make good choices. Subjects tend to be integrated. Different ways of understanding and interpreting the world are emphasized. Competition between students is discouraged (Cuban & Shipps, 2000).

These schools, according to Cuban, "have clear and shared purposes; they believe that all children can learn; each school staff has developed a working culture that embodies these common beliefs and enjoys collective action; and parents are deeply involved with the school" (Cuban & Shipps, 2000, p. 152). Which school do you think is better?

The answer, of course, depends on what you value, and what you expect the outcome or purpose of education to be. For parents who have very strong religious beliefs and feel that religion needs to be closely connected to every aspect of their children's learning, neither school A nor B would be "good." For parents who value obedience and time on task over creativity and freedom, school A might seem better. On the other hand, parents who want to encourage personal freedom and self-discovery in their children might consider school B superior.

What should a good school want to accomplish? More than a hundred years ago, John Dewey argued, "What the best and wisest parent wants for his own child, that must the community want for all of its children. Any other ideal for our schools is narrow and unlovely; acted upon, it destroys our democracy. All that society has accomplished for itself is put, through the agency of the school, at the disposal of its future members" (Dewey, 1907, 1980). Dewey's argument suggests that the "good" school is the one that best serves our children and the ideals of our democracy.

Do schools necessarily serve the needs of all children equally well? Do they always serve the ideals of a democracy? Some people would say no. Others might maintain that they do some of the time. Much depends on the perspective and experience of the individual who is asked. For the parents of an upper-middle-class suburban neighborhood in a major urban area whose children are on a college-bound track, the answer is probably yes. For a recently arrived immigrant child, the answer may also be yes. Interestingly, the schools these parents consider "good" may serve each student differently. The elite suburban school may direct students toward high-paying jobs with a great deal of status—jobs that allow them to maintain the same social and professional status as their parents. Immigrant children may be given the means by which to assimilate into American culture and achieve greater economic independence than their parents. Both goals may be desirable for the students each school serves.

SOCIOLOGICAL MODELS OF SCHOOLING

What is the purpose of school? What is the relationship between the school and the larger society? Historically in the United States there have been two widely different opinions about what should be the role and purpose of schooling. The first maintains that schools should primarily be sites for educating people to be competent and productive workers. The second argues that schools are instruments for the creation and promotion of equality (Labaree, 1994).

Should schools primarily produce good workers, or should they be mostly concerned with creating greater equality? Or should schools be more concerned with other issues—such as the creation of good citizens? Can the creation of good workers, greater equity, and good citizens be accomplished at the same time? Do these goals necessarily contradict each other? There are many different approaches to answering this question. Three interpretations are the functionalist model, the conflict theory model, and the interpretivist model.

Many people argue the real purpose of schools. Do schools serve the needs of all children equally?

● **Functionalist Model**   According to the **functionalist model**, schools have the *function* of socializing students to be part of the social, economic, and political institutions of a culture. Schools represent an essential element in the machinery of the social system. Students are shaped to assume the roles required of them by the cultural and social system.

How does a functionalist model potentially affect you in your work as a teacher? Within the functionalist model, as a teacher you are shaping students to hold specific values and beliefs and to assume specific roles in the culture. This is not necessarily a bad thing. We want to create good citizens, people who are polite and fair with one another, who believe in the American values of democracy and fair play. Of course the question arises as to what values and beliefs should be promoted, and what role should teachers play in promoting them. Should a teacher promote points of view that are unpopular or not consistent with the values of the local community? Imagine being White and teaching in segregated schools in the South in the 1940s. Would it have been right for you to support the local community and school board's argument that Black and White students needed to be sent to separate schools? What if you strongly disagreed? What would have been the right thing to do?

● **Conflict Theory Model**   **Conflict theory** argues that schools reproduce and maintain the existing class and social power structures in a society. In other words, wealthy and influential segments of the culture create privilege and opportunity through the schools that specifically benefit their social and economic class. The power and privilege associated with this "class" of society may conflict with conditions of the working class and lower economic class. In this way, the schools reflect the competition between different groups for power and status.

Have you noticed that in American society we are reluctant to talk about social and economic differences? We act as if they exist only in other countries such as Great Britain or France. Social class exists in the United States, just as it exists elsewhere. You may find yourself teaching in settings where social class plays an important role. For example, if you teach in a wealthy suburban high school or private preparatory school, your students will have much more of a tendency to assume that they are entitled to political, social, and economic power. Going on to college and university—often very expensive schools—will be considered an automatic thing to do, not a privilege but a right.

In contrast, you may find yourself teaching in a lower-middle-class or lower-socioeconomic setting. Going on to higher education, even among your most capable students, may be a dream that just doesn't seem possible to many of them, even with scholarships and supplementary funding. What can you do to help these students? If the school system has modest expectations for its students—expectations that you think underestimate the students' potential—how do you act?

According to conflict theory, schools become instruments and sites of conflict for control of the society. Recent years, for example, have seen considerable debate over whether urban school districts such as Oakland, California, should recognize "Black Language" or "Ebonics" as a valid linguistic system. The issue focuses on whether the use of nonstandard English by Black schoolchildren should be recognized as a valid way of speaking and expressing themselves. The argument is not about Black Language superseding or taking the place of English, but whether the two languages could mutually function within our society.

The Ebonics debate "has absolutely nothing to do with language itself but with the role of language" (Baldwin, 1998, p. 67). If the use of Black Language is rejected, then advocates of Ebonics maintain that the Black cultural and historical experience is also being rejected. For Baldwin, the rejection of Black Language represents the imposition of English as a dominating linguistic system—one that has often been oppressive and worked against the needs of African Americans. According to him, "It is not the Black child's language that is in question, it is not his language that is despised: It is his experience" (Baldwin, 1998, p. 70).

The debate over Ebonics represents, from a conflict theory perspective, not just the issue of how children learn the language they use in school. It also addresses the questions of who has power in American society and how we define what it means to be an American.

● **Interpretivist Model**   Finally, the **interpretivist model** argues that we must understand schools in the context of the communities and cultures in which they are located. In a certain sense, this means that we must constantly analyze, revise, and reinterpret what we see based on our position or location in the culture. There are not necessarily clear-cut answers, but only different ways of understanding what is going on. A strict disciplinary policy in an inner-city high school, for example, may represent, from the perspective of school administrators and local community members, a way of maintaining order and discipline while providing a safe learning environment. For others, it may represent the imposition of an oppressive and discriminatory system, intended to constrain individual freedom and to encourage students to accept a subordinate and inferior position in the culture. The interpretivist perspective requires careful analysis and interpretation from multiple perspectives of what occurs in schools.

As a teacher, you may find the interpretivist model an exciting but demanding context in which to work with students. Essentially, it requires that you be sensitive to the community in which the school you teach is located, including the historical and social forces that shape it. Thus, if you are teaching in a school located in a traditional Chinese community in San Francisco or an Orthodox Jewish neighborhood in New York City, you may need to be responsive to local traditions and religious beliefs.

In reality, one finds in most schools evidence of all three models at work. How each affects various students may differ based on their socioeconomic class or other similar factors.

Who am I?   **What do I believe?**

"School should be a place where you can leave your problems behind, where you can find good, regular activity, a structured place . . . "

MS. PAYTON, SEVENTH GRADE SCIENCE TEACHER

THINK ABOUT THIS:

Everyone has an opinion about schools and what they think makes a school good. These opinions are formed by a number of things: their own upbringing, their interpretations of what children will need to be able to do in the future, and their own personal biases about society and education. What do you think makes a good school? How did the school you attended reflect forces at work within your local community? Do you think that they reflected forces at work within the larger culture or society? Can you describe the type of school you would like to work in as teacher?

SHARE and **COMPARE:**

Using the three models discussed in this section, identify the approach taken at your school. As a class, tabulate the responses of all students and determine which approach was most common.

HOW DOES SCHOOL CULTURE AFFECT A LEARNING COMMUNITY?

Working as a teacher in the schools assumes that you are also part of a learning community. Think about your own experience as a student. How close was the relationship between the community and the school? Think about the "personalities" of each of the schools within

INTASC

Principle #10

Partnerships: The teacher fosters relationships with school colleagues, parents, and agencies in the larger community to support students' learning and well-being.

EDUCATION MATTERS

Homeless Students

The Denver, Colorado, public schools are taking a step to support their homeless students. Threads, a teen boutique, is making it possible for homeless students to go to school. The store, which opened in October 2003, is available to middle and high school students who spend their nights in shelters, motels, or other makeshift housing. Nearly 900 students in the 72,000-student district have been identified as homeless, and volunteers want to help them come to school.

The school system's homeless liaison states, "These kids have told me flat out, 'Well it was snowing this morning and I don't have a coat.' How can you focus on school when you are freezing?" The grant-funded project is a key to breaking the cycle of poor attendance by homeless kids. The store location is secret and students come by appointment to select clothes that have been donated. Name brands such as Abercrombie, Nike, and Tommy Hilfiger are on the racks. New underwear and hats have been donated. Boys head straight for the pants ranks. Staffers notice that these boys have outgrown their own pants, which ride up to show bare legs when they sit in class. Everyone in the project knows that these students will be more confident in school now and will do much better.

The Education Issue: How schools can address the educational needs of homeless students

Teachers notice students who come to school with less than other students. Students notice as well. The pressure students feel about how they dress, how they look, and whom they hang around with is as much a part of the informal social culture of a school as the personal interactions between students, faculty, and administration. Education for all students is the goal in schools, but when poverty and neglect are involved, some students may make fun of others.

Homelessness is a major problem in the United States that doesn't affect just adults. The U.S. Department of Education reports that from 1997 to 2000, the number of homeless youth (pre-K–12) increased from 841,700 to 930,200. Of this group, preschool and elementary age children compose the largest number of homeless students.

School systems face a great challenge in meeting these children's educational needs, with the greatest challenge being getting the students to attend. Besides the social pressure of fitting in with their peers, homeless students face some serious barriers: transportation to and from school, lack of proper documents required for enrollment, and high rate of mobility.

Schools see the results of this misfortune and can influence the lives of these students by creating ways to support them, such as the Threads clothing center in Denver. Passage of the McKinney-Vento Homeless Assistance Act of 2001 ensures the educational rights of homeless children and youth, providing school districts with special assistance to address the educational needs of homeless children in their communities. Check out the following Web sites for more information on programs addressing the needs of homeless students:

- Urban Peak Denver (www.urbanpeak.org)—a homeless shelter for teens

- National Runaway Switchboard (www.nrscrisisline.org)

- National Coalition for the Homeless (www.nationalhomeless.org)

- Directory of State Coordinators for the Education of Homeless Children and Youth (http://nch.ari.net/EHCY.html)

- Homeless Students and School, Maryland People's Law Library (www.peoples-law.org/education/homeless-students.htm)

What's Your Opinion?

What are the benefits of the Threads program? What would you do if you had a homeless child in your classroom? Investigate the Web sites listed here to find out more about homeless youth and what you can do as a teacher to help.

Source: N. Mitchell, "New Threads for Homeless Students," *Rocky Mountain News*, p. 1 (September 25, 2003); U.S. Department of Education. *Education for Homeless Children and Youth Report to Congress.* (Washington, DC: U.S. Government Printing Office, 2000).

the district. Was your school known for its athletics or fine arts programs? Can you identify the "rough" school in the district? Schools develop identities based on characteristics that exist or reputations that evolve over time. Because schools are places where students of all ages and adults interact for more than 6 hours a day for at least 180 days a year, they create a profound impact on teachers and the way they complete their work.

DEFINING SCHOOL CULTURE

School culture is created by interactions among and between teachers, students, and other school personnel. As a student, you have experienced many classrooms and different types of teachers and have been part of a school culture from elementary through the secondary level. Some of your experiences may have been very positive; others may not have been as rewarding for you. Schools are often categorized as "successes" or "failures" based on various criteria established by local, state, or national standards. Some people say they can tell whether a school is successful by the "feel" of the school when they walk in the door or walk through the hallways. How would you describe the schools in which you have been enrolled?

School culture is the set of norms, values and beliefs, rituals and ceremonies, symbols, and stories that make up the "persona" of the school. These unwritten expectations are created and evolve over time as teachers, administrators, parents, and students work together, solve problems, deal with challenges, and, at times, cope with failures. For example, every school has a set of expectations about what can be discussed at staff meetings, what constitutes good teaching techniques, how willing the staff is to change, and the importance of staff development (Deal & Peterson, 1999). Some school culture is clearly observable and explicit to beginning teachers. It is written in policies and other documents you will receive at the beginning of the year, such as a school mission statement or vision plan.

Formal school culture is generally recorded in documents that the school makes available to the public. These may include the student manual, dress or conduct codes, permission letters, or other formal communications between the school and students' homes. Less familiar to parents, but still part of formal school culture, are documents such as teachers' master contracts, state curriculum guidelines, school board policies, and pertinent state and national laws regarding education and the rights and privileges of students. Often educators are not familiar with all aspects of these documents, so it is easy to see why many parents are not aware of them. Even if students or parents consult one of these documents, the language they contain (formal English) may not always be understandable.

It is important that teachers and other school personnel explain the rationale behind school policies. Even though everyone may not always agree once the reasons have been explained, the effort to explain is often seen as recognizing the importance of students and families. Culturally sensitive teachers work to make formal school culture more democratic and accessible to all of the school's constituencies.

The culture of the school, both formal and informal, can greatly affect the classroom environment and the quality of learning.

INTASC

Principle #9

Professional Commitment and Responsibility: The teacher is a reflective practitioner who continually evaluates the effects of his/her choices and actions on others (students, parents, and other professionals in the learning community) and who actively seeks out opportunities to grow professionally.

INTASC

Principle #10

Partnerships: The teacher fosters relationships with school colleagues, parents, and agencies in the larger community to support students' learning and well-being.

Informal school culture, on the other hand, is hidden and more difficult to observe. By its very nature, informal school culture is known only to school insiders and shared by those insiders with individuals they choose. One example of informal school culture is the circle of people the school principal relies on for advice before making decisions. Two principals may have an identical amount of formal authority, but one may be more willing to share it with members of the faculty and rely on a wide circle of teachers, parents, and staff for advice. Another principal may have only one or two people who are "really consulted" before decisions are made. The difference between these two situations could not be determined by looking at the two schools' organizational charts, because the two charts may be identical. Perhaps there may be an expectation to have faculty meetings every Tuesday as part of normal routine, part of the valued shared time in a school. However, it may be unspoken, but known by faculty, that no one speaks honestly at these meetings. How that belief or ritual started would be difficult to track.

Understanding informal school culture can be perplexing and time-consuming. Yet educators cannot know the total culture of schools unless they know both the formal and informal school cultures. The task of learning about formal and informal school cultures is a significant one for new teachers and can take years to master. If a beginning teacher steps out of a norm, there may be a response from the teachers in the school. How do you identify the hidden culture norms? What can you do to prepare yourself for them? The National Staff Development Council identifies three variables, or behaviors, that help define the culture of a school: professional collaboration, collegiality, and efficacy/self-determination (Wagner, 2002). Figure 6.1 identifies 13 characteristics that define these three behaviors.

SCHOOL MISSION STATEMENTS

School **mission statements** can often reveal a great deal about a school and its culture or climate. A mission statement is defined as a relatively short written document (a few paragraphs at most) that states in clear and succinct terms the fundamental values and beliefs of the school. The mission statement is considered the guiding force that oversees the school and it is often posted prominently for all to see as they enter the building. A typical mission statement might look like this one from Franklin High School in Franklin, Massachusetts:

Franklin High School exists as a covenant among students, parents, staff, and community. This collaboration promotes a rigorous yet safe and nurturing environment in which students are responsible and passionate learners. In an atmosphere of equality, tolerance and respect, students prepare to contribute to our democratic society and an interdependent world.

Where do mission statements like this come from? In the case of the Franklin High School mission statement, a committee of teachers worked together to craft the statement and then presented it to the faculty for consensus. The statement then became part of the school's disposition and approach for creating a caring community of learners. This public statement serves as an important point of reference for individual classroom teachers. Sometimes schools write these statements and then they are filed away and never seen again because it was an exercise for a committee to complete, not a part of real school life.

Writing the statement, although it can be difficult in a group, is not the hard part of a school mission. What is hard is actually making it real in the day-to-day practice of the school. What would a mission like Franklin High School's really look like in the school? In a classroom? Evidence that the statement is alive in the school usually can been seen when a visitor walks through the front door of the school. Is student work displayed? Are students engaged? Are classrooms organized for learning? Some ways schools can bring their mission statements into action include the following:

- Schools should examine their current mission statements word by word to analyze what each word actually means.

- Schools' guiding statements lead to action when they address specific instructional practices.

FIGURE **6.1**

Observing School Culture

INDICATORS AND CHARACTERISTICS OF SCHOOL CULTURE

Professional Collaboration

- *High expectations of self and others.* Excellence is acknowledged; improvement is celebrated, supported, and shared

- *Experimentation and entrepreneurship.* New ideas abound and invention occurs.

- *Tangible support.* Improvement efforts are substantive, with abundant resources made available by all.

- *Shared vision.* Participants understand what's important and avoid trivial tasks.

Collegiality

- *Collegiality.* The way adults treat each other: respect and harmony versus disrespect and discord.

- *Trust and confidence.* Participants believe in the leaders and each other based on the match between creeds and deeds.

- *Appreciation and recognition of improvement.* People feel special and act special.

- *Humor.* Caring is expressed through "kidding" or joking in tasteful ways.

- *Traditions.* The school has identifiable celebrations and rituals that are important to the school community.

- *Open and honest communication.* Information flows throughout the organization in formal and informal channels. Everyone receives information on a "need-to-know" basis.

- *Metaphors and stories.* There is evidence of behavior being communicated and influenced by internal imagery.

Efficacy/Self-Determination

- *Efficacy.* Feeling of ownership or capacity to influence decisions; do people tend to live with or solve problems?

- *Shared decision making by all participants.* Those affected by a decision are involved in making and implementing the decision.

Source: Adapted from C. Wagner, *School Cultural Assessment.* (Bowling Green, KY: The Center for Improving School Culture, Western Kentucky University, 2000). www.schoolculture.net

- Schools must continue to discuss the mission statement to deepen their reflection and understanding of the beliefs and practices.

- A school's work in all areas, including assessment, mentoring, teacher evaluation, and communicating with parents, must be aligned with the guiding statement.

- Effective principals use guiding statements to guide their actions and those of their teachers.

- Schools need a systematic way to gather information about how people are using the guiding statement and how well they understand it. (Allen, 2001)

When you visit schools, ask to read the mission statement, find out who was part of developing the statement, and see whether you can find "observable behaviors" in the school that illustrate this statement. At some point during your teacher preparation, try to observe a mission statement committee meeting. Your observations will give you inside information about the energy, beliefs, and values of the faculty and the school. You may want to talk with the principal about the school's mission or guiding statement and see whether the principal is using any of these recommendations. The success of a mission statement is highly dependent on the engagement of a school's administration in its goals and purposes.

CLASSROOM CLIMATE VERSUS SCHOOL CULTURE

What is the difference between the terms *classroom climate* and *school culture?* The term *school climate* is often used interchangeably with *school culture;* however, it does have a different slant. **Classroom climate** refers most often to the tone of the classroom and the teacher's effect on students, whereas school culture encompasses more of the school as a whole, including the way groups of teachers and staff members work together in the school.

Each classroom in a school has a climate based on the interactions between that teacher, other adults in the room, and students. Characteristics of a positive classroom culture might include the following:

- The teacher interacting with humor and enthusiasm for the topic
- Students engaged with the content
- Students respectful of each other
- Students willing to ask questions and actively seek help when they need it

The physical arrangement of a classroom can also help promote a positive classroom culture. Which of the two classroom floor plans in Figure 6.2 do you think would promote a more positive learning environment? A school with classrooms that operate with a positive dynamic—happy, productive students and teachers who are learning—would often be described as a "successful" school with a positive school culture that enhances student learning.

As you enter schools this year, and in the future, observe the interactions of adults in the school and the impact of school culture on classroom teachers. Continue to observe individual classrooms to observe the impact of the classroom climate on the students and their learning.

SCHOOL CULTURE IN PRACTICE

Following are two case studies of schools. Note in each case indicators of school culture and classroom climate. Do you notice anything in the following descriptions that indicate that the school culture would positively or negatively affect student learning? What do you notice about the classroom climate and the teacher student interactions?

Case I: Anytown High

Joe, a student teacher, was placed at Anytown High School for his full practicum student teaching. He walked into the school and read a large sign that said, "Do Not Enter this Building without a Pass. See the Police Officer to Get One!" Unable to find the officer, Joe went to the main office. The person at the desk didn't look up when he arrived and Joe waited for 5 minutes to ask if he could meet Mrs. Jones, his cooperating teacher. The school secretary asked, "Where is your pass? You can't be in this building without one! Didn't you read the sign?" Joe stammered and got red in the face and said he didn't know where to find the officer on duty since this was his first time in the school.

The pass was written out and Joe proceeded to his classroom at the end of the school corridor. On the way to Mrs. Jones's class he noticed that the school was silent. Not a sound was coming from the classrooms! All the students were sitting in rows facing the

FIGURE 6.2

Two Classroom Layouts

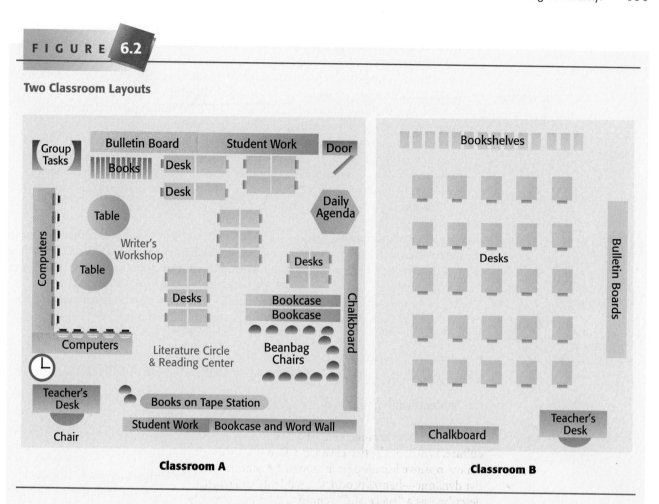

Classroom A

Classroom B

teachers. One classroom had a teacher outside the door pointing a finger at a student. He overheard her saying, "If I ever hear you say that again, you will be expelled! You are a rude, nasty boy!" Joe walked quickly past that classroom.

The corridors were dark. There were no photos, student work, or posters. The windows had screens and bars over them and the floors were dusty and had paper and candy wrappers strewn about. "If you didn't know it was a school, it might be a prison," he thought. Joe found Mrs. Jones and she opened the door to him. She said, "Well, you finally got here. I have been waiting for you for an hour. I don't have time to talk now, I have to prepare these students for the test, so sit down in the back and watch. Don't expect anything exciting. I gave up being creative years ago when they mandated these state tests."

Case II: City High

Susan was placed at City High for her student teaching. She drove up the long driveway and saw a large billboard outside the school that said Welcome to Our School. It was autographed by every student at the high school and there were flowering bushes next to it. She walked to the front door and pressed the bell and was greeted by a voice that said, "How may I help you?" She stated her name and that she was here to meet Mr. Smith, her cooperating teacher.

She was buzzed into the building and given directions to the main office, where she signed in as a guest and put on a nametag. She was asked to write her name as Ms. Harris to appear as one of the teachers. Susan liked that, because she was just a senior in college and looked like some of the high school students.

INTASC

Principle #5

Classroom Motivation and Management: The teacher uses an understanding of individual and group motivation and behavior to create a learning environment that encourages positive social interaction, active engagement in learning, and self-motivation.

Susan was greeted by the principal and introduced to the secretary and the department chair. They gave her a welcome packet with general guidelines for the school, and the department chair escorted her to Mr. Smith's classroom. On the way she saw student posters from the art room hanging in the hallway as well as some original poetry. She hoped her teacher would let her do some poetry teaching.

The door to Room 7 opened and she saw the teacher walking around the room as students worked in groups on some kind of creative writing assignment. There was another teacher in the room. It looked like they might be co-teaching the lesson. When Mr. Smith noticed her, he stopped and introduced her to the class as Ms. Harris from University College. He explained she would be working with them this term. He invited her to join a group and observe the activity. He whispered, "Let me finish this and then we can talk after class. I am so glad you are here."

Figure 6.3 identifies five "lenses" through which to observe school culture in action. Use the five lenses to examine what is going on in the two preceding case studies. Be clear about the distinction between school culture and classroom climate. What do you notice about each school?

Each school likely has a mission statement, yet their implications for teaching and learning are quite different as encountered by their students and teachers. How does this happen?

DETERMINING THE CHARACTER AND CULTURE OF A SCHOOL

Numerous factors come together to determine the character and culture of a school. For example, consider the community in which a school is located, the character and cultural and historical experience of the people who attend it, the type of people who are on the school board that control and shape its policies, and so on.

● **Schools as Vehicles That Promote Democracy**   In the United States we value the idea that our schools contribute to the promotion of a broader and more inclusive democracy. Schools do indeed provide individuals with important opportunities. Schools can shape students in significant ways as well. But schools can actually limit the potential of the students who attend them.

To a significant degree, schools must be understood in the context of the communities in which they are situated. Recent efforts at school reform have ignored this idea by empha-

---

FIGURE 6.3

Observing School Culture through Different Lenses

As you begin to visit and observe in schools, consider the following four aspects of school culture that inform what is going on in classrooms, and what the school is or is not accomplishing through its educational programs:

1. The school's mission statement, core values, and philosophy.
2. The school's social, historical, political, and organizational context.
3. The school's demographics and resources, including its students and the community in which it is located.
4. The methods, programs, and procedures used to assure effective teaching and learning.

Also think about the different lenses through which to observe school culture:

1. the student's lens
2. the parent's lens
3. the school district's lens
4. the legislator's lens
5. the teacher's or your lens.

Source: Friedman, A. (2000). *Facilitator's manual for undergraduate inquiry.* Chestnut Hill, MA: Boston College. Reprinted by permission.

sizing a top-down approach in which curriculums and models for teaching are passed down from the federal government, state legislature, or a central office in a state department of education. Often these reforms demonstrate little understanding of the significance of their implementation at the local level.

On the surface, we can argue that a school is a school, and the children who attend it simply need to be taught. This idea is reinforced by the fact that schools look pretty much the same, as do students and teachers. On closer examination, however, the culture of a school and the individual challenges faced by schools are very different, depending on where they are located, whom they serve, and how many students they teach.

During the 2001–2002 school year, there were 47,688,000 million students in the United States (National Center for Educational Statistics,2004a). Five states (California, Florida, Illinois, New York, and Texas) had more than 2 million students enrolled in their public schools. Wyoming, on the other hand, had fewer than 100,000 students (National Center for Educational Statistics, 2004a), or slightly more than one-fourth the number of students in a large urban district such as the Miami/Dade County public schools, with 370,000 students and nearly 20,000 teachers (MDCP, 2004).

The average number of students in American primary schools in 1999–2000 was 446. Middle schools had an average of 595 students and high schools 752 students. Rural western states such as Montana, North Dakota, and South Dakota averaged less than 300 students in their high schools, whereas states such as Florida and Hawaii averaged 1,400 students or more (National Center for Educational Statistics, 2004c). In many urban and suburban school districts, student numbers are much larger. In the Miami/Dade County public school system, for example, some high schools have more than 6,000 students. These high schools are two to three times the size of many small colleges around the country. Based on enrollment alone, how might the culture in these schools differ than the culture in a school of 500? Table 6.1 on page 180 and Figure 6.4 on page 181 further explore the breakdown of enrollment in schools across the country.

● **Schools and Their Connection to Local Communities** Reading researcher Patricia Edwards has concluded that success in teaching children to read is profoundly connected to the literacy of the communities in which they live, as well as to the literacy of their parents. If parents have low reading skills, they tend not to reinforce reading as an important and valued skill. Nor, do these parents necessarily support the efforts of the school in teaching their children how to read. In settings where students have parents with limited reading skills, schools need to teach its students how to read as well as also help their parents improve their own reading skills. Such a model would not be necessary, or desirable in an affluent setting, where most parents are not only literate but college educated as well (Edwards, Pleasants, & Franklin, 1999).

Literacy among parents may not depend on prior education and ability, but rather on the availability of jobs and economic opportunities. It is no accident that illiteracy is related to poverty. An economically poor community is likely to struggle more with literacy issues than an affluent one. American society needs to understand more clearly that the quality of life in local communities profoundly affects the quality of schooling in those same communities. The two are inevitably interdependent.

Since schools are closely connected to the local community in which they are found,

INTASC

Principle #10

Partnerships: The teacher fosters relationships with school colleagues, parents, and agencies in the larger community to support students' learning and well-being.

The extent to which parents value reading affects children's success in learning to read. In addition, there is a clear connection between quality of life of a community and the quality of that community's schools.

TABLE 6.1

Distribution of Regular Public School Districts and Students, by District Membership Size, 1999–2000 School Year

DISTRICT MEMBERSHIP SIZE	NUMBER OF DISTRICTS	PERCENTAGE OF DISTRICTS	PERCENTAGE OF STUDENTS
United States	14,571	100.0	100.0
100,000 or more	25	0.2	12.4
25,000–99,999	213	1.5	19.7
10,000–24,999	579	4.0	18.7
7,500–9,999	320	2.2	6.0
5,000–7,499	716	4.9	9.4
2,500–4,999	2,068	14.2	15.6
2,000–2,499	806	5.5	3.9
1,500–1,999	1,087	7.5	4.1
1,000–1,499	1,564	10.7	4.2
800–999	807	5.5	1.6
600–799	1,007	6.9	1.5
450–599	920	6.3	1.0
300–449	1,161	8.0	0.9
150–299	1,489	10.2	0.7
1–149	1,809	12.4	0.3

Note: Table includes the 50 states and the District of Columbia, and excludes 357 regular school districts for which no students were reported in membership. Percentages are rounded to the nearest tenth and may not add to 100.
Source: U.S. Department of Education, National Center for Education Statistics, Common Core of Data, "Local Education Agency Universe Survey." (Washington, D.C.: 1999–2000).

teachers and others working in the schools must be able to work across different cultural settings. The United States is defined by the diversity and complexity of its people. Teachers often work in settings that are very different from their own background. Thus, to be effective, they must become border crossers (Giroux, 1992).

Chapter 1 discussed how teachers must function as border crossers by adopting skills similar to those of anthropologists or sociologists. Like anthropologists, for example, they must go into cultural settings and derive understanding from observation and reflection. In this sense, they would follow the interpretivist model described earlier in this chapter.

Such an approach recognizes that schools are cultural and social institutions. They are connected to the larger community of which they are a part. Without understanding the social and cultural context in which a school functions, teachers will find it hard to understand the variables that shape and define the learning process for their students. Part of what you will need to understand as a teacher is how power functions in the community where you are working. Much of what you will need to know will be subtle and hard to detect. A great deal will be very visible. As a border crosser you will have to carefully observe the forces at work in the local community in which you teach, and act in ways that are consistent with the reality that is there.

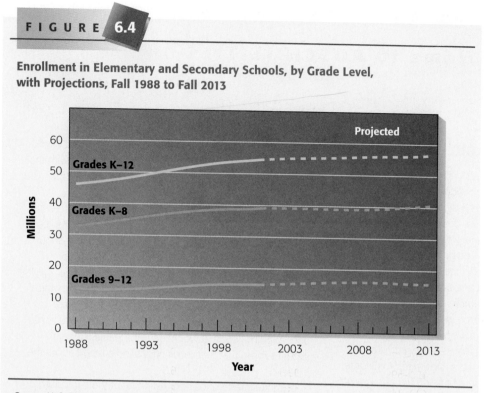

FIGURE 6.4

Enrollment in Elementary and Secondary Schools, by Grade Level, with Projections, Fall 1988 to Fall 2013

Source: U. S. Department of Education, National Center for Education Statistics, Common Core of Data, "State Nonfiscal Survey of Public Elementary/Secondary Education," various years; Private School Universe Survey (PSS), various years; 1985 Private School Survey; and National Elementary and Secondary Enrollment Model.

WHO CONTROLS THE SCHOOLS?

In theory, as part of the democratic process, schools are controlled by the members of the community where the school is located. This control is exercised primarily through elections, in which local voters choose board members who set educational policy at the local level. Approximately 90% of school board members are elected. In a small number of settings, approximately 10% of all schools, however, they are appointed by the local government. School boards are expected to set policy for school administrators to carry out, not to run the schools. This job is the responsibility of the superintendent and other administrators they hire. In addition, the typical school board sets the school calendar, approves broad curriculum aims, develops a salary schedule for teachers and administrators, acts on the recommendations of administrators for the hiring and firing of teachers, and when appropriate, negotiates with the teachers' union.

FEDERAL, STATE, AND LOCAL CONTROL OF EDUCATION

While schools in the United States function largely at a local level, they also work at the state and federal levels. Most decisions, such as the hiring of teachers, the maintenance of buildings, and the purchase of materials such as textbooks, are made at the local level. At the state level, decisions are made on a broader basis, such as establishing the minimum training standards a person must need in order to work as a teacher. At the federal level, until recently, involvement in K–12 public education has been largely limited to collecting

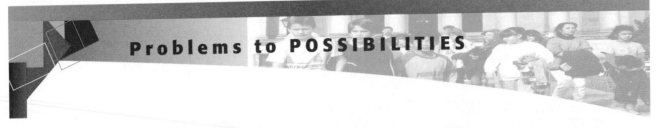

Problems to POSSIBILITIES

DEFENDING A COLLEAGUE

George Newcombe was in his second year of teaching Social Studies at Branford High School. When he started at the school a year earlier, he was assigned a mentor, Mrs. Kennedy, a 10-year veteran in the department. She and George hit it off immediately, and Mrs. Kennedy proved to be a valuable resource during George's first year. She was always there for George when he needed help, whether it involved ordering supplies and textbooks, deciding what to teach, or determining how to handle an unruly student. Mrs. Kennedy's friendship and mentorship continued to be valuable during George's second year.

One afternoon after school, Mrs. Kennedy came to George's classroom, clearly upset, and confided to George, "I have been accused by a student of being biased against her religious beliefs." "Based on what?" George asked, "Is there any basis to the charge?" "Of course not!" said Mrs. Kennedy. "This all started when I stated in class that the upcoming school Christmas concert wasn't about Christmas anymore, since it now includes Hanukkah and Kwanzaa songs, as well as some traditional carols. A student told her parents what I said and now they are quite upset, feeling that I was minimizing the importance of a significant Christian holiday. They contacted the principal and some school board members. I have to meet with the girl's parents and the principal later this afternoon. You know I don't have a biased bone in me. Do you mind coming with me to the meeting, and helping me explain that this is all a big misunderstanding?"

Discussion Questions

Should George go to the meeting with Mrs. Kennedy? Does he have any special obligation to help Mrs. Kennedy? If so, what is the best way for him to help?

Possibilities

George is in a difficult position, but one that is fairly clear-cut. On the one hand, he wants to help someone who has always been there for him. But he has no way of truly knowing whether Mrs. Kennedy has been insensitive to the student and her family. George wasn't present for the initial discussion; therefore, he is in no position to determine right or wrong or to pass judgment on what happened. It would be inappropriate for George to attend the meeting with the principal and the parents unless invited by the principal. The meeting is a closed administrative affair.

What George *can* do is be available in the hall after the meeting to show moral support for Mrs. Kennedy. He could also suggest that they both speak with the principal about how George might be able to help in the conflict. For example, as Mrs. Kennedy's mentee for the past year, George is in a perfect position to speak to her character and ethical positions. Mrs. Kennedy may see George's actions as reflecting a lack of support on his part after "all that she has done for him," but that would be unfortunate. George should explain that he cannot offer blind support about the incident.

Parental interference or questioning of the curriculum or concepts discussed or taught in the classroom can be very unsettling and can result in adversarial stances and expectations. In schools in which parents, teachers, and administrators see each other as adversaries, members of each group may feel pressure to provide blind support. Such school cultures can undermine collaborative and collegial relationships and, ultimately, learning. Striving for an environment that encourages three-way communication among parents, teachers, and administrators benefits all parties—most of all the students. The following resource may provide helpful hints for turning Problems into Possibilities.

- Visit the Northwest Regional Educational Laboratory (http://www.nwrel.org/scpd/sirs) to read about their School Improvement Research Series, which includes materials for improving school culture.

- Questia Online Library (http://www.questia.com/library/education) offers a wide array of journal articles and links, including discussions on parent-teacher relationships, teacher-administrator relationships, and transforming school culture.

Ethical Question: When should teacher unions or professional groups get involved in conflicts over parental or community objections about what is taught in the schools?

Title IX opened the doors for many girls in education and sports by making the opportunities available to them equal to those of boys.

statistics, doing research about schools, and making sure that people had equal access to schooling in their local communities.

According to the Constitution, the control of schools is supposed to be a state and local function. Why, then, does the federal government have any involvement in public schooling in the United States? This is a complicated issue that has been subject to considerable debate throughout much of American history.

THE GROWTH OF FEDERAL INVOLVEMENT IN SCHOOLS—1950s TO THE PRESENT

Since the mid-1950s, the federal government in the United States has become increasingly involved in education. Essentially, the federal government can intervene in education at the state level and the local level when the individual rights of students need to be defended. In other words, the federal government has a legitimate Constitutional claim for being involved in schools when doing so reinforces or supports some aspect of the rights guaranteed under the Constitution. Thus, in 1957 the federal government was able to intervene on the behalf of African American students in Little Rock, Arkansas. These students' civil rights were being violated because they were not being given equal access to public schooling. As a result, President Eisenhower had the legal right to mobilize federal troops to help protect African American students as they attended public schools as part of the integration process.

Similarly, the federal government can intervene with laws that provide greater access to schooling for selected—and often discriminated against—segments of the population, as was discussed in Chapter 5. This was the case, for example, with the passage of Public Law 94–142 (Education of All Handicapped Children Act) in 1975. Under this law, Congress required that in order to receive federal funding, state and local systems of government had to develop and implement policies that assured a **free appropriate public education** to all children with disabilities. In doing so, the federal government was defending the civil rights of disabled children.

In a similar way, the passage of Title IX of the Educational Amendments of 1972, which stated, "No person in the U.S. shall, on the basis of sex be excluded from participation in, or denied the benefits of, or be subjected to discrimination under any educational program or activity receiving federal aid," represented the federal government's getting involved in state and local education in order to protect the civil rights of women.

When President Bush signed into law the No Child Left Behind Act in 2002 it represented the culmination of a major effort to establish accountability and standards for elementary and secondary education that began in the mid-1980s. The act links academic standards to federal funding, the lifeblood of all public schools.

NCLB has had a great deal of support from a public concerned with making sure students learn as much as possible while they are in school. Critics of the accountability and standards movement argue, however, that the federal government has unreasonably imposed itself on local schools, and that it has taken control away from teachers in the classroom by creating a curriculum of "teaching to the test," rather than having meaningful learning take place in the classroom.

The issue of accountability and standards is, in fact, a continuation of the debate between progressivism and social efficiency outlined in Chapter 5 that has dominated American education since the early twentieth century. The debate is essentially about who should control education, what the purpose of schools should be, and how we define what it means to be educated.

THE ROLE OF STATE GOVERNMENT IN EDUCATION

As mentioned earlier, public schools in the United States are controlled largely at the state and local level, which is different from most other countries around the world, where schools are organized and controlled at the national level through a bureau or ministry of education. Local control of the schools is a result of traditions dating back to the colonial period, as well as a provision under the 10th Amendment to the Constitution that all duties not specifically assigned to the federal government (the president and Congress) are assigned to the local level. Since education and the administration of the schools is not mentioned anywhere in the Constitution, the control of the schools reverts to the state and local level (Eisner, 2001). State governments control selected aspects of public education, such as the certification of teachers, which is regulated by the state department of education. Through the legislature, laws can be passed that determine issues such as standards for graduation, rules for the construction of schools including health and safety regulations, and policies concerning what curriculum to teach. State legislatures provide funding to local school districts through administration of federal grants, and collection and distribution of state sales taxes. Because states and local communities are assigned the duty of administering the public schools, there are 50 state departments of education and approximately 100,000 different school districts in the United States (Eisner, 2001).

● **State Boards and Departments of Education**   State boards of education are political appointees and have largely an oversight function with relatively little political power. In the state of Florida, for example, the board consists of seven people who meet on a monthly basis. In New York State the state board is called the board of regents; it was created more than a century ago by Governor Theodore Roosevelt to unify the educational system in the state for "greater efficiency, economy and harmony." The board of regents, with the assistance of the state department of education, governs education from prekindergarten to the graduate level. State departments of education typically function as agents of the state's education board and the state's legislature. The functions of state boards of education vary greatly across the country. To find out more about how your state's department of education functions, visit its website as listed in Appendix C.

● **Chief State School Officers**   Each state also has a chief state school officer, who is typically given the title of state superintendent or commissioner. They are selected to serve by different methods. In Florida, the commissioner of education is elected in a statewide elec-

Do school boards serve students and teachers, or vested political and social interests?

tion. In Ohio and Louisiana, the officer is appointed by the state board of education. In states such as New Jersey and Maine, officers are appointed by the governor. State commissioners and superintendents can wield a great deal of political power and often move on to other positions, including governorships and congressional and Senate seats.

LOCAL OVERSIGHT OF SCHOOLS

Historically, Americans have been proud of their schools and the tradition of local control. On a day-to-day basis schools are administered by several different people who are part of a highly stratified bureaucratic and hierarchical system. Most are organized around a centralized structure, with a superintendent of schools at the top of the structure along with associate superintendents; principals, vice principals, department heads, and teachers within the schools are in the middle; under them are the students. The overall school system is under the control of a school board made up of members of the community. The administration of any local school system will depend largely on the size of the district itself. Figure 6.5 on page 186 shows the flowchart of the Medford public schools in Oregon.

● **Superintendents and Principals**   School districts vary in size and number of schools. No matter what their size, however, they will always be headed up by a **superintendent** of schools, whose primary job is to oversee all aspects of the entire school district, much as a CEO would for a business. In large school districts, the superintendent may have associate or assistant superintendents who oversee specialized functions, such as facilities, curriculum, or transportation. They may also head up special areas such as exceptional citizen education.

Anyone who has attended school in the United States is familiar with how schools are administered. The basic unit of most school systems is the classroom. Next, at least in high schools, comes the department and then the school. The **principal** oversees all matters involving a specific school, while staying within the guiding principles of the entire district. Very large schools with several thousand students may have several assistant principals, each with specific duties, as well as a large specialized staff.

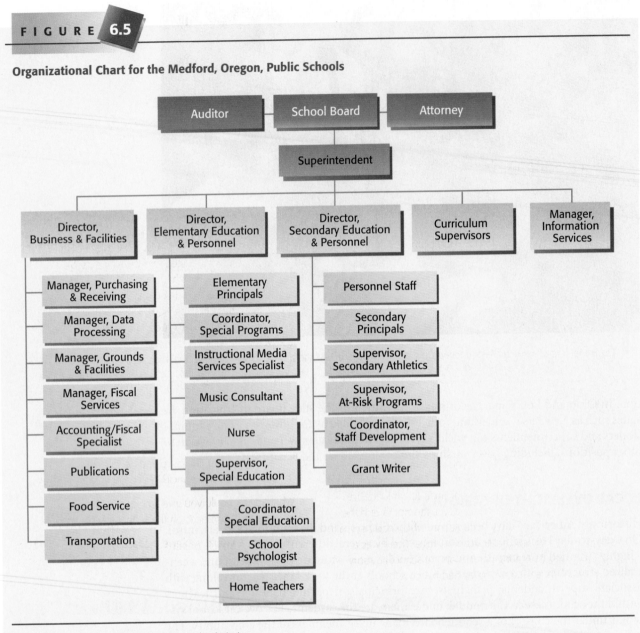

FIGURE 6.5

Organizational Chart for the Medford, Oregon, Public Schools

Source: Courtesy of the Medford, Oregon, School District.

Technically, the administration of the schools, whether it is at the building or superintendent's level, is under the control of a school board. In an effectively functioning school system, the board should have largely oversight functions, letting local administrators and teachers accomplish their work.

● **School Boards** School boards represent the most basic level of the American political system. Most school boards are elected in the United States. In a few cities, school boards are appointed by the political power in control. School board members often use their positions as a stepping stone to a larger political career.

School boards tend to be conservative and often represent vested political and social interests. The regulation and control of school boards varies widely throughout the country,

Through the Eyes of
Culturally Sensitive Teachers

Cultural Changes at Juarez High School

Benito Juarez High School is located in a section of Tucson, Arizona with a high Mexican and Mexican American student population. Over time, the composition of the neighborhoods from which Juarez drew its students began to change. Older buildings and warehouses around Juarez were renovated and property around the school began to increase in value. As this occurred, many Hispanic families moved to other sections of the city where property was more affordable and the ethnic and socioeconomic mix of Juarez's students changed significantly. Eventually Hispanic students dropped to less than a quarter of Juarez's population. A similar shift occurred among the parents on the school advisory council.

Francisco Reyes and Kevin Green were English teachers at Juarez and members of the school advisory council. Over the years, they had watched the council's deliberations become more contentious. One group of non-Hispanic parents suggested that the bilingual program at Juarez should be ended and replaced with English-only instruction for native Spanish speakers. Another effort was an attempt to end the Cinco de Mayo (Fifth of May) celebration, which had been a Juarez tradition celebrating Mexican heritage. There was a contentious debate among parents on the school advisory council over "whose school Juarez had become."

Francisco and Kevin suggested that the bilingual program could expand to include native English speakers who wanted to become proficient in Spanish; these students would profit from being in the same program with fluent Spanish speakers. They also suggested that the Cinco de Mayo celebration did not have to be cancelled but could include additional groups that populated Arizona besides those who originally came from Mexico. Some parents from all communities were willing to support the compromise, but others were not. While relations among parents on the school advisory council have improved somewhat, tensions still remain.

Points To Ponder

1. How does a change in the nature of a school's population affect school culture and governance?

2. Do you agree with Francisco and Kevin's suggestions to the school advisory council? Why or why not?

3. What advice would you give Francisco and Kevin to improve circumstances on the school advisory council?

4. What advice would you give the faculty and administration at Juarez?

as do the length of terms served and the number of members. Being a school board member in a small suburban or rural school district is very different from serving on a school board in a large urban area such as New York or Los Angeles, where members can easily be responsible for administering a budget of hundreds of millions of dollars each year.

School board members typically reflect the power structure of their community and tend to be overwhelmingly male and White, similar to the traditional power structure seen in government and business. Most board members tend to be businesspeople or professionals most of whom work without a salary or any form of compensation. Besides tending to be White and male, they are also middle-aged and wealthier than the general population. It is likely that their children have already completed school, and they see their work on the school board as a service to their community.

School boards tend to perpetuate themselves. Because of this fact, many school boards have limited minority representation. As minority groups have demanded greater power in recent years, their membership on school boards—particularly in large urban districts—has increased dramatically.

As part of the struggle for reform of our schools, communities have protested for the implementation of a voucher system that distributes funds to parents and allows them to use those vouchers toward the tuition to a school of their choice.

INTASC

Principle #10

Partnerships: The teacher fosters relationships with school colleagues, parents, and agencies in the larger community to support students' learning and well-being.

● **Sources of Conflicts in Local School Systems**   Bureaucratic systems, including public schools, by their very nature operate according to rules—rules that are often unspoken, but nonetheless present. Principals, not teachers, for example, have responsibility for their schools. The director of elementary education and personnel is not responsible for secondary teachers, and so on. Expertise is highly valued in such systems with a chain of command for getting things done. Standardization of time schedules, grading guidelines, disciplinary procedures, professional standards, and texts and curriculum are often part of the bureaucracy of modern school systems.

While the rules and procedures often found in schools are necessary in large complex social systems, they also force the day-to-day functioning of the school to be rule-bound and often very conservative. In the process of setting up appropriate procedures, the needs of individuals at the school level—particularly those of teachers and students—can get overlooked, resulting in conflicts.

School boards typically mediate the many potential sources of conflict that develop in local school systems. For example, parents who do not want their child taught particular curricular content may file a complaint. If the issue cannot be resolved at the classroom (teacher) or the school (principal) level, the issue may end up being reviewed by the superintendent and then the school board.

Often parents may not be particularly vocal about issues that concern them. This may not necessarily be because of apathy on their part, but because they do not feel empowered to act. Thus, recently arrived immigrant and possibly illegal alien parents may not have the time, language skills, or experience to lobby the school system about issues that they believe are important. As a result, affluent and educated members of the community are typically much more influential in shaping school policy than other groups.

Religious issues and the First Amendment rights of students are probably the main sources of conflict that develop at the local level. Are religious activities such as prayer meetings going to be allowed in the schools? Is the curriculum appropriate in terms of students' religious beliefs? Do discussions in biology courses include only reference to evolution and not to creationism? Sometimes issues arise over taxation when parents who send their children to parochial schools feel that they are being unfairly taxed for public education. Property taxes that support the schools are some of the only taxes that local communities have any control over. As a result, local citizens (particularly those without a vested interest in the schools, such as retirees and people without children) may protest increased funding for the schools.

What do I believe?

"I think it's a shame when the first step in becoming a politician is serving on the local school board."

MARIA C., PARENT

THINK ABOUT THIS:

People's motivation for serving on a school board can vary a great deal. Of course we would all like to think that the primary reason for serving is to ensure that all children have the best opportunity to learn. But sometimes the motivation, just as this parent suggests, is as a stepping-stone to a political career. The administration of schools is a highly politicized environment these days, one in which students and teachers often become pawns. Why do you think this is so? How might this affect your work in the classroom? Why do you think Maria thinks using the school board as a stepping-stone is a shame?

SHARE and COMPARE:

School board meetings are public. Attend a local school board meeting and report your observations back to the class. What was the most controversial subject of the meeting? Did members seem to agree on issues?

HOW ARE SCHOOLS FINANCED IN THE UNITED STATES?

American schools are complex social systems with many factors determining what they are like. They also have certain things in common, whether they are in Florida, Alaska, a rural state such as Idaho, or an urban area such as Washington, D.C. All public schools are bureaucratic systems. In addition, they are all funded through local property taxes.

Funding for the public schools comes primarily through the collection of local property taxes. Significantly, these are collected at a local level, thus making it possible for different levels of funding to be available in different communities. Wealthy suburban communities with high property values and relatively few children, for example, may have much more money available for school funding than poorer communities with low property values and many more children living in them.

Some funding comes from the federal government to support schools. In most cases this funding is connected to a group with special needs, or as part of a compensatory funding program. In the case of **compensatory funding,** the federal government can provide funding as part of an effort to overcome past social injustices or inequity. Thus, schools with high numbers of minority students in poor inner-city schools often receive funding to compensate them for past social injustices.

Total expenditures for schools in 2002 were approximately $350 billion for prekindergarten through Grade 12. These funds paid the salaries of nearly 3 million people and also covered the costs of buildings, textbooks, transportation, and other resources. Total expenditures per pupil averaged $7,500 (National Center for Educational Statistics, 2002). Such figures can be misleading, however. Keep in mind that the per-pupil expenditures in rural

BUILDING ON EDUCATIONAL FOUNDATIONS

Commercializing Public Schools

In 1998 a student at a high school in Georgia made national news when he was suspended for wearing a Pepsi T-shirt during a promotional photo shoot for the school's "Coke in Education Day." The "Coke in Education Day" was part of the school's participation in a national contest sponsored by the Georgia-based soft drink company. As part of the contest, teachers created an entire curriculum around the soft drink and students were encouraged to distribute promotional Coke discount cards in their local communities. Coke executives visited the school to promote the day's activities, which included analyzing the chemical properties of Coke and discussing marketing tactics for the soft drink as part of Economics classes.

According to school officials, the student was suspended because he was disruptive and rude during a school activity. Gloria Hamilton, the school's principal, explained the issue in the following way: "It's not a Coke-Pepsi war issue. It has nothing to do with that. It was a student deliberately being disruptive and rude" (Saltman, 2000, pp. 57–58)

This incident raises the question of the extent to which advertising and commercial promotion should take place in public school settings. School administrators across the country face serious financial crises and find themselves being more and more creative to come up with ideas for alternative financing of school programs. In turn, many corporations consider schools

ideal places to promote their products. Brand loyalty established with children often follows them through their lives. Students are also important consumers, not only purchasing for themselves but often influencing purchases by their families. Corporate sponsorships and connections can raise as much as $100,000 each year for large schools—a significant number in these tight economic times.

In addition to soft drink companies and athletic apparel companies that lock in exclusive rights with a school's athletic teams, corporations such as Channel One have gone into schools and provided free televisions and educational broadcasts on condition that students listen to a certain number of advertisements. Arguments in favor of Channel One include the fact that a service is being provided for "free" that would otherwise not be available, and that it does not really interfere with what students learn.

What do you think? Should students be required to watch advertisements in order to receive access to educational broadcasts? Should the student who wore the Pepsi T-shirt have been suspended? Is this practice ethical, or is it simply necessary? What might be a solution to avoiding corporate commercialism of schools? Does the practice represent a conflict of interest?

states may be as low as $3,000–$4,000 per year, and as high as $8,000–$9,000 per year in more affluent states.

Raising taxes for schools is often a difficult process. It is easier for citizens to object to raising the level of local property taxes than to oppose statewide taxes or the federal income tax. As a result, tax increases are often voted down. In states such as Florida and Arizona, which have large elderly populations, it is no surprise that proposals to increase property taxes to benefit schools are often strongly opposed.

PRIVATE SCHOOLS AS AN ALTERNATIVE

While there has been a general consensus in American society that public schools serve the general good, many people believe that students should have the freedom to attend **private schools.** Private education is, in fact, guaranteed by the Supreme Court as a Constitutional right. In 1922 an Oregon law was passed that required children to attend public school and prohibited their attendance at religious or parochial schools. The law was overturned by the U.S. Supreme Court in the 1925 decision of *Pierce v. Society of the Sisters.* The court's decision held that the Oregon law interfered with the rights of a private school—in this case, a religious school—and students and parents by compelling public attendance.

The *Pierce* decision maintained the right of private schools to exist in competition with the public system, and the right of parents to send their children to these schools. It did not, however, exclude such schools from limited control by the government. Thus, private schools can be held to limited standards of accountability in terms of curriculum, as well as basic standards involving health and human rights.

There are many different types of private schools in the United States. They include religious schools, independent day schools, boarding schools, and schools for students with special needs or academic interests. In recent years there has been a great deal of public debate about whether private or semiprivate schools should receive public funding.

CHARTER SCHOOLS

Charter schools are sectarian public schools that operate independently from many of the regulations of more traditional public schools. Educators, parents, community leaders, and entrepreneurs create them, and parents send their children to these schools by choice. Under a charter, an independent group contracts with a public school system to achieve certain goals, and then is granted a contract to achieve those goals, typically within a specified time of 3 to 5 years. Charter schools are financed through public funding and their operators are accountable to their sponsor—usually a state or local school board. The assumption underlying charter schools is that they have greater autonomy and flexibility than traditional public schools and that they can do the following:

- Increase opportunities for learning and access to quality education for all students

- Create choice for parents and students within the public school system

- Provide a system of accountability for results in public education

- Encourage innovative teaching practices

- Create new professional opportunities for teachers

- Encourage community and parent involvement in public education

- Leverage improved public education broadly (U.S. Charter Schools, 2004)

Minnesota passed the first statewide charter school law in 1991. By 1999, 36 states, Puerto Rico, and the District of Columbia had passed charter school legislation. As of the fall of 2002, there were 2,700 charter schools operating in 36 states and the District of Columbia, serving more than 575,000 students (Center for Educational Reform, 2002).

Charter schools are highly controversial, as critics maintain that they draw resources away from public school systems. Advocates argue that they meet the special needs of students and their parents and provide an alternative to large and often unresponsive public school systems. The issue of charter schools is, in fact, part of a larger debate over school choice: Should public funds be used to support schools outside the traditional public school system?

"I made a Valentine's Day card for you. The school has no art supplies so I wrote the color in."

Courtesy of Aaron Bacall, *The Lighter Side of Teaching*, p. 7. Copyright 2003 by Aaron Bacall. Reprinted by permission of Corwin Press Inc.

VOUCHERS

Vouchers have been proposed by many people as an alternative the traditional funding of education in the United States. The typical voucher program would distribute funds to parents (usually somewhere between $2,500–$5,000) to purchase education for their children on the open market. These vouchers can be used toward the cost of tuition at private schools and even schools that are church affiliated.

Opposition to voucher programs has been very strong among public school advocates. Many people believe that vouchers will undermine public schooling, as well as subvert the constitutional principle of the separation of church and state. Supporters of vouchers, particularly parents sending their children to privately funded religious schools, maintain that they should be able to draw on tax funds to help educate their children in the manner that they consider appropriate.

Providing public funds for the support of private schools is done in many different countries throughout the world. In Canada, for example, religious schools often receive public funds to help finance their operation. In the United States, religious schools have not been funded because of the constitutional principle of separation of church and state. As a result of our having many different and often competing religious beliefs in American society, we have constructed a system that deliberately separates the functions of the government from those of our religious systems.

In an 1802 letter Thomas Jefferson stated the need for a "wall of separation between church and state." Jefferson felt that maintaining such a separation was essential to protect the rights of all Americans. In presenting his argument, he referred to the **establishment clause** of the Constitution, which guarantees all citizens the right to follow their personal religious faith. The logic follows that if any single or selected group of religious practices were supported through government institutions such as the schools, the rights of those who followed other beliefs (including nonreligious or nonbelieving individuals) would be violated. This is why tax vouchers (with the exception of a few programs in cities such as Milwaukee and Cleveland) and other types of financial support for religious schools have not been provided in the United States. In addition, many people believe that funding alternatives to the traditional public schools will undermine the integrity and strength of public schools. Thus, government funds are not typically provided to religious or nonreligious private schools. In the few instances in which public funding is provided for private schools, it is in the form of "direct aid" to students—such as secular textbooks or bus transportation.

Who am I? What do I believe?

"The object of the education is to prepare the young to educate themselves throughout their lives."

ROBERT M. HUTCHINS

THINK ABOUT THIS:

Helping students become better thinkers requires creating a good learning environment. Some people believe that private schools are better able to accomplish this because they don't have to deal with the same administrative red tape or financial issues as public schools. Are there public and private schools in your community? What are these schools known for—that is, why do parents send their children to these schools? Do some of the public schools have better or worse reputations than others?

SHARE and COMPARE:

What was the reputation of the school you attended? What social forces shaped the schools in your community and the educational experiences of the students who attended them? Compare your experience with those of a classmate or friend. How are they different or the same?

FINAL THOUGHTS

Schools—both public and private—are an important part of the landscape of American society. We tend to take their existence and continuance for granted. In general, both public and private schools have served American culture and society well.

Yet despite this fact, in recent years, public schools in particular have come under increasing criticism. We need to ask ourselves, why? Whose needs are met by public schools? How do they promote the values of a democratic culture? What role will you play in them as a teacher? Why is their traditional role and function in American culture being challenged? Are innovations such as charter schools and vouchers really needed, or are they simply attempts on the part of special-interest groups to have their needs met?

These are complex and often emotional questions. Their answers will determine much of the future of American education and the type of work you may be doing in the schools as a teacher. Few professions face such enormously challenging issues.

Who am I? **What do I believe?**

REFLECTIONS

Professional Plan for Understanding the Social Context of Schools

1. Three things I learned from this chapter about the social contexts of schools are:

2. Two things in this chapter I would like to learn more about are:

   a. _____

   b. _____

3. I plan to investigate these two areas and learn more about topics in this chapter by:

   _____ Reading some of the selections from the Read On section

   _____ Reading sources referenced in the chapter that interest me

   _____ Visiting the following schools and taking note of their school culture using the criteria identified in Figure 6.1:

   a. _____

   b. _____

   _____ Exploring the Web sites listed in the Log On section

4. Three ways that I can learn more about the politics of education in my hometown and in the community where I go to school are:

5. I will include the following in my Touch the Future Portfolio.

SUMMARY

What Makes a Good School?

- Schools imply the idea of an institution or organization.

- There are different definitions of what makes a good school. Different types of schools may suit different needs.

- There are three main sociological models of schooling—functionalism, conflict theory, and indepretivism.

How Does School Culture Affect a Learning Community?

- Numerous factors determine the character of a school.

- What takes place in schools is closely connected to the communities in which they are located.

- As border crossers, teachers can work across various cultural settings to help students and families adapt to the formal and informal culture of schools.

Who Controls the Schools?

- According to the Constitution, control of education is supposed to be largely under the control of state and local government.

- Federal involvement in education has grown over the past 50 years.

- State boards and departments of education play a significant role in the educational system.

- School boards reflect class and power structures in their communities.

- Accountability is a subject of debate in many communities.

How Are Schools Financed in the United States?

- Financing of schools is based on local taxes.

- People are allowed to pursue private education as a constitutional right.

- The separation of church and state is an ongoing issue affecting American public education.

Visit the **Touch the Future . . . Teach!** Companion Website at www.ablongman.com/diaz for additional opportunities.

KEY WORDS

charter schools   191

classroom climate   176

compensatory funding   189

conflict theory   170

establishment clause   192

formal school culture   173

free appropriate public
  education   183

functionalist model   170

informal school culture   174

interpretivist model   171

mission statements   174

principal   185

private schools   190

school culture   173

superintendent   185

vouchers   191

CONCEPT REVIEW

1. Explain the difference between schooling and education, and describe the characteristics that might make a good school.

2. Identify the main characteristics of the functionalist, conflict theory, and intepretivist models of schooling and describe examples of each.

3. Discuss the factors that determine the character and effectiveness of a school, and explore the role that local communities play in influencing the school.

4. Describe how teachers, as border crossers, can help influence the culture of a school and what they can do to help others navigate that culture.

5. Explain what a mission statement is and why it is an important document for understanding the character of a school.

6. What are the main means by which local schools are administered at the local level?

7. Discuss the federal government's involvement in public school education in recent years, and explain why it has created conflict among educators, administrators, and community groups.

8. Describe how schools are administered at the state, district, and building level, and the roles that state boards and departments of education play in the educational system.

9. What are some of the potential sources of educational conflict in most communities?

10. Identify how schools are financed and identify at least two possible alternative funding sources to which schools might turn.

11. Explain why the separation of church and state is an important principle in the American education system and consider some contemporary actions that might cause some conflict over this principle.

12. Explain how the establishment clause in the Constitution might serve as a protection of an individual's rights in education and how some might use it in a conflict over the separation of church and state.

TOUCH THE FUTURE . . .

Read On

School and Society
John Dewey (Chicago: University of Chicago Press, 1991)
This modern edition of Dewey's classic essay, originally written in 1900 explores the role of school and society by one of America's greatest educational philosophers. Although *School and Society* has been published in various editions over the years, this edition restores a "lost" chapter that had been edited out of the original back in 1915.

Education and the Cult of Efficiency
Raymond Callahan (Chicago: University of Chicago Press, 1962)
A groundbreaking study of the organization and control of schools in the early twentieth century.

Tinkering toward Utopia: A Century of Public School Reform
David Tyack and Larry Cuban (Cambridge, MA: Harvard University Press, 1995)
An analysis of the role of reform in American public education.

The Power of Their Ideas: Lessons for America from a Small School in Harlem
Deborah Meier (Boston: Beacon Press, 1995)
One of the United States' most innovative educators talks about reform and her work in schools, offering an optimistic picture of the possibilities of public education. The author offers lessons grounded in her own experience.

The Manufactured Crisis
David C. Berliner and Bruce Biddle (Reading, MA: Addison-Wesley, 1995)
A controversial and critical analysis of recent criticisms of American education, including an exploration of issues surrounding accountability and student achievement.

Log On

A Certain Logic: Selected Works of John Dewey
http://spartan.ac.brocku.ca/~lward/Dewey
> As part of The Mead Project at Brock University, an extensive collection of some of the greatest foundation documents in history, A Certain Logic includes the writings of some of Dewey's greatest works, including *School and Society.*

American School Board Journal
www.asbj.com
> The website for the National School Board Association's monthly journal, an invaluable resource for those interested in exploring contemporary issues facing schools.

Council of Chief State School Officers
www.ccsso.org
> The Council of Chief State School Officers is a national organization for state school officers. This site provides information on policy, standards in teacher education, available resources, opportunities for special funding, and much more.

National Association of State Boards of Education
www.nasbe.org
> The National Association of State Boards of Education is the main organization in the United States for state boards and departments of education. Its website provides links to state boards throughout the country, as well as valuable policy information.

National Center for Educational Statistics: Quick Tables and Figures
http://nces.ed.gov/quicktables
> The National Center for Educational Statistics offers many useful resources online. One of the most useful is its search engine, which provides quick access to more than 17,000 tables and figures identifying basic demographic trends in American education.

School District Demographics
http://nces.ed.gov/surveys/sdds/index.asp
> This site provides geographic and demographic data at the K–12 level for every school district in the United States. Besides general population profiles, the site provides access to maps of school districts. Among the most useful features of the site is the ability to automatically compare the demographic profiles of different school districts from across the country.

Write On

> *"We raise cattle in Nebraska, and one thing that we've learned is that you can't fatten cattle by putting them on a scale. You have to pay attention to the diet."*
> —Nebraska woman, at a speech given by Elliott Eisner

Think for a moment about this comment made to Elliott Eisner, a professor of education at Stanford University, after he gave a lecture in Nebraska on evaluation and the standards movement. In your journal, explain what point this woman is trying to make. What does her comment have to do with the accountability and standards movement?

OBSERVATION GUIDE

TEACH: LINKING THEORY TO PRACTICE

Linking Theory to Practice

Objective: To explore school culture

School (use code name): _____   Observer: _____

Grade Level Observed: _____   Date: _____

Subject Taught: _____   Time In: _____   Time Out: _____

Directions: In this observation activity you will conduct a general observation of a school. Your purpose will be to identify the general characteristics of the school and the influence of the community in which it is located. Before you visit the school, see whether the school has a Web site you can visit. Also see whether a profile of the school is available online through a school or district Web site. Use these questions as a guide and create some of your own, using this chapter to assist you. Use your findings to write a brief summary describing the school and its social characteristics.

1. What is the general neighborhood in which the school is located like?

2. Who primarily attends the school? What is the racial, ethnic, social, and economic background of those attending the school?

3. Is the character of the school influenced by the community in which it is located? If so, how?

4. Describe the physical characteristics of the school. Is it well kept and orderly? Do you see any problems?

5. Would you enjoy attending the school? Might you like to teach there? Explain your reasons.

Connecting with INTASC: Principle 5

Classroom Motivation and Management: The teacher uses an understanding of individual and group motivation and behavior to create a learning environment that encourages positive social interaction, active engagement in learning, and self-motivation.

Based on your observations of the schools and surrounding communities, how would you rate the culture of the schools? Do you feel they've created a positive learning environment for the students? Arrange to speak with one or two teachers and ask them how they set up their classrooms to motivate learning.

7

The Professional and Ethical Context of Teaching

Who am I? What do I believe?

THINK ABOUT THIS:

Have you ever thought about what it would be like to be a lawyer or a nurse? Have you ever tried to imagine what it would be like to be a movie producer or the president of a large corporation? You probably have some general ideas about what it might be like to have these jobs but have very little actual knowledge about what it is really like to work in these fields. If you were asked what it is like to be a teacher, you would probably have a much clearer idea. This is because almost all of us have been attending schools for years and have been able to see firsthand the work of teachers. What do you think teachers actually do? What is their work actually about?

> "Teachers teach because they care. Teaching young people is what they do best. It requires long hours, patience, and care."
>
> Horace Mann

Anyone who has attended school regularly has had the chance to observe teachers on a firsthand basis for thousands of hours over the normal 12 years spent in elementary and secondary school. You have seen teachers formally and informally. You have seen them work with different age groups and teach different subjects. Yet, there is much that you probably do not know about some of the things teachers must deal with behind the scenes. In the following chapter we will look at the role of teachers in American society. In doing so, we will try to answer the following key questions:

Key Questions

1. What is the history of teaching?
2. What is good teaching?
3. What ethical issues do teachers face?
4. What are the legal rights of teachers?

t may surprise you to learn something about the attitudes that the public, and even teachers themselves, have about the teaching profession. To some extent, you need to step back from your own experiences in going to school and regularly observing teachers in your classrooms. You need to think about teaching in different settings with students who are different from the cultural and social groups you are most familiar with. It may help to learn about the history of teaching and about the forces that currently shape and define the profession. You need to know about the stereotypes that exist about teaching. While all teachers at the kindergarten through high school level share certain things in common, there are many different teaching experiences in the United States and many different definitions of what it means to be a teacher.

WHAT IS THE HISTORY OF TEACHING?

Teaching is among the oldest of all professions. Records identify teachers as far back as 3000 B.C. in the ancient Sumerian city of Erech (Kramer, 1989). While technologies and curricular content have changed profoundly since antiquity, the actual act of teaching has probably changed very little. Teachers have always been dispensers of knowledge. They are responsible for communicating fundamental values about the culture in which they live and teach. Typically they teach groups of students rather than individuals. As a result, they have often been concerned with issues of discipline and management. Teachers are usually involved in the evaluation of their students. Ideally they are concerned not only with providing instruction, but also with learning themselves through the process of sharing and dialogue.

TEACHING AND THE COMMON SCHOOL MOVEMENT

During the seventeenth and eighteenth centuries, teaching was dominated by men. With the industrialization of states such as Massachusetts and Connecticut during the first half of the nineteenth century, people became interested in setting up *Common Schools* that would be open to everyone. They would provide basic skills in reading, writing, and arithmetic, as well as a foundation in civic values and history. Such goals were extremely important to a new country with a constant flow of new immigrants, as well as the need to develop businesses and manufacturing.

Universal common schooling—that is, public schools—were in place throughout the North, and much of the Midwest, by the beginning of the Civil War (1861–1865). Not only did the establishment of these schools require the creation of an infrastructure of buildings and administrators, but also large numbers of teachers had to be hired. Many young women were recruited into the profession.

These young women were encouraged to become teachers for a number of reasons. To begin with, they were an inexpensive source of labor, since women could be hired for far less money than men. Employment opportunities for women during the nineteenth century—particularly professional options—were limited. Besides nursing, teaching was one of the few professions open to women. Many women entered the profession through an apprenticeship. In rural schools, for example, a young girl, twelve or thirteen years of age, would work as an assistant to the regular teacher. If she proved talented, on graduation she would be given her own class to teach. Typically, she herself had had only 6 to 8 years of schooling.

The first *normal school* for training teachers was opened in Lexington, Massachusetts, in 1839. Normal schools, which derived their name from the French *école normale* or "model school," provided students a year or two of training beyond elementary school.

THE NEW SCHOOL-MISTRESS.—[DRAWN BY MISS JENNIE BROWNSCOMBE.]

Along with nursing, teaching was one of the very few career options available for women in the 19th century. They were encouraged by society to become teachers because of the inexpensiveness of their labor.

They were set up to train young students—mostly women—to become elementary school teachers. Many normal schools evolved into colleges and schools of education, becoming the foundation for the development of larger colleges and universities.

TEACHING AS A FEMINIZED PROFESSION

Public schoolteaching at the elementary level was a feminized profession by the end of the Civil War, when it was dominated numerically by women. Historically, in the United States, feminized professions have reflected patterns of gender discrimination. As a result, teacher salaries have been kept relatively low—reflecting the devaluation of women's work. This situation began to change in the 1960s with the civil and women's rights movements. As the status of women in American society has changed, so too has the status of teachers changed.

Approximately 75% of all teachers in public and private schools are women, more than in most other countries (Grant & Murray, 1999). Throughout much of the country, until the late 1940s, female teachers were required to resign from their work if they got married. Today, three-fourths of American teachers are married (Grant & Murray, 1999). Until the late 1960s, female teachers were usually supervised by male administrators.

While 32% of all students in American schools are African American, Hispanic, Asian American, or Native American, only about 12% of teachers come from minority populations, as Whites dominate teaching. This fact has important consequences, as many teachers are culturally mismatched with the students they teach. This situation contributes to the phenomenon of American teachers teaching "other people's children" (Delpit, 1995).

According to the American Federation of Teachers (AFT), the average teacher salary in 2000–2001 in the United States was $43,250. Connecticut had the highest average salary at $53,507 per year, followed by California with an average salary of $52,480. The lowest average salary of $30,265 was in South Dakota (AFT, 2001). Health and retirement benefits typically add 25% to these figures. For 2000, the average family income in the United States

"Instead of observing your teaching, I'm going to install a Web cam in your classroom."

Courtesy of Aaron Bacall, *The Lighter Side of Technology in Education*, p. 2. Copyright 2003 by Aaron Bacall. Reprinted by permission of Corwin Press Inc.

was $42,228. Thus a teacher who is the sole worker in his or her family is at the center of the average middle-class income in the United States (DeNavas-Walt & Cleveland, 2002). While salaries have risen slightly since 2000 (see Table 2.2, p. 33), health insurance costs have risen four times as much, leaving less disposable income (AFT, 2004).

TEACHER EMPLOYMENT CYCLES

Teacher supply and demand has always been an important issue for the profession, and the teaching profession has been characterized in the United States by relatively easy entry and exit. Throughout much of the twentieth century a common employment pattern for female teachers was to teach for a few years after completing an education program, then drop out to marry and have children. They often returned to teaching once their children reached school age. This model, while beneficial to many women, also tended to deflate their salaries because salary levels in the professions are usually correlated to the number of years of work and experience. The easy-entrance-and-exit model is becoming less common among female teachers in the United States. Although they continue to marry and have children, fewer women are dropping out of the profession to raise their children, or at least are doing so for shorter periods of time.

During the 1960s, a large shortage of teachers followed the population explosion after World War II, the period known as the "baby boom." As children born after 1945 entered the schools, they created an increased demand for teachers. This population bubble burst, however, in the early 1970s, and there was an oversupply of teachers.

A teacher shortage exists when there are not enough certified teachers to teach a specific subject in the public schools. Teacher shortages are the direct result of rising student enrollments, retirements, high rates of teacher attrition, and increased demand for improved student performance and reduced class size. As has been discussed in earlier chapters, government estimates indicate that there will be a need for approximately 2 to 2.5 million teachers in the United States by 2010. Subject areas in the greatest demand include math, science, special education, and multicultural education. Urban and rural schools, in particular, will face a serious shortage of qualified teachers (U.S. Department of Education, 1998).

INTASC

Principle #9

Professional Commitment and Responsibility: The teacher is a reflective practitioner who continually evaluates the effects of his/her choices and actions on others (students, parents, and other professionals in the learning community) and who actively seeks out opportunities to grow professionally.

WHAT IS GOOD TEACHING?

In the 1989 movie *Dead Poets Society*, set in 1959, Robin Williams plays a young teacher at an elite college preparatory school called Welton Academy, a very traditional school. In a speech to the students at the beginning of the school year, the school's headmaster greets the students at the opening assembly, "One hundred years ago in 1859, 41 boys came to this school and were asked the same question that now greets you at the start of this semester: 'What are the four pillars?'" To the question, the students answer in unison: "Tradition. Honor. Discipline. Excellence." The headmaster then tells them, "The key to your success rests on our four pillars. These are the bywords of this school and they will become the cornerstones of your lives."

Although teacher John Keating (played by Williams) attended Welton as a student, he does not subscribe to many of its conservative and traditional educational models. He teaches in a nontraditional fashion that encourages students to reject the rote and uncreative models of learning at the school and to follow their dreams and live life to its fullest. Neil Perry, more than any other student, embraces Mr. Keating's approach, and a conflict

Education Matters

Schools Designed for Teachers?

What would a school designed for teachers actually look like and why would it make a difference? Schools in this country haven't changed in design since the turn of the last century. The average school in America is 40 years old; as recently as 1990 more than 60% of schools have been renovated or replaced, but they are only newer versions of the old building structures. The old cookie-cutter building with teachers in separate rooms repeated all over the building actually keeps teachers and students separated from each other all day. A few districts in the country are rethinking the old schoolhouse format and experimenting with an architectural style that brings teachers together. This newer concept has teachers in Aurora, Illinois, excited.

The idea is that the school becomes more of a laboratory setting, with clear glass between classrooms and open access to other groups of students. This breaks down teacher isolation and promotes collaboration and sharing. A new middle school in Roseville, California, included office space for every teacher in a centralized location and a planned staff lounge. A professional library with computer worktables and desks with seminar rooms are all part of the design.

The Education Issue:　Can the design of a school change teacher behavior?

How Schools Designed for Teachers Affect Teachers and Students

Does school design make a difference to teachers? Absolutely! Morale is high and student performance continues to improve. The staff report that it is a bit scary at first for teachers to be out in the open, but the classrooms of the future will be more like architectural design studios than the classrooms of today. Proponents of the work agree that buildings can help foster staff development and collaboration. If teachers are happy and productive they will work harder with students. Professional development ties to student learning. If rooms are designed for teachers to sit in a circle and share student work, they are more likely to do so consistently. Analyzing student work is a first step in correcting teaching and setting new goals for students.

What's Your Opinion?

1. What did your classrooms look like?

2. Would you like to work in open space or glass areas?

3. Why might teachers not like this design?

4. How could this design actually change behavior?

---

over Neil's guidance emerges. Neil's father is sending him to the school at great personal sacrifice to help him get into a good college and begin a course of study to become a doctor—something his father wants, but Neil does not. When Neil pursues his interest in acting and participates in a school play, against his father's wishes, a major conflict ensues between Neil and his father, as well as the school, Mr. Keating in particular. Neil is so conflicted by the internal and external struggles that he is moved to take drastic action and a tragedy results.

In opposing the dictates and traditions of the school, was Mr. Keating a bad teacher? Did he serve Neil's best interests? Neil's actions suggest that Keating, Neal's father, and the school, all failed Neil in one way or another. Likewise, an argument could be made that Neil failed himself. Was the school bad? Whereas Keating may have been a bad teacher for Neil, could he have been good for other students? Could he have been a good teacher in another school?

MODELS OF TEACHING

How the local community, and society in general, perceives the roles of teachers and the respect the community gives teachers varies a great deal depending on a number of factors, including personal expectations, individual experiences, and professional backgrounds to name just a few. People want and expect different things from teachers, which means teachers wear a number of different hats, both in the classroom and in the community.

INTASC

Principle #1

Knowledge of Subject Matter: The teacher understands the central concepts, tools of inquiry, and structures of the subject being taught and can create learning experiences that make these aspects of subject matter meaningful for students.

- **The Teacher as Expert**   The "teacher as expert" model, in which the teacher is primarily a conveyor of information, is just one of several models of teaching that define a teacher's work. This model is commonly found in higher education, in which knowledge of subject matter is extremely important, and people recognize the work and effort required to obtain an advanced degree. In general, all teachers have been recognized for their knowledge expertise to some degree. After all, parents turn over the responsibility for their children's education to teachers. Therefore, even at a most basic level, there is some recognition of the teacher, and the school system as a whole, as an "expert" in this undertaking. Teachers of certain disciplines, in particular, may command more respect for their expertise. For example, high school science and mathematics teachers often fit this model. Teachers in other disciplines, such as kindergarten, may be recognized or valued less for their academic expertise but more for other qualities that define other models of teaching (Grasha, 1994).

- **Teaching as a Moral Craft**   Educator Alan Tom argues that teaching is a "moral craft" in which teachers need to be "reflective, diligent and skillful" (Tom, 1984). The nature of their work requires that they become involved in the lives of the students they teach. For Tom, scientific and artistic models of teaching are inadequate to explain what teachers really do. Teachers make complex and moral judgments involving expert knowledge and reflection, as well as on-the-spot judgments—much the same way that craftspeople such as carpenters and cabinetmakers constantly evaluate and reassess their work.

  Related to the idea of teaching as a moral craft is the concept of **teaching as a vocation.** Underlying this concept is the idea that teaching is a "calling"—something people are drawn to or compelled to do. Describing teaching as a vocation puts a different spin on the occupation than when it is described as a "job," "work," a "career," or a "profession." The concept of vocation "presupposes public service" (Hansen, 1995). The idea of public service is fundamental to how most teachers define their work.

INTASC

Principle #2

Knowledge of Human Development and Learning: The teacher understands how children learn and develop, and can provide learning opportunities that support their intellectual, social, and personal development.

- **Teaching as an Act of Caring**   Teachers are expected to be sympathetic and friendly to students. Part of their role is that of mentoring and coaching. But simply caring about students is not enough. For the educational philosopher Nel Noddings, the main goal of teaching and the schools should be to nurture children—to help them grow and develop. In her book *Caring: A Feminine Approach to Ethics and Moral Education* (1984), Noddings argues that teaching should focus on the act of caring. Caring represents an interaction between people in which an individual (in this case the teacher) puts personal needs aside in favor of the needs of another (students).

  Noddings describes teachers as "all caring," which means that the teacher cares more about students than about the content of instruction. The teaching of skills and knowledge, however, is not necessarily disregarded by Noddings' caring teacher. A **caring teacher,** by definition, is concerned with the transfer of knowledge, but the needs of students come above all else.

- **The Teacher as Authority Figure**   In this model, the teacher sets standards and ways of doing things. To some extent, this model can be seen as rule driven. Subject matter is studied because it is required by the curriculum. Strict rules are followed. While this may seem an oppressive and unthinking model sometimes, it is probably necessary in certain fields. For example, a teacher working in driver education needs to have students follow precise guidelines, as does a chemistry laboratory teacher.

- **The Teacher as Personal Model**   The concept of "teacher as personal model" involves the teacher instructing by means of direct example. This model could be represented by an art teacher who shows a student how to draw a precise curve in a drawing or how to throw a pot on a potter's wheel. It could be a religious teacher who sets a personal model or standard for behavior. Coaches and physical education teachers often must demonstrate techniques required for successful performance of a skill. In this way, they are modeling the behavior they seek from their students.

- **The Teacher as Facilitator**   "Teachers as facilitators" guide and facilitate the process of learning. This model is also associated with the idea of mentoring. An example of a facilitating teacher would be an English teacher showing students how to be a creative writer, or a university professor showing students the process of research.

- **The Teacher as Delegator**   In this model, the teacher assigns tasks for students to complete. They are pointed in the appropriate direction and expected to do the work on their own. A professor providing a reading course for a student would fit this model. A high school teacher overseeing a student's work in an independent literature course would be delegating the workload and expectations, but the bulk of the responsibility falls on the student. The teacher monitors the student's progress.

    None of these models functions separately from the others; they are typically merged together. Good teachers learn to employ each model like a tool used for different purposes or at different times. The best teachers draw on all of these models depending on the needs of their students and the classrooms where they work.

DEFINING A PERSONAL PHILOSOPHY OF EDUCATION

Every teacher needs to define a personal **philosophy of education**. For the ancient Greeks, the term *philosophy* literally meant "love of wisdom." A philosophy of education can therefore be conceived of as thinking wisely about education, or more specifically, about the act of teaching.

- **Deciding on a Personal Philosophy of Education**   At the graduate level you may take a specific course in the philosophy of education. In Western culture, hundreds of great authors have written about the key concepts and questions that are fundamental to the field of education, from the ancient Greeks Plato and Aristotle to the French Enlightenment thinker Jean-Jacques Rousseau. The American John Dewey, the Brazilian Paulo Freire, and the American Nel Noddings have all written about a philosophy of education. Each of these theorists may be able to help you determine your own philosophy of education and teaching.

    Do you believe, for example, that children should be left largely to their own devices and unencumbered by the values and beliefs of the larger society? If so, then the ideas of the philosopher Jean-Jacques Rousseau (1712–1778) would interest you. In his book *Émile*, first published in 1762, Rousseau argued that education should not be primarily about imparting knowledge to the child, but about drawing out of the child what is naturally there. Teachers should act as guides and encourage their students to follow their own interests in learning, rather than be tyrants who cram knowledge and information into their students. Rousseau believed that if children were raised in a more natural environment, ours would be a more just and natural society.

- **Dewey's "My Pedagogic Creed"**   Rousseau influenced many educational thinkers, including philosopher John Dewey (1859–1952). In 1897, Dewey wrote an article for *The School Journal* titled "My Pedagogic Creed." Dewey's piece is divided into five sections, or articles. In Article I, "What Education Is," he wrote:

> I believe that all education proceeds by the participation of the individual in the social consciousness of the race. This process begins unconsciously almost at birth, and is continually shaping the individual's powers, saturating his consciousness, forming his habits, training his ideas, and arousing his feelings and emotions. Through this unconscious education the individual gradually comes to share in the intellectual and moral resources which humanity has succeeded in getting together. He becomes an inheritor of the funded capital of civilization. The most formal and technical education in the world cannot safely depart from this general process. It can only organize it or differentiate it in some particular direction. (Dewey, 1897)

I N T A S C

Principle #9

Professional Commitment and Responsibility: The teacher is a reflective practitioner who continually evaluates the effects of his/her choices and actions on others (students, parents, and other professionals in the learning community) and who actively seeks out opportunities to grow professionally.

BUILDING ON EDUCATIONAL FOUNDATIONS

Teaching and Popular Culture

Americans get many of their ideas from the media, including impressions we may have about the nature of schools and the teaching profession in general. This is particularly true in terms of what they understand teachers do in their day-to-day work. The film *Stand and Deliver* is a typical example of an influential "teacher movie" based on the life of a real-life teacher.

In *Stand and Deliver* (1988), Jaime Escalante leaves a job in the corporate world to become a high school mathematics teacher in East Los Angeles. Working against all odds, Escalante demands, and gets, excellent work from his students—helping them to eventually succeed on the advanced-placement exam in calculus.

In the movie, Escalante is driven by a vision of his students succeeding in his course at all costs. But this "mission" leaves his personal life a mess, with no time for his family. It also shows us that he disregards the fact that students are taking courses other than his and that he refuses to cooperate with other teachers and the administration in his school. Escalante eventually has a heart attack after a few years of teaching and leading his students to high scores in mathematics.

While Escalante may have succeeded in teaching his students mathematics, his approach was both idiosyncratic and ultimately self-destructive. His is not a model you should follow if you intend to have a long and effective career as a teacher. While his passion and aspirations for his students was admirable and certainly inspiring, his methods were breakneck and ultimately unrealistic.

Escalante continues to be involved in education today, running workshops on math and science. His story, and the stories found in other teacher films, are indeed messages about the impact one person can have on the lives of young people. But as you watch films about teachers and the work they do in schools, you need to keep in mind that films are about entertainment and not necessarily about reality. As with all programs, watch with a critical eye. Films often distort and misrepresent the realities of teaching. The average teacher in the average school district in America would never be able to take some of the steps or measures with students that Escalante did. This was a special situation that called for special actions.

In Article II, "What the School Is," Dewey argued that "the school is primarily a social institution. Education being a social process, the school is simply that form of community life in which all those agencies are concentrated that will be most effective in bringing the child to share in the inherited resources of the race, and to use his own powers for social ends." Dewey further argued that "education, therefore, is a process of living and not a preparation for future living." Schooling fails because it neglects the idea of the school as a form of community life:

> It conceives the school as a place where certain information is to be given, where certain lessons are to be learned, or where certain habits are to be formed. The value of these is conceived as lying largely in the remote future; the child must do these things for the sake of something else he is to do; they are mere preparation. As a result they do not become a part of the life experience of the child and so are not truly educative. (Dewey, 1897)

Dewey's "My Pedagogic Creed" is a long, formal document written in an earlier historical period. Yet it remains an important educational document that questions, in fundamental ways, how and why we educate people and what is the fundamental purpose of schooling.

● **Formulating Your Own Philosophy of Education**   As a teacher, and as part of your general program in education, you will be asked to create a personal philosophy of education. Your credo or philosophy should not be confused with an objective or professional mission statement, which is related but different. A personal objective or mission statement is much shorter and essentially defines what you want to do as a professional—the types of students you want to work with, your professional goals, and so forth, for example, "I want to work with students with special needs" or "I am interested in teaching high school history and doing coaching on the side."

Your philosophy-of-education statement will not be based on state or federal regulations; instead it will be informed by your past experiences, your personal beliefs, and your personal disposition. In formulating it, you will seek answers to the following types of questions and then articulate those answers as part of your philospohy: "What do I believe?" "Why am I becoming a teacher?" "What do I wish to accomplish in the classroom?" "Based on my knowledge, training, and experience, what do I believe are the best methods for teaching? Why?" Take this assignment seriously; ask yourself difficult questions and allow yourself the luxury of reflecting on these questions. The purpose of this assignment is to uncover your own beliefs and dispositions so you can examine them before entering the classroom. Your philosophy will affect how you interact with students and set up your learning environment.

As you formulate your philosophy, think back on your own experiences. How did your experiences in school and in your family setting help shape your ideals? All of these experiences are part of your memory bank and will influence the ways in which you operate in your own classroom.

You can turn to many sources for help when developing your personal philosophy. You may take a philosophy of education course, in which you will review the major theories that educators have developed over the years about children, teaching, and learning. In your studies you may focus on the work of a single educator, such as Maria Montessori or John Dewey, or a more contemporary figure such as Nel Noddings. You also will further explore the fundamental educational philosophies of education introduced in Chapter 5 throughout your preparation program.

As you prepare to become a teacher, it is important to recognize how your own thoughts and beliefs, in combination with theories and practices you learn along the way, will coalesce to form your own belief system. Taking time to reflect on how this affects who you are will influence what you bring to the profession. Figure 7.1 on page 208 provides an example of the philosophies of two student teachers.

What do I believe?

"The mediocre teacher tells; the good teacher explains; the great teacher demonstrates; the excellent teacher inspires."

WILLIAM ARTHUR WARD

THINK ABOUT THIS:
Determining the characteristics that make a teacher "good" is a difficult process. Every parent has expectations for what teachers can or will do with their child. Sometimes all that can be asked of a teacher is to make a difference in a child's life, in some way, because every child needs something. The difficult task is discovering what each child needs.

SHARE and COMPARE:
Think about the things you consider important as a teacher. What do you hope to accomplish? What influence do you want to have on children's lives? As you work through your thoughts, share them with one other student in your class and see what you have in common.

FIGURE 7.1

Philosophies of Education

EDUCATIONAL PHILOSOPHY

If ever there were a teacher,
As perfect as could be,
She would strive to make a difference
In the children that she sees.

Reading, writing, history
Science, art and math,
All important subjects
That starts them on their path.

As well as all the others
Like social skills and play,
These too are important
To get them on their way.

Modeling behavior,
Making kids aware
That with a little effort,
They too will learn to care.

She'll be the one to make them see
Their efforts surely pay.
All kids can learn things every day
At different rates, in different ways.

She'll have them think outside the box,
Set expectations high,
Some may not think they're capable
But she expects them all to try.

These individuals have different needs,
Are surely very smart.
Although at different levels,
They'll be growing from the start.

Since experience is crucial,
Varied it will be,
But hands-on is one way she'll go
For it is something kids can see.

A community of learners
Is something she will stress.
The whole class will contribute
And she'll expect no less

Remember they are children first,
This she can't forget.
They must enjoy it as they learn,
She'll take care of all the rest.

She must remember to believe
In all children and herself,
Since this belief will carry through
Her teachings and all else.

Not only will the children learn,
But she will learn as well,
For a teacher who pursues learning,
Shows growth, as time will tell.

On top of all things she does,
There is a hidden fact . . .
That what goes on behind the scenes
Is a truly selfless act.

If ever there were a teacher
As perfect as could be
She would strive to make a difference
And this teacher would be me.

—Renee N. Cachuela, M.Ed.

MY TEACHING PHILOSOPHY

It's as easy as ABC . . .

A ctive; teacher must move around the room, get involved, be curious.

B e prepared

C atch them being good. Focus on the positive; do not point out the negative.

D iscipline with dignity. Use the long talk; show the child respect, not shame.

E quity: Be aware of culture, sex, ethnicity, religion. Learn from differences.

F lexibility: Not everything goes as planned. Look for "teachable moments."

G roup collaboration: With parents, students, and teachers.

H umor: He who "Laughs, Lasts!"

I nnovative, interesting, and intriguing instruction

J ob goes beyond the classroom: Constant learning, research, and seminars.

K nowledge of curriculum & students. Be honest if unsure of answers.

L east restrictive environment.

M odel: "Practice what you preach." Children learn through observation.

N ever give up on a student, only the practice.

O pen minded, organized, order, observation.

P rofessionalism, problem solving: "Sorry isn't enough."

Q uality education: Meet the standards and needs of self and students.

R einforcers: "Fit the child": Social, tangible, positive, negative, and PRAISE!

S mile: Teaching is a joy. If you stop smiling, *evaluate* the situation and change.

T alk and communicate with parents, teachers, and students.

U nderstand students; look for cues to their thoughts and actions.

V alue the student: Student-centered classroom and learning.

W ho are we? Celebrate diversity: What makes each of us unique?

X ercise power: Attractive, rewarding, expert, legitimate, and coercive.

Y esterday is in the past: Start each day off with a blank slate.

Z ip-a-dee doo da: Teaching is FUN; make sure learning is too!

—Amy Tavaras

WHAT ETHICAL ISSUES DO TEACHERS FACE?

Establishing a personal philosophy of education will also help you when faced with ethical issues as a teacher. All individuals face ethical issues and dilemmas in their personal lives. Teachers face additional ethical issues in the classroom and in their profession in general. All professionals (physicians, attorneys, educators) have a fair amount of discretionary authority that they must exercise in order to practice their professions. Society grants professionals the latitude to use their own judgment in exercising authority because years of study by the profession are reflected in meeting licensing requirements.

Society assumes that professionals will exercise their judgment in an ethical manner. Teachers are expected to reflect honesty, trust, confidentiality, fairness, responsibility, and respect for others in their decision making. Although state laws and school board policies regulate certain decisions that teachers may or may not make, every aspect of professional behavior cannot be regulated by an external rule; that is the nature of a profession. Teachers, like other professionals, are trusted to make decisions affecting students and curriculum fairly and ethically. However, instruction in **professional ethics** is still not included in most teacher preservice curricula (Campbell, 1997).

ETHICS IN THE CLASSROOM

Students of education find it easy to understand what behavior by a teacher is illegal. Sexual harassment of students is illegal, and school board policies or state law detail what constitutes this behavior. Teachers know that if they are convicted of a felony crime they will lose their teaching licenses. What constitutes ethical versus unethical behavior, however, is often much more complicated for future teachers to understand. For example, teachers frequently receive small gifts from students at the end of the school year. If these are ethical for teachers to accept, however, is it appropriate for a teacher to accept a $500 gift from the parents of a student who is doing poorly in a class shortly before grades are issued? What if the parents stipulate that the gift is not intended to influence the teacher's judgment? Should this affect the teacher's decision to accept the gift?

● **Making Ethical Judgments as a Teacher**
Making ethical judgments is not easy. It involves the application of values to real-life situations and being able to resolve some measure of ambiguity. For example, suppose a well-meaning teacher tells the parents of a 7-year-old ESL student to speak only English to the child at home. What are the ethical dimensions of this request? The teacher logically feels that the outcome of this advice would be good for the student. While the teacher's intention may be good, has the teacher thought about what this may do to the dynamics of parent/child communication when parents feel forced to communicate only in their second (weaker) language? The parents may sound like adults in their first language, but may be able to communicate only with a child's vocabulary in English. How will this affect the parents' image in the eyes of the child? If the parents comply with the teacher's request, will the child be able to maintain the non-English language and grow up to be bilingual?

What was apparently a simple, commonsense request by the teacher may turn out to have a num-

As a teacher you have authority and the rights that come with it. Students also have rights, and you need to be respectful of them. Always approach your work with students with an attitude of professionalism, responsibility, confidentiality, and fairness.

INTASC

Principle #9

Professional Commitment and Responsibility: The teacher is a reflective practitioner who continually evaluates the effects of his/her choices and actions on others (students, parents, and other professionals in the learning community) and who actively seeks out opportunities to grow professionally.

ber of ethical ramifications. Yet teachers in schools in the United States give out this advice to parents on a daily basis. Often, the full ramifications of such requests haven't been analyzed carefully. What if teachers were to learn that Hispanic students in U.S. schools who speak Spanish at home academically outperform Hispanic students who speak English at home (Soto, 1997; Gándara, 1995; Zentella, 1997)? Would knowing the results of this research affect the advice teachers give parents of English language learners?

Teachers who practice their profession without a clear understanding of the moral and ethical dimensions of teaching are playing the role of "technicians" (Ewing, 2001). In this role, teachers carry out classroom routines that are unconnected to their students' lives. While there may be legitimate questions regarding how much involvement teachers should have in their students' lives, they should practice Nel Noddings' "ethic of caring" (Noddings, 1988, 1990). To do this, teachers need to know enough about their students to help them construct personal meaning out of the material they learn and to establish a climate that lets students know that their futures really matter.

● **Codes of Ethics for Teachers**   Major professional organizations such as the **National Education Association** and the **American Federation of Teachers** provide codes of ethics to guide decision-making by their members. (See Figure 7.2.) A **code of ethics** is a statement of principles that teachers must interpret and apply to daily situations. Therefore, codes of ethics do not specifically address the details of an ethical dilemma teachers may face. Codes of ethics are helpful guidelines, but teachers cannot escape taking personal responsibility for their own ethical decision making.

Ironically, no code of ethics exists for teacher educators (Freitas, 1999). College and university teacher education programs vary a great deal in their examination of ethical issues teachers face. As a result, there is no guarantee of fundamental agreement among future teachers about what constitutes ethical behavior. Two researchers found that the education majors they taught were not at all in agreement that "teaching is a profoundly moral and ethical behavior" (Broidy & Jones, 1998, p. 3). When they asked their students to identify ethical issues in a case study involving a censorship dispute in a junior high school, many responded with puzzlement; they did not see any ethical issues at all.

All teachers face ethical dilemmas sooner or later in their professional lives. These dilemmas occur "when teachers have to take action that benefits one party at the expense or inconvenience of another" (Freeman, 1998, p. 31). What values do teachers bring to bear in resolving these issues? How does the moral/ethical climate of the times affect how teachers behave?

● **Moral Reasoning**   The ability to engage in sound moral reasoning does not guarantee that a teacher will behave ethically, but it increases the probability of such behavior. In examining the moral reasoning of preservice and in-service teachers, Bloom (1976) found that moral reasoning among education majors was lower than among college students with other majors. After reviewing thirty studies, Diessner (1991) found that teachers were reasoning at the "principled" level 30% to 50% of the time. What is the practical impact of having teachers in classrooms with high or low levels of moral reasoning? Chang (1994) suggests the following:

Teachers with High Levels of Moral Reasoning:

1. Have a more democratic and humanistic view of student discipline.

2. Are better able to consider and accommodate different viewpoints.

3. Can better perceive students' feelings and needs.

4. Are more admired by their students and perceived as more friendly/cheerful.

5. Understand educational concepts more broadly and deeply.

FIGURE 7.2

NEA Code of Ethics

Code of Ethics of the Education Profession

Preamble

The educator, believing in the worth and dignity of each human being, recognizes the supreme importance of the pursuit of truth, devotion to excellence, and the nurture of the democratic principles. Essential to these goals is the protection of freedom to learn and to teach and the guarantee of equal educational opportunity for all. The educator accepts the responsibility to adhere to the highest ethical standards.

The educator recognizes the magnitude of the responsibility inherent in the teaching process. The desire for the respect and confidence of one's colleagues, of students, of parents, and of the members of the community provides the incentive to attain and maintain the highest possible degree of ethical conduct. The Code of Ethics of the Education Profession indicates the aspiration of all educators and provides standards by which to judge conduct.

The remedies specified by the NEA and/or its affiliates for the violation of any provision of this Code shall be exclusive and no such provision shall be enforceable in any form other than the one specifically designated by the NEA or its affiliates.

PRINCIPLE I—COMMITMENT TO THE STUDENT

The educator strives to help each student realize his or her potential as a worthy and effective member of society. The educator therefore works to stimulate the spirit of inquiry, the acquisition of knowledge and understanding, and the thoughtful formulation of worthy goals.

In fulfillment of the obligation to the student, the educator—

1. Shall not unreasonably restrain the student from independent action in the pursuit of learning.

2. Shall not unreasonably deny the student's access to varying points of view.

3. Shall not deliberately suppress or distort subject matter relevant to the student's progress.

4. Shall make reasonable effort to protect the student from conditions harmful to learning or to health and safety.

5. Shall not intentionally expose the student to embarrassment or disparagement.

6. Shall not on the basis of race, color, creed, sex, national origin, marital status, political or religious beliefs, family,

social or cultural background, or sexual orientation, unfairly
   a. Exclude any student from participation in any program
   b. Deny benefits to any student
   c. Grant any advantage to any student

7. Shall not use professional relationships with students for private advantage.

8. Shall not disclose information about students obtained in the course of professional service unless disclosure serves a compelling professional purpose or is required by law.

PRINCIPLE II—COMMITMENT TO THE PROFESSION

The education profession is vested by the public with a trust and responsibility requiring the highest ideals of professional service. In the belief that the quality of the services of the education profession directly influences the nation and its citizens, the educator shall exert every effort to raise professional standards, to promote a climate that encourages the exercise of professional judgment, to achieve conditions that attract persons worthy of the trust to careers in education, and to assist in preventing the practice of the profession by unqualified persons.

In fulfillment of the obligation to the profession, the educator—

1. Shall not in an application for a professional position deliberately make a false statement or fail to disclose a material fact related to competency and qualifications.

2. Shall not misrepresent his/her professional qualifications.

3. Shall not assist any entry into the profession of a person known to be unqualified in respect to character, education, or other relevant attribute.

4. Shall not knowingly make a false statement concerning the qualifications of a candidate for a professional position.

5. Shall not assist a noneducator in the unauthorized practice of teaching.

6. Shall not disclose information about colleagues obtained in the course of professional service unless disclosure serves a compelling professional purpose or is required by law.

7. Shall not knowingly make false or malicious statements about a colleague.

8. Shall not accept any gratuity, gift, or favor that might impair or appear to influence professional decisions or action.

Source: National Education Association. Retrieved May 6, 2005, from http://www2.nea.org/code.html

Teachers with Lower Levels of Moral Reasoning:

1. Hold a custodial-authoritarian view of student discipline.

2. View social issues only from their own or the school's viewpoints.

3. Are less able to discern student feelings and have poorer classroom climates.

4. Are less favorably perceived by their students.

5. Have a less profound grasp of educational concepts and are more likely to perceive teaching as benefiting groups rather than individuals.

It is important to have teachers in our classrooms who have high levels of moral/ethical reasoning. Is it fair, however, to ask why teacher preparation programs in the United States generally do not assess their candidates for these abilities and why curriculum to develop higher levels of moral/ethical reasoning is not more common? Moral reasoning can be significantly improved when these skills are taught and reinforced in the curriculum. When teachers function at lower levels of moral/ethical reasoning, "their moral thinking is subject to change depending upon school leaders or the atmosphere of the schools in which they serve" (Chang, 1994, p. 72).

ETHICS AND THE CURRICULUM

As you progressed through school, you probably expected teachers to provide a wide array of knowledge about the curriculum and to explore pertinent values and perspectives. While teachers cannot provide all the information that is germane to a subject, it is reasonable to expect that students receive a representative sample of the appropriate facts and information. An American literature class should include exposure to some works by African, Asian, Hispanic, and Native American authors. Teachers of American literature should include this content because failure to do so would deprive students of a well-balanced course in American literature. A literature course with significant selections by authors from these backgrounds will provide students with perspectives they would not necessarily be exposed to otherwise because these authors write about themes that are less prevalent in the mainstream literature. These authors also bring values and perspectives to bear on these themes that students may not otherwise obtain. But what if a teacher of American literature is not well versed in the works of authors from minority-group backgrounds? Is it ethical to omit this content from the curriculum simply because the teacher is unfamiliar with the minority works? One thing is certain: the gaps in the teacher's education on these literary topics will now be passed on to the students.

● **Values and the Curriculum**   There has always been some conflict in education circles between those who want to provide a value-free education (in order to avoid any chance of indoctrination) and those who want to teach a set of values (generally their own) to the nation's students. In examining this issue, two Australian educators note that "education itself is not neutral, but a value-laden, political act" (Andrew & Robottom, 2001, p. 778). They found the following:

1. Values are the object of study.

2. Values influence what is selected for study.

3. Values are the result of study.

Since societal values affect what is selected for study, they also affect what is omitted from the curriculum and what emphasis is given to various subjects. For example, most Western industrialized nations require high school graduates to have minimal conversational fluency in another language. This skill is often tested as one condition for college/university entrance. Is this true for students in the United States? If not, what values

A Student Teacher's Ethical Dilemma

Mary Davis had just completed her last semester prior to student teaching at State University. She was looking forward to her school assignment. She received a letter assigning her to Buttonwood Elementary School with Susan Torrey as her cooperating teacher. When Mary went to the school, Susan told her that she wanted Mary to watch a "master teacher" work for a week before giving her any class responsibilities. Mary was also told to "take notes" while Susan taught.

Dutifully, Mary began her observation week with notebook in hand. The first thing she noticed was that Susan was using whole-group instruction with her third graders for periods of almost an hour. This went against what Mary had learned in her educational psychology class about the attention span of young children. The students sat quietly because when there was any breach of classroom discipline, Susan would discipline that child in front of all of the others. Mary soon learned that nearly all of the students characterized Susan as a "mean teacher." Mary also noticed that Susan did not pay nearly as much attention to students of color as to the rest of the class.

After the week of observation, Susan told Mary that she would allow her to take over one subject per week for 6 weeks, after which Mary would have primary responsibility for all subjects. Susan told Mary that she would be observing Mary in the class and going over her plans with her, since she would have to write up an evaluation for the university at the end of the semester as the cooperating teacher.

At the end of the conference with Susan, Mary felt as if her stomach were tied in knots. She didn't want to alienate Susan or to receive a bad recommendation. Mary knew that the cooperating teacher's report was very important in determining her student teaching grade, and it would also be in her files that schools would want to see when she was looking for a job. But a great deal of what Susan described as "model teaching" was very different from many of the things Mary had learned in her university courses. Mary was concerned that if she modeled a teaching style significantly different from Susan's, it would be regarded as a rejection of Susan's approach to teaching.

Discussion Questions

Should Mary adopt Susan's teaching style for the semester and later use her own when she gets her first job? If Mary uses a teaching style derived from her university courses, how do you suggest that she approach a likely conflict with Susan?

Possibilities

It is not at all unusual that Mary would find herself working with a teacher whose teaching style might be different from what Mary learned in her college courses. Mary has been in Susan's class for one week; Susan has been in the classroom for several years and has developed a style that works for her in her classroom. Mary needs to be open to new ideas, even if they may actually be "old" ideas. Book knowledge does not always translate to the schoolroom as smoothly as it might seem while sitting in a university class.

On the other hand, having just been in a university setting, Mary may have greater access to the latest trends and research findings. As one cooperating teacher stated in a workshop, "We look to the student teachers as a resource of new information and ideas." Cooperating teachers expect their student teachers to have questions. Mary needs to speak openly with Susan and ask her about her methods, why she does things the way she does, and explore the possibility of trying some new strategies when she takes over some of the classes. It's important that Mary establish a good rapport with Susan to maximize her benefits from the experience. Student teaching is an opportunity for both parties to learn from each other. A good teacher has to be a communicator. This challenge is an opportunity for Mary to work on her communication skills.

Most important, Mary can't be changing her style just for the sake of getting a good recommendation. That's no different from a teacher who "teaches to the test" so students score well on state exams and the school looks good. The point of student teaching is to learn under the watchful eye of an experienced teacher. The cooperating teacher has been selected by the university student teaching program as someone they consider to be a good model. If Mary continues to be conflicted over her experience with Susan, then she needs to speak with her university's student teaching supervisor, who may have some helpful advice.

A couple of Web sites offer a venue for student teachers to share thoughts and ideas while working through the experience:

Teacher.Net—Student Teaching Chatboard
(http://teachers.net/mentors/student_teaching)

I Love Teaching (www.iloveteaching.com/steacher/)

Ethical Question

Do you see an ethical conflict between what may cause the fewest problems for Mary and what is best for her students during the student teaching semester? Why or why not?

influence the curricular differences and why are expectations of U.S. students different from those of their counterparts in the rest of the industrialized world?

All students in U.S. schools are required to take classes that explain their nation's history at various points in the curriculum before they graduate from high school. Given the redundancy of this curriculum, how many important Hispanic Americans can most U.S. high school graduates name after 12 years of study? How many can you name? If the answer is none, one, or two, has the curriculum (and those who taught it) been chosen and taught in an ethical and professional manner? How does this affect Hispanic and non-Hispanic students if both groups come away from 12 years of formal education with little or no knowledge about this nation's largest minority group?

● **Parental Pressures on Teachers**   Teachers may also be pressured by parents or administrators to provide recommendations for students to enter gifted education or advanced-placement courses. Accelerated education is seen by many parents as a desirable goal for their children. They may urge teachers to provide access to an accelerated curriculum even though the child may not be able to assimilate material at an accelerated rate. Should teachers go along with these requests to satisfy parents when the student is floundering or facing undue academic pressure?

Another ethical classroom dilemma may be posed if special needs students are mainstreamed into a classroom, and resources (teacher aides) that are generated by these students do not follow them into the mainstream classroom. National law requires that special-needs students be placed in the least restrictive environment that will provide for their academic needs. Sometimes teachers are thrust into situations in which they may want to provide for special-needs students as well as the rest of the class. They often find, however, that satisfying the requirements of both in a mainstream classroom with limited resources is beyond their abilities. They don't want to choose among their students, but ethically they find themselves in an untenable position.

● **Teaching as Helping**   People go into the teaching profession for a variety of reasons, but ideals and a desire to help humankind are generally high on their list of priorities. A study of British and American education majors found that both groups were idealistic and

Use a cooperative approach with parents to create relationships that are beneficial for the student.

believed in a universal set of moral principles to guide teaching. The British sample, however, tended to believe that in order to achieve "good," some individuals may be harmed. The American sample was more likely to believe that all individuals could achieve "good" without anyone being harmed (Deering, 1998, p. 356).

How we achieve the goal of training teachers who have high levels of moral reasoning and who behave ethically is open for discussion. Freeman (2000) suggests that the ethical dimension of a teacher preparation curriculum should not be left to chance. "Students benefit most from regularly planned, intentional, focused opportunities to apply ethical codes" (Freeman, 2000). Yet most teacher preparation programs do not give high priority to activities that stress ethical reasoning. It is comforting to note that when students are given ample opportunities to engage in moral and ethical reasoning activities as part of their college courses, their abilities improve significantly.

One dilemma for teacher educators is to maintain the idealism of students who want to enter teaching, while simultaneously presenting a curriculum that explores ethical issues and presents the reality of classrooms so that graduates do not enter teaching naively. Striking a balance between these two goals has always been a challenge. Current and future schools in the United States need teachers who are subject-matter competent and who have versatile pedagogical skills. It is equally important that teachers have high levels of moral/ethical reasoning and the behavior to match, in order to meet the needs of classrooms in the twenty-first century.

Who am I?

What do I believe?

"You're molding young people's minds. You're giving them an idea. . . . You're shaping their minds and their thought processes. You're seeing them change— become more social with society."

OSCAR, JUNIOR HIGH SCHOOL MATH TEACHER

THINK ABOUT THIS:

Being a teacher is not just about teaching subject matter, but also about shaping and molding children. When one teaches, one inevitably promotes different values and ways of looking at the world. In American schools, we teach children to be "good Americans," something that obviously would not be done in another country such as Canada or Cuba. Through schools we pass on the values and beliefs of the society.

SHARE and COMPARE:

Think for a moment about being a teacher and how you will shape and influence what children believe and what they understand about the world. What ethical issues will you face? What do you need to avoid? What will you need to do to accomplish your job? Discuss this issue with a friend or classmate.

INTASC

Principle #9

Professional Commitment and Responsibility: The teacher is a reflective practitioner who continually evaluates the effects of his/her choices and actions on others (students, parents, and other professionals in the learning community) and who actively seeks out opportunities to grow professionally.

WHAT ARE THE LEGAL RIGHTS OF TEACHERS?

Teachers, like students, do not lose their constitutional rights when they enter the classroom. As a result, teachers have the right to be politically active and even to publicly criticize the school system in which they work. If they do so, they must make sure that what they are saying is accurate. In the 1968 Supreme Court case of *Pickering v. Board of Education,* an Illinois high school teacher, John Pickering, was dismissed for writing a letter to a local newspaper that criticized the school board's use of funds to support athletics. According to the school board, numerous statements made by Pickering in his letter were false. The school board claimed that the publication of his letter was "detrimental to the efficient operation and administration of the schools of the district."

The Illinois court reviewed the proceedings to determine solely whether the board's findings were supported by substantial evidence and whether the board could reasonably conclude that the publication was "detrimental to the best interests of the schools." The court upheld the dismissal, rejecting Pickering's claim that his letter was protected by the First and Fourteenth Amendments. The court stated that as a teacher he had to refrain from making statements about the schools' operation "which in the absence of such position he would have an undoubted right to engage in." Pickering eventually appealed his dismissal to the Supreme Court.

The Supreme Court concluded that Pickering had been unfairly dismissed, and that his right to free speech concerning a public issue had been violated. Even though Pickering had made several inaccurate statements about the school board and its policies, he had not done so intentionally. Since his actions did not interfere with his effectiveness as a teacher or with the operation of his school, there were no grounds for his dismissal.

TEACHER TENURE

In general, the law protects teachers from arbitrary actions by school officials. In most school districts, teachers, if they perform satisfactorily, are **tenured** after a 3- to 5-year probationary period of employment. This means that they cannot be fired without cause. The concept of tenure guarantees that teachers are free to express their opinions without the fear of dismissal. This does not mean that tenured teachers can say whatever they want, but it does mean that teachers can be dismissed only for a cause defined by the law.

Tenure can be broken when "cause" can be shown that teachers are not fulfilling their duty. Illinois law states, for example, that a local school board has the power to dismiss teachers for "incompetency, cruelty, negligence, immorality or other sufficient cause and . . . whenever, in its opinion, the interests of the schools require it" (Fischer, Schimmel, & Kelly, 1999, p. 43). Incompetence, as grounds for firing a teacher, must be carefully documented. In other words, if a teacher is observed by a supervisor as having a serious problem with discipline, it must be demonstrated that this is a consistent problem, and not just a situation in which the teacher was "having a hard day." Teachers are expected to know the subjects that they teach. They can be dismissed for teaching inaccurate information or for being inadequately prepared. Once again, this situation must be shown to be an ongoing problem.

In the past, teachers could be fired by local communities for what was considered immoral conduct. Today, immoral conduct, as a cause for dismissal, must be shown to affect a teacher's effectiveness on the job. Thus, a female teacher could live out of wedlock with a man—a practice that might be objectionable to a majority of the community—and not be dismissed unless her living arrangement can be shown to interfere with her work. While this scenario is far less likely to arise today, the same cannot be said for gay or lesbian teachers living with their partners. A teacher's sexual orientation remains a very sensitive subject in

The principal or department chair will often observe your class instruction in order to offer feedback that will help you grow as a teacher. Good administrators use these opportunities to ensure quality instruction.

Through the Eyes of
Culturally Sensitive Teachers

Ethics and Cultural Sensitivity at River Shore Middle School

Myra Jones was one of the few African American teachers at River Shore Middle School in Canton. River Shore Middle students were mostly of middle to high socioeconomic status. One notable exception to this trend were African American students who were bused in from the neighboring community of Delmore. Myra brought her sixth-grade students to the orientation assembly for sixth graders held during the first week of class. It was run by Mr. Hobson, the assistant principal in charge of sixth graders. After the usual explanation of the campus map, school lockers, and policies for hall passes, the assembly took a very unusual turn. Mr Hobson stopped and said, "Now, I would like to turn my attention to you Delmore kids." (All teachers and most students realized that "Delmore kids" was synonymous with "African American students.") "You are in Canton now and I would like you to act civilized like the people in Canton. Look at the kinds of cars people in Canton drive. You need to act like Canton people while you are in this school." Myra was flabbergasted! She looked around at her fellow teachers to see if there was any look of surprise on their faces but saw little out of the ordinary.

After the assembly, she approached various sixth-grade teachers and asked about the propriety of Mr. Hobson's remarks toward the "Delmore kids" but they responded that it was just the way Mr. Hobson spoke, and he probably didn't mean much by it. Another teacher admitted that Mr. Hobson's statements had clear racist implications but advised Myra not to "make waves." After much soul searching, Myra decided to approach the principal and ask for some workshops provided by local university facility on multicultural issues for the administration and faculty. The workshops were eventually held with mixed results. While many faculty and staff participated with enthusiasm, an offer to have the university faculty help the River Shore Middle staff conduct a school-wide survey of classroom and school climate was politely declined.

Points to Ponder

1. Do you think Myra was right in bringing Mr. Hobson's comment to the principal's attention? If so, why? If not, why not?

2. Do you agree with the teacher who advised Myra to "not make waves" by bringing this matter to the principal? Explain the reason behind your answer.

3. What ethical framework were teachers adhering to when they said nothing about Mr. Hobson's remarks?

4. What ethical principles guided Myra in her decision to bring the remarks to the principal's attention?

many parts of the country, forcing many gay teachers to keep their orientation private. Would tenure protect these teachers?

Tenured teachers can also be dismissed during periods of financial crisis, a practice known as **riffing** (reduction in force). When teachers are riffed because of financial problems, seniority is typically used as the criterion to determine who is released. As a result, untenured teachers are let go first, and then individuals with less experience and time in the system. Teachers can also be laid off because of the elimination of a program (for example, if a school district decides to no longer offer a subject) or as a result of school consolidation or reorganization (as when two school districts are merged and only one teacher is needed in a particular subject area).

PERSONAL CONDUCT OF TEACHERS

What is considered appropriate or inappropriate personal behavior on the part of a teacher has changed over the years. In the 1930s in Dade County, Florida, public schoolteachers could not wear lipstick. Up until the end of World War II, in many school districts across the country female teachers could not marry and keep their jobs. Such rules are considered ridiculous today and demonstrate how appropriate behavior is redefined from one generation to the next.

Today the personal conduct of teachers is usually considered their own business. Generally speaking, teachers cannot be dismissed for their moral behavior unless they break a law or their actions affect their work in the classroom. Recent court cases, for example, have guaranteed female teachers the right to bear a child out of wedlock, despite moral objections from the local community. In a 1986 Illinois court decision, a judge maintained that a single female teacher "had a substantive due process right to conceive and raise her child out of wedlock without unwarranted . . . School Board intrusion" (Fischer et al., 1999, p. 301). In a 1991 federal district court decision, it was determined that an unmarried Ohio teacher had the constitutional right to conceive by artificial conception and give birth to and raise a child (Fischer et al., 1999, p. 301).

Teachers cannot engage in sexual activities with their students. In most cases, such a relationship is a violation of the rights of a minor, but even if the student is of age (18 or older), it can be argued that such involvement interferes with the effectiveness of the teacher on the job. Likewise, a teacher can be dismissed for making sexual advances toward students or participating in drug use with them. In terms of personal behavior, the general rule is that while teachers cannot be dismissed for private conduct that does not conform with the values of the local community in which they live, they can lose their jobs if they are committing an illegal act, or if it can be shown that their action is affecting their ability to do their work (Fischer et al., 1999).

PROTECTING TEACHERS

There are two major professional organizations for teachers in the United States: the National Educational Association (NEA) and the American Federation of Teachers (AFT). The NEA began as a teachers' organization in 1857 and became a union in the 1960s. The AFT was founded as a labor organization in 1912. In addition to teachers, both the NEA and AFT enroll other school-related workers such as bus drivers, cafeteria workers, and secretaries.

Teachers' unions grew rapidly during the 1960s. Declining salaries and poor working conditions encouraged teachers to become union members. In 1972, the National Education Association established its first political action committee. In 1979, largely as a result of union lobbying, the U.S. Department of Education was founded. Interestingly, while both the NEA and the AFT primarily support the Democratic Party, teachers, as a group, are divided almost equally between the two main political parties in the United States.

● **Teacher Union Membership**   More than 80% of all teachers belong to a professional organization; some teachers belong to both. The National Education Association, for example, has more than 2 million members. The American Federation of Teachers has approximately half a million members. Teachers are constitutionally guaranteed the right to belong to a union. At the same time, teachers cannot be forced to join. In most states, the law requires the local school board to negotiate with whatever organization represents the largest majority of teachers in the district.

The NEA and the AFT have similar purposes. Besides improving working conditions and salaries for teachers and protecting teachers' rights, they also have an interest in improving the quality of education in the United States. The single most important role of the teachers' unions is to negotiate contracts for their members. In a large urban district, teacher contracts can run several hundred pages in length, addressing salary, supervisory issues, tenure, and conditions of work. Teachers have a limited right to strike in about half

As a teacher, you have a constitutionally guaranteed right—but not an obligation—to belong to a union or professional association. Agreements between the teachers union and state governments vary among the states. For example, in some states teachers are not permitted to form a legal strike. Do you think teachers should be able to strike?

of the states in the United States. In general, striking is discouraged because of the welfare and educational needs of the students whom teachers serve.

● **Collective Bargaining**   School systems in 34 states in the United States are required by law to engage in **collective bargaining,** which means that the group is represented in negotiations with a district school board and the final agreement reached applies to everyone in the group. Collective bargaining avoids independent negotiating by individual employees and results in a fair and equitable pay scale for individuals of equal education and experience. It does not, however, allow for bonus pay for outstanding service, unless otherwise outlined in negotiations. In most states where collective bargaining procedures are in effect, the majority of teachers unions negotiate the contract in a local school district.

Collective bargaining mostly gives teachers greater power and influence over their working conditions, class size, salaries and benefits, transfer policies, and so on. In other words, collective bargaining has been used to deal with the working conditions of teachers. Generally speaking, teachers have not used collective bargaining as a means by which to initiate school-level curricular reform and improvement. This is a potentially rich area for development in the future. Imagine teachers, for example, exerting political power to reshape the curriculum. Many teachers believe that there is too much emphasis on standardized testing in the schools. It is possible that teachers could begin to negotiate, as part of their contracts, not to be involved in overintrusive testing and evaluation methods. To what extent do you believe that teachers should use their collective bargaining power in this way? Is this an appropriate role for teachers?

The time will come when you will have to decide whether to join a teachers' union. It's important to know that the union does more than negotiate your contract. Besides negotiating your contract and monitoring the conditions under which you work, the union will defend you if you become involved in a legal problem such as a liability lawsuit, a complaint by a parent, or wrongful termination. Suppose, for example, that a student falsely accuses you of discrimination. The union will provide legal help and support as part of your union membership.

While certain rights of teachers are the same across the country, based on federal and state laws that protect all individuals, some things may vary based on local laws and customs of specific communities. Teachers are hired by school systems to perform a specific type of work. Local school systems can establish standards for the teachers who work for them, as long as they do not violate their constitutional rights.

"I find it infuriating to work in a profession where people think that just because they WENT to school that they are capable of making up the policies. I also believe that parents should [not] be involved in any decisions that affect the teacher's contract."

CAROL C., READING SPECIALIST

THINK ABOUT THIS:

Some people feel that professional organizations such as AFT and NEA have become *too* politically involved in the daily events of schools. Many teachers, however, argue that the professional association protects them from the numerous sources of pressure they face on a daily basis, including those from parents with opinions about the best ways to teach. A major irritation to many teachers is the political conflicts that interfere with their daily work with students. Why do you think teachers are particularly vulnerable to such interference? What do you think of Carol's concern over parent involvement in setting salaries?

SHARE and COMPARE:

How would a teacher's work be affected if there were no unions? Find out what other members of your class think about the presence of teacher unions.

FINAL THOUGHTS

Teaching is a complex profession that has been shaped by many different historical forces. As a profession, teaching is service oriented. Situating yourself, in terms of your ethical practice and personal philosophy, is critical if you are interested in "touching the future" through teaching.

In addition, you need to know how teaching is situated as a profession in American society. If you are to be successful in your work, you will need to be familiar with the role of professional groups such as teachers' unions and the legal rights you are guaranteed, not just as a teacher but also as a citizen. Mastering this knowledge is ultimately an essential part of being a professional who can truly succeed as a teacher.

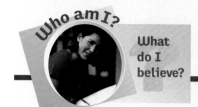

Who am I?
What do I believe?

REFLECTIONS

Professional Plan for Understanding the Ethical Contexts of Being a Teacher

1. The three main ideas I learned in this chapter about being a teacher are:

2. Two things in this chapter that I would like to learn more about are:

    a. _____

    b. _____

3. I plan to investigate these two areas and learn more about topics in this chapter by:

    _____ Reading some of book club choices

    _____ Reading sources referenced in the chapter that interest me

    _____ Interviewing teachers and asking them to identify two common ethical conflicts they face

    _____ Observing classrooms and taking notes on issues mentioned in this chapter that occurred and how teachers responded to them

    _____ Exploring the websites listed in the Log On section

4. I will include the following in my Touch the Future portfolio:

    _____ My first attempt at a personal philosophy of education

    _____ Responses to Who Am I? activities

    _____ A brief essay on my thoughts about Problems to Possibilities

    _____ Responses to the Observation Guide

    _____ Other (materials assigned by your instructor):

SUMMARY

What Is the History of Teaching?

- An extensive public school system had come into being by the middle of the nineteenth century.
- The Common School movement was a major force in opening up teaching to women.
- Teaching has been a relatively easy career to enter and exit.
- A growing teacher shortage will hit some regions of the country more severely than others.

What Is Good Teaching?

- Teachers wear many different hats, depending on community needs and expectations. Models of teaching include *teaching as a moral craft* and *as an act of caring*, and the teacher *as expert, as authority figure, as personal model, as facilitator,* and *as delegator.*
- Noddings' model of teaching as caring maintains that schools are concerned with helping children grow and develop.
- Defining a personal philosophy of education helps teachers identify their internal motivation for teaching and establish goals they wish to accomplish.
- John Dewey's "My Pedagogic Creed" influenced many educational thinkers and encouraged people to think about the fundamental purposes of schooling.

What Ethical Issues Do Teachers Face?

- Teachers are expected to reflect honesty, trust, confidentiality, fairness, responsibility, and respect for others in their decision making.
- Making ethical judgments involves the application of values to real-life situations and being able to resolve some measure of ambiguity.
- It is important to have teachers in our classrooms who have high levels of moral/ethical reasoning.
- There has always been some conflict in education circles between those who want to provide a value-free education and those who want to teach values.
- Individuals with a higher level of moral reasoning are more likely to practice ethical behavior.
- Teachers' ethical makeup affects all aspects of their work, including decisions about what to teach and how to teach it.

What Are the Legal Rights of Teachers?

- School systems can establish standards for teachers who work for them, as long as they do not violate their constitutional rights.
- The personal conduct of teachers is usually considered their own business, although there are definite limits on teacher behavior.
- There has been a major growth in teachers' unions since the 1960s. Today more than 80% of all teachers belong to teachers' unions. Professional organizations or teachers' unions help establish the salary scale for teachers and negotiate conditions that protect teachers' rights.
- Collective bargaining is an important source of power for teachers.

Companion Website

Visit the **Touch the Future . . . Teach!** Companion Website at www.ablongman.com/diaz for additional opportunities.

KEY WORDS

American Federation of
    Teachers   210
caring teacher   204
code of ethics   210
collective bargaining   219

National Education
    Association   210
philosophy of education
    205
professional ethics   209

riffing   217
teaching as a vocation   204
tenured   216

CONCEPT REVIEW

1. Describe the origins of the teaching profession in the United States and explain how the profession has evolved.

2. Discuss the significance of teaching as a feminized profession and the impact this has had on the profession.

3. Define various models of teaching and explain how teaching differs according to various settings.

4. Describe the purpose of professional teacher organizations and the benefits they provide their members.

5. Contrast the pros and cons of the fact that teaching is a relatively easy career to enter and exit.

6. Describe how values are reflected in the content of curriculum taught by teachers.

7. Develop a personal philosophy of education and describe what is involved in doing so.

8. Identify various ethical issues faced by teachers.

9. Define moral reasoning and explain how it affects a teacher's work.

10. Identify the major teachers' unions in the United States and explain their basic characteristics.

11. Describe the legal and constitutional rights of teachers.

12. Explain how teacher tenure works and why some people might oppose it.

13. Identify what might be considered acceptable public and private behavior for teachers.

TOUCH THE FUTURE . . .

Read On

Schoolteacher: A Sociological Study (2nd ed.)
Dan C. Lortie (Chicago: University of Chicago Press, 2002)
Originally published in 1975; considered the classic text in the sociology of teaching.

The Call to Teach
David T. Hansen, with a foreword by Larry Cuban (Teachers College Press, 1995)
A study of urban teachers working in urban public and private schools and a valuable source on understanding the forces shaping teachers in their day-to-day work.

Images of Schoolteachers in America
Pamela Bolotin Joseph and Gail E. Burnaford (Mahwah, NJ: Lawrence Erlbaum, 2001)
A very readable description of teachers and their portrayal in American society.

The Courage to Teach: Exploring the Inner Landscape of a Teacher's Life
Parker Palmer (San Francisco: Jossey-Bass, 1998)
An exploration of the self and teaching by a skilled practitioner concerned with understanding the joy and frustration of being a teacher.

The Courage to Teach: A Guide for Reflection and Renewal
Rachel V. Livsey and Parker Palmer (San Francisco: Jossey-Bass, 1999)
A work focusing on the meaning of being a teacher, with a special emphasis on the teacher as engaged in a process of reflection and renewal.

Log On

National Education Association
www.nea.org/

American Federation of Teachers
www.aft.org

The two main teachers' unions in the United States, include not only detailed information about their respective organizations, but also up-to-date information about political and social issues affecting teachers.

My Pedagogic Creed (The Pragmatism Cybrary)
http://dewey.pragmatism.org/creed.htm

The full text of Dewey's "My Pedagogic Creed."

The Center for Dewey Studies
www.siu.edu/~deweyctr/

Located at Southern Illinois University in Carbondale, the Center for Dewey Studies provides a complete list of information about Dewey and his teachings.

Center for the Study of Ethics
www.uvsc.edu/ethics/curriculum/education/

Offers a series of case studies involving ethical conflicts whose outcomes you can consider.

Write On

"It is the supreme art of the teacher to awaken joy in creative expression and knowledge."

—Albert Einstein

As part of your work in education you will read a lot of platitudes about what it means to be a good teacher, as well as the purposes of teaching. Is the quote by Albert Einstein just another platitude, or is there an important sentiment at work in what he has said? In your journal, write a brief essay describing what you feel it means to be a good teacher.

OBSERVATION GUIDE

TEACH: LINKING THEORY TO PRACTICE

Linking
Theory to
Practice

Objective: To interview a teacher about the challenges of teaching

School (use code name): _____   Interviewer: _____

Grade Level Observed: _____   Date: _____

Subject Taught: _____   Time In: _____   Time Out: _____

Directions: In this observation activity you will interview a teacher about his or her work. Find a teacher whom you think will be willing to be interviewed, and whom you think will be interesting to talk to. Some suggested questions follow. Add your own questions as you think appropriate.

1. How long have you been in the classroom? How long do you plan to teach?

2. What would you say is your philosophy of education?

3. What are you trying most to achieve with students? What goals do you hold for students? What methods and strategies do you use to achieve these goals?

4. What is your greatest satisfaction in teaching? What is your greatest frustration in teaching?

5. How involved are parents with the activities at the school? What level of autonomy do you have in your classroom?

6. To what degree do you think the context of the school affects what you do in the classroom?

7. What about the community do you have to consider when deciding on your curriculum?

8. How active is the union in your school? Is there a good working relationship between the teachers and the administration?

Connecting with INTASC: Principle 9

Professional Commitment and Responsibility: The teacher is a reflective practitioner who continually evaluates the effects of his or her choices and actions on others (students, parents, and other professionals in the learning community) and who actively seeks out opportunities to grow professionally.

When speaking with the teacher, find out what the teacher does to meet Principle 9. What does the teacher do to seek out opportunities for personal and professional growth? When attending conferences, what does the teacher look to gain from them? Present the "models of teaching" and then ask, "Which of these models of teaching would you say best explains who you are as a teacher?"

8

Diversity and the Cultural Context of Teaching

Who am I?

What do I believe?

THINK ABOUT THIS:

Students of all cultural, religious, ethnic, and socioeconomic backgrounds attend public schools together, and it is often assumed that they receive similar treatment. At the end of 12 years of school, they have compiled a grade point average and standardized test scores that will affect the rest of their lives. Students, however, don't always receive the same training and treatment for various reasons. How do you think academic performance might be affected if you attend a school where you aren't comfortable? How might this affect the validity of test results or other measures of student performance? What can you as a future teacher do to ensure a fair classroom climate for students you will teach in the future?

> "A child cannot be taught by anyone who despises him, and a child cannot afford to be fooled."
>
> James Baldwin (author)

You are preparing to become a teacher in schools that are more culturally, linguistically, and racially diverse than those that you or your parents attended. Increasing diversity can be seen as something to be concerned about or as positive change. Clearly, effective teachers in the future need to be culturally literate just as much as they need to know their subjects or master effective teaching techniques.

In this chapter we explore diversity issues and how teachers and schools respond to students of diverse backgrounds. We examine many dimensions that affect educational opportunities and point out some barriers to equitable treatment of all students. At the conclusion of the chapter, you should have a good idea of how effective teachers can make a difference in today's diverse classrooms. The material is organized to answer the following key questions:

Key Questions

1. How does socioeconomic status affect learning?
2. What effect does race have on schools?
3. How do ethnicity and language differences affect learning?
4. How do gender and sexuality issues affect schools?
4. What role does religion play in schools?

"**W**elcome to our school. At this school we treat all of our students equally." This phrase is often heard by parents and students at the first parent-teacher organization meeting of the year. Many students, parents, and educators accept this statement as an article of faith. We assume that a diverse population of students attending the same school will be treated similarly.

How do we know that this is really true? Do principals and teachers typically have research performed in their schools to support this assertion, or is it wishful thinking? Does it make sense to treat all students equally (that is, identically)? Perhaps a better goal for educators is to provide *equitable* rather than *equal* treatment. It is easy to see whether teachers are treating their students identically. Equal treatment may meet the needs of some students, but it will very rarely address the needs of all students. Equitable treatment, on the other hand, does not treat all students in the same manner but rather in a way that is appropriate to meet their academic needs.

Despite the egalitarian sound of equal treatment, if you treat students identically, you can easily regard them as a single category instead of the individuals they are. Simply put, it is far easier to treat students equally than it is to treat them equitably. If schools are to be the vehicles for socioeconomic mobility and enlightenment that most people in the United States expect them to be, it seems reasonable that access to effective teachers, opportunities for critical thinking, and high-status knowledge be available to every student.

HOW DOES SOCIOECONOMIC STATUS AFFECT LEARNING?

Many attitudes that people hold are influenced by their social class. In describing the "hidden rules" that exist in the lower, middle, and upper classes, Payne (2001) notes that attitudes toward possessions, education, time, and money are deeply influenced by social class standing. For example, the driving forces for people in poverty are survival, relationships and entertainment. For the middle class they are work and achievement. The wealthy are driven more by financial, political, and social considerations. A significant component of American culture holds that people should be judged on their own merits without regard to their family or social class background. But does this actually happen? Often, people judge each other based on tangible things—where they live, the cars they drive, the clothes they wear, and other visible indicators of socioeconomic status. These judgments can carry over to many facets of daily life, including schools.

Many time-honored assumptions in American culture, such as "Save your money for a rainy day" or "Parents should help teachers drive on field trips or raise money for the school," are heard by students of all social classes. "Saving money for a rainy day," however, assumes that there is some disposable income at the end of a week to be saved. This is not always the case. Getting parental help for field trips assumes that parents are available during school hours because they don't have to work outside the home. Raising money for the school requires time and is important only after families have raised sufficient money to support their own homes. All of these common suggestions are rooted in assumptions about the student's social class.

Most Americans see themselves as middle class, even those who have incomes that would place them well above or below any broad definition of the middle class. As first noted in Chapter 3, approximately 20% of children in the United States live below the poverty line (Hodgkinson, 2000/2001). Table 8.1 on pages 230–231 shows the distribution of poverty across the country. For some it is the result of **situational poverty,** which is temporary and caused by circumstances such as divorce, death, or illness. Too many families, however, experience **generational poverty,** which is defined as lasting two generations or longer (Payne, 2001). Two students in the same school may come from equally poor families, but attitudes may vary depending on the circumstances that have caused their poverty. For example, children who have been raised in a middle-class home may find themselves suddenly in poverty as a result of a divorce. They are at particular risk if the parent without custody stops making child support payments and the family is often left with less than half of the income it previously enjoyed. In generational poverty, attitudes are rooted more deeply and the effects on individuals and the schools can also go pretty deep.

As a general rule, the higher the average socioeconomic status of a school's student population, the more favorably it will compare with the following criteria. However, some schools with low-socioeconomic student populations also fare well when measured by the same criteria. The social class of a school will affect the following:

- The proportion of high-status (advanced-placement) courses available to students

- The proportion of the faculty holding temporary or emergency teaching credentials

- The average level of per-pupil funding the school has available, which affects the books, materials, and field trips available to students

- The expectations students have for success in college preparatory courses

- Teacher expectation of high student achievement (Lutz, 1995)

ACCESS TO RESOURCES

Since nearly all public schools in the United States draw their student bodies from neighborhoods located reasonably close to the school, students' social class is the primary determinant of their place of residence and also determines which public school a student will attend. While there are some exceptions, rarely do poor students go to the best-funded public schools. Students attending low-income public schools almost always find conditions more detrimental to learning than their peers in more affluent schools. Schools in low-income areas tend to have more of the following characteristics:

- Less likely to be connected to the Internet

- Lower teachers' salaries

- Less parental involvement

- Less money spent per pupil for instruction and improvement of the physical facilities

- More faculty and administrative time focused on discipline issues, leaving less time for instruction (U.S. Department of Education, 1997)

- **Funding**   How much quality education is influenced by available money and how much is due to the effort of individual students has been argued for years. Public schools can vary significantly in the resources available to them for facilities as well as to pay high-quality teachers. This can be true whether comparing public schools in different districts within a state or districts in different states.

Degrees of funding inequality of schools within public school districts appear to be related to racial, educational, or metropolitan lines in some, although not all, states (Burke & White, 2001). Students attending

I N T A S C

Principle #3

Adapting Instruction for Individual Needs: The teacher understands how students differ in their approaches to learning and creates instructional opportunities that are adapted to diverse learners.

"I got tattoos to make a statement, but my teacher said I could do the same thing by joining the debating team."

Courtesy of Aaron Bacall, *The Lighter Side of Teaching,* p. 72. Copyright 2003 by Aaron Bacall. Reprinted by permission of Corwin Press Inc.

TABLE 8.1

Concentration of Poverty by School District Urbanicity: Number (in Thousands) and Percentage of Related Children Ages 5–17 in Poverty, by Urbanicity and Region, 1999

TYPE OF STUDENT	TOTAL	URBANICITY		
		CENTRAL CITY OF LARGE MSA	CENTRAL CITY OF MIDSIZE MSA	URBAN FRINGE OF LARGE MSA
TOTAL				
ALL STUDENTS	51,696	8,654	6,661	16,814
POOR	8,188	2,108	1,314	1,763
NONPOOR	43,508	6,545	5,347	15,050
PERCENT POVERTY	15.8	24.4	19.7	10.5
NORTHEAST				
ALL STUDENTS	9,410	1,889	1,032	3,355
POOR	1,420	541	263	297
NONPOOR	7,990	1,348	769	3,058
PERCENT POVERTY	15.1	28.7	25.5	8.8
MIDWEST				
ALL STUDENTS	11,971	1,679	1,632	3,573
POOR	1,471	408	266	237
NONPOOR	10,499	1,271	1,366	3,336
PERCENT POVERTY	12.3	24.3	16.3	6.6
SOUTH				
ALL STUDENTS	18,236	2,496	2,199	4,989
POOR	3,265	555	466	584
NONPOOR	14,971	1,941	1,734	4,406
PERCENT POVERTY	17.9	22.2	21.2	11.7
WEST				
ALL STUDENTS	12,080	2,590	1,798	4,896
POOR	2,032	604	319	646
NONPOOR	10,048	1,986	1,479	4,250
PERCENT POVERTY	16.8	23.3	17.7	13.2

Note: MSAs denote metropolitan statistical areas and are geographic areas containing a large population nucleus together with adjacent communities having a high degree of social and economic integration. To define poverty, the Bureau of the Census uses a set of money income thresholds, updated annually, that vary by family size and composition to determine who is poor. If a family's income is less than the family's threshold, then that family, and every individual in it, is considered poor.

public schools in this nation have a better opportunity to access a quality education if their school is located in a community with an affluent tax base. To offset these disparities, the funding formulas of many states include revenue sources other than the local tax base. Some communities and special-interest groups have tried to level the playing field for poorer communities by challenging the disparities as unconstitutional. Results of such efforts have been mixed. Substantial funding disparities in public schools within the same state have been upheld by cases such as *San Antonio School District v. Rodriguez,* in which the U.S. Supreme Court ruled that these disparities did not violate any elements of the Constitution. However, at the state level, out of 34 states where funding systems have been challenged in court, 16 state supreme courts have declared their state's funding system unconstitutional, while 18 state supreme courts have upheld their state's approach to funding public education (Dayton, 1998).

Equity in public school funding has been a particularly difficult issue for rural school districts in the United States, where property taxes are relatively low and communities are

		URBANICITY		
URBAN FRINGE OF MIDSIZE MSA	LARGE TOWN	SMALL TOWN	RURAL OUTSIDE MSA	RURAL WITHIN MSA
		TOTAL		
5,310	661	4,895	4,572	4,130
711	123	903	838	427
4,599	537	3,992	3,734	3,703
13.4	18.7	18.5	18.3	10.3
		NORTHEAST		
1,023	32	497	425	1,157
92	5	70	63	89
931	27	427	362	1,068
9.0	16.4	14.0	14.8	7.7
		MIDWEST		
862	207	1,468	1,441	1,108
72	30	185	196	78
790	178	1,284	1,245	1,029
8.4	14.2	12.6	13.6	7.1
		SOUTH		
2,614	221	2,088	2,134	1,494
429	51	501	469	211
2,185	171	1,587	1,666	1,283
16.4	22.9	24.0	22.0	14.2
		WEST		
811	200	842	572	371
117	38	149	111	48
694	162	693	461	323
14.4	19.0	17.7	19.4	13.0

Source: U.S. Department of Education, NCES, Common Core of Data (CCD), "Local Education Agency (School District) Universe Survey," 2000–01, Table 3.1; and U.S. Department of Commerce, Bureau of the Census, *Current Population Survey* (CPS), Small Area Income and Poverty estimates, Title I Eligibility Database, 1999, previously unpublished tabulation (December 2002).

declining in population. As populations decline, student enrollments decline as well, and schools find themselves unable to provide basic educational services to the students they do have. For many schools facing significant decreases in students, the only solution may be closure of the school and consolidation with a school in the nearest community. These mergers generally result in enough students to justify the costs of basic educational services, but students often must commute longer distances to obtain them.

● **Teachers** In an ideal world, students with the greatest academic needs would have the greatest access to qualified teachers. Every student should have a highly qualified teacher. However, this assumes that there are enough highly qualified teachers to meet the needs of all of the nation's students. Reality falls short of this ideal. When highly qualified teachers are in short supply, they are less likely to be found teaching in low-income schools (Viadero, 2000). When public schoolteachers choose to leave their schools, the three major reasons they give for their decisions are opportunity for a better teaching assignment (40%), dissat-

significance can easily carry over to our schools, in which ethnic diversity is increasing, as shown in Table 8.3.

Schools are not only places for learning, but also critical places where identity formation in youth occurs. Adolescents of all backgrounds often struggle with identity issues, but White adolescents rarely have race as their primary identity. In her book *Why Are All the Black Kids Sitting Together in the Cafeteria?*, Tatum (1997) notes that "Black youths, in par-

---

TABLE 8.3

Racial/Ethnic Distribution of Public School Students: Percentage Distribution of Public School Students Enrolled in Grades K–12 Who Were Minorities, 1972–2000

	WHITE	MINORITY ENROLLMENT			
		TOTAL	BLACK	HISPANIC	OTHER
1972	77.8	22.2	14.8	6.0	1.4
1973	78.1	21.9	14.7	5.7	1.4
1974	76.8	23.2	15.4	6.3	1.5
1975	76.2	23.8	15.4	6.7	1.7
1976	76.2	23.8	15.5	6.5	1.7
1977	76.1	23.9	15.8	6.2	1.9
1978	75.5	24.5	16.0	6.5	2.1
1979	75.8	24.2	15.7	6.6	1.9
1980	72.8	27.2	16.2	8.6	2.4
1981	72.4	27.6	16.0	8.7	2.9
1982	71.9	28.1	16.0	8.9	3.2
1983	71.3	28.7	16.1	9.2	3.4
1984	71.7	28.3	16.1	8.5	3.6
1985	69.6	30.4	16.8	10.1	3.5
1986	69.1	30.9	16.6	10.8	3.6
1987	68.5	31.5	16.6	10.8	4.0
1988	68.3	31.7	16.5	11.0	4.2
1989	68.0	32.0	16.6	11.4	4.0
1990	67.6	32.4	16.5	11.7	4.2
1991	67.1	32.9	16.8	11.8	4.2
1992	66.8	33.3	16.9	12.1	4.3
1993	67.0	33.0	16.6	12.1	4.3
1994	65.8	34.2	16.7	13.7	3.8
1995	65.5	34.5	16.9	14.1	3.5
1996	63.7	36.3	16.6	14.5	5.3
1997	63.0	37.0	16.9	14.9	5.1
1998	62.4	37.6	17.2	15.4	5.1
1999	61.9	38.1	16.5	16.2	5.5
2000	61.3	38.7	16.6	16.6	5.4

Note: Percentages may not add to 100.0 due to rounding.
Source: U.S. Department of Commerce, Bureau of the Census, *October Current Population Surveys, 1972–2000.* Table 3.1.

ticular, think of themselves in terms of race because that is how the rest of the world thinks of them" (p. 53). It is common for children from diverse racial backgrounds to play and interact together in elementary schools. However, by sixth or seventh grade, racial grouping begins to occur. African American students often use self-segregation to cope with stress, social rejection, and outright racism in a school setting (Tatum, 1997).

If African American students sense alienation in schools, they may develop an **oppositional identity** to the school setting. This oppositional identity often defines doing what the school wants as "acting White." Unfortunately, some youth define high academic achievement as "acting White" and do not realize that no culture has ownership of school success. Some African American students look for ways to play down their achievements if doing so means greater acceptance among their African American peers. To gain acceptance among their White peers, they may adopt a strategy of "racelessness" that diminishes their African American characteristics.

Any time students have to develop an identity for school purposes that is at odds with their authentic identity, stress can result. This stress is not conducive to learning or to healthy identity development.

CREATING RACIAL EQUITY IN SCHOOLS

Delpit (1995) examines another dimension of race in schools called the **silenced dialogue**, which refers to both students and teachers of color who become frustrated trying to be heard in a school culture they rarely control. When discussions with those in the "culture of power" prove fruitless, a common response is to "silence the dialogue." In order to have a fruitful dialogue, Delpit suggests that educators "learn to be vulnerable enough to allow our world to turn upside down in order to allow the realities of others to edge themselves into our consciousness. In other words, we must become ethnographers in the truest sense."

The question has long been raised about the correlation between student performance and the relationship between a student's background and that of the teacher. Do students benefit academically by seeing someone of their own ethnic or cultural background in the

I N T A S C

Principle #5

Classroom Motivation and Management: The teacher uses an understanding of individual and group motivation and behavior to create a learning environment that encourages positive social interaction, active engagement in learning, and self-motivation.

I N T A S C

Principle #3

Adapting Instruction for Individual Needs: The teacher understands how students differ in their approaches to learning and creates instructional opportunities that are adapted to diverse learners.

Whites protest as black students enter school under police protection during desegregation in Arkansas. De facto segregation still exists in public schools as a result, in part, of residential patterns.

front of their class? One study of elementary pupils in Tennessee (Project Star) showed some interesting results. Students who had a teacher of their own race for at least one of the 4 years of the study tended to score higher on standardized tests of reading and mathematics. These effects tended to be particularly strong for children from lower-income families (Viadero, 2001). All of the reasons behind why a teacher's race affected students' scores are not yet fully understood. One concern shared by many, however, is that such findings could be used to support school segregation.

When U.S. public schools have had very high levels of racial segregation, they have rarely been equal. Many Americans tend to assume that racial segregation in public schools is a thing of the past. After all, the *Brown v. Board of Education* decision abolished legal (de jure) segregation in 1954. However, racial segregation in public schools that is caused by residential patterns—de facto segregation—is alive and well. In 1974, the Supreme Court ruled in *Swann v. Charlotte-Mecklenberg* that public schools should explore a variety of options to desegregate. If no option other than transportation was viable, school districts were permitted to transport students in order to end racial segregation, often called *court-ordered busing*. Careful reading of the court's decision finds that the justices recognized the potential inconvenience of busing, but felt that inconvenience could not be used as an excuse to prolong racial segregation.

U.S. public schools are becoming more segregated as a result of **white flight** to the suburbs and federal courts, which have ended strong desegregation plans. The average African American student attends a school in which 55% of the students are also African American (Zehr, 2001). There has been a great deal of controversy regarding the effectiveness of public school desegregation efforts in the United States. Critics of court-enforced desegregation plans have charged that these efforts were responsible for the white flight to suburbia that followed. Proponents of school desegregation have often been disappointed with the lack of long-term commitment to this goal. Ultimately, Americans must decide whether they truly believe in Horace Mann's notion of the Common School and whether they are willing to make all public schools "common."

Ladson-Billings (1994) suggests, however, that African American students need better, not necessarily separate, schools that:

1. Provide educational self-determination.

2. Honor and respect the students' home culture.

3. Help African American students understand the world as it is and equip them to change it for the better.

Teachers who use culturally relevant pedagogy and incorporate African American traditions in their classrooms serve as "dreamkeepers" for African American students. These teachers may come from any racial, ethnic, or cultural background but are united in the idea that African American students are capable of high academic achievement and deserve effective teaching and exposure to a challenging curriculum. Teachers can make a significant difference working with students that mainstream education would consider "at risk."

NEW DEFINITIONS OF RACE

Another small but rapidly growing category of students is composed of people from biracial or multiracial backgrounds. These students often encounter unique challenges in the schools because they feel that they are being asked to "declare" a single racial identity when doing so would deny the rest of their background. Biracial or multiracial students may choose a variety of identities. Some may want to be classified solely as "human," fearing that any classification other than White would subject them to racism. Others may choose to identify as biracial or multiracial and feel equal pride and identity with all facets of their backgrounds. Some may come from families who want to foster an identity with the racial

Problems to POSSIBILITIES

High-Stakes Testing and Multicultural Teaching

Kristel Jones is a sixth-grade teacher in Boston, Massachusetts. Most of her students are African American and Latino, and more than two-thirds of her class qualifies for free or reduced lunches. She has been teaching at the same elementary school for 5 years; last year the school got a new principal, Dr. Anderson, who made it clear to all teachers that raising scores on the state's high-stakes test (the MCAS) was not just the top priority, it was his only priority. To pursue this goal, Dr. Anderson decreed that of the 30 hours per week available for instruction in the regular classroom, 27 of those hours had to be spent focusing on MCAS skills. He also made it clear that, even if students didn't think it was "fun," he was going to monitor classrooms very closely. He also told teachers that he didn't want to hear any criticism that they were "teaching to the test," because test scores were what the superintendent wanted raised and that was the reason he was appointed principal. He "knew" that the best way to raise MCAS scores was to teach those specific verbal and quantitative skills on the test even if that left little time to teach anything else. Kristel didn't disagree that her students' verbal and quantitative skills needed improvement. Her major concern was how she was going to find time to teach science and social studies which were subjects she also was responsible for teaching and for which she had to issue grades.

Discussion Questions

What might Kristel do to resolve the dilemma between what she is being asked to do by the school principal and her own beliefs about good teaching?

Possibilities

Kristel approached her colleague, Mary Decker, a 25-year veteran teacher, for ideas. Together they reasoned that verbal and quantitative skills found in the MCAS could be taught in the traditional mathematics and language arts context, but they could also be taught in a science or social studies context. They set out to revamp the way they taught science and social studies to incorporate MCAS skills. Reading comprehension strategies were applied to the science and social studies texts. Student essays were focused on scientists and historical figures. Assignments were evaluated according to grammar, writing style, and content.

These approaches were written into detailed lesson plans, which were submitted to Dr. Anderson. After initial hesitation on how his directions had been interpreted by Kristel and Mary, Dr. Anderson thought about it further and approved the lesson plans.

Ethical Question

What is the major ethical consideration in this dilemma? To whom do teachers answer—administrators, students, the community, or society?

---

background that children resemble most. The role of educators is not to help decide the identity of biracial or multiracial students, but to affirm the identity that students have selected for themselves (Schwartz, 1998).

Many students that schools label as Hispanic are biracial or multiracial in origin. Hispanics are often a mixture of African, Indian, and Spanish ancestry. The term *Hispanic* refers to linguistic/cultural background, not to physical appearance.

Biracial or multiracial students may feel the sting of rejection not only from members of the mainstream culture, but from members of racial/ethnic minority groups whose heritage they share. Marta Cruz-Janzen (2000) speaks of the trials of biracial or multiracial students in public schools by sharing the following example of the emotional stress these children can feel: "A second grader of Mexican American and African American parentage would cry and cry in my office unable to tell me why except that she had no friends and nobody liked her either" (p. 64). Teachers of these students need to be especially vigilant and sensitive to make sure that the identities of biracial and multiracial students are being respected by school staff as well as by fellow students.

Cruz-Janzen also notes that "clearly Latinos present a dilemma for the US—what to do about a rapidly increasing population of mixed racial ancestry that defies categorization" (2002, p. 88). She also points out that many **Latinegros,** Latinos with African ancestry, "realize that the stringent black versus white dichotomy of the U.S. is widening the racial divide that has existed among Latinos" (p. 89). Biracial or multiracial immigrant students may be further confused by a racial classification structure in the United States unlike that in their home countries. They may be uncomfortable declaring themselves to be strictly White, African American, or Asian and thus need extra support from their teachers.

WHITE RACIAL IDENTITY

A final theme when examining race and schooling concerns the racial identity of White teachers and students. As members of the majority group in the United States, many don't see themselves as having a racial identity apart from their national identity as Americans. Racial identity is often seen as applicable only to people of color. Whites typically have the advantage of having language and cultural norms that are very similar to the language and behavioral norms of most American public schools. The average White child attending a public school in the United States does not have to become conversant in a new language as does the average Mexican immigrant child. The cultural and behavioral patterns of public schools are quite familiar to White students; they are often much less familiar to Native American, Black, and Hispanic students, and those of other racial backgrounds.

Being native to the United States and being White carries with it distinct advantages, in and out of school, that many people with these characteristics have not considered, although not all Whites enjoy the same advantages. White students who live in poverty, for example, do not enjoy much **white privilege.** McIntosh (1990) has pondered this question by noting, "I have come to see white privilege as an invisible package of unearned assets that I can count on cashing in each day, but about which I was supposed to remain oblivious."

White privilege is like "an invisible weightless knapsack of special provisions, maps, passports, code books, visas, clothes, tools and blank checks" (McIntosh, 1990). The following are just some of the attributes of white privilege:

1. I can turn on the television or open the front page of the paper and see people of my race widely represented.

2. When I am told about our national heritage or about "civilization," I am shown that people of my color made it what it is.

3. I can be sure that my children will be given curricular materials that will testify to the existence of their race.

4. I am never asked to speak for all of the people in my racial group.

5. I can do well in a challenging situation without being called a credit to my race.

6. I can remain oblivious to the language and customs of people of color, who constitute the world's majority, without feeling in my culture any penalty for such oblivion.

7. I can criticize our government without being seen as a cultural outsider. (McIntosh, 1990)

For many people of color, advantages that Whites take for granted are still elusive in the United States of the twenty-first century. Educators and policymakers need to become more aware of this dynamic. Scholar Gary Howard (1999) observes that "Whites need to acknowledge and work through the negative historical implications of 'Whiteness' and create for [themselves] a transformed identity as White people committed to equity and social change" (p. 112).

Occasionally educators may claim "colorblindness" in an effort to underscore their lack of bias. When students of color are told by their teachers that "they don't see color," their most common reaction is feeling invisible. The claim of colorblindness is often a fig leaf behind which people who do not want to address the intricacies of race in America may hide. Students of all colors are often quick to see this. Teachers need to see students as students first, but they also need to acknowledge their students' racial identity and honor it. Colorblindness is not the answer; respect is.

Another element involving White identity and schooling is that some Whites look at culture and ethnicity as belonging to other groups, not themselves. Sleeter (2000) observed the following about her teacher education university students: "most have little knowledge of any group other than the one into which they were born. And schools have been inducting them since kindergarten into that culture—which they regard not as a culture but as a given. Without some depth of knowledge of at least one other cultural group and how another group views one's own taken-for-granted culture, teachers will probably oversimplify the meaning of culture" (p. 127).

Race and schooling in the United States interact in a number of complex ways. Current and future teachers should understand these dynamics if they are going to provide students with equitable opportunities to learn.

"We need to put ourselves in the shoes of others. We must have a broader view, appreciate differences, convey tolerance."

JOYCE, ADULT EDUCATION TEACHER

THINK ABOUT THIS:

Some teachers approach the area of race and schooling by simply saying, "I don't see color." Do you think teachers mean this literally and they don't actually perceive racial differences? If not, what do you think they really mean?

SHARE and COMPARE:

Choose a classmate and discuss the "color blind" position with the view that teachers must "see color" in order to understand their students' backgrounds and teach them effectively.

How Do Ethnicity and Language Differences Affect Learning?

While race and ethnicity are often intertwined, public schools represent cultures, structures, and ways of doing things that are fairly comfortable for students of certain ethnic backgrounds, but less so for others. The culture of a school can make all students who attend it feel a sense of ownership or it can leave some students feeling like residents while others feel like guests. Teachers and school administrators can do a great deal to promote school and classroom climates in which students of all backgrounds feel comfortable.

Depending on how schools are run, they can be places of accommodation or settings where high levels of conformity are required for students from ethnic minorities.

CULTURAL DIFFERENCES AND SCHOOL PRACTICES

When schools require high degrees of conformity of students, the reason often given is that these students need to assimilate to mainstream U.S. culture and they learn that conformity in public schools. All schools and classrooms must have rules for functioning effectively, but to what extent do these policies, which are culturally neutral on the surface, benefit some over others?

Does the school rule banning headwear apply to the Orthodox Jewish student wearing a yarmulke? Are requirements to wear shorts in physical education or face a grade penalty fair to female Arab American students who may consider such dress immodest? What should teachers do if parents object on religious grounds to their child reading a required book in a literature class? On the other hand, a valid point can be made that rules and expectations must apply to all students. Educators often wrestle with these questions to determine how much consistency is required and how much accommodation is necessary when working with students of different backgrounds.

A point to remember when making such decisions is that you can negotiate process, but you don't negotiate product. *Process* refers to timelines for assignments, methods of learning, and ways in which students prefer to study or complete assignments. After all, human beings do not learn identically and cultural background can affect the ways students learn best. *Product* refers to the academic outcome of a class or learning assignment. Teachers may provide occasional alternate assignments for students who may have a cultural or religious objection to the standard assignment. Some students have objected to dissections in a biology class but have been allowed to learn the same concepts by engaging in a virtual dissection on a computer. When alternatives are provided, the goal should be that students gain the same knowledge. Expectations should always remain high for all students; those who encounter difficulty should receive additional assistance, not a lowering of goals.

INTASC

Principle #3

Adapting Instruction for Individual Needs: The teacher understands how students differ in their approaches to learning and creates instructional opportunities that are adapted to diverse learners.

Every child in your class will present you with the opportunity and inspiration to promote an appreciation of diversity. What kinds of activities might you be able to incorporate into your teaching that would honor the cultural backgrounds of your students?

SCHOOL CULTURE AND CURRICULUM

The impact of ethnicity in schools can be seen primarily in two places: the treatment that students receive from school staff and fellow students and the representation of diverse ethnic content and perspectives in the curriculum.

● **Culture**   During your childhood or adolescence, did you ever move and have to attend a new school? How long did the feeling of being in a strange situation last? For some culturally different students, that feeling can last for years. Students from outside the mainstream culture sometimes experience difficulties in schools, but other times do quite well. Ogbu (1995) argues that some minority students have more difficulty adjusting than others, depending on why they are living in the United States. Students from **voluntary minority groups,** immigrants who moved to the United States willingly, often compare their experiences in the United States with those in their country of origin. Even if the U.S. experiences involve problems, these experiences are compared with those in the countries they came from. If the U.S. experience is better, and it often is, the problems are given less importance. After all, they were willing immigrants.

Students from **involuntary minority groups,** groups that were initially brought into the United States against their will, do not have experiences in other nations to contrast with their lives in the United States. Therefore, their adjustment to American schools is more difficult. The consideration that their experiences are better than where they came from is not appropriate. Therefore, involuntary minorities such as African or Native Americans tend to compare their lives and experiences, in and out of school, with those of mainstream Americans. They expect their lives and treatment to compare favorably with those of fellow Americans. When they don't, students from involuntary minority groups are likely to feel disappointed or upset.

In general, the more students' ethnic backgrounds differ from the mainstream U.S. culture, the more difficulties they will encounter in public schools. This principle holds even when the group has been fairly successful academically (Ooka Pang, 1995). African American students are widely underrepresented in gifted programs, but overrepresented among students suspended from school. Ethnic-minority students generally receive a lower quantity and quality of attention from their teachers than do their mainstream peers. Schools rarely survey students to measure differences among ethnic groups' perceptions of school and classroom climate. Yet any visitor to a diverse school who questions students on how they view their status in that school can readily see that important differences often exist.

● **Curriculum**   In the past two decades, U.S. schools have increased the inclusion of diverse perspectives in the curriculum. However, cultural content pertaining to ethnic minority groups is still at the **cultural additive stage,** which means content is placed in separate courses or units rather than being fully integrated into the mainstream curriculum. For example, African American content often is emphasized in February, women's history in March, and Hispanic topics in October rather than regularly integrated into the curriculum. There are no monthly designations for mainstream curricular content; apparently, every month is equally appropriate.

When students are learning a largely monocultural curriculum but live in a multicultural world, they often see what they are learning as being disconnected from reality. Students who rarely see people like themselves reflected in the

INTASC

Principle #8

Assessment of Student Learning: The teacher understands and uses formal and informal assessment strategies to evaluate and ensure the continuous intellectual, social, and physical development of the learner.

Not everyone agrees on the benefits of bilingual education. People often tend to ignore the fact that students with dual language knowledge have linguistic skills that most Americans do not have.

curriculum are learning the subtle lesson that people like themselves did not do much that is worthwhile of study. When all students see people like themselves in the curriculum, it gives them a more representative view of the subject as well as greater motivation to learn.

LANGUAGE DIFFERENCES

INTASC

Principle #6

Communication Skills: The teacher uses knowledge of effective verbal, nonverbal, and media communication techniques to foster active inquiry, collaboration, and supportive interaction in the classroom.

In a perfect world of education, every child would start a U.S. public school in kindergarten, speak the same language, and begin school ready to learn. That world has never existed. Today's schools must enroll ever-increasing numbers of students who don't speak standard English at home or who speak a language besides English. (See Figure 8.1.) These students are enrolled in public schools where a significant number of teachers and administrators have not had much exposure to the research or literature on second language acquisition. Considering the following situation:

> A second-grade teacher who had studied second-language acquisition but spoke only English got a new class with six English language learners (ELLs) who spoke Spanish as their first language. The other second-grade teacher had one Spanish-speaking ELL. There were two aides; one was bilingual in Spanish and English and the other spoke only English. The teacher with the six ELLs suggested to her principal that she would take the lone ELL student in the other class and requested the bilingual aide. The principal denied the request on the basis that she did not want ELL students to "have a crutch in the classroom."

This anecdote reflects the widely believed myth that any use of a child's native language retards English-language acquisition. The reality is quite the opposite. Children who are literate in their home languages learn a second language more quickly than those who do not. By supporting native-language proficiency, we indirectly support English-language acquisition (Cummins, 2000). Cummins (2000) notes that the practice of ignoring the use

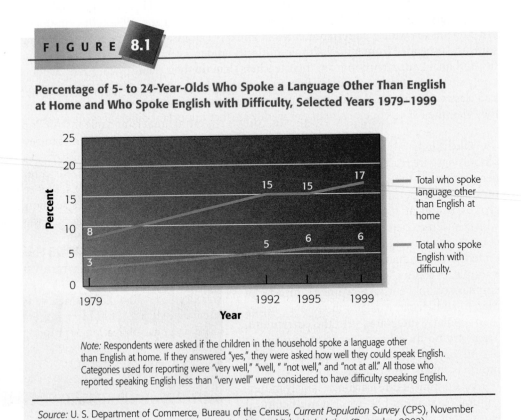

FIGURE 8.1

Percentage of 5- to 24-Year-Olds Who Spoke a Language Other Than English at Home and Who Spoke English with Difficulty, Selected Years 1979–1999

— Total who spoke language other than English at home

— Total who spoke English with difficulty.

Note: Respondents were asked if the children in the household spoke a language other than English at home. If they answered "yes," they were asked how well they could speak English. Categories used for reporting were "very well," "well," "not well," and "not at all." All those who reported speaking English less than "very well" were considered to have difficulty speaking English.

Source: U. S. Department of Commerce, Bureau of the Census, *Current Population Survey* (CPS), November 1979 and October 1992, 1995, and 1999, previously unpublished tabulation (December 2002).

BUILDING ON EDUCATIONAL FOUNDATIONS

Lau v. Nichols

The landmark case of *Lau v. Nichols* involved some interesting legal arguments on both sides. The attorneys for the San Francisco Unified School District argued that Lau had been treated "just like every other student" when he had been provided with an education solely in English. Lau's attorneys argued that the equal treatment Lau had received produced discriminatory results because if a student cannot understand what the teacher is saying, little else matters. While the U.S. Supreme Court did not mandate instruction in the student's home language, it did state that schools had to provide "understandable instruction" through either home-language instruction or adapted English instruction. Failure to do so

would be tantamount to "creating entry standards into the first grade."

- Is "understandable instruction" a reasonable standard to apply to schools when determining whether they are teaching English language learners properly?

- Since both home-language instruction and adaptive English approaches may be used to achieve understandable instruction, why have schools that have chosen to teach students in English as well as their home languages typically generated more controversy?

---

of languages other than English at home "is frequently exacerbated by the temptation for teachers to encourage students to give up their first language and switch to English as their primary language of communication; however, the research suggests that this retards rather than expedites academic progress in English" (p. 131). Although it may not sound logical at first, supporting ELL students' first language in schools helps English acquisition.

- **Legal Issues Involving Language and Schools**   Getting understandable instruction for English language learners in U.S. schools has been a long struggle and continues to be a difficult process. *Lau v. Nichols,* a landmark Supreme Court decision in 1974, involved a Chinese American student (Lau) who sued the San Francisco Unified School District for failure to provide him with understandable instruction, because Lau was not fluent in English and all instruction was in English (Provenzo, 2002). The Supreme Court's decision, while not mandating bilingual education, stated that understandable instruction was required for limited or non-English-speaking students.

In 1991, Multicultural Education Training Associates (META), a California-based Hispanic advocacy group, successfully sued the State of Florida to provide training in five areas of teaching English to speakers of other languages. In 2004, an extension of the META decree required training in these areas for administrators and school counselors. This training continues today as new teachers continue to arrive in Florida schools. An important question to explore is if school districts have a legal and ethical obligation to properly educate *all* of their students, why do some groups, such as English language learners, have to resort to the courts to get districts to meet their basic responsibilities?

- **Language Fluency and School Achievement**   In analyzing the relationship between native-language fluency and school achievement, Nieto (2001) finds that schools which view students who speak a language other than English as "handicapped" actually retard their academic progress. If languages were money and schools were banks, English would be the only

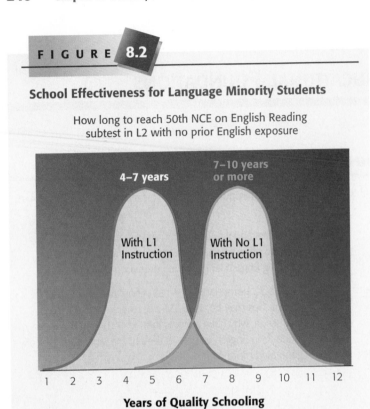

FIGURE 8.2

School Effectiveness for Language Minority Students

How long to reach 50th NCE on English Reading subtest in L2 with no prior English exposure

4–7 years

7–10 years or more

With L1 Instruction

With No L1 Instruction

1 2 3 4 5 6 7 8 9 10 11 12

Years of Quality Schooling

Source: W. Thomas, & V. Collier. *School Effectiveness for Language Minority Students.* (Washington, DC: National Clearinghouse for Bilingual Education, George Washington University, 1997). Copyright 1997 by Wayne P. Thomas. Adapted with permission.

currency accepted in most U.S. schools. There is no mechanism of exchange to spend another currency until students acquire academic English. Students first develop **basic interpersonal communication skills (BICS)**, which allow students to communicate with their peers and teachers. But BICS is not the language of textbooks, essays, or standardized tests, which Cummins refers to as **cognitive academic language proficiency (CALP)**. Most students can learn BICS in a year. Learning CALP at a level equal to their peers in the same grade takes at least 5 to 7 years (Cummins, 1984). (See Figure 8.2.)

Most English language learners do not spend 5 to 7 years receiving mediated language instruction in an ESL or bilingual program. Therefore, when "mainstreamed" into the general student population in 2 or 3 years, these students can converse in English but often have deficiencies in reading and writing the English language that will hinder them academically. Some English language learners today receive no mediated language instruction, especially if they attend school in areas where there are few English language learners.

How long would it take you to learn a language you don't currently know in order to be able to function without any handicap as a student in that language? After careful consideration, 5 to 7 years may be a conservative estimate for most of us. In addition, one also has to consider that English is one of the more difficult languages to master.

● **Approaches to Teaching English Language Learners** Public opinion in the United States toward the education of English language learners has typically been to teach these children English as fast as possible with little or no regard for their native-language literacy. At first, this makes intuitive sense. If you want students to simply learn English, just immerse them in English. This view would favor an **English immersion** approach—sink or swim— as was done with early-twentieth-century immigrants. The problem with this approach is that most students subjected to it sink.

Another approach is an **English for Speakers of Other Languages (ESOL)** program in which the use of complex English is minimized and students are brought along slowly in the new language. The challenge comes in helping these students keep up with their peers in all of their subjects when all subjects are instructed in a language they barely understand, much less read or write. How well do you think American students would keep up with Hungarian students in science or geography if both were instructed in Hungarian with few or no accommodations made for U.S. students? ESOL approaches work best when the topic of instruction is concrete and can be easily illustrated with visuals. These techniques are less successful when teachers are trying to get across abstract subjects.

The third and least common approach to teaching English language learners is **bilingual education**. In this approach, students are given intensive English instruction while their other subjects are instructed in the native language. In many programs, English-language instruction is added to the subject areas as students' English abilities increase. But bilingual education generates a great deal of controversy even though the literature

Though the Eyes of
Culturally Sensitive Teachers

Advocating for English Language Learners

Lisa is a former middle school English teacher who received her master's degree with a concentration in multicultural education. After she earned her degree, the school district for which she works offered her a position as a resource teacher focusing on the needs of low-income and limited-English-speaking students. The following are some of Lisa's observations, in her own words, after working as a resource teacher for some years:

We are still convincing teachers on a regular basis to use varying strategies with students who are learning English as a second language. There are high school teachers who stand up in the middle of your presentation and say, "I'm sorry, this person is in my class like everybody else and he learns like everybody else, period." Another teacher challenged me by saying, "No, English language learners do not need any modifications."

You have to explain to those teachers why this group learns better cooperatively, why this group cannot listen to you standing and lecturing for 60 minutes in a row. If you

are just lecturing for 60 minutes every day, how many students besides the English language learners are you missing? In these situations, I love to show teachers guided reading approaches, small-group instructional techniques and research on effective teaching and second-language acquisition.

Points to Ponder

1. Why do you think Lisa is meeting some resistance when she suggests to teachers that students who are learning English as a second language need alternative teaching approaches?

2. How difficult do you think it is for Lisa to change teaching habits that have been in place for years? Why?

3. Should teaching practices be determined by what teachers prefer to do or by what is most effective with students?

4. Would you follow Lisa's approach with experienced teachers who resist change? Why or why not?

---

strongly supports such programs (Collier & Thomas, 2004). If late-exit (lasting 7–8 years) bilingual programs are successful, they produce bilingual/biliterate students in a society in which such people do not abound.

Most high school graduates in the United States are not bilingual or biliterate as are high school graduates in many European nations. If they were, there would likely be considerably less controversy surrounding bilingual education because the graduates of bilingual programs would have similar dual-language skills to those of most Americans. With the current curriculum, bilingual programs produce bilingual/biliterate graduates who have language abilities not shared by most of the U.S. population.

The concept of bilingual programs often seems "counterintuitive" to some Americans. It requires considerable explanation to understand why nurturing the first language is beneficial to acquiring the second one.

As the number of English language learners increases in U.S. schools, issues that previously affected large urban districts are being faced in suburban and rural schools. Providing understandable instruction for students who speak languages other than English is a challenge. This challenge must be met for the sake of these students as well as the nation's future.

How Do Gender and Sexuality Issues Affect Schools?

"Boys will be boys." This statement has been used for generations in the United States. What does it really mean in the context of schools? Should teachers overlook certain behaviors they would correct in girls when boys behave that way? Few teachers would admit that they favor boys over girls in the classroom. Fewer yet would admit that if they did so, they did it knowingly. When parents send their children to school, they expect that boys and girls will be given equal nurturing, attention, and opportunities to learn and take leadership positions in the classroom. But research on the education of males and females has revealed some interesting findings:

- Sex differences in mathematics become apparent at the middle school level. Male superiority increases as the level of mathematics becomes more difficult.

- Although women achieve better grades than men, they are less likely to believe they can do college work. Females exhibit lower self-esteem than do males during secondary and higher education.

- Girls are more likely to be invisible members of classrooms. They receive fewer academic contacts, less praise and constructive feedback, fewer complex and abstract questions, and less instruction on how to do things for themselves.

- Boys are more likely to be scolded and reprimanded in classrooms. Also, they are more likely to be referred to school authorities for disciplinary actions than girls.

- Boys are more likely to be identified as having greater reading and learning disabilities and are also more likely to receive lower grades and be grade repeaters.

- Girls who are gifted, especially in math and science, are less likely to participate in special or accelerated programs to develop their talents (Sadker, Sadker, & Long, 1997).

These findings strongly suggest that American education still has some improving to do before it produces school environments in which gender expectations do not play a significant role in the education of students.

GENDER

Classroom interaction patterns between teachers and students typically favor students who are very quick to respond to teachers' questions and are verbally assertive. Most of these students are boys. Teachers call on boys more frequently than they call on girls, and they also provide more encouragement and fuller responses to male students. Female students are also more likely to be interrupted while making comments in class than their male counterparts.

Why do these patterns exist when most teachers are women, and few if any teachers would admit that they favor one gender over the other? Teachers make a large number of decisions every hour they are in the classroom. When teachers interact more often or more fully with male students than with female students, it is generally not a conscious effort to deny educational opportunities to girls or boys. Rather, most teachers are following a habit they may not be aware they have, a practice sometimes called **institutional sexism**. This form of sexism is not necessarily malicious, but rather develops as a result of commonly held misconceptions about socially appropriate male and female behaviors. These misperceptions have been reinforced by society over the course of many years and are difficult to break. It takes an observer in the classroom to accurately code and categorize teacher inter-

I N T A S C

Principle #5

Classroom Motivation and Management: The teacher uses an understanding of individual and group motivation and behavior to create a learning environment that encourages positive social interaction, active engagement in learning, and self-motivation.

actions with students. Frequently, when teachers are presented with data showing that their questions and comments favor boys over girls, they express amazement.

As boys and girls mature to young adulthood, their communication patterns evolve. Young men generally tend to communicate to exchange information and establish social standing. Their speech is often categorical or competitive. Young women often use their communication to establish a connection or rapport with the person with whom they are speaking (Tannen, 1994). While there are certainly young men and women whose communication styles vary from these trends, teachers should be aware of the general patterns. This knowledge can prevent a high school teacher from inadvertently encouraging or discouraging a student's aspirations based on institutionalized misconceptions.

Teachers who are familiar with the research on gender and communication patterns in the classroom know that communication patterns should not be regarded as inferior or superior, but merely as different. An example of the difference in communication styles is found in the results of a study in which men and women were asked to describe a flood that devastated their community. Women's accounts of the flood focused on stories they heard from other people emphasizing how community and human spirit overcame the tragedy. Men's accounts of the flood focused much more on information involving details, objects, and the time frame that related to the flood (Johnson, 1993).

As the people responsible for establishing a fair and equitable climate for all students in the classroom, teachers need to be aware of who is speaking, how often, and at what length. Male and female students should share equitably in being the "voices of the classroom" and teachers should create learning environments where this may occur. Traditional gender roles may suggest that being outspoken in the classroom is unfeminine for girls but normal for boys. If girls internalize this belief, they often silence themselves in school and this interferes with effective learning. An interesting finding concerning Latina girls differs from the pattern found in most of the literature. Third-grade Latina girls in bilingual classrooms took on the responsibility for helping other students accomplish the group's tasks. While they related well to all of their peers, they showed greater concern for girls' actions (Cook-Gumperz & Szymanski, 2001).

- **Balanced Curriculum**   A significant element of gender-fair education concerns how women are portrayed in the curriculum. A gender-balanced curriculum goes far beyond mentioning Marie Curie in science, Susan B. Anthony's role in procuring women's right to vote, or Eleanor Roosevelt's influence on Franklin Roosevelt's policies. This "contributions approach" to curriculum keeps women and their roles in academic disciplines on the edge of knowledge. Tetreault (1997) defines a gender-balanced curriculum as one that examines the intersections of men's and women's experiences. Additionally, a gender-balanced curriculum does not view men's or women's experiences as the same; they are affected differently by social class, race, and many other factors. It is important for all students, but particularly for female students, to see people like themselves as shapers of knowledge in the school curriculum. A gender-balanced curriculum presents mathematics and science as human domains, not just male domains. Women and men are each given significant attention in the social science and literature curriculum and questions are raised that examine gender roles in each discipline.

- **Teaching Techniques**   Gender-balanced teaching techniques examine new knowledge and relate this information to people and society. Girls generally prefer to have information connected to human activity, rather than having important facts taught in isolation. When pedagogy is balanced, varied, and focused on inquiry, there is a much better chance that both girls and boys are learning.

Young men and women experience an average drop in academic self-concept during the middle school years; however, this drop is more pronounced for girls than for boys. (See Figure 8.3 on page 250.) Perhaps the most publicized academic gender gap in the United States is the one in mathematics and science; however, this gap is small and closing. In an analysis of

INTASC

Principle #3

Adapting Instruction for Individual Needs: The teacher understands how students differ in their approaches to learning and creates instructional opportunities that are adapted to diverse learners.

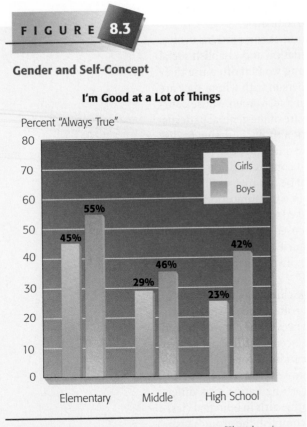

FIGURE 8.3

Gender and Self-Concept

I'm Good at a Lot of Things

Source: American Association of University Women, "Shortchanging Girls," *Shortchanging America: Executive Summary* (p. 9). (Washington, DC: Author, 1994). Retrieved May 6, 2005, from http://www.aauw.org/research/SGSA.pdf. Copyright 1994 by the American Association of University Women. Adapted with permission.

gender differences on various tests of the National Assessment for Educational Progress, Coley (2001) found that females outscored males across all racial and ethnic groups in reading and writing in Grades 4, 8, and 12. In science, white males scored higher than white females in Grade 4. No gender gaps were found in other groups. Other research notes that current trends indicate that the mathematics and science gap will disappear in 30–40 years (Nowell, 1998).

In order to overcome gender differences in academic achievement, some educators have advocated for single-gender schools. Historically, some traditional private schools were restricted to one gender. One argument for same-sex education is that, when educated separately, boys and girls worry less about having to impress the opposite sex and focus more on their academics. Critics of same-sex education point out that the real solution lies in making coeducational classrooms gender fair. They also argue that, ultimately, young men and women graduate from high schools to interact in a mixed-sex world. Therefore, coeducational schools provide the best preparation for life after graduation.

The interaction between gender and education is a complex one. Some areas of school practice favor males (such as classroom discourse) while other areas (such as discipline) tend to favor females. On balance, the areas of teaching and school practice that most affect learning tend to favor boys. Research on gender and schooling, while disturbing at times, does not suggest that educators are willingly trying to deny a gender-fair education to all students. If gender-fair education is to take place, educators cannot rely on their habits. Teachers should consciously evaluate school and classroom climates, instructional practices, and curricula to provide equitable opportunities for all students regardless of gender.

SEXUAL ORIENTATION

Some educators have argued that students' sexual orientations are irrelevant to the educational process. For heterosexual students, the norm in American society, that is very likely the case. For lesbian, gay, bisexual, and transgendered (LGBT) students, especially those whose sexual orientation is known within a school, it is anything but irrelevant. Isolation and fear remain the unfortunate companions of many LGBT youth in U.S. public and private schools. Some data to consider:

- Ninety-seven percent of students in public high schools report regularly hearing homophobic remarks from their peers.

- The typical high school student hears anti-gay slurs 25.5 times a day.

- Eighty percent of gay and lesbian youth report severe social isolation.

- Forty-five percent of gay males and 20% of lesbians report having experienced verbal harassment and/or physical violence during high school.

- Forty-two percent of adolescent lesbians and 34% of adolescent gay males who have suffered physical attack also attempt suicide (Planned Parenthood of Connecticut, 1998, 1–2).

Issues around gender development and sexual orientation are very relevant to the educational process. Gay, lesbian, bisexual, and transgendered students often deal with prejudice, discrimination, and isolation at school, and sometimes at home as well. What can a teacher do to promote a balanced and positive environment?

When students who come from racial or ethnic minority groups encounter prejudice in schools, they generally go home to parents or family members from the same racial/ethnic groups who provide advice, comfort, and support. When LGBT students encounter prejudice or discrimination in school, there is no assurance that they will find support at home. They may encounter additional hostility from family members who are homophobic.

Programs to combat discrimination based on sexual orientation in schools are scarce. Equally scarce are components in the teacher preparation curriculum that address these issues. One major reason for the relatively mystical nature of this topic in educational circles is the degree of controversy that sexual orientation still generates in American society. Educators who advocate for equity in schools on the basis of race, culture, or gender may do so without having their own backgrounds questioned. People will rarely suggest that you are African American, Puerto Rican, or a woman if you are not. However, supporting equitable treatment for students irrespective of sexual orientation could risk questions about one's own sexual orientation. Given the negative stereotypes often attached to this label, educators may opt for silence as the risk-free alternative. When educators are silent in the face of harassment of gay and lesbian students, students suffer doubly—once because of the harassment and again because trusted adults turned their backs.

A number of noteworthy efforts to address the needs of LGBT students in public schools exist, and more are arising each year. More than two decades ago, the Harvey Milk School was started in New York City to offer lesbian, gay, bisexual, and transgendered youth a safe environment in which to pursue their education. This approach has been copied in a few large city school districts. The effort seen more commonly in schools around the country are the formations of gay/straight alliances (GSA) with varying degrees of support from school administrators. This group, as the name implies, assumes that all people are responsible for creating climates that discourage homophobia. Ten years ago, fewer than 100 schools sponsored gay/straight alliances. Today, more than 3,000 schools have GSA or other clubs that address LGBT issues (Gay, Lesbian, and Straight Education Network,

FIGURE 8.4

States with Safe Schools, Laws, and Policies

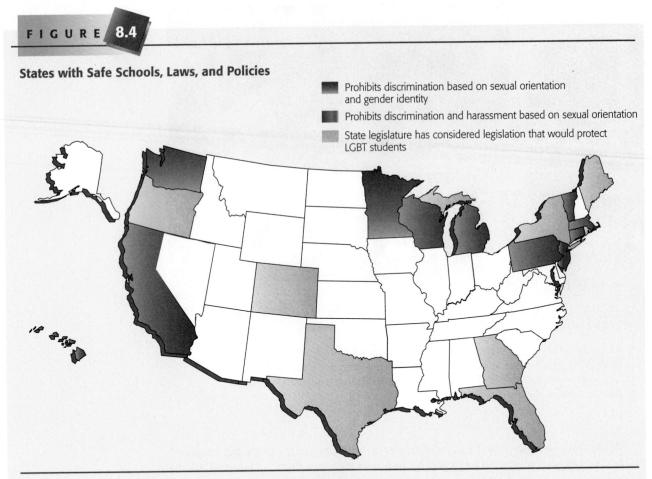

■ Prohibits discrimination based on sexual orientation and gender identity

■ Prohibits discrimination and harassment based on sexual orientation

■ State legislature has considered legislation that would protect LGBT students

Source: Gay, Lesbian, and Straight Education Network (GLSEN), "Laws and Policies Impacting LGBT Youth in Schools." (New York: Author, 2002): 4. Retrieved May 6, 2005, from www.glsen.org/binarydata/GLSEN_ATTACHMENTS/file/338-3.pdf. Copyright 2002 by GLSEN. Adapted with permission.

2005). Figure 8.4 identifies states that have established policies and laws to ensure that students are safe from discrimination and harassment in school based on sexual orientation and gender identity.

Whatever personal opinion an educator may hold toward LGBT orientation, one thing remains irrefutable—educators have the same legal and ethical responsibilities to educate LGBT students as any other category of students. To this end, educators must create schools and classrooms that are safe places for lesbian, gay, bisexual, and transgendered students to learn. Homophobic remarks by faculty, staff, or other students have no place in a safe learning environment and should be regarded with the same seriousness as racist, sexist, or religiously offensive comments. All degrade the learning environment. Homophobic remarks are sometimes made when the speaker perceives that there are no LGBT people within hearing distance, without realizing that many LBBT people have not divulged their sexual orientation in public for fear of negative consequences.

As a future teacher, you may very well have fellow teachers who are lesbian or gay. You may or may not be aware of your colleagues' sexual orientation, depending on their desire to let others know and the comfort level they feel in the school. It may be that you are that future gay or lesbian teacher. In any case, a collegial relationship among faculty is certainly undermined if teachers hear insulting remarks about themselves, even when such remarks may not be meant seriously.

In a professional setting such as a school, the topic of sexual orientation should be taken seriously by all professionals and is not an appropriate subject for humor. In relating to students, the teacher's sexual orientation, whether straight, lesbian, gay, bisexual, or transgendered, is not an appropriate component of the teacher/student relationship.

Teachers and school administrators have a professional obligation to play more active roles in securing safe learning environments for lesbian, gay, bisexual, and transgendered students. The issue here should not be framed in terms of supporting or not supporting a sexual orientation. Like physicians who provide professional health care for all patients, educators have the ethical and legal responsibility to provide a safe school environment for all students and teachers regardless of their sexual orientation.

Who am I?   **What do I believe?**

"Through education, backed by research, we can make a difference."

CAROL, RESOURCE TEACHER

THINK ABOUT THIS:

In order to make a difference in students' lives, you need to examine your own attitudes first. Do you feel you are a good role model for demonstrating tolerance? Write down the first five words that come to your mind associated with the term *poverty*. Now do the same for the term *diversity*. Are these words positive, negative, or a combination of the two?

SHARE and **COMPARE:**

As a teacher, what could you do in your class to make sure that all students have access to high-quality education? Discuss with a classmate what teachers can do to balance inequities, based on the various characteristics discussed throughout this chapter.

WHAT ROLE DOES RELIGION PLAY IN SCHOOLS?

When Americans were polled with the question, "When it comes to your outlook, do you regard yourself as . . . ?" 37% answered religious, 38% responded somewhat religious, and only 16% answered secular or somewhat secular (Kosmin, Mayer, & Keysar, 2001, p. 19). Clearly, teachers in U.S. schools interact with a significant majority of students for whom religion plays a major role in their lives. With regard to religious preference, 76.5% of Americans polled said they were Christian, with Catholics (24.3%), Baptists (16.3%), Methodists (6.8%), and nondenominational Christians (6.8%) making up the largest four Christian groups. Jews (1.3%) and Muslims (0.5%) were the largest of the non-Christian religions, with 19.5% saying they belonged to no religious group or failing to answer (Kosmin, Meyer, & Keysar, 2001). The exact mixture of religions that you may encounter in your classroom depends on where you teach. Although people of all faiths live throughout the country, certain areas have become enclaves for some groups more than others. For example, teachers in New York City or in South Florida will have higher proportions of Jewish students than would teachers in rural Iowa; those teaching in rural Georgia will have more Baptist pupils; faculty in Dearborn, Michigan, will encounter many more Muslim students; and those who teach in Utah will have many students from the Mormon faith.

Understanding the basic religious belief systems of your students and the surrounding community will be very helpful in your efforts to become an effective teacher.

RESPECTING DIFFERENCES

An example of the value of this knowledge is illustrated in a situation in which a Christian teacher was approached by a Jewish student said she had to miss the next two days because she was "sitting shiva." The teacher responded by saying, "Please give my condolences to your family." The student was quite surprised that a teacher who was not Jewish knew that "sitting shiva" is a traditional act of mourning someone who had passed away. The teacher demonstrated interest and respect in this case. Knowledge of and respect for other religions can generate tremendous goodwill for teachers from students and their families.

While public schools are prohibited from advancing specific religions, they must teach students who come from a variety of religious viewpoints. Therefore, teachers and other school professionals need to be knowledgeable about religions, especially those of students that attend their schools. Students from certain religions may require accommodations in the curriculum or school schedule. Most Jewish students will not attend classes on Yom Kippur. Observant Muslims will not eat or drink throughout the day during Ramadan. Jehovah's Witnesses do not pledge allegiance to the flag. Should schools respect these religious views or attempt to force these students to conform to the traditions of the majority? Decisions of the U.S. Supreme Court, as shown in Figure 5.1 on pages 142–143, generally side with the right of students to follow their religious views in schools without fear of punishment.

Religious beliefs sometimes require accommodations from public schools (Haynes, 1999). In one case, a math teacher announced the date for the midterm exam to his mathematics class. After class, he was approached by one of his students who told him that the exam was on Rosh Hashanah and he couldn't take the test that day. He asked for a later makeup test day, and the teacher agreed. Some of the other students heard this conversation and complained that it wasn't fair to them if their classmate got more time to study. What would you do if you were the teacher in this situation? What factors should you consider when making this decision?

As a veteran of 12 or more years of schooling, have you ever been asked to take an exam on a Sunday or on Christmas Day? How would you react if you were asked to do so and it conflicted with your religious beliefs? Christian students in U.S. public schools are not generally put in this position. While the school calendar is officially nonreligious, major Christian holidays and Sunday, the Christian day of worship, never conflict with classes or exams. Therefore, Christian students do not have to face the dilemma presented previously.

Another side of this discussion is that some students have no religious affiliation or may be agnostic or atheist. These students can often feel uncomfortable if they attend a public school where most students, faculty, and staff come from a religious background. These students have as much of a right to not have religious beliefs and still feel comfortable in their public schools as do students who come from religious homes. Teachers are in a key position to try to make all students sensitive to religious diversity in both schools and society.

CURRICULUM EFFECTS

Religion affects how people view social issues that are discussed in classrooms. Students' views on topics that may arise in the curriculum, such as gay marriage, abortion, evolution, separation of church and state, or even foreign policy issues, may be affected by their religious affiliations. Muslim and Jewish students may have very different opinions about conflicts in the Middle East. Students who belong to liberal religious denominations may have very narrow grounds to justify U.S. involvement in a war. In some denominations, such as the Mennonites or the Amish, war cannot be justified.

The religious views of students and their families may also influence other aspects of education. Students from conservative Christian backgrounds may object to studying Dar-

I N T A S C

Principle #3

Adapting Instruction for Individual Needs: The teacher understands how students differ in their approaches to learning and creates instructional opportunities that are adapted to diverse learners.

I N T A S C

Principle #7

Instructional Planning Skills: The teacher plans instruction based upon knowledge of subject matter, students, the community, and curriculum goals.

Informing yourself about the religious traditions of your students will help you be more culturally sensitive and accommodating of their specific needs.

winian evolution in a biology class and ask for exemption from the topic or for alternate assignments. On occasion, parents who object to certain topics in the curriculum for religious reasons try to have that topic removed from the curriculum for all students. Parents from some religious backgrounds may object to their children's participating in sex education because they feel that the topic is strictly for discussion at home or because they feel that such education may encourage sexual activity among teenagers.

An important concept to grasp in order to understand religions is the concept of **orthodoxy,** which refers to the degree to which someone is a strict or literal believer in a faith. Therefore, strict followers of three of the major religions in the world could be referred to as orthodox Muslims, Christians, or Jews. In general, orthodox followers of a religion believe in more strict gender roles and that women's primary role is in the home while men have the responsibility to provide for their families.

How is this knowledge practical to the average teacher? Suppose you have a female student who comes from an orthodox religious background. She is the top student in your chemistry class. You inquire about scholarships to top universities and contact a few chemistry departments to inquire on her behalf. You learn that she has an excellent chance of getting a full scholarship, but, if successful, she would have to go to another state to study. How might her family feel about your encouraging her to apply for a scholarship? They may be proud of their daughter's academic accomplishments but not want her to relocate away from the family in order to pursue a degree. As the teacher, you have to be careful or you could be viewed by the student's parents as meddling in family affairs where teachers don't belong.

PERSONAL BELIEFS

Educators also come from all segments of the spectrum of religious diversity. Whether public schoolteachers are highly religious or have no religious beliefs at all, their role in the classroom is the same. You may address religious topics when those issues are appropriate to the curriculum, but you need to avoid trying to impose your religious views on students.

Teachers cannot explain the Crusades without discussing the religious motivations of both Christians and Muslims. Christianity, Judaism, Islam, Buddhism ,and Baha'i must be discussed in detail as components of a comparative religions class. After all, students in such a class need to know what followers of each religion believe (Haynes, 1999). What teachers cannot do, however, is advocate one religion over another. A number of court cases throughout history have examined the role of religion in public schools, in particular *McCollum v. (Champaign County, Ill.) Board of Education* (1948), *Abington School District v. Schempp* (1963), *Epperson v. Arkansas* (1968), and *Wisconsin v. Yoder* (1972). You have to remain objective when you examine religious beliefs/topics in a public school classroom.

People often feel strongly about their religious beliefs, and these emotions can affect classroom discussions on a variety of subjects. Some conservative Protestant faiths feel that the *Abington School District v. Schempp* (1963) Supreme Court decision, which disallowed prayer in public schools, was a mistake and public schools should return to the practice of beginning each day with a prayer. But in a religiously diverse nation, would students of minority faiths be expected to bow their heads and listen politely to Christian prayers? Would Christian students occasionally do the same and listen to Muslim, Jewish, or Buddhist prayers? This issue remains controversial more than four decades after the *Abington* decision.

Teachers in today's schools need to have significant knowledge about religion as well as the court decisions and laws that govern the place of religion in schools. For instance, students may conduct prayer sessions in public schools as long as they occur outside school hours. They also may have religious clubs that meet in public school classrooms (Anti-Defamation League, 2001). However, students may not use public schools as a place to try to convert fellow students, and teachers are also barred from engaging in this activity. One of the responsibilities of teachers is to ensure that students enjoy the benefits of a public education without feeling uncomfortable for their religious beliefs or lack thereof.

FINAL THOUGHTS

This chapter has examined the effects of social class, race, ethnicity, language, gender, religion, and sexual orientation on what occurs in American schools. The issues covered by each topic should not be interpreted as an all-inclusive list, but rather as an introduction to a discussion on each subject. U.S. public schools are becoming more diverse with each passing year. Current and future teachers can view this increasing diversity as a trend that creates an insurmountable challenge, or as a demographic fact that is making our schools more interesting human communities. One thing is certainly clear: effective teachers in the twenty-first century need to be much more than subject-matter competent. You will need to be multiculturally and globally literate in order to effectively teach an increasingly diverse student population. Becoming highly knowledgeable on the issues raised in this chapter takes considerable time. Nobody does it in one college course or after reading one book. Your investment in learning more about these topics will pay great dividends in the future because teachers who are effective "border crossers" to other cultures reach more students and also derive more satisfaction from teaching.

The chapter began by distinguishing between *equal* and *equitable* treatment of students. A single example used by a teacher does not work equally well with all students, but you could argue that the teacher has treated all students equally if they all heard the same example. Teachers concerned with equitable treatment present different examples until every student has grasped the idea. Without question, striving for equitable education requires more effort and imagination and represents a greater challenge than treating all students identically.

Americans have always relished a challenge. How well American education meets the needs of a diverse student population will affect this nation's future for generations to come.

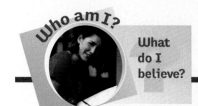

REFLECTIONS

Professional Plan for Diversity and the Cultural Context of Teaching

1. Three main ideas I learned in this chapter about diversity issues and schools are:

2. Two things in this chapter that I would like to learn more about are:

   a. _____

   b. _____

3. I plan to investigate these two areas and learn more about topics in this chapter by:

   _____ Reading some of the book club choices

   _____ Reading sources referenced in the chapter that interest me

   _____ Interviewing teachers about diversity issues they have encountered in their careers

   _____ Exploring the websites listed in the Log On section

   _____ Observing classrooms and taking notes on what issues mentioned in this chapter occurred and how teachers responded to them

4. I will include the following in my Touch the Future portfolio:

   _____ Responses to Who Am I? activities

   _____ A brief essay on my thoughts about Problems to Possibilities.

   _____ Responses to the Observation Guide

   _____ Other (materials assigned by your instructor):

SUMMARY

How Does Socioeconomic Status Affect Learning?

- Median family incomes affect which public schools students attend and which academic tracks they are likely to follow.
- The socioeconomic status of students influences the average level of funding in public schools.
- Students' socioeconomic backgrounds often affect teachers' academic expectations and the quality of instruction available.
- Students' social class has an influence on placement in special education and gifted classes.

What Effect Does Race Have on Schools?

- Race has no biological significance, although it has the social significance society chooses to give it.
- Self-segregation is sometimes used by students of color as a means to cope with stress or racism.
- Biracial and multiracial students are a small but rapidly growing segment of the student population.
- White racial identity brings with it benefits that are often unrecognized.

How Do Ethnicity and Language Differences Affect Learning?

- Schools require varying degrees of conformity that influence some students' cultures more than others.
- In general, the more students' cultures vary from mainstream U.S. culture, the more difficulties they will encounter in schools.
- Students who speak English as a second language are an increasing proportion of U.S. students.
- Students who are literate in their first language learn English more quickly than those who are not.
- Bilingual programs are often controversial because many people do not understand why it is beneficial to nurture a first language in order to teach English as a second language.

How Do Gender and Sexuality Issues Affect Schools?

- Classroom interaction patterns show that teachers tend to give more attention to boys than to girls.
- There are differences in the communication patterns of males and females.
- During the middle school years, girls have a greater decrease in academic self-concept than boys.
- Lesbian, gay, bisexual, and transgendered students experience significant prejudice in schools.
- The issue of teaching lesbian, gay, bisexual, and transgendered students should not be framed on the basis of supporting or not supporting a sexual orientation.
- Teachers have the legal and ethical responsibility for providing a safe environment and quality education for LGBT students.

What Role Does Religion Play in Schools?

- Students from some religious backgrounds may require some accommodation in school procedures.
- Supreme Court decisions generally support the rights of students to follow their religious beliefs in public schools without fear of punishment.
- U.S. public school calendars, while officially nonreligious, do not intrude on Christian holidays or days of worship.
- Orthodoxy, or strict religious interpretation, may be found in nearly all faiths.
- Religious affiliation may affect students' perceptions on a variety of topics in the curriculum.

Companion Website

Visit the **Touch the Future . . . Teach!** Companion Website at www.ablongman.com/diaz for additional opportunities.

KEY WORDS

basic interpersonal
 communication skills
 (BICS)   245
bilingual education   246
cognitive academic language
 proficiency (CALP)   245
cultural additive stage   243
English for Speakers of Other
 Languages (ESOL)   246

English immersion   246
generational poverty   229
institutional sexism   248
involuntary minority groups
 243
Latinegros   240
Lau v. Nichols   244
oppositional identity   237

orthodoxy   255
silenced dialogue   237
situational poverty   228
voluntary minority groups
 243
white flight   238
white privilege   240

CONCEPT REVIEW

1. Distinguish between equal and equitable treatment.

2. Understand how the socioeconomic status of a community influences the quality of education that is typically available.

3. Understand why some students of color may self-segregate while others may adapt a strategy of "racelessness."

4. Identify the landmark Supreme Court cases in the area of school segregation and integration.

5. Identify the dilemmas often faced by biracial and multiracial students.

6. Explain the characteristics of white privilege.

7. Understand how first-language literacy affects the acquisition of second-language literacy.

8. Distinguish between basic interpersonal communication skills (BICS) and cognitive academic language proficiency (CALP).

9. Summarize research findings on how boys and girls are treated differently in schools.

10. Explain what is meant by a gender-balanced curriculum.

11. Identify factors that contribute to LGBT students feeling isolation and fear in public schools.

12. Explain how students' religious views may affect their opinions on various topics in the curriculum.

TOUCH THE FUTURE . . .

Read On

Amazing Grace: The Lives of Children and the Conscience of a Nation
Jonathan Kozol (New York: Harper Perennial, 1996)
By the author of *Savage Inequalities* (also recommended); filled with first-person narratives of students and the people who nurture them, a powerful narrative of how children in the South Bronx deal with difficulties.

Teaching Strategies for Ethnic Studies (7th edition)
James A. Banks (Boston: Allyn and Bacon, 2003)
Authored by the founder of the field of multicultural education; an excellent source for readers who want to increase their knowledge about ethnic groups in the United States; chapters also contain lesson plans as well as annotated bibliographies for teachers and students.

Affirming Diversity: The Sociopolitical Context of Multicultural Education (4th ed.)
Sonia Nieto (Boston: Longman, 2004)
Helps explain the "why" behind issues of race, language, ethnicity, and equity in public schools; the author, a well-known scholar in multicultural education, also provides some stimulating case studies in many chapters.

Log On

National Association for Multicultural Education
www.nameorg.org
> The major professional organization in the United States concerning multicultural issues in schools; the site contains links to publications, position papers, and resources in the field.

North Central Regional Educational Laboratory
www.ncrel.org
> Provides links to topics such as No Child Left Behind legislation, teacher quality, and school improvement.

Electronic Resources on Diversity
http://www.scu.edu/diversity/esources.html
> Link to general information on ethnicity, as well as specific links to information on African Americans, Asian Americans, European Americans, Latinos, Middle Eastern Americans, and Native American groups.

National Clearinghouse for English Language Acquisition
http://www.ncela.gwu.edu/
> Contains information about language issues and education, technical assistance, and a link to job searches.

Public Broadcasting System
www.pbs.org/race
> A website that accompanies the PBS documentary series, *Race: The Power of an Illusion;* contains various links to timelines, human diversity, and quick facts about race and explains how race has been used to justify social inequalities as natural.

Write On

"What we want to see is the child in pursuit of knowledge, not knowledge in pursuit of the child."
—George Bernard Shaw

In your journal, write a short essay explaining what you think Shaw meant in this statement. How do you think this idea compares with the emphasis on high-stakes testing? How well do teachers have to know individual students to enact Shaw's idea?

OBSERVATION GUIDE

TEACH: LINKING THEORY TO PRACTICE

Linking Theory to Practice

Objective: To observe classroom interactions

School (use code name): _____   Interviewer: _____

Grade Level Observed: _____   Date: _____

Subject Taught: _____   Time In: _____   Time Out: _____

Directions: In this observation activity you will observe typical classroom patterns of communication between the teacher and students, as well as among students. Try to observe "the sociology of the classroom." Answer as many of the following questions as your observations permit. Afterward, use these answers to write a brief essay explaining the patterns of interaction in the classroom or classrooms you observed and include it in your Touch the Future portfolio.

1. Notice the seating pattern in the classroom. Are students of a similar racial/ethnic background or gender concentrated in a section of the room?

2. Who chose the seating pattern? Was it the teacher or students?

3. Make a T chart in your notes and label one side *Boys* and the other *Girls*. Make a mark whenever the teacher addresses a student. Are students of each gender receiving the amount of teacher attention that corresponds to their numbers in the classroom?

4. Notice the degree of suggestion or encouragement in the teacher's responses to students. Are girls receiving the same as boys?

5. Make another T chart and label each side regarding another characteristic of diversity present in the classroom (such as ethnicity or native- or second-language learners of English). Repeat steps 3 and 4, using the characteristics you chose.

Connecting with INTASC: Principle 3

Adapting Instruction for Individual Needs: The teacher understands how students differ in their approaches to learning and creates instructional opportunities that are adapted to diverse learners.

After observing the class, find out what the teacher does to meet Principle 3. Ask what classes or professional development workshops the teacher has taken that focused on dealing with diversity issues. Ask how useful these classes were and what diversity issues the teacher wishes had been covered more thoroughly. Finally, explore what the teacher's school does to adapt to the changing diversity, and what the teacher does to adapt instruction to meet the needs of students.

9

Curriculum: What to Expect in American Schools

Who am I?

What do I believe?

THINK ABOUT THIS:

Everything you learned in school was part of a larger curriculum. Some of what you learned was formally presented to you in textbooks and as part of your classroom instruction. Much of what you learned, however, was informally taught to you by your teachers and classmates.

How were you shaped by the curriculum that you learned in school? To what extent are the values that you hold today a result of what you were taught? What do you believe should be the role of the schools, and more specifically, the role of the curriculum in shaping who and what students are?

> "Curriculum . . . resides at the very core of education."
>
> Elliot W. Eisner (1984)

This chapter explores the different forces of curriculum—both formal and informal—that shape and define the content of public education and schooling in the United States. By the time you have completed this chapter, you will have learned the answers to the following key questions:

Key Questions

1. What is curriculum?
2. How does curriculum represent cultural values?
3. What are the historical roots of curriculum in the United States?
4. What roles do teachers play in the curriculum?
5. What roles do textbooks play in the curriculum?

The communication of ideas and information about ways of living and understanding the world is seen by many people as the primary purpose of schooling. As a teacher, you are in the classroom to guide students through the process of learning. In order to do this you will have to have content, or a curriculum, to teach. Curriculum comes in many shapes and forms and is influenced by many different forces. One of the most important tasks you will have as a beginning teacher is to understand the curriculum that you will be required to teach. Being an effective teacher involves implementing a formal plan of study, maintaining standards, and working with students informally, but in important ways that go beyond what is included in textbooks and the guidelines provided by your school district.

WHAT IS CURRICULUM?

At first, defining the meaning of **curriculum** is simple. The *American Heritage Dictionary* (1982), for example, defines it as "1. The aggregate of courses of study given in a school, college, etc. 2. The regular or a particular course of study in a school, college." *Roget's Thesaurus* (1963) lists *syllabus, content,* and *learning* as synonyms for *curriculum.*

Definitions like these, however, don't really explain how the curriculum functions and what role it plays in shaping American public education. You need to understand the concept of the curriculum as a technology, a system, and a cultural phenomenon.

THE FORMAL AND INFORMAL CURRICULUM

Learning in the schools takes place on both a formal and an informal level. Too often, we tend to think of the curriculum only in a formal context. It is important to understand that the curriculum is more complex than this. In kindergarten you probably learned to recite the alphabet, to read simple words, and to count with numbers. Perhaps you used a simple textbook or primer. The things you learned were almost certainly part of a **formal curriculum.** If you went to a public school, the curriculum that you learned had probably been formulated at the state level, and was designed to meet specific learning or behavioral objectives. A good example of the formal curriculum is what you find in textbooks.

At the same time, as you were learning the formal curriculum, you were also being taught an **informal curriculum.** The informal curriculum is never actually defined. It often involves social things. Think again about your experience in kindergarten. Your teacher likely taught you certain social behaviors, such as how to line up to go out on the playground and how to interact with your fellow students. Perhaps you learned something about gender roles. Almost every adult woman in the United States, for example, probably has a memory of being told to "act like a lady" at some point in her life. Or perhaps she was told, "That's not the way a girl is supposed to behave." Young boys are informally taught "to be strong" and never to cry. These are good examples of the informal curriculum.

When talking about the informal curriculum, two related concepts are often introduced—the hidden curriculum and the null curriculum. Each is an important means of shaping and defining what children know and the social values they hold.

● **The Hidden Curriculum** Phillip Jackson in his book *Life in Classrooms* (1968) first developed the concept of the **hidden curriculum,** which he defines as curriculum that promotes cultural mores and values that "each student (and teacher) must master if he is to make his way satisfactorily through the school" (Jackson, 1968, pp. 33–34). McLaren (1998) calls it the "unintended outcomes of the schooling process" (p. 186) that take place

INTASC

Principle #5

Classroom Motivation and Management: The teacher uses an understanding of individual and group motivation and behavior to create a learning environment that encourages positive social interaction, active engagement in learning, and self-motivation.

Recognizing the limitations of the general curriculum and adopting special curriculum devices allows you to avoid the trap of a dominant discourse tendency that ignores topics and subjects related to cultural diversity.

in classrooms beyond the teaching of official subject matter, outside the course materials and the scheduled lesson content.

The hidden curriculum often reflects dominant ideologies in the schools and community. As educational theorist Elliot Eisner (1985) explains, "schools teach far more than they advertise" (p. 92). Think about your own experience in school. What lessons about life did you learn outside the structures of course instruction?

● **The Null Curriculum**   Closely related to the concept of the hidden curriculum is the concept of the null curriculum. The **null curriculum** refers to the lessons that are taught as a result of *not* teaching something. Eisner (1985) categorizes the null curriculum along two major dimensions: the *cognitive processes* that are stressed or disregarded and the *subject matter* included or excluded in the curricular content of the schools. Cognitive processes are how information is communicated or taught. Are students in elementary schools taught to spell by memorizing, by oral drill and repetition, or by copying down long lists of words? Is one thing being taught by not teaching another thing? For example, are students taught that group work is not important if a spelling lesson focuses on individual memorization? Think about the unspoken messages children hear every time a teacher praises another child as "a prize student." What is the hidden message here? If that child is a "prize," then what am I?

In the case of *subject matter,* excluding certain topics or books from the curriculum—that is, what is taught—teaches students that a particular subject is not important or worth the attention of those who are learning. Thus, the systematic exclusion of Black history and women's history from high school American history textbooks until the late 1960s "taught" that these subjects were not important or worthy of inclusion in the curriculum. The existence of the null curriculum has profound consequences: "ignorance is not simply a neutral void; it has important effects on the kinds of options one is able to consider, the alternatives one can examine, and the perspectives from which one can view a situation or problem" (Eisner, 1985, p. 97). Teachers have to be aware at all times of the potential for unintended messages to be hidden in their lessons.

Through the Eyes of Culturally Sensitive Teachers

Architecture and the Hidden Curriculum

Juliet Hart recalls being a beginning special education teacher of students with severe emotional disturbances:

I was both excited and anxious about my first teaching assignment. I learned I would be teaching a diverse group of elementary students in grades K–5. I was looking forward to working with the general education content-area teachers of subjects such as music, physical education, and art because of my firm conviction that at least some of my students, given appropriate behavioral management supports, would be able to be mainstreamed for these subject areas, thus maximizing the benefits they could experience due to contact with their nondisabled peers. In addition, I was looking forward to coordinating my class schedule for activities such as lunch, library visits, and recess with the general education teachers so that my students could be included to the greatest extent possible in the realm of activities of the school in general.

During the preplanning period for teachers, I arrived at the school and was given information about where my classroom was located. To my surprise and dismay, portable #58 was quite a trek from the school's office, and was an even greater distance from the cafeteria, library, recess area,

and most important the general education classroom wing where I hoped many of my students would be mainstreamed for instruction with regular education students. Throughout the four years I taught in portable #58, my students lost valuable instructional time because of time spent traveling to and from various locales around the school. In addition, the physical distance my students experienced from the central locations of the school site sent a strong, yet hidden message. The physical structure of the school functioned as a hidden curriculum that sent a message of exclusion of students with disabilities from the school's most basic and critical activities.

Juliet's description points to how physical space operates as part of the hidden curriculum. In her case, students with special needs are taught that they are different from mainstream students and do not warrant special attention.

Points to Ponder

1. Can you think of examples from your own experience as a student in which you saw a hidden curriculum at work?

2. Considering the definition of a null curriculum, what message is being sent in Juliet's case?

3. What are the potential ramifications of Juliet's situation?

PHYSICAL SPACE AS CURRICULUM

INTASC

Principle #6

Communication Skills: The teacher uses knowledge of effective verbal, nonverbal, and media communication techniques to foster active inquiry, collaboration, and supportive interaction in the classroom.

Some educators argue that the curriculum is everything that goes on in the schools (Winch & Gingell, 1999). Thus we can say that the physical design of a school is a curriculum. Have you ever noticed that there are windows in the doors of most public school classrooms? In older buildings, typically, there is a 3-by-3-foot window at the top of most doors. In newer buildings there is often a solid door with a 6-inch-wide window that goes the entire length of the door. These may seem like trivial design features, but in fact, they represent a powerful part of a curriculum of observation and control that is physically set into the school building.

Windows in classroom doors are used to observe in rather than out. Principals and other administrators look in on classrooms as they walk by. As they move by, their perspective changes and they are able to observe different parts of the classroom. The teacher or students inside the classroom, unless they are moving, can only see out to one fixed point. As a result, teachers and students become aware that they are subject to surveillance as part of their day-to-day activity.

Therefore, curriculum can literally be embedded in the design of a building. It is no accident that in the nineteenth century many schools were designed to look like temples and churches—because they were meant to be temples or cathedrals of knowledge. The design of a school building tells you something about the environment in which the school is set, as well as the type of learning that goes on in it. In this sense, the design of the school building is part of the curriculum. What do you think the design of contemporary schools suggest? New schools being built today now incorporate more outside light and provide more internal open space that encourages collaboration and cooperation.

"I entered the classroom with the conviction that it was crucial for me and every other student to be an active participant, not a passive consumer . . . education that connects the will to know with the will to become."

bell hooks

THINK ABOUT THIS:

All of us have had classes in school in which we were expected to simply learn what was taught and not think or reflect on what we had learned. Are there situations in which just learning the facts is all that a student needs to do?

SHARE and **COMPARE:**

Make a list of when just "learning the facts" might be justified. If you think that just learning the facts is never justified, explain why. Talk to a classmate or friend about what it means to be an "active" learner, and the benefits of being an active versus a passive learner.

HOW DOES CURRICULUM REPRESENT CULTURAL VALUES?

INTASC

Principle #7

Instructional Planning Skills: The teacher plans instruction based upon knowledge of subject matter, students, the community, and curriculum goals.

In 1860, the English social philosopher Herbert Spencer (1820–1903) wrote his famous essay "What Knowledge Is of Most Worth?" In this piece Spencer asked the perennial question, to what knowledge should we devote ourselves to as a culture, and by inference, what should we teach in the schools? Spencer asked what is perhaps the most important question, and certainly one of the most interesting questions, in education: "What should we teach?" Determining what is taught is ultimately a political process, one that involves the investment of cultural capital.

Cultural capital refers to the idea that a society such as the United States invests in teaching certain knowledge or information to its students. According to Henry Giroux, "Just as a country distributes goods and services, what can be labeled as material capital, it also distributes and legitimates certain forms of knowledge, language practices, values, modes of style and so forth, or what can be labeled cultural capital" (Giroux, 1988, pp. 5–6). What is selected to be included, or not included, in the curriculum of our schools becomes an extremely important issue. Not only does it reflect who has power and influence, but also whose voice and beliefs are heard in our culture. In this sense, the curriculum represents cultural capital.

TEXTBOOKS AS CURRICULUM

Textbooks are also a form of cultural capital. This can be seen by looking at textbooks published during different historical periods.

● **The New England Primer** *The New England Primer,* for example, first published at the end of the seventeenth century, contains a curriculum dominated by issues of religion and death. The beginning of the book includes lists of one-, two-, three-, four-, five-, and six-syllable words. In the list of words with six syllables you will find *A-bo-mi-na-ti-on, Gra-ti-fi-ca-ti-on, Be-ne-fi-ci-al-ly, Hu-mi-li-a-ti-on, Con-ti-nu-a-ti-on, I-ma-gi-na-ti-on, De-ter-mi-na-ti-on, Mor-ti-fi-ca-ti-on, E-di-fi-ca-ti-on, Pu-ri-fi-ca-ti-on, Fa-mi-li-a-ri-ty,* and *Qua-li-fi-ca-ti-on.*

These are not the types of words used today to teach students how to read. But *The New England Primer* was intended to be the first book used to teach colonial children how to read. These words reflected a culture concerned with religious issues and values consistent with the historical period in which the book was written and used. In the rhyming alphabet also included in *The New England Primer,* references are made not only to death and mortality, but to specific stories and episodes from the Bible.

Think about how different the content of a book such as *The New England Primer* is from the books you would use to teach children how to read in a classroom today. Textbooks, both historically and in contemporary times, reflect the dominant values of our culture. As culture changes, its values and traditions change as well. Thus, a textbook that worked well in the nineteenth century—even for a subject as basic as reading—would have little relevance today.

● **The McGuffey Readers** If *The New England Primer* reflects the values of late-seventeenth-century colonial society, then the McGuffey readers provide a similar insight into the nature and purpose of mid-nineteenth-century American culture. First published in 1836 by Professor Willam Holmes McGuffey (1800–1873) while he was president of Cincinnati College, the series included six basic readers that took students through a process of basic instruction at the elementary level in reading and language arts.

McGuffey's textbooks were enormously popular and were widely used in American schools throughout the nineteenth century. The readers heavily emphasized the idea of hard work and personal achievement. They also reflected and promoted democratic values. Chase Osborn, the governor of Michigan just prior to World War I, recalled how the first schoolbook that he remembered was the speller from the McGuffey series:

> It had a picture of a good dog Tray getting a beating because he was caught in the company of a bad dog. "Evil communications corrupt good manners" was the lesson.

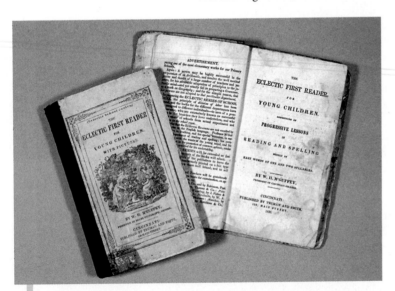

A staple of nineteenth-century American education, the McGuffey Reader promoted democratic values, as well as values such as hard work and personal achievement.

Osborn also describes the fable of a boy up in an apple tree stealing fruit. The tree's owner, an old man, threatens him with a big stick, telling him to get out of the tree. The boy ignores him, thinking that the old man cannot reach him and dares him in an effort to stop him from taking the fruit. The old man proves much more of a threat than the boy realizes, knocking him out of the tree. He runs away having received a sound beating. It turns out that the story served as the inspiration to Teddy Roosevelt's phrase "Speak softly and carry a big stick," which became the metaphor for his plan for the United States to police the Western Hemisphere as an expansion of the earlier Monroe Doctrine.

● **The Dick and Jane Readers** By the beginning of the twentieth century, other textbooks had taken the place of the McGuffey readers in the schools. Probably the most famous single textbook series to come out the first half of the twentieth century was the Dick and Jane readers—which included *Fun with Dick and Jane, Our New Friends, Fun Wherever We Are,* and many more.

First published in the 1930s, the Dick and Jane readers incorporated not only new methods of reading instruction, but also a very specific vision of what it meant to be an American. The books portray a "typical" American family. Mother stays at home and raises the family, while Father goes off to work in the city at an office. Mother and the two girls (Jane and Sally) are blond-haired and imitate their mother and her interests. Dick, the eldest child, is manly and, like his father, likes to take command of projects and get them done. Mother and the girls mostly help.

The early editions of the book did not include Black characters, nor did they include ethnic minorities. Not until the mid-1960s did a middle-class Black family move in next door to Dick and Jane and their family. Their inclusion reflected changes that were taking place in American culture as a result of the civil rights movement and were beginning to redefine the curriculum of the American schools.

Works such as the McGuffey readers and the Dick and Jane readers clearly conveyed specific social and political values—ones that reflected what was seen as important by mainstream American culture during their respective historical periods.

This idea of textbooks reflecting the society and culture of which they are a part is essential to understanding one of the basic functions of the culture, which is to reproduce the culture. Thus a high school American history textbook includes discussions of the Constitution of the United States, and not very much about the constitutions of other countries. Likewise, American literary and historical figures will be emphasized, rather than the literatures or traditions of other people and cultures. This makes perfect sense, except for the fact, as discussed earlier, that our culture is becoming increasingly more diverse and more equitable. So what should be the content of the curriculum found in the textbooks use in our schools?

Penny said, "Look at this little dog. See what it will do for me. I want this one."

Pam said, "Oh, this is fun. I like the three little dogs. I want a little dog."

Textbooks reflect larger social changes in the culture, as in the case of the Dick and Jane readers, which included a Black family for the first time in the mid-1960s.

CULTURAL LITERACY

During the last 15 to 20 years, there has been considerable debate over what should or should not be taught in the schools. E. D. Hirsch, Jr., set off a huge debate with the 1987 publication of his book *Cultural Literacy*. In this work, as well as in books such as *The Schools We Need and Why We Don't Have Them* (1996), and through his efforts with the Core Knowledge Foundation, Hirsch has argued that schools—both public and private—should teach a core curriculum based largely on the Western cultural tradition. In order for citizens to be literate and able to engage in a common conversation, Hirsch maintains that certain ideas and information need to be held in common across the culture.

Among the most controversial aspects of Hirsch's *Cultural Literacy* was the inclusion of a list of 5,000 things "every American needs to know." Most of the items on the list are perfectly reasonable things for an educated citizen to know. Under the letter *Q*, for example, he includes *quadratic equation, Quaker, quantum leap, quantum mechanics, quarantine, quark,* and *quasars.* Examples of Q words he does not have in his list, however, are *quantum computer, queer, quilt,* and *Quetzalcoatl.*

Is knowing the meaning of the word *Quetzalcoatl,* an ancient pre-Columbian god from the region now known as Mexico, less important than knowing the meaning of *Quaker*? Are you more culturally literate or more able to communicate with other Americans if you know the meaning of one term versus the other? Which term is more important?

If you come from Philadelphia and your relatives date back to the colonial period, then perhaps knowing about the Quaker tradition in North America is more important than

I N T A S C

Principle #7

Instructional Planning Skills: The teacher plans instruction based upon knowledge of subject matter, students, the community, and curriculum goals.

EDUCATION MATTERS

Values: The Implicit Curriculum

At River School in California the school culture includes an implicit curriculum of values called the four R's: responsibility, respect, resourcefulness, and responsiveness, according to Adlerian psychologist Raymond Corsini. The school's message to teachers is, "You are not teaching subjects, you are teaching who you are." The school rarely *talks* about character; teachers just model the values they want to see in their students by example. The school's mission is to help students develop a strong sense of self through demonstrations of personal and social responsibility.

Conflicts in the community become opportunities to grow and deal with differences, as well as how to solve real problems. The school wants students to be able to voice their opinions and share their ideas so they feel empowered to participate fully. The message at this school is clear. Teachers respect their students because they are human beings. They admit that their ideas are not new; the school has just applied them to everyday situations. Everything they do and say is about character.

The Education Issue: Is there a place for teaching and modeling values in schools?

How Does a Values Curriculum Impact Teachers and Students?

Teachers in some school districts may say they are hired to teach content, and values have no place in schools. This is the job of the parents. It becomes one more thing for teachers to do. On the other hand, teaching students how to respond appropriately may reduce discipline and management issues teachers typically have in schools, which could make their lives easier. Could a values curriculum be in conflict for religious reasons?

What's Your Opinion?

1. Did your school experience include a focus on values education? If yes, how did it affect you as a learner?

2. Would you be comfortable working in a school that used a values curriculum? How could it help you in the classroom?

Source: L. Inlay, "Values: The Implicit Curriculum," *Educational Leadership,* 60(6) (2003): 69–71.

---

knowing about *Quetzalcoatl*. If you are Mexican American or Native American and live in the Southwest, however, then perhaps *Quetzalcoatl* is more important for you to know if you want to be culturally literate. Whose culture needs to emphasized? What is American? What is essential or **core knowledge?**

In a highly diverse culture such as the United States, there is intense disagreement over what the content of the curriculum should be. Hirsch's emphasis on a predominantly Western curriculum tends to reflect his own background and interests, but many other equally important topics could be taught. There needs to be a constructive democratic dialogue concerning the curriculum included in our schools. Perhaps just as important as *what* is taught is the dialogue that people need to engage in concerning what *should* be included in the education of our children so that they become culturally literate.

THE MYTH OF A VALUE-FREE CURRICULUM

There is a widespread belief in education that it is possible to create a totally objective and value-free curriculum. However, every curriculum is culturally specific and represents a very specific and selective way of viewing the world. This may seem obvious when discussing a subject such as history, but not so clear with a subject such as mathematics. Teaching history obviously includes the selection of specific social and political themes, but mathematics is just formulas and operations, right? Think for a minute: What system of mathematical notation is used? In Western culture we notate mathematics using a system based on ancient Arabic models. The Mayans and Romans, just to mention a few different cultures, used different notation systems. Let's take another example from mathematics: What is the content of word problems? What subjects do they focus on, and so on? Do word problems in mathematics have the potential to be culturally biased? Or is mathematics an essentially neutral or value-free curriculum?

No. All curricula carry with them the values of the people who created them. If no curriculum can be entirely neutral, can it be reasonably objective? The answer is yes. Teachers in the classroom, and the textbooks they use in instruction, need to make clear what perspectives they hold and how those perspectives shape the way they view the world. While there is no such thing as neutral knowledge and teaching, you should be aware enough of your own personal feelings and beliefs to be objective. Suppose, for example, you are a high school health teacher personally opposed to abortion. You should be able to discuss abortion issues as part of the curriculum with your students while not imposing your personal values on the discussion. You can, however, help your students understand what issues underlie the abortion debate in American society. Likewise, the textbooks you choose to use should be as objective and fair as possible as well.

WHAT ARE THE HISTORICAL ROOTS OF CURRICULUM IN THE UNITED STATES?

The American curriculum has always been shaped by politics, the educational needs of children, and the social values at work in the culture. These influences can be seen in more than just the content of our textbooks but also in the philosophical models that guide teaching and in the reform movements that arise.

PHILOSOPHICAL FORCES THAT GUIDE THE CURRICULUM

A number of philosophical forces have come together to shape the curriculum found in American schools over the last hundred years. Some have been social in nature; others have been psychological.

● **Sociocultural Forces**   Social and cultural forces were spearheaded by the work of John Dewey (1859–1952) and John Franklin Bobbitt (1876–1952). Both were university professors who taught for at least part of their careers at the University of Chicago. Each had a very different definition of the role and function of curriculum.

John Dewey   Dewey came out of a liberal/progressive tradition that emphasized social improvement and reform. Dewey was primarily a philosopher. While teaching at the University of Chicago in the early 1890s, he began to formulate a theory of education based on the point of view of the child. He became interested in this issue because he was concerned about the education of his own children. Dewey came to the conclusion that schools were social centers where children learned by doing. At the **laboratory school** that Dewey and his colleagues established at the University of Chicago in 1896, he developed a model of elementary education in which the school functioned as a small collaborative society, and teachers and students joined together to solve real problems. Laboratory schools are schools that are run by a college or university to serve as demonstration schools. They often model best teaching practices, test new strategies, and offer the college or university age-appropriate subjects and environments in which to test new theories and observe children and their development. Lab schools incorporate the latest ideas in education and generally offer challenging and progressive curricula.

> **INTASC**
>
> **Principle #9**
>
> *Professional Commitment and Responsibility:* The teacher is a reflective practitioner who continually evaluates the effects of his/her choices and actions on others (students, parents, and other professionals in the learning community) and who actively seeks out opportunities to grow professionally.

For Dewey, it was imperative that schools become vital and meaningful social institutions. He felt that schools should represent an "embryonic" version of community. They should be:

> active with the types of occupations that reflect the life of the larger society, and permeated throughout with the spirit of art, history and science. When the school introduces and trains each child of society into membership within such a little community, saturating him with the spirit of service, and providing him with the instruments of effective self-direction, we shall have the deepest and best guaranty of a larger society, which is worthy, lovely, and harmonious." (Dewey, 1907, pp. 43–44)

Dewey believed that developmental, intellectual, and social goals were intertwined in the process of schooling, and therefore in the curriculum. Cooking, for example, was included as part of the school's curriculum. Children learned not only to cook, but to measure and interact with other people, as well as to test different foods for the presence of proteins, fats, and carbohydrates. Cooking thus became part of a science lesson as much as an experience in home economics (Tanner, p. 27).

Dewey's work at the laboratory school influenced him throughout his career. His ideas about education—what have come to be known specifically as progressive education—had a profound influence on the development of K–12 schooling, both public and private, throughout the twentieth century. Dewey's work is often misunderstood, however, and considered nonacademic and lacking in substance. He was opposed to children's learning "inert facts" that had little or no meaning in their lives. He promoted a highly rigorous and academic curriculum, nonetheless, which emphasized experimentation, cooperative learning, and shared social responsibilities.

John Franklin Bobbitt A competing and in many respects more successful model than Dewey's was promoted by educational administrator John Franklin Bobbitt. Like Dewey, Bobbitt was a professor of education at the University of Chicago in the early 1900s. Unlike Dewey, Bobbitt was part of the **social efficiency movement** in the United States. At the beginning of the twentieth century, believers in this movement tried to increase industrial productivity through scientific management. Educators, including Bobbitt, tried to apply its principles to increase the effectiveness of schools.

In 1918, Bobbitt wrote what many consider to be the first modern textbook in curriculum, *The Curriculum*. Bobbitt applied an industrial and scientific management model to the schools and the curriculum that they taught. In the preface to *The Curriculum*, Bobbitt defined what he meant by curriculum:

> Human life, however varied, consists in the performance of specific activities. Education that prepares for life is one that prepares definitely and adequately for these specific activities. However numerous and diverse they may be for any social class, they can be discovered. This requires only that one go out into the world of affairs and discover the particulars of which these affairs consist. These will show the abilities, attitudes, habits, appreciations, and forms of knowledge that men need. These will be the objectives of the curriculum. They will be numerous, definite, and particularized. The curriculum will then be that series of experiences which children and youth must have by way of attaining those objectives. (Bobbitt, 1918, p. 11)

The curriculum, according to Bobbitt, was "that series of things which children and youth must do and experience by way of developing abilities to do the things well that make up the affairs of adult life; and to be in all respects what adults should be" (Bobbitt, 1918, p. 11).

On the surface, Bobbitt's model of curriculum may sound somewhat like Dewey's. In fact, particularly as each curriculum was implemented, they were profoundly different. Bobbitt's model was based on a supposedly scientific analysis of what a child needed to learn to become a productive member of the culture. What the child was interested in was of no importance. The curriculum of the schools would be determined by surveying what "successful" adults did. The results of this process would be to construct a set of educational objectives that the student would have to meet.

Bobbitt's model emphasized curricular content that had a direct and, ideally, a measurable payoff in adult life. Subjects such as history, literature, and geography were not very important to him, since it was hard to show that they had much of an effect on producing good workers for the industrial system. In addition, the impact of humanistically oriented subjects was difficult to measure. Bobbitt, along with behavioral psychologists such as Edward Lee Thorndike, believed strongly in testing students in the interest of eliminating waste and improving educational efficiency (Flinders & Thorton, 1997, pp. 2–3).

Progressivism versus Social Efficiency Dewey's curricular and educational model emphasized serving the child. Bobbitt's emphasized serving the society. In Dewey's model, children engaged in curricular activities that met their immediate needs and interests. In Bobbitt's model, children were evaluated to determine what "treatment" or "instruction" would most efficiently develop the skills needed to assume a useful role in the society. Bobbitt's model emphasized testing and tracking of students, while Dewey's emphasized development of children's skills in the context of their interests.

At a very general level, the history of American schooling in the twentieth century involved an ongoing competition between Dewey's and Bobbitt's models. While many of Dewey's ideas have been incorporated into the basic fabric of American education, Bobbitt's ideas have predominated. Today, American schools are closely linked to the interests of business. Students are carefully tracked and their knowledge is increasingly measured by standardized tests. We desire to create a series of measurable educational objectives that all students can achieve. While on the surface this may seem to be a desirable goal, such an approach limits a student's potential to learn and turns schools into places where things are more often memorized than learned. We are reminded of Dewey's argument at the beginning of *The School and Society* (1907):

> What the best and wisest parent wants for his own child, that must the community want for all of its children. Any other ideal for our schools is narrow and unlovely; acted upon, it destroys our democracy. All that society has accomplished for itself is put, through the agency of the school, at the disposal of its future members. All its better thoughts of itself it hopes to realize through the new possibilities thus opened to its future self. Here individualism and socialism are at one. Only by being true to the full growth of all the individuals who make it up, can society by any chance be true to itself. (Dewey, 1907, pp. 19–20)

While Dewey's philosophy of education and curriculum does not mean that schools cannot have high standards or that children should not be tested to see what they know, it does emphasize that the ultimate goal of the school and the curriculum is to serve children and their development and growth. What do you think?

- **Psychological Forces** The curriculum of American schools has been influenced not only by social and cultural forces, but also by psychological movements. Perhaps the two most important of these movements have been behaviorism and constructivism.

Behaviorism Behaviorism dates back to the beginning of the twentieth century when J. B. Watson, drawing heavily on the work of the Russian psychologist Ivan Pavlov, argued that human behavior was not so much dependent on mental states, but was based more on the response of a subject to external stimuli. In the 1950s and 1960s, theorists such as B. F. Skinner extended Watson's theories.

Experimenting with animals, Skinner used a method called **operant conditioning** to train pigeons to do specific tasks by rewarding them with food. Skinner's methods of

INTASC

Principle #2

Knowledge of Human Development and Learning: The teacher understands how children learn and develop, and can provide learning opportunities that support their intellectual, social, and personal development.

reinforcement to increase and shape behaviors were soon widely applied to education, in which systems of rewards, negative reinforcement, and punishment were used to shape desired behavior in classrooms and to encourage motivation.

Behaviorism is very important in special education, in which teachers of students with special needs break down learning tasks into small and teachable units. The completion of these units is based on a system of behavioral reinforcements that condition the learner. Inherent in Skinner's method, however, is a philosophical position that views students as objects who can be shaped and controlled if provided with the appropriate behavioral stimuli.

Constructivism In contrast to behaviorism, **constructivist** models of learning are based primarily on the work of the Swiss psychologist Jean Piaget (1896–1980). Piaget began his work as a biologist interested in how different organisms adapt to their environment. Piaget described this adaptation process as intelligence. One's ability to adapt to one's environment is controlled through mental organizations called **schemes**. Piaget hypothesized that humans are born with schemes that operate from birth, called reflexes, that control the behavior of most animals throughout their lives. Human beings, in contrast, operate differently from animals. According to Piaget, human beings adapt to their environment by replacing their reflexes with constructed schemes of the world. Constructivist approaches in education, therefore, encourage students to actively construct their learning. It provides much more freedom for learners, who essentially come to understand the world by inventing or constructing it for themselves. Table 9.1 provides a comparison of the two models.

It is not the purpose of this book to outline in detail the work of psychologists such as Skinner and Piaget, which you will learn more about in courses in child development and educational psychology. What is important is to understand that each represents a very different model of how children learn and should be taught. You will find both models employed in the schools in which you observe and eventually teach.

THE STRUGGLE FOR THE AMERICAN CURRICULUM

The differences between Dewey's and Bobbitt's beliefs about curriculum are part of what the educational historian Herbert M. Kliebard describes as "the struggle for the American curriculum." This struggle has been going on throughout history; the American curriculum has constantly evolved as the American people have been shaped by forces such as the economy, war and national defense, and the civil rights movement. During the Great

---

TABLE 9.1

Behaviorist versus Constructivist Models of Instruction

	BEHAVIORIST MODEL	CONSTRUCTIVIST MODEL
STUDENT'S ROLE	The student is positively or negatively reinforced to respond in certain ways. The stimuli provided to the student and how they are manipulated determine what the student learns.	Students are seen as needing to understand and integrate the world around them. Learning becomes a process of personal invention and discovery.
TEACHER'S ROLE	The teacher regulates and controls a carefully prescribed curriculum. The idea is to provide the student with an effective treatment by which to learn or behaviorally reinforce the curriculum.	The teacher guides students to discover and understand the world around them.
PHILOSOPHICAL MODEL	Prescriptive—essentially modern.	Phenomenological—essentially postmodern.

Depression of the 1930s, for example, very few jobs existed for young people, so more students than usual attended the public schools. As a result, the high school curriculum became less elitist and more practical. By the beginning of World War II, people had become used to staying in school longer. Compulsory school attendance had become nearly universal for most students through age 16.

● **Life Adjustment Education**   Following World War II, a national movement developed that was known as **Life Adjustment Education.** The purpose of Life Adjustment Education was to provide the 60% of high school students who were not part of college preparatory or vocational programs the skills necessary to become useful members of society. The curriculum under the Life Adjustment movement emphasized citizenship, family life, health and hygiene, and leisure.

Many critics argued that the curriculum represented a watering-down and reduction of standards. In 1952, Arthur Bestor, Jr., a history professor at the University of Illinois, wrote a scathing article critiquing the Life Adjustment movement. The article was expanded into a 1953 book titled *Educational Wastelands: The Retreat from Learning in Our Public Schools.* Bestor's work set off a national debate that in many regards is still going on today. The debate is over the extent to which the public schools should emphasize the development of academic skills in the curriculum over developmental and personal life skills.

● **The National Defense Education Act**   The postwar debate about curriculum took a significant turn on October 4, 1957, when the Soviet Union launched an artificial satellite called *Sputnik I.* As a result, many people and educators in the United States feared that we had fallen behind the Russians in scientific and technological development. The rhetoric of the postwar period insisted that we were engaged in a battle against the Soviet Union, and a large part of that battle was fought in the classrooms of the public schools and in our colleges and universities.

The furor over *Sputnik* and the "crisis in education" resulted in a number of responses at the federal level. In 1958 Congress passed the **National Defense Education Act (NDEA),** which provided more than $1 billion in federal funds in scholarships, as well as funds to improve the academic quality of the schools, to provide vocational training, and to build new classrooms. In addition, the National Science Foundation became involved in secondary school curriculum development in fields such as mathematics, biology, chemistry, and the social sciences. Eventually a wide range of innovative curricula were developed, including the "new math," the "new social studies," and innovative natural and physical science programs (Ravitch, 1983).

During the 1960s the promise of the *Sputnik* reforms were partially swept away as a result of the demand for greater equity on the part of African Americans and other minorities, including women (Ravitch, 1983). Further changes were made in the curriculum. The history and literature of African Americans and women, as well as other minorities, were recognized for the first time as being worthy of inclusion in the curriculum. Attempts to provide minority students with compensatory education intended to overcome past social

The Soviet Union's launch of Sputnik in the 1950s serves as a milestone in American Education. Fearing the country's educational programs were falling behind its rivals in science and math, the federal government instituted a significant reform of America's education curriculum and allocated significant funding for scholarships and special programs to promote science and math development. These efforts continue today.

discrimination were, as in the case of the Dick and Jane readers mentioned earlier, also introduced into the curriculum.

Debate over what should be included in the curriculum was ongoing. Should math, biology, and physics be taught using traditional methods, or should the innovative curricular approaches developed by the National Science Foundation be used? Should evolutionary theory be included as part of the biology curriculum? How should minority groups such as African Americans and various ethnic groups be represented in textbooks and other curricular sources?

During the 1970s there was an increasing consensus that the schools should play a role in the reform and improvement of American society. Sometimes this took the form of emphasizing innovative curricula, and sometimes a return to "basics."

● **A Nation at Risk**   By the early 1980s, it was clear that there was, at best, a limited consensus throughout the country as to what the goals of education should be. In April 1983, the rhetoric of war was once again introduced into the debate about the curriculum in the United States when the U.S. Department of Education released the report *A Nation at Risk* (1983). The report argued that the mediocre quality of the public schools in the United States was reducing American economic competitiveness and placing the country in severe jeopardy. The rhetoric of *A Nation at Risk* is clear in its opening lines:

> If an unfriendly power had attempted to impose on America the mediocre educational performance that exists today, we might well have viewed it as an act of war. As it stands, we have allowed this to happen to ourselves. We have even squandered the gains in achievement made in the wake of the Sputnik challenge. Moreover, we have dismantled essential support systems [that] helped make those gains possible. We have, in effect, been committing an act of unthinking, unilateral educational disarmament. (*A Nation at Risk,* 1983, p. 5)

A Nation at Risk represents the first stage of the conservative educational movement that dominated the 1980s and 1990s and continues into the first decade of the new century.

Were the schools as bad as the educational conservatives said? Numerous studies, ranging from the work of Berliner and Biddle to Bracie and Rothman, offered little evidence that the public schools in the United States were worse in 1983 than they had been in the past. Nor is there evidence that they have been in a decline in the decades since *A Nation at Risk* was issued. In fact, there is considerable evidence to suggest that, at present, the schools are serving a wide a population as well as they have at any time in American history and that students are achieving high standards of learning. This is not to say that the public schools work as well as they should; however, they are presently functioning no worse, and probably better, than they have at any other point in our history.

"My teacher said the school has tough new standards and I need to improve my vocabulary. What's 'vocabulary'?"

Courtesy of Aaron Bacall, *The Lighter Side of Teaching,* p. 54. Copyright 2003 by Aaron Bacall. Reprinted by permission of Corwin Press Inc.

● **The Standards Movement and the Curriculum**   The debate over what should be the curriculum of American public schools continues today. We are currently caught up in a national standards movement that focuses on increasing the level of accountability for students in schools across the country, an outgrowth of the 1983 *A Nation at Risk* report. It emphasizes that schools focus their curriculums on the development of demonstrable skills.

While few can object to schools being held accountable for what they teach children, there is considerable debate over how this should be done. As discussed in Chapter 5, high-stakes testing is increasingly being implemented in schools across the country as a result of the implementation of the No Child Left Behind legislation. In many states, schools are evaluated and then provided funding on the basis of how their students score on a statewide exam. Many educators feel that such tests are artificial and particularly unfair to students who come from minority and lower-economic backgrounds. Teachers often find themselves teaching to the test rather than the subject matter at hand.

Federal legislation, in the form of the No Child Left Behind Act of 2001, represents a sweeping overhaul of the government's efforts to support elementary and secondary education in the United States. It emphasizes school-level accountability, creating a system of education based on scientific research, expansion of parental options, and increased local flexibility and control. According to the U.S. Department of Education:

> Under *No Child Left Behind,* each state must measure every public school student's progress in reading and math in each of grades 3 through 8 and at least once during grades 10 through 12. By school year 2007–2008, assessments (or testing) in science will be underway. These assessments must be aligned with state academic content and achievement standards. They will provide parents with objective data on where their child stands academically. (U.S. Department of Education, n.d.)

Critics maintain that the No Child Left Behind legislation represents an unreasonable intrusion of the federal government into the lives of teachers and the students they teach. More specifically, it represents a continuation of the debate over progressive versus social efficiency models of education that has dominated American public education for more than a hundred years.

Who am I? What do I believe?	"I think kids are concerned with what goes on in their day-to-day lives, and not much about what goes on in the future. We need to keep that in mind when we're teaching them."
	MARGO, HIGH SCHOOL SCIENCE TEACHER

THINK ABOUT THIS:

The French philosopher Michel de Montaigne (1533–1592) wrote that as individuals we should be more concerned with the journey than with its goal. How does this potentially affect the type of curriculum we teach in the schools? How does Montaigne's idea relate to the preceding quote from the teacher, or to John Dewey's statement that "education is a process of living and not a preparation for future life"?

SHARE and **COMPARE:**

Identify two incidents in your life that involved important steps in learning. Why were these experiences important? What did they mean to you? Compare your experiences with those of a classmate or friend.

INTASC

Principle #9

Professional Commitment and Responsibility: The teacher is a reflective practitioner who continually evaluates the effects of his/her choices and actions on others (students, parents, and other professionals in the learning community) and who actively seeks out opportunities to grow professionally.

WHAT ROLES DO TEACHERS PLAY IN THE CURRICULUM?

Teachers play the critical role of delivering the curriculum used in the schools. Whatever is taught is filtered through their perception and way of teaching, for both formal and informal curriculum. Curriculum theorists such as Gail McCutcheon maintain that "Teachers

Problems To POSSIBILITIES

Freedom of Expression

David Sandler is a young eleventh-grade English teacher. Several of his students have come to him about getting extra credit for creating an online literary magazine. Not wanting to discourage them, he responds, "Sure, show it to me when you've got it done." David is excited to see that his students are showing the initiative to create something and to find a way to have their voices heard.

A week later David is called into the school's main office. Mr. Ransom, his principal, is furious. "I don't think it's even a little bit funny what you and your students have done, and claiming free speech and the Constitution simply isn't going to cut it as far as I am concerned."

David has no idea what Mr. Ransom is talking about. "What do you mean?" he asks.

"Me, in a dress and a lampshade on my head," explains Mr. Ransom. "It makes me look ridiculous. I don't appreciate your having encouraged the students with their online humor magazine. Not only is my picture circulating on the Internet, but students in the computer labs have been printing up my picture and posting it on all of the bulletin boards in the school. I want it to stop, and stop now!"

Discussion Question

Can Mr. Ransom do anything to "stop" the students' online literary magazine? If you were David, how would you respond?

Possibilities

School oversight of student postings on the Internet represents a relatively new, but controversial, legal area for schools. Over the years, the courts have generally sided with a student's right to free expression. In one of the earliest cases, *Tinker v. Des Moines Independent Community School District* (1969), the court found that a student doesn't lose the right to free speech "at the schoolhouse gate."

Since *Tinker,* many other cases have further helped outline the parameters of expression, allowing the school to interfere if material is considered vulgar or lewd or if school regulation is necessary for educational purposes. But Internet expression is stretching the parameters. To date, the U.S. Supreme Court has provided no definitive guidelines, although a few individual state cases have taken on the issue—some siding with the students, others siding with the schools. A couple of key issues arise when determining legal rights in these cases:

- Can school officials interfere if the website is created on offsite school computers?

- What if the material is created as part of a school curriculum, as a school assignment?

Students have easy access to powerful technologies. Often Internet services include more than enough space to publish a newsletter and flyer with pictures. Once posted, it is there for the whole world to see. David not only should have talked with the students about what type of online magazine they were creating for extra credit, but should also have made it clear that before anything was published to the World Wide Web, he would need to review and approve it.

Ethical Question

1. Does the First Amendment of the Constitution protect the students' freedom of expression? Does it protect David?

2. Go to the First Amendment Center at www.firstamendment center.org/Speech/index.aspx and visit the area on "K–12 public school student expression" to read more about students' rights. How far can a school go to monitor or regulate students' material online?

are the filters through which the mandated curriculum passes. Their understanding of it, and their enthusiasm, or boredom, with various aspects of it, color its nature. Hence, the curriculum enacted in classrooms differs from the one mandated by administrators or developed by experts" (McCutcheon, p. 193). Early curriculum theorists such as John Franklin Bobbitt, on the other hand, believed that the curriculum could be managed at the upper levels of the administrative system and delivered according to specific administrative instructions by the teacher in the classroom.

The process envisioned by Bobbitt has been described to as a **teacher-proof curriculum.** Such a model represents a failure to understand the highly contextual nature of teaching and the extent to which good teaching represents more of an art than a science. While a teacher needs a good curriculum to work from, the delivery of that curriculum is always a highly individual process. Talking about the Cuban missile crisis and the role of Fidel Castro in international politics in a Miami high school classroom is going to elicit very different responses from students and parents than it would in a Minneapolis school. Even in Miami, the discussion of Castro will elicit different responses from various students, depending on the part of Miami in which the school is located. The response you receive will also depend upon how you teach the curriculum.

HOW TEACHERS SHAPE THE CURRICULUM

Teachers have little control over the hidden curriculum of a school because it comes through many sources, including parents, students, and even the media. Often, the hidden curriculum of a school is shaped and delivered simultaneously by widely different groups. Among teenagers, for example, there may be specific lessons at work about what to wear or not wear in order to be "cool." Learning about what is "in" or "out" may involve watching—but not necessarily discussing—what other students wear, responding to a television or print advertisement, and so on. Teachers may, or may not, have influence over this aspect of what is learned in schools.

What a teacher *can* influence is a school's formal curriculum. According to McCutcheon, teachers have enormous power to shape and control the delivery of the formal curriculum:

> [I]t is up to them to understand what is to be taught and then conceive of ways to enact it and make it accessible to students. Teachers must also make sense of the context—the neighborhood, their students, parents' hopes and dreams, the social setting within the school, as well as the shape of the nation itself—and fit the objectives into these understandings. In this manner, such decisions are moral ones, going beyond an objective management activity. It is also the teachers who contend with policies and other phenomena within which the curriculum operates. (McCutcheon, p. 193)

It is extremely likely that as a teacher you will eventually serve on some type of curriculum committee. Their purpose is to identify the content that needs to be taught in order to meet state curriculum guidelines, but also to consider issues involving testing and evaluation of students. Committees usually meet year round, but the bulk of the work is often done over the summer once the school year is finished. Many school districts pay an extra stipend to teachers who serve on a curriculum committee. These committees come in many shapes and sizes and serve different purposes in different schools. Curriculum committees may contain only teachers or teachers and administrators; sometimes they include parents. At the Ivanhoe School, a public elementary school in Los Angeles, the curriculum committee is made up of two parents and two teachers. The committee's purpose is to discuss "implementing new curriculum, adoption of state and district standards, and intervention programs. Specific curriculum decisions that are the realm of educators and the principal are not decided by this committee" (Ivanhoe School, 2000).

Following is the description of the work of the Bethpage Union Free School District's K–5 social studies committee located in Long Island, New York. The members of the committee include the district's director of social studies as well as a dozen teachers from three different elementary schools in the district. The description provides a good sense of the type of issues you might find yourself involved with as a member of a school's curriculum committee:

> The New York State Education Department has revised the K–12 Social Studies Curriculum. Perhaps the biggest change will be the increased emphasis on the use of documents in the teaching of Social Studies at all levels. A dedicated committee of

Serving on a curriculum committee offers you the opportunity to influence formal curriculum. How does this put you in a position to affect change?

Bethpage teachers has been volunteering to write curriculum and assessments that will provide our teachers and students with the materials needed to achieve success on the new 5th Grade Social Studies Assessment to be given annually in November. That test covers Grade 3/4 content and Grades K–4 Social Studies skills. It will include a Document Based Question essay, 35 Multiple Choice and 3–4 Constructed Response Questions (interpreting charts, pictures, quotes). (Bethpage Union Free School District, n.d.)

Visit the websites of your local schools to see whether you can learn more about how curriculum committees work. Check out the subject areas that you are interested in teaching and examine the expectations and objectives for these areas.

IMPLEMENTING STANDARDS

INTASC
Principle #9

Professional Commitment and Responsibility: The teacher is a reflective practitioner who continually evaluates the effects of his/her choices and actions on others (students, parents, and other professionals in the learning community) and who actively seeks out opportunities to grow professionally.

The No Child Left Behind Act of 2001 represents a standards-based model of school reform. As explained earlier, the standards movement calls for measurable results in terms of school improvement. Specifically, it calls for students to meet carefully defined state standards of excellence. In its report *Making Standards Matter* (1996), the American Federation of Teachers called for the development of clear and meaningful standards on the part of state and local districts. Specifically, it outlined 10 criteria it felt were necessary if the standards movement was to succeed:

1. Standards must focus on academics.

2. Standards must be grounded in the core disciplines.

3. Standards must be specific enough to ensure the development of a common core curriculum.

4. Standards must be manageable given the constraints of time.

5. Standards must be rigorous and world class.

6. Standards must include "performance standards."

7. Standards must define multiple levels of performance for students to strive for.

8. Standards must combine knowledge and skills, not pursue one at the expense of the other.

9. Standards must not dictate how the material should be taught.

10. Standards must be written clearly enough for all stakeholders to understand. (Jones, n.d.)

INTASC

Principle #8

Assessment of Student Learning: The teacher understands and uses formal and informal assessment strategies to evaluate and ensure the continuous intellectual, social, and physical development of the learner.

Implementing standards such as those outlined here is something you will almost certainly have to do as a teacher. At its best, the standards movement is trying to ensure that all students learn. Such an ideal is commendable. Making it actually happen, however, is a different matter. Well-developed standards conform to what we feel children should learn in the curriculum. Thus, having standards on learning to do addition and subtraction in the first grade is perfectly reasonable. Standards should not, however, drive the curriculum. The goal should not be to pass a test, but rather to become educated. In many school districts people are teaching to the test, rather than the needs of children and the curriculum. To do so is ultimately an educational failure. But today's climate of standards-based education makes it difficult for a teacher to maintain this stance, as pressure to "meet the standards" comes from many directions.

As the educational reformer Jonathan Kozol (2000) has pointed out, the question is not whether we should have standards in our schools: "It is, rather, how and where they are determined, and by whom, and how they're introduced, and how we treat or penalize (or threaten, or abuse) the child or the teacher who won't swallow them." Standards can be very helpful, but they should not drive the curriculum.

You will need to learn about the standards for your state and the local school district where you eventually work. Standards for different grade levels and subjects are normally found at state department of education websites as well as on the websites for local school districts. You can also search on the Internet for "educational standards" to find websites listing educational standards that relate to your interests.

"The most extraordinary thing about a really good teacher is that he or she transcends accepted educational methods."

MARGARET MEAD

THINK ABOUT THIS:

Good teaching has a certain degree of magic, art, and chance to it. Why a lesson works with one class and not another is often inexplicable. Think about the extent to which we can prescribe how to teach a particular subject or group of students. Is it possible to simply have teachers teach a curriculum they are given by others, or do good teachers somehow make it their own?

SHARE and **COMPARE:**

Talk to a classmate or friend about how good teachers that you have had made the curriculum they were teaching their own. Explore how you can do the same yourself.

WHAT ROLES DO TEXTBOOKS PLAY IN THE CURRICULUM?

While the United States does not have a national curriculum administered from a central federal office in Washington, D.C., we do have a curriculum that has informally evolved over the years as part of custom and tradition. In the first grade, for example, we traditionally teach addition and subtraction. This is done before we teach children to multiply and divide. In this case, the curriculum evolved largely out of the cognitive and developmental needs of children. This curriculum is roughly the same as that found in Israel, Venezuela, or China.

As we proceed further in the schooling process, the curriculum becomes more distinctive and more "American." Textbooks create uniformity in the American curriculum, as do standards established by professional organizations and groups and requirements for admission into colleges and universities. Technically, state and local school systems ultimately determine the curriculum of schools in the United States. Powerful steering forces, however, can influence the creation of a relatively uniform curriculum across the country.

TEXTBOOK ADOPTIONS

While the look of textbooks has changed over the years, reflecting the changes in the country, interested parties continue to struggle over control of the curriculum. The textbook selection process in some states can get volatile as various interest groups question the content of texts, particularly with regard to topics such as sexuality, religion, and politics.

Roughly half of the states in the United States are textbook **adoption states.** This means that for any textbook to be purchased for use in the public schools using state money, the text must first be reviewed and approved, or adopted, by a committee from the state education department. This is done to guarantee quality, keep costs competitive, and make sure that curricular guidelines for that particular state are being met. Needless to say, no two states review textbooks in exactly the same way, and some wield more influence on the content of texts than others simply because of their potential purchasing power. States such as Texas, California, and Florida, because of their large populations, have enormous influence in the textbook development process. Getting a textbook approved by one of these states represents a major step toward the success of the book. As a result, according to Michael Apple, publishers:

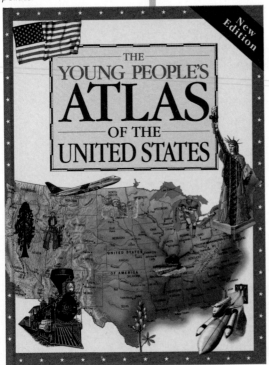

simply because of good business practice, must by necessity aim their text publishing practices toward those states with such state adoption policies. The simple fact of getting one's volume on such a list can make all the difference for a text's profitability. Thus, for instance, sales in California and Texas can account for over 20 percent of the total sales in any particular book—a considerable percentage in the highly competitive world of elementary and secondary school book publishing and selling. Because of this, the writing, editing, promotion, and general orientation and strategy of such production is quite often aimed toward guaranteeing a place on the list of state-approved material. (Apple, 1989, p. 107)

Every state, whether or not it is an adoption state, looks for textbooks to support the statewide curriculum, but states can often have very differing perspectives on what they feel should be taught in their schools. Imagine, for example, developing a text that would meet the needs of both California and Missouri. As a result, textbooks—particularly those used in subjects such as social studies and literature—tend to be fairly neutral in order to appeal to as large a population as possible.

Approximately 90% of classroom instruction is accomplished through textbooks and related instructional materials (Honig, 1991, p. 106). Textbooks are, in fact, the basis for instruction in

BUILDING ON EDUCATIONAL FOUNDATIONS

Whose Content Is Taught in Schools?

The question of what content is taught in classrooms is a constant issue in American education. Often parents object to reading material based on its religious content. For example, fundamentalist Christian parents who believe in creationism may object to a book being used with their children that talks about dinosaurs that lived millions of years ago. (Many Christian fundamentalists, based on evidence from the Bible, believe the world was created several thousand—not millions—of years ago.) An important instance of parents objecting to seemingly harmless curriculum content took place in Tennessee in the mid-1980s. A new reading series from a major publisher included selections that referred to magic and evolution, as well as other materials that some parents found objectionable. An alternate reading program was requested and provided by the school.

Trouble arose when the school board voted to eliminate all alternative reading programs and to require every student to participate in the reading program using the adopted series. Parents' requests to reinstate the alternative reading program were rejected by the school system. As a result of the decision, many parents decided to home-school their children or send them to private schools. Eventually they brought a lawsuit against the school system, *Mozert v. Hawkins County Public Schools,* 582 F. Supp. 201 (ED. Tenn. 1984), arguing that by being forced to have their children use what they considered

objectionable material, their rights to the free exercise of religion protected by the First and Fourteenth Amendments to the U.S. Constitution were violated.

In 1987, the U.S. District Court of Eastern Tennessee ruled against the public school district and in favor of the fundamentalist Christian parents. The court ruled, "Plaintiffs sincerely believe that the repetitive affirmations of these viewpoints is repulsive to the Christian faith. . . . They have drawn a line and it is not for us to say that the line they drew was an unreasonable one." The court's decision reinstated the alternate reading program and financial damages were awarded to the plaintiff families in order to pay for their legal costs and having had to provide alternate education for their children.

Mozert v. Hawkins is an important court case because it says that when designing a curriculum, schools must take into account the religious rights of students. If students can demonstrate that certain materials included in the curriculum are objectionable on the grounds of their religious beliefs, then they must be provided an alternative.

How does a court decision such as *Mozert v. Hawkins* potentially influence your work as a classroom teacher? In what ways do you need to carefully listen to the concerns and questions of parents?

American schools. Therefore, their content is extremely important. According to Apple and Christian-Smith, "Conflicts over texts are proxies for wider questions of power relations" (1991, p. 3).

TEXTBOOK AND CURRICULUM CONTROVERSIES

Textbooks and their content have the potential to trigger major controversies in local communities. In the mid-1970s, for example, Kanawha County, West Virginia, was torn apart by conflicts over the content of textbooks being used in the public schools. It must be realized that textbooks and their curricular content represent specific constructions of reality. In this sense, they are part of a selective tradition of knowledge and information that is taught to the children in our schools (Apple & Christian-Smith, 1991).

When the content of what is taught impinges on religious or political beliefs of the local community, then people take particular notice of what is being taught in the schools. Books and films that you might think are entirely appropriate to include as part of the curriculum in your classes may not be considered suitable by parents or other members of the

INTASC

Principle #7

Instructional Planning Skills: The teacher plans instruction based upon knowledge of subject matter, students, the community, and curriculum goals.

community. Protests regularly arise, for example, over the content in health education classes. Some communities encourage a very broad curriculum that includes open discussion about HIV, AIDS, sexuality, abortion, and condom use. Other communities restrict discussion about some of these topics and limit discussion about sexuality to abstinence-only programs. The health education curriculum has become one of the most closely monitored and hotly contested subjects in schools and communities across the country in the past 20 years.

Informal activities that are not part of the formal curriculum may cause problems with parents. During the last couple of years the huge popularity of the Harry Potter books has led many teachers to use them in their classes—often as supplemental reading or as books that are read aloud by the teacher. Because of the books' emphasis on wizardry and "the Dark Arts," some conservative religious groups have objected to their use in public school classrooms. According to these people, the books are not just harmless fantasies, but have the potential to encourage children to reject Christianity in favor of the occult.

If you add supplementary materials to the required curriculum you teach in your classes, be sensitive to the values and beliefs held in the community in which you are working. J. D. Salinger's classic American novel of coming of age, *The Catcher in the Rye*, has been pulled from schools and libraries in the past because its main character, prep school student Holden Caulfield, visits a prostitute (even though nothing actually happens between him and the woman).

While you should feel free to introduce ideas and materials into the curriculum—which is part of what teaching is all about—it is best to do so carefully. Consult with your principal, assistant principal, or department head to make sure there are no potential problems with the content of what you want to teach or are adding to the curriculum.

CHOOSING THE RIGHT TEXTBOOKS FOR YOUR CLASSROOM

Typically, the textbooks used by most teachers are selected by a curriculum planning group in the school district's central office or by a committee of teachers from across the district or in an individual school. Sometimes teachers have little or no input on what books are used in their classroom. This is particularly the case with major **basal textbook** programs in large school districts. Basal textbooks provide basic grade-appropriate information in various K–8 subject areas. For example, a K–8 reading program would include grade-appropriate materials—student texts, teacher's text, and learning aids—for each grade level. Because all the materials are from the same series, the content and strategies build off each other from one year to the next. In small school districts, individual teachers might have more input on the selection of the series than teachers in large school districts with multiple elementary schools and multiple classrooms for each grade.

A single purchase of beginning elementary reading books or basal readers will be used for multiple classes typically 5 to 6 years—generally until they wear out or the content is outdated. It is highly likely that when you begin teaching, you will inherit a set of texts to use from the previous school year.

When a new set of teaching materials is chosen, teachers are often given a choice between several textbooks they can use. You may also be able to select a text from a centralized book depository. Large school districts will have a central textbook facility with a library where you can review different works.

If you are able to choose your own text or are on a teacher review committee, keep the following questions in mind:

1. Is the textbook you are selecting consistent with the goals of the course you are teaching?

2. Does the textbook you are interested in provide multiple ways of delivering information to your students?

3. Is the textbook culturally sensitive in terms of issues of race, gender, religion, and ethnicity?

4. Does the textbook and its content match the educational level of the students you are teaching?

5. Is the textbook you are considering logical in its organization and presentation of materials?

6. Is the textbook affordable?

7. Are there useful supplements that come with the textbook, such as multimedia support and teacher's guides?

8. Is the material found in the textbook potentially interesting for students?

Other things to consider as you select textbooks or other types of instructional material are how clearly the content is written; the layout and design of the work; how well illustrations, charts, and photographs are used; the implied pedagogical content; and finally, the research and knowledge underlying the overall work. Texts often serve as the core of your curriculum; therefore, your choice is an important one that you will have to live with for years. Tread carefully and responsibly.

FINAL THOUGHTS

If you are like most people, you have never given much thought to the curriculum that you learned in school. You probably took it for granted that what you were being taught was what everybody else was learning and that it was what you needed to know to get an education. But as we have tried to demonstrate in this chapter, the issue of what curriculum we include in our schools not only is complex, but also reflects a wide range of forces that are at work in the larger society.

We began this chapter with a set of questions. In order to teach effectively you will need to continue to explore not only these questions, but other ones as well. What counts as legitimate information or knowledge for the curriculum? How is such knowledge or information produced? How is this knowledge communicated in the classroom? What role does the teacher have in mediating the knowledge provided by the curriculum? Who has access to legitimate forms of knowledge? Whose interests does this knowledge serve (Giroux, 1988, pp. 17–18)?

Curriculum is value-laden. There is no such thing as a neutral or totally objective curriculum. Instead, the curriculum we find in our schools is part of a complex set of social factors. These factors define not only our schools, but also our society as a whole. Understanding the role of curriculum in shaping what goes on in schools is essential to what we do as teachers. There are few more interesting topics in education.

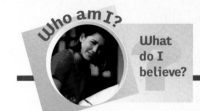

REFLECTIONS

Professional Plan for Understanding the Role of Curriculum in Your Teaching

1. The three main ideas about curriculum that I learned in this chapter are:

2. Two things in this chapter that I would like to learn more about are:

    a. _____

    b. _____

3. I plan to investigate these two areas and learn more about topics in this chapter by:

    _____ Reading some of the book club choices

    _____ Reading sources referenced in the chapter that interest me

    _____ Interviewing one or more teachers about curriculum development and considerations they make when creating a plan for each subject they teach

    _____ Exploring the websites listed in the Log On section

    _____ Observing classrooms and taking notes on issues that seemed to influence the curriculum in the classroom and school

4. I will include the following in my Touch the Future portfolio:

    _____ Responses to Who Am I? activities

    _____ A brief essay on my thoughts about Problems to Possibilities

    _____ Responses to the observation guide

    _____ Other (materials assigned by your instructor):

SUMMARY

What Is Curriculum?

*   The curriculum works on both formal and informal levels.
*   Every school has an informal curriculum that involves hidden and null factors. A successful teacher needs to be aware of all the factors that influence a school's informal curriculum and work to overcome their potential negative influences.
*   Many things encompass the curriculum, including the design of a classroom and the way certain groups are dealt with or treated.

How Does Curriculum Represent Cultural Values?

*   The curriculum is a deeply cultural phenomenon.
*   The curriculum represents a type of cultural capital that society invests in knowledge in much the same way that a banker invests in certain financial investments.

- Hirsch's concept of cultural literacy stresses the importance of a shared core of knowledge.
- There is no such thing as a neutral curriculum.

What Are the Historical Roots of Curriculum in the United States?

- Sociocultural and psychological forces have produced competing models of what the curriculum should be in American society.
- Many of the reform struggles in American education are rooted in the struggle between progressive and social efficiency models.
- Constructivism is based on Jean Piaget's work on how organisms adapt to their environments.
- Educational struggles in the United States have often arisen out of a perception of deficiency.

What Roles Do Teachers Play in the Curriculum?

- Teachers have enormous potential to shape the meaning of curriculum and its effect on students.
- Teachers have greater control over the formal curriculum than over the hidden curriculum.
- Reform movements such as the standards movement cause teachers to constantly revise their curricula.

What Roles Do Textbooks Play in the Curriculum?

- Textbooks play a critical role in implementation of curricula, as they serve to provide uniformity.
- Teachers often must supplement textbooks in order to add personal meaning and flair.
- Teachers must be careful when choosing textbooks that meet with the needs and values of the local community.

Visit the **Touch the Future . . . Teach!** Companion Website at
www.ablongman.com/diaz for additional opportunities.

KEY WORDS

adoption states   282

basal textbook   284

behaviorism   273

constructivist   274

core knowledge?   270

cultural capital   267

curriculum   264

formal curriculum   264

hidden curriculum   264

informal curriculum   264

laboratory school   271

Life Adjustment
    Education   275

National Defense Education
    Act (NDEA)   275

null curriculum   265

operant conditioning   273

schemes   274

social efficiency
    movement   272

teacher-proof
    curriculum   279

CONCEPT REVIEW

1. Compare and contrast the differences between the formal and informal curriculum and explain how they function differently from one another.

2. Identify elements that make up the curriculum of the schools.

3. Explain what is meant by the null curriculum and the hidden curriculum.

4. Provide at least three examples of cultural capital.

5. Explain how textbooks such as *The New England Primer,* the McGuffey readers, and the Dick and Jane readers function as cultural documents.

6. Identify intellectual traditions that have shaped and defined the development of the curriculum in the United States.

7. Describe the role of textbooks in the American curriculum.

8. Discuss the concept of a neutral curriculum and explain the difference between a curriculum being *neutral* and *objective.*

9. Explain how the standards movement is helping shape the curriculum of the schools.

10. List some key factors that you need to take into account when you create personal materials or review textbooks and other formal curriculum for use in your classroom.

TOUCH THE FUTURE . . .

Read On

Struggle for the American Curriculum, 1893–1958
Herbert M. Kliebard (New York: Teachers College Press, 1995)
A classic read for anyone studying the American curriculum; provides a historical overview of educational reform in the United States up to 1958.

Understanding Curriculum: An Introduction to the Study of Historical and Contemporary Curriculum Discourses
William Pinar, William M. Reynolds, Patrick Slattery, and Peter M. Taubman (New York: Peter Lang, 1995)
An encyclopedic work covering all aspects of curriculum and contemporary culture.

The Curriculum Studies Reader
David J. Flinders and Stephen J. Thorton, eds. (New York: Routledge, 1997)
An outstanding collection of key historical and contemporary works on the curriculum and American schools.

Changing Course: American Curriculum Reform in the 20th Century
Herbert M. Kliebard (New York: Teachers College Press, 2002)
An overview of American curriculum reform in the twentieth century.

Log On

Educational Resources Organizations Directory
http://bcol02.ed.gov/Programs/EROD/
Are you interested in finding out about education in the state where you live? The U.S. Department of Education through its online Education Resource Organizations Directory provides links to not only state department of education websites, but also a wide range of educational and school-related sites.

University of Chicago Laboratory Schools
www.ucls.uchicago.edu/about/
John Dewey's lab school at the University of Chicago was one of the first in the nation and still exists today. Visit the school's website to learn more about Dewey's early work in establishing the school.

Association for Curriculum Supervision and Development (ASCD)
www.ascd.org
ASCD is an international organization representing school superintendents, supervisors, principals, teachers, professors of education, and school board members. The website provides information on all aspects of education, including outstanding resources on curriculum and contemporary educational reform.

Core Knowledge Foundation
www.coreknowledge.org
Founded by E. D. Hirsch, Jr., explores curricula, develops books and other resources for parents and teachers, offers workshops for teachers, and helps schools develop a curriculum based on the 4 S's of core knowledge: solid, specific, shared, and sequential.

Write On

"There is nothing wrong with America that cannot be cured by what is right with America."
—William Jefferson Clinton

What does former president Bill Clinton suggest about where we should obtain the content for what we teach in the schools? In your journal, write a brief essay identifying characteristics that are essentially American and that should be included in what all children learn in school.

OBSERVATION GUIDE

TEACH: LINKING THEORY TO PRACTICE

Objective: Observing the use of curriculum in the classroom

School (use code name): _____   Observer: _____

Grade Level Observed: _____   Date: _____

Subject Taught: _____   Time In: _____   Time Out: _____

Linking Theory to Practice

Directions: In this observation activity you will observe how the curriculum works in a typical classroom setting. After you are cleared to conduct your observation, enter the classroom and be as unobtrusive as possible. Answer as many of the following questions as possible. Summarize your findings once you have finished your observation.

1. What is the basic content of the courses being taught?

2. What kinds of instructional materials are being used? What direct sources, text or curriculum packages developed by external sources, and curriculum packages developed by the district, the school, or the classroom teacher are being used? How many different kinds of materials are used?

3. Do the content and materials seem appropriate in terms of students' knowledge level, skill level, and interest level? Is there evidence of bias (sexism, racism, or classism) in the materials?

4. To what degree do current societal forces seem to influence curriculum? Is there, for example, a strong standards emphasis?

5. Does the teacher appear to have a strong background and grasp of the subject being taught? Is there any evidence of interdisciplinary teaching?

6. Does the teacher appear to be strongly invested in or interested in the curriculum? How does the teacher convey this enthusiasm to the class? What is the interest of the students in the materials being taught?

7. Does the teacher appear to have strong sense of self in terms of the ability to influence the curriculum, or is he or she simply repeating material from textbooks and other sources?

Connecting with INTASC: Principle 1

Knowledge of Subject Matter: The teacher understands the central concepts, tools of inquiry, and structures of the subject being taught and can create learning experiences that make these aspects of subject matter meaningful for students.

After observing the class, find out what the teacher does to meet Principle 1. Ask how the teacher incorporates the district's academic scope and sequence into the daily lessons. Find out what the hot issues are in this school's community and how they influence the curriculum.

10

Planning, Delivering, and Assessing Instruction

THINK ABOUT THIS:

Learning is not automatic. Teachers, curriculum specialists, and program developers in schools spend many hours planning instruction in order to help students learn and reach their full potential, and perhaps beyond. How do you incorporate the planning skill into your life? Would you describe yourself as a planner? If planning does not come naturally to you, it will become a learned skill as you begin to develop lessons and routines for completing a school day. Advance planning for any task helps the process go more smoothly and makes change easier to adjust to. Effective teachers know their students' needs and different learning styles and develop instructional plans to meet those needs and learning styles. But how do they know whether they're successful?

> "The pupil who is never required to do what he cannot do, never does what he can do."
>
> —John Stuart Mill

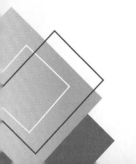

Good Morning!
Today is Tuesday

An experienced teacher always asks:
How do I know my students are learning? What can I do to help those students who did not understand what was taught in class? How do I challenge some students while accommodating the special needs of others? How can I best accommodate *all* of my students?

Planning is a critical component of teaching. It allows teachers to map out how they will teach each unit, week by week and day by day. An effective plan ties lessons to the curriculum dictated by the school district, to which each school is accountable, and assesses the success of that plan on a daily basis in order to make adjustments when necessary. Once a comprehensive lesson plan is in place, effective teaching will follow. This chapter will address four major components of teaching and at the end of the chapter you will know the answers to the following key questions:

Key Questions

- How do teachers plan?
- How do teachers deliver instruction?
- How do teachers assess student progress?
- How do teachers communicate student progress to parents?

Have you ever had a teacher who was brilliant but could not seem to engage students? Did you sense that this teacher was just saying whatever came to mind? Perhaps the teacher had a wealth of knowledge, but no plan for conveying that knowledge to the students. Knowing the material and actually being able to plan a lesson that engages students in learning are two different things. Without a plan in place, effective teaching is very difficult.

HOW DO TEACHERS PLAN?

Planning is a powerful skill that allows teachers to manage curriculum by deciding what is being taught, to whom, for how long, and when. It allows them to look at the big picture, unit by unit, and break it down into manageable teaching segments. Because the composition of each class varies from year to year, a successful *lesson plan* also takes into account mitigating circumstances that will affect each classroom, such as how to accommodate students with special needs, students who are gifted, and students from other cultures. While an effective plan does not guarantee that each lesson will be flawlessly delivered, it dramatically increases the chances of success.

WHY PLANNING IS IMPORTANT

Teachers are accountable for implementing districtwide goals established for each grade level. While curriculum developers in school districts are responsible for mapping out where skills and content are taught, teachers are the architects who actually design the daily lesson plans that foster successful learning. These plans can then be used for purposes of accountability, as they become the ultimate blueprint for what has been taught in classrooms on a daily, weekly, and monthly basis.

Lesson plans are written plans that teachers devise to help them stay organized and focused. They allow teachers to document the purpose of each lesson, explain the rationale for using certain teaching strategies and learning theories, and note any special considerations that may need to be taken into account for certain students. In addition to planning individual lessons, solid lesson plans incorporate information on how to best engage students in order to achieve district goals. By thinking through each lesson prior to teaching each class, teachers can anticipate any problems that may arise and determine how to resolve them. This dynamic reflects the ongoing cycle of teaching that is perpetuated from one lesson plan to the next.

Beginning teachers often comment that experienced teachers seem to be teaching without written lesson plans. This common misperception is understandable. What these beginning teachers do not see is that the teacher has planned the lesson and thought it out carefully, but because it has been taught so many times, a written plan is no longer needed. For beginning teachers, it is important to write the detailed plan on paper as a guide for teaching as well as a record of accountability.

HOW LEARNING THEORIES RELATE TO PLANNING

Understanding how students learn is essential to being able to create a lesson plan that reaches all of them. Theorists have proposed a number of learning theories over the years to explain how students learn, but most teachers find that no one theory applies in every case. Consequently, most teachers use a combination of these learning theories to create workable teaching plans. Four particular theories include Howard Gardner's theory of multiple intelligences, Anthony Gregorc's styles delineator approach, brain-based learning theory, and

INTASC

Principle #2

Knowledge of Human Development and Learning: The teacher understands how children learn and develop, and can provide learning opportunities that support their intellectual, social, and personal development.

Bloom's taxonomy. As you read the theories described here, think about your own learning preferences and how you will use this information to inform your future teaching.

- **Theory of Multiple Intelligences** Howard Gardner's **theory of multiple intelligences** has had a visible impact on teachers' thinking in recent years. This theory states that each person possesses not one, but eight intelligence: visual/spatial, musical, verbal, logical/mathematical, interpersonal, intrapersonal, bodily/kinesthetic, and naturalist intelligences (Gardner, 1993). In devising his theory, one of Gardner's goals was to acknowledge that intelligence goes beyond math and verbal skills; it incorporates many other talents and skills as well. The implication for teachers is that looking at students' abilities in these various categories allows them to create more effective lesson plans to accommodate their students' diverse skills and talents.

Courtesy of Aaron Bacall, *The Lighter Side of Technology in Education*, p. 74. Copyright 2003 by Aaron Bacall. Reprinted by permission of Corwin Press Inc.

- **Gregorc's Style Delineator Approach** Anthony Gregorc's **style delineator approach** looks at how students perceive information. He breaks perceptual qualities into two categories: *concrete* and *abstract*, with *concrete* focusing on fact-based, physical information and *abstract* focusing on logical, deductive reasoning. He also categorizes students' ability to order information into a *sequential* or organized sequence and a *random* or disorganized sequence. Understanding these learning styles may help teachers understand how students prefer to approach certain tasks. This understanding, in turn, allows teachers to build this approach into their lesson plans.

- **Brain-Based Learning Theory** **Brain-based learning** theorists believe that traditional schooling and lesson plans often inhibit learning by discouraging the brain's natural process because of the way the learning is structured and delivered. To best engage students, they encourage teachers to use three instructional techniques that could easily be incorporated into any lesson plan: *immersion*, creating learning environments that immerse students in learning; *relaxed alertness*, making students feel safe and academically challenged; and *active processing*, allowing students to consolidate and internalize information (Brooks, 1999).

- **Bloom's Taxonomy** **Bloom's taxonomy** is an approach that has been used by teachers for decades to elevate learning and discussions beyond the knowledge level (Bloom, 1956). Bloom identified six levels of thinking, as shown in Table 10.1 on page 294. This approach promotes the use of specific words and actions to encourage certain student behaviors and to develop their ability to think critically. Being aware of the levels and consciously using the levels as a planning resource encourages teachers to move students to higher levels. As you sit in your own college classes, think about how many levels of learning you are accessing. Are you thinking only at the knowledge level or are you moving to analysis and synthesis?

These are just some of the theories that teachers consider when designing their lesson plans. The more that teachers understand how their students learn, the better they will be at meeting the needs of their classrooms. Without this knowledge, teachers could become rote messengers instead of reflective, thoughtful, engaging teachers. Lesson planning that incorporates these theories is crucial to student learning.

INTASC

Principle #7

Instructional Planning Skills: The teacher plans instruction based upon knowledge of subject matter, students, the community, and curriculum goals.

PLANNING INSTRUCTION FOR STUDENT LEARNING

The teacher's lesson plan is a critical part of a teaching cycle that includes teaching, assessing, reteaching, and modifying the initial plan. Each daily lesson plan focuses on the purpose of the lesson, what students should achieve, how to assess what students learn, and

TABLE 10.1

Bloom's Taxonomy: Levels of Thinking

LEVEL	SKILLS	WORD CUES
KNOWLEDGE	Basic recall of dates, events, places, major ideas, and key concepts of subject matter.	list, define, tell, describe, identify, show, label, collect, examine, tabulate, quote, name, who, when, where
COMPREHENSION	Understands information and is able to grasp meaning and translate information into new context. Can use inference to identify causes and predict consequences.	summarize, describe, interpret, contrast, predict, associate, distinguish, estimate, differentiate, discuss, extend
APPLICATION	Uses information and learned techniques to solve problems.	apply, demonstrate, calculate, complete, illustrate, show, solve, examine, modify, relate, change, classify, experiment, discover
ANALYSIS	Breaks down information by identifying patterns and organizational structures and recognizing hidden meanings. Able to develop conclusions to support generalizations.	analyze, separate, order, explain, connect, classify, arrange, divide, compare, select, explain, infer
SYNTHESIS	Creatively uses information to create new ideas; able to predict and draw conclusions using information from multiple sources.	combine, integrate, modify, rearrange, substitute, plan, create, design, invent, what if?, compose, formulate, prepare, generalize, rewrite
EVALUATION	Able to assess value of material based on theories, personal input, and reasoned arguments and to recognize subjectivity and personal bias.	assess, decide, rank, grade, test, measure, recommend, convince, select, judge, explain, discriminate, support, conclude, compare, summarize

Source: Benjamin S. Bloom et al., *Taxonomy of Educational Objectives.* Published by Allyn and Bacon, Boston, MA. Copyright © 1984 by Pearson Education. Adapted by permission of the publisher.

where they need to go next. Teachers must also track how each lesson relates to standards dictated by state and federal initiatives.

● **Teaching for Understanding**   Effective teaching offers evidence of student skill development and understanding. Teachers must first create the foundation for thinking and learning and then build on that foundation. Teachers who use well-designed lesson plans present information tailored to their particular classroom. Questions for teachers to consider when creating lesson plans include the following:

● What are my goals for this lesson or unit?

● What do I want students to learn?

● Are these goals realistic for all students?

● What do I need to motivate my students?

● What will the students be doing in class today?

When you ask questions such as these, you take an important step toward planning lessons that will reach your students. Your students, in turn, will reap the benefits by developing a thorough understanding of their lessons. To ensure that all students are at the same place in the lesson, lesson plans must incorporate time for assessing where students are in the lesson. For those who fall behind, you need to allow for time to reteach portions of the lesson. This may require modifying lesson plans. Not all of the lesson-planning content, however, is at a teacher's discretion.

● **Aligning Plans to Standards**   Have you ever surprised yourself by scoring well on a test that covered content you didn't completely understand? You might have memorized concepts, definitions, or theories that a week later were erased from your memory. How well do you think that test gauged your understanding of the topic? This scenario is increasingly common these days as the emphasis on teaching shifts toward **curriculum frameworks,** which are statewide content standards that must be adhered to at each grade level.

With the implementation of the No Child Left Behind Act of 2001, the federal government determined to make high-stakes testing a mandatory measurement of students' yearly progress. This testing has forced school districts to plan accordingly. District goals and state curriculum frameworks are organized around sets of skills and knowledge that guide the curriculum. Districts determine the **scope and sequence** for when topics and skills will be taught and at which grade level. Then, at three separate grade levels, standardized tests are given to assess student knowledge. For example, state tests such as the Massachusetts Comprehensive Assessment System (MCAS) test guide the curriculum in Massachusetts. Other states across the United States have similar tests that play the same role. Figure 10.1 illustrates a cycle for planning and teaching using standards.

This national testing initiative has influenced the daily planning of classroom teachers across the country. Accommodating these prescribed standards has meant that teachers have fewer choices with regard to the content they can teach. There is also an urgency to present material that will be on the test prior to the test. These artificial timelines often create problems for students who need more time to grasp concepts and for teachers who need more time to teach them. For these teachers, a necessary challenge has been finding a middle ground between test preparation and teaching for student understanding. With

I N T A S C

Principle #7

Instructional Planning Skills: The teacher plans instruction based upon knowledge of subject matter, students, the community, and curriculum goals.

I N T A S C

Principle #1

Knowledge of Subject Matter: The teacher understands the central concepts, tools of inquiry, and structures of the subject being taught and can create learning experiences that make these aspects of subject matter meaningful for students.

F I G U R E 10.1

Teaching to Standards Cycle

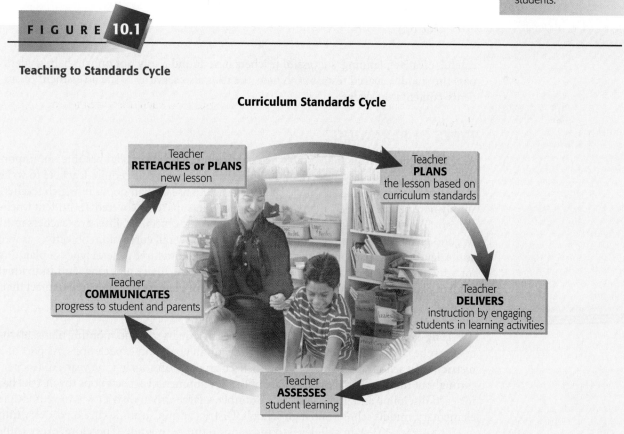

Curriculum Standards Cycle

Teacher **RETEACHES or PLANS** new lesson

Teacher **PLANS** the lesson based on curriculum standards

Teacher **COMMUNICATES** progress to student and parents

Teacher **DELIVERS** instruction by engaging students in learning activities

Teacher **ASSESSES** student learning

BUILDING ON EDUCATIONAL FOUNDATIONS

Teacher-Proof Curricula

Many people think that teaching should be carefully regulated and controlled. Under such conditions, teachers would simply deliver the curriculum, the content of which is determined by someone other than teachers. An opposing model has the teacher as an active agent in the classroom, shaping the curriculum, determining its content, and planning for its introduction and discussion.

In the first model, it is relatively easy to establish guidelines and standards that need to be met. In doing so, however, the real needs of students may not be addressed. Teaching can become highly formulaic, especially when directed toward students doing well on assessments (learning to the test). In the second model, the teacher functions as a professional and

reflective practitioner, adapting the curriculum to meet the specific needs of the students and the community.

How much do teachers need to be regulated in terms of what they teach? How much freedom should they be given to shape their instruction? Is the answer to these questions different in different types of communities, and with different types of student populations? For example, in Special Education, should the curriculum be highly controlled and regulated, or does the teacher need to be given latitude in terms of meeting the individual needs of students?

What do you think? How much should teachers function independently, and how much should they be regulated and controlled in terms of the content they teach?

careful, creative planning, successful teachers have found a way not only to help students pass the standardarized tests, but to have the tests also serve as a true assessment of students' content knowledge.

TYPES OF PLANNING

As teachers move through an established curriculum, the lesson plan becomes an important piece of a much larger curriculum objective. Some districts require teachers to write plans tied to state objectives; other districts allow the use of plan books in which teachers simply note page numbers and basic objectives for lessons to be covered. In student teaching most programs require long plans with very specific objectives. Effective teachers must be good planners, as their plans take into account the overall curriculum objectives as well as the day-to-day classroom activities. Lesson plans fall into three general types of planning for which teachers are responsible: long-range planning, daily planning, and individual student planning. Teachers equipped with each type of plan are well prepared to meet their immediate and long-range goals.

● **Long-Range Planning**   In order to create yearly, quarterly, and monthly plans, teachers must be cognizant of the district and curriculum goals and expectations. As part of a district, each school must meet certain district expectations during the year. All teachers throughout the district have to be aware of the developmental expectations the district has for each discipline and grade level. For example, a large urban district will have multiple elementary, middle school, and high schools. District administrators will expect every fifth grader to reach a certain skill level to move on to the sixth grade. Therefore, every fifth-grade teacher in the district needs to be aware of these expectations in order to prepare the students for that move. Teachers also must take into account any preparation for standardized tests that may be given and assume responsibility for expectations and district goals for these standardized tests. Some teachers do **back planning,** which means they create a long-range plan that indicates where they want to be at the end of the year, and then work backward to determine what they need to do first to meet their end goal.

Most teachers divide their year into **unit plans.** Creating a unit plan involves mapping out content instruction based on thematic units. For example, an elementary teacher's yearlong plan for math instruction might include units on long division and multiplication. Reading might be broken up into content-area reading, main ideas and supporting details, or reading for comprehension. Integrated into these plans might be some stand-alone lessons that can be inserted at various places in the overall unit. For example, if a guest speaker is scheduled or if there is a field trip scheduled as part of the unit, such events may need to revolve around availability of the speaker or field trip destination. Breaking up the year into thematic units provides organization for the teacher and the students.

Planning is at the heart of effective teaching: As the adage says, "Failure to plan is planning to fail." What are some steps you can take now to make sure you learn to plan well?

● **Daily Planning**   Daily lesson plans represent the nuts and bolts of teaching. They establish the agenda teachers use to map out the daily learning objectives. In elementary schools, where teachers must teach all subjects, planning can be intensive as they fit in all of their lessons in concert with their students' electives such as art, physical education, music, and computers. In secondary and middle schools, where teachers focus on specific content, lesson plans are designed around concepts and skills to be taught or reviewed that fit into the larger unit plan. Review the sample lesson plan in Figure 10.2 on page 298. What do you notice about teacher planning? For example, a history teacher might plan a unit around a specific event, such as the Civil War. A single plan for one or two days of the unit might focus on the Battle of Gettysburg. Because this teacher may have several classes of students, each class must have a plan of its own to accommodate the different levels and mix of students.

● **Individual Student Planning**   In addition to creating long-range plans and daily plans, some students may require teachers to create modified plans. These modifications may be designed to cater to students who are ahead of or behind the rest of the class, or students with behavioral issues who require individual hands-on plans and activities. When teachers anticipate potential behavioral problems and work them into their lesson plans, they can revise their plans to handle disruptions and avert potential disaster.

Beginning teachers often don't have a conceptual framework for the different types of planning required throughout the year. While they are most familiar with daily lesson planning, they don't yet see how further, detailed planning can make their jobs easier. While some student teaching programs require student teachers to prepare long-range plans, their objectives are very different from those of teachers. As you observe and interview teachers throughout your teacher preparation program, be sure to ask them how they do their long-range planning. Where do they start? Where do they end?

Although not all teachers prepare every type of lesson plan presented here, many planning options are available to help you structure your year, your units, and your classes. You need to take time, experiment, and gain experience to determine what works best.

PLANNING FOR THE DIVERSE CLASSROOM

Look around you. How many of your classmates do you think share your background? How many grew up in a similar environment? Go to the same place of worship? Have the

F I G U R E **10.2**

Sample Daily Lesson Plan Format

Subject or skill: _____ Date: _____

Lesson topic: _____(content area)_____ Time: _____

Why am I teaching this lesson and how does it relate to school, district, and state standards?

Curriculum framework number (or title): _____

Behavioral objectives (What will the students know and be able to do as a result of this lesson?)

1. _____
2. _____
3. _____

Key vocabulary terms	Key questions to guide discussion (Bloom's taxonomy)

Materials, resources, technology:

Anticipated student behavior issues:

Is differentiated instruction required for any students?

Procedures

Opening motivator

What the lesson will cover

How lesson will close (summary activity)

Assessment (How will I know students have learned?):

Reteaching (What will I need to do next?):

Homework or enrichment work assigned:

Teacher Self-Assessment (What would I do differently the next time I teach this lesson?):

I N T A S C

Principle #4

Multiple Instructional Strategies: The teacher uses various instructional strategies to encourage students' development of critical thinking, problem solving, and performance skills.

same family dynamic? Chances are, you will find that your life experiences are unique, as are those of every member of your class. This becomes an integral part of a teacher's lesson planning. Getting to know each and every student should be a primary focus for a teacher whose goal is to meet all of the expectations for each class. How students learn, who they are, where they come from, their cultural backgrounds, their familial backgrounds, and their past and current living environments are all important aspects of planning for successful student learning.

As you plan for a diverse classroom, you will need to acknowledge three key factors:

1. *Your students' diverse communities*—By acknowledging the different needs of different kinds of communities, you can best plan lessons to accommodate students' needs, interests, and environments.

2. *Your students' diverse cultures*—By acknowledging your classroom's cultural diversity and the particular makeup of the classroom, you can integrate the richness of the classroom community in your lessons.

3. *Your students' diverse academic skills and abilities*—By acknowledging the wide range of academic abilities in your classroom, you can plan to accommodate the various levels of skills and abilities of each student.

As you learn more about your students, you will gain a better understanding of their backgrounds, approaches to learning, and personal expectations. This understanding will inform your overall classroom agendas.

- **Acknowledging Students' Communities** As teachers get to know their students, they grow to understand each of the social and environmental contexts that influence their behavior, motivation, talents, and skill sets. Students moving through an urban classroom may have different learning styles from students moving through a rural or suburban classroom.

Students in urban classrooms in city schools may have very different needs from students in rural classrooms. Safety is a concern that other types of schools may not think about. When teachers are exposed to experiences such as one teacher describes—"when I entered the building [I] saw a police officer and a scanner for weapons. . . . When he found out I was a student teacher he let me go around"—the context in which they engage students will be different from the context of a teacher from a more sheltered environment.

Suburban classrooms may have their own set of issues and challenges for teachers. While teachers in urban schools may find that parental involvement is minimal, some teachers in suburban schools find that parents are too involved in that they want to have more input into how and what their children are learning. In addition, unlike urban schools where school supplies and resources are often minimal, suburban schools often have a wealth of resources, but so many initiatives and new projects in the district that it is difficult to get things done. The pressure for students to all be high achievers may affect the way the teachers approach their lesson plans.

Because rural schools are located in more sparsely populated areas, some schools may have multiple grades in one classroom because there are few teachers. Other rural schools may be so far from students' homes that they are forced to arrive late and leave early every day. These students also may have trouble focusing in school because, in reality, their days are longer than those of their classmates. (See Education Matters.) These issues present a number of challenges to teachers planning to accommodate statewide curricular frameworks. In addition to meeting the needs of diverse age groups or part-time students, these teachers tend to be isolated from other adults in the district.

- **Acknowledging Students' Diverse Cultures** The social groups and activities in which students participate tell teachers a lot about who they are. Some of their social context is dictated by their cultural backgrounds. For example, some students sharing the same ethnicities form friendships based on the fact that they share the same native language and many of the same cultural traditions. These students are labeled as **English language learners (ELLs)** because English is not their first language.

Other aspects of this context are dictated by students' interests. Figure 10.3 provides some questions teachers might ask students at the beginning of the year to help them get to

INTASC

Principle #7

Instructional Planning Skills: The teacher plans instruction based upon knowledge of subject matter, students, the community, and curriculum goals.

FIGURE 10.3

Interest Survey

1. What is your favorite subject in school?
2. What do you like to do after school?
   (If high school) Do you have a job? What are you saving your money for?
3. Have you been to another country?
4. What language do you speak at home?
5. What is your favorite hobby or sport?
6. Do you play an instrument? Sing? Dance?
7. What do you wish you could do in school?
8. How do you learn best?
9. What can your teacher do to help you learn?

EDUCATION MATTERS

Why Sleep Matters

There is growing evidence that a chronic lack of sleep can lead to obesity, mimic symptoms of attention deficit disorder, and contribute to depression. Brown University's Mary Carskadon studies sleep and says tired kids get lower grades, don't do well in sports, and have more emotional problems than kids who get enough sleep. Sleep deprivation has also been cited as a cause of car accidents. According to a survey by the National Sleep Foundation, only 15% of students reported sleeping 8.5 hours on school nights, the minimum doctors think they need.

Some say school days are organized for the wrong populations of students. Elementary students who go to bed early and get up early have late start times of 8:30 or later. Meanwhile many high school students who work after school, play sports, and generally stay up later have to be in class at 7:15 or 7:30. One school district in Minnesota experimented with changing the start time of the high school day from 7:20 A.M. to 8:40 A.M. for its 12,000 students. The results were so encouraging, with more alert students in early classes and fewer depressed students, that 34 districts in 19 states have followed suit by starting the school day later. Adolescents' natural body clocks keep them up to at least 11:00, so this system is working to give them the sleep they need to be successful in school.

The Education Issue: Do students need more sleep to be successful?

How Does a Lack of Sleep Affect Teachers and Students?

Teachers can't teach students who have their heads on their desks or are tired. Secondary classrooms often have had very high tardy rates for first-period classes, leading to lower academic achievement by students who are always late. Students who are always late or who are nodding off all day are not getting the most out of school and run the risk of dropping out of high school. Changing the starting time of a school day can affect students and teachers positively.

What's Your Opinion?

1. How much sleep do you need to be alert and at your best?

2. How do you think sleep affects learning?

3. Why do you think schools continue to start their days so early if the research shows that students are less productive?

---

know more about each student. These questions focus on students' cultural backgrounds as well as their self-identified strengths. Teachers can then integrate what they learn about their students into their lesson plans. For instance, if a teacher knows that a student grew up practicing a particular custom that relates to a lesson, the teacher can ask that student to share this firsthand knowledge with the class. In planning for diverse classrooms, teachers need to understand their students' cultural backgrounds in order to understand expectations or practices that may differ from expected classroom practice.

Teachers who create and plan for an inclusive classroom that integrates all social and cultural contexts should achieve success. Even in situations in which teachers may be assigned new students who have moved from one context to another—whether from a different town or a different country—these students may have difficulty adjusting. Good teachers work these students into their plans. They make sure that they get to know these students, their needs, and their backgrounds and interests in order to better integrate them into the classroom.

- **Acknowledging Academic Diversity**   Planning for academically diverse classrooms holds a number of challenges beyond those that have already been discussed. If a classroom runs the gamut from very slow learners to accelerated learners, with most students demonstrating a range of academic skills somewhere in the middle, this will give you some idea how comprehensive a solid lesson plan should be.

INTASC

Principle #3

Adapting Instruction for Individual Needs: The teacher understands how students differ in their approaches to learning and creates instructional opportunities that are adapted to diverse learners.

Many states have enacted **special-needs legislation,** which provides funding for programs that offer additional support to students who need remediation as well as to students who excel and need special projects and accelerated work in order to remain challenged in the classroom.

Gardner's theory of multiple intelligences reminds us that all students have certain gifts. For example, students who are identified as needing academic support also may be gifted musicians or artists. To accommodate students who may have special needs within their school districts, teachers and school counselors meet with the students' parents and create **individualized education programs** (IEPs) that outline the support the students need to be successful in schools. These plans list these students' goals and objectives for the school year. Teachers' lesson planning must take these IEPs into consideration and modify the lessons for each student's specific needs. Teachers who recognize the individuality of their students learn about their students and use their strengths in the classroom.

Just as special-needs students need additional support, so do students identified as **gifted and talented.** These students may finish the assigned work early and need more challenging or different types of assignments. Gifted and talented programs are defined differently in various school districts. Some of these programs involve pulling students out of their classes to participate in special projects. Others receive additional work within their classroom. For students who finish their work early, teachers need to plan for providing additional work in order to keep them interested and motivated.

Throughout this section, you have learned about the importance of preparing a comprehensive lesson plan for effective teaching. You have also learned why it is important to integrate a number of learning theories in your plans in order to accommodate the different learning styles of your students. While state and federal initiatives and standardized testing have informed teachers' lesson plans nationwide, creative teachers find a balance in their plans to teach to the standard and teach for understanding. As important as these steps are to good teaching, getting to know your students and their diverse backgrounds and needs is critical to planning and executing effective lesson plans that will guide your students to success.

"The hardest part of student teaching is the PLANNING! I hate planning. I hated it when I first started, and I hate it now. However, it is the single most important thing. There were days when I did not have time to plan. Those days were awful. The anxiety that came along with the knowledge that I had not planned was stifling, and the classes were chaotic. I hated those days. . . . I hated them more than I hated planning."

STUDENT TEACHER

THINK ABOUT THIS:

Think of a time when you had to create a plan either in your personal life or for school. Perhaps you were planning a party or a class presentation. How did you organize your plan? Did you have to change it at some point? Planning comes naturally for some people; others have to really work at it. Whether it comes easy or hard for you, good planning is critical for a teacher.

SHARE and COMPARE:

With a classmate, discuss why planning is such an important skill for teachers to learn. What do you think would be the consequences of not having an effective lesson plan?

How Do Teachers Deliver Instruction?

Although important, understanding one's chosen discipline is not enough to ensure classroom success. One must also appreciate the developmental stages and learning styles of students; apply learning theory in individual and group contexts; balance classroom management needs with the nurturing and respect that all children need; model values required for good citizenship; evaluate, design, and select motivating tasks; communicate effectively to students and parents; and help students understand the connections among their subjects. And that's the short list.

Robert Feirsen, Principal, Westbury, New York
What Matters Most: Teaching for America's Future (p. 6)

There is a point in teaching when you know that you're doing what you were meant to do. You might be in the middle of a lesson looking at a flurry of hands shoot up when you pose a question. It might be when you're working with a student who has been struggling with a concept that she finally understands. It might be while you're researching information for presenting a standard lesson in an innovative way. This is the magic of teaching, when all the intrinsic rewards materialize that first time you see that you are facilitating learning in your classroom.

In earlier chapters, the INTASC principles were introduced as a guide for what effective teachers should know and be able to achieve. These principles offer specific criteria and standards for new teachers. Charlotte Danielson has taken these principles and organized them into four domains: Domain 1, Planning and Preparation; Domain 2, The Classroom Environment; Domain 3, Instruction; and Domain 4, Professional Responsibilities. Domain 3, Instruction, constitutes the core of teaching. To deliver meaningful instruction, teachers need to give clear directions, make the lesson meaningful, maintain student attention, and use higher-order thinking. These domains provide a framework for teaching (Danielson, 1996).

Teaching is a complex process that requires more than having content knowledge, masterful skills, and the ability to articulate. Teaching requires a drive to impart knowledge, an ability to understand children, a willingness to adapt to any situation, and an openness to ideas.

Teachers use a variety of teaching styles to engage their students. While some students may learn more easily from lectures, others may get more out of working in small groups, while others still may be more visual learners. Your own teaching style, your willingness to differentiate instruction to accommodate a range of learning styles and abilities, and your insights into potential behavioral problems will all help you become an effective teacher. This section provides an overview of key factors and considerations that influence how teachers deliver instruction.

INDICATORS OF EFFECTIVE TEACHING

INTASC

Principle #7

Instructional Planning Skills: The teacher plans instruction based upon knowledge of subject matter, students, the community, and curriculum goals.

In some schools where the main focus is on test scores, signs are posted that read, "We dispense knowledge. Bring your own container." Distinguished professor Martin Haberman believes this approach to be the wrong way to teach students and suggests that effective teachers should "draw out" knowledge from students, not stuff it in (Haberman, 1996).

How does this philosophy manifest itself in the classroom? Think about students who sit passively listening to lectures for hours, and then use their study halls to memorize definitions and concepts. Are they recipients of effective teaching? What about students who are asked to research a subject and then present a report on that subject to the class? Are they recipients of effective teaching? Figure 10.4 illustrates that when teachers are able to foster student involvement, positive student interactions, mutual respect, independent thinking, self-responsibility, and curiosity and thinking beyond the classroom, they have practiced good teaching.

FIGURE 10.4

Indicators of Good Teaching

How you know good teaching is going on . . .

Students are involved with issues that are important to them . . . like advocating for school issues that are real and relate to their interests

Students are discussing issues of human differences in classrooms . . . like why are there rich and poor people, why do stores have parking for disabled drivers? Why do women make less money than men?

Students are engaged in big ideas . . . like how did our civilization evolve? What lessons have we learned from history?

Students are planning their own learning . . . like what they would like to study and how they will present their learning to their classmates.

Students are involved in applying issues of fairness and social justice . . . like discussing democratic ideas in school or investigating health care issues.

Students are actively involved in their own learning . . . by doing the experiments in class not just watching the teacher demonstrate the concept.

Students are involved in real life activities . . . like field trips and internships in places where real people are working.

Students are asked to think and challenge stereotypes and commonly agreed upon assumptions . . . like how students who don't speak English learn.

Students are involved in editing and polishing their work to make it better . . . like using conferencing skills and sharing ideas with others.

Students are using technology to enhance their learning . . . like internet searches to find primary research documents or the latest news.

Students are reflecting on their own lives and what they believe . . . writing autobiographies and sharing their lives with others.

Source: Adapted from M. Haberman, "The Pedagogy of Poverty versus Good Teaching," in *City Kids, City Teachers,* N. Press (Ed.). (New York: New Press, 1996).

Good teaching does not always require teachers to be at the head of the classroom. As long as teachers plan and orchestrate the learning environment, it presents many opportunities for students to engage and learn. For example, in a **student-centered community** where teachers provide students resources for experimenting and investigating, it may appear to an outsider that the students are doing all the work as teachers sit by idly. However, while teachers ensure order and accountability, students are honing their critical thinking skills, demonstrating responsibility, learning to work cooperatively with others, and becoming independent thinkers (Haberman, 1996).

● **Teaching Styles**   As with learning styles, there is no one-size-fits-all approach to teaching. Earlier in this chapter you learned how important it is for teachers to get to know all students in their classrooms. Knowing your students and understanding how they learn is key to being able to engage them. This often requires teachers to adopt a variety of teaching styles in their classrooms.

As a student, what type of teaching do you find most accessible? Do you prefer lectures? Charts and graphs? Classroom discussions? Learning by doing? All teachers have their preferred way of learning, which inevitably informs their own teaching styles. Being able to combine your preferred learning styles with teaching formats that will reach your students is essential. For example, teachers who tend to lecture without the help of visual aids will have a hard time reaching the visual learners in their classrooms. Conversely,

INTASC

Principle #6

Communication Skills: The teacher uses knowledge of effective verbal, nonverbal, and media communication techniques to foster active inquiry, collaboration, and supportive interaction in the classroom.

teachers who rely heavily on the chalkboard and charts and graphs will have a hard time reaching students who are better listeners.

As you get to know your students, you can start to shape your method of delivering information. Your best way to determine what works best for each student is keen observation. You can also learn more about how your students prefer to learn by having them complete a simple questionnaire from which to extract important information. For instance, are the majority of students concrete thinkers (see Gregorc's style delineator approach earlier in the chapter) or abstract thinkers? Do they like to passively absorb information or are they more interested in learning by doing? Most likely, there will be a mix of learning styles. To accommodate these differences, you need to create classrooms rich in all styles of learning, as students' preferred styles may change as they grow and develop their skills. If you are creative, involved, flexible, and open to adapting instruction to the needs of your students, you will likely be effective. If students remain curious, involved, motivated, and stimulated, your methods are sound.

● **Differentiated Instruction**   The best way to keep students involved is to vary the instruction. Carol Ann Tomlinson's work (1999) in **differentiated instruction** has informed teachers and given them specific strategies to use in response to the diverse needs of their students. Differentiated instruction basically encourages the use of multiple instructional options in order to meet the needs of each student. Being able to modify instruction by explaining something differently or analyzing a task so that it becomes a manageable skill are necessary adjustments that teachers must make. The three principles of differentiation are *respectful tasks, flexible grouping,* and *ongoing assessment and adjustment* of any work assigned. (See Figure 10.5.)

To manage the range of needs in differentiated classrooms, teachers must assess their students' readiness to learn, ability levels, interests, and learning profiles, all of which influence how you will connect with them. If students are not ready to learn, it doesn't matter how they are taught. Understanding students' learning expectations at their different stages is necessary in order to apply the principles of differentiated instruction. Teachers using differentiated instruction are able to group their students by interests, need, and ability and

Adjust the teaching plan, not the child. A differentiated instruction approach and individual work with students allows you to address their specific needs and interests.

FIGURE 10.5

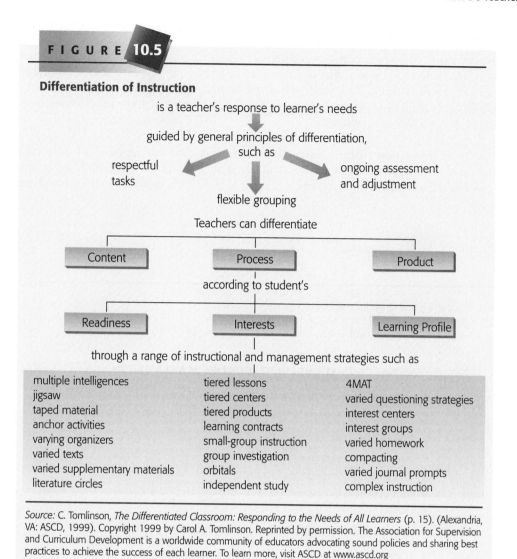

Differentiation of Instruction

is a teacher's response to learner's needs

guided by general principles of differentiation, such as

respectful tasks

flexible grouping

ongoing assessment and adjustment

Teachers can differentiate

Content   Process   Product

according to student's

Readiness   Interests   Learning Profile

through a range of instructional and management strategies such as

multiple intelligences	tiered lessons	4MAT
jigsaw	tiered centers	varied questioning strategies
taped material	tiered products	interest centers
anchor activities	learning contracts	interest groups
varying organizers	small-group instruction	varied homework
varied texts	group investigation	compacting
varied supplementary materials	orbitals	varied journal prompts
literature circles	independent study	complex instruction

Source: C. Tomlinson, *The Differentiated Classroom: Responding to the Needs of All Learners* (p. 15). (Alexandria, VA: ASCD, 1999). Copyright 1999 by Carol A. Tomlinson. Reprinted by permission. The Association for Supervision and Curriculum Development is a worldwide community of educators advocating sound policies and sharing best practices to achieve the success of each learner. To learn more, visit ASCD at www.ascd.org

to use various methods for the different groups. These classrooms are vibrant, active places that foster learning.

● **Anticipating Behavior Problems**   As teachers get to know students and their particular strengths, weaknesses, and unique characteristics, they also learn to anticipate when students might become disruptive in class. To avoid common misbehaviors and disruption, teachers need to acknowledge potential misbehaviors in their plans so that they will be prepared if and when the behaviors occur. In some cases, disruption may occur when students finish early and need more enrichment. Teachers who are prepared may have specific procedures in place for all lessons if students finish early, such as reading a book, or they may arrange for these students to go to an activities center, where their restlessness will be alleviated.

Disruption is not always brought on by individuals, however. Classroom management strategies and routines can help minimize most potential mishaps in a classroom. For example, when teachers bring up for discussion potentially controversial topics that might incite arguments or anger, it is important that they have a protocol in place to deal with diverse opinions. Some classrooms might adopt a policy to agree to disagree after a certain period of time, or others might have their students resolve their anger by presenting their arguments in essay assignments or Web logs. By having a solution in place, teachers ensure that their classroom will not get out of hand and that students will get the most out of their school day.

INTASC

Principle #5

Classroom Motivation and Management: The teacher uses an understanding of individual and group motivation and behavior to create a learning environment that encourages positive social interaction, active engagement in learning, and self-motivation.

DIVERSE MODELS FOR DIVERSE LEARNERS

Teachers with diverse learners must be prepared to use many different models of instruction (see Table 10.2). Tomlinson's differentiated instruction model encourages teachers to use a variety of methods. Direct instruction, the constructivist approach, and guided teaching all have a place in a teacher's repertoire. It is up to teachers to determine which methods to use in particular circumstances.

● **Direct Instruction**   Direct instruction is a teacher-centered approach to conveying information to students. This type of instruction is most successful when introducing new topics or skills at beginning levels of thinking; it is most often delivered to the whole class

---

TABLE 10.2

Effective Lesson Practices

Teachers structure their days around class periods that range from 30 to 120 minutes. Effective teachers build structural frameworks within the time frame of the lesson so that they can maximize student learning. As you observe teachers in real classrooms, look at these key areas and see how they actualize them in the classroom.

TEACHING PRACTICE	EXAMPLES OF WHAT THIS MIGHT LOOK LIKE IN A CLASSROOM
Assessing students' prior knowledge	● Asking students what they already know about the topic at the beginning of the class ● Giving a pretest and checking for understanding prior to teaching the lesson
Gaining students' attention	● Reviewing the agenda for the class ● Sharing a funny story that relates to the topic ● Asking a student to begin the lesson ● Asking students to look at the teacher ● Writing on the overhead ● Writing on the board and inviting students to read the topics
Giving clear directions	● Using the overhead to write the directions for visual learners ● Saying the directions and repeating them ● Allowing questions about the directions ● Creating a model of what the completed product might look like and showing students
Using a well-designed lesson plan that engages all learners in meaningful activities that promote higher order thinking and meet curriculum standards	● Referring to a written lesson in a plan book ● Writing the concepts on the board that will be part of the lesson and making outcomes clear to students ● Using a variety of materials and methods to meet diverse learners' needs
Maintaining attention and order throughout the class period	● Walking around the room while students are working ● Answering questions ● Maintaining enthusiasm for the topic ● Responding to inappropriate behavior as it happens
Assessing student learning throughout and at the end of the lesson	● Asking students questions as a group or individually to determine understanding ● Giving a written or verbal quiz ● Reviewing completed products
Assigning homework or enrichment	● Putting assignment on the board ● Handing out a sheet

(although it can be delivered one-on-one). Examples of direct instruction include teacher-directed lectures, presentations, and demonstrations. In these classroom situations, students sit passively listening. The length of time a student can stay engaged as a listener in whole-class direct instruction varies by grade level and students' needs.

A direct instruction method that perpetuates learning involves using workbooks, computer program drills, practice programs, and other educational games that emphasize skills or knowledge mastery. Classrooms receiving this type of instruction are often set up with the desks in rows, teachers' desks up front, and all teaching materials behind the teacher's desk to be distributed, as needed, when students reach certain curriculum benchmarks.

- **Constructivist Approach**   The **constructivist approach** to teaching is the opposite of direct instruction in that it encourages teachers to create an environment that allows the students to direct their own learning. This approach draws from the psychologist Jean Piaget (1896–1980) and constructivists such as Lev Vygotsky (1896–1934), who believed that knowledge cannot be simply transmitted directly from the teacher to the learner, as stated in the direct approach, but it must be *constructed* by the learner and *reconstructed* as new information becomes available. Teachers who practice this approach believe that knowledge is built on students' prior knowledge.

In constructivist classrooms, teachers actively engage students in learning through real life situations with a focus on what the students think and how they perceive the world. Process and understanding are emphasized over product and test outcomes. Constructivist teachers use questions and inquiry to motivate students to think about what they are learning. This student-centered classroom often allows students to select what they want to learn, how they believe they would best learn, and how they would like to share what they learn. Because solving problems and creating systems for the ways in which students learn is integral to the constructivist approach, teachers create problem-solving activities and processes that promote learning new material and skills. This type of classroom is often structured with a number of separate areas within the classroom such as a computer station, a quiet reading area, and clusters of desks for small groups of students. An array of materials is available for students to access.

Constructivist teachers usually are less concerned with curriculum standards; instead they are committed to providing students freedom to explore and create activities, to read books of their choosing, and to learn about topics that interest them. They encourage hands-on experiential work based on students' prior knowledge. Instruction in these classrooms focuses on allowing students to make connections and fosters understanding through open-ended questions and discussions that require high-level thinking skills such as interpretation and analysis. This type of instruction does not use a standardized grading system or testing. Instead, students' self-assessments are an integral part of the whole learning process (Popham, 1999).

- **Guided Teaching: A Balanced Approach**   **Guided teaching,** or balanced teaching, uses both teacher-centered and student-centered approaches to learning. This approach is sometimes referred to as the *eclectic* or *integrated* approach. Teachers using this approach in their classrooms are well versed in a variety of theories and approaches, allowing them to tailor their instruction to individual students' needs. For example, for students having difficulty learning the alphabet, teachers might elect to work with them on mastering their letters, using a direct approach, one-on-one. For students in these same classrooms who have mastered their letters, teachers may start the class standing up front and use the blackboard to illustrate how to use the letters being discussed for a period of time, but then allow students to work in small groups reading to each other or by themselves. This guided approach can also be seen in math instruction when teachers stand in front of the class and present concepts, but then leave students time to work independently applying what they have just learned in class. With guided instruction, teachers often end the class by directing students to summarize what they have learned. This brief period allows teachers to revisit the objectives stated at the beginning of the lesson.

INTASC

Principle #6

Communication Skills: The teacher uses knowledge of effective verbal, nonverbal, and media communication techniques to foster active inquiry, collaboration, and supportive interaction in the classroom.

WORKING WITH STUDENTS WITH SPECIAL NEEDS

As of 2004, almost every general education classroom across the United States included students with special needs (NEA, 2004). As discussed earlier in the chapter, teachers must account for these students in their lesson plans. This allows them to ensure that they are addressing the needs of all students during class time. There are two approaches to working with students with special needs: *inclusion classrooms* and *pull-out programs.*

Typically inclusion classrooms contain some special education students with moderate special needs. Some schools, however, have been able to include students with severe disabilities as well. These schools are identified as **full inclusion** schools. Students with severe disabilities usually require special teacher's aides who are assigned to work with them in the classroom. Special education teachers, teachers' aides (when necessary), and classroom teachers must collaborate to make sure that their students' goals, as established in their IEPs, are being met and that students are feeling successful.

Pull-out programs pull students with special needs out of the regular classroom setting to learn and practice skills one-on-one with a special education teacher. **Reading recovery programs** for struggling readers, for example, provide direct instruction to students in separate rooms and have met with significant success in teaching nonreaders how to read. The cost of paying a reading recovery teacher and the extra time required, however, have left some districts without these valuable programs. Schools vary on the procedure they use with their special education students, and often decisions are based on funding.

MAXIMIZING AVAILABLE RESOURCES

In the United States, according to a 2004 NEA study, as of fall 2003 an influx of nearly 400,000 additional children was entering our countries' classrooms, yet funding for these students remained stagnant (NEA, 2004). Unfortunately, because not all schools are created equal, many schools in low-socioeconomic areas suffered larger class sizes and no new resources. Consequently, schools in wealthier communities have money available for supplies and resources, while schools in poorer communities have limited resources and supplies. Where does this leave those teachers with limited resources?

Teachers in these classrooms clearly face more challenges than those with resources at their fingertips, yet effective teaching is still possible. For example, when schools cannot provide the most current textbooks, one elementary school teacher from New York suggests using the community newspaper. She states, "It arrives before the students and we use it to teach reading." Another creative middle school teacher offers, "I use the media center in our school and log on when I have outdated textbooks." Solutions such as this allow teachers to supplement old material with more current information and examples. A high school chemistry teacher explains, "I ordered examination copies from publishers and used these new ideas to supplement the ideas I was using in my old textbooks."

There are a myriad of other ideas on which teachers can capitalize. Each year private and federal grant opportunities are announced for the purpose of helping school districts obtain additional and necessary resources. With an open mind and determination, teachers can find creative solutions to the obstacles posed by having limited resources.

Grant funding has been particularly helpful for teachers and schools seeking to improve their access to technology. According to a report on school technology issued by an education department, "Virtually all U.S. schools are connected to the Internet, with about one computer for every five students" (Associated Press, 2005). Many teachers are taking advantage of this in their instruction by using computers to demonstrate concepts, create simulations, teach students to conduct research, have students create independent and/or group projects, or have students use computers to do practice drills or creative problem solving.

The number of computers in classrooms and access to computers, however, dictate the ways in which teachers use technology to enhance learning. Although today's children are growing up during the technological revolution, schools still have a limited supply of computers. For classrooms with only one computer, the teacher is mostly limited to using it as a tool for presenting information, and student access to the computer is also limited. In classrooms with more than one computer, or in schools with computer labs, teachers can more fully integrate technology into their instruction. One concern that many teachers encounter, especially in schools with limited student access, is ensuring that all students have equal opportunity to use the computer.

HOW DO TEACHERS ASSESS STUDENT PROGRESS?

Teachers plan lessons for effective instruction and create environments where students can learn through direct, constructivist, or guided teaching approaches, but all is wasted if the teacher does not know how to **assess,** or evaluate, students' progress and then use that information to set new goals for learning. Assessment of student progress has always existed in the field of education, as teachers need benchmarks throughout the school year to help them determine how individual students are progressing. Figure 10.6 identifies good practices for assessing student learning.

In the past decade, the emphasis on assessment has intensified, creating what some consider a "testing culture." Driven by national educational reform and supported by state policies that have adopted standards approaches to curriculum and instruction, the outcomes-based environment requires us to find out whether students are actually learning.

The debate about what today's children are learning and how they are being assessed is raising important questions for parents, teachers, and the public. They are questioning the value of the content appearing on the tests, how tests relate to overall curriculum standards, whether teachers are exclusively teaching to the tests, how tests are constructed, and whether these tests really measure what students need to know.

Some educators argue that too much testing is being done. They feel that valuable instruction time is being compromised as teachers prepare students for testing. Consequently, instead of creating learning experiences in which students would be engaged and

INTASC

Principle #8

Assessment of Student Learning: The teacher understands and uses formal and informal assessment strategies to evaluate and ensure the continuous intellectual, social, and physical development of the learner.

FIGURE 10.6

Principles of Good Practice for Assessing Student Learning

1. The assessment of student learning begins with educational values.
2. Assessment is most effective when it reflects an understanding of learning as multidimensional, integrated, and revealed in performance over time.
3. Assessment works best when the programs it seeks to improve have clear, explicitly stated purposes.
4. Assessment requires attention to outcomes but also and equally to the experiences that lead to those outcomes.
5. Assessment works best when it is ongoing not episodic.
6. Assessment fosters wider improvement when representatives from across the educational community are involved.
7. Assessment makes a difference when it begins with issues of use and illuminates questions that people really care about.
8. Assessment is most likely to lead to improvement when it is part of a larger set of conditions that promote change.
9. Through assessment, educators meet responsibilities to students and to the public.

Source: Adapted from A. W. Astin et al., *AAHE Assessment Forum.* (Washington, DC: American Association for Higher Education, 2003). Retrieved May 6, 2005, from http://www.aahe.org/principl.htm. Copyright 2003 by the AAHE. Reprinted with permission.

interacting, they are learning testing techniques and focusing specifically on material that will yield successful test scores. Conversely, proponents of the testing movement believe that schools need to be held accountable. Teachers, as well as students, need to be held to certain performance standards in order to move to the next level. These educators feel that test outcomes are valid indicators of student progress.

Whatever your perspective on this weighty issue, teachers need to assess students' progress to ensure that they are learning throughout the year. Measuring how much a student knows is complicated.

EDUCATION REFORM AND HIGH-STAKES TESTING

Before the implementation of NCLB, other types of **standardized tests** were administered as part of state initiatives for education reform. Standardized tests incorporate "standard methods of developing items, administering the test, scoring it, and reporting the scores" (Woolfolk, 2004, p. 516). Standardization allows results to be compared across schools, districts, and states. Most states have already been using different types of assessment instruments such as achievement tests, minimum competency tests, developmental screening tests, aptitude tests, performance tasks, and authentic assessments. NCLB has simply augmented that commitment to education reform on a national level.

● **State Tests**   In response to NCLB, state and federal agencies have raised the bar for all students by setting world-class standards instead of minimum competencies. Many policymakers have attached rewards to high-performing districts and sanctions to schools that don't make the grade (Stiggins, 2002). This system of reward and punishment further emphasizes the insistence on establishing high achievement standards. Many states have created their own standardized tests to measure student performance based on these state-mandated standards.

By transforming these standards into rigorous assessments, educators are finding themselves accountable for student outcomes as reflected in student test scores. The importance of districtwide outcomes, in fact, is such that outcomes are publicly reported to par-

The focus on accountability and standards has placed a great deal of pressure on schools. Are standardized tests the best way to evaluate students' intellectual skills and the quality of teaching?

ents and the community in the local newspapers. Some educators feel this is unfair, as these outcomes do not truly measure how much students learned. Stiggins takes this one step further by asserting that we need to go beyond the measures *of* learning and look to assessment *for* learning. Districts and schools need to use test results to identify and communicate where more work is needed rather than to highlight failed classrooms and call out teachers or principals for failed results. Tests that are used as weapons to hurt schools and districts often fail the students because teachers and principals hesitate to teach there, knowing that they are in the public spotlight for criticism.

● **Concerns over High-Stakes Testing**   Most state-mandated tests are used to determine students' participation in extracurricular activities or qualifications for advancement or graduation. In many states, teachers' pay and promotion status also ride on the test outcomes, thus creating a high-stakes environment.

There has been widespread concern over the misuse of test results and the equity of how and where they are administered. Many variables are not taken into account when evaluating test scores. For instance, for many urban school districts, the student body is much more culturally diverse than that of suburban schools. In addition, class sizes tend to be larger, resources are scarce, economic standards are lower, and they have a higher ELL population. As a result, there may be fewer students reading at grade level and fewer resources available to support these schools. Teachers and principals in these districts protest that being held to the same standards as more privileged, homogenous populations is not fair and equitable. Proponents of the tests, however, respond that they are pushing for these tests in order to advocate for these students. For example, they believe that low test scores for ELL students indicate that they need to speak English to pass these tests, forcing reform on these schools.

Not all students taking the test approach it with the same degree of seriousness. For instance, high school students who know that these tests determine whether they graduate feel more pressure when taking these tests than some fourth graders, who don't fully understand the purpose of the tests. (See Problems to Possibilities for other problems related to high-stakes testing.) Yet even fourth graders can feel the pressure of high-stakes testing. One fourth-grade student teacher noted that the anxiety levels prior to a state-mandated test impeded the students' learning. The cooperating teacher prepared the students in a variety of ways prior to the test day, with sample tests, pep talks, and support sessions. All students participated in these activities in school, but their reactions to the preparation and upcoming test differed. Despite the teacher's support and test preparation, some students still demonstrated extreme anxiety prior to the test week. These students believed that the tests would identify them as being smart or not smart. Other students seemed to keep the test in perspective (Flecca, 2002). What was the difference? This limited study of one classroom showed that the parents were the key. When the test was overemphasized at home, the students tended to have more anxiety.

A number of salient issues drive the debate about the value of high-stakes testing. This issue will not find a solution any time soon. For now, the tests will continue and teachers will try to find a balance between preparing students for these tests, teaching students in a way that is engaging, and assessing students' understanding based on methods other than standardized tests.

ONGOING CLASSROOM ASSESSMENTS

Most student assessment takes place on a daily basis in the classroom as part of a teacher's routine. Because teaching for understanding and having students demonstrate what they have learned is the purpose of teaching, the process by which we assess student learning is critical. Lesson plans designed by teachers must match classroom, school, and district goals as well as the appropriate assessment tools.

To assess students' progress appropriately, most teachers use a number of tools to evaluate students at different points throughout the year. While teachers design some of the

INTASC

Principle #8

Assessment of Student Learning: The teacher understands and uses formal and informal assessment strategies to evaluate and ensure the continuous intellectual, social, and physical development of the learner.

Problems to POSSIBILITIES

How Do Teachers Handle Issues of Cheating?

As a first-year math teacher at Johnson High School, Karen Syndocki's goal is for all of her students to pass the district math exam and be able to attend at least the local community college. She wants them to have the option to attend college and she knows that math majors have a lot of opportunities. She has been preparing all of her classes every day for the "big test," which will be held on Friday.

Friday comes and the students seem prepared. When the test scores are tallied, Karen is thrilled by the outcomes. Even the students who had been struggling did well. Her least motivated and one of her lower-performing students, Susan, even got 100! She feels like the best teacher in the district. It wasn't as tough as they told her it would be. She showed her critics that even a first-year teacher can teach these kids.

After Karen finishes correcting the papers, she reviews them once again. She suddenly gets an awful feeling when she looks at Susan's paper again. She notices that Susan's test looks remarkably similar to Joe's, whom she was sitting next to. Karen didn't question Joe's results as he showed his work; she could see that he understood how to arrive at the right answer. Susan didn't show her work. She can't believe it. It is obvious to her that Susan cheated on the test. Did she do this on her own, or did Joe knowingly help her?

Discussion Questions
When can an incident of cheating be handled in the classroom, and when should parents and the principal become involved? What would you do if you caught a student cheating?

Possibilities
Cheating is a serious offense and teachers need to be alert to prevent it from happening in their classrooms. You may have been aware of students who cheated on tests or quizzes

when you were in school. If it is easy to cheat, some students will cheat. Cheating can take several forms. It may be one individual or sometimes a whole group of student who steal a test. Plagiarism, the act of using other people's words and making them your own, is a growing form of cheating, made even more common now by easy access to the Internet, where prewritten reports are readily available.

You need to be vigilant about the possibilities of cheating and take steps to prevent it in advance. Keep tests hidden before exams so they can't be stolen. Many teachers create multiple versions of a test for use with different sections of the same class. When giving a test, walk around the room to let students know you are watching.

While this may seem like an untrusting situation, students who are not motivated to work hard may still want good test scores and have trouble resisting the temptation to cheat. In addition, high-stakes testing has created an atmosphere in which some students either have such strong test anxiety or feel such a need to succeed that cheating becomes a viable option.

When students are caught cheating, a letter usually goes into their file at the guidance office, which may affect college admission. Some schools also suspend students for a period of time. Students need to be made aware of the short- and long-term consequences. Always be aware of the policies in your school to find out what teachers do when they discover students cheating. Most important, if someone breaks the rule, you must stand firm, because a consistent and strict policy is the best deterrent of all.

Ethical Question
In many schools and universities, plagiarism or cheating on exams can result in automatic expulsion. Do you think this is a fair punishment for a one-time offender?

---

assessment tools themselves, others might use prewritten tests created by publishers as part of the textbook program being used. A key to assessing student progress is making sure the students know ahead of time what is being assessed. Stating clear objectives at the beginning of each lesson has the dual purpose of establishing teaching objectives for teachers and learning objectives for students. This also helps teachers and students track what has been covered and what students should know.

● **Formal Assessments**   Formal assessments refer to systematic approaches to evaluating student learning that result in the assignment of a grade to the students' work. Formal assessments often require students to memorize end-of-chapter terminology, complete skills worksheets, and take formal tests at the end of the chapters on specific sections and at the end of lesson units. However, they can also include projects and assignments for which a teacher has developed a **rubric** to use to grade the work.

A rubric is a scoring guide that clearly defines the criteria for grading performance. It answers the question, "Why did you give me that grade?" Rubrics let students know what the expectations are for successful completion of a task. Figure 10.7 portrays a sample rubric from a reading lesson. Rubrics may be preconstructed or designed by the classroom teacher. Numerous sites on the Internet offer assistance with writing rubrics, but the best rubrics are those written by classroom teachers, who know their students best. Formal assessments may include traditional quizzes and tests, even the statewide assessments, as well as performance-based projects and portfolios.

Authentic Assessments **Authentic assessments** are less concrete, more subjective measures of students' knowledge in that they require students to apply knowledge in a variety of ways. Unlike tests and quizzes, which are graded based on the number of correct responses, authentic assessments are graded on a number of other factors such as effort,

FIGURE 10.7

Rubric for a Narrative Essay

Name: _____   Class: _____   Date: _____

	BACK TO THE DRAWING BOARD	SCHOOL NEWSPAPER	NATIONAL MAGAZINE	PULITZER PRIZE FOR WRITING
Focus	Tells 2 or more events	Has extra intro and follow-up that do not match event	Tells one event but has extra intro or follow-up	Tells one event
	Multiple people tell the event	Shifts between narrator and character	Two characters tell the event	One character tells the event
Details and Elaboration	Incorrect details	Few details	Several details	Many details
	No emotions	1–2 emotions	2 emotions	3 or more emotions
Organization	No paragraphs	Some paragraphs	Mostly paragraphed correctly	Paragraphed correctly
Length	Less than one page typed size 12	One page typed	One and a quarter pages typed	At least one and a half pages with no extra spacing
English Conventions	No spellcheck	Spell checked	Some grammar or sentence errors	Few errors
	Many run-on or incomplete sentences	Many run-on or incomplete sentences		No run-ons

✔ Plan   ✔ Draft

1. Choose ONE event from your book.
2. Reread that section so you know all of the details and can retell the event correctly.
3. Make a list (sequential plan) of all that happened in the event.
4. Write a draft retelling the event from one character's point of view.
5. Ask your partner to listen to the draft to judge if it tells only one event and if the details are correct.
6. Make the changes and corrections you wish to make. Consult the rubric above for requirements.
7. Write a final draft.

Source: M. F. Graves & Juel Graves, *Teaching Reading in the 21st Century*, 2/e. Published by Allyn & Bacon, Boston, MA. Copyright © 2001 by Pearson Education. Reprinted by permission of the publisher.

execution, creativity, and the ability to accurately convey knowledge of a subject area. Some examples include designing a poster, writing and presenting a skit, writing an essay, designing a model, creating a video, reading a play, and mapping out an experiment. Students often prefer this type of proactive assessment tool over tests and quizzes. For teachers, this type of assessment looks beyond not just what students have learned, but how they can apply it. For this reason, authentic assessments can be used both formally and informally to assess student progress.

Portfolios A **portfolio** is a collection of students' work in any content area that exemplifies and documents their learning over time. Teachers often require students to place certain items in their portfolios for later review. In some cases, students select what they want included in their portfolios. In these cases, teachers often recommend that students write why they included particular pieces. For example, students in an English class may be asked to select an essay that they are most proud of and to explain why. Teachers can learn as much about their students by reading the rationale as they can from reading the assignment.

- **Informal Assessments** Teachers also include **informal assessments** as a way to monitor student progress. Based on their findings, they may make adjustments to their lesson plans, which, in turn, result in adjustments to their instruction. There is no one type of informal assessment. These assessments may be administered in the form of homework assignments, periodic observations of student participation in the classroom, or small, informal meetings between teachers and individual students. The daily feedback a teacher receives using informal assessments serves a valuable purpose.

Observations Baseball legend Yogi Berra once said, "You can observe a lot by watching." Teachers observe students all day long. These thoughtful observations allow them to attribute meaning to their students' behavior, a skill that sharpens with experience. Recording progress on observation forms or in notebooks is often part of teachers' routines. Many also keep a record of what a student is learning. For instance, to keep track of what students are reading and how well they understand it, teachers may record students' progress by tracking them in reading groups, then noting how much they participate in group discussions and how well they can answer questions.

Many teachers find that observation is most effective when combined with student interviews. This format allows teachers to sit down with students, discuss what they have learned, and note their reactions. By having these one-on-one sessions, teachers can get the best sense of where students are making the most progress and where they may be lagging behind. To help students see how they are progressing weekly, teachers may set up visuals such as progress charts with bar graphs that illustrate progress in skill areas. Teachers look at the students' charts weekly. While this may be the most time-consuming type of assessment, especially for teachers with very large classes, it also provides the most complete information about individual students as well as instructional feedback. For example, a teacher who keeps a daily log of student participation and notes when they seem puzzled by a concept may realize that additional time needs to be spent on the lesson. In this way, teachers assess their own teaching as well as student progress and make adjustments along the way.

Assessing Students' Work Determining what students know and what they are able to do may be easier in some subject areas than in others. Looking at student work can be useful in a number of ways. For example, in evaluating students' math abilities, checking their work is somewhat helpful when there is one right answer; however, if teachers are asking students for multiple ways to solve a problem, the *way* they work out the problems becomes very telling. If students are using the wrong operations to solve the problem, they may have a fundamental misunderstanding of a math concept. However, if students are solving the problem using several different solutions, but are coming up with some right and some wrong answers, it may indicate that the students understand the concepts, but are just executing the problem carelessly. Assessing students' writing samples can be more challenging because the level of skill may be open to interpretation. Some students may have strong analytical abilities, which enable them to articulate complex interpretations; however, they may not be good at putting their ideas in writing. Conversely, some students may be very good at organizing and communicating their thoughts, but their thoughts may be less sophisticated than those of other students.

In schools where students have multiple teachers, many schools have adopted the practice of having teachers review samples of students' work cooperatively. These meetings can be effective in cases such as those just mentioned because students' work is evaluated from a variety of perspectives. In these meetings, all teachers bring samples of students' work and discuss how well these students have met course objectives and how to grade them. By looking at the students' work together, they

Not a nine-to-five career path, teaching requires dedication and time even after the last bell for the day rings.

can discuss what they can each do to best meet their students' needs. If all of their students seem to be grasping all of the concepts, then they determine that they are ready to move ahead. However, if one or two students need additional support to master concepts, the teachers rework their lesson plans to accommodate those students' need. Evaluating students cooperatively affords teachers the opportunity to analyze the effectiveness of their own teaching. It also allows teachers to help each other to better provide for their students. As an example, consider the case of a second-year teacher, Bernadette, who worked with her mentor to review her students' papers from a recent assignment. Bernadette had asked her students to extract some information from their textbook and write about what they found. When she and her mentor went through the papers together, they determined that while students were able to pull out details from the text, few were able to grasp the main ideas. This realization indicated to Bernadette that she would have to modify her lesson plan, reteach the lesson, then give students another assignment. She and her mentor believed that this process would enable her students to better understand their learning goals. To ensure that her revised strategy worked, Bernadette planned to reassess her students' and her own progress the following week (Boyle, 2001).

A controversial issue for students, parents, and teachers has always been the role of homework in how students learn. Students often complain that homework is merely busy-work, while some parents complain that teachers don't take into account their children's busy schedules outside the classroom. However, in an article in *The Washington Post,* "Not Quite Piling On the Homework" (Mathews, 2003), the author cites a national study that concluded that American students should be spending *more* time doing homework. The article refuted the notion that students are overburdened with homework, stating that that claim is largely a myth. While some schools have specific policies that dictate how much and when homework should be assigned, many schools leave this up to their teachers.

Teachers who succeed with homework do so because their assignments are relevant, interesting, and creative. Just as teachers must engage students in the classroom, they must also have students engaged in their homework. Teachers who purposefully design and plan homework that ties back to classroom instruction, but that also requires students to use critical-thinking skills to "investigate," have more success in having students turning it in than teachers who assign drills (Murray, 2003).

Student work is one of the key indicators of students' progress throughout the year. It is critical that you consistently check students' work to ensure that you and your students are meeting the respective objectives.

THE STUDENT'S ROLE IN ASSESSMENT

There are two schools of thought regarding what students' roles should be in assessing their own or other students' progress. Those who believe students should be involved in their own assessments feel that it is part of the learning process. They believe that students learn more when they are engaged in the process of identifying and correcting their own or others' mistakes than they do when they receive a paper with corrections a week after completing the work. Those who oppose this kind of student involvement object less to students correcting their own work than they do to students' correcting the work of their peers. These opponents feel that when students correct others' work, it opens up the opportunity to ridicule students who do not perform well on their assignments (Riggins & Erikson, 2002).

- **Self-Assessment**   Teachers tend to use self-assessments in classes where students are actively engaged in their own learning. They want to grow and they are curious about new ideas. Peter Airasian's ToolKit provides teachers assessment instruments to use with students, some of which relate to behavior as well as academics. These assessments can be completed individually or in small groups. Or a teacher can simply have students answer the question, "What did you learn today?" This type of self-assessment can provide students and teachers with useful information.

- **Students Correcting Papers**   In 2002 the Supreme Court ruled that teachers do not violate any laws when they allow students to correct each other's papers (Starr, 2002). But is this good practice? Teachers have different points of view. In a debate written for *NEA Today*, two teachers shared opposite points of view. One argued that correcting each other's work is a positive and natural part of the learning process. While not advocating that students correct each other's tests, this teacher felt that correcting each others' homework is useful and does not have to embarrass students who don't do well because everyone has weaknesses. When students correct each other's work, it creates a team environment in which the class helps each other meet goals. Another teacher strongly disagreed with this perspective arguing that it is important to keep students' work as private as possible in order for students to maintain their self-worth if they are not doing well in school. Students who receive X's on their papers from other students often get upset. Correcting their own work helps students learn from their mistakes, but correcting each other's work invades privacy. What do you think?

ASSESSING STUDENTS WHO NEED EXTRA SUPPORT

Many teachers have students who are easily distracted or struggle with learning. Some students just need a little nudge to get on track if they are not paying attention, and others may have more serious learning issues. As a teacher you need to know the difference and adapt your practices to accommodate your students as much as possible. There are a myriad of reasons why students struggle. They may be bored; they may have difficulty with the language; or they may have a disorder that makes learning difficult. Teachers need to pay attention to these students and respond accordingly.

- **English Language Learners**   Many teachers have found that authentic assessments are particularly effective tools for ELL students. They find that by allowing students to demonstrate their knowledge in alternative ways, they can get a good sense of how well their students are grasping subject matter. Because more traditional forms of assessment are difficult for these students due to the language barrier, and because cultural differences may cause these students to have a different knowledge base from their peers, teachers often look to alternative, more informal types of assessment. Authentic assessment and informal measures allow teachers to see progress on a daily basis rather than on a one-time

INTASC

Principle #8

Assessment of Student Learning: The teacher understands and uses formal and informal assessment strategies to evaluate and ensure the continuous intellectual, social, and physical development of the learner.

INTASC

Principle #3

Adapting Instruction for Individual Needs: The teacher understands how students differ in their approaches to learning and creates instructional opportunities that are adapted to diverse learners.

test. In the classroom, where teachers use differentiated instruction strategies to work with these students, their assessment tools ideally tie back to their teaching strategies. Teachers can also work with the bilingual teachers to assess what content students understand and where they may be struggling.

SPECIAL-NEEDS STUDENTS

Should students with learning disorders be held to the same expectations as other students? If not, on what basis should teachers assess these students? Decisions about student progress are not made in isolation. Classroom teachers often consult with other specialty teachers or school personnel to assess students' overall performance. If a teacher is co-teaching or working on a team in a middle school, the teachers often assess students as a team. If students are presenting consistent concerns, teachers will take special measures to ensure that these students' needs are met.

For students who have been identified as having special needs and are receiving support from the district, the teacher needs to meet with the core evaluation team to review the goals for the student and to assess progress. Modifications to assessment instruments may be designed for individual students.

What happens when students with serious learning difficulties do not meet the standards for their grade levels? There has been great debate on this issue. In older grades, with states creating high school graduation exit exam requirements, educators are concerned that more students could drop out of school. In response to this concern, some schools are considering working harder to retain students in earlier grades, which may entail postponing more formal tests for a year until students have mastered the requisite content area.

HOW DO TEACHERS COMMUNICATE STUDENT PROGRESS TO PARENTS?

A key to planning and assessing student progress is making sure students know ahead of time what is being assessed. Stating clear objectives at the beginning of the lesson as part of the objectives for teaching is critical to effective assessment. Evaluating student progress is an important component of teaching, but communicating it to both students and parents is equally critical.

Communicating with parents and guardians is an integral part of teachers' jobs. Various opportunities for such communication exist throughout the school year, including progress reports, report cards, and conferences. Teachers can encourage home involvement by asking parents and guardians to check their children's homework, especially in the lower grades. Sometimes extenuating circumstances require additional communication between teachers and parents, such as when children are having problems in school, when children are excelling, or when children are misbehaving. Parents and guardians can help their children with remedial work that might be necessary along the way and can help them focus on and comprehend the lessons.

HOME COMMUNICATION

Communication with the home can take many forms. Usually beginning teachers think about calling parents when their children misbehave in class. As you will come to learn, teachers need to communicate with parents in a variety of ways on an ongoing basis. Frequent communication makes it much easier to communicate with parents when there is a difficult situation. Teachers don't always deliver bad news, however; there are ways to communicate positive feedback as well. Following are some ways parents can stay apprised of their children's academic progress:

E-mail serves as an informal, yet efficient way to stay in touch with parents and to keep them informed about the progress of their children. As one teacher stated, "E-mail has enabled parents and teachers to communicate daily about the child's progress. Although we cannot discuss grades, we can discuss habits and missed work. E-mail also allows me to send a positive note that I might not have taken the time to give in the past."

● **Homework**   Homework is an important means of communicating with parents. When students are younger, parents usually review the homework with them. As they progress through school, parents may just check to see that homework was completed. When homework requires students to be creative or analytical, they tend to ask parents for input more than they do if assigned repetitive drills. Getting parents involved keeps them apprised of what their children are learning and their commitment to doing a good job. One technique some teachers use to get parents involved is to write letters to families explaining the homework assignment and explaining how parents can work with their children to complete it.

● **Progress Reports**   Midterm progress reports and end-of-term report cards are typically sent to parents. These reports indicate whether there are any areas in which teachers feel their students may be having problems. They also indicate any behavioral issues of which parents should be aware.

When students are failing a subject area, warning notes or academic progress slips may be sent home with the student or mailed directly to the parent. In these notes, teachers may indicate how they intend to address the issue and how they intend to follow up with parents.

● **Report Cards**   The most traditional means of gauging a student's progress is the report card. Although typical report cards in middle schools and high schools assign letter grades in each subject area, such as A, B, C, D, and F, many school districts use a different type of grading for elementary school students. Many of these report cards present grids that list tasks for each subject area; teachers rate students' mastery of these tasks according to a particular scale, (such as, Unsatisfactory, Satisfactory, Satisfactory +, or Below Average, Average, Above Average or Superior). In addition to the ratings teachers assign on report cards, they also typically write comments as to whether a student is doing well or needs encouragement. Sometimes report cards are delivered in person at parent conferences; other times they are mailed to students' homes.

CONFERENCES

Conferences, whether called for a particular reason or prescheduled, are powerful and necessary communication tools. Before teachers meet with parents or guardians, many teachers first meet with students so that they will know how they are progressing and get a sense of what their teachers will be discussing with their parents. From there, teachers may opt to meet with parents or with parents and students together. Teachers should be well prepared for all conferences by having available any assessments they have conducted regarding their students as well as samples of their students' work.

● **Student and Teacher Conferences**   Teachers use a variety of methods to communicate with students on a daily basis. One such method is to establish specific locations for students to pick up or drop off papers at any time. These may take the form of student mailboxes and teacher mailboxes or in and out boxes. Students can also use these dropoff

Through the Eyes of
Culturally Sensitive Teachers

Finding Solutions That Work

Guadalupe Valdes was a shy and frightened second grader when she enrolled at Tedder Elementary in Dodge City, Kansas. Her family had recently moved from Mexico to work in the meat-packing industry. Guadalupe had gone to school for one year in rural Mexico, but that small school in her hometown was nothing like Tedder. Her second-grade teacher was Cynthia Halstead, who had been at Tedder for 10 years. Cynthia did not speak Spanish, and Guadalupe spoke only a few words of English. Guadalupe spent one and a half hours a day with the ELL specialist and the rest of the time she was in Cynthia's room. While Cynthia had some training in English as a Second Language, Guadalupe presented a challenge because she was the only non-English speaker in the class. Cynthia decided to seat Guadalupe next to Maria Reyes, another student who was fairly bilingual in Spanish and English, and she asked Maria to translate as much as possible.

For the first few months in class, Guadalupe seemed to be listening to everything, but she was very hesitant to speak. Cynthia recognized this as the "silent period" often experienced by English language learners. She encouraged Guadalupe to participate as much as she wanted, but Cynthia didn't push. By December, Guadalupe was venturing to speak a little more. Cynthia decided to ask for a parent conference to provide Guadalupe's parents with a progress report. She had a Spanish-speaking colleague with her as she met with Mrs. Valdes. At first, Mrs. Valdes assumed she had been called to the meeting because something was wrong. Cynthia reassured her that nothing was wrong and Guadalupe was making reasonable progress. Mrs. Valdes sighed with relief. She told Cynthia that in Mexico a child's teacher was *la segunda madre* (the second mother) and that she trusted Cynthia completely

to do what was right for Guadalupe. Cynthia was thrilled at being granted that type of parental support.

One morning, Mary Rasmussen, Cynthia's assistant principal, paid a surprise visit to Cynthia's class. She came in through the rear door of the classroom, where Guadalupe and Maria sat. Mary heard Maria translating some of Cynthia's science lesson in Spanish to Guadalupe. After a brief stay, Mary asked to see Cynthia after school.

Mary questioned the practice of having Spanish spoken in the classroom by one student to another when the goal of the school was to have all students do well on the Kansas state standardized test. "How will hearing Spanish help Guadalupe with the English section of the standardized test?" Cynthia explained that the Spanish being used was not the focus of the lesson, but she had asked Maria to translate any content that Guadalupe didn't understand in English. Cynthia posed the question, "What good is any lesson in any language if the student doesn't understand it?" The meeting ended with an uneasy truce and Mary saying that she would watch Cynthia's classroom closely.

Points to Ponder

1. Do you think Cynthia acted properly in seating Guadalupe with Maria and asking Maria to do some translating for Guadalupe? Why or why not?

2. Why do you think the assistant principal objected to hearing a non-English language used in the classroom?

3. What should Cynthia do at this point? Should Cynthia involve the principal and/or Guadalupe's mother at this point, or just wait and see what happens next? Why should she follow the action you suggest?

locations to leave notes for teachers; teachers, in turn, can use them to give students assignments or to leave notes for students to bring home, as necessary.

Many teachers also communicate with students regarding their progress in one-on-one conferences. In these meetings, teachers may discuss the students' achievement as well as any concerns the teacher may have about the students' progress. In turn, teachers can use these opportunities to find out what students might be struggling with both in and out of school.

● **Parent Conferences** All schools schedule some type of formal, preset conference two to four times a year in which parents and guardians are invited to come in and meet with their children's teachers for a progress report. At these meetings, parents/guardians and teachers review the children's work, discuss areas of needed improvement, and identify strategies that both parties can cooperate on to encourage improvement. In a perfect setting, the teacher and parents/guardians work as a team and stay in constant contact with each other, all in the child's best interest. Most often, however, the parent conference may offer the only opportunity for a teacher to sit down with parents to discuss a child's progress. Sometimes conferences are held during the day; sometimes they're held in the evening to best accommodate working parents. Unfortunately, teachers often point out that the parents most likely to attend conferences are those whose children have the fewest problems.

When a student displays consistent problems that interfere with learning, a teacher and other personnel may call a special conference with parents or guardians. The purpose of these meetings is to intercept problems before they get worse and enlist the help of the home. One-on-one meetings offer a good opportunity for parents and teachers to gain an understanding of where each side is coming from.

In her book *The Essential Conversation: What Parents and Teachers Can Learn from Each Other* (2003), noted sociologist Sara Lawrence-Lightfoot estimates that parents sit down with their children's teachers to hear how their kids are doing in school more than 100 million times a year. Too often, Lawrence-Lightfoot points out, these meetings are adversarial, identifying teachers and parents as "natural enemies." She explains, "when parents say 'I want you to be fair to my son,' they are saying I want you to give him special attention. When teachers say 'I have to be fair to all the children,' they are saying, 'I have to share the resources of my energy among all my children'" (Lawrence-Lightfoot, 2003).

School conferences can be stressful for parents, as they often serve as a reminder of their own school days. Overcoming this anxiety and getting parents and guardians to recognize the value of these meetings is important. Lawrence-Lightfoot (2003) suggests that students always be included in the conference because students are invested and want to know what the teacher is saying about them, and the student can also become actively involved in the final solution.

● **Student-Led Conferences** Some schools are moving to student-led parent conference sessions. In this type of conference, instead of having teachers tell parents what their children are learning in their classes and how well they are progressing, the students tell their parents what they have learned and how they would like to improve. Students typically share samples of their work with their parents during these conferences. At the end of these conferences, teachers have a chance to highlight academic areas they will be covering as the year progresses. These are replacing the more traditional parent nights with teachers to include students.

Noted educator Lois Brown Easton (2002) describes how another type of student-led conferences work at one alternative school in Eagle Rock, Colorado. In these meetings, students are required to give three presentations a year to a school panel that illustrate what they have learned. These presentations allow students to "make a case" that they have learned both academically and personally. In these presentations, students must reflect on their learning, connect it to previous learning, and project new learning goals.

Does it make a difference? Their teachers think so. They feel that the written statements that students prepare for these presentations give voice to the students. The teachers at the school read all the learning packets and learn from their students. One student wrote, "Growth is a constant cause for struggle and celebration." Student voices can be powerful forces in school reform. All we have to do is ask and listen.

● **Special Meetings** You have read earlier that students with special needs require special team meetings that include a variety of adults and support services. These conferences are scheduled by the special education coordinator in the school or district. Special education meetings are required by law and must include all members of the team who work with special-needs students and at least one parent or guardian. In these meetings, teachers and the student's guardians go over the student's IEP that was established earlier in the year to evaluate whether the goals are being met in the classroom.

While ELL students are often designated to receive additional support through schools' special education programs, in many cases they do not need these services for learning and are not, by all accounts, students with special needs; they simply have a language barrier. Treating these students as special-needs students may not best serve their needs or the needs of the schools. When bilingual teachers and classroom teachers work together on these students' behalf and meet with the parents as a team, this may be the best format to accommodate these children and their families.

Parents, particularly parents of special-needs students and ELL students, often express discomfort about coming to school for a variety of reasons. Some teachers share their suggestions for better accommodating these parents:

> I let the parents set the meeting time so they can come even if it's at 7:00 in the morning. I know they don't want to lose their jobs and if we have it at 10:00 they can't come. I also learned some Spanish so I can say a few words in the meeting and whenever I see the parents in town.
>
> Brian, Washington

> If parents need a babysitter I say bring the baby and we'll get a sitter.
>
> Susan, Pennsylvania

> I know that parents often feel outnumbered with such a big team of teachers and school people, so I always start the meeting with questions and comments from the parent first and then we list the child's strengths.
>
> Mary, Minnesota

> I meet the parent first before the IEP meeting and explain everything alone so they understand it all before they see the full team.
>
> Marjorie, Tennessee

Who am I? What do I believe?

"Not all students will make the same journey as they learn, but this diversity of learning styles enriches the classroom community."

JENNIFER, STUDENT TEACHER

THINK ABOUT THIS:

Imagine that every student in your classroom has a different style of learning. How would this affect your ability to create a lesson plan that reaches all students? What learning style best describes how you learn?

SHARE and COMPARE:

Compare how you like to learn with your classmates' preferences, using any of the theories described in this section. How do all of these various styles enrich this classroom community?

FINAL THOUGHTS

This chapter highlighted how teachers plan and deliver instruction, assess student progress, then communicate their progress to parents. Thorough, comprehensive lesson planning is necessary to facilitate effective teaching. These plans must take into account districtwide curriculum goals and objectives, as well as the needs of students with diverse backgrounds and intellectual capabilities.

National and state education reform influences the daily life of teachers through state curriculum frameworks and testing initiatives. Because teachers understand that students have different skills, talents, and abilities that affect how they learn, it is critical that teachers get to know their students. Students' learning styles, teachers' teaching styles, and the social and cultural context of the classroom all inform how teachers deliver instruction, assign homework, and use technology in their classrooms. Effective teachers prepare a variety of lessons with their diverse students' abilities and interests in mind.

Assessing student progress is a complex endeavor. It is also essential to effective teaching. Teachers must understand how much students are learning and where they may be faltering in order to plan future lessons. With educational policy setting national and statewide standards, state-mandated testing, and diverse classrooms comprising students at different learning levels with different cultural backgrounds, teachers use a variety of assessment tools to evaluate student progress. All assessments are based on the goals and objectives established in teachers' lesson plans and instruction. Types of assessments include informal assessments, formal assessments, authentic assessments, and self-assessments.

Connecting with parents and guardians is a key component to enhancing the home–school collaboration. Teachers communicate with parents at specified intervals, unless extenuating circumstances dictate more frequent communication. To keep parents informed about what students are learning in school, teachers encourage parents to view their children's homework. They convey how students are progressing through progress reports, report cards, and parent or student-led conferences.

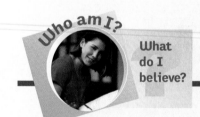

Who am I?

What do I believe?

REFLECTIONS

Professional Plan for Understanding the Importance of Planning

1. Three things I learned from this chapter about planning, delivering, and assessing instruction are:

2. Two things in this chapter I would like to learn more about are:

   a. _____

   b. _____

3. I plan to investigate these two areas and learn more about instructional planning and assessment by:

_____ Reading some of the book club choices

_____ Reading sources referenced in the chapter that interest me.

_____ Interviewing one or more teachers about considerations they make when planning lessons and how they assess students' progress.

_____ Exploring the websites listed in the Log On section

_____ Observing classrooms and taking notes on techniques that teachers use to assess and encourage students' learning on an ongoing basis

4. I will include the following in my Touch the Future portfolio:

_____ Responses to Who Am I? activities

_____ A brief essay on my thoughts about Problems to Possibilities

_____ Responses to the Observation Guide

_____ Other (materials assigned by your instructor)

SUMMARY

How Do Teachers Plan?

- Planning instruction for students includes teaching for understanding, aligning plans to curriculum goals and districtwide standards, and being aware that you are teaching *all* students.

- Designing effective plans requires applying a combination of learning theories to accommodate diverse learners. These theories include Gardner's theory of multiple intelligences, Anthony Gregorc's style delineator approach, brain-based learning theory, and Bloom's taxonomy.

- Planning for instruction through daily and long-term plans, teaching for understanding, modifying plans for diverse learners, and anticipating behavior problems are all part of good teaching.

- Planning for all students means that a teacher acknowledges the students' communities, academic diversity, cultural diversity, and special needs.

How Do Teachers Deliver Instruction?

- Good teachers tap into students' prior knowledge, gain and maintain student attention, provide clear instruction, use higher-order questions and thinking, assign relevant homework, integrate resources and technology, and summarize what students have learned.

- Teachers use a variety of teaching styles to accommodate students' different learning styles.

- Teachers may group students in cooperative, discussion, and ability groups to accommodate diverse learners.

- Teachers use models of teaching that may include direct, constructivist, and balanced instruction.

- Teachers accommodate students with special needs by working with special education instructors to create special plans designed to lay out goals and objectives for these students.

- When teachers have limited resources, they look for alternative resources that will allow them to provide engaging and timely instruction.

- To ensure that students complete their homework, teachers must assign homework that is relevant and engaging. They also must let students know that their homework will be considered as part of their overall grade.

- Technology can be used to teach diverse learners, adapt and modify lessons for special needs, or provide advanced opportunities for talented students.

How Do Teachers Assess Student Progress?

- State-mandated standardized tests are used to evaluate students for accountability purposes tied to education reform. All students must pass these tests in order to graduate or participate in other activities such as after school sports.

- Teachers maintain records to document progress in skill and content areas. To gather this information, they use a variety of assessment tools, including standardized test scores; information assessments that involve observations, evaluation of student work, and meetings with students; formal assessments; rubrics; and portfolios. Informal assessments and records are maintained by teachers to document student progress in skill and content areas.

- Authentic assessments are alternative assessments that teachers use to allow students to demonstrate learning in ways other than tests and quizzes. Examples include researching and writing reports, creating videos, designing models, designing posters, writing essays, performing a play, or writing a speech. Authentic assessments are valuable tools for evaluating ELL students' understanding.

- Some teachers feel that having students involved in assessment is part of the learning process. While some have students correct each other's papers, others feel that it may be counterproductive for students who do not do well in school. Many teachers, however, feel that student self-assessments are valuable, as is the practice of having students correct their own work.

How Do Teachers Communicate Student Progress to Parents?

- Teachers communicate with students and parents through homework, progress reports, report cards, and conferences.

- Parents of students with special needs meet with teachers and a team of other specialists involved in their children's education. While ELL students are often identified as special-needs students, most of these students do not have learning disabilities; their only obstacle to learning is the language barrier.

Visit the **Touch the Future . . . Teach!** Companion Website at www.ablongman.com/diaz for additional opportunities.

KEY WORDS

assess   309

authentic assessment   313

back planning   296

Bloom's taxonomy   293

brain-based learning   293

constructivist approach   307

curriculum framework   295

differentiated
   instruction   304

direct instruction   306

English language learners
   (ELL)   299

formal assessment   312

full inclusion   308

gifted and talented   301

guided teaching   307

individualized education
   program (IEP)   301

informal assessment   314

lesson plans   292

multiple intelligences   293

portfolio   314

pull-out program   308

reading recovery
   program   308

rubric   313

scope and sequence   295

special-needs
   legislation   301

standardized test   310

student-centered
   community   303

style delineator
   approach   293

theory of multiple
   intelligences   293

unit plan   297

CONCEPT REVIEW

1. Explain the theory of multiple intelligences and how it can be used in the classroom to enhance student learning.

2. Select either brain-based learning theory or Bloom's taxonomy and describe how they influence learning.

3. Explain the difference between urban, suburban, and rural teaching.

4. Articulate academic and cultural diversity and how they are alike and different.

5. List several components of an effective lesson plan and explain why they are important to instruction.

6. Describe three models of instruction and explain how they differ.

7. Discuss ways to identify diverse learners and set goals for learning.

8. Describe four kinds of assessments used in a classroom.

9. Summarize all of the ways a teacher communicates with students and parents.

TOUCH THE FUTURE . . .

Read On

Understanding by Design and *The Understanding by Design Handbook*
Jay McTighe and Grant Wiggins (Alexandria, VA: Association for Supervision and Curriculum Development, 1998)
Effective tools for planning lessons to enhance student learning based on standards and outcomes

The Skillful Teacher: Building Your Teaching Skills
Jon Saphier and Robert Gower (Acton, MA: Research for Better Teaching, 1997)
An extensive offering of practical strategies based in research for student teachers and in-service teachers.

The Differentiated Classroom: Responding to the Needs of All Learners
Carol Ann Tomlinson (Alexandria, VA: Association for Supervision and Curriculum Development, 1999)
A thorough discussion of the value of differentiated instruction with specific practical examples of what to do in your classroom. These techniques are particularly helpful for working with culturally diverse students who are English language learners.

Log On

Teaching Ideas for Primary Teachers
www.teachingideas.co.uk
Hundreds of websites exist for the purpose of helping teachers share lesson ideas; this site provides ideas for primary teachers, lesson plans, and links to other helpful sites.

Discovery School
http://school.discovery.com/lessonplans/
Sponsored by the Discovery Channel, this site offers hundreds of lesson plans written by teachers for teachers for Grades K–12.

Teachers Helping Teachers
www.pacificnet.net/~mandel/
An outstanding website of shared lessons and discussions covering issues from across the curriculum; written up in *Education Week* and *Teacher Magazine* as an outstanding resource for teachers.

Understanding by Design Exchange
www.ubdexchange.org/
Based on the works of Grant Wiggins and Jay McTighe, this website offers a template to assist with unit design as well as a rich database of unit plans that can be adapted for individual classroom use.

Rubistar
http://rubistar.4teachers.org/index.php
> A great website for teachers who wish to develop their own rubrics but have limited time, practice creating your own rubrics following step-by-step instructions.

Write On

I had the opportunity to participate in parent-teacher conferences during student teaching. One meeting was intimidating for me because the parents I met were concerned about their child being able to graduate from high school. My cooperating teacher was with me and we calmed the parents and the conference ended positively. In retrospect, I would have sent a note to each parent at the beginning of student teaching letting them know I was a student teacher so I wasn't meeting them for the first time at the conference. I learned how important parent support is. . . .

High School Student Teacher

When you student teach, you will be responsible in some classes for student work. How you assess student progress could affect a student's graduation. Working with your cooperating teacher and the students' parents is essential. Do you agree with this student teacher's point about communicating with parents? Why or why not? Write a short response to this comment in your journal.

OBSERVATION GUIDE

TEACH: LINKING THEORY TO PRACTICE

Linking Theory to Practice

Objective: Observing the purpose of instructional planning

School (use code name): _____ Observer: _____

Grade Level: _____ Date: _____

Subject(s): _____ Time In: _____ Time Out: _____

Directions: In this observation and interview activity, think about the topics of planning, delivering, and assessing instruction as well as other issues you have read in this chapter. Ask to speak with the teacher after class to ask a few follow-up questions. Use these questions as a guide and create some of your own. Write a brief summary of your observation and interview to submit to your instructor and include it in your Touch the Future portfolio. You may choose to complete this observation with a variety of teachers and write a comparison instead of visiting just one teacher.

1. Before the lesson, ask for a copy of the lesson plan or to look at the teacher's plan book so you understand the objectives, state standards, and expected outcomes for the students. If this is not possible, try to predict what they are by observing.

2. As you begin, draw a floor plan of the classroom with student desks and teacher desk. Make a note on the plan about anything that stands out for you about the way the classroom is set up and organized. What is your first impression of the classroom climate? What aspects of the classroom most inform your impression? List data to support your opinion.

3. How does the teacher begin the lesson? Does the teacher provide any motivation or hook for the students? Does the teacher seem to be basing instruction on students' prior knowledge? Were there any "housekeeping" issues (attendance etc.) that needed to be done prior to the start of the lesson?

4. What is the teacher teaching? Write the directions as you heard or saw them.

5. What was the procedure for learning? Groups? Independent work?

Ask the Teacher: Interview Questions after the Observation

1. Did you meet your objective for the lesson? Why or why not?

2. What are some suggestions you have for me as a potential teacher for teaching a lesson like this?

3. What three important bits of advice should I know about planning, delivering a lesson, and assessing students?

Connecting with INTASC: Principles 4, 7, and 8

Multiple Instructional Strategies: The teacher uses various instructional strategies to encourage students' development of critical-thinking, problem-solving, and performance skills.

Instructional Planning Skills: The teacher plans instruction based on knowledge of subject matter, students, the community, and curriculum goals.

Assessment of Student Learning: The teacher understands and uses formal and informal assessment strategies to evaluate and ensure the continuous intellectual, social, and physical development of the learner.

After observing the class, find out what the teacher does to meet Principles 4, 7, and 8. How did the teacher assess the success of the lesson? In your opinion, did the students learn? What considerations about the students did the teacher incorporate into the lesson plan? Did the teacher make any modifications for ELL students or special-needs students? Explain.

11

Classroom and Behavior Management: Creating a Positive Learning Environment

Who am I? What do I believe?

As you reflect on your own education, do you recall having both positive and negative classroom experiences? From your perspective as a future teacher, think about what your teachers did to create a positive classroom *community of learners.* How did these efforts support your learning? Now, think about negative classroom situations you experienced. What, in your opinion, contributed to creating this negative classroom environment? What do you think your teacher could have done to shift the negative classroom to a positive community of learners? As a teacher, what steps will you take to prevent your classroom from becoming a negative environment?

"Communities of learners seem to be committed above all to discovering conditions that elicit and support human learning and to providing these conditions."

Roland Barth

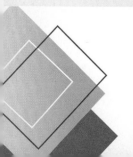

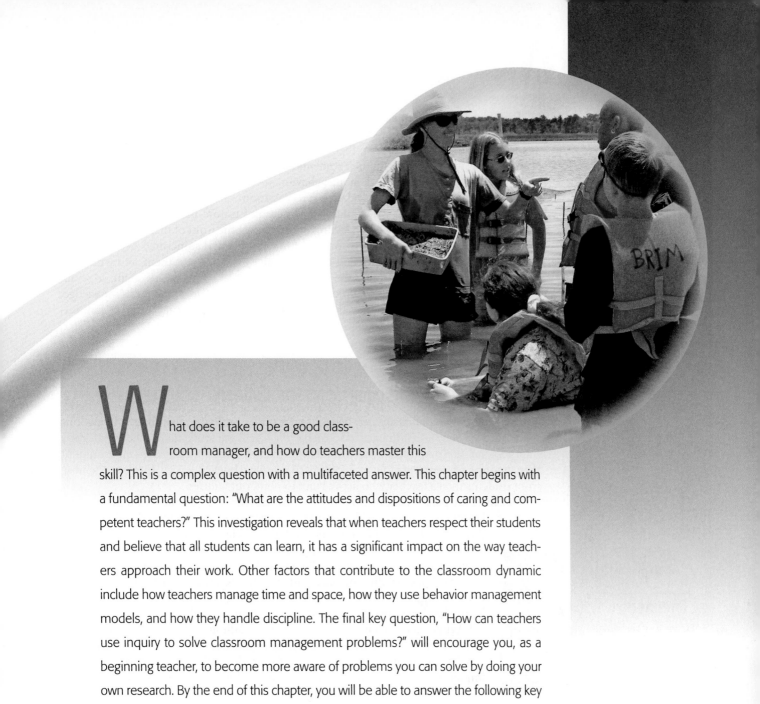

hat does it take to be a good classroom manager, and how do teachers master this
skill? This is a complex question with a multifaceted answer. This chapter begins with
a fundamental question: "What are the attitudes and dispositions of caring and competent teachers?" This investigation reveals that when teachers respect their students
and believe that all students can learn, it has a significant impact on the way teachers approach their work. Other factors that contribute to the classroom dynamic
include how teachers manage time and space, how they use behavior management
models, and how they handle discipline. The final key question, "How can teachers
use inquiry to solve classroom management problems?" will encourage you, as a
beginning teacher, to become more aware of problems you can solve by doing your
own research. By the end of this chapter, you will be able to answer the following key
questions:

Key Questions

- What are the dispositions of caring teachers?
- How do effective teachers manage their classrooms?
- What are different approaches to behavior management?
- How do teachers respond to inappropriate behavior in the classroom?
- How can inquiry help solve classroom management problems?

When the term *management* is used in reference to schools, it often implies how teachers "manage the misbehavior" of students or how they "control" the class. In fact, **classroom management** is an umbrella term that refers to how teachers arrange their classrooms for learning, how they interact with their students and encourage their students to interact with each other, how they handle student misbehavior, how they establish and enforce rules, and how they manage their time (Secada, 2002). Classroom management is a concern for all teachers, but it is also an issue that affects school administrators, parents, and students.

For beginning teachers who are taking their places at the front of the classroom for the very first time, managing the classroom is a fundamental and sometimes overwhelming responsibility. As these teachers stand there with all eyes looking at them, and with their students filled with anticipation of the coming year, the reality of the task begins to set in, bringing excitement, hope, and trepidation. When teachers are armed with knowledge, insight, and a positive attitude, they are well equipped to begin shaping a positive community for learning.

WHAT ARE THE DISPOSITIONS OF CARING TEACHERS?

Teachers' underlying philosophies, beliefs, and attitudes influence their daily interactions with students. They also influence how teachers instruct their students. Teachers with good interpersonal skills are those who will be most likely to create a classroom environment that supports student learning. A teacher with a smile will elicit a very different response from students than a teacher who uses a ruler to point out failures.

Teachers' **dispositions,** or prevailing moods, are informed by their values, commitments, and professional ethics, which in turn influence how they treat their students, families, colleagues, and communities. When teachers' dispositions are positive, it sets the tone for student learning, motivation, and development, as well as their own professional development. For example, caring teachers who value fairness, honesty, responsibility, and social justice will pass these beliefs on to their students. At the same time, when teachers believe that all of their students can learn, they implement high standards for all students.

While there are no tests to measure the relationship between teachers' belief systems and student learning, there are indicators of success. Teachers who project and inspire positive attitudes foster motivation and interest, which are immensely important to the productivity in the classroom. This often leads to successful test outcomes.

RESPECT *ALL* STUDENTS

Teachers who establish routines, organize seating plans, and create consequences in classrooms are shaping an environment in which students have clear guidelines and expectations. With a structure and purpose in place, teachers can use class time to foster mutual respect among the classroom community. According to Sara Lawrence-Lightfoot, noted professor of education at Harvard's School of Education, "respect is the most powerful dimension in defining successful relationships in schools" (Lawrence-Lightfoot, 2002). Teachers convey respect in how they look at, interact with, talk with, and greet all students every day. In classrooms with students from many cultures and students with disabilities, teachers serve as role models, demonstrating the importance of embracing all people from all cultures. Some teachers may even go so far as to learn a second language well enough to be able to understand their English language learners. Showing this effort creates a tone for the classroom community. Respect nourishes relationships between teachers and students.

INTASC

Principle #5

Classroom Motivation and Management: The teacher uses an understanding of individual and group motivation and behavior to create a learning environment that encourages positive social interaction, active engagement in learning, and self-motivation.

Students recognize when a teacher cares genuinely. Sharing laughs and an overall positive disposition encourage learning, build trust, and enhance student motivation.

In recounting her experiences visiting hundreds of schools in culturally and economically diverse communities over the past 25 years, Lawrence-Lightfoot explains:

> In all of these schools, I've asked students to identify their good teachers and to tell me why they think they are good. The students' answers across all these settings are always the same. "Why do we think Mrs. Browning is a good teacher?" they ask me incredulously as If I should know the answer. "Because," they say, "she respects us." I pushed further, trying to discover what they mean by respect. Again, there is no reluctance or ambivalence in their responses. They feel respected by teachers who make them feel visible and worthy, who are demanding, who hold high standards for them and who insist they learn. And they feel disrespected, or "dissed," by teachers who never bother to get to know them, who let them off easy, who do not take them seriously, or believe they can be successful. Respect grows in relationships of expectation, challenge, and rigor. It is diminished by inattention, indifference, and empty rituals. (Lawrence-Lightfoot, 2002)

● **Classrooms for Social Justice** To promote respect in the classroom, teachers create classrooms for **social justice**, which focus on equality and fairness. Sonia Nieto, noted author and researcher and a former junior high school and elementary school teacher, has spent her career working with multicultural students and writing about issues of social justice. Her work has led her to ask profoundly multicultural questions that address issues regarding equal access to resources and quality education and fairness toward all students. For example, in asking questions such as, "Who's taking Calculus?" Nieto is asking which students have access to and are up to the task of taking highly challenging courses. In asking questions such as, "Which classes meet in the basement?" Nieto is trying to ascertain whether all students and courses are being treated equally, or whether certain classes, such as multicultural classes, are being relegated to the basement. In asking, "Who's teaching the children?" she is questioning all students' access to high-quality teachers. According to Nieto, "Multicultural education needs to be accompanied by a deep commitment to social justice and equal access to resources" (Nieto, 2003). Think about your own school experience and how the experiences of multicultural students you knew relate to these questions.

INTASC

Principle #9

Professional Commitment and Responsibility: The teacher is a reflective practitioner who continually evaluates the effects of his/her choices and actions on others (students, parents, and other professionals in the learning community) and who actively seeks out opportunities to grow professionally.

BUILDING ON EDUCATIONAL FOUNDATIONS

What Is a School?

More than a hundred years ago, John Dewey argued, "The school is primarily a social institution," whose central purpose is not "science, nor literature, nor history nor geography . . . but the child's own social activities." According to Dewey, children learn best by doing things that are real and meaningful for them. Second graders, generally speaking, are not interested in learning something for use in the future. Instead, they are interested in what is around them in the present.

Many critics feel that Dewey's approach fails to address the needs of society. It is seen as a permissive model, one in which students are allowed to have their own opinions, to voice their own concerns, and to go in whatever direction they feel appropriate in terms of their own learning.

As a teacher, you will, in fact, be responsible for engaging students in the learning process. Your major challenge will be how to actually make this happen. Can you meet the natural needs and interests of students, while at the same time teaching them about the things society considers important? Are the two necessarily incompatible? Does it make any sense to try to teach students if they are not personally engaged in the learning process? Will students learn things simply because they are told to do so?

What do you think? What motivated you to learn as a student? What do you think will work best for you in your own classroom?

● **The Democratic Classroom**   As mentioned in earlier chapters, John Dewey (1859–1952) stressed that classrooms are a part of life, not merely preparation for it. He believed that in order to make society more democratic, students must participate in classrooms that are themselves democratic societies. To perpetuate this belief, Dewey recommended that teachers cultivate rules that would support **democratic classrooms.** The democratic classroom, according to Dewey, gives students a chance to learn how their own actions affect the group and how to "do one's part" in contributing to classroom projects (Dewey, 1938/1976).

Teachers today who welcome diverse students from many cultures, as well as those with special needs, into their classrooms are carrying out Dewey's vision. Dewey viewed diversity as a resource for all in a democratic society. His desire for such integration started to materialize as the civil rights movement of the 1960s demanded equal treatment and access for students of all races and cultures.

The democratic classroom works best when teachers organize the classroom space in a way that facilitates a *community of learners* who will work together; a democratic classroom is not one in which teachers exert power and control. Teachers, no matter how benevolent, can be in the role of "oppressors" in the classroom, controlling and manipulating students to do what they want them to do. They can "control" students by using authority, charisma, language, or other means to force or persuade students to comply. Teachers need to be in a constant dialogue with their students, examining choices and decisions (Freire, 1995), a theme many current education theorists also espouse today.

● **Shared Leadership in the Classroom**   Classrooms in which teachers share the leadership role with the students by creating rules and accountability systems together create effective learning environments for all students. Giroux's **resistance theory** suggests that many lower-class students behave badly in school as an expression of healthy resistance (Giroux, 1981). Because of this, some students may be targeted and labeled as troublemakers. Giroux's research showed that students who resisted authority knew that the school was limiting their chances to succeed and in a sense, dooming them to failure. Instead of just passively accepting the rules, these students responded. Students' responses, labeled as bad behavior by some teachers and principals, however, may actually be good for the students who are protecting their rights. When teachers respect all of their students and have a democratic classroom that practices social justice, they are more likely to understand the intent behind the students' resistance. Instead of reacting with anger to these students, these teachers talk with students before reacting to the resistant behavior they may have observed in a hallway or classroom (Giroux, 1996).

The concept of a caring classroom that is democratic and that practices social justice is worthy; the real challenge to teachers is in how to implement them. Urban educator Gloria Ladson-Billings suggests that teachers ask *culturally relevant questions* of themselves as a guide to creating a caring classroom. Figure 11.1 describes what culturally relevant teachers look like. Classrooms that implement caring and inclusive practices for all students become **culturally relevant** places for learning (Ladson-Billings, 1994). Through the Eyes of Culturally Sensitive Teachers provides further insights into ways culturally relevant teachers can work with all students.

No one would argue the value of cultural relevance in today's diverse classrooms. While many teachers want to embrace their multicultural classrooms, they recognize that they are doing so from their own myopic perspective. How can they identify with and relate to a variety of cultures that are different from what they know? As discussed throughout this book, it becomes particularly important that teachers know their students—their interests, concerns, special culturally relevant customs, and unique talents. This will help you develop an appreciation for the diversity within the classroom and to encourage students to appreciate that diversity. It is critical to successfully managing a democratic and respectful classroom.

F I G U R E 11.1

What Do Culturally Relevant Teachers Look Like?

✓ Have high self-esteem and a high regard for others.

✓ See themselves as part of the community, see teaching as giving back to the community, and encourage their students to do the same.

✓ Believe that all students can succeed.

✓ Help students make connections between their community, national, and global identities.

✓ See teaching as "digging knowledge out" of students.

✓ Have "humanely equitable," fluid relationships with students.

✓ Cultivate relationships with students beyond the classroom.

✓ Demonstrate a connectedness with each student.

✓ Encourage a community of learners.

✓ Encourage collaborative learning, expecting students to teach each other and take responsibility for each other.

✓ View knowledge critically.

✓ Are passionate about knowledge.

✓ Help students develop necessary skills.

✓ See excellence as a complex standard that takes student diversity and individual differences into account.

✓ Honor and respect the student's home culture.

✓ Help African American students (and others) understand the world as it is and equip them to change it for the better.

Source: G. Ladson-Billings, *The Dreamkeepers: Successful Teachers of African American Children.* (San Francisco: Jossey-Bass, 1994). Copyright 1994 by Gloria Ladson-Billings. This material used by permission of John Wiley & Sons, Inc.

Through the Eyes of Culturally Sensitive Teachers

Getting Kenyon to Pay Attention

Kenyon Williams was a bright African American student in the sixth grade attending Washington Middle School in Chicago. He had always liked his teachers in elementary school and was looking forward to the new adventure of changing classes in middle school. He was assigned to the "blue" sixth-grade team, which meant that this team of students would all have the same English, mathematics, science, and social studies teachers for the year. After two months in school, Kenyon liked his science teacher, Ms. Delgado, most but he was having some problems with Mrs. Fallon, his English teacher.

One day, Kenyon came into Ms. Delgado's class looking quite dejected. She immediately noticed this and asked Kenyon what was wrong. "That woman, she just doesn't like me," uttered Kenyon. "What woman?" asked Ms. Delgado. "You know, Mrs. Fallon, the English teacher," responded Kenyon. Eventually Kenyon related that in class Mrs. Fallon had asked him a question he couldn't answer. Mrs. Fallon then responded, "Well, class, as you can see, some of us aren't paying attention because we have better things to do." Kenyon felt like digging a hole and crawling into it. He thought every set of eyes in the room was on him and that time had stopped. "Honest, Ms. Delgado, I was paying attention, but I just didn't know the answer, and that teacher made me look like a fool! I'm not going to learn for her!" he said angrily.

Ms. Delgado tried to calm Kenyon and suggested that by not learning in his English class, he would only be hurting himself. Kenyon was still angry by the time that school day ended. Ms. Delgado went home to ponder the situation. Should she approach Mrs. Fallon and tell her that Kenyon had been humiliated that day? How would Mrs. Fallon take this? After all, she was far more experienced than Ms. Delgado.

A meeting of "blue team" teachers was scheduled in two days, so Ms. Delgado decided to wait until the meeting. Toward the end of the meeting, the topic turned to discipline. Ms. Delgado used the opportunity to talk about how humiliation or embarrassment of students should never be used in a classroom, or as a discipline technique. She ended her remarks by saying, "Even when our students have failed to study or have done something wrong, they should be able to hang on to their dignity." Ms. Delgado hoped that, without mentioning any student or teacher by name, the message had been received by Mrs. Fallon.

Two weeks went by and Ms. Delgado spoke again with Kenyon and asked him how things were going in his English class. "The teacher has been nice to me lately. I think I'll give her a second chance," Kenyon responded. Ms. Delgado had been resigned to speak to Mrs. Fallon directly if Kenyon had still been having problems or felt uncomfortable in English class. She was glad that this conversation was no longer necessary.

Points to Ponder

1. Do you think that Mrs. Fallon was fully aware of the impact of her comments on Kenyon? If humiliation causes such agony in students, why do you occasionally see it used?

2. Should Ms. Delgado become involved in trying to make Kenyon's situation better in another teacher's class? Why or why not?

3. How might Ms. Delgado have approached Mrs. Fallon in Kenyon's case if the topic had not come up at the teachers' meeting?

4. Can you think of another way Ms. Delgado could have advocated for Kenyon?

BELIEVE THAT *ALL* CHILDREN CAN LEARN

One of the most important notions that came out of the education reform movements of the last decade is the idea that *all children can learn*. Based on this belief, schools and teachers should provide the resources and environment that will encourage successful learning. Yet this goal has not been universally realized. According to a report by the National Commission on Teaching and America's Future titled "What Matters Most: Teaching for

America's Future" (Darling-Hammond, 1996), the number one barrier to successful learning and the biggest challenge for schools is teachers' and principals' low expectations for student performance. This report has influenced state legislatures, districts, and schools of education as they try to create a system of education that will provide the best for all children. The first premise of the commission states, "What teachers know and can do is the most important influence on what students learn." Federal legislation has been enacted to ensure that all teachers exert a positive influence over what students learn.

● **The Role of Federal Reform in the Classroom**   The most current education reform is the No Child Left Behind Act of 2001 (NCLB), a revised version of the federal Elementary and Secondary Education Act of 1965 (ESEA). The premise of this act is that too many of the neediest children are being left behind because schools have not been focused on these students. It supports the philosophy that all children can learn and *will* learn. NCLB also set new teacher quality benchmarks to ensure that highly qualified teachers certified in all core academic areas are in every classroom by 2006. The stakes are high for schools and teachers because failure to meet specific goals specified in the act may result in reduced funding for the school and being labeled as a "failed school."

The work of the National Council for the Accreditation of Teacher Education (NCATE) also reinforces the belief that all children can learn. By establishing standards that shape curriculum in schools of education, NCATE helps ensure that prospective teachers will come to understand the importance of entering their profession with a disposition that will foster learning. For example, NCATE's Standard 1 states: "Candidate knowledge, skills, and dispositions are all important aspects of this preparation" (NCATE, 2001). It is the job of education programs to help teachers acquire the necessary knowledge and skills to pass on to their students.

In addition to the national standards, state standards and mandates influence the current focus on how teachers manage their classrooms. All states grant teachers' licenses and provide a list of expectations for learning. Among these expectations is classroom management. Most state regulations include something like the following:

Manages Classroom Climate and Operation
The teacher:

● creates an environment that is conducive to learning.

● creates a physical environment appropriate to a range of learning activities.

● maintains appropriate standards of behavior, mutual respect, and safety.

● manages classroom routines and procedures without significant loss of instructional time

You should always be aware of the state standards against which you will be assessed when managing a classroom. Pay attention to the language. How is it worded? Be aware of the expectations. Watch for key words such as *respect* and *social justice*. Keeping these things in mind will help you stay focused and meet expectations.

● **The Role of Personal Philosophies in the Classroom**   Although federal reform and state standards influence how schools and teachers design their own classroom communities, it is the teachers' personal philosophies and experiences that shape the classroom. Within this framework, teachers ensure that requisite standards are met.

As you begin your preparation to become a teacher, your own thoughts and beliefs will integrate with the theories and methods you learn. Taking time to reflect on who you are and what you bring to the profession is important. As a beginning teacher it is important to get in touch with what you bring to the profession and to the classroom, especially as it relates to management and behavior. All of these experiences, whether as a student or an observer, are part of your memory bank and will influence the ways in which you operate in your own classroom. The judgments you have made about how teachers maintain their environment and how they should respond to students will make a difference in how you

INTASC

Principle #9

Professional Commitment and Responsibility: The teacher is a reflective practitioner who continually evaluates the effects of his/her choices and actions on others (students, parents, and other professionals in the learning community) and who actively seeks out opportunities to grow professionally.

create your learning community. When you are able to articulate your philosophy, you will be one step closer to being in a position to start managing a classroom of your own.

"Good teachers are those who can transmit a passion for learning. They believe all children can learn—some may take a little longer, but they will not stop until they have tried everything they can, and then some."

JOANNE L., PARENT, SANTA MONICA, CALIFORNIA

THINK ABOUT THIS:

Caring teachers respect all students and believe that all students can learn. Do you believe that all students have the ability to learn? Do you think that all people believe that all students can learn? What role should federal and state government play in dictating how students should be taught?

SHARE and COMPARE:

In your class, discuss the possible consequences when people in charge of learning—teachers, administrators, politicians—give up hope on the learning potential of some children.

INTASC

Principle #5

Classroom Motivation and Management: The teacher uses an understanding of individual and group motivation and behavior to create a learning environment that encourages positive social interaction, active engagement in learning, and self-motivation.

How Do Effective Teachers Manage Their Classrooms?

Results from the 36th Annual Phi Delta Kappa/Gallup poll of the public's attitude about education today have forced educators to take notice. For the third consecutive year, in response to the question, "What do you think are the biggest problems the public schools of your community must deal with?" lack of control or discipline in schools has registered as the second biggest concern (Rose & Gallup, 2004). (See Table 11.1.) Table 11.1 also lists reasons people give for why students fail to learn. As you can see, "lack of student interest" and "lack of discipline" are among the top perceived reasons for failure. Regardless of the poll or the respondents, classroom management is repeatedly ranked as one of the top concerns among educators.

In light of these findings, today's teachers have a formidable task. They must manage their classrooms, engage students' interest, and enforce disciplinary procedures in their classrooms while adhering to state and federal standards. The biggest challenge is how to do this while showing students respect, maintaining high standards in the classroom, and keeping order.

Recall from earlier in the chapter that classroom management is viewed as a broad umbrella concept that addresses techniques for controlling behavior as well as the academic climate in the classroom. This is typically the most challenging aspect of teaching for new teachers. Because creating a classroom in which all of the elements work together can be a trial-and-error process at the start, new teachers often need to spend time acclimating themselves to a new school, a new class, and a new profession. It may be more accurate and productive to think of classroom management as "the orchestration of classroom life so that all children can maximize their learning potential" (Dudley-Marling, 1993).

Harry K. Wong, an educational consultant, compares teaching to managing a store or a restaurant. "Just because you know how to cook a steak does not make you a successful

TABLE 11.1

Public Attitudes about Education (shown in percentages)

What do you think are the biggest problems the public schools of your community must deal with?

	NATIONAL TOTALS			NO CHILDREN IN SCHOOL			PUBLIC SCHOOL PARENTS		
	'04	'03	'02	'04	'03	'02	'04	'03	'02
Lack of financial support/funding/money	21	25	23	22	26	23	20	24	23
Lack of discipline, more control	10	16	17	10	17	18	8	13	13
Overcrowded schools	10	14	17	9	12	14	13	16	23
Use of drugs/dope	7	9	13	7	10	14	7	7	11
Fighting/violence/gangs	6	4	9	6	3	9	6	5	9

How much does each of the following reasons contribute to learning failures in the public schools in your community?

	GREAT DEAL PLUS FAIR AMOUNT	GREAT DEAL	FAIR AMOUNT	NOT VERY MUCH	NOT AT ALL	DON'T KNOW
Lack of home or parental support	93	74	19	5	1	1
Lack of interest by the students themselves	90	60	30	8	1	1
Lack of discipline in the schools	84	60	24	10	5	1
Lack of good teaching	81	47	34	13	6	*
Lack of funding	78	45	33	14	7	1
Lack of community emphasis on education	78	43	35	15	6	1

*Less than one-half of 1%.
Source: Phi Delta Kappan (September 2003): 44, 51.

restaurant owner. Just because you have a college teaching degree, does not make you a teacher" (Wong & Wong, 1991). In keeping with the comparison of a well-managed class-room to a well-managed store, the teacher is the ultimate "store manager" or classroom manager.

ORGANIZING CLASSROOM SPACE

The layout of a classroom can play an important role in classroom management and requires purposeful consideration. An effective arrangement maximizes student visibility during a lesson, promotes discussion and student involvement, allows for breakouts into smaller groups, and keeps all students in clear eyesight of the teacher. Sometimes special considerations have to be made for students with special needs, such as a student in a wheelchair, or visually or hearing-impaired students.

Teachers organize their classrooms to facilitate certain types of instruction. The organization is often dictated by grade level because of the different instruction required. For example, middle schools and high schools usually seat their students in rows facing the front of the classroom where there is a whiteboard or a blackboard. This setup implies that the teacher is directing the lesson and the students are there to listen. However, many teachers vary this arrangement by having students move their desks into groups or pairs in order to work on assignments or to have small discussions. Elementary and early childhood

Flexible arrangements of the classroom setting allow you to accommodate different activities and student needs at the same time.

classrooms sometimes do not even have individual desks; many classrooms have learning stations where students work in groups.

Once the classroom organization has been established, the next step is for teachers to identify all of their students and their students' needs. This requires taking the time to learn about each and every student. Students from other countries or cultures add to the fabric of the class, but they may also have issues related to being different to which teachers must be sensitive. When teachers are sensitive to their students' concerns and make an effort to spend some individual quality time with these students, it goes a long way toward making them feel part of the classroom community. Armed with this knowledge, teachers can connect students to each other.

This process can also help teachers identify those with special needs as well as those who have special skills or gifts to add to the class. Recall from Chapter 10 how a teacher sat an ELL student next to another student who had a familiarity with the ELL student's native language. This seating decision was deliberate. By using the strengths and skills of the students in a classroom, you can create a democratic community of learners based on what each student brings to the classroom. This strategy allows you to foster the attitude that everyone in the room makes some contribution to the community. As Education Matters illustrates, the organization of the classroom as well as other design decisions can have a significant impact on student learning.

In your career as a student, consider the wide variety of classroom arrangements in which you have taken classes. Science classes may have been organized in small groups. Language arts may have also been organized by group, whereas history class may have been arranged in rows. The key to thinking about physical room setup is to think about why it is organized this way. How will it affect the management of the classroom? Will more or less learning take place for students?

ESTABLISHING CLASSROOM ROUTINES

In addition to organizing classroom space and noting students' needs, teachers need to create daily routines that will establish an order to the day. Two types of routines are those that relate to general day-to-day management details and those that organize lesson presentations. Routines are important for maintaining consistency, establishing expectations, and moving students through their day. Procedures such as writing the agenda on the board or listing the activities that will be covered that day or week are simple, yet invaluable vehicles for communicating class goals and expectations.

A key factor in engaging students is not how long a teacher has been teaching, but how effectively a teacher begins the lesson and engages the students (Berliner, 1985). Students respect teachers whose classrooms are organized because it shows that they are well prepared. This organization allows teachers to increase instructional time, which in turn improves student achievement. Students want to succeed. When teachers demonstrate conscious acts of planning by creating routines for processes throughout the day, it allows them to move students smoothly from the beginning to the end of a day (Saphier & Gower, 1997). The goal is to move from one task to another—lessons, lunch breaks, attendance, in-class projects—"without significant loss of time," a primary goal for all teachers!

Establishing effective routines is not an easy task, and is one that all teachers struggle with—even those with years of experience. In Jon Saphier's books *Activators* and *Summarizers* (Saphier & Haley, 1993a, 1993b), he discusses the importance of having routines in place and offers effective strategies for engaging students throughout the lesson. These effective teaching tools, when integrated into teachers' planning processes, enhance stu-

EDUCATION MATTERS

Can Feng Shui Aid Learning?

Can the shape of a hallway discourage bullying in schools? Can more windows or a change in paint color raise test scores? Can carpeting turn the class clown into a math whiz? According to a *New York Times* article, "The Feng Shui of Schools," the idea that the way a school looks could make a difference with learning is being revisited. Feng shui is defined as an Asian art of design that changes uses of space to bring positive energy. Business and home decorators have been using it with clients for several years. Could this art be used in schools to improve learning?

Teachers in Rhode Island are trying feng shui. A veteran teacher who began using feng shui says, "People make fun and joke about this all the time. Some people think it is some big crazy thing." She has no proof that her students are smarter because she incorporates feng shui, but she notices, "I am more conscious of how I interact with them. I am more open to listening and more focused on my questioning and responding, trying to be more nurturing."

The Education Issue: Does it matter how schools and classrooms look and feel?

How Do School Buildings and Classrooms Affect Teachers and Students?

Teachers spend their whole day and career in a building with students. For some teachers this could mean 30 or more years in the same classroom. Yet they are called on to create more interesting and motivating educational experiences, often for reluctant learners in dreary spaces. Architects, educators, and environmental psychologists point to research between elements of design that say how a classroom feels will influence student achievement. With the need for more than 6,000 new schools before 2006, how classroom space is used will be an important question to discuss.

What's Your Opinion?

1. What did your school and classrooms look and feel like?

2. Did you feel that they helped or hindered your learning?

3. How does the concept of design and feng shui make you more aware of classroom environment?

Sources: "The Feng Shui of Schools," *The New York Times* (August 5, 2001); S. B. Coleman, "Flowing to School," *The Boston Globe* (September 5, 2001).

---

dents' focus on the lesson. Problems to Possibilities demonstrates what happens when routines are not yet established.

There are many ways to integrate routines in the classroom that will motivate and engage students. This, in turn, will result in successful student learning. How routines are implemented in the classroom will vary by grade level. For example, elementary school teachers may collect homework by having students place it in an "in box" on their desk. High school teachers may call the students' names and check them in a grade book to be sure all students have done the assignment. Others may simply have students pass in their work. All are examples of routines. Figure 11.2 on page 340 presents typical routines that may be necessary on any given day. If they work for teachers and students, they will be maintained. If they do not help teachers and students achieve their goals, however, the routines will need to be changed.

As you visit schools, pay attention to the types of routines the teacher has established, or the lack of routines if you notice chaos. Allow the following questions to inform your observations:

1. Are the students familiar with the routine? How do you know?

2. How does this teacher reinforce any student who is not participating properly?

3. What other skills are students learning by using this routine?

4. How are these observed routines saving time for other teaching activities?

As teachers become comfortable with setting the structure for their classrooms, they will notice that there are times in the day when it may be difficult to motivate students; in

FIGURE 11.2

Examples of Routines Teachers Need to Create in a Typical Day

OPENING THE CLASS	TRANSITIONS	EXPECTATIONS FOR BEHAVIOR	CLOSING THE CLASS OR DAY
Attendance	Walking in the halls	Rules and rewards	Collecting work
Lunch count	Fire drill procedures	Materials	Putting materials away
Homework	Restroom passes	Talking in class	Leaving the building
Welcome	Passing in papers	Working with other students	Closing activity

particular, early morning and right after lunch. Teachers need to take this into account as they plan their days. Incorporating certain routines into the day can help maintain students' motivation to learn. In a national education survey, teachers from around the United States were asked for ideas on what they incorporate into their days to maintain students' interest:

> I let students take a short break to get drinks and go to the restroom. Then I begin reading an ongoing chapter book aloud. This motivates the children to be on time.
>
> Third-Grade Teacher, Pennsylvania

> To get my Spanish classes going we begin with oral conversations. I walk around the room and ask questions and ask for responses. Students then have to ask questions of other students and call on their classmates. Some days we do relay races with words, have scavenger hunts, or sing songs!
>
> Spanish Teacher, Tennessee

> I have very sleepy early classes. I have tried many tactics, but my students' favorite is playing Simon Says. I go through the motions in double time so they have to engage their minds to keep up. This is a fun wake-up activity and it only takes a few minutes of class time.
>
> Elementary Teacher, Illinois

> To begin the morning we start the day by doing the calendar routine. Students participate by counting together, reading words at the chart, and singing. We skip and hop to get the blood flowing and warm us up for the day.
>
> English Immersion Teacher, California

INTASC

Principle #5

Classroom Motivation and Management: The teacher uses an understanding of individual and group motivation and behavior to create a learning environment that encourages positive social interaction, active engagement in learning, and self-motivation.

CREATING RULES, REWARDS, AND CONSEQUENCES

When teachers are caring and show respect to all students, their rules, rewards, and consequences reflect that philosophy. In democratic classrooms, students have a voice in creating the rules and doling out consequences to their classmates. Rules vary by grade levels, yet most classrooms have a universal rule: "Be respectful to all in the room."

Teachers offer a range of rewards for good behavior or for following rules and meeting academic goals; these rewards vary according to students' grade level. For example, one reward might grant students free time to work on computers, to read, or to sit next to a friend for a day. If an entire class meets its academic goals or does something noteworthy, a reward might be a class pizza party.

When students do not follow rules, or when they do not meet their goals, some teachers may implement the use of **student contracts,** a document that states that a student is

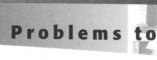

Problems to POSSIBILITIES

How Does a Teacher Gain Students' Attention?

The beginning of the school year has been difficult for Eric. As a first-year teacher in an urban high school, he has had many frustrating days beginning his classes and it is only the end of October. He doesn't get it. He was well prepared at his university, and he passed all of his content tests for history at the top of his class. He loves history and just assumed that he would pass his enthusiasm on to all of his students, who would just come into the classroom ready to learn.

Some days are a little better than others. Yesterday was worse. Yesterday he just couldn't get the students to sit down and pay attention. He had planned what he thought would be a great group lesson—staging an ancient Roman election—but he just couldn't get the students to listen to the directions or even care. He had stayed up late preparing overheads, group posters, and an innovative, fun, creative summary sheet that would help them study for the test. Nothing was working. After 15 minutes of talking to individual students and trying to get them to sit and cooperate, Eric shouted, "All right, that's it! We won't have the election! We won't go over the summary sheet. Forget the groups, you can't even let me give directions! Just open your books to page 20 and write the answers to the questions. You will be graded on your answers. What's the point in trying to have a little fun in class? Clearly you don't want to learn anyway! I give up!" He then went back to his desk and sat down. Eric had thought teaching was going to be a lot easier.

Discussion Question

What can Eric do to capture and maintain his students' attention and control misbehavior?

Possibilities

Teachers may romanticize the reality of their profession. Many new teachers, like Eric, may think teaching will be easy because they believe that students will all want to learn as much as they did. Eric could be any beginning new teacher or student teacher. He may have been in a great education program, and he knows his content inside and out, but if he can't convey his knowledge to his students in an engaging fashion, then he needs to find another strategy for managing his classroom.

Eric could start by getting to know his students as individuals. This step is often overlooked in formal preparation, yet it is one of the most important. Once Eric gets to know his students, he will see that it will go a long way toward motivating and engaging them as a group. Developing in students a desire to learn is an important skill that is often overlooked in formal preparation.

Eric also needs to give more thought to the opening and closing routines he establishes at the beginning and end of lessons. Most beginning teachers think about the lesson plan, the skills, and the assessment process, but forget to plan how to *begin* the class by engaging the students' attention. Without opening and closing routines, there may not be any lesson because teachers spend class time trying to diminish students' frustration and to curb their own frustration without showing it to the students. Opening "motivators" help capture the students' attention and set the stage for learning. Routine wrap-ups help summarize the message of the lesson for students.

Once teachers know and understand their students, and once routines are in place, teachers will be able to move students effortlessly through lessons and events each day, positively affecting the quality of the education. As part of their classroom management strategy, teachers need to establish student expectations based on rules, rewards, and consequences. However, before creating rules and giving rewards or doling out consequences, you need to be able to stand up in front of students and respectfully motivate them to "want" to listen and learn the information.

The following resources may provide helpful hints:

- *Activators: Activity Structures to Engage Students' Thinking Before Instruction* and *Summarizers: Activity Structures to Support Integration and Retention of New Learning,* by Jon Saphier and Mary Ann Haley (Acton, MA: Research for Better Teaching, 1993).

- *Classroom Activators: 64 Novel Ways to Energize Learners,* by Jerry Evanski (Sterling Heights, MI: Center for Creative Learning and Teaching, 2003).

Ethical Question

How far can a teacher go to maintain control in the classroom? How will you learn how to do this prior to your student teaching and your first year in the classroom?

Student Contract

Student's name _____

    I will change (list the behavior)_____. I will measure my
success by (how the change in behavior will be noted) _____.
    For successful demonstration of the appropriate behavior my reward will be _____
_____.

Signed _____ Teacher

Signed _____ Student   Date _____

I N T A S C

Principle #6

Communication Skills: The
teacher uses knowledge of
effective verbal, nonverbal,
and media communication
techniques to foster active
inquiry, collaboration, and
supportive interaction in
the classroom.

agreeing to commit to specific terms with the teacher. Figure 11.3 shows an example of a
student contract. Student contracts are often used as a tool to modify behavior. How do
you think a student feels about using a contract? What are the other students thinking?
How does the teacher influence the students?

    Many beginning teachers assume that all students will adhere to the rules established at
the beginning of the year, and as a result, they don't create consequences up front. As they
will come to learn, and as experienced teachers know, establishing clear and reasonable
consequences for breaking class rules is a necessary component of classroom management.
Implementing them equitably and ensuring that students understand them is essential for
setting a tone of equality. For example, if all students know that forgetting homework
means missing recess, then they won't be surprised when it happens (Pelletier, 2002). Likewise, if students know that being disrespectful toward classmates means writing an essay
about how they should have behaved, they may be able to censor themselves before behaving disrespectfully.

    When you visit schools, ask teachers how they deal with consequences for common
class disruptions such as forgetting homework, not having a pencil, or walking in late to
class. Ask them how well they feel these consequences work in motivating students to comply with their rules.

TIME MANAGEMENT STRATEGIES FOR BUSY TEACHERS

Another critical piece of classroom management is using time management strategies to
seamlessly move through each day. Necessary tools to help teachers budget their time and
their students' time wisely include daily "to-do lists," weekly planning books, monthly
organizers, and yearlong unit planners.

    Teachers who are aware of time and space and how they affect students often have
fewer discipline issues in their classrooms. While creating routines is invaluable, it is essential to develop them within a workable time frame. These time frames must allow for the
fact that not all students learn at the same pace. They must also allow for the fact that not
all students will always adhere to the rules, so certain measures may need to be taken that
could affect how time is allotted. Taking such factors into account when planning your
time will allow you to create a structure and system for teaching and learning. For example,

Pleased with your students' achievements and behavior? Reward them—positive reinforcement is a powerful motivator!

if you have students with different levels of ability in one class, you might allow those who work well independently to work on their own or in small groups. If you have the resources available, you could have students who are struggling in a certain area work with a specialist. This frees you up to work with the remainder of the students in a small group. This type of planning makes good use of time while promoting learning at all levels.

When visiting schools, notice the various strategies teachers use to maximize their time. Because class composition differs, no one strategy works across the board. Teachers need to find what works best for their needs and for the needs of their classes, and they need to be flexible, as circumstances warrant. How will you know whether your classroom management strategies are successful? Ask yourself, "How would an observer walking by a classroom know whether it is was well managed?" It is well managed if:

- Students are deeply involved with their academic work.

- Students know what is expected of them and are generally successful.

- There is relatively little wasted time due to confusion or disruption.

- The climate of the classroom is work-oriented, but relaxed and pleasant. (Wong & Wong, 1991)

When you begin your student teaching or set up your first classroom, you will appreciate the importance of these basic components of classroom management. Give yourself time and understand that some trial-and-error is involved. You will likely find that you will need to create routines or rules for processes that you had never even considered. First-time teachers and student teachers often exclaim in the beginning, "I didn't realize there were so many routines to think about! I didn't know I had to tell the students how to pass in the papers!" Now that you appreciate the underlying structure of classroom management, you need to explore managing student "behavior."

INTASC

Principle #4

Multiple Instructional Strategies: The teacher uses various instructional strategies to encourage students' development of critical thinking, problem solving, and performance skills.

INTASC

Principle #5

Classroom Motivation and Management: The teacher uses an understanding of individual and group motivation and behavior to create a learning environment that encourages positive social interaction, active engagement in learning, and self-motivation.

WHAT ARE DIFFERENT APPROACHES TO BEHAVIOR MANAGEMENT?

Classroom management is often used interchangeably with **behavior management** because often, if space and time are not organized effectively, behavioral problems result (Pelletier, 2004). However, even when teachers organize their classes in a way that makes efficient use of time and space, there may still be behavioral issues that require discipline.

All beginning teachers agree that knowing how and when to discipline a student is a very challenging aspect of teaching. Even when you organize the classroom, establish routines, and create rules, rewards, and consequences, students will sometimes misbehave. Knowing how to respond to these students while keeping your classroom focused on learning is critical to gaining your students' respect. The attitude and disposition you bring to your class, as well as the knowledge you have of successful behavior management models and theories, will enhance your chances of success.

Teachers use a combination of models with varying amounts of success. Most beginning teachers find the daily routine and pace of teaching initially overwhelming, leaving them little time to think about the theories they learned. However, effective teachers find a balance between theory and practice. Once you find this balance, you will be able to use this information to continue your own inner reflective dialogue, which will lead you to create your own behavior management philosophy.

THEORY INFORMING PRACTICE

Just as *behavior management* and *classroom management* are often used interchangeably, so too is *behavior management* used interchangeably with **discipline.** If you consider that discipline is described as the action required by teachers or school administrators toward individual students or groups of students who disrupt the educational process or who do not adhere to established rules, you can trace the connections.

Many discipline models are based on the degree of power or control that teachers wield over students to effect adherence to the rules. Some teachers find that a minimal amount of power—through the use of verbal cues or gestures—can curb inappropriate behaviors. However, in extreme cases, when students' behavior is highly inappropriate or dangerous, teachers may need to exert a maximal amount of power by using physical intervention (Wolfgang, 2004). How teachers respond to misbehavior is largely a reflection of their teaching philosophy and disposition toward students. However, the type of student misbehavior also dictates how teachers will respond. For example, forgetting homework will elicit a very different response than will hitting another student in class.

Table 11.2 presents seven traditional models of behavior management. As you will discover, these theoretical models offer a knowledge base that will help you create your own approach for responding to students and for ensuring that all of your students understand your responses. When teachers take time to clearly communicate guidelines and expectations, and when they make sure that students understand, then they can apply behavior management models. Consistency is the key to using any model. This list is by no means exhaustive; your professors may provide you with additional models as well. While teachers find that some models resonate with their beliefs more than others, each model provides a distinct way to think about behavior. Many teachers use a combination of models as they develop their own approach to handling behavioral issues in their classrooms. Following are two of the most common approaches to behavior management, both of which are informed by multiple research.

• **With-It-Ness.**   One basic principle of classroom management comes from Jacob Kounin's work. The concept of **with-it-ness** refers to teachers' awareness of students' behavior and work performance in the class. Kounin found that when high school students

TABLE 11.2

Behavior Management Models

MODEL	THEORY	MAIN POINTS
The Kounin model	The teacher is "with it," alert, and able to manage the group effectively.	• Teacher is able to address off-task behaviors while continuing instruction of group. • Teacher provides a smoothness of learning and does not go on tangents. • Teacher keeps class momentum and keeps students alert.
The Neo-Skinnerian model	Behavior can be shaped to desired outcome.	• Behavior is conducted by consequences: strengthened if reinforced, weakened if not reinforced. • In the beginning stages of learning, regular reinforcement provides the best results.
The Ginott model	Situations must be addressed with clear messages.	• Teacher self-discipline is important. • Address student's actions. Do not attack student personally. • Invite cooperation rather than demand it.
The Glasser model	Good behavior comes from good choices.	• Focus on class meetings as a means of developing classwide discipline. • Do not accept excuses for bad behavior. • Reasonable consequences for both good and bad behavior.
The Dreikus model	The teacher confronts mistaken goals.	• Misbehavior is result of student's belief that it will gain them peer recognition. • Misbehavior is directed at mistaken goals (attention getting, power seeking, etc.). • Discipline is not punishment. It means self-control.
The Canter model	The teacher assertively takes charge of the classroom.	• Assertive rather than passive or hostile. • Expectations stated early. • Insist on responsible behavior. • Use calm, firm voice and make eye contact.
The Fred Jones model	The teacher emphasizes learner motivation and classroom behavior.	• Teacher informs students about desired structure in the classroom (simple and clear). • Teacher uses effective nonverbal act to stop misbehavior. • Lost classroom time can be avoided if classroom is managed properly.

know that their teachers are aware of what is going on throughout the class, they become more involved in their work and tend not to misbehave. For example, teachers who display with-it-ness would notice if a student is listening to a headset or poking another student and would recognize a facial expression that might indicate failing to understand a concept (Kounin, 1970).

I N T A S C

Principle #2

Knowledge of Human Development and Learning: The teacher understands how children learn and develop, and can provide learning opportunities that support their intellectual, social, and personal development.

Teachers show they are "with it" by (1) being aware of students and responding to their misbehavior or confusion; (2) asking a question of students who are misbehaving or not paying attention, and (3) walking near students who may be bothering their classmates. Conversely, when teachers ignore misbehaviors and continue teaching, the misbehavior persists, other students see their classmates get away with the behavior, and the other students start to misbehave as well, spreading the inattentiveness throughout the class. If teachers are not "with it" and end up reprimanding the wrong student, students become frustrated, convinced that the teacher is not aware of what is *really* going on.

Experienced teachers who are effective in the classroom can do and see many things at once, but it takes a certain amount of experience and comfort before this becomes natural. When teachers are comfortable moving around the room, looking at all students, and using eye contact and other cues to maintain attention, they tend to have control of the class. This control is not punitive; it is the result of teachers' ability to convey respect and a mutual understanding about how the room is managed, as well as how students and the teacher interact on a daily basis. Teachers who are "with it" and can multitask can manage a classroom and move the business of learning ahead efficiently and effectively. When student teachers or beginning teachers try to model their mentor teachers' approach, they often become frustrated because they cannot seem to multitask with ease. This may occur for a number of reasons. It may simply be that beginning teachers are not always "with it," and as a result students may not behave well because they can sense that the teacher is not confident. Other times, student teachers may be so attached to their lesson plans and to the front of the classroom that they find it difficult to move around or even look beyond the first row of students. With time and experience, many of these beginning teachers will become more comfortable veering off their established lesson plan when necessary and moving around the classroom with ease. Alternatively, they may find that another model better suits their approach to teaching.

● **The Responsive Classroom**   The *responsive classroom* model of behavior management was developed in the early 1980s by classroom teachers who wanted "an approach to teaching and learning that fosters safe, challenging, and joyful classrooms and schools, kindergarten through eighth grade" (www.responsiveclassroom.org). Based in theory and tested in practice, this model is being used in classrooms across the country. Seven guiding principles define the responsive classroom:

- Social and academic curriculum are equally important to student growth.

- Social interaction is integral to student growth.

- The process by which students learn is as important as what they learn.

- To achieve success, students must exhibit cooperation, assertion, responsibility, empathy, and self-control.

- Teachers must know their students as well as they know their content.

- Teachers must develop relationships with their students' families.

- All adults in the school must work together as a community.

To execute these principles, teachers use many of the strategies that have been discussed throughout this chapter, such as arranging the classroom in a fashion that best suits instruction, establishing clear rules and consequences, providing consistent and fair discipline for misbehavior, and promoting learning that engages and interests students. Having the additional element of family involvement in students' education encourages social and academic learning in and out of the classroom. To further this relationship, schools are setting up classes to explain the rules to which students should adhere in and out of school. The hope is that parents will also use these systems at home and there will be consistency

FIGURE 11.4

Classroom Management Advice

STUDENT

"Don't be a mean teacher. Have a sweet voice so the students will feel good."

Amina, second-grade student

"Make some rules and put them somewhere in the classroom where everyone can see it."

Lia, third-grade student

"If a child has a problem, don't scream at them or anything. Listen to what they have to say."

John, fourth-grade student

"I think a good teacher is a person that does not lose his or her patience very quickly."

Paul, third-grade student

"The teacher should go around the class to help everyone with things that the students do not understand."

Eliz, fourth-grade student

STUDENT TEACHER

"Never get into a power struggle with your students. Always listen to both sides with a nonjudgmental and nonconfrontational attitude."

"Have a good balance of discipline and humor with the children. In order to gain their respect, you need to convey your genuine enjoyment to be with them."

"In terms of behavior management there are three key principles I always try to keep in my mind: Make sure not to hold grudges from the day before, introduce a positive reinforcement schedule, and compliment each child at least once a day."

---

between home and school systems. In Figure 11.4 students and student teachers offer some helpful advice.

● **Other Research** Evertson, Emmer, and Worsham (2000) suggest that effective teachers must have systems in place to prevent student misbehavior. In ascertaining whether elementary and secondary schoolteachers have similar or different behavioral issues to contend with in their classrooms, the authors found more similarities than differences among teachers working at different grade levels (Evertson, Emmer, & Worsham, 2000). When teachers break down the rules to very specific behaviors that are expected of students and teach them how to follow these rules, they will prevent confusion, miscommunication, and frustration that can result in misbehavior. Evertson and colleagues determined that the most effective teachers prevented behavioral issues from disrupting their classrooms by doing the following:

● Breaking down classroom tasks into specific rules and procedures that are easy for students to follow,

● Teaching students rules and procedures as an important classroom lesson at the beginning of the year and then following up later in the year to ensure that students have absorbed them.

● Predicting where students will have the most difficulty with procedures and then emphasizing and clarifying the material for better student understanding.

● Monitoring and handling all problems immediately and directly.

Critics of Evertson and colleagues' work argue that it is based on the wrong premise. By looking at student compliance in teacher-controlled classrooms, what is really being measured is the effectiveness of the power a teacher has in the room over students. "Now if a good classroom is simply one where students do what they're told, we shouldn't be surprised that a teacher is more likely to have such a classroom when students are aware that she can quickly spot noncompliance" (Kohn, 1998). Researchers wonder whether the research promotes understanding, continuing motivation to learn, and having concern for others, or merely perpetuates a practice that enforces obedience to authority.

Teachers who mix and match models of behavior management may have conflicting methods operating in the same classroom. How teachers use the research to build the classroom community in combination with the attitudes they bring will be the biggest influence on the classroom environment. If teachers believe in power over respect, they will create a classroom based on compliance. If they believe in respect over power, they will create a classroom based on mutual respect and cooperation.

PRACTICE INFORMING THEORY

Practitioners have always created their own models of discipline in their own classrooms using research, theory, and their own experiences of what works. Following are different approaches to practicing discipline in the classroom. They represent a small sample of different approaches teachers take to behavior management.

As a prospective teacher, you may be drawn to these practical approaches, especially if you are concerned about how to handle behavioral issues in your classroom. It is important, however, to remember that these approaches are not miracle cures. They are simply possible approaches that work for some situations. Most teachers find that they achieve the most success using a combination of many different approaches to classroom discipline.

● **Teaching Discipline**   According to Harry K. Wong, the first thing a teacher needs to remember about classroom management is, "You were hired to take a group of possibly disinterested, howling, and unruly people and turn them into interested, disciplined, and productive learners in a well-managed environment" (Wong & Wong, 1991). Wong considers the primary reason for behavior problems in the classroom to be teachers who fail to create procedures and routines for discipline. Teachers need to present their rules clearly and provide reasonable explanations for each. They must invest classroom time in teaching discipline by creating a **discipline plan,** which lists rules, rewards, and consequences. These would be clearly stated to the students and consistent with the school's mission or guiding goals (Wong & Wong, 1991).

● **Community Building**   A second approach to practicing strategies for controlling behavior in class highlights community building rather than discipline. In *Authentic Classroom Management, Creating a Community of Learners,* Barbara Larrivee (1999) endorses taking a reflective approach to behavior management issues. She bases her approach on the assumption that effective classroom and behavior management strategies require teachers to be proactive in how they approach students who misbehave. This serves to empower students because they are not made to feel defensive and to provide teachers the opportunity to engage in conversation with these students.

Teachers who do not engage in proactive strategies can experience burnout as a result of being unable to comfortably deal with student misbehavior. Figure 11.5 presents the Burnout Cycle and Renewal Cycle, which illustrate how teachers' responses to students' misbehaviors can create a cycle of frustration or a cycle of renewal. Teachers who respond to student misbehavior effectively remain enthusiastic about teaching.

In the multicultural classroom, promoting acceptance of students from all cultural and social backgrounds is the responsibility of all teachers (Larrivee, 1999). Managing behavior in the multicultural classroom may include allowing behavior, intervening, or accommodating the behavior. Teachers have to make conscious choices based on the students and the classroom culture as to which response should be used with which students. The rationale for choosing the approach is an important reflective process for the teacher.

FIGURE 11.5

Teacher Burnout and Renewal Cycles

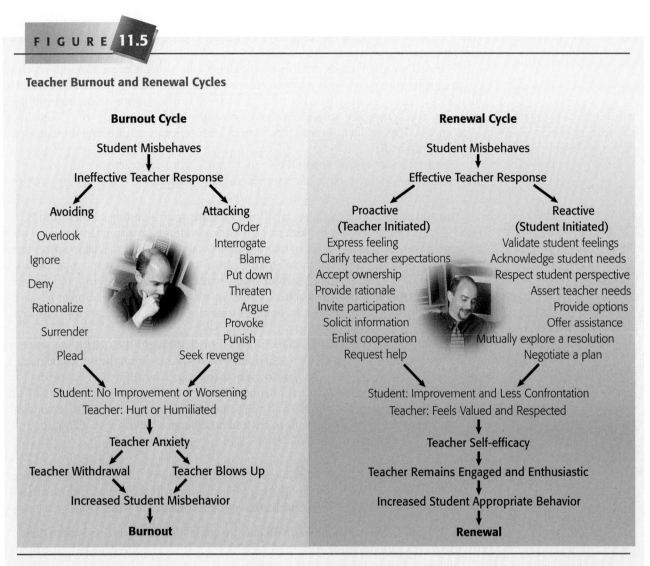

Burnout Cycle

Student Misbehaves

Ineffective Teacher Response

Avoiding
Overlook
Ignore
Deny
Rationalize
Surrender
Plead

Attacking
Order
Interrogate
Blame
Put down
Threaten
Argue
Provoke
Punish
Seek revenge

Student: No Improvement or Worsening
Teacher: Hurt or Humiliated

Teacher Anxiety

Teacher Withdrawal   Teacher Blows Up

Increased Student Misbehavior

Burnout

Renewal Cycle

Student Misbehaves

Effective Teacher Response

Proactive
(Teacher Initiated)
Express feeling
Clarify teacher expectations
Accept ownership
Provide rationale
Invite participation
Solicit information
Enlist cooperation
Request help

Reactive
(Student Initiated)
Validate student feelings
Acknowledge student needs
Respect student perspective
Assert teacher needs
Provide options
Offer assistance
Mutually explore a resolution
Negotiate a plan

Student: Improvement and Less Confrontation
Teacher: Feels Valued and Respected

Teacher Self-efficacy

Teacher Remains Engaged and Enthusiastic

Increased Student Appropriate Behavior

Renewal

Source: B. Larrivee, *Authentic Classroom Management: Creating a Community of Learners.* (Boston: Allyn & Bacon, 1999). Copyright 1999 by Pearson Education. Reprinted with permission.

In order to ensure equity among students in the classroom, teachers need to be proactive in creating learning and in providing consequences for misbehavior in the classroom. They need to ask themselves the following questions:

1. During group work, do I ensure that students from different cultural and social backgrounds have the same responsibilities as other students?

2. What do I do to ensure that students from different backgrounds will participate in group work?

3. What strategies do I use to raise the academic image of students from different cultures in the eyes of all students?

4. What strategies do I use to bridge the gap between the culture and the school and classroom community? (Larrivee, 1999)

● **Preventing Problems**   A third approach includes practical ideas for preventing problems. Both the National Education Association (NEA) and the American Federation of

Teachers (AFT) have designed workshops and specialized training for their members. The NEA's I Can Do It program focuses on the teacher's style and the practical ways in which problems can be prevented.

The AFT model focuses on antisocial behavior by using a preventive approach to working with students who have serious emotional and social issues. Teachers first need to identify students who are labeled "at risk" in order to provide support and improve their behavior. Teachers record students' behaviors to gather concrete evidence of behavioral benchmarks. This evidence can then be used to help define areas in which these students need the most help.

Based on research and current theory, both models provide teachers with tools necessary for improving classroom situations with difficult students.

I N T A S C

Principle #6

Communication Skills: The teacher uses knowledge of effective verbal, nonverbal, and media communication techniques to foster active inquiry, collaboration, and supportive interaction in the classroom.

● **Bringing Out the Best in Students**   Ron Clark, an award-winning teacher from North Carolina and former teacher in Harlem, New York, developed an approach based on what he calls "55 essential rules" for bringing out the best in his students. This practice-based approach, created through trial and error in his own classrooms, revolves around the importance of respect in the classroom perpetuating students' thinking and learning (Clark, 2003). To experienced teachers, the rules may seem like common sense, but to beginners with little time in the classroom, they make good sense. All relate to very specific behaviors expected of the students.

To implement his rules in his classrooms, Clark first taught the rules to his students and followed up immediately if a student did not follow a rule. From the outset, he made it clear that the purpose of the rules was to make them successful students. His success with students in Harlem made him a national hero. In an interview, one student stated, "Mr. Clark gave me the strength to hold on and be somebody. He is the one who believed in me. He told me not to give up. He told me to try, and no other teacher did that." Clark's 55 rules include the following:

- *Rule #2: Make eye contact.* Looking people in the eye shows that you have confidence and gives you a better chance of getting what you want. Because Clark believes that making eye contact is difficult, he has his students practice in pairs.

- *Rule #4: Congratulate a classmate.* To encourage classmates to feel good about their progress, Clark has students clap (three times) for students who deserve praise for a high test score or for completing a task.

- *Rule #5: If you win, do not brag; if you lose, do not show anger.* Teaching students how to lose gracefully and to not be cocky when they win a game is important.

- *Rule #8: Do not show disrespect with gestures.* This means no rolling of the eyes, smacking of the lips, or *tsk* sounds when other students are talking.

- *Rule #48: If anyone is bullying you, let your teacher know.* This is the big rule for building morale and a family bond in the classroom. He asks the students not to take matters into their own hands.

- *Rule #55: Be the best person you can be.* Learn from your mistakes, try hard, and be the kind of person other people want to be around.

According to Clark, the key to this model is actually teaching the rules and following up when the students adhere to them. Although this takes a lot of time in the beginning of the year, it pays off in the end.

● **The Positive Discipline Approach**   A fifth approach to behavior management relates to common problems that confront new teachers. These problems are discussed in *Positive Discipline: A Teachers A–Z Guide* (Nelsen, Escobar, Ortolano, Duffy, & Owen-Sohocki, 2001).

Topics cover how to handle students dealing with issues such as arguments, blaming, cheating, depression, divorce, failing, gangs, homework, jealousy, lying, parent involvement, sex, stealing, tantrums, tardiness, and whining. The guide suggests that teachers look at and learn about each issue separately, then deal with each problem individually.

Using positive models suggested in this guide, such as encouragement, self-esteem, kindness, and positive time-outs, the authors provide useful solutions to common problems. It is up to teachers to identify problems and then find them in the A–Z list to find relevant solutions.

The A-to-Z approach is about understanding children and the beliefs that motivate their misbehavior. It reinforces the concept of treating students with respect and dignity and having faith in their abilities. The problems in the book become learning opportunities in the positive discipline approach.

● **Reaching Out** Beginning teachers who have completed their student teaching offer a final approach to behavior management. They point to the importance of talking with teachers, observing student teachers, and spending time in schools. These measures will allow you to get closer to students and more familiar with the real issues of classroom management.

As a prospective teacher, you may be getting a bit nervous about all of the components that teachers need to balance to successfully manage a classroom. Keep in mind that there is a learning curve. You don't have to remember every approach and theory now—you just need to get a sense of what's involved and how it all fits into the big picture. Keep this text and use it when you are closer to student teaching to remind you of the big picture. While this is just an overview of the issues related to discipline in theory and in practice, the real value is learning *how* to handle situations with students who don't behave.

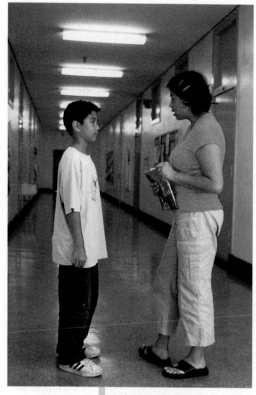

Using a positive and respectful approach to discipline allows you to understand your students' motivations and to work with them proactively to change their behavior. You also serve as a positive model.

How Do Teachers Respond to Inappropriate Behavior in the Classroom?

Teachers have so much to do in the classroom, and misbehavior of students can prevent them from meeting their goals. One student can disrupt the entire class and make learning difficult. Some students come to school with difficult circumstances and need additional help to get through their lives; however, students do not need to be removed to make the class work more smoothly. Beginning and experienced teachers alike struggle with issues of misbehavior and lack of motivation. Parents, school principals, and the students themselves often have different and sometimes conflicting perspectives about how each situation should be handled.

This will be one of the most challenging and complicated issues you will face as a beginning teacher. How you approach discipline and how you show your respect for rules, social justice, and all other people in the school will set you apart. A good place to start is to look at ways in which you can prevent problems from happening in your classroom.

PREVENTING COMMON MISBEHAVIORS

The bottom line to classroom management and behavior management will be how you as a teacher use the research and opinions of others to establish your own community of learners. In theory, if teachers organize effective classrooms, design motivating lessons that

INTASC

Principle #5

Classroom Motivation and Management: The teacher uses an understanding of individual and group motivation and behavior to create a learning environment that encourages positive social interaction, active engagement in learning, and self-motivation.

meet the needs of the students, and present information in engaging ways, they should not have any student acting out in class. In practice, however, all teachers encounter cases in which students break the rules and become disruptive.

● **Understand the Causes**   Rudolph Dreikurs (Dreikurs & Stolz, 1964) proposed that much misbehavior relates to students choosing *mistaken* ways of meeting the primary social needs to belong and to feel significant. Children choose mistaken behavior because they either aren't aware of more positive approaches or have given up on positive behavior. The four most common goals of misbehavior are as follows:

- Attention—"I belong and am significant only when I have your attention."

- Power—"I belong and am significant only when I am winning, or at least when I don't let you win."

- Revenge—"It hurts when I don't belong or feel significant, but at least I can hurt back."

- Assumed inadequacy—"I give up; it is impossible to belong" (Gold & Chamberlin, 2000).

Dreikurs emphasizes the importance of using encouragement with students who misbehave or are disruptive, as he believes that "a misbehaving student is a discouraged student." A simple problem-solving strategy will help you get at the root of the student's problem:

1. Define the problem individually with the student.

2. Brainstorm possible solutions—without criticizing.

3. Choose one approach—review all solutions and write the one that will be used.

4. Evaluate the effectiveness of the approach, and revise the plan if needed.

You Can Handle Them All (www.disciplinehelp.com), a website with behavior and management resources for teachers, presents a similar model of misbehavior as Dreikurs's, listing four key reasons that students misbehave:

1. *The need for attention.* Students who need attention commonly are those who speak out, arrive late, or make noise in class to get attention. When attention is the cause of their misbehavior, they feel frustrated when they don't get it.

2. *The need for power.* Students who seek power usually feel threatened. Their response to the threat is to openly dissent or to stir up controversy in some other way.

3. *The need for revenge.* Students who define themselves by being disliked, feared, or even hated are those who seek revenge. Repeated failure has made them fearful and angry, and as a result they have given up trying to gain attention or power via socially acceptable methods. These are the students who write on desks, bully classmates, threaten younger students, mark on restroom walls, and damage others' personal property.

4. *The lack of self-confidence.* Students who lack self-confidence expect failure. They frustrate their teachers because they can do the work, but fail to actually complete anything. For these students, only academic success of some kind can change their self-image (Master Teacher, 2002).

● **Apply Discipline**   There will be times and situations during teaching when issues will need to be addressed and discipline must be handed out. Three types of discipline can be

---

INTASC

Principle #8

Assessment of Student Learning: The teacher understands and uses formal and informal assessment strategies to evaluate and ensure the continuous intellectual, social, and physical development of the learner.

INTASC

Principle #2

Knowledge of Human Development and Learning: The teacher understands how children learn and develop, and can provide learning opportunities that support their intellectual, social, and personal development.

applied, depending on the type of student misbehavior and on your overall philosophy with regard to discipline.

"My teacher said that if I disrupt the class one more time, she's putting your work number on speed dial."

Courtesy of Aaron Bacall, *The Lighter Side of Technology in Education*, p. 34. Copyright 2003 by Aaron Bacall. Reprinted by permission of Corwin Press Inc.

- **Preventive discipline** promotes positive behaviors, much like Clark's "55 rules" mentioned earlier in the chapter. When students learn how to show courtesy, model good behavior, and make eye contact, they learn how to behave according to their teachers' and classmates' expectations.

- **Supportive discipline,** in which teachers help students gain control through agreed-on signals, helps students channel their own behaviors productively. Your goal in these cases is not to control as much as to support students and encourage them to control themselves. For example, when you make eye contact with a student who is about to hit another student, this signals to the student that the behavior is inappropriate. When the student responds appropriately, it saves the student from having to be corrected.

- **Corrective discipline** requires correcting students' behavior if all other attempts at discipline have been exhausted. If corrective discipline is required, teachers or administrators must correct the behavior expeditiously using the school or classroom guidelines and consequences with which students are familiar. The purpose is to correct, not to intimidate or punish. If you correct the behavior in a calm and even voice, students tend to respond favorably. However, when you lose your temper or yell at students, the situation often worsens.

Prior to the 1997 Individuals with Disabilities Act, teachers often disciplined students on individualized education programs (IEPs) differently from mainstream students. Complaints about students whose behaviors threatened teachers and staff led Congress to clarify the current law. In 1997, an amendment was added that stated that the only disciplinary procedure that applies exclusively to special education students is when teachers and administrators determine that long-term suspension or removal from school and placement in an alternative setting is required. Proponents of the amendment stated that a discipline policy is for all students and to meet federal standards, schools need a humane and just administration of discipline that respects and protects all students' rights to a free and public education. The plan must not just correct problems resulting from student disruption, it must prevent it and support positive behavior (Charles, 1999).

You need to understand what actually causes a misbehavior, how you can cool students down when they do get upset, and what to do to prevent a situation from getting worse. Many beginning teachers with little experience may walk into a situation or use language that could trigger misbehavior. A sound piece of advice to keep in mind at all times is, "Think before you act or respond to any student."

Master Teacher Tips lists types of phrases teachers sometimes use that may cause more tension and make a bad situation worse:

1. *Interfering phrases* such as "Here's what you have to do . . ." or "It would be best if you . . ."

2. *Accusing phrases* such as "You started the mess . . ." or "You never listen."

3. *Categorizing phrases* such as, "You're always trying to get attention."

These phrases may be true, but they will not yield the positive results (DeBruyn, 2001).

No matter how difficult conflict may feel, such situations are learning experiences that will help you in the long run. In *Back Off, Cool Down, Try Again: Teaching Students How to Control Aggressive Behavior*, Rockwell (1995) identifies five "Characteristics of Effective Behavior Managers" that encourage teachers to do the following:

1. Respect their own strengths and weaknesses as seriously as they respect those of their students.

2. Understand that social-emotional growth is a never-ending process.

3. Clearly communicate rules, goals, and expectations to students.

4. Respond to behaviors consistently and predictably.

5. Discriminate between issues of responsibility and problem solving.

Using these strategies is a good starting point for addressing some student misbehaviors. Here is some advice from practicing teachers (*NEA Today*, 2002–2005):

- One high school teacher tells of receiving a phone call from a neighbor who heard a group of students arguing. They heard one of the students say that she was going to damage the teacher's house because of a situation in school. The teacher explains: "I talked with the school psychologist, the principal, and the girl's mother about what I had heard. I talked with the mother and assured her that I had no grudge against her. It all worked out and I ending up forming a relationship with the student."

- A middle school teacher tells of a situation in which a sixth-grade student lost control in class. The teacher explains: "He threw chairs and picked one up to throw at me. I maintained eye contact and spoke calmly. I didn't say 'Put it down,' or 'Don't throw that chair'; instead, I said, 'Think carefully, I understand that you are angry and hurt.' I kept talking calmly until he put it down."

- A third-grade teacher talks about a student who needs frequent reassurance and support. The teacher states, "I have a student who is taller than me with a lot of emotional problems. Whenever she loses it she threatens me. I look up right in her eyes and call her by name. I say, 'What can I do to help you? I am on your side.' This calms her down. I tell her I love and respect her and expect her to treat me with the same respect."

Each of these stories shares a common element: All of these teachers prevented a situation from getting worse. These provide good examples of how putting theory into practice can be effective, a skill that takes time to develop, as English teacher Margaret Metzger explains in a letter of advice to prospective teachers:

Dear New Teachers,
No one is born knowing how to control 125 adolescents for five hours a day and teach curriculum at the same time. Learning to discipline takes years. Mostly, it's trial and error. Nothing works all the time, and what works well in one class has no effect on another.

However, over time, our repertoire of responses grows; we learn what we can tolerate; we gain a sense of timing; we make alliances within a school. Trust me, you will improve.

When I began teaching, I struggled to control my classes. I didn't understand the difference between classroom discipline and classroom management. (Metzger, 2002).

Learning to become a *manager* of your classroom will come with experience. Sometimes, however, students have issues that cannot be addressed by traditional administrative corrective discipline. In these cases, you need to identify these students and help them and their families get the help they need.

GETTING STUDENTS THE HELP THEY NEED

As a classroom teacher, your main objective is to keep the classroom safe and productive for the entire community of learners. When students misbehave continually, teachers may notify the principal or the parents. Depending on the school protocol and the classroom teachers, the response may depend on how many misbehaviors will be tolerated. Parents often want to know what their child did and what they can do to prevent the behavior. You need to be prepared to meet with parents and have a report ready that outlines the issues, as well as have a list of suggestions to change the behavior. If this cannot be achieved through individual intervention with parents, the school may have to intervene and provide more individualized attention to the student.

● **Student Referrals**   When you have students who are persistently disruptive and you have exhausted all behavior management strategies, you need to take the next step. To start the process that will get students the individual support they need, you must first meet with the school principal or department chair to apprise them of the situation. From there, a meeting with other teachers, guidance counselors, and school psychologists may be arranged. Figure 11.6 on page 356 outlines questions you need to ask yourself to determine your response to a situation that requires disciplining a student.

Once you have met with teachers, parents, administrators, and school counselors, you can then formally request additional support for the student. In some states this is called a **student referral process**. As part of this process, you must write a report providing specific details about the situation that warranted initiating the referral. A dated log that clearly notes the date, time, and location of the incidents as they arise is a valuable tool. Record what the student did and how you responded to the behavior. This type of information should be kept in all discipline cases, but it can be especially important when meeting about students who repeatedly act out as a way of illustrating specific problems or patterns of behavior. It is important to depersonalize the situation and record only the facts.

● **Enlisting the Help of Parents**   Communicating with parents is critical. Be prepared, however, because often parents view their children's behavior differently from the teacher. A best-case scenario for students with behavioral issues is when parents and teachers work together. Parents may have certain expectations from teachers about how they want their child treated in school. They will also have concerns about their child's progress. Parents want to know answers to questions such as the following:

"Will my child be successful?"

"How does the system work?"

"Why do I feel as if I'm standing alone?"

"Will teachers listen to me?"

"Am I doing the right thing?"

"What will the teacher think of me?" (Benjamin & Sanchez, 1996)

By communicating honestly and compassionately with parents whose children exhibit inappropriate behaviors in school, you will have a better chance of getting their children the help needed to ensure success in school. In some cases, students may be involved in these conferences, depending on school policy and the teacher's expectation for the meeting. If parents do not speak English or have difficulty getting to school to meet with school officials, it can affect the successful resolution of the problem. Schools need to access all the available resources to provide the support a student requires.

● **Advocating**   Beginning and experienced teachers often complain that it takes a long time for students to get the help they need. Students with serious problems may be left in

INTASC

Principle #9

Professional Commitment and Responsibility: The teacher is a reflective practitioner who continually evaluates the effects of his/her choices and actions on others (students, parents, and other professionals in the learning community) and who actively seeks out opportunities to grow professionally.

INTASC

Principle #10

Partnerships: The teacher fosters relationships with school colleagues, parents, and agencies in the larger community to support students' learning and well-being.

FIGURE 11.6

Things to Think about Before Disciplining a Student

- Who is the student?

  Does this student have a prearranged plan when disruptive (e.g., sent to guidance, principal, or resource or learning center classroom)?

  Is this the first offense or is this repeated misbehavior?

  Does this student have a special need that has not been addressed?

  Are there other adults that need to be notified when this student is disruptive?

- What rule did the student break?

  Is it a major offense (e.g., hitting someone or possessing a weapon)?

  Is it a minor offense (e.g., chewing gum or wearing a hat)?

  Is it related to academic work (e.g., not doing homework or cheating)?

  Is it related to work habits (e.g., not listening in class)?

- What did the student specifically do or say?

- Is this misbehavior appropriate for the student's age?

- Where did the misbehavior take place?

  In the classroom?

  On the playground, in a hallway, in the cafeteria, en route to class?

  Off school grounds but near school?

- Is this behavior a common occurrence?

  For this student?

  For others in the school?

- Do you have personal feelings about this student?

  Have you interacted positively or negatively before this?

  Do you know this student at all?

- What are your legal rights when dealing with disruptive students?

  State and local guidelines for restraining students, searching lockers, etc.?

  School policies related to alcohol, drugs, weapons?

  Students with educational plans?

Source: C. M. Pelletier, *A Handbook of Techniques and Strategies for Coaching Student Teachers,* p. 118. (Boston: Allyn & Bacon, 2004). Copyright © 2004 by Pearson Education. Reprinted by permission of the publisher.

classrooms because the funding to move them to another school or a private setting is not available. Money is always a factor in providing services to students. For the benefit of students who need support and for students who are affected by their classmates' disruptions, you need to be an advocate for students who need help. This requires getting to know how the system works in your school and district and where the funding comes from, which may help you find opportunities and possible solutions for all of your students.

Some districts require that a **building-based support team (BBST)** be created to review referral requests and analyze options for classroom teachers. These problem-solving teams work with parents, teachers, and administrators to brainstorm possible solutions for teachers before the student is formally referred. It is the last effort to solve the problem in the school.

If teachers have tried every means possible to help students who are behaving inappropriately in school, all to no avail, they need to realize that they have not failed. Some students need and deserve special assistance. Districts are required to provide that support to families and their children.

The purpose of schooling is to provide a safe learning environment that holds high standards for learning, self-esteem, and knowledge. Teachers play an enormous role in the lives of students and therefore should be well respected by students and the school community.

LORI, STUDENT TEACHER

THINK ABOUT THIS:
How do teachers keep their classrooms safe and focused on learning? Why is it important to have a system for recording information when students behave inappropriately in class?

SHARE and COMPARE:
When you visit schools, ask for samples of documents they use to record student behaviors. Compare your samples with those that your classmates have collected. Are they different? If so, how? What are the most critical components of these documents?

HOW CAN INQUIRY HELP SOLVE CLASSROOM MANAGEMENT PROBLEMS?

Inquiry is a systematic process of data collection used to answer specific questions. Teachers often apply these data to help explain and resolve classroom or behavior management problems. As a beginning teacher, when informed by data, you will be able to learn more about your own practices and what works best with your students. Teachers use inquiry to discover strategies for handling different situations. For example, did students seem to get more out of their lessons when they worked in small groups after the initial instruction, or were they best served when assigned independent reading following instruction? While this type of research may not translate into more formal studies, it is a useful tool.

REFLECTING ON PRACTICE

Teachers can make a difference in shaping their classroom environment when they take time to reflect on the issues that arise in the classroom, collect data on a variety of events and situations, and analyze that data to guide their own practice. Reflection on practice takes time and energy. But when teachers make this reflection a priority, they have a better chance of improving the classroom environment and ensuring that all children will learn.

Reflection can take many forms. Some teachers use journals to record details of their day; others participate in **peer coaching**, an arrangement that allows two teachers to work together, sometimes observing each other's classroom, and exchanging feedback. Some teachers use feedback from administrators or curriculum coaches to improve their classroom instruction. The common denominator in all of these forms of reflection is the use of the feedback and information to inform teachers' approaches toward managing their classes and changing practices that may not be effective.

● **Keeping a Journal**   Education programs often require student teachers to keep journals during their student teaching or their field observation courses because they are such a valuable and reliable tool. *Reflective journals* or *inquiry journals* are more than just a log

INTASC

Principle #1

Knowledge of Subject Matter: The teacher understands the central concepts, tools of inquiry, and structures of the subject being taught and can create learning experiences that make these aspects of subject matter meaningful for students.

INTASC

Principle #9

Professional Commitment and Responsibility: The teacher is a reflective practitioner who continually evaluates the effects of his/her choices and actions on others (students, parents, and other professionals in the learning community) and who actively seeks out opportunities to grow professionally.

listing dates of particular events or misbehaviors; they are a record of questions, feelings, problems, dilemmas, and other concerns that arise as they relate to a certain student or classroom issues. It is important that student or beginning teachers record their assumptions, beliefs, and thoughts about teaching. This important exercise allows them to see how their own thinking has evolved based on their experiences over the course of a semester. As one student teacher stated at the end of the semester after rereading all of his journal entries, "Did I think *that* at the beginning of the semester? Did I write that? Wow! I have changed!"

● **Peer Coaching**   Inquiry does not have to be a solitary activity and often is more interesting in pairs. Peer coaching is often used when there are problem areas that teachers would like to improve on. In many cases, for beginning teachers, the problems they want to improve relate to classroom management issues. Peer coaching sessions are set up for a prescribed number of meetings. During these meetings, peers share ideas and give each other feedback based on their observations.

At the New Teacher Center in Santa Cruz (Moir, 2003) teachers use an approach similar to peer coaching. Teachers use a Collaborative Assessment Tool to organize meetings between mentor teachers and first-year teachers in the required mentor program. This tool contains a series of questions ("What is working?" "What isn't working?" and so on) that helps guide new teachers' reflections on their practices and uses feedback from their "collaborative conversation" to change their routines or approaches to teaching. The mentor teachers also reflect on their role and meet with other mentors to exchange feedback on how they can provide more support to new teachers. Their goal is to have new teachers *reflect* and come to the insights themselves, rather than having mentors *tell* them what they can improve on. The mentors then offer the teachers support by helping them determine how to best improve any difficult situations.

● **District Evaluation**   Journal writing and collaborative discussion are both based on teachers' reaching their own insights about how to improve situations in the classroom. These insights are based on measurable data as opposed to just feelings or intuition. The

Peer coaching allows your students to share ideas, to give and receive feedback, and to improve upon problem areas with the help of other students. What life lessons can children learn from serving as a peer coach?

next approach relies on district evaluation and observation to *tell* the teacher what is and what is not working.

A teacher who continually sends students to the front office or refers students for special services may need more support. In scheduled observations, principals or department chairs will observe firsthand how the teacher handles the class. They then provide recommendations for change, which may be in the form of a written report or a personal meeting outlining helpful changes. This type of feedback can be very instructive.

Unlike reflective approaches that allow teachers to develop insights and implement changes over time, positive district evaluations can be a condition of employment. If teachers are not able to organize time and space for effective learning, and if they are unable to keep misbehaviors at a minimum, they may not be rehired. Teaching academic subjects and testing for learning outcomes is clearly the objective of all schools; ensuring that these expectations are met in a safe environment is the job of all teachers.

USING A SYSTEMATIC APPROACH TO PROBLEM SOLVING

The first step in your inquiry process as a new teacher will be to determine your own beliefs and values in a systematic way. By keeping a journal of your thoughts, you will amass evidence and rationales for why you think the way you do. As you work with other teachers and share ideas, their thoughts and beliefs will play a role in your belief system as well.

While inquiry is not used exclusively to deal with problems or behavioral issues, new teachers find that these are the most pressing issues that they want to resolve. As you begin the inquiry process, you start by identifying a dilemma or problem that needs to be addressed. The next step involves creating a question to study that will improve your management or discipline skills. There are many ways to collect data to provide evidence for the question. Observations, interviews, surveys, videotapes and audiotapes, student work, and tests all can be used to answer your question. Some examples of questions student teachers have used include the following:

- How does behavior intervention change a student's achievement?

- Does motivation and on-task behavior improve when an incentive program is used?

- How do classroom organization and the implementation of a variety of instructional strategies affect the behavior of students in the classroom? (Friedman, 2003).

These questions help you focus your research and allow you to learn something new about a specific aspect of your teaching. It is important to frame your questions in a way that produces data that can be easily organized and analyzed (Shagoury Hubbard & Miller, 2003).

Consider the case of a student teacher using an inquiry approach to solve behavior problems in her classroom. Her question, "What are the social and academic impacts of using the guided reading approach with two first-grade special education students?" was framed to allow her to see how successful her students were in class. She thought that perhaps their inability to read well was affecting their social interaction with other first graders and causing misbehavior.

Once she had formulated her question, she selected a variety of data sources that would provide her with information about the question. A sample of the data sources she used included student interviews, teacher interviews, high-frequency word lists, an oral retelling checklist, a writing rubric, a conversational speaking checklist, and an oral reading rubric. Results and analysis of her data proved her hypothesis correct. Using a new reading method increased student success in all areas she measured and, in turn, boosted students' self-confidence and reduced the incidence of misbehaviors.

What does this all mean? Teachers need to take time to collect and interpret data based on classroom practices and the social context in which it was collected. To aid in the interpretation of data, you can consider different ways to present it, such as written reports or graphic depictions such as line graphs, pie charts, bar graphs, and tables. However you choose to present it, your analysis of the data will allow you to identify practices that are working and those that need to be changed.

I N T A S C

Principle #9

Professional Commitment and Responsibility: The teacher is a reflective practitioner who continually evaluates the effects of his/her choices and actions on others (students, parents, and other professionals in the learning community) and who actively seeks out opportunities to grow professionally.

USING DATA TO CREATE A POSITIVE LEARNING ENVIRONMENT FOR ALL STUDENTS

Effective teachers understand that inquiry into practice is ongoing, as they are constantly learning from their students, their colleagues, and their own experiences (Hobson, 1996). The information they gather empowers them to make informed decisions about various aspects of their teaching. Because much of their research is based on their classrooms, teachers have the opportunity to respond to their students in a social context.

You have learned how teachers can use inquiry and data analysis to measure the success of teaching practices in the classroom; inquiry can also be used to measure social and emotional issues as well. Classroom research can be used to make recommendations to administrators to improve school conditions for students and teachers. Teachers who can support requests and recommendations with data have a much better chance of being heard.

Who am I? What do I believe?

Each and every child has the ability to learn. It is my responsibility as a teacher to determine how that child will learn. I feel that experimentation is the key to uncovering that child's secret.

ANDREA, ELEMENTARY STUDENT TEACHER

THINK ABOUT THIS:

Think about some of the teachers you have had throughout your academic career—good teachers as well as those who were not so good. How do you think their beliefs and values shaped how they applied discipline as well as the overall classroom environment? Think of two examples that illustrate your response. Knowing what you know now, how might these teachers have used their past experiences to inform their current practices?

SHARE and COMPARE:

Compare your recollections with your classmates. How did their experiences compare with yours? Compare how you believe your belief systems will shape your teaching style.

FINAL THOUGHTS

Surveys have indicated that classroom management and discipline are two key challenges that face classroom teachers today. How teachers take on this task will depend on their dispositions and belief systems. If they are able to show respect to all students and if they believe that all students can learn, this will set a tone and standard for classroom achievement.

Teachers need to coordinate a number of factors to effectively manage their classrooms. How they organize their classroom, establish routines to begin and end lessons, and establish and implement rules, rewards, and consequences will all help shape the classroom dynamics.

Think about how theory influences practice and how practice informs theory. As you begin to think about becoming a teacher, pay attention to how teachers you observe set up their classrooms for learning as well as how they implement behavior management strategies.

What you personally believe about teaching, learning, and students' abilities will affect how you organize your space and create a learning environment for your students. Using inquiry as a way to gather information will help you analyze what works best and what doesn't work in the classroom. By using inquiry and analysis, you will create a tool that will help you solve classroom management problems that will benefit you and your students.

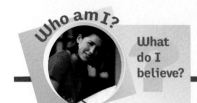

REFLECTIONS

Professional Plan for Classroom and Behavior Management

1. Three things I learned from this chapter about organizing a classroom and managing behavior.

2. Two things in this chapter that I would like to learn more about are:

   a. _____

   b. _____

3. I plan to investigate these two areas and learn more about classroom and behavior management by:

   _____ Reading the following book club choices

   _____ Reading sources referenced in the chapter that interest me

   _____ Interviewing several teachers about their classroom management and discipline strategies

   _____ Reading the selections listed in the Read On section

   _____ Exploring the websites listed in the Log On section

   _____ Observing several classrooms and taking notes on the specific strategies teachers use that work for them

4. I will include the following in my Touch the Future portfolio:

   _____ Responses to Who Am I? activities

   _____ A brief essay on my thoughts about Problems to Possibilities

   _____ A brief response to Education Matters

   _____ Responses to the Observation Guide

   _____ Other (materials assigned by your instructor):

SUMMARY

What Are the Dispositions of Caring Teachers?

- Teachers who respect all students create socially just and democratic classrooms.
- Teachers who believe all students can learn.
- Teachers who are able to create democratic classroom, instill high standards, and adhere to federal and state standards.

How Do Effective Teachers Manage Their Classrooms?

- Designing a plan for using time and space to enhance learning.
- Getting to know their students and use their strengths.
- Establishing routines, rules, rewards, and consequences.
- Using time management strategies.

What Are Different Approaches to Behavior Management?

- Theory informs practice from many traditional models and research studies.
- Practice informs theory from a variety of practitioner models.

How Do Teachers Respond to Inappropriate Behavior in the Classroom?

- Preventing misbehavior is easier when the teacher understands why students misbehave.
- Teachers need to record misbehaviors, question their responses, communicate with parents, and refer students for extra support when necessary.

How Can Inquiry Help Solve Classroom Management Problems?

- Reflecting on practice includes journal writing, peer coaching, and mentoring, as well as feed-back from district evaluators.
- A systematic approach to problem solving requires a question, data sources, and results to be analyzed.
- Teachers can use inquiry results to create positive learning environments and share recom-mendations with other teachers and administrators.

Visit the **Touch the Future . . . Teach!** Companion Website at www.ablongman.com/diaz for additional opportunities.

KEY WORDS

CONCEPT REVIEW

1. Explain how a teacher builds a community based on trust and democratic principles and why it is important.

2. Identify state and national initiatives that support all children learning.

3. Recall philosophy statements written by student teachers.

4. Summarize classroom management strategies for organizing a classroom.

5. List ways a teacher can save time to maximize instruction through classroom routines.

6. State rules, rewards, and consequences used in caring classrooms.

7. Paraphrase major discipline theories for behavior management.

8. Describe ways to avoid discipline problems.

9. Discuss common classroom misbehaviors and how to respond to them.

10. Reflect on steps to think about before disciplining a student.

11. Explain how to use inquiry to solve your own classroom problems.

TOUCH THE FUTURE . . .

Read On

The Essential 55
Ron Clark (New York: Hyperion, 2003)
A firsthand approach to motivating students in urban schools, by the 2001 Disney Teacher of the Year.

Dreamkeepers: Successful Teachers of African American Children
Gloria Ladson-Billings (San Francisco: Jossey-Bass, 1994)
Discusses how to create wonderful democratic caring communities within an inner-city school and offers an awareness of working with African American children using questions and strategies.

Positive Discipline: A Teacher's A–Z Guide
Jane Nelsen, Linda Escobar, Kate Ortolano, Roslyn Duffy, and Deborah Owen-Sohocki (New York: Random House, 2001)
Provides the positive discipline fundamentals as well as an A–Z guide of common problems a teacher may encounter in schools and specific strategies for dealing with them.

Log On

You Can Handle Them All
www.disciplinehelp.com
A helpful website providing tips and resources in discipline and behavior management; information is provided for misbehaviors at school as well as at home.

Tips for Successful Discipline
www.pdkintl.org/kappan/k0209met.htm
Margaret Metzger's full letter of advice to new teachers; she provides insight and practical strategies, especially for secondary teachers.

About.com
www.k-6educators.about.com
Offers information and sample lessons for educators on all topics, including classroom management.

University of Manitoba
http://home.cc.umanitoba.ca/~fboutin/frame.html
Educators France Boutin and Chris Chinien offer an interactive website on classroom management. Visitors can read about real classroom management issues, write about how they would handle the situation, read how a professional did handle the situation, and then reflect on both.

Write On

"As a new teacher, it is important to recognize and accept that I will make mistakes. I cannot let fear of failure stand in the way of trying out creative ways to teach my students. A teacher cannot make a child learn, but a good teacher should spark something within a child to make him or her want to learn."

—Stephanie, Student Teacher

In your journal, write a short explanation of what this quote means to you. How does it relate to classroom management and behavior issues discussed in this chapter? How can a teacher create ways for a student to want to learn?

Linking
Theory to
Practice

OBSERVATION GUIDE

TEACH: LINKING THEORY TO PRACTICE

Objective: To observe effective classroom management strategies

School (use code name): _____   Observer: _____

Grade Level: _____   Date: _____

Subject(s): _____   Time In: _____   Time Out: _____

Directions: In this observation and interview activity, you will consider some of the classroom management and behavior management topics you have read about in this chapter. Ask to speak with the teacher after class to follow up your observation. Use these questions as a guide and create some of your own, using this chapter to assist you. Write a brief summary of your findings. You may submit your paper to your instructor, as well as include it in your Touch the Future portfolio. You may choose to complete this observation with a variety of teachers and write a comparison paper.

1. How is the physical space in the classroom organized? Draw a floor plan and attach it to your essay.

2. What are the routines for passing in papers? Leaving your seat? Answering questions? Attendance? How well do they work for this teacher?

3. Would you describe this environment as a caring community of learners? Why or why not?

4. Do you notice any routines for opening and closing lessons? Explain.

5. Does the teacher appear confident, competent, and caring? How is this expressed with students?

Interview Questions after the Observation

1. Can you explain your philosophy of behavior management to me? Why do you use this approach?

2. Can you explain why you set up your room and your routines this way? Did your decision relate to reducing behavior problems?

3. What is the most difficult behavior you have had to handle? How did you do it?

4. What advice do you have for me about classroom organization and behavior management as I begin my teaching program?

Connecting with INTASC: Principle 5

Classroom Motivation and Management: The teacher uses an understanding of individual and group motivation and behavior to create a learning environment that encourages positive social interaction, active engagement in learning, and self-motivation.

What strategies does the teacher use to create a positive learning environment in the classroom? Are all students actively involved in lessons, or do some get "lost" as a result of misbehavior? How does the teacher motivate students to participate actively, and how do these efforts help control the learning environment of the classroom?

12

Technology and Teaching

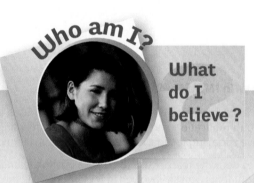

Who am I?

What do I believe?

THINK ABOUT THIS:

Technology shapes our lives in many different ways. Computers in particular play an increasingly important role in our lives. Think about how different your life would be without access to cell phones, the World Wide Web, or cable or satellite television. All of these are computer-based technologies. Think about getting treatment at a hospital. What medical technologies depend on computers?

> "But what . . . is it good for?"
>
> Engineer at IBM, 1968, commenting on the microchip

Just as computers are changing our day-to-day lives, they are also affecting the educational system at all levels. Computer-assisted instruction is common in many schools. Teachers and students have access to extraordinary information resources via the Internet and World Wide Web. Students with special needs can use adaptive or assistive technology to help them read and write. What role will computer technology play in your work as a teacher? How important is the use of this and other technologies for effective teaching?

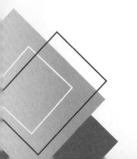

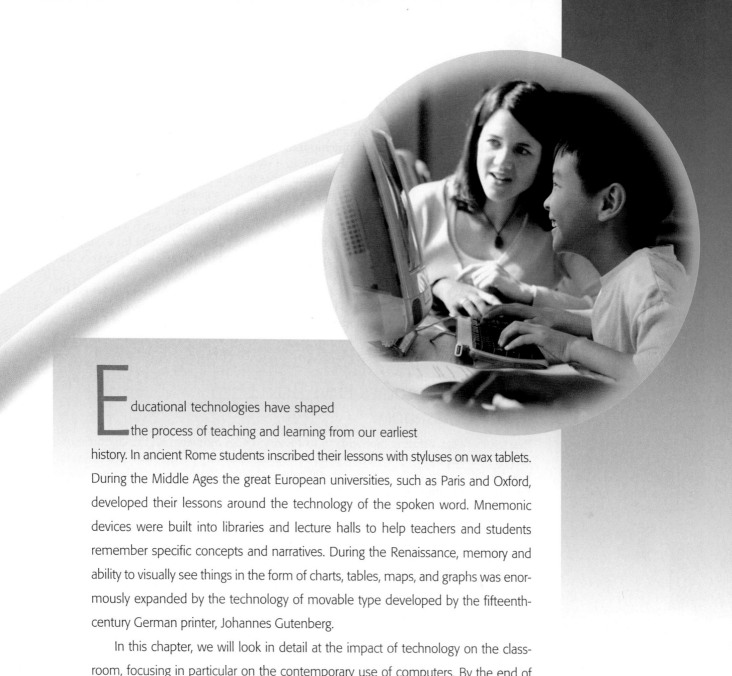

Educational technologies have shaped the process of teaching and learning from our earliest history. In ancient Rome students inscribed their lessons with styluses on wax tablets. During the Middle Ages the great European universities, such as Paris and Oxford, developed their lessons around the technology of the spoken word. Mnemonic devices were built into libraries and lecture halls to help teachers and students remember specific concepts and narratives. During the Renaissance, memory and ability to visually see things in the form of charts, tables, maps, and graphs was enormously expanded by the technology of movable type developed by the fifteenth-century German printer, Johannes Gutenberg.

In this chapter, we will look in detail at the impact of technology on the classroom, focusing in particular on the contemporary use of computers. By the end of this chapter you will be able to answer the following key questions:

Key Questions

1. What technologies have been used in the classroom?
2. How do television and the Internet shape and influence children?
3. How can computers change the teaching environment?
4. What should teachers know about technology?
5. How widely do teachers and students use technology?

In his book *The Children's Machine: Rethinking Schools in the Age of the Computer*, Seymour Papert (1993) proposes a thought experiment in which he asks the reader to imagine a group of surgeons transported in a time machine from a hundred years ago to the present. Visiting the operating room of a contemporary hospital, most of what the surgeons would see would be totally new to them. In general, it would be almost impossible for them to function with the new technologies and techniques that are essential to modern medicine.

Papert then asks the reader to imagine that, instead of a group of surgeons, a group of teachers are transported from the past into the present. If they were to visit a classroom, most of what they would see would be familiar. If they were asked to teach a basic history lesson, or a reading lesson, most could probably do a credible job. Except for a couple of technologies such as television, videotape players, and computers, there would be very little in the classroom that was different from their classrooms in the past.

Changes in technology that occur in education can have a profound impact on the work of teachers in the classroom. The introduction of computers into the classroom, for example, represents a defining moment in the experience of teaching.

INTASC

Principle #6

Communication Skills: The teacher uses knowledge of effective verbal, nonverbal, and media communication techniques to foster active inquiry, collaboration, and supportive interaction in the classroom.

WHAT TECHNOLOGIES HAVE BEEN USED IN THE CLASSROOM?

Every society has defining moments in its history. These moments set the character of a culture and shape its future. In European culture the discovery of what was then called the New World was one of these moments. Of course, the New World was certainly not new to the native populations who already lived here.

MOVABLE TYPE AND PRINTING AS AN EDUCATIONAL TECHNOLOGY

In the history of education, the introduction of movable type during the late fifteenth century by printers such as Johannes Gutenberg was another such moment. Moveable type made it possible to produce inexpensive and precisely reproduced books. Books had, in fact, existed for many centuries in medieval European culture, but they were handwritten books—not only expensive to reproduce, but often subject to considerable variation and error.

The New York Times
expect the world®
nytimes.com

Themes of the Times

Expand your knowledge of the concepts discussed in this chapter by reading current and historical articles from the *New York Times* by visiting the "Themes of the Times" section of the Companion Website.

The Gutenberg revolution represented a technology that transformed education and learning. Inexpensive books made it possible to educate greater numbers of people. It was no longer necessary to memorize information when you were trying to learn something. The reference book was literally invented at this time. The Gutenberg revolution brought about a revolutionary reinvention of the meaning of text and what constituted a book (Eisenstein, 1983).

The invention of movable type and modern printing made possible the introduction of new types of learning materials. In Johannn Amos Comenius's *Orbis Sensualium Pictus,* first published in 1658, for example, detailed illustrations were integrated with virtually every major concept. Thus, a pictorial subtext was provided for each concept included in the work. According to Eisenstein, "Within the Commonwealth of Learning it became increasingly fashionable to adopt the ancient Chinese maxim that a single picture was more valuable than many words" (1983, p. 37). The modern illustrated textbook had been created.

THE TEXTBOOK AS AN EDUCATIONAL TECHNOLOGY

As discussed in Chapter 6, textbooks such as reading and spelling books came into widespread use throughout Europe at the end of the seventeenth century. Books like the *New*

England Primer were mass-produced, making it possible for textbooks to be used in new ways. For example, they could be used to teach religious values to an entire population of learners. In the case of Noah Webster's 1781 three-volume *The Grammatical Institutes of the English Language* (the first volume of which was later known as the *Blue-Back Speller*), they could be used to teach political values to a new nation.

As the most important educational technology of the early modern period, textbooks created "a new discursive space"—quite literally a new way to teach and to learn. Textbooks were organized from beginning to end (Provenzo, 2000). Their pages were numbered. They had tables of contents, indexes, and special features, including illustrations and highlighted sections. Over the years, these features, which define the technology of the textbook, have become more sophisticated.

Illustrations, figures, and special features in contemporary textbooks promote active learning

TOYS AS TECHNOLOGIES FOR LEARNING

Historically books, and more specifically textbooks, have been the single most important technology to be used in education. Other technologies, however, have also been used in classrooms, as shown in the timeline of instructional technologies in Figure 12.1 on page 371. In 1692, the English philosopher John Locke (1632–1704) discussed the use of educational toys such as a forerunner to the alphabet blocks in *Some Thoughts on Education*. In the early nineteenth century, the German educator and founder of the concept of kindergarten Frederick Froebel (1782–1852) introduced a series of educational toys called "Gifts" and "Occupations." These toys included several systems of blocks, parquetry tiles, weaving exercises, and even a primitive set of Tinkertoys (Provenzo & Brett, 2000). Italian physician Maria Montessori (1870–1952) introduced similar types of "hands-on" learning materials that were used in what came to be known as the **Montessori method.**

OTHER EDUCATIONAL TECHNOLOGIES

There are many different educational technologies that have been used as tools for teachers since the nineteenth century. Some are extremely simple.

- **Slates and Chalkboards** Slates and chalkboards were introduced during the early nineteenth century. The chalkboard is seemingly a trivial technology, but in fact much more valuable than it may at first appear. Chalkboards are cheap, easy to use, flexible, virtually foolproof, and fairly unobtrusive. They are widely used by teachers—much like the textbook—because they fulfill the needs of instruction in the classroom. As the educational researcher and policy analyst Larry Cuban explains, "The tools that teachers have added to their repertoire over time (e.g., chalkboards and textbooks) have been simple, durable, flexible, and responsive to teacher-defined problems in meeting the demands of daily instruction" (Cuban, 1986, p. 58).

- **Early Media** New educational technologies frequently have a revolutionary effect on education and learning. Movable type and printing are examples of this fact. Some new educational technologies turn out to be less important than their early advocates anticipated. At the beginning of the twentieth century, for example, many educators believed

BUILDING ON EDUCATIONAL FOUNDATIONS

Appropriate Use of Computers

Computers and related technologies have the potential to profoundly change us as human beings. An increasingly important ethical issue is how much we should allow computers to change who and what we are. This is a particularly sensitive issue in reference to people with special needs.

Almost all of us have seen science fiction programs on TV or in the movies in which characters are able to do things using technologies that seem unbelievable to us, but that's why the programs are called *science fiction*. Like so much in science fiction, what is predicted in old science fiction programs was not that far off from what has actually happened (think about cloning, for example). Such devices are already under development. Should they be used? The answer is not as clear as you might think.

For example, cochlear implants are becoming very common. A cochlear implant is a device that is surgically implanted in the inner ear and activated by a device worn outside the ear. It is not a hearing aid. In other words, it does not make sound louder or clearer. Instead, it bypasses damaged parts of the user's auditory system and directly stimulates the auditory nerve, making it possible for the person to hear. The technology is still limited and provides less than perfect results.

Critics in the Deaf community have raised numerous objections to cochlear implants, arguing that children may grow up dependent on the medical community to maintain a device that can easily become obsolete. They also argue that deafness should not be considered a disability to be "fixed" by a

mechanical device, but rather just a different way of living. For some people in the Deaf community, what may seem like a positive use of technology to help people hear is an expensive, imperfect technology that interferes with their community and roboticizes and controls human beings.

The argument can be made that we use technologies such as hearing aids, so why not cochlear implants? If we object to devices such as these, why not object to eyeglasses, or crutches and wheelchairs for people who cannot walk? But let's take the argument a bit further. Hans Moravec, one of the country's leading robotics researchers, predicts that at some point in the next 20 to 30 years we will be able to download a human consciousness into a computer. Suppose that this does indeed become possible. Then it would theoretically be possible to transfer a paralyzed individual's consciousness into a robot, thus allowing the person to move around. Would the consciousness still be human?

In the novel *The Ship that Sang,* a terribly deformed newborn baby's brain is connected to a spaceship's computer before the baby dies. The spaceship is then sent into deep space, where it is navigated with the help of a human pilot. A problem arises when the spaceship's consciousness falls in love with her pilot. Science fiction, to be sure, but perhaps a brief glimpse into a possible future.

What do you think? Are computer technologies neutral? What concerns should we have, as prospective teachers, about this issue?

INTASC

Principle #6

Communication Skills: The teacher uses knowledge of effective verbal, nonverbal, and media communication techniques to foster active inquiry, collaboration, and supportive interaction in the classroom.

that the gramophone and records would revolutionize learning by bringing music and the spoken word of plays and great speeches into every classroom. In the 1920s and 1930s, educational radio was the rage. Educational films and filmstrips were very popular during the 1940s and 1950s as was educational television in the 1950s and 1960s. While useful, none of these technologies brought about the revolution in education their supporters anticipated.

INSTRUCTIONAL TECHNOLOGY

The concept of **instructional technology** was well established in the schools by the early 1950s, when it was thought that film and television would revolutionize instruction. Instructional technology did not meet the expectations of many educators, however. Why not? As new media such as film and television pervaded popular culture and entertain-

FIGURE 12.1

Timeline of Instructional Technology

1816	The first photographic negative is made on paper.
1877	Thomas Alva Edison invents the phonograph.
1890s	Silent films are made available commercially.
1895	The Italian inventor Guglielmo Marconi sends the first radio transmission.
1904	The first modern audiovisual department is begun by the St. Louis Public Schools. Objects from the Louisiana Purchase Exposition that had taken place in the same year in St. Louis were put on display.
1911	Edison releases a series of historical fims for use in the classroom. At about this time films begin to be introduced for use in a limited number of educational settings.
1912	The 16-mm film projector is introduced.
1920	Station KDKA in Pittsburgh goes on the air as the first commercial radio station in the United States.
1920s	Instructional technology begins to be introduced as a subject of study in teacher education programs in American colleges and universities.
1923	Vladimir Zworkin invents the technology for the television.
1933	Filmstrips are introduced at the Century of Progress Fair in Chicago.
1937	The technology for the xerographic machine or copier is invented.
1946	ENIAC, which many people consider the first modern computer, is built.
1948	Commercial television is introduced in the United States.
1951	Videotape is invented.
1968	The Children's Television Workshop creates the program *Sesame Street*.
1969	The Public Broadcasting System is established by Congress.
1973	The first personal computer, the Alto, is developed at the Xerox Palo Alto Research Center.
1977	Apple introduces its first microcomputer.
1984	CD-ROM players are introduced for computers.
1990	The protocol for the World Wide Web is developed by Tim Berners-Lee.
1993	The first widely used Internet browser, Mosaic, is released for use.

ment, their novelty for use in the classroom was lost. Cuban argues that by the mid-1980s, "radio, film and instructional television met only marginally most problems that teachers define as important" (Cuban, 1986, p. 67).

Perhaps part of the answer also lies in the fact that a large part of what is most important in classroom instruction has to do with what actually takes place between teacher and learner. This argument suggests that learning may involve a much more social and personal dimension—one in which new knowledge needs to be more than just transferred, as it often was through the instructional technologies.

Film and television were the dominant forms of instructional technology until the late 1970s and early 1980s. At that time, new technologies such as videotape and computers came into widespread use. DVDs followed a few years later. Each has become increasingly less expensive and sophisticated in the past 20 years. These are the technologies, besides the textbook, that you will make the greatest use of in your classroom. Many educators believe that they represent a revolution in teaching and learning similar to the one that took place after Johannes Gutenberg introduced modern printing at the end of the fifteenth century.

During the 1970s and 1980s and before the Internet became widespread, videocassette recorders (VCRs) served as technological innovations in the classroom. Teachers were able to customize their lessons with programs readily available on television. What sort of innovative technologies are used in classrooms today?

Others feel that these technologies—especially the computer—have been vastly overrated in terms of their potential impact on the classroom.

Think about your own life for a moment. What would it have been like without television, computers, or the Internet? How does television, as a form of media, shape and affect the lives of children you know? How do you think today's technologies affect students and the attitudes and knowledge they bring into the classroom?

Who am I?
What do I believe?

"Technology such as computers keeps me from doing what I do best as a teacher."

JUNIOR HIGH SCHOOL SOCIAL STUDIES TEACHER

THINK ABOUT THIS:

Technology, in the form of computers, can expand our potential as teachers. It can also limit our effectiveness by introducing another layer of complexity into the classroom. When is the use of computers in the classroom desirable? When does it serve as a distraction?

SHARE and COMPARE:

Make a list of how computers can make teaching more effective. Make a second list of how they can interfere with what needs to be done. Talk to a classmate or friend about what you consider the best uses of computers in education and why. Talk about how computers and other technologies may potentially help you in your work as a teacher.

HOW DO TELEVISION AND THE INTERNET SHAPE AND INFLUENCE CHILDREN?

Television is so widespread in our culture that we tend to take it for granted. Commercially broadcast television was first introduced in 1948. If you have grandparents who are over 70 years old, they grew up without television. Their world growing up would have been very different from that of most children today. They would have played more in their neighborhoods with other children, they would have been involved in different types of activities, and they probably would have known much less about the world.

TELEVISION AS CULTURE

Television creates an extraordinary window with which to view the world. Theorist Neil Postman argues that television has, in fact, become our culture—that it is our main source of knowledge. It is the single thing that we share with each other more than anything else (Postman, 1984). Postman's point is well

Courtesy of Aaron Bacall, *The Lighter Side of Technology in Education*, p. 2. Copyright 2003 by Aaron Bacall. Reprinted by permission of Corwin Press Inc.

taken. Not every child knows who Teddy Roosevelt was or when the Civil War was fought, but they probably do know who Ronald McDonald is or what the Eiffel Tower looks like. This is a new type of literacy, not so much based in traditional texts, but instead in visual and auditory sources—ones that are often linked to advertising and consumption.

Television is universal in our culture. In 1999, 98.2% of all households had a television. The average home had 2.4 televisions, and 67.5% of all households had a cable subscription. In 1999, 84.6% of all households had video recording and playback machines (VCRs). In 1980 only 1.1% of the same households had such devices (U.S. Census Bureau, 2000). No class, race, ethnic, or social group seems to be without television.

How much of a role does television play in the life of the average child? The typical child in the United States watches 3 to 4 hours of television every day. Television is the number one after-school activity for children 6 to 17 years old. Annually, children spend about 1,500 hours in front of the TV and 900 hours in the classroom. The average American child who has completed the sixth grade will have seen more than 100,000 acts of violence on TV, including 8,000 murders. The average child sees more than 20,000 commercials each year, and by age 21 will have viewed approximately 1 million commercials (Center for Media Education, 2002).

Television profoundly changes the experience of childhood. Children see many of the same programs as adults. Few secrets are kept from children anymore as a result of television. Explicit sexual references, violence, and megaconsumerism are a regular part of what children see on the screen. Some would argue that television has reduced the distance between the world of children and the world of adults (Postman, 1982; Winn, 1983).

BRINGING THE WORLD TO THE CHILD THROUGH TECHNOLOGY

If television has come to be a major force in the experience of our culture, specifically for children, then the Internet and the World Wide Web are similarly an increasingly important force. The origins of the Internet can be traced back to the 1960s and government networks established by the military. Its widespread use, however, was a result of the introduction of the World Wide Web in the early 1990s. In December 1990, Tim Berners-Lee, who was working at the European particle physicis laboratory (CERN) in Switzerland, developed a graphically oriented computer browsing system that would make it easier to communicate over the Internet. When he posted it on the Internet in the summer of 1991, he began a revolution in networked computing.

I N T A S C

Principle #6

Communication Skills: The teacher uses knowledge of effective verbal, nonverbal, and media communication techniques to foster active inquiry, collaboration, and supportive interaction in the classroom.

I N T A S C

Principle #2

Knowledge of Human Development and Learning: The teacher understands how children learn and develop, and can provide learning opportunities that support their intellectual, social, and personal development.

I N T A S C

Principle #1

Knowledge of Subject Matter: The teacher understands the central concepts, tools of inquiry, and structures of the subject being taught and can create learning experiences that make these aspects of subject matter meaningful for students.

Essentially the World Wide Web makes it possible to easily navigate the Internet. It connects different sites by *hyperlinks* in the form of a piece of text or image. Clicking a hyperlink connects you to another point in a website or to a separate site. Thus, you could be writing about a piece of computer software and point the reader to its manufacturer. Or you could point to a historical site. For example, suppose you have a website devoted to the Great Depression of the 1930s. On your site you might include a photograph from a series of photos taken by photographer Dorothea Lange in 1936, in Nipomo, California. Lange recalled in 1960 how she saw the woman and took her picture:

> I saw and approached the hungry and desperate mother, as if drawn by a magnet. I do not remember how I explained my presence or my camera to her, but I do remember she asked me no questions. I made five exposures, working closer and closer from the same direction. I did not ask her name or her history. She told me her age, that she was thirty-two. She said that they had been living on frozen vegetables from the surrounding fields, and birds that the children killed. She had just sold the tires from her car to buy food. There she sat in that lean-to tent with her children huddled around her, and seemed to know that my pictures might help her, and so she helped me. There was a sort of equality about it. (Library of Congress, 2005)

You could use the preceding quote as part of lesson plan for a high school American history course. On your website you could not only provide the quote, but you could also link it to the full collection of photographs Lange took of the woman that are available online at the Library of Congress. Students could be put in direct connection with the Library of Congress and its vast collection of artifacts documenting the history of the United States. Not that long ago, such an experience would have required a field trip to Washington, D.C.

Students using the Internet and World Wide Web, whether at home or in school, have resources from around the world at their fingertips. They can visit libraries and museums and have electronic pen pals. They can also be exposed to materials that are not necessarily considered suitable for people their age. Like television, the Internet and World Wide Web, and computers in general, radically redefine the experience of those who have access to it, often creating totally new problems for educators.

For example, bullies have always been a problem in schools, but bullying has taken on new aspects as a result of the introduction of technologies such as instant messaging. Victims of bullying can now be harassed electronically as well as physically. A *New York Times* article reported the story of an eighth-grade girl new to her school who had reported the theft of her makeup case by some school bullies. No sooner had she reported them to the office than messages started appearing on her instant message program accusing her of being tattletale and a liar. Typing back to the thieves, she wrote: "You stole my stuff!" The bullies responded by calling her names. Shaken, the girl pulled away from her computer to go to a family outing and had her messages forwarded to her cell phone. By the time the situation was over, she had received 50 nasty messages from the bullies—the maximum her phone service could receive (Harmon, 2004).

Technology enabled these school bullies to impose themselves on the girl outside school. Access to instant messaging has changed the nature of a more traditional problem that teachers and schools must face. Examples like this point out how technologies are changing the experience of students and their teachers.

How does the new computer technology—the most recent of all educational technologies—potentially shape the work of

Using images and other resources readily available on the Internet can help you place knowledge in context. A lesson on the Great Depression of the 1930s, for example, can be reinforced with historical photos from national archives, such as those of photographer Dorothea Lange.

EDUCATION MATTERS

Cyber Worlds as Multiple-User Dimensions (MUDs)

They might not show up on school construction budgets, but tomato greenhouses, river towns grappling with epidemics, and Star Trek spaces are showing up in schools. These educational spaces of a special sort:—multiple-user dimensions (MUDs), worlds that exist only in cyberspace—are keeping teens interested in school. Many students have grown up on video games in which these dimensions have been commonplace. Now, as part of an initiative, educators and researchers along with Internet entrepreneurs have begun to construct MUDs for educational purposes. The use of MUDs is in its beginning stages, with no evidence that they work in classrooms.

MUDs are visual and interactive computer simulations, allowing students to be part of three-dimensional landscapes. They use avatars, which are digital personages, to move through a computer-controlled game. Some educators have long thought this could be a tool for education. If game worlds can keep kids interested for hours at home, can this world keep them interested for a 50-minute social studies class? To what extent are technologies such as MUDs of use in learning?

The Education Issue: Should game technology be used in school?

How Do Games Affect Teachers and Students?
Could a game world actually help teachers create options for simulations and interaction with content area? Most games are not designed to teach content, so the challenge of this initiative will be to see how new learning would actually take place. The benefit to this idea is the interest on the part of the students. However, designers and teachers will have to see if girls and boys are affected equally. The amount of money this project would require to develop solid academic ideas will be a challenge, and then good research would have to be done to test whether it really makes a difference at all.

What's Your Opinion?
1. Do you like to play video games? Do you learn things by playing them?

2. How do you think this type of technology would have helped you in school?

---

teachers working in the classroom? The following section explores how computing affects teachers' work and what they can or cannot accomplish by using it in the classroom.

HOW CAN COMPUTERS CHANGE THE TEACHING ENVIRONMENT?

Just as the introduction of the book into European culture in the late fifteenth century changed the work of teachers and the meaning of literacy, so too does computing change the experience and work of teachers at all levels of the educational system. At the K–12 level the computer becomes an extraordinary tool for record keeping, for communicating across distances, for assisting students with special needs, and so on.

COMPUTERS AS TOOLS FOR LEARNING

The idea of the computer as a tool for learning is extremely important. Traditionally computers have been seen primarily as efficiency and productivity tools. Computers are, in fact, much more than this. They are tools for learning.

Just as a carpenter has a tool chest with hammers and saws and screwdrivers, computers have the potential to function as a set of tools for learning. The computer can function

INTASC

Principle #4

Multiple Instructional Strategies: The teacher uses various instructional strategies to encourage students' development of critical thinking, problem solving, and performance skills.

Through the Eyes of
Culturally Sensitive Teachers

Overcoming Obstacles to Using Technology

Marta Thompson, a recent education graduate of a small liberal arts college, has just been hired to teach fifth grade at an inner-city school. She has received excellent training in the use of computers in the classroom. Not only is she skilled using multimedia presentation systems such as PowerPoint, but she has also done extensive research online, using electronic library resources as well as the Internet.

Marta believes that computers have tremendous potential for use in the classroom and is very excited at the idea of having her fifth-grade students use the computer as a tool to do creative writing, to research science and social topics online, and to have e-mail exchanges with students overseas.

During the planning week before she began her school year, Marta sat down with the technology specialist in her school. Marta was told not to "get too fancy" using the computers in the school's media center, or her classroom. "Look, we don't expect too much out of these kids. They

need to work as much possible on their basic verbal and mathematical skills that will be tested as part of the state assessment."

Marta responded by saying, "I was taught at the university that computers aren't just simply tools for skill and drill, but also tools for creating."

"That's fine, but not for most of the kids here. They can't be creative until they learn their basic skills; then we can let them loose."

Points to Ponder

1. How should Marta respond to the technology specialist?

2. Why do you think the technology specialist is giving such advice?

3. What do you think would occur if Marta follows the advice of the technology specialist? What would be the result if she followed the advice of her university professors?

I N T A S C

Principle #9

Professional Commitment and Responsibility: The teacher is a reflective practitioner who continually evaluates the effects of his/her choices and actions on others (students, parents, and other professionals in the learning community) and who actively seeks out opportunities to grow professionally.

as a calculator, a word-processing system, a portal to the Internet and World Wide Web and the great libraries and museums of the world, and a grade book for a teacher.

More and more university and college teachers are making use of computers in their instruction. In many ways it makes their work as instructors much easier; it also complicates their work in unexpected ways. For example, using PowerPoint to present lectures creates a structured way for presenting materials, allowing lectures to be posted online or e-mailed. On the surface these are good things. However, the relatively rigid format of a PowerPoint presentation makes it more difficult to be spontaneous and explore important side issues raised by students in the class. Students do not have to take notes as carefully if a lecture is available online. This means that more time can be given to classroom interaction and discussion with the instructor and other members of the class. What seems to happen, quite often, is that the academically strongest students listen carefully in class and review materials afterward online. They also take limited notes on particularly important issues. The weakest students take almost no notes and seem to spend little or no time reviewing the online lectures.

With the widespread introduction of e-mail, students come to office hours less and less, using e-mail instead to communicate with the professor. Many professors find they have less opportunity to interact informally with students—learning about their families, interests, and aspirations. These things come up naturally when students stop by the office, and they contribute to a professor's better understanding the students. Such things are not discussed in e-mail.

This effect translates to K–12 educators as well. Research from the mid-1990s found that teachers felt that their work in the classroom was significantly changed as a result of introducing computers into their classrooms. In a national survey of 608 teachers, 73% of those surveyed had been using computers for at least 5 years. Ninety percent of the teachers surveyed felt that their teaching had changed as a result of using computers in their classrooms. Approximately three-fourths, for example, reported that they expected more work from students when computers were available for their use in creating and editing their work (Office of Technology Assessment, 1995).

● **Computers as Tutor, Tool, or Tutee**   Computers can be used in many ways different in the classroom. Robert Taylor has divided computer use in the classroom into three useful categories: tutor, tool, and tutee.

A **tutor** function, according to Taylor, involves using the computer to drill students in ways that are typical of rote memorization and learning exercises. Programmed instruction fits this type of category, as well as a program such as Math Blaster, a game about invading spacecraft, which drills students in addition, subtraction, multiplication, and division.

In a **tool** function, students use the computer as a tool for going on the Internet to do research or using the computer to type a paper or create a spreadsheet.

In a **tutee** context, students program a machine to do particular tasks. A program such as Lego/Logo, for example, has the user construct a machine using Lego pieces that include not only traditional Lego building bricks but gears, motors, and sensors as well. Users then hook their machines to a computer and write a computer program to control the machine. A user might build a house with lights that turn on and off at a specific time or a garage door that opens whenever a sensor is tripped (Taylor, 1980; MIT Epistemology and Learning Group, 2002).

● **Type I and Type II Uses of Computers**   The special educator Claburne Maddux talks about **Type I** and **Type II applications** of the computer in the classroom. In a Type I use of the computer, the computer is used to complete a task more efficiently or effectively than it has been done before. Thus, using a word processor in place of a pencil or typewriter is an example of a Type I application of the computer. A Type II application is a totally new use of the computer to expand a lesson in a way unique to the technology. Having students play a simulation game such as Sim Earth, in which they take charge of the Earth at its creation and guide it through billions of years of evolution, represents an almost totally new use of the computer in the classroom (Maddux, 1986).

The computer profoundly changes the dynamics of the classroom. It is not a neutral technology, but instead is profoundly value laden. Computers make many aspects of the instructional process easier, but they can also add complexity to classroom settings and activities.

● **Computers as Adaptive or Assistive Technology**   In a piece for the *Harvard Education Letter,* Karen Kelly described a 12-year-old dyslexic boy with a familial tremor in his hand. While he loves to tell stories, he cannot hold a pencil or effectively use the keyboard on a computer. He could not complete school assignments and found himself very discouraged. After someone suggested the use of a voice-recognition typing system, the boy soon was able to dictate stories and edit them on the computer (Kelly, 2000).

This boy was using the computer as an **adaptive technology**, also called **assistive technology**. It augmented his ability to write, much as glasses help some of us to read. Other examples of adaptive technology would be a program that takes text from the computer and reads it

Assistive technology encourages and allows students with special needs to participate in all activities and assignments.

aloud to someone who is blind, or an electronic calculator that helps someone multiply or divide. The concept of the computer augmenting or enhancing human intelligence was first introduced by the American engineer Douglas Engelbart in 1963, the inventor of the computer mouse as well as computer screen interfaces such as icons and windows.

● **Computers as Augmentation Devices**   The idea of a computer augmenting human intelligence potentially opens new ways of knowing and learning. In the seventeenth century, augmentation devices such as telescopes and microscopes opened new scientific vistas and experiences. While technologies such as these typically expand human experience and possibilities, there are often hidden costs. Look, for example, at the benefits and limitations of the automobile. While we have greater speed and mobility, we also have pollution and deaths from accidents, and the character of our towns and cities has been redefined. Technologies carry with them certain benefits and certain limitations.

Many people have trouble spelling. A spell-check system on a word processor can help search for errors in spelling. Of course, in order to use a spell-check system effectively, we must be able to distinguish when a word is actually misspelled. Many words that show up as misspelled in the spell checker's dictionary are simply foreign or obscure in their use or meaning. Therefore, we still must have the critical insight and skill to determine whether the computer and its spell-checking system is helping us or misleading us.

COMPUTING AS A VALUE-LADEN TECHNOLOGY

C. A. Bowers argues in *The Cultural Dimensions of Educational Computing* that computers are not a neutral technology, but they shape and define the experience of both teaching and learning (Bowers, 1988). Think for a moment, as discussed earlier, about how e-mail has changed the typical professor's interactions with students. E-mail has cultural and educational ramifications of a much greater consequence than one would assume. Think about some of the new words that have come into our language in recent years as a result of computing: *cyberspace, e-mail, hacker.* These words represent not just new words, but new values and cultural orientations as well.

According to the German philosopher Martin Heidegger (1889–1976), technologies such as the automobile, radio, television, airplanes, and computers mediate the experiences of individuals by selectively *amplifying* or *reducing* certain characteristics (Bowers, 1995). Thus, in the case of the classroom, the computer changes how we teach and learn.

LIMITATIONS OF THE TECHNOLOGY REVOLUTION

A number of critical questions about the effect of using computers in educational settings arise. What, in the sense raised by Heidegger, gets amplified and what gets reduced? How is instruction changed or altered? How does the use of computing change the opportunities to learn? What is positive about the use of computers in the classroom? What is negative?

Computers have tremendous potential to help teachers, but while using them, you must also recognize their limitations and how they can potentially shape you. Like any technology, the computer has its disadvantages and advantages, and it can profoundly direct the process of teaching and learning.

● **Computers and the Hidden Curriculum**   The use of new technologies in education—especially computers—is based on a number of assumptions including the devaluing of local knowledge, the rise of globalism (the Internet and World Wide Web), the emphasis on instrumental and scientific ways of knowing and the devaluing of group over individual activities (Bowers, 1988, 2000). Often what is promoted by computers and computer software involves a hidden or null curriculum. For example, the Internet and World Wide Web may be a wonderful way of making information available on a global basis, but it has a way of devaluing local knowledge and expertise. English is the language of the Internet and tends to push out other languages and traditions. Scientific and technological knowledge is emphasized over other ways of knowing.

Simulated educational games can help bring lessons to life for students. Why do you think some students respond well to this type of instruction?

Such problems are not simply limited to the Internet and World Wide Web, but can be found in educational software as well, just as in textbooks. The extremely popular educational simulation Oregon Trail II, for example, provides an interesting but highly value-laden experience for elementary school children. Native Americans in the original version of the program, released in 1975, were not identified by their tribes and functioned in the program as a problem to be overcome as students simulated the experience of making their way West. A male perspective predominates throughout the simulation, as well as a general assumption that Native American ways are inferior to European models. In the process, students are taught little about the actual folkways and culture of Native American people. They are simply obstacles to be overcome.

Other types of educational software also promote very specific ways of knowing and interpreting the world. Look, for example, at the following description of the program SimLife found in the game's instruction manual:

> *SimLife* is the first genetic engineering game available for personal computers. It lets players manipulate the very fabric of existence, giving life to creatures that defy the wildest imaginations. Players create exotic plants of various shapes, sizes and temperaments, and turn them loose into a custom-designed environment in which only the best-adapted species survive! With *SimLife,* the budding mad scientist can people the landscape with mutagens (agents that cause mutation and, indirectly, evolution). Or change the individual genetics of one creature and see what effects its offspring have on the long-term survival of its species and the ecosystem as a whole. (Bowers, 2000B, pp. 136–137)

SimLife is what is known as a "God Game." It assumes that it is alright for human beings to shape and manipulate nature. Although a huge international debate is currently underway concerning whether cloning and gene manipulation is amoral, SimLife assumes that students can learn about the issue as part of a game—one that assumes that such practices are not only acceptable, but also fun. How many future genetic researchers and physicians will have had the moral and ethical grounding for their professions formed for them while playing games like this?

● **The Significance of the "Digital Divide"**   Many people have been concerned that there is a "digital divide" based on factors such as race, ethnicity, and social class. Access to the Internet and World Wide Web represents a reasonable proxy for computer access and use. (See Figure 12.2.) While the number of households with Internet access has increased each year, use is clearly more concentrated in wealthier and more educated segments of the population. Computer access rises considerably among households earning a minimum of $35,000. As of 2000, more than two-thirds of all households earning more than $50,000 had Internet connections (60.9% for households earning $50,000 to $74,999 and 77.7% for households earning $75,000 or more) (U.S. Department of Commerce, 2000).

Significant differences in Internet use occur in terms of different races and ethnic groups, as well, as you can see in Figure 12.3. Across all socioeconomic levels, Asian Americans and Pacific Islanders have the highest level of Internet access in their homes, at 56.8%. Blacks and Hispanics have the lowest rate of access to the Internet in their homes, at 23.5% and 23.6%, respectively. While behind other ethnic and racial groups in their use of the Internet, Blacks increased their access to the Internet in the 20 months from December 1998 to August 2000 from 11.2% to 23.5%. Hispanic access during the same period increased from 12.6% to 23.6% (U.S. Department of Commerce, 2000).

A person with a disability is half as likely to have access to the Internet as someone without a disability: 21.6% compared to 42.1%. People with impaired vision and problems with manual dexterity have particularly low levels of use (U.S. Department of Commerce, 2000).

If computers, as many people argue, are critical to new models of learning and access to information and possibilities for jobs in the years to come, then questions of access are very important. Just as access to equal schooling is an equity issue, so is access to high-speed com-

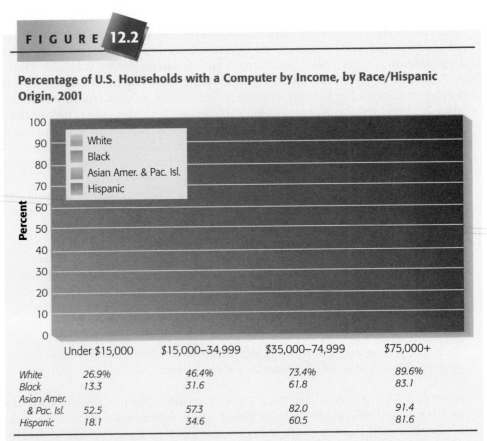

FIGURE 12.2

Percentage of U.S. Households with a Computer by Income, by Race/Hispanic Origin, 2001

	Under $15,000	$15,000–34,999	$35,000–74,999	$75,000+
White	26.9%	46.4%	73.4%	89.6%
Black	13.3	31.6	61.8	83.1
Asian Amer. & Pac. Isl.	52.5	57.3	82.0	91.4
Hispanic	18.1	34.6	60.5	81.6

Source: NTIA and ESA, U.S. Department of Commerce, using U.S. Bureau of the Census *Current Population Survey* supplements.

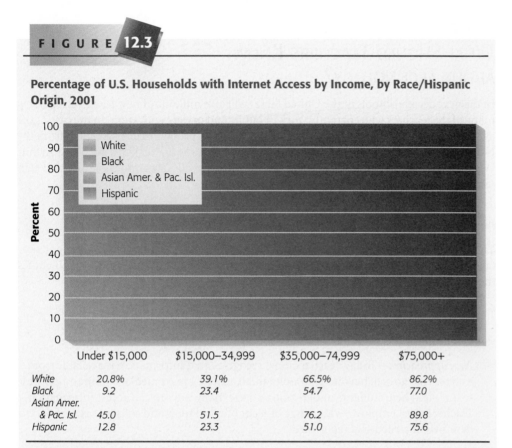

FIGURE 12.3

Percentage of U.S. Households with Internet Access by Income, by Race/Hispanic Origin, 2001

Legend:
- White
- Black
- Asian Amer. & Pac. Isl.
- Hispanic

	Under $15,000	$15,000–34,999	$35,000–74,999	$75,000+
White	20.8%	39.1%	66.5%	86.2%
Black	9.2	23.4	54.7	77.0
Asian Amer. & Pac. Isl.	45.0	51.5	76.2	89.8
Hispanic	12.8	23.3	51.0	75.6

Source: NTIA and ESA, U.S. Department of Commerce, using U.S. Bureau of the Census *Current Population Survey* supplements.

puting. In communities where resources are scarce, computer access may be particularly important. With a single Internet connection, for example, a school in an impoverished part of the country can access resources from the Library of Congress or the Louvre Museum.

Who am I?

What do I believe?

"Technology is overwhelming even for me. And I have been working with these devices since they came out. There are so many different devices, and so many different levels and upgrades for each one."

CAROL FARRELL, SPECIAL EDUCATOR

THINK ABOUT THIS:
Keeping up with changes in technology is a constant challenge. New software and improved hardware constantly becomes available. What are the essentials that a teacher needs to know?

SHARE and COMPARE:
Talk to a classmate or friend about what you consider the necessary skills with computers that you will need to have to be an effective teacher. Explore how you will get these skills and keep them up to date.

WHAT SHOULD TEACHERS KNOW ABOUT TECHNOLOGY?

In the next decade schools in the United States will hire millions of new teachers, replacing many of the teachers who currently work in public and private education. In the case of the existing teacher population, computer literacy is highly problematic. In a report from the National Council for the Accreditation of Teacher Education (NCATE), president Arthur Wise expressed wonder over whether these new teachers will "be comfortable and skilled in using technology" (NCATE, 1997).

NCATE GUIDELINES

The NCATE report developed a set of general guidelines that teachers adapt to take advantage of technology for instruction. These guidelines provide a useful model that includes the realization of:

- *New understandings*—Teachers need to understand the deep impact technology is having on society as a whole: how technology has changed the nature of work, of communications, and of our understanding of the development of knowledge.

- *New approaches*—Today, teachers must recognize that information is available from sources that go well beyond textbooks and teachers—mass media, communities, and so on—and help students understand and use many ways to can access information. Teachers must employ a wide range of technological tools and software as part of their own instructional repertoire.

- *New roles*—Teachers should help students pursue their own inquiries, using technologies to find, organize, and interpret information, and to become reflective and critical about information quality and sources.

- *New forms of professional development*—Teachers must participate in formal courses, some of which may be delivered in nontraditional ways, such as via telecommunications; they must also become part of ongoing informal learning communities with other professionals who share their interests and concerns.

- *New attitudes*—Finally, teachers need an "attitude" that is fearless in the use of technology, encourages them to take risks, and inspires them to become lifelong learners (NCATE, 1997).

ISTE STANDARDS

At a much more specific level the **International Society for Technology in Education (ISTE)** established a set of standards in 1993 for training teachers in the use of computers in their day-to-day work in the classroom. The ISTE standards have been revised three times since their introduction and have been adopted by the NCATE. A school or college of education that applies for NCATE accreditation must follow the ISTE standards for the technology component in its program. In doing so, it must demonstrate a "commitment to preparing candidates who are able to use technology to help all students learn; it also provides a conceptual understanding of how knowledge, skills, and disposition related to educational and information technology are integrated throughout the curriculum, the instruction, field experiences, clinical practice, assessments, and evaluation" (NCATE, 2000).

The ISTE standards used by NCATE, found in the document *National Educational Technology Standards for Teachers* (NCATE, 2000), include 23 indicators organized into six categories. (See Figure 12.4)

FIGURE 12.4

International Society for Technology in Education National Educational Technology Standards (NETS) and Performance Indicators for Teachers

ISTE STANDARDS

All classroom teachers should be prepared to meet the following standards and performance indicators.

I. **TECHNOLOGY OPERATIONS AND CONCEPTS** Teachers demonstrate a sound understanding of technology operations and concepts. Teachers:

   A. demonstrate introductory knowledge, skills, and understanding of concepts related to technology (as described in the ISTE National Educational Technology Standards for Students).

   B. demonstrate continual growth in technology knowledge and skills to stay abreast of current and emerging technologies.

II. **PLANNING AND DESIGNING LEARNING ENVIRONMENTS AND EXPERIENCES** Teachers plan and design effective learning environments and experiences supported by technology. Teachers:

   A. design developmentally appropriate learning opportunities that apply technology-enhanced instructional strategies to support the diverse needs of learners.

   B. apply current research on teaching and learning with technology when planning learning environments and experiences.

   C. identify and locate technology resources and evaluate them for accuracy and suitability.

   D. plan for the management of technology resources within the context of learning activities.

   E. plan strategies to manage student learning in a technology-enhanced environment.

III. **TEACHING, LEARNING, AND THE CURRICULUM** Teachers implement curriculum plans that include methods and strategies for applying technology to maximize student learning. Teachers:

   A. facilitate technology-enhanced experiences that address content standards and student technology standards.

   B. use technology to support learner-centered strategies that address the diverse needs of students.

   C. apply technology to develop students' higher-order skills and creativity.

   D. manage student learning activities in a technology-enhanced environment.

IV. **ASSESSMENT AND EVALUATION** Teachers apply technology to facilitate a variety of effective assessment and evaluation strategies. Teachers:

   A. apply technology in assessing student learning of subject matter using a variety of assessment techniques.

   B. use technology resources to collect and analyze data, interpret results, and communicate findings to improve instructional practice and maximize student learning.

   C, apply multiple methods of evaluation to determine students' appropriate use of technology resources for learning, communication, and productivity.

V. **PRODUCTIVITY AND PROFESSIONAL PRACTICE** Teachers use technology to enhance their productivity and professional practice. Teachers:

   A. use technology resources to engage in ongoing professional development and lifelong learning.

   B. continually evaluate and reflect on professional practice to make informed decisions regarding the use of technology in support of student learning.

   C. apply technology to increase productivity.

   D. use technology to communicate and collaborate with peers, parents, and the larger community in order to nurture student learning.

VI. **SOCIAL, ETHICAL, LEGAL, AND HUMAN ISSUES** Teachers understand the social, ethical, legal, and human issues surrounding the use of technology in PK–12 schools and apply that understanding in practice. Teachers:

   A. model and teach legal and ethical practice related to technology use.

   B. apply technology resources to enable and empower learners with diverse backgrounds, characteristics, and abilities.

   C. identify and use technology resources that affirm diversity.

   D. promote safe and healthy use of technology resources.

   E. facilitate equitable access to technology resources for all students.

HOW WIDELY DO TEACHERS AND STUDENTS USE TECHNOLOGY?

To what extent are teachers and students actually using computers in the classroom? According to the National Center for Educational Statistics (NCES), as of 2001, 99% of all schools had access to the Internet (see Figure 12.5) (NCES, 2002). In a 1999 survey, 39% of public school teachers with access to computers or the Internet in their classrooms indicated that they used the technology "a lot" to create instructional materials, 34 percent said they used it "a lot" for administrative record keeping (NCES, 2002).

COMPUTER USE BASED ON TEACHER COMFORT

Table 12.1 indicates that younger or newer teachers tend to make greater use of computers. Teachers with 3 or fewer years of teaching, for example, used computers or the Internet "a lot"—30% of the time—to communicate with colleagues, while teachers with 20 years or more of experience used it "a lot"—19% of the time. Teachers in schools that were poor tended to use computers less often than their counterparts in wealthier settings (U.S. Dept. of Education, 1999).

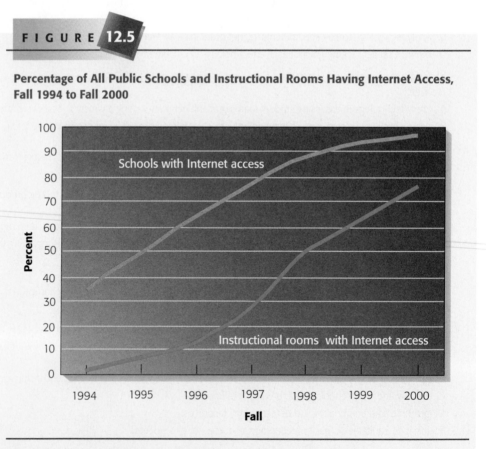

FIGURE 12.5

Percentage of All Public Schools and Instructional Rooms Having Internet Access, Fall 1994 to Fall 2000

Source: U. S. Department of Education, National Center for Education Statistics, Fast Response Survey System, *Internet Access in Public Schools and Classrooms: 1994–2000.*

TABLE 12.1

Percentage of Teachers Indicating They Use Computers or the Internet a Lot at School to Accomplish Various Objectives, by School and Teacher Characteristics, 1999

SCHOOL AND TEACHER CHARACTERISTICS	CREATE INSTRUCTIONAL MATERIALS	ADMINSTRATIVE RECORD-KEEPING	COMMUNICATE WITH COLLEAGUES	GATHER INFORMATION FOR PLANNING LESSONS	MULTIMEDIA CLASSROOM PRESENTATIONS	ACCESS RESEARCH AND BEST PRACTICES FOR TEACHING	COMMUNICATE WITH PARENTS OR STUDENTS	ACCESS MODEL LESSON PLANS
All public schoolteachers with access to computers or the Internet at school	39%	34%	23%	16%	8%	7%	7%	6%
Teaching experience								
3 or fewer years	43	38	30	21	10	11	6	11
4–9 years	47	38	30	22	8	10	10	8
10–19 years	38	35	22	14	9	7	6	6
20 or more years	35	30	19	11	6	5	5	5
School instructional level								
Elementary school	37	29	25	14	7	7	7	6
Secondary school	44	47	21	19	8	8	6	7
Percentage of students in school eligible for free or reduced-price school lunch								
Less than 11%	52	43	31	20	11	9	9	8
11–30%	42	37	27	19	7	9	8	8
31–49%	35	36	23	13	6	5	6	4
50–70%	35	30	15	10	8	5	4	4
71% or more	32	24	19	15	8	7	5	8

Source: U.S. Department of Education, National Center for Education Statistics, Fast Response Survey System, "Survey on Public School Teachers' Use of Computers and the Internet," FRSS 70, 1999.

Sixty-six percent of public schoolteachers used computers or the Internet during class time, while 41% assigned students work that involved the use of applications such as word processing or spreadsheets, 31% reported assigning practice drills and 30% assigned research using the Internet (Table 12.2, U.S. Department of Education 2000).

TABLE 12.2

Percentage of Teachers with Access to Computers or the Internet at School According to the Level of Preparedness They Feel to Use Computers and the Internet by School and Teacher Characteristics, 1999

SCHOOL AND TEACHER CHARACTERISTICS	NOT AT ALL PREPARED	SOMEWHAT PREPARED	WELL PREPARED	VERY WELL PREPARED
All public school teachers with access to computers or the Internet at school	13%	53%	23%	10%
School instructional level				
Elementary school	12	55	23	10
Secondary school	15	50	23	12
Percent of students eligible for free or reduced-price school lunch				
Less than 11 percent	10	53	25	12
11–30%	13	52	25	10
31–49%	14	51	24	10
50–70%	16	58	16	10
71% or more	13	55	22	10
Teaching experience				
3 or fewer years	10	46	31	13
4–9 years	10	49	28	13
10–19 years	14	55	21	10
20 or more years	16	58	19	8
Hours of professional development				
0 hours	32	46	15	6
1–8 hours	19	55	20	6
9–32 hours	4	61	25	10
More than 32 hours	1	32	37	29
Type of work assigned to a moderate or large extent				
Use computer applications such as word processing, spreadsheets, etc.	4	45	33	19
Practice drills	4	54	27	14
Research using the Internet	4	43	34	19
Solve problems/analyze data	3	49	29	19
Research using CD-ROM	3	42	33	21
Produce multimedia reports/projects	5	38	33	24
Graphical presentation of materials	4	38	35	22
Demonstrations/simulations	2	34	37	28
Correspond with experts, authors, students from other schools, etc., via e-mail or Internet	4	32	34	30

Source: U.S. Department of Education, National Center for Education Statistics, Fast Response Survey System, "Survey on Public School Teachers' Use of Computers and the Internet," FRSS 70, 1999.

ACCESS TO COMPUTING

Availability of the Internet in public schools became widespread in the 1990s. At the beginning of the decade, Internet availability in most schools was less than 5%. By the end of the decade it was more than 90% in most schools across the country (U.S. Department of Education, 2001). It is hard to believe, but the Internet's World Wide Web was invented in the early 1990s—yet it has redefined how we use computers, communicate, and conduct our work as educators.

COMPUTER USE IN DIFFERENT TYPES OF SCHOOLS

An important issue that has been raised with the increasing introduction of computers in our educational system and culture is, who has access to computing? On the surface, the United States has done a very good job of providing computers and Internet access to students in public schools. In 1999, 94% of all public elementary schools had Internet access, and 98% of all high schools (U.S. Census Bureau, 2000). On February 8, 1996, President Clinton signed the **Telecommunications Act of 1996,** which represented the first comprehensive revision of the country's communications laws in more than 60 years. Under the universal section of the law, schools and libraries are provided access to state-of-the-art services and technologies at discounted rates. By 2000, after 2 years of operation, the program committed $3.65 billion to more than 50,000 schools and libraries. As a result, the "E-Rate" made it possible for 1 million public school classrooms to be connected to modern telecommunications networks. In addition, 13,000 community libraries and 35,000 private and 45,000 Catholic school classrooms were able to gain access to the Internet and World Wide Web (Kennard, 2000).

Such figures are impressive. Of course they only tell part of the story. Because a computer is available in a classroom does not mean that good use is being made of it. As the journalist Maisie McAdoo has argued, "The issue of equity now centers not on equality of equipment, but on quality of use" (McAdoo, 2000, p. 143). How effectively is the computer being used in instruction? What type of instruction is emphasized—skill and drill, critical thinking, or online research? What type of training have teachers had in integrating computers in their classrooms? Do students have access to computing outside school? Can they use them in their homes or in local community centers?

COMPUTERS AND ACCEPTABLE USE POLICIES

The widespread introduction of computers into schools, particularly when combined with connections to the Internet and World Wide Web, have created both opportunities and problems for schools. While filtering software can block student access to many undesirable sites, such as hate sites and pornographic sites, such blocking programs are imperfect. Students will inevitably be curious and test the limits of what they can do online.

Schools and libraries have increasingly adopted policies that specifically define appropriate uses of computers. Most large school district or state departments of education have an explicit policy, called an **acceptable use policy (AUP),** that defines precisely how computers may or may not be used in the schools. The Virginia Department of Education (n. d.) outlines the following components as key to any successful acceptable use policy for K–12 classrooms and library media centers:

- a description of the instructional philosophies and strategies to be supported by Internet access in schools

- a statement on the educational uses and advantages of the Internet in your school or division

- a list of the responsibilities of educators, parents, and students for using the Internet

- a code of conduct governing behavior on the Internet

INTASC

Principle #6

Communication Skills: The teacher uses knowledge of effective verbal, nonverbal, and media communication techniques to foster active inquiry, collaboration, and supportive interaction in the classroom.

INTASC

Principle #7

Instructional Planning Skills: The teacher plans instruction based upon knowledge of subject matter, students, the community, and curriculum goals.

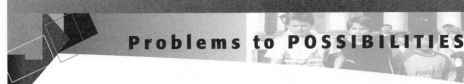

Problems to POSSIBILITIES

Students Abusing the Use of Computers

Mr. Arthur, the media center's director, had been working in the media center with the students from Ms. de Silva's class for about 45 minutes when a normally rambunctious pair of students, Clyde and John, suddenly got suspiciously quiet. A moment later one of their friends exclaimed: "You guys are gross beyond belief!" Figuring something was up, Mr. Arthur quietly walked over to the two boys and checked out their computer screen. "Anything I should know about?" asked Mr. Arthur, to which the boys said, "No, we were just doing our English assignment."

In fact, on the screen was a website for The Scarlet Letter. *Having a good bit of experience teaching tenth graders, Mr. Arthur said to the two boys, "You won't mind if I look at the website you're visiting for moment, will you?" Clyde didn't answer and John nervously answered, "Sure have a look."*

There was indeed a website on the computer screen about Nathaniel Hawthorne and his writing. Taking the computer mouse, Mr. Arthur clicked on the browser's address box, only to find that the previous address visited had been a well-known pornography site. He asked the boys if they had visited the site and then gone back to the Hawthorne site. Both denied knowing anything about it. "Somebody must have been visiting the pornography site before we got the machine," said John. "Yeah," said Clyde, "That's what must have happened."

Discussion Question

If you were Mr. Arthur, how would you deal with John and Clyde?

Possibilities

The Internet and World Wide Web have made the process of regulating and controlling information increasingly difficult in school settings. Obviously, certain types of websites are not suitable for minors or appropriate for sharing in public places. These include websites with extreme violence, pornography,

or those that include racially, sexually, or ethnically offensive material. Most school districts have acceptable use policies in place that provide very explicit guidelines for computer use. Such policies typically include a list of the responsibilities of educators, parents, and students for using the Internet; a code of conduct on computer use; an explanation of the consequences of violating the policy's code of conduct; and so on.

Before Mr. Arthur can deal with John and Clyde, he will need to verify with other students that they were looking at a pornographic site. This will be difficult, and students most likely will not want to "rat" on their classmates. The situation presents a good opportunity for Mr. Arthur to review the school's acceptable use policy with the entire class. In doing so, he can create a teachable moment and be fair to the two boys while he ensures that they understand why looking at pornography in a public setting is inappropriate.

The following resources may provide helpful hints:

- The Pew Internet and American Life Project (www .pewinternet.org) explores the impact of the Internet on daily life, including its effect on education.

- Monroe County Library in Indiana provides a special "Internet Advocate" page (www.monroe.lib.in.us/ ~lchampel/netadv3.html) that offers assistance and information on acceptable use policies.

- The North Central Regional Educational Laboratory (www.ncrel.org) offers materials from rubrics to preparation guides for using technology in the classroom appropriately.

Ethical Question

Did Mr. Arthur invade the students' privacy by taking command of the computer and tracking their online usage?

- a description of the consequences of violating the AUP

- a description of what constitutes acceptable and unacceptable use of the Internet

- a disclaimer absolving the school division, under specific circumstances, from responsibility

- a statement reminding users that Internet access and the use of computer networks is a privilege

- a statement that the AUP is in compliance with state and national telecommunication rules and regulations

- a signature form for teachers, parents, and students indicating their intent to abide by the AUP

As either an observer or an associate or beginning teacher, make sure you know what the acceptable use policy is for the school in which you are working, and be ready to use it should a problem with computer use arise when you are teaching.

PLAGIARISM AND THE INTERNET

On a practical day-to-day level the availability of technology for students increases the potential for certain types of problems in the schools and in the classrooms where you teach. The example of students being harassed by bullies through instant messaging was discussed earlier in the chapter. **Plagiarism** is another problem that is increasingly made possible by students' having access to the Internet and being able to cut and paste materials that are posted online.

Teachers need to spend more time in their already busy schedules letting students know how materials can be acceptably used and what is involved with using quotes and properly citing where materials are acquired. This is by no means an impossible task, but represents an additional challenge for teachers and the work they do in the classroom.

SUCCESSFUL USES OF COMPUTERS IN THE CLASSROOM

We are approximately 25 years into using computers in the classroom, and their use has been enormously successful . . . and highly problematic. Computers have not, as many people predicted, taken the place of classroom teachers. They have functioned most effectively as a tool to support the traditional aims and purposes of instruction.

Computers clearly do certain things very well. There is little doubt that they can take the place of traditional workbook and drilling systems, freeing time for teachers to do other things with students. They provide the means to access worldwide information in ways that have never been possible, just as they make the process of writing easier and more efficient. Presentation systems such as PowerPoint greatly expand the capacity of teachers to present information in engaging and interesting ways.

Much of the most important use of computers for teachers probably remains hidden—that is, as a tool for organizing one's work and communicating with others. Like other technologies such as the telephone, the full implementation and use of computers will probably take at least a generation or possibly as long as a generation and half to be fully realized. This process, of course, is further complicated by the fact that computers and software are constantly being upgraded. Who would have predicted the extraordinary potential of the Internet and World Wide Web 10 or 15 years ago. It is likely that similar advances will be made in the future, ones that will have profound influences on education and the work of teachers.

"I'm prepared to bring technology resources to my students that I wouldn't have dreamed of a year ago. I'm not teaching students to use computers—I'm using computers to help them develop critical thinking skills."

SHERYL BOND, HIGH SCHOOL TEACHER

THINK ABOUT THIS:

Most people think of computers as tools for efficiency. The tendency is not to think about them as tools for thinking. How might the computer be a tool for thinking?

SHARE and **COMPARE:**

Talk to a friend or classmate about the different ways in which you use computers. Explore the ways you use them, or could use them, that go beyond simply using them as productivity or efficiency tools. Consider how important they may be to encouraging creativity and new ways of thinking.

FINAL THOUGHTS

Technology has always played an important role in the work of teachers and the experience of students. Whether in the form of a book, television, freestanding computers, or the Internet and World Wide Web, technology shapes the settings where it is found. Contrary to popular assumptions, technology is not neutral, but shapes and influences the environment in which it is used. While technologies may be very valuable, they tend to emphasize certain models or approaches while deemphasizing others.

As educators, we need to be aware of the limitations and possibilities of the use of technology. Such an approach requires educators to be skilled not only at using technology, but also at using it critically. To do anything else is to find ourselves at a disadvantage. In this context, it is worth recalling the philosopher Martin Heidegger's idea of reflecting on what a technology *amplifies* and *reduces*. In doing so, we will ultimately best serve not only our own needs as educators, but also those of our students and society at large.

Who am I? **What do I believe?**

REFLECTIONS

Professional Plan for the Use of Technology in Your Teaching

1. Three things I learned from this chapter about diversity issues and schools are:

2. Two things in this chapter that I would like to learn more about are:

   a. _____

   b. _____

3. I plan to investigate these two areas and learn more about topics in this chapter by:

_____ Reading some of the book club choices

_____ Reading sources referenced in the chapter that interest me

_____ Interviewing teachers and exploring how they use technology in their classrooms

_____ Exploring the websites listed in the Log On section

_____ Observing classrooms and speaking with teachers to explore how they use technology in their classrooms

4. I will include the following in my Touch the Future portfolio:

_____ Responses to Who Am I? activities

_____ A brief essay on my thoughts about Problems to Possibilities

_____ Responses to the Observation Guide

_____ Other (material assigned by your instructor)

SUMMARY

What Technologies Have Been Used in the Classroom?

- Many technologies have been used in the classroom, from the book, and the blackboard, to the computer.
- Historically, textbooks have been the single most important technology used in the classroom.
- New technology, including videotape players and computers, has played an increasingly important role in schools in recent years.

How Do Television and the Internet Shape and Influence Children?

- Television creates an extraordinary source of information for children.
- Television is essentially universal in our culture.
- The average child in the United States watches 3 to 4 hours of television a day.
- Television redefines the experience of childhood.
- The Internet and World Wide Web are becoming increasingly important forces in shaping the experience of children.
- Access to the Internet and World Wide Web makes it possible for students and teachers to have extraordinary information resources easily available to them.

How Can Computing Change the Teaching Environment?

- Computing redefines the work of teachers at all levels of the educational system.
- According to Taylor, computers are used in three different ways in the classroom: as tutor, tool, and tutee.
- Type I uses of computers represent using them to do traditional tasks, while Type II uses involves their being used in totally new ways.
- Computers are not a neutral but a value-laden technology.
- Computers mediate the experience of people.

- Adaptive computer technologies have the potential to augment human intelligence.
- Computers have the potential to promote a hidden or null curriculum.
- Access to computers is significantly influenced by factors such as race, ethnicity, and social class.
- Access to computers is an important social issue.

What Should Teachers Know about Technology?

- The use of new technologies such as computers in the classroom requires new models for educating teachers.

How Widely Do Teachers and Students Use Technology?

- Internet use is becoming widespread if not almost universal in the schools.
- The rapid growth in the adoption and use of the Internet and World Wide Web is even more remarkable in light of the fact that the technology is so new.

Visit the **Touch the Future . . . Teach!** Companion Website at www.ablongman.com/diaz for additional opportunities.

KEY WORDS

acceptable use policy (AUP)   387

adaptive technology   377

assistive technology   377

instructional technology   370

International Society for Technology in Education (ISTE)   382

Montessori method   369

plagiarism   389

Telecommunications Act of 1996   387

tool   377

tutee   377

tutor   377

Type I application   377

Type II application   377

CONCEPT REVIEW

1. Identify some of the major educational technologies that have shaped classroom practice.

2. Explain how textbooks represent a type of educational technology.

3. Describe how different forms of media have shaped the lives of children.

4. Identify potential uses of technology in the classroom and why the Internet and World Wide Web can be significant technology for educators.

5. List examples of computers functioning in the classroom as tutor, tool, and tutee, as well as Type I and Type II uses of the computer.

6. Explain how a computer is a value-laden technology.

7. Discuss why adaptive or assistive technology is such a promising area for students with special needs.

8. Explain how technologies such as computers potentially devalue local knowledge and traditions and why this is an important issue.

9. Explain what is meant by the "digital divide" as it relates to equity.

10. Identify "acceptable and appropriate" uses of computers by students in classroom and school settings, as well as their limitations.

TOUCH THE FUTURE . . .

Read On

Brave New Schools: Challenging Cultural Illiteracy through Global Learning Networks
Jim Cummins and Dennis Sayers (New York: St. Martin's Press, 1995)
An outstanding work discussing computers and the Internet in the transformation of schools, of particular interest is the authors' discussion of computers and multiculturalism.

The Digital Classroom: How Technology is Changing the Way We Teach and Learn
David Gordon, ed. (Cambridge, MA: Harvard Education Letter, 2000)
A useful collection of essays about how we can better prepare teachers to use new technologies in the classroom, as well as what can be done about problems such as the digital divide.

Oversold and Underused: The Cost of Educational Computing
Larry Cuban (Cambridge, MA: Harvard University Press, 2001)
Cuban questions whether the cost of computers is justified in terms of their actual improvement of instruction, arguing that schools might be better served by focusing on civic moral issues instead.

Log On

Classroom Connect
www.classroom.com
Longtime web resource whose goal is to help K–12 teachers use technology to become better teachers.

National Educational Technology Standards for Teachers
http://cnets.iste.org/teachers/
The International Society for Technology in Education's (ISTE) website for educational technology standards for teachers.

Teacher Talk
http://education.indiana.edu/cas/tt/tthmpg.html
Interesting ideas and resources to help teachers to be more productive and creative in their classrooms.

Kathy Shrock's Guide for Educators
http://school.discovery.com/schrockguide/index.html
One of the best teacher sites available, sponsored by the Discovery Channel; an outstanding source for lesson plans, resource materials (clip art and so on) and links to educational sites for teachers.

T. H. E. Journal Educator's Roadmap to the Web
www.thejournal.com/highlights/roadmap/
Technological Horizons in Education, one of the leading journals in educational computing, provides a superb portal to websites of interest to educators.

U.S. Department of Education Office of Technology
www.ed.gov/about/offices/list/os/technology/index.html
Learn about the federal government's efforts to improve education through the use of technology.

Write On

"The goal is to give to the computer those tasks which it can best do and leave to man that which requires (or seems to require) his judgment."

—Joseph Weizenbaum

In your journal, write Weizenbaum's quote down and then develop a brief essay that describes what you think is essential about teaching, and how computers and other technologies can either help or hinder you in your work.

OBSERVATION GUIDE

TEACH: LINKING THEORY TO PRACTICE

Linking
Theory to
Practice

Objective: To observe computer use in a classroom setting

School (use code name): _____   Observer: _____

Grade Level: _____   Date: _____

Subject Taught: _____   Time In: _____   Time Out: _____

Directions: In this observation activity, observe how teachers use computers as part of their instruction. Make general notes on all that you observe. Answer as many of the following questions as your observations permit. Afterward, use these answers to write a brief essay explaining how the computer influenced and shaped the classroom you observed. You may submit the essay to your instructor as well as include it in your Touch the Future portfolio.

1. Notice how computers are located in the classroom. Are they assigned a special space? Do they have furniture that is specially designed for them, or are they placed on regular classroom tables and desks? Are there signs or posters that indicate how the computers are supposed to be used?

2. For what types of activities do the students use the computers: skill-and-drill, individual research, collaborative projects?

3. Do the computers encourage individual or shared work activities among students, or do they isolate them from one another?

4. If both boys and girls are working at computers, can you identify any patterns? For example, do boys spend more time at the machines than girls? Are boys considered expert about using computers?

5. Do all students, regardless of racial or ethnic background, use the computers equally?

6. Do students always stay on task using computers, or are they involved in things that would be frowned on by the teacher or the school in general?

7. Does the time spent using computers in the classroom you observed seem well spent?

Connecting with INTASC: Principle 6

Communication Skills: The teacher uses knowledge of effective verbal, nonverbal, and media communication techniques to foster active inquiry, collaboration, and supportive interaction in the classroom.

Meet with the teacher after your observation and find out what the teacher does to use technology to enhance instruction. Does the teacher communicate with parents via e-mail or by posting homework on a class website? What does the teacher do to link more general classroom activities with students' uses of the computer? Find out whether the teacher is familiar with the ISTE standards and, if so, how these standards inform the teacher's instructional planning.

13

Becoming a Teacher: Next Steps

Who am I?

What do I believe?

THINK ABOUT THIS:

In Chapter 1, the question "Am I a teacher?" was posed to you and you were asked to think about it as you completed this course. Think about your answer to the question now. Use what you have learned through your observations, interviews, personal reflections, and class discussions to guide you. How would you describe your passion for teaching? How will *you* touch the future as a teacher?

Throughout the practicum experience I grappled with the question of who I was as a teacher. What I found at the end was that I was the best teacher when I was myself. When I allowed my passion to shine through, the students responded."

Student Teacher

T aking this course has given you the opportunity to think about becoming a teacher. As you have
seen throughout this text, becoming a teacher is a developmental
process that begins here, in your first education course. It is here where you begin to
reflect on your assumptions and beliefs about teaching. This reflection will continue
through early field experiences and culminate as you student teach during your senior
year. This early preparation will influence how you approach your professional life as a
teacher.

This chapter provides you with information pertaining to the next steps that will
take you closer to becoming a teacher. It will discuss early field experiences, student
teaching, induction into the profession during your first several years, professional
development, teacher leadership opportunities, and new roles in education. As you
read this chapter, envision yourself as a teacher and think about how these topics
will affect you.

The end of this chapter leaves you with the concept of teachers as heroes.
Christa McAuliffe was a shining example of a teacher making a difference in the
world when she was chosen to be the first teacher to fly into space in 1986. She left
us with the credo: "I touch the future, I teach." This will be your legacy. At the end of
the chapter, you should know the answers to the following key questions:

Key Questions

- What's next?
- What can you expect in your first year of teaching?
- How will you continue to grow as a teacher?
- What does it mean to teach for life?

WHAT'S NEXT?

As you prepare to launch your teaching career, it is important that you understand what is involved in the process. Whether you are receiving your certification through a four-year teacher education program or a special certification program, there will be a process to taking charge of your own classroom. A number of essential stages make up this process, including "practice," searching for jobs, applying for a license, and signing your first contract.

PREPARING FOR SUCCESSFUL FIELD EXPERIENCES IN SCHOOLS

Even though you have 2 or 3 more years of coursework ahead of you, you should be aware that most of your methods courses will require you to work in schools to develop your skills and to gain experience.

● **Early Field Experiences** As part of your undergraduate education program, you will most likely be required to complete early field experiences, sometimes called prepracticum experiences, which may include observing classrooms and doing some teaching. You also may become a volunteer in a school to gain classroom experience. For undergraduates, these early experiences typically begin in the sophomore year and involve attending a school one or more days a week. The in-school experience is usually linked to methods courses. Having practical experience as the main vehicle for coursework allows professors to assign activities based on your in-school experience. Some schools teach methods courses in addition to prepracticum work. This allows students to apply some of the theoretical information they learn to the classroom. These in-school experiences are invaluable because they give you a context in which to apply the knowledge you are learning in your courses.

To prepare for your early field experiences, it is important to understand some of the following guidelines:

1. *Be clear about the purpose of the visit to the school.* Is it to complete an assignment for a course? Is it volunteer work? Is it for this course as an observation and interview? Is it for your own experience?

2. *Understand that you are a guest in the school and in a teacher's classroom.* Gain permission for the visit. Contact the principal's office secretary to find out how to set up a school visit. Do you need to sign in? Do you need a note from the professor? Do you need to have identification and name tags on at all times?

3. *Be prepared to assist the teacher.* Are you willing to help out if asked? Would you be comfortable volunteering to work with a student who seems to need help? Are you shy or bold? Can you talk to teachers?

4. *Be professional.* Teachers are very busy focusing on their students. They may not have extra time for early field observers, or they may not be available for interviews. Make appointments with busy teachers to show that you understand their time constraints.

5. *Record what happened the day of the visit.* It is important to record what you observe and what you think at the time of the visit. Your memory may fade and things may look different several days later.

6. *Show appreciation for the teacher's time.* Take time to write a thank-you note or e-mail to any teacher who spends time with you. Teachers appreciate the acknowledgment and will often spend more time with you in the future if you show that you understand how busy they are.

● **Student Teaching** The capstone experience of your teaching program is your full practicum, often known as *student teaching*. While this may seem very far away right now, it will arrive sooner than you think. Whereas your prepracticum involved spending one or two days at school, student teaching will place you at school full-time for an entire semester or a school year. This usually takes place during your senior year or at the end of your graduate program. Some accreditation programs may set it up as an internship. Student teaching is the culminating experience that will provide you the opportunity to work with a teacher full-time and to apply what you are learning in your university courses to your student teaching.

Students often rank the practicum as *the most valued component* of a teacher preparation program. Why do student teachers value this experience so much? Most say that it is the first time they really put into practice what they have learned in their theory and methods classes. The practicum is, in fact, practice for new teachers and preparation for having their own classrooms.

Each teacher education program designs field experiences to provide student teachers with opportunities to develop skills, think about their assumptions, and interact with students. If you have not already done so, make an appointment to talk with your advisor to learn about the field experiences offered in your program. These experiences will enrich your knowledge in your classes as well as your in-class experience.

Becoming a teacher takes practice. Your opportunity to practice during early field experiences or student teaching is much like a medical internship in which medical students work at a hospital. Your work in schools with students and teachers will begin in small increments. You may begin by tutoring one student or by observing a class. Even though your actual teaching may be several years away, it is important to start thinking about the skills required to be a teacher. Do you feel uncomfortable with the idea of speaking in front of groups of students? Does the thought of communicating with parents or administrators make you edgy? As you begin to enter classrooms, you will become more comfortable with students and your role as a student teacher. As issues and questions arise, don't be afraid to discuss them with your professors and classmates. It will help you anticipate and resolve concerns that you will no doubt have to face when you have your own classroom. Keep in mind that all student teachers have questions. Following is some advice from student teachers who have completed the practicum experience:

> Enjoy each day in the classroom. Live each moment to the fullest. Your experience will be filled with wonder and struggles, laughter and frustrations. But each morning the sun will come up and you will stand before a new day with an opportunity to change lives. It's hard to ask for more than that.

> You are embarking on a difficult journey. It is tough to get up each morning long before your roommates are even thinking about hitting the snooze bar. It is hard when the students challenge your authority and put you on the spot. Chances are you will feel guilty when you raise your voice to a student for the first time. Your supervisor will expect your work to be high quality, demanding the best from you. You will want to take a nap when you go home every day, but will have to prepare lessons. Your will, integrity, and patience will be tested. And it's all worth it!

> It feels as if it were yesterday that I was feeling a bit nervous and excited about what lay ahead. I am telling you to hold on and enjoy the ride. There will be many moments when you feel you are drowning in work and are too overtired to think, but in the end it is all worth it. There will be times when you think, "Why am I doing this?" "Do I really want to teach?" To be honest, that is how I felt. I was incredibly unsure whether I was taking the right life path. I promise you student teaching will let you know. Look at the children in your classes. They look up to you. Let them pull you through.

> My advice is not to take yourself so seriously. Take the experience seriously, but learn to laugh at yourself and your mistakes. You must enter your practicum with a sense of humor and an abundance of humility. If your ideal lesson bombs, don't worry. Chances are it will be followed by a successful lesson. There are lots of ups and downs during this experience. Capitalize on your mistakes and learn from them.

INTASC

Principle #9

Professional Commitment and Responsibility: The teacher is a reflective practitioner who continually evaluates the effects of his/her choices and actions on others (students, parents, and other professionals in the learning community) and who actively seeks out opportunities to grow professionally.

Every mountain is climbed one step at a time. As you climb the steps of your practicum experience, you might wonder when you will reach the top. But it is the journey up the mountain that changes us and helps us grow. So enjoy the journey, and don't worry about reaching the top just yet. Before you know it, you'll be there.

● **Filtering Information**   As you begin to observe classrooms in the next year or two, you will inevitably see some things that teachers do that you do not agree with or that conflict with what you've learned in your program. When this happens, you may feel some dissonance as a result. For example, if you observe a teacher scolding a child in front of an entire class in a classroom that you had understood to be a democratic classroom, you might instantly judge that teacher negatively. But what if the student had thrown something at another student and injured that student? What if the student had said something highly offensive to another student? Perhaps the teacher's response was not as the class model called for, but it may be more understandable in the proper context. In these types of circumstances, you may start to question what you really believe, or you may still determine that the teacher's response is wrong, or you may try to stay out of it altogether and decide not to make any judgments because you're new to the field and you don't feel you know enough yet. Often there is no definitive right and wrong, but it is important that you understand the situation that led to the behavior in question. Don't be afraid to ask questions at these times. This will help you clarify your beliefs throughout your field experiences.

When you first enter someone else's classroom as an observer or a student teacher, it may feel awkward. After all, you are a guest in another teacher's class. This may not be easy for the teacher either. Because this is not your classroom, you will not be responsible for making the final decisions about curriculum or rules for conduct. The key to a successful experience and to making yourself a welcomed guest is communicating respectfully, openly, and honestly with your cooperating teacher.

At the end of any field experience, especially student teaching, you will find that you are doing things you never expected you would ever do. One student teacher said it this way: "'Did I just do all that?'" you will say to yourself as you walk out the door for the final time. Did I help a child learn to read? Was that little boy I worked with all semester really

During the interview, school officials will be looking to see if you will fit in with their school culture, but you are also interviewing them to see if they meet your needs. What will your needs be?

not able to do that work when I started my student teaching? Did I really hear all of those kind words from parents? Is this portfolio in my hand really full of all my hard work and memories? Did I really come into an empty building during vacation to feed turtles, guinea pigs, and an iguana? How on earth did I manage to get up so early each morning?" His words ring true for many other education students as well. You too will realize that you did it because of the amazing relationships you formed with so many wonderful children.

Preparing yourself for field experiences in schools, whether they are early on or in your senior year when you are student teaching full-time, will enrich your journey to becoming a teacher. Take notes, observe, ask questions, and integrate what you learn with what you see and experience firsthand. This process will help you establish your belief system, which will inform your decisions when you enter the classroom as a teacher.

THE JOB SEARCH

It is never too early to think ahead and begin to plan for the time when your job search will begin. Unlike many college graduates who are not sure of their next steps, you know that you want to teach. The most common questions you will have are: How do I find out what jobs are available? How do I apply for these positions? How do I prepare for an interview? How do I use my teaching portfolio in an interview? What do I do if I am asked to demonstrate a lesson? If I have more than one job opportunity, how do I know which is best? What does it mean to sign a contract? What do I do after accepting a position?

Whether on paper or as an electronic resource, your professional portfolio is an important representation to potential employers of your professional preparation. They will be looking for progress in your development.

- **Resources**   A good first step in preparing for a job search is to visit the career center at your college or university to find out what services they offer their graduates. As you finish up your student teaching your senior year, you may find that the school where you do your student teaching provides a network. Speak with teachers with whom you work during your various field experiences as well as school administrators for advice and any potential contacts. Newspaper advertisements, state employment websites, and retirement newsletters are also good resources for discovering where there may be openings for teachers. Those going to other states can use the Internet to connect to district openings across the country and the world.

Many publications on the market can help you organize your materials for the job search. One such book is *The Job Search Handbook,* published by the Association for School, College, and University Staffing (ASCUS), a free booklet that outlines specific suggestions for cover letters and résumés and practical strategies for interviews. Your school's career center or field experience coordinator likely will have a copy of this publication or at least know how to obtain a copy. This might be a good resource to get you started. Many others are available as well. Visit your bookstore or go online and search for books related to finding teaching jobs. When looking for books online, you can often view user reviews that will help you assess how useful the book may be.

- **Preparing for the Interview**   The interview will be an important aspect of the job search. Prepare yourself for this time by practicing responding to questions you may be asked. A good strategy is to create a support group of students who are all interviewing and role-play the interviews. You might consider videotaping each other so you can see how you look when you respond to an interviewer. While this can be intimidating, it can also be a very useful tool for perfecting your interviewing skills. Whether you use the videotape or not, review Figures 13.1 on page 402, Top 10 List for Interviewees, and Figure 13.2 on page 403, Commonly Asked Interview Questions. These questions will be helpful for your interview for student teaching placement as well as for interviews after graduation.

FIGURE 13.1

Top 10 List for Interviewees

1.
COME PREPARED.

Do research in advance about the school. Interviewees who do their homework find themselves more confident and better prepared to answer questions about the responsibilities of a current open position.

2.
BRING A CLEAN COPY OF AN UP-TO-DATE RÉSUMÉ.

Résumés should list major accomplishments and results achieved. Résumés should be no more than two pages. Bring a separate folder to the interview containing examples of your work, references letters, and so on.

3.
DRESS THE PART.

At least one day before your interview, examine your outfit you plan to wear to the interview (including shoes). Leave strong perfume and cologne at home. It's better to be conservative than flashy during interviews.

4.
PLAN TO ARRIVE TEN MINUTES EARLY.

Make sure you know how to get where you are going and allow for enough time to collect your thoughts before your appointment.

5.
KNOW WHY YOU WANT THE JOB.

Be prepared to answer the questions, whether asked directly or indirectly, why you want this particular job and why you would be the best choice for it.

6.
LISTEN TO YOUR INTERVIEWER'S QUESTIONS CAREFULLY.

Be prepared to answer difficult questions under pressure. If you need an extra few seconds to prepare your answer; it is okay to ask the interviewer to repeat and/or clarify the question.

7.
ANSWER WITH ENTHUSIASM AND PROFESSIONAL VOCABULARY.

Avoid slang. Highlight appropriate aspects of your education, work experience, and continuing education (seminars, training, and so on). Convey enthusiasm. Body language is important. Make eye contact with the interviewer.

8.
BE PREPARED TO DISCUSS AREAS YOU NEED TO STRENGTHEN IN YOUR WORK EXPERIENCE AND KNOWLEDGE.

It is hard to trust an interviewee who expresses no limitation in his or her performance. Avoid trying to present a perfect image.

9.
BRING QUESTIONS OF YOUR OWN.

The interviewee who asks informed questions about the school and the position is set apart from the crowd. Don't be afraid to ask information about what the school has to offer you.

10.
FOLLOW UP AFTER THE INTERVIEW WITH A THANK-YOU.

Within 24 hours, send a postcard or a brief letter thanking the interviewer for the opportunity to interview for the job. Include something specific that was discussed during your time together. Call 5 to 10 days later and the interviewer know you are still interested in the job.

Source: Lani Williams Parker, Director of Advancement, Western Seminary, Portland, OR.

FIGURE 13.2

Commonly Asked Interview Questions

1.
TELL ME ABOUT YOURSELF.

Keep your answer brief. The interviewer is interested in your experience, interests, and communication skills.

2.
WHAT ARE YOUR STRENGTHS/WEAKNESSES?

Emphasize your good traits and those that relate to the job for which you are interviewing. You can mention an area that you are working to improve, or one in which you have recently made great strides.

3.
WHY DO YOU WANT TO WORK HERE?

This is a good chance to mention how you can apply your skills, interests, and goals to the job.

4.
WHY SHOULD WE HIRE YOU?

Take this opportunity to highlight the unique qualities you can bring to the job.

5.
WHAT WOULD YOU DO IN (A PARTICULAR SITUATION)?

Don't be afraid to say that you would ask questions of your supervisor and approach each challenge as a learning opportunity.

Source: Adapted from MetLife Consumer Education Center, *About. . . . Getting Your First Job.* (New York: Metropolitan Life Insurance Company, 1996). Copyright 1996 by Metropolitan Life Insurance Company. Adapted with permission.

● **Documenting Your Professional Preparation**   You will create many kinds of portfolios throughout your college experience. Some may be hard copies of documents that you assemble for a course; others may be electronic summaries of field experiences. This class is a good time to begin collecting materials for your Touch the Future portfolio, reflecting on thoughts you've reached throughout the course. You may find yourself changing your perspectives during the course of your training, and your portfolio can help you record those changes. Whatever type of portfolio you create, the goal of the process will be to compile evidence of your competency as a teacher. Your portfolio should demonstrate that you have met the skills required. Some college programs require students to start their field portfolios in their sophomore year and build on them until graduation. As a result of this lengthy process, these portfolios may become so large and cumbersome that it is difficult to find anything. So what do you do for the job interview when you have 2 or 3 years' worth of information?

Professional Portfolio   School districts advise students to pare down their portfolios to create a small, streamlined **teacher portfolio** or **professional portfolio** (Wolf, 1996). This abridged portfolio is usually a smaller subset of the many documents or **artifacts** you will collect during your teacher preparation. An artifact is a document that demonstrates or shows evidence of a skill or competency. It may be a photo, a sample of your work, a lesson plan, or a variety of other products. You will have an opportunity to select artifacts and think about why you want to highlight these particular lessons or skills. Professional portfolios are important to take with you to interviews; they are also a useful tool to share with parents and other teachers in the school.

A streamlined portfolio typically includes a philosophy statement, a sampling of student work, one or two lessons, and perhaps some photos. Some students make several copies of this mini-portfolio and leave it with the members of interview committees.

Electronic Portfolios Many teacher education departments now require students to prepare **electronic portfolios,** or electronic documentation that represents your in-class experiences and projects. Figure 13.3 presents some sample pages from an electronic portfolio. While electronic portfolios should not entirely replace professional portfolios, they may be used as a pre- or postinterview introduction or follow-up. You will still want hard-copy documentation to bring with you to interviews.

Electronic portfolios have both advantages and disadvantages. On the plus side, electronic portfolios allow you to collect documents over a long period of time without taking up any physical space as compared to unwieldy hard-copy portfolios. The disadvantage, however, is that even in this age of technology not all schools are wired for sharing these portfolios. To allow for both options, many education majors find a balance between the paper portfolios and e-portfolios and include some aspect of technology in their job interviews. For example, you could bring to interviews both a hard copy of your professional portfolio and a disk or CD with sample units or lesson plans, samples of student work, and some of your own comments that you can leave with the interviewer for review after the meeting. To see a sample of an actual student teacher portfolio, turn to the Log On section at the end of the chapter.

Be aware that you could put many hours into selecting documents for your professional portfolio only to have it ignored at an interview. This happens quite often; nevertheless, you should always bring your portfolio with you to interviews, as teachers and administrators will expect you to have it in your interview. Also keep in mind that creating your portfolio allows you to think about issues and reflect on practices as you compile artifacts that illustrate what you have learned. Education majors agree that the *process* of creating the portfolio is equally important. It made feel them confident and well prepared to answer interviewers' questions (Pelletier, 2004). Just as you might review quizzes you have taken in order to prepare for a test, reviewing your work prepares you for answering the interviewers' questions on any topic.

Creating a Brochure An alternative or supplement to creating a portfolio is creating a small brochure that provides an overview of your skills and experience. This type of document may leave a unique impression with the interview committee. Choose the approach that will highlight your skills and share your passion for teaching.

APPLYING FOR YOUR FIRST TEACHING LICENSE

I N T A S C

Principle #9

Professional Commitment and Responsibility: The teacher is a reflective practitioner who continually evaluates the effects of his/her choices and actions on others (students, parents, and other professionals in the learning community) and who actively seeks out opportunities to grow professionally.

Applying for your teaching license from the state department of education (DOE) and signing a teacher's contract will be important milestones in your career as a teacher. Depending on the state where you are looking for jobs, you will need to find out whether you have to take any content tests for licensure and whether passing these tests is a requirement of your student teaching program. Each state has its own requirements and procedures for applying for a license. Some states call the license a **teacher certificate.**

● **Reciprocity** If you are planning to teach in a state other than the one in which you completed your student teaching, you should contact that state's certification/licensure office as a first step. Appendix B includes a list of websites from the *Job Search Handbook* (AAEE, 2004) to get you started. You may also find links to specific states and those with an **interstate agreement,** a document between various states indicating reciprocity and licensure transfer. The U.S. Department of Education website also contains links and lists of school districts looking to hire teachers. Applications are usually available online. Many states require that you mail in proof that you have completed an "approved program" in

FIGURE 13.3

Electronic Portfolios

This is an example of an electronic portfolio home page. The home page should include a brief introduction to your portfolio and a navigation system. The links in the table of contents allow the reviewer to quickly access the documents in each area. If the portfolio reviewer wanted to learn about your classroom management, he or she would click the Classroom Management link, which would then take them to a menu of categories related to your classroom management artifacts. This example illustrates what the reviewer might see if he or she clicked on the category of seating arrangement.

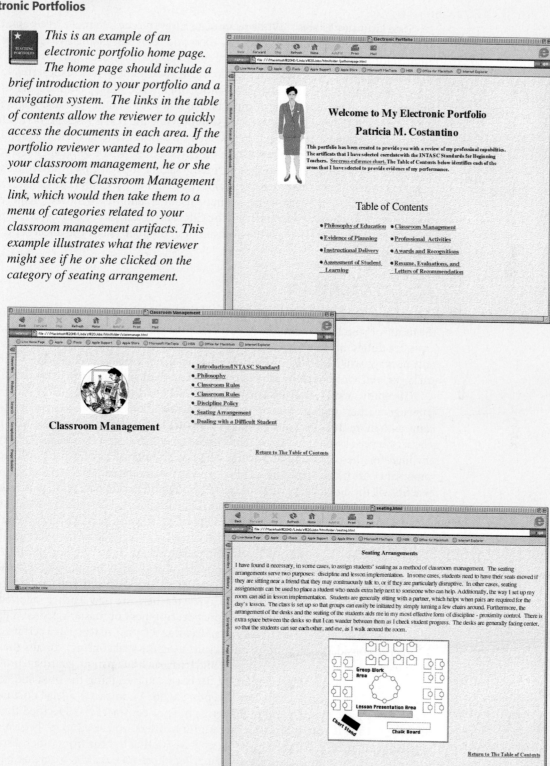

teacher education. Preparing to become a teacher through a college teacher preparation program generally earns you a more advanced teaching license, making it easier to qualify for reciprocity. Teaching candidates who enter through alternate pathways may find it more difficult to qualify for reciprocity.

● **State Licensure Exams**   While reciprocity allows teachers to move freely among states with an interstate agreement, it does not allow you to bypass taking any tests that may be required for licensure. Most states require some type of licensure exam for preservice and beginning teachers. The most common licensure assessment is the **Praxis Series.** Licensure exams measure literacy skills as well as some content knowledge. Different states require different assessments, so it will be important to talk with your advisor about specific state requirements as they pertain to your job search. While the Praxis assessments are transferable from state to state, several states have their own entrance tests; therefore, applicants in these states would still be required to take the entrance test before being eligible for a teaching position. Always do your homework before taking any tests; you want to be sure you are taking the right ones. For example, California requires the California Subject Examination for Teachers (CSET) for its beginning educators, and Massachusetts requires applicants to take the Massachusetts Tests for Educator Licensure (MTEL) in content and literacy. Once you take and pass the licensure test, the state issues you a teacher certificate or license.

SIGNING A CONTRACT

Upon accepting a teaching position, you will be required to sign a **contract** that outlines the terms of your agreement. These terms include your salary, your benefits package, and any extra duties that may be part of your agreement with the school. Included in your benefits package will be health insurance, sick days, dental plans, life insurance, retirement packages, and allowances for professional development and support.

Currently, math and science teachers, special education teachers, and some foreign-language teachers are in demand. Because these positions are in high demand, they may come with more attractive offers from the districts. Teachers licensed in these areas will have a better chance of being able to pick and choose their districts, and since salaries are not usually high for the profession as a whole, the benefit and retirement packages become an important part of the decision-making process. For example, what percentage of health benefits will the district pay? How much will that require you to pay? How good is the health plan coverage? These will be very important details that you will want to seriously consider before committing to a school or district. Often a good health benefit package with a higher percentage of the premium paid by the district will outweigh the salary offering.

Other factors to consider before signing a contract include whether a mentoring program exists for new teachers. Are there opportunities to collaborate with other teachers? Are there reduced class sizes for beginning teachers, and are beginning teachers given students who are more likely to respond to a new teacher? Are new teachers allotted time to prepare lessons and offered free professional development or master's degree support? All of these issues should be considered when deciding whether to teach in a certain district.

As you consider your options with regard to a potential contract, discuss the terms of the agreement with someone you respect and trust, such as a parent, guardian, professor, or advisor. This is an extremely important decision, and weighing the pros and cons is an important part of the process before accepting a job. A contract is a legal document, and once you sign it you are bound to the terms of your contract for a specified time period (usually a year). If you are considering multiple offers, you need to be honest with the potential employer. It is okay to say that you are waiting to hear from other districts and that you need a little time before responding. This honesty saves you from possibly having to break a contract, which could have detrimental effects on the district. While it is not unheard of, many districts consider breaking a contract to be unethical.

WHAT CAN YOU EXPECT IN YOUR FIRST YEAR OF TEACHING?

When asked about their first year of teaching, beginning teachers usually express elation over surviving the first year and are excited to begin the next year with the knowledge they gained the first year. It is difficult to explain to someone who has never taught what it is really like to be in charge of your very first classroom. Just like sailing a boat or skiing down a slope, it is an "experience" you have to feel. You have prepared for it for years—but still, when you're in front of the class for the first time without a mentor (or safety net), you are on your own. Following is some advice from first-year teachers that may make a difference and help you avoid some common pitfalls.

ADVICE FROM FIRST-YEAR TEACHERS

A panel of first-year teachers was asked several questions related to their preparation as teachers (Massachusetts Coalition, 2002). These questions included the following: What happened your first year that you did not expect? What do you wish you had learned more about in college? What advice would you give to future first-year teachers?

These new teachers all were excited, energetic, and proud to be teachers. They wanted to share these bits of advice, not to make prospective teachers fear teaching, but rather to prepare them for the classroom. Their responses should be enlightening, as they will help you understand some of the key issues that concern first year teachers.

- **What Happened Your First Year That You Did Not Expect?**   Some beginning teachers explained that they didn't anticipate what it would be like to be "on" all day in front of a group of students. While they had some taste of this when they were student teaching, as first-year teachers they realized that when they were student teachers they had actually taken breaks when their cooperating teacher taught the class. While the beginning teachers all loved their classrooms and students, they agreed that they slept very well at the end of the school day.

All the teachers couldn't believe how much paperwork was involved in teaching. While they had thought student teaching required filling out a lot of forms, they found even more paperwork as first-year teachers. For example, they mentioned that there were forms for lunch, attendance, enrollment reports, book clubs, annual reports, diversity reports, testing, and special education reports. Filling out all of these forms became part of their daily routines. All those forms, on top of all of the homework that they assigned and then had to grade, made for an enormous amount of paper. Many stated that once they got into a routine for addressing the paperwork, it all became very doable.

Responsibilities above and beyond their classroom teaching had not registered on the radar screens of many beginning teachers when they had been student teachers. All first-year teachers found themselves fulfilling duties unrelated to teaching, yet required by the school. A **duty** is defined as something a teacher is assigned by the school that is outside their own classroom. Examples include playground monitoring, cafeteria duty, duty outside the bathroom (in high schools, usually), or study hall. Most of these teachers agreed that while these responsibilities were not always fun, they were necessary to the smooth operation of the school.

Two other areas that surprised these new teachers related to how much time they spent on committee work and faculty meetings. As student teachers, they hadn't been tuned into the fact that professional activities were also part of a teacher's routine. Even as first-year teachers, many had been invited to join curriculum committees and meet after school with other teachers. This unexpected time was often not planned for them and they wanted to let new teachers know to factor this in. They also didn't understand the culture of the faculty meetings and often did not speak for fear of saying something that might offend someone.

Problems to POSSIBILITIES

How Do You Make Life Easier for a New Teacher?

Mike had just accepted his first teaching position and was excited to begin. When he arrived for his orientation, he picked up his class assignment. Some of the other teachers in the school looked at it and warned that it could be a difficult combination of students. This made Mike nervous, but he figured he'd just do the best he could. He walked to his classroom to begin setting it up before students arrived for the start of school, and the room was completely empty! His textbooks were not in the room, and the teacher before him had taken all her supplies and materials from 20 years of teaching and given them to a new teacher at another school who was a friend of the family.

Mike didn't know where to turn for help. He had met the principal in his interview and very briefly at orientation, but to be honest, she appeared busy and unapproachable. His mentor was in another grade level in the school, but he had made it clear that "you young people need to earn your stripes." His mentor had laid the ground rules—they could schedule meetings during the school day, but after school, the mentor had to get to his part-time job. Mike stood in the classroom door looking at the empty room with the class list in his hand. This was not what he was expecting.

Discussion Questions

What would you do if you were Mike? How will you anticipate possible problems as you enter the profession your first year? How would you like to be mentored?

Possibilities

Schools are busy places. Principals, mentors, and other teachers often are pulled in many directions. Class lists are often made up at the end of the previous school year and sometimes even over the summer. New teachers who need special consideration with student management and discipline issues need to meet with their mentors and principal to bring these issues to the forefront.

New teachers are often told to ask their mentors for help when they need it, but often they don't know what kind of help they need until a situation or problem presents itself. In Mike's case, he needs to find materials and needs to review his "problematic" class list with someone who can either move some students out of his class or give him advice as to how best to prepare for the situation. If the teachers

reviewing the list already know these students, they can help address some of the potential issues.

Other teachers in the building can also assist new teachers. In fact, it is often the *informal mentor,* such as the teacher next door, who becomes the easiest advisor because that person is right there. New teachers need to ask questions, ask for advice, and be available to listen to a variety of points of view before deciding the best approach to a situation. Problem solving is a way of life for teachers. As a beginner, you need to be able to quickly assess the situation, know where to go for help, and try a variety of solutions. And remember, it does get easier with time! The following helpful hints from experienced teachers may help:

- Ask experienced teachers to tell you of the possible pitfalls you can expect in your first year. Make a list of these pitfalls. Anticipating situations makes them easier to deal with. Make time to discuss them with the teachers as they happen.

- Ask your mentor to brief you on all types of procedures in the school—how to get to buses, fire drills, and so on—to make sure you know what you are doing.

- Meet with the principal or department chair about students in your class and review the class list. Ask whether teachers can help you with these problem students up front before the students act out.

- Find out where all the other new teachers are in the building or in the district. Network with them socially and in school to share ideas and coping techniques.

- Find out whether you have a supply budget. If not, find free and inexpensive materials in the community to set up your empty classroom. Share with other new teachers. If you create a social studies unit and another teacher purchases science units, you can switch and share later.

- Be available to be mentored! Your mentor may be making time for you, but are you there to listen? You don't have to take all the advice, but respectfully listen and use what you can to improve your teaching.

BUILDING ON EDUCATIONAL FOUNDATIONS

Establishing Authority

When you enter a typical classroom as a new teacher, you will be confronted with the problem of establishing authority with 25 or 30 students who may or may not wish to be there. Essentially, any classroom teacher is in command of a small social system in which lines of authority and command are very real.

Sociologists have identified three types of authority that work in classrooms. The first is *charismatic authority,* which arises from the devotion of a group to a particular individual. Charismatic authority is gained through trust and is an almost inexplicable quality that certain individuals have to provide leadership.

Authority can also function in classrooms as *traditional authority.* In this type of authority, students obey teachers simply because they are teachers and occupy a specific position in the educational system.

The third and final type of authority that operates in classrooms is *legal–rational authority.* This is literally the authority of the law. Students accept the authority of the rules provided by a coach for playing a sport such as baseball. They cannot change the rules and still play the game. In the classroom, teachers employ legal–rational authority when they enforce attendance, a specific dress code, or a grading requirement.

Of course, in most classrooms probably all three types of authority are at work. It is interesting to determine which one predominates and why.

What types of authority are likely to be at work when you are a teacher? Do you think certain types of authority will come into play more often in certain types of educational settings or at different times in your career?

They recommend that you learn about all types of meetings early in your education program so you are better prepared when you are a first-year teacher.

- **What Do You Wish You Had Learned More about in College?** First and foremost, beginning teachers advised education majors to learn more about how schools work during early field experiences and student teaching.Specifically, they stated that they wished they had known more about how decisions are made and how a beginning teacher can navigate the complicated nature of schools. No one on the panel, representing seven colleges, felt their schools had sufficiently prepared them for the real school culture. While all agreed that their schools were quite different, they did find some common themes that could have been addressed. See Problems to Possibilities for a possible scenario that any new teacher could encounter.

As beginning teachers, they felt that although they possessed knowledge about curriculum, strategies for teaching, learning theories, and behavior and classroom management, they were surprised at how difficult it was to make decisions about how to handle certain children or even how difficult it was to do something as simple as order new books. The elementary teachers wished their college programs had provided them with more information about various types of curriculum. They found themselves faced with district programs for reading and math with which they were unfamiliar. They wished they could have reviewed many kinds of curriculum in all areas instead of just focusing on areas that particular professors found to be the best approaches for teaching. Even though the new teachers agreed with these approaches from their college preparation, they had to *teach* the district programs and because they were unfamiliar with them, it took enormous amounts of time each night not only learning the material, but then trying to modify it to meet the needs of all learners.

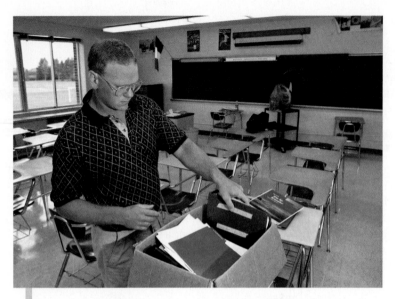

Once you have that first job, the classroom is yours, and every child who enters it becomes your responsibility. Although you will be part of a larger system, you determine the learning that takes place in that room.

I N T A S C

Principle #9

Professional Commitment and Responsibility: The teacher is a reflective practitioner who continually evaluates the effects of his/her choices and actions on others (students, parents, and other professionals in the learning community) and who actively seeks out opportunities to grow professionally.

The new teachers also wished they had gone into their jobs knowing more about education reform and the language dominating faculty meetings. As No Child Left Behind and other state testing initiatives were driving their classroom curriculum, these teachers didn't feel that they had enough background to understand the rationale and the big ideas behind these legislative decisions. Some said that they had heard of them in college, but didn't pay as much attention as they should have because they didn't really understand the impact of state and federal mandates on their own classrooms. They also wanted to know more about how education reform worked in practice. Members of the panel said they found it difficult to understand the big picture of why tests were being given to students who couldn't speak the language or who had special needs. Consequently, they just didn't understand how these mandates would affect their teaching.

While many teacher education programs teach creative approaches and new ways to engage learners, they do not explain how to do this working within the frameworks dictated by district, state, and federal initiatives. Some beginning teachers stated that they wished they had better understood how to mesh creative lesson preparations with the prescriptive curriculum tied to high-stakes tests. They were passionate and committed to students, but felt that their teaching programs didn't really explain how difficult it would be to juggle state and federal mandates and creative teaching.

Many beginning teachers had trouble figuring out where they fit into the culture of the school. Starting at the top, some said they weren't sure what the principal expected of them as first-year teachers. They also didn't know how they were to fit in with their colleagues, who spanned a variety of ages and experience. Figure 13.4 identifies some common expectations new teachers have for teaching. They learned, however, that collaboration is necessary in working with colleagues. Some first-year teachers on the panel discussed being "forced" to work with another teacher whom they didn't choose; they felt awkward and pressured to conform to how more experienced teachers did things even when they didn't agree. They wished that these types of scenarios had been discussed in some of their courses or seminars so they would have felt more prepared to deal with some difficult situations. Instead, many first-year teachers said that being among the youngest teachers in the building sometimes made them feel that they could not speak up because they didn't have enough experience. Later in this chapter you will read about ways to think about working with other adults in a school.

Classroom and behavior management continued to be a priority for all first-year teachers on the panel. While they understood theoretical constructs as applied to classroom management, they also realized that they needed a context for understanding how to implement their own routines, arrange their classrooms, manage their time, and handle behavioral issues. They pointed out that reading a case study of a difficult student was a lot different from experiencing the problem firsthand.

Finally, all the new teachers expressed a need for more strategies for connecting with parents and the community. They did not feel that this topic was given enough emphasis for them to implement their own course of action.

● **What Advice Would You Give to Future First-Year Teachers?**   Many teachers said that if they could have done some something differently when they were in school, they would have observed more teachers. They would have then kept a log of methods, ideas, and

Voices of New Teachers: Seven Things We Wish We Had Learned in College

- How to navigate the culture of schools . . . where to go to get questions answered, how decisions about students are made, how to get supplies, and so on.

- What the principal really expects of a new teacher . . . how to be evaluated, when to meet with the principal, how to follow up after an observation, and so on.

- What the most current curriculum programs are . . . especially for elementary, balanced literacy, hands-on math, science companies, and so on.

- How education reform is influencing the daily work of classroom teachers . . . especially No Child Left Behind and state and district initiatives, how to learn more about the district prior to starting the job, and so on.

- How to collaborate and be a colleague with older teachers . . . how to speak up when the teacher is experienced, how to fit collaboration in, what to do when you have to work with another teacher that you may not have selected, and so on.

- What to do to connect with parents in the first year . . . how to introduce yourself, what to do at parent conferences, how to get into the community, and so on.

- How to manage time, routines, and behavior more effectively and efficiently during the first year . . . time management techniques for collecting papers, correcting, setting up the classroom to avoid behavior problems, dealing with difficult students, and so on.

Source: Massachusetts Coalition. (2002). Panel Presentation: New Teachers Share Expectations at the Title II Conference, Sturbridge, Massachusetts.

materials pertaining to each of the teachers they observed. They also said they would have co-taught and collaborated much more during senior student teaching. They felt that this would have given them even more ideas and models for lessons.

As a future teacher, the panel suggests, find out as much as you can before beginning your first year. Ask questions in all college courses so that you can engage in authentic discussions about these issues. To their college professors who are teaching education courses, they recommend visiting schools more often, inviting teachers to classes so they can share with prospective teachers what is happening in schools today. They also suggest that professors touch on all of the topics discussed in this section in all aspects of course and field experiences. While all first-year teachers agreed that college programs can't provide the beginner with information on every topic and issue that comes up, and teaching requires lifelong learning, they do agree that more discussion would help. They warn students: Be prepared for a steep learning curve your first year, but also be assured that you will have a lot of support, and in your second year you will be doling out advice to prospective teachers.

Everyone on the panel agreed that teaching is at once challenging and rewarding. The most experienced educators agree that if you really want to teach, "hang in" for the first year; it will get easier. Beginning teachers who completed their first year in an urban district were asked to respond to the question, "What do we need to do to keep you here for another year?" Their responses, presented in Figure 13.5 on page 412, will give you some insight into some of the challenges this group experienced and how they would like to grow as professionals.

ADVICE FROM STUDENTS

Beginning teachers agree that students are their best guides for improving their teaching practice. One new teacher explained, "I listen more to my students to learn more about my

I N T A S C

Principle #2

Knowledge of Human Development and Learning: The teacher understands how children learn and develop, and can provide learning opportunities that support their intellectual, social, and personal development.

FIGURE 13.5

What Do We Need to Keep Us Here?

- Less administrative red tape

- Opportunities to continue coursework in order to raise our salary

- Opportunities to take on challenges that can make positive changes

- Positive recognition and encouragement from the principal to help us reach our goals

- Better balance between the union and non-union perspectives and intentions

- Financial support for pursuing further education

- Respect

teaching." We have all been students and know what we like in a teacher. Think about what you have liked about your teachers over the years. What would you like to emulate? Consider the following student suggestions and how you would apply them. Even though these are college students responding to a professor's survey, most of these responses can be adapted to pre-K–12 students.

1. *Make the class interesting.* Use the elements of variety and surprise occasionally. If it is a lecture, be animated.

2. *Show true enthusiasm and pride in the content and the students in the class.* If you are excited, the students will be more likely to be excited and want to learn.

3. *Relate the content/activity to the real world.*

4. *Be clear about the purpose of the lesson.* What do you want the students to get out of the lesson?

5. *Know where the students are coming from.* How much did they know before the start of the class and where they are going after this course?

6. *Emphasize and repeat key points.*

7. *Let your students see that you're a person.* Let them know something about your life.

8. *Be empathetic.* Let students know that you appreciate and understand that they have personal problems, course loads, and limited skills (not to lower standards, but to be understanding).

9. *Make adequate time to meet with students.*

10. *Make tests and assignments, fair, valid, and consistent, and make sure directions are clear.*

11. *Seek meaningful feedback from students.* (Adapted from Hawkes, 1995)

As a student in the college courses in which you are currently enrolled, what kind of feedback would you give to your professors? How many teachers or professors have ever asked for your feedback?

TRANSITIONING INTO THE PROFESSION

Many school districts offer new teachers support to help them make the transition into their own classrooms. In this section, we will look at some programs including mentoring programs, induction programs, and the New Teacher Center.

● **Mentoring Programs** Working with a **mentor** is an important aspect of your learning in your first year because your mentor can fill in the gaps that may be missing from your college program. The role of the mentor is to support you in learning district curriculum as well as to orient you to the school and district. Mentors who are trained in supervising new teachers or student teachers might observe you in class and then provide helpful feedback. In most districts, however, mentors do not have anything to do with the evaluation process or decide whether to rehire a new teacher.

This relationship between new teachers and mentors is similar to the relationship between student teachers and their cooperating teacher. Mentors may help new teachers set up their classroom, find resources, and design the curriculum for the first day of school. If you do not have an assigned mentor, ask the principal whether someone in the school could work with you informally. Seek out help and support. It is important to realize that you do not have to do this all by yourself. As one first-year teacher said of his mentor teacher:

> The mentor teacher has acted as a lifeline to me this year . . . Although she is not aware of this, I could not have made it without her support this year.

In *Mentoring Programs for New Teachers* (Villani, 2002), the author highlights programs from around the United States that serve as models for districts. In the United States, mentor program designers are learning key lessons from their new teachers and using the feedback they get to improve their programs. For example, by using data to track the relationship between mentors and new teachers, the district is trying to measure how many interactions mentors and **mentees** (those being mentored) have during the year and what kind of and how many interactions are needed. These interactions include observation visits as well as time devoted to analyzing student work and team teaching. These programs are designed with five focus areas in mind: beginning teachers, classroom and behavior management, lesson planning, ensuring that discussions have a purpose consistent with beginning teachers' needs, and district goals. By tracking data with regard to these five focus areas, districts are better able to measure the effectiveness of their mentoring programs.

Three methods that help new teachers and mentors work together in more formal ways are cognitive coaching, collaborative consulting, and evaluating. Review Figure 13.6 on page 414 to learn the differences between these models. How could each of these models be useful to you as a beginning teacher? How could these models benefit experienced teachers as well?

● **Induction Programs** The purpose of district **induction programs** is to retain highly qualified effective teachers in their classrooms. Many induction programs, besides offering their teachers a mentor, offer an orientation session at the beginning of the school year or at the end of the summer, before school begins. This provides new teachers with an overview

INTASC

Principle #9

Professional Commitment and Responsibility: The teacher is a reflective practitioner who continually evaluates the effects of his/her choices and actions on others (students, parents, and other professionals in the learning community) and who actively seeks out opportunities to grow professionally.

INTASC

Principle #10

Partnerships: The teacher fosters relationships with school colleagues, parents, and agencies in the larger community to support students' learning and well-being.

You are not alone! Collaborating with colleagues and participating in a mentoring program will allow you to get helpful advice and answers to any questions you might have as a beginning teacher.

FIGURE 13.6

Three Services That Help New Teachers

COGNITIVE TEACHING

A colleague–colleague relationship

Purpose

- To mediate or to develop self-directed learning
- To maximize effectiveness of actions toward goals
- To build capacity for professional effectiveness

COLLABORATIVE CONSULTING

A mentor–colleague relationship

Purpose

- To provide information or technical assistance
- To teach, guide, and share expertise
- To improve teaching effectiveness

EVALUATING

An authority figure–employee relationship

Purpose

- To assess performance based on external criteria
- To generate data for personnel decisions
- To have teachers internalize teaching standards

Source: Reprinted with permission of the National Staff Development Council, www.nsde.org, 2004.

of the school district's expectations. It also allows new teachers to meet the other new teachers. Tours of the district and schools, meetings with parent groups, and lunches with mentors may be part of your orientation.

Induction programs often also offer professional development workshops to beginning teachers to educate them about district curriculum and goals. These workshops may focus on topics such as how to apply district curriculum and standards in your classrooms, how to work with special-needs students, and the most popular topic, behavior management. Make every attempt to attend these sessions with new colleagues and use the information you learn to apply the skills in your classroom. Because the most challenging issues in the first year relate to time management, establishing classroom routines, and managing behavior, attending workshops that offer helpful strategies and taking the opportunity to talk with other teachers is extremely useful.

Researching Better Practices Administrators in districts and individual schools focus on supporting and retaining new teachers. In their efforts to offer this support, districts use technology and professional resources to keep high-quality teachers in the profession.

Typically higher education's role in the induction of new teachers has been as researchers of the process—studying new teachers, what they think, what is missing for them, and how they perceive their first years of teaching. Researchers have spent considerable time studying new teachers, their roles in schools, and the act of teaching instead of just the obstacles to teaching (Feiman-Nemser, 2001b). Induction needs to go beyond orientation and must include serious new teacher development to close the gap between preservice preparation and continuing professional development (Feiman-Nemser, 2001a). Using exemplary examples of mentoring, Feiman-Nemser shares with others how to help new teachers improve their classroom practice. The mentors identified two aspects of teaching that they felt could help beginning teachers: helping them find ways to express themselves, and helping them develop a practice that is responsive to the community and to what we know about children and learning. Mentors provided their support by demonstrating lessons and by teaching their mentees what to look for.

More recent projects have higher-education programs working hand-in-hand with school districts to find better ways to retain highly qualified effective teachers for their classrooms. Harvard University is working with Milwaukee school leaders to tackle their problem of new teacher retention. The urban district of 105,000 students and 165 schools loses 10% of its teachers annually (Dede, 2002). Education sociologist Pedro Noguera, professor of communities and schools, Steinhardt School of Education at New York University, is guiding administrators via Internet2, an enhanced version of the Internet, to educate school leaders about the best support strategies for new teachers. This project is designed to allow virtual and face-to-face professional development courses in a number of areas. As you move through your program, think of how you can use technology to support your knowledge of teaching and to connect to other new teachers.

The New Teacher Center Instead of just researching new teacher issues, the University of California at Santa Cruz takes a hands-on approach to support new teachers. The **New Teacher Center (NTC)** was created to allow Santa Cruz higher-education faculty to work with teachers and mentors (advisors) directly and document their work for later use (Moir, 2003a). Using funds from state and other professional resources, the center provides training and professional development to mentors and new teachers.

The NTC uses the beginning teachers' real challenges and dilemmas to create workshops and follow-up sessions that will help them manage issues that arise in their classrooms. The center, which began in 1998, has been consistently revised to respond to teachers' needs. The center promotes the importance of listening to new teachers' issues. Because one size does not fit all, mentors are instructed to tailor their work to meet the needs of the beginners (Moir, 2003a). Moir and her colleagues talk with new teachers about the phases they should expect to go through during their first year; their purpose in describing these phases is to ward off any disillusionment they may feel. (See Figure 13.7 on page 416.)

Teachers for a New Era Schools As first discussed in Chapter 2, the Teachers for a New Era project, funded by the Carnegie Corporation, was created to allow higher-education schools of teacher preparation to follow their graduates into their beginning years of teaching. In this ongoing project, each of the 11 participating universities has developed its own program for working with graduates to ensure their success in the schools. Boston College, one of the universities, has created a support program for its graduates called Project SUCCESS (School University Collaborative Committed to the Educational Success of all Students). Under the direction of a clinical practice team, which includes teachers, education and arts and sciences professors, and researchers, the Boston College Lynch School of Education is studying ways to support graduates of its program. The project provides not only practical support, but measurable data to track graduates' success. Find out whether your teacher preparation program is going to be following you into the profession and how they will track your progress.

"This is our real-time chat room."

Courtesy of Aaron Bacall, *The Lighter Side of Technology in Education*, p. 86. Copyright 2003 by Aaron Bacall. Reprinted by permission of Corwin Press Inc.

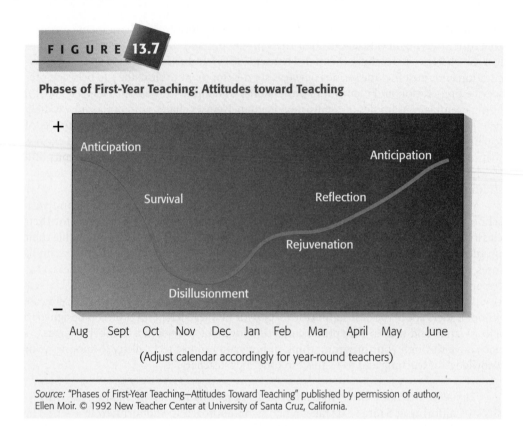

FIGURE 13.7

Phases of First-Year Teaching: Attitudes toward Teaching

Source: "Phases of First-Year Teaching—Attitudes Toward Teaching" published by permission of author, Ellen Moir. © 1992 New Teacher Center at University of Santa Cruz, California.

BECOMING A COLLEAGUE

INTASC

Principle #10

Partnerships: The teacher fosters relationships with school colleagues, parents, and agencies in the larger community to support students' learning and well-being.

In some ways, teaching can be an isolating profession in that the much of the work teachers do is on their own time, behind closed doors. It is important for teachers to stay connected to other teachers in order to learn from each other. Your colleagues will consist of teachers at your grade level, teachers in your department, specialist teachers who may co-teach with you, specialists who may pull your students out for special services, and specialty teachers in art, music, and foreign languages. How you interact with your colleagues and how your students move from one class to another will affect your day. Through collaboration, sharing ideas with others, and getting to know the school staff, you will find that most obstacles are surmountable.

● **Collaborating and Co-Teaching**   While some teachers find that collaboration is not always easy, the benefits of working with others usually outweigh the challenges. Collaborating and co-teaching are often expected of first-year teachers. **Collaborating** involves working with other teachers cooperatively to create a positive learning environment or to address issues that may threaten that environment. **Co-teaching** refers to sharing instructional responsibilities with another teacher and thereby capitalizing on each other's strengths. For example, interdisciplinary co-planning sessions in which English and history teachers map out a curriculum unit that allows students to integrate knowledge from two classes are becoming more common. Math and science are handled in a similar fashion.

Control   A challenge of collaboration is determining who is in control. If you are collaborating with a special education teacher (or if you are a special education teacher collaborating with a regular education teacher), your issue may be, "Who controls the student's curriculum?" If you are collaborating with a specialist who pulls a student out of the classroom, your issue may be, "Who decides when the student should be pulled?" If you co-teach, your issue may be, "Who decides who does what?" If you take your students to

Through the Eyes of
Culturally Sensitive Teachers

Meeting Whose Standards?

Rosa Cruz had always been at the top of her class. As an elementary school student in Bayamon, Puerto Rico, she was always on the principal's honor roll. Her family moved to New York City when Rosa was 11 and despite the difficulty of having to study in her second language, Rosa would study late into the night to maintain her position as one of her school's top students. It was a matter of personal pride to Rosa. She had always earned *sobresaliente* (superior) and she wasn't going to settle for anything less in New York than she had achieved in Puerto Rico.

Rosa went on to graduate third in her high school class of more than 2,000 and received a full scholarship to Cornell University, where she decided to become a teacher. After 4 years of study and a cumulative 3.8 average, Rosa graduated and got a job teaching fifth grade in a wealthy suburban New York City school district.

In her first year, Rosa shared a pod containing two fifth-grade classrooms with Kim Thomlinson, a veteran of 15 years teaching at the school. Kim quickly realized Rosa's great potential and set out to help in every way she could. After 2 months, the school had an open house. Kim warned Rosa that many parents were professionals who were highly driven and had great expectations of their children. On occasion, they expected too much and a few did not have all of the necessary courtesies with teachers. The open house was going well and Rosa explained the year's curriculum to parents. After the bell rang to end the open house, Rosa said she would be willing to stay late to answer any additional questions. One parent, Mrs. Carlton, began to question Rosa about her background and preparation. To Rosa, it seemed as if Mrs. Carlton was engaging in a job interview. Kim overheard the conversation but felt that she shouldn't interrupt. Mrs. Carlton asked Rosa whether her Spanish accent might be a

barrier to teaching language arts. Rosa assured her that English had been one of her best subjects, and fifth graders had already a fairly well-developed pronunciation. As the questions wore on, they sounded more judgmental of Rosa's qualifications. Mrs. Carlton ended the session by saying she would "think over" keeping her son in Rosa's class, which shocked Rosa.

As soon as Mrs. Carlton left, Kim came to counsel Rosa, who was quite upset. She assured Rosa that her qualifications to be a fifth-grade teacher were outstanding. Rosa was wondering out loud whether she had chosen the right profession or the right school. Kim assured her that both were correct choices and not to let Mrs. Carlton's callous attitude shake her confidence.

Rosa continued to devote herself to her teaching, and at the end of the year Mrs. Carlton's son had the highest verbal totals for any fifth grader on the standardized test required by the state. On the last day of school, Mrs. Carlton's son brought Rosa a present with a card. The card read, "I am very sorry I ever doubted your abilities."

Points to Ponder

1. Why do you think that Mrs. Carlton was particularly prone to doubt Rosa's teaching abilities?

2. How important was Kim's reassurance to Rosa when she was being questioned by Mrs. Carlton?

3. Are teachers of some backgrounds more likely to have their abilities doubted by parents than teachers of other backgrounds? If so, why?

4. Do veteran teachers have an ethical obligation to help newer teachers succeed? If so, why? If not, why not?

---

another room for a specialist program, your issue may be, "How do I get the specialist to use the same rules I use with my students?" These concerns can lead to tension between you and your colleagues and pose obstacles to sharing ideas, resources, and information about students. As a beginning teacher, be aware of the complex nature of schools and teacher interactions. Think about the ways in which you interact with adults in the school and how your interactions support or hinder your students' growth.

Sharing Ideas Collaboration can also be very rewarding. Learning new perspectives and approaches to working with students is a professional role you will play as a teacher. By comparing and contrasting your ideas with those of other teachers, you can enhance your own interactions with your students and colleagues.

Teachers share information and learn from each other every day through their interactions in meetings, conversations in the hallway, informal conversations during breaks, and when they ask for assistance. You may find also yourself among a group of teachers before and after school. This is another opportunity to collectively share ideas and solve problems.

Whether or not you have a mentor, you will find ways to create relationships with teachers in your school. You might engage in peer coaching (see Chapter 11) or you might informally consult with colleagues. You might select several coaches in your school to work with you in different areas. For example, you might try to arrange for a peer coaching relationship with a teacher whose classroom management ideas you admire. If there is another teacher whose teaching of science seems exciting and interesting, you might arrange to share ideas with that teacher as well. Other first-year teachers may even serve as coaches. Keep your options open.

Many new teachers who work in the same school now organize support groups, study groups, inquiry groups, book clubs, and sharing circles for new teachers. These informal groups provide new teachers with professional and social support. Collaborating with other first-year teachers is an excellent way to feel supported by others who are sharing a similar experience with you.

INTASC

Principle #10

Partnerships: The teacher fosters relationships with school colleagues, parents, and agencies in the larger community to support students' learning and well-being.

● **Getting to Know School Staff**   You have read how important it is to learn about your school and understand the school's culture. Some key players can help you better navigate your way around the school and the system. Most are members of your school staff. Only the superintendent is not; however, superintendents are rarely involved in the day-to-day operations of the school.

It is important that all new teachers have a clear understanding of the roles of all school administrators. Superintendents of schools are in charge of entire school districts. They do not usually get involved in the daily operations of schools in their district; they delegate these responsibilities to their administrative teams. Administrative teams could include principals, directors of curriculum, deans of discipline, department chairs, guidance counselors, and other advisors. Human resources departments handle the paperwork for beginning teachers in large school districts. Principals are the school leaders in charge of faculty and the school curriculum. While they may be responsible for evaluating teachers, they often delegate this responsibility to department chairs or other administrators.

In addition to getting to know other teachers with whom you can collaborate and share ideas, who you should get to know other staff members at your school. Two very important people in the school are the school secretary and the custodian. The secretary, in many cases, "runs the school" in that all of the daily operations go through the front office. The custodian, meanwhile, knows the ins and outs of the school, manages the keys to the classrooms and storage areas, and can often be helpful in other ways as well. If you need help moving around the furniture in your room, having the custodian on your side is helpful. If you need access to a storage area or need to borrow equipment or furniture, the custodian can help you out. During your full practicum, observe the ways in which these important people contribute to the lives of the teachers!

An unfortunate mistake some beginning teachers make is to underestimate the power of the secretary and the custodian. These teachers don't see how they relate to their "real work" of teaching in the classroom. As a beginning teacher, introduce yourself to the school secretary and the custodian. Show that you respect the work that everyone in the school does to keep it running smoothly. Establishing relationships with nonteachers will not only foster mutual respect, but it will also build a bigger network of people with whom you can collaborate.

BEING EVALUATED AND REHIRED

At the end of the school year you will be evaluated and either you will be rehired or you will not. Throughout the year, your principal or a designated administrator will observe and rate your classroom performance. You may also have to complete a beginning teacher portfolio or attend meetings with the administrative team to chart your progress. The following guidelines will help you navigate the assessment process.

- Make sure you clearly understand the professional standards and how you will be evaluated.

- Ask for copies of the assessment tools that will be used.

- Talk about assessments with your mentor or another knowledgeable colleague.

- Practice being observed using the tools by asking a colleague to come in and try them out.

- Find out whether you will have a formative assessment program in addition to your summative report from the evaluator. Make sure you know the difference.

You are probably getting the sense that the first year will be pretty stressful. In many ways, it will be the most difficult year of your professional career. There is so much to learn and so many routines to establish. Always keep in mind that you are a lifelong learner; you don't have to learn everything all in one year! This is just the beginning. Take care of yourself. You know how to do that. Take time to monitor your stress levels. Sleep, eat healthily, and share your frustrations. Don't try to pretend that you are perfect and that you should have learned everything in college. This is not possible.

You will also experience a lot of excitement your first year, from teaching someone how to read to the joy of watching students share in class; all of these achievements offer satisfying rewards. As you move through your career, you will continue to learn and grow every day of every year. The next key question will highlight components of professional development.

"I was so stressed when I started and then I realized I didn't need to be a perfect teacher, I needed to be a good teacher. I tried to teach the best I could every day and to learn from my students. I knew that I would get better at this next year. I feel so much more confident at the start of this year."

FIRST-YEAR TEACHER

THINK ABOUT THIS:
The stress leading up to and throughout that first year of teaching is very real, but it is also something very normal. Your desire to do well and to do right by your students drives that stress. How do you think colleagues and other staff can help alleviate some of that stress? How does careful preparation help?

SHARE and COMPARE:
Share your concerns at this point in your preparation with another classmate. Do you have any that sound familiar?

How Will You Continue to Grow as a Teacher?

After completing your student teaching and your first year as a teacher, do not expect that you will be equipped with everything you need to know about teaching and learning. If you have been enrolled in a teacher education program, you will enter the profession with a strong foundation and some experience; however, you need to see yourself as a lifelong learner in order to meet the continually changing needs of your diverse students. Professional development affords you a vehicle for continuous learning and growing throughout your career. These opportunities are provided in a number of settings and formats, such as in-service education opportunities, professional development workshops and conferences, recertification, and teacher leadership programs.

IN-SERVICE EDUCATION

In-service education or professional development, as opposed to preservice education—what you are doing as you prepare to become a teacher—refers to the ongoing process of applying new skills and knowledge while you are teaching. To keep you up to date on new information, standards, or methods, the district usually offers after-school workshops, courses, and seminars throughout the year and during the summer.

As discussed, many induction programs offer a series of workshops designed specifically for beginning teachers. These in-service programs are designed to prepare beginners for their daily work. The first three years are often "catch-up" times for beginners who need to quickly learn district curriculum and approaches to teaching that have already been established in the district.

More traditional in-service education is often offered to all teachers in the districts. After-school workshops are the most common format for conveying information relating

The education landscape changes constantly, requiring teachers to adjust to those changes as well. Take advantage of the numerous professional development opportunities available to you for improving the quality of your work.

to district or state curriculum frameworks. Because policies, curriculum, and content areas continually change, teachers within districts need to stay apprised of new approaches. As a student teacher, you may have an opportunity to attend some of these workshops. You will most likely find that they are similar to classes in your college program. Speakers for the sessions may be in-service teachers sharing information they learned from attending workshops off site, or they may be college professors or consultants hired by the district.

These sessions are sometimes offered during the school day when teachers can attend sessions together. Sometimes they are offered after school. When the activities are offered during the school day, substitutes are assigned to the classrooms. There are pros and cons to after-school and school-day in-service workshops. At the end of the day, many teachers are so tired that it is difficult to learn new things; on the other hand, during the day, many teachers prefer not to leave their students. These dilemmas are not easily resolved.

When school districts are facing budget cuts, professional development is often the first thing to be cut. This means that teachers need to go outside the district to remain current. Teachers often attend these outside courses and workshops at their own expense.

PROFESSIONAL DEVELOPMENT AND TEACHER QUALITY

Because teaching is a dynamic profession, new information is always available and the chance to learn and grow is a constant. For this reason, professional development is critical to effective teaching. Several types of professional development opportunities exist outside the school. In addition to workshops, teachers can continue to learn and grow by keeping up with current literature related to teaching in their particular grade level and subject matter. Teachers also need to find ways of keeping up with federal initiatives and current theories on teaching. Joining professional organizations offers opportunities for expanding teachers' professional networks by attending meetings and conferences outside their school districts.

With the enactment of No Child Left Behind, teacher quality initiatives have influenced the role of professional development options for teachers. Improved teacher quality has become an objective for every district across the United States. To ensure that this objective is met, federal funding is being provided for increased professional development for teachers, such as workshops, courses, and professional conferences.

There is a constant flow of literature and journals on teaching. To further enhance your own knowledge base, you should read as much as possible as you begin to develop your own professional library. See Figure 13.8 on page 422 for a list of books with which to get started.

Joining professional organizations is another way to foster your professional growth. Many organizations have their own journals, offer workshops, and sponsor conferences. A complete list of organizations is located in Appendix B of this book. Popular professional organizations that offer journals include the Association of Curriculum and Development (ASCD), Phi Delta Kappa, the National Staff Development Council, and the National Council of Teachers of English. Beginning teachers often like to read journal articles that focus on issues that they may encounter in their own classrooms. Secondary education teachers may be more inclined to focus on articles that focus on content in their own subject area, such as math, English, science, or history.

Attending conferences and workshops sponsored by professional organization is a good way to connect with other professionals with a common focus or interest. However, attendance may require a registration fee and traveling to another state for national conferences. Depending on the registration fee and location, attending these conferences may not be feasible for new teachers. They may prefer to stay closer to home and attend local workshops offered by state affiliates of these national groups. Teachers often find out about conferences by reading the journals, checking their websites, or reading *Education Week*. Most principals or curriculum directors receive one or more of these papers or journals. As a beginning teacher you may not want to spend the money to join right now, but ask to read the copies available in your school to find the organization that you feel most comfortable. The school library will also have copies of these important professional sources.

FIGURE 13.8

Recommended Readings in the Profession

Keys to the Classroom: A Teacher's Guide to the First Month of School (Moran, Stobbe, Baron, Miller, & Moir, 2000)
A guide for the first month of elementary teaching that offers hundreds of practical ideas to get started in the classroom. Letters to parents and other activities in English and Spanish are included.

Tips from the Trenches (Chase & Chase, 1993)
Includes specific practical advice from practicing classroom teachers. Divided into elementary and secondary and provides ideas at all grade levels. One tip about getting along with colleagues is to refuse to be part of gossip about your colleagues or their classrooms.

The First-Year Teacher: Teaching with Confidence (Bosch & Kersey, 2000)
Highlights how to get started on the very first day of school. Provides explanations for connecting with parents and how to organize those meetings.

If You Don't Feed the Teachers They Eat The Students (Connors, 2000)
A humorous guide for principals and teachers interested in making a difference in their school by improving school culture by positively "feeding" the teachers. M.E.A.L.S. (Meaningful Experiences Affecting Long-Term Success) are listed throughout.

Oops: What We Learn When Our Teaching Fails (Power & Hubbard, 1996)
A book of essays written by new and experienced teachers about lessons they have learned from students.

From Surviving to Thriving (Bromfield, Deane, & Burnett, 2003)
Journal exercises to prompt your thinking as you move through your student teaching or your first year. Keeping you in the center of the reflection will mean your needs will be met. The authors encourage partnerships with families and give specific ways to do it.

Still Teaching after All These Years: Survival Lessons to Keep You Sane (Fuery, 2001)
One teacher's journey and inside tips to organizing a classroom and staying self-fulfilled even on the bad days.

Another option for professional development is to take additional college courses in specific subject areas to enhance your knowledge base. Teachers who are teaching a particular grade level or content area that they would like to learn more about may register for a course related to that level or content. Many college programs offer evening classes, summer institutes, and workshops. Many universities offer **distance learning** courses for busy classroom teachers, in which teachers can learn new information at their computers in the comfort of their own school or home. Some states may require a master's degree as a licensing requirement. Such master's degrees often require 8–10 courses and can be taken part-time over several years. Teachers who receive a master's degree will qualify for a higher salary level in their district.

Writing, sharing, and publishing ideas is a high form of professional development. To promote writing and publishing within schools, districts, and communities, writer's support groups are usually available, such as the National Writing Project. These writing groups create writers' retreats, in-service courses, and workshops that help practicing teachers write about their practice. Writing groups allow all teachers to share ideas and explore publishing options. By encouraging practicing teachers to submit articles to journals, these groups are helping to bring the voices of teachers to state and national audiences. When possible, partnering with a university professor who has an entrance into publishing can help unpublished teachers gain some recognition.

Your ongoing professional development will influence the way you teach. Staying current, connecting with other teachers, and making new professional contacts will keep you energized and help you focus on your primary goal—teaching and engaging all of your students.

RECERTIFICATION

Many states require that teachers **recertify,** or have their license renewed, every five years. The goal of recertification is to ensure that all teachers are up on current teaching strategies and content. This, in turn, ensures that students have access to a high-quality education.

Many college or university programs provide information about recertification. As you reach the end of your teacher education program, talk to the certification officer or licensing officer on staff to learn more about certification and recertification requirements. This officer will endorse you as you finish your program and will verify that you have met all requirements. The websites for certification offices across the United States (See Appendix C) will most likely have recertification information too. It is important to check the requirements for each state so you are clear about how long your license is valid.

TEACHER LEADERSHIP

There are always professional development opportunities for teachers at all levels of experience. For veteran teachers who have made teaching a career, **teacher leadership** learning opportunities are offered by the district (Lieberman, 1998). These programs, in many cases, are more advanced versions of the same workshops that less experienced teachers attend, or they may be independent study activities that promote reflection and collegiality at grade level. These workshops are often centered on practice and may include information about portfolios, peer coaching, study groups, book clubs, and teacher research. The use of inquiry and the creation of "questions" to investigate real classroom issues are becoming more popular as teachers learn how to solve their own classroom problems. While this method may not be practiced in all districts, it is becoming increasingly recognized as a useful teaching and problem-solving strategy.

Another option that many veteran teachers find invaluable is being a cooperating teacher, a mentor teacher, or a peer coach to student teachers. Many veteran teachers find that the opportunity to work with preservice teachers allows them to share their expertise as well as to learn new strategies from student teachers. Many cooperating teachers cite working with a student teacher as powerfully rewarding. Many state that they feel they learned as much as their student teacher during the experience.

National Board for Professional Teaching Standards (NBPTS) certification provides an opportunity for experienced teachers to enhance the status of their school district while receiving recognition for their contribution to the school community. This national certification process is an intensive reflective program that requires teachers to be videotaped, to write about their experiences teaching and learning, and to complete a portfolio. Because teachers with National Board Certification increase the status of their district, the application fee is sometimes paid by the district to encourage teachers to complete this professional process. Once they receive their National Board Certification, many teachers are often asked to take on other leadership roles in the school and/or the community. When you visit schools, ask if any National Board Certified teachers are available to talk with you.

Teachers exhibit their leadership qualities by taking on roles in the local, state, or national teachers' unions. Being part of the teachers' union gives a collective voice to teachers in a district or state. These unions often provide professional development for beginning teachers as well as veterans. In Massachusetts, an extensive statewide professional program is offered to any Massachusetts Teachers Association (MTA) member. Teacher leaders teach all the sessions and provide follow-up mentoring to beginning teachers. Beginning teachers tend to participate in sessions on classroom management, discipline strategies, content frameworks, assessment, and dealing with parents.

Teachers also exercise their leadership skills by working with students in capacities beyond the classroom. For example, teachers may be invited to coach a team, advise the yearbook, or direct the school band. Clubs and extracurricular activities also offer teachers opportunities to work with students in new ways during the school year. Students and administrators alike view these teachers as leaders.

INTASC

Principle #9

Professional Commitment and Responsibility: The teacher is a reflective practitioner who continually evaluates the effects of his/her choices and actions on others (students, parents, and other professionals in the learning community) and who actively seeks out opportunities to grow professionally.

EDUCATION MATTERS

Delaying Retirement

Teachers in Coral Springs, Florida, are back in the classroom. Teachers who had signed off on an early retirement plan several years ago now are being asked to stay. Why? To fend off an impending teacher shortage, something being felt throughout the state and the country. Their original plans to leave teaching at age 60 have been changed due to special offers from districts and the legislature allowing them to defer their retirement. The Deferred Retirement Option Program (DROP), will allow teachers to continue to teach *and* get their retirement payouts agreed to in their original plan.

One veteran teacher who has taught for 22 years says he is basically not burned out and wants to stay. With a shortage in certain districts, having experienced teachers stay on has been a win–win situation for both. In Broward County, where 2,000 new teachers were needed, 40 retiring teachers opted to stay. School officials see this as "good for our district."

The Education Issue: Are new options for retiring teachers a good thing?

Should teachers just leave when their retirement time has come or should these new options be instituted in states where there is a need for so many new teachers? Students interviewed in Florida who had a returning teacher come back said, "She lets you be an individual." The teacher said the opportunity to keep inspiring "future artists" outweighs the perks of a quiet retirement. Can students benefit from an experienced teacher instead of a new one?

What's Your Opinion?

1. What do you think of this solution to the need for teachers?

2. Do you think teachers should have to leave after a certain number of years or by a certain age?

Source: "Some Teachers Shun Retirement and Go Back to Class," CNN.com, September 19, 2003.

REFLECTING ON TEACHING

INTASC

Principle #9

Professional Commitment and Responsibility: The teacher is a reflective practitioner who continually evaluates the effects of his/her choices and actions on others (students, parents, and other professionals in the learning community) and who actively seeks out opportunities to grow professionally.

No matter how long you've been teaching, you can always learn from your mistakes. Many teachers create support groups to analyze their mistakes and turn what they perceived as problems into new possibilities for the future. Many teachers also find it useful to write down their thoughts about their teaching experiences over the past year and consider what they might do differently the following year.

In the book *Oops: What We Learn When Our Teaching Fails* (Power & Hubbard, 1996), veteran and beginning teachers share experiences of how they learned from their mistakes through humorous essays such as "I Wonder If Real Teachers Have Problems" and "New Teacher Blues: How I Survived My First Year." These essays remind us that even experienced teachers fail from time to time and that reflection is the key to moving forward and learning. For new teachers these stories are particularly empowering, as they learn from insiders that all teachers are lifelong learners.

Like the teachers who captured their "oops" moments in essays, you should also keep track of your "oops" moments and write them down. Let them inform your teaching. Of all the professional development and learning that goes on outside your classroom, these experiences will have the greatest impact on your teaching. Don't be shy about sharing them; others will learn from them as well. When you can articulate these moments and find ways to talk about them, you'll find that they will lead to some shining moments and revelations. Perhaps you may even consider writing and publishing your thoughts. Beginning teachers appreciate the fact that everyone makes mistakes. It takes courage to write them down and share them with others.

WHAT DOES IT MEAN TO TEACH FOR LIFE?

What would it be like to stay in the profession for 20 or 30 years? That is probably very hard to imagine from where you are sitting right now. Talk with veteran teachers and find out what it has been like for them. Be prepared for the difficult stories, the "oops" moments that they learned from, and the regrets they may have about not doing something else. Then really listen to their stories, which will reveal what you may not hear them say directly—why they are still in teaching. There is something in between the complaints about the day-to-day operations and the real passion that keeps good teachers in the classroom.

MAINTAINING A PASSION FOR TEACHING

At a recent teacher gathering, a third-grade teacher close to retirement stated, "I just don't want to leave. I love teaching! I have always loved it and will really miss it." The other teachers at the table just groaned. Many were counting the days to retirement after serving for more than 30 years, many of them at the same grade level and in the same schools. What makes some teacher race to the door and others not want to leave, like the retired teachers in Education Matters? Passion is difficult to describe but easy to see.

What keeps people in this profession fulfilled? As you interview experienced teachers, ask them what has kept them in their profession for so long and try to notice the passion that motivates them to stay in the classroom. Think about your own passion. How do you express it?

Figure 13.9 asks you to create a career map that reflects the course of your journey as a teacher. As you complete this map, think about the question "Am I a teacher?" as opposed to the question "Do I want to teach?" Let your response to this question serve as your guide.

FIGURE 13.9

Career Map: Touching the Future

AM I A TEACHER?

Complete the answers. Draw a map on a piece of paper to document the journey. Use your vision of where you would like to be to answer the ending questions! Compare this to My First Professional Plan that you wrote at the end of Chapter 1 at the beginning of this course.

1. When I first decided to teach:

2. How people responded:

3. First goal I set to get my teaching career in motion:

4. What I have done this year to further my goal:

5. When I plan to do early field experiences:

6. When I plan to student teach:

7. Other things I plan to do to forward my skills as a teacher:

8. My first teaching job will be (be as specific as possible in your vision):

9. Plans after I teach for a few years: (such as stay for career, move to another role in a district, become an administrator, teach at a university, write books about teaching)

EDUCATION OPTIONS

Many educators stay in the profession but leave the classroom as they seek to grow professionally and find a new role in education. A number of options are open to you. You may consider administrative positions such as principal, department chair, or the director of a department, or perhaps opt for specialized positions within the school. If you want a new experience and environment, you might partner with a higher-education institution to teach college courses, or you may opt to leave teaching K–12 altogether to teach at the college level.

- **Administration** The most common move, however, is to an administrative position. There is a need for qualified principals. Teachers who want to become principals enter graduate programs that will provide them with the license to do the job. Becoming a principal is a natural leadership step for veteran teachers. The attraction to this position is that they may have the opportunity to create a vision and guide a school to new heights. The downside to the position, however, is the paperwork, as well as frequent meetings with faculty and other administrators who may not share the vision. Principals also have to grapple with other concerns such as financial constraints, building issues, and discipline problems. Those who feel up to the job welcome these challenges. You may already know that you aspire to administration and may have indicated that goal on your career map.

  Another administrative position that offers leadership opportunities without the overarching responsibilities of a principal is becoming a department chair in a secondary school or even for an entire district. In most cases, this position involves a reduced teaching load or a stipend for taking on additional duties. Duties typical of this position include directing a department, being a liaison to the principal, and providing support to students and beginning teachers. Department chairs most frequently oversee the program for a discipline (such as English, math, science, or physical education) at a single secondary school. However, some districts may have discipline coordinators who oversee the curriculum for the entire district. For example, a district science coordinator or chair would be responsible for making sure the grade- and developmentally appropriate skills and content outlined in the scope and sequence of the science curriculum is taught as planned. During your field experiences and school visits, interview a department chair about these duties and what led to this professional decision.

- **Specialists** Most larger school districts have a number of specialist positions including curriculum directors, technology specialists, reading specialists, and content coaches. These roles take teachers out of the classroom, and provide important scaffolding for district planning and professional development. As teachers who had their own classrooms enter these roles, they make decisions that influence classroom practice in ways that administrators without classroom experience may not.

- **Higher-Education Opportunities** Teacher leadership roles in schools that partner with higher-education institutions offer veteran teachers new opportunities. In the past, being a cooperating teacher was the only way teachers could interact with a college program. Increasingly, however, more partnerships are being developed between higher-education institutions and lower grades. The Professional Development School (PDS) movement has created a path that allows teachers to teach courses for student teachers on-site, or to teach other in-service teachers at the college level. In some cases, this affiliation allows teachers to collaborate with professors who are teaching related courses. It also may forge relationships that lead to teachers and professors co-writing articles, pursuing research, and planning innovative ways to support preservice and in-service teachers. In each of these roles, experienced teachers help professors who want to bridge the gap between theory and practice. It also allows teachers to both stay in the classroom and connect with higher-education institutions.

Some teachers ultimately decide to leave the classroom altogether to work in higher education at a college or university. To become a college professor to teach courses such as the one you are currently enrolled in, teachers would need to complete a doctoral program. The professors who are working with you right now may have been practicing classroom teachers before moving into higher education. Ask your professors how they decided to teach at the college level and whether it was part of their original professional plan. Mapping out your career plan early on will guide your decisions as you begin your career.

What do I believe?

"Enhance the human condition
Expand the human imagination.
Make the world more just."

**MISSION STATEMENT, LYNCH SCHOOL
OF EDUCATION, BOSTON COLLEGE**

THINK ABOUT THIS:

What kind of professional development do you think would be most useful in your first year of teaching? Why do you think you can make a difference in children's lives?

SHARE and COMPARE:

With a classmate, identify online classes, workshops, and other types of programs available to in-service or preservice teachers that sound like they would help "keep the fire burning."

FINAL THOUGHTS

This chapter moves you closer to the end of your introductory journey into the teaching profession. The beginning of the chapter offered you practical information related to your next steps as you enter the world of teaching—early field experiences, student teaching, your first job search and licensing process, and then going into the classroom as a beginning teacher. First-year teachers, university students, and K–12 students offer advice you may or may not find helpful. Think about what they have had to say and use their voices to find your own.

Teaching is filled with challenges. Even the most experienced teachers admit this. With new students, new situations, and new reforms, this dynamic profession requires energy, dedication, and diligence. Beginning and veteran teachers all agree that the first year is the most difficult. In recognition of this fact, more universities and districts are supporting their alumni and newcomers as they transition from their education programs into the professional world. Most school districts are also supporting new teachers by providing professional development opportunities such as induction programs, mentoring programs, and professional workshops. This chapter also addresses the importance of getting to know your colleagues as well as the staff at your school such as the school secretary and the custodian. All of these connections help you to become an effective, collaborative teacher.

Only you know whether you have the passion that is the "fire in your belly" to do what it takes on a daily basis to contribute to America's future. If you decide that the classroom is not for you, there are many other opportunities to be part of the profession. If you decide that you belong in the classroom, relish that knowledge, allow yourself to make mistakes, and learn every day. This lifelong learning process will make you a better teacher.

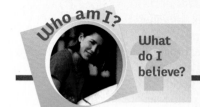
REFLECTIONS

Professional Plan for Becoming a Teacher

1. Three things I learned from this chapter about teachers are:

2. Two things in this chapter that I would like to learn more about are:

   a. _____

   b. _____

3. I plan to investigate these two areas and learn more about topics in this chapter by:

   _____ Reading some of the book club choices

   _____ Reading sources referenced in the chapter on topics that interest me

   _____ Interviewing several teachers about their professional goals and aspirations and advice for planning my future

   _____ Exploring the websites listed in the Log On section

   _____ Observing several classrooms and taking notes on the specific strategies teachers use that work for them in practice

4. I will include the following in my Touch the Future portfolio:

   _____ Responses to Who Am I? activities

   _____ A brief essay on my thoughts about Problems to Possibilities

   _____ Responses to the Observation Guide

   _____ Other (materials assigned by your instructor)

SUMMARY

What's Next?

- Early field experiences and student teaching are important ways to learn about schools and practice what you are learning in education courses.

- There are steps to a job search: visiting your career center, checking newspaper ads and state employment websites, and reading literature about the job search are good first steps.

- When preparing for interviews, prepare professional portfolios as well as electronic portfolios that you can leave with your interviewer.

- A contract is a legal document that maps out specific terms to which you will be committed when you sign it. A signed contract obligates you to work in a school district for a specified period of time.

What Can You Expect in Your First Year of Teaching?

- The first year of teaching may be challenging, but mentoring and induction programs provide support to new teachers.
- Becoming a colleague is an important aspect of your first year of teaching. Benefits of collaborating with other teachers include reducing isolation and improving your teaching as the result of collegial conversations.
- Mentors are coaches who support you and work with you in the classroom; however, they have nothing to do with your evaluation to determine whether you will be rehired. Evaluators such as your principal or department chair will decide whether you will be rehired based on your performance in the classroom.

How Will You Continue to Grow as a Teacher?

- In-service professional development is one way to learn new techniques and practices. Teachers participate in workshops and courses on-site or in the district.
- You may need to recertify after several years of teaching. Check the requirements in your state.
- Teacher leadership opportunities exist in schools for teachers who would like more responsibility and experience beyond the classroom.
- Learning from your mistakes and "oops" moments will make you a stronger, more experienced teacher.

What Does It Mean to Teach for Life?

- Passion for teaching is measured in many ways. Teachers express their passion and enthusiasm from their beginning years to retirement.
- Education skills are transferable to many other professions.
- Teachers are ordinary people doing extraordinary work as heroes in America's classrooms every day.

Visit the **Touch the Future . . . Teach!** Companion Website at www.ablongman.com/diaz for additional opportunities.

KEY WORDS

artifacts 403	in-service education 420	New Teacher Center
collaborating 416	interstate	(NTC) 415
contract 406	agreement 404	Praxis Series 406
co-teaching 416	mentee 413	professional portfolio 403
distance learning 422	mentor 413	recertify 432
duty 407	National Board for	teacher certificate 404
electronic portfolio 404	Professional Teaching	teacher leadership 423
induction program 413	Standards (NBPTS) 423	teacher portfolio 403

CONCEPT REVIEW

1. List seven steps that will create a successful student teaching experience.
2. Summarize aspects of the job search.
3. Describe a professional portfolio and an electronic portfolio.

4. Articulate the importance of signing a teaching contract.

5. Explain the issues first-year teachers wished they had learned in college.

6. State what first-year teachers wished they had done during student teaching.

7. Describe the issues that surface in a typical first year of teaching.

8. Summarize what it means to be a colleague.

9. Define professional development and in-service education and give examples.

10. Present several teacher leadership opportunities for career teachers.

11. Share what "teaching for life" means to you.

TOUCH THE FUTURE

Read On

Stories of the Courage to Teach: Honoring the Teacher's Heart
Sam Intrator, with foreword by Parker Palmer (San Francisco: Jossey-Bass, 2002)
A book of essays written by teachers in classrooms all over the United States; their stories offer an inside view of what it takes to teach and the potential rewards.

Being Mentored: A Guide for Protegées
Hal Portner (Thousand Oaks, CA: Corwin Press, 2002)
Offers some insight into being mentored and how you can get the most out of your relationship by taking responsibility for your learning.

101 Answers for New Teachers and Their Mentors: Effective Tips for Daily Classroom Use
Annette L. Breaux (Larchmont, NY: Eye on Education, 2003)
A practical tip guide for new teachers, including discussion of classroom management, planning, and motivating students.

Portfolio Handbook: Developing a Professional Teacher Portfolio
Patricia Constantino and M. De Lorenzo (Boston: Allyn & Bacon, 2002)
Provides ideas for different options when creating your portfolio.

Log On

Association of Supervision and Curriculum Development
www.ascd.org
Learn about current issues in education. This professional organization covers all topics for all grade levels and offers a daily e-newsletter and a journal, *Educational Leadership,* with membership.

National Staff Development Council
www.nsdc.org
Provides members with the *Journal of Staff Development* and newsletters with current information about in-service topics; a national conference offers many sessions on induction and mentoring.

New Teacher Center (University of California at Santa Cruz)
www.newteachercenter.org
Dedicated to teacher induction, the center offers practical ideas, materials, workshops for districts, and summer conferences for mentors, new teachers, and principals. The center also offers new teachers the opportunity for e-mentoring.

First Year Teaching Strategies: A Collection of Student Views
http://aci.mta.ca/MtATeach/FirstYear.html
Dr. Bob Hawkes of Mount Allison University offers sound advice for first-year teachers.

Student Teaching Portfolio
www2.bc.edu/~gibsonjc
See an example of a student teacher's e-portfolio. You can also visit his teaching website at www.mr-gibson.com.

Write On

When elementary students were asked to respond to the prompt, "How does someone become a teacher?" one student said, "By working hard and studying kids."

What will you do to study kids as you prepare to become a teacher? Write your short response in your journal.

OBSERVATION GUIDE

TEACH: LINKING THEORY TO PRACTICE

Linking Theory to Practice

Objective: To observe a faculty meeting being held in a school

School (use code name): _____   Observer: _____

Meeting: _____   Date: _____

Attendees at Meeting: _____   Time In: _____   Time Out: _____

Directions: For this observation and interview activity, see if you can attend a faculty meeting. While there, consider what it will be like to enter the profession as a student or beginning teacher. How do you see yourself in your role as a colleague? After the meeting, ask the leader (principal or teacher leader) a few questions to follow up on what you observed. Use the following questions as a guide and create some of your own, using this chapter to assist you. Once you have finished your observation and interview, write a brief summary of your findings, which you may submit to your instructor as well as include in your Touch the Future portfolio.

1. How is the physical space in the meeting room organized? Are there refreshments and materials? How and where are teachers sitting? Where is the principal or teacher leader sitting? Draw a diagram and put a check mark next to the names of the people who speak during the meeting.

2. Would you describe this meeting as a caring community of learners? Why or why not?

3. What is the purpose of the meeting? Was the purpose met at the end of the session? Explain.

4. Does the tone of the meeting seem to be collegial?

Interview Questions after the Observation

1. Did you meet your objective as the meeting leader today? If yes, explain. If no, explain what your next steps will be.

2. How can new teachers or student teachers participate in teacher meetings? What should they do or say?

3. If this is the principal, ask, "Can you share your views of teacher leadership in your school?" If the meeting was run by a teacher leader, ask, "How did you become a teacher leader? What do you most enjoy about it?"

4. What advice do you have for me as I begin my teaching career? How can a new teacher become a colleague when there is an established school culture?

5. If I said I was not sure I wanted to be a teacher for life, what would you say to me?

Connecting with INTASC: Principle 9

Professional Commitment and Responsibility: The teacher is a reflective practitioner who continually evaluates the effects of his or her choices and actions on others (students, parents, and other professionals in the learning community) and who actively seeks out opportunities to grow professionally.

When speaking with the meeting leader, find out what efforts school leadership takes to meet Principle 9. What does the school do to encourage personal and professional growth in its teachers? Are teachers encouraged to attend conferences? If so, does the district help financially? What types of in-service workshops are held to help teachers develop their skills with regard to decision making in the classroom, parent and community interactions, and ethical challenges?

14

How Will the Teaching Profession Change?

Who am I?

What do I believe?

After reading the quote at left by Albert Einstein, think about schools in the United States 25 years from now. What will our students need to know then that may be different from what they are taught now? What role will knowledge play in the future of education when compared to imagination? Write down what you think the five major goals of education are today. Then, look at these goals as if it were 25 years from now. Will all five goals still be as important? Are there some goals you would want to add or subtract?

"Imagination is more important than knowledge. Knowledge is limited. Imagination encircles the world."

—Albert Einstein

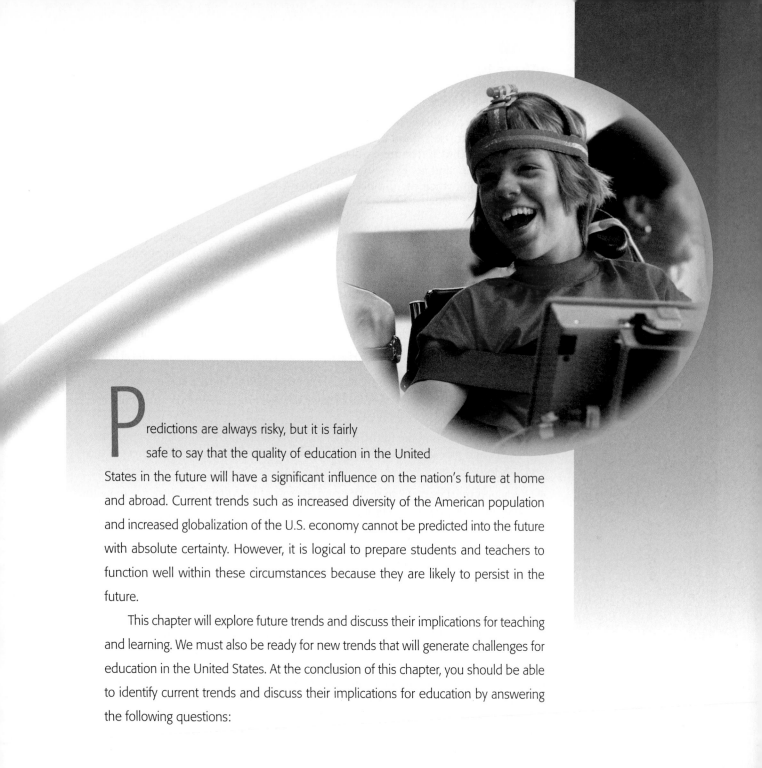

Predictions are always risky, but it is fairly safe to say that the quality of education in the United States in the future will have a significant influence on the nation's future at home and abroad. Current trends such as increased diversity of the American population and increased globalization of the U.S. economy cannot be predicted into the future with absolute certainty. However, it is logical to prepare students and teachers to function well within these circumstances because they are likely to persist in the future.

This chapter will explore future trends and discuss their implications for teaching and learning. We must also be ready for new trends that will generate challenges for education in the United States. At the conclusion of this chapter, you should be able to identify current trends and discuss their implications for education by answering the following questions:

Key Questions

1. What is teaching likely to look like in the future?
2. What are students going to look like in the future?
3. Why are multicultural and global perspectives necessary for future teachers?
4. Should teachers be leaders and agents for change?

WHAT IS TEACHING LIKELY TO LOOK LIKE IN THE FUTURE?

Any attempt to completely predict the future of American education is bound to encounter a number of surprises. About the only prediction about the future of education that can be made with certainty is that there will be change. However, a number of trends have already begun to surface and are likely to continue into the foreseeable future. No crystal ball is needed to identify their significance now or in the years ahead. Among these trends are the following:

- Multicultural awareness and knowledge will become more important to understand the population of the United States, teach its children, and conduct business successfully.

- Global literacy and fluency in more than one language will give Americans a greater competitive edge in international business, diplomacy, and cultural pursuits.

- Technology skills will increase in significance in academic as well as work settings.

- Educational requirements will rise in the United States, even for entry-level jobs.

- Schools will be expected to provide skills beyond basic literacy and mathematical abilities to all students. These skills will involve thinking critically and being able to work cooperatively with others.

- Citizenship skills in the future will involve a greater understanding that the duties, rights, and privileges we insist on for ourselves must be a reality for the rest of the U.S. population.

- Teachers must be ready to step beyond the role of providers of knowledge to youth; they must be prepared to be leaders in schools and communities.

This is certainly not an all-inclusive list, but it contains food for thought and challenges that go beyond those met by most schools today.

EVOLVING GOALS OF EDUCATION

Traditionally, one of the most important roles of education was to enable students to enter the workforces in their communities. One hundred years ago, educators did not worry much about how the education provided in their schools would prepare students for life in other states, regions, or nations; most Americans didn't move. **Portability of education** was not a significant issue. Today, most Americans move several times in their lifetime. Americans educated in one community are commonly found throughout the nation as well as abroad. No matter where you teach, you must keep this point in mind. Will you be preparing students to be functional in other venues?

Another concept that was implicitly taught in the curriculum, especially in the elementary social studies curriculum, was that the significance of places and events lessened as they became more geographically distant. It still is not uncommon for students to say, "Why must we learn about that place? We don't have any of those people around here." Few Americans could have located Afghanistan or Iraq on the map a few years ago. Today, many know someone in the armed forces who went or is there. Events around the world can affect lives in many Americans' homes. Educators have the responsibility to see that current and future generations of Americans do not see themselves as residents of an "island continent," but as citizens of an interdependent world who have a significant understanding of that world and can exercise their responsibilities as

BUILDING ON EDUCATIONAL FOUNDATIONS

What Is Teaching Going to Be Like in the Future?

If you were a teacher and got into a time machine and went back 100 or 150 years ago, classrooms would probably look a lot like they do today. You probably would see students at desks, a single teacher working with them in the front of the class, a class of perhaps 20 to 40 children, and so on. But what things would be different in a contemporary classroom? What is likely to be different in the future?

Teachers from 100 years ago would probably find classrooms today much more racially and ethnically diverse than the classrooms they taught in in the early twentieth century. Technologies such as computers, television sets, and video recorders would be totally new to them. Their students would

almost certainly have walked to school. Even something like a bus picking up students and taking them home each day would be new. At a personal level, they would find that more principals are women and that it is permissible to teach and be married.

How have schools and the work of teachers changed since you were an elementary school student? Are there important changes that you have seen that you can describe?

What changes do you think will take place in schools in the near future? Will schools change over the course of what will be, for many of you, a 25- to 30-year career? How? What do you think?

citizens appropriately. Future decisions made by American voters will affect citizens in other parts of the world in ways that we cannot currently predict.

On average, states spend more than 45% of their budgets on the education of elementary and secondary students in their public schools (Morgan, Matranga, & Peltier, 1998). Given the significant position that education occupies as a public policy issue, what are some additional trends for the future of education and teaching?

ACHIEVEMENT AND EQUITY AS PUBLIC POLICY GOALS

One study asked the Council of Chief State School Officers (CCSSO) what were the major issues in education at the beginning of the twenty-first century. Their three top responses were the following:

1. Student preparation for the workplace (81%)

2. Utilization of instruction (79%)

3. Providing a safe learning environment (79%) (Morgan, Matranga, & Peltier, 1998)

These same chief state school officers listed the following topics as not likely to be very important:

1. Equity in funding capital projects and school operations

2. Site based decision making

3. Educator preparation and licensure

Problems to POSSIBILITIES

Whose Version of History?

Richard Erlaq was a second-year social studies teacher at Central High School. His colleague, Padraig Williams, had been teaching social studies at Central for 24 years. One day they were discussing the social studies curriculum when Richard stated that he felt the social studies curriculum needed an overhaul. Clearer connections had to be made between the U.S. and world history courses. Richard felt that too many students were simply banking information in short-term memory, repeating the facts on the test, and promptly forgetting the material. He also felt that U.S. history had to be presented from multiple perspectives so that the voices of all of the nation's citizens could be heard in the curriculum. He felt this would motivate some students of color who had privately complained to Richard that they were still waiting to study about "people like them" in more than token ways.

Richard also felt that a more thematic approach could help balance the chronological approach that dominated history teaching at Central. Richard recalled studying that people remembered better if new facts were centered around concepts.

Padraig listened politely and said, "Young man, you are still fresh out of the university and green behind the ears. These students don't need that deep understanding you suggest. If they need to know about multicultural heroes, they can find them on the Internet at the click of a mouse. The "theme" they need to know is what happened after what, period. I know that our students often don't remember much a few days after the test, but they simply have to try harder. In my class, I present the information: if they get it, they get it; if they don't, they don't."

Richard was dejected to hear this but decided not to contradict his more senior colleague for now.

Discussion Questions
How common do you think this type of exchange is between veteran and new teachers? What suggestions do you have for Richard? Do you agree with Richard or with Padraig?

Possibilities
Richard decided to discuss this matter with another new social studies teacher, Jana Perez. Together, they decided that the thing to do was not to contradict the other senior colleagues, but to lead by example. Together they decided to collaborate to try something new. Jana would develop a series of curriculum units to incorporate multicultural and global perspectives in history. Richard would write some thematic units with concepts and critical-thinking questions included and share them with Jana. Over the next semester, the two young teachers tried all of the units in their classes. Students participated a great deal more because each unit limited lecturing to 10 to 15 minutes. Students read short passages the two teachers had selected and discussed them in small groups and then as a class. Word began to get around the social studies department about the students' positive reaction to the units, greater participation in classes, and the culturally relevant information Jane and Richard were sharing with students.

One day after classes were over, Richard got a knock on his classroom door. It was Padraig Williams. He said, "Richard, I'm sorry to bother you, but could I make some copies of those new units you have been using lately?"

Stepping into a culture in which routines and procedures have already been established can be difficult for new teachers, especially when the "message" in their teacher preparation program has been about progressive ways to teach and strategies for doing so. The following resources can help:

- Teacher Quality (www.teacherquality.us/Public/PublicHome.asp), a Department of Education website, shares information on a number of initiatives to help teachers, including state induction and mentoring initiatives.

- Teachers Network (www.teachersnetwork.org) offers a connection for new teachers to help get them started, as well as putting teachers in touch with each other.

- Beginning Teacher's Toolbox (www.inspiringteachers.com) from Inspiring Teachers offers resources and guidance to student teachers and first-year teachers.

Ethical Question
Do veteran teachers have a moral obligation to help new teachers? Do they have an obligation not to discourage new teachers from exploring innovative ideas? Would you have shown the same initiative as Richard and Jana? What if you were the only one trying to initiate something new?

Skills that are not strictly academic, such as interpersonal skills, critical thinking, and leadership, are as important for your students' personal development as is academic knowledge.

Some of these officials noted that achievement is likely to have a much higher priority than equity issues. A question to raise at this point is, "Should equity and achievement in education be seen as opposite or complementary goals?" It is entirely possible to provide high-quality education for a few students or for all students. The quality of education is not enhanced by an increased dropout rate, although a school's failure rate has sometimes been cited to students who succeed as a sign of excellence in the education they are receiving. While it is difficult to contest that students should be able to be productive in the marketplace upon graduation, should the market determine the entire content of the curriculum? Casanova (2000) suggests two types of education: education for those who conceptualize and education for those who carry out routine tasks of work. In democratic societies education must serve the needs of the many and not just the needs of a few. Teachers have a critical role to play in deciding whether high-status knowledge will be more available to all students in the future than it is today (Casanova, 2000).

Privatization and increasing consumerism are trends that have established themselves in public education. Some public school districts have delegated the management of public schools to private individuals through charter schools or by turning over the administration of a regular public school to a private corporation. The theory is that market forces will work in public education much as they do in the private economy and students will be better served. These trends are relatively recent and the research is not yet conclusive on whether the gains hoped for by the advocates of privatization of public education will occur. Some public school principals have made business arrangements with companies that allow them access to schools as a marketplace in return for badly needed financial support. When a high school signs a contract to allow the sales of only a particular soft drink on its campus, is this in the best interest of all of the school's students or education in general? These practices also raise some questions about equity in public education between public schools who have found corporate sponsors or contracts and those who have not. However, this trend shows little sign of slowing in the near future.

Another trend for you to think about as a future teacher is that students need to develop skills that make them effective as members of groups, not simply as individuals.

I N T A S C

Principle #6

Communication Skills: The teacher uses knowledge of effective verbal, nonverbal, and media communication techniques to foster active inquiry, collaboration, and supportive interaction in the classroom.

The top qualifications preferred by potential employers are oral communication skills, written communication skills, interpersonal skills, proficiency in the field of study, teamwork, and leadership (Davis & Miller, 1996). Three of these skills—interpersonal skills, teamwork, and leadership—could be defined as "nonacademic," but very important. Being an effective member of a group is a necessity in most jobs today. However, the educational system that prepares students is essentially a "go-it-alone" enterprise. Where do students get the exposure and experience to acquire these skills? Sports, clubs, and extracurricular activities provide some exposure, but not all students engage in these activities. Students who are consistently socialized in schools to do their own work may have difficulty in being part of a team in which the collective product is what matters. More important, schools almost always evaluate students on their individual work. After years of becoming accustomed to only individual evaluations in schools, graduates often find themselves in a workplace where the results of the group they belong to matter also. Students must learn how to adjust their views and egos to better cooperate with others in order to achieve group goals before they reach a point where failure to do so may cost them their jobs. This is an area in which schools of the future may look to provide students with more experiences.

TECHNOLOGY LITERACY AS A GOAL

Another trend that has already influenced teaching and is likely to continue to do so in the future is the use of technology. Technology infusion in education is not a cure-all, and educators should look at it as simply a tool. The computer can be incorporated into the classroom in ways that make it no more than an "electronic blackboard," or in highly creative ways such as the Electronic Mentoring Project, in which Native American professionals serve as resources and mentors to students via the Internet (Allen, Christal, & Perrot, 1999). Certainly, new teachers being prepared today must enter schools with a significant amount of technological literacy, and veteran teachers who did not obtain technology proficiency in their teacher preparation programs have to obtain it through professional development. Figure 14.1 shows some of the trends regarding the growth of computer use in schools. One of the difficulties in this area is that "what has really changed is the speed at which things are changing" (Lord, 1998). This is particularly true in technology, in which a computer or a computer program may be obsolete in 2 or 3 years.

I N T A S C

Principle #4

Multiple Instructional Strategies: The teacher uses various instructional strategies to encourage students' development of critical thinking, problem solving, and performance skills.

Gillingham and Topper (1999) point out the following dilemma in preparing teachers in the field of technology: "Although technology keeps advancing into the culture of classrooms and the students who attend them, faculty in programs that prepare teachers are unsure what to teach future teachers or how to use technology in instruction" (p. 303). For the foreseeable future, keeping up with technology in schools is going to be like painting the Golden Gate Bridge; by the time you finish painting at one end, it is time to start at the other.

Besides the ongoing challenge of teachers keeping up with technology, there are other issues to consider. If educators develop Internet courses or computer-based instructional modules that have commercial value, who owns the rights to these products (Ludlow & Duff, 1998)? Most school systems today would argue that if the product was developed on their time and with their equipment, the rights are theirs. Educators who have the abilities to produce these products often feel that they should profit from any commercial application of products they develop. This potential conflict needs to be resolved in advance so that educators who are active in technology-based instruction feel more comfortable in this pursuit.

While the application of technology has great promise when properly used in all settings, it holds particular attraction for rural schools in the United States. Programs such as the Star Schools Project operated by the University of Oklahoma offer courses in foreign languages, mathematics, and sciences taught by college professors to schools across the country (Ludlow & Duff, 1998). A number of electronic and Internet schools also exist in various locations in the United States: Moab, Utah; Orange, Virginia; and Perris, California (Kidd, 1996; Van Horn, 1997). While schools like these are accessible from anywhere with an Internet link, they are particularly useful for students in rural areas wishing to take courses that would have low enrollment if taken in conventional classrooms. A student in a high school in rural South Dakota could take a high school course in Japanese through an

FIGURE 14.1

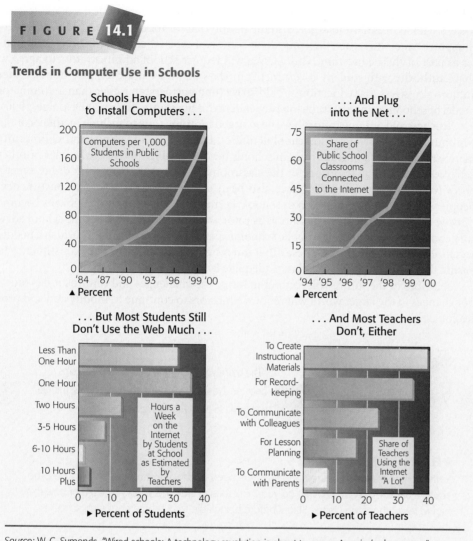

Trends in Computer Use in Schools

Schools Have Rushed to Install Computers . . .

Computers per 1,000 Students in Public Schools

. . . And Plug into the Net . . .

Share of Public School Classrooms Connected to the Internet

▲ Percent

. . . But Most Students Still Don't Use the Web Much . . .

Hours a Week on the Internet by Students at School as Estimated by Teachers

Less Than One Hour
One Hour
Two Hours
3-5 Hours
6-10 Hours
10 Hours Plus

▶ Percent of Students

. . . And Most Teachers Don't, Either

To Create Instructional Materials
For Record-keeping
To Communicate with Colleagues
For Lesson Planning
To Communicate with Parents

Share of Teachers Using the Internet "A Lot"

▶ Percent of Teachers

Source: W. C. Symonds, "Wired schools: A technology revolution is about to sweep America's classrooms," *BusinessWeek.* Copyright 2000 by The McGraw-Hill Companies Inc. All rights reserved.

electronic high school if the local high school does not have a Japanese teacher or lacks sufficient enrollment even if a teacher is available locally.

Technology may also be used to further open the dialogue in conventional classrooms. Bowman (1996) argues that "computers will permit dialogues with diverse audiences on problems and hypotheses that relate to class activities" (p. 305). When used in this manner, computers can help bring "multiple voices" into today's classrooms as well as classrooms of the future. Students could communicate with students from other states, regions, and nations to engage in an academic dialogue on issues being studied. Technology can help humanize rather than dehumanize the classroom when used properly. However, technology should be viewed as assisting, not replacing, quality teaching.

STUDENTS' VOICES IN THE FUTURE OF EDUCATION

A number of scholars suggest that in the future students will have a greater voice in their education. Dixon (1994) suggests that student governments in public schools be given real responsibilities, stating that "student government has never been taken seriously by school reformers" (p. 363). Dixon suggests that all school rules be issued from and enforced by student government committees and that students be encouraged to assume all classroom roles including teaching. While this is a significant departure from typical student roles in today's schools, it is hard to argue with the notion that for today's students to have leadership potential in the future, they must have some real experience deciding things that matter as part of their education. This change will require school administrators to agree to share authority with student governments in ways that have not been traditional. Other authors also stress that education should strive for a partnership rather than a dominator model of schooling and stress the interdependence of humanity (Eisler, 2000; Mabie, 1996).

Teachers and administrators have been urged for some time to include members of the community in classroom and school activities. Parents, grandparents, and community members can play significant roles in schools beyond raising funds at bake sales or other activities. They can be resources for the classrooms as they share their work or life experiences with students. Educators have also been urged to involve a larger constituency: people who do not have children in school (Ferrandino, 2000). As more citizens become directly involved in the work of schools as tutors, volunteers, members of the school advisory committee, or other roles, public schools expand their base of support, which can only enhance academic programs. These other interested adults can form a key constituency to ensure that school funding remains at adequate levels.

Teaching in the future will contain many of the challenges and rewards it has today, but changes in the larger world will require educators to continue to modify and add professional skills.

Who am I?

What do I believe?

"The more you know, the clearer the problems become. Now that you have the credentials, people will listen to me. I feel energized!"

MARGARET, SECONDARY TEACHER

THINK ABOUT THIS:

Reflect on what type of background teachers need to educate students who will become adults a decade from now. What do you think foreign students at your college or university had to learn about the United States before being able to graduate from high school in their country.

SHARE and **COMPARE:**

Choose a classmate and share your responses with each other. Is this more or less than what U.S. students have to learn about other nations? Discuss with your classmates why there are differences, if any, in the curriculum in each nation.

WHAT ARE STUDENTS LIKELY TO LOOK LIKE IN THE FUTURE?

American students in the future will increase on at least two variables: numbers and diversity. Between 1996 and 2006:

- Total public and private school enrollment will rise from 51.7 to 54.4 million students.

- Public high school enrollment will rise by 15% with the western states experiencing an almost 30% increase in the number of high school graduates.

- College enrollment is projected to increase by 14%.

- Just to maintain current K–12 services in 2006, we will need to build 6,000 additional schools and invest about $15 billion in additional revenues (Riley, 1997).

More than 60% of U.S. population growth will come from "nonwhite" populations. Most of this population will be absorbed in the states of California, Texas, Florida, and New York, but everyone in the nation will live with expanded racial and ethnic diversity. The United States is more segregated by income than by race, and 20% of our students live below the poverty line, a statistic unchanged in 15 years (Hodgkinson, 2000). By the end of the twenty-first century, a projected 90 million students will be enrolled in the elementary and secondary schools of the United States (Malveaux, 2000).

Another characteristic of students of the future is already evident: high mobility. Forty-three million Americans move every year (Hodgkinson, 2000). The combination of a growing, more diverse, and highly mobile student population suggests that schools of the future will need more resources and greater articulation among schools. Student records may one day be placed on secure Internet sites so they may be accessed from any school in the nation. One of the key issues affecting students in the future is whether steps will be taken to eliminate, or at least narrow, the significant funding differences in U.S. public schools. If top-quality students are to be a national priority, Malveaux (2000) suggests that we need to look for ways to narrow the funding differences in U.S. public schools. Currently, public schools rely very heavily on local property taxes. In 1999, 63% of all schools had access to the Internet, but only 39% of schools in high-poverty areas had Internet connections (Malveaux, 2000). This situation, if not corrected, helps maintain a "digital divide" among students of different socioeconomic classes. You may recall from the discussion in Chapter 12 that all ethnic and socioeconomic groups show a rise in Internet access, but significant differences across groups still exist.

ACCOUNTABILITY AND DEMANDS ON STUDENTS

It is difficult to predict whether students in the future will face the same, lesser, or greater accountability demands than students face today. While the major purpose of high-stakes testing is to guarantee that all students have minimal skills, these tests will have other less desirable effects if they continue to increase in importance. Given the significance of high-stakes tests to students, teachers, administrators, and schools, it is no surprise that preparation for them often tends to dominate the curriculum and overshadow other subject matter that, while important, does not get much instructional time simply because it is not on the high-stakes test. Students and their parents have already begun to question whether it is good public policy to have significant outcomes such as passing to the next grade or graduating from high school based on the results of a single test. Bauer (1999) suggests, "It may be necessary for teachers to have some latitude with alternative assessments in their classrooms without accountability pressures from the district" (p. 168).

Reliance on high-stakes testing is accompanied by a standards movement that requires strict adherence to a statewide curriculum that is aligned with the high-stakes test. Many teachers have expressed concern that overemphasizing a standardized curriculum has taken some of the creativity out of teaching. Time will tell whether future political forces will make the curriculum more standardized or more flexible.

Another factor that current and future teachers must consider is the overall demand on students' time from all sources. Dixon (1994) notes, "Millions of high school students are working 55 hours a week or more when school, home, and paid hours are totaled." (p. 362). But nobody has bothered to create, let alone control, a "total job description." Educators

INTASC

Principle #8

Assessment of Student Learning: The teacher understands and uses formal and informal assessment strategies to evaluate and ensure the continuous intellectual, social, and physical development of the learner.

"Our school computers are one year old. How can they expect us to be competitive in the job market if we're being trained on obsolete equipment?"

Courtesy of Aaron Bacall, *The Lighter Side of Technology in Education*, p. 25. Copyright 2003 by Aaron Bacall. Reprinted by permission of Corwin Press Inc.

must understand the total demands on students' time and work to create learning environments that are flexible and yet demand high-quality work from students. It is unlikely that demands on students' time will decrease in the years ahead.

WHY ARE MULTICULTURAL AND GLOBAL PERSPECTIVES NECESSARY FOR FUTURE TEACHERS?

In the decades ahead, circumstances will likely demand that students know more than they do today to be considered minimally educated. The high school diploma is considered the minimum educational achievement to be employable in many entry-level jobs today. However, this credential does not often give the diploma holder entry into additional jobs with high levels of responsibility. It is likely that in the future, the associate degree, requiring 2 years of college, will become that minimum educational credential. As the world moves forward into the twenty-first century, well-paid jobs that require only a high school diploma are diminishing, and those that remain for high school graduates tend to be relatively low-paid. Blue-collar jobs once held by a significant portion of people in the United States will make up only about 10% of the workforce in the future. Manufacturing jobs, once the staple of middle-class support for Americans with high school diplomas, are commonly being lost or "outsourced" to cheaper labor in other nations. The jobs replacing them require skills that were previously taught to only a few students (Pepper & Rowland, 2000).

Even traditional jobs that remain in the United States change in their educational requirements. Automobile mechanics trained decades ago are fairly obsolete today if they cannot work with autos or engines that integrate computer technology. As other occupations continue to rely more and more on computer integration, people trained to repair or maintain equipment in those areas will need more education. This same pattern is being felt in education, medicine, finance, and nearly every other sector of the economy in industrialized nations, and increasingly in developing nations.

GLOBAL ECONOMIC AND POLITICAL TRENDS

As transportation and technology continue to shrink the world, educational systems must adapt to that changing reality. In a fourth-grade class in Pocatello, Idaho, today, approximately a third or more of the students will eventually have jobs working directly or indirectly with the global economy. The question arises, which third? Since we can't predict that today, the only solution to ensuring that the appropriate third is prepared is to expose all students to an elementary curriculum that will give them a good foundation for future work in the global economy. It could also be argued that the entire fourth-grade class must be prepared for a job they will all share: U.S. citizen. In order to carry out the duties of citizenship and cast intelligent votes, these fourth graders need to understand the world at a level that is unprecedented in American education. They are citizens and future voters of the world's only economic and military superpower. As such, not only will their political decisions affect their fellow U.S. citizens, but Americans have much more influence in the world than the voters of any other nation. With such influ-

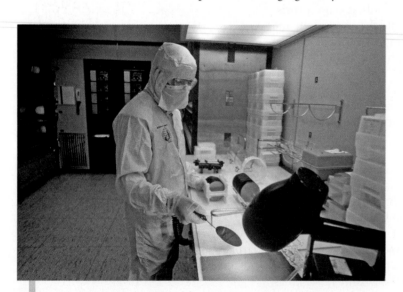

The emergence of a global economy has resulted in a more global curriculum as well. As knowledge and technology evolve rapidly, the focus in schools will continue to adapt.

ence comes the responsibility to understand international issues so that policymakers in the United States view their decisions in the international arena as items the public cares about and understands. Such accountability cannot occur if the educational system does not empower the average American with the tools to understand foreign affairs and international economic and military matters as well as local issues. These skills go beyond the traditional definition of what American educators have defined as the "basics" in reading, writing, and mathematics. However, for this democracy to continue to flourish, domestic and global civic literacy will have to be added as a "fourth basic" in American education.

Many U.S. school districts have tried to fill shortages in certain specialties in teaching by recruiting teachers from other nations. A student in Belle Glade, Florida, may have a Spanish teacher whom the school district recruited in Spain and a mathematics teacher recruited from the Philippines. These international teachers may be a sign of a greater trend in the future: a global marketplace for U.S. teachers.

The world has become much more interdependent in the past few decades, and education should reflect this. Financial and currency markets are not only national, but international. Nations have grouped together into economic units. In the European Union, products are sold across borders of member nations without paying additional taxes for importation. A citizen of Portugal, a European Union member, may seek employment in Germany or Denmark without needing special permission from those governments. The United States, Mexico, and Canada have formed the North American Free Trade Agreement (NAFTA), which allows products to be sold from one country to another without paying tariffs. While NAFTA does not currently cover free movement of workers, it could be amended to do so. This could result in an even greater influx of foreign workers and their families, with children who would need to be educated. However, poll findings indicated in Figure 14.2 show that the U.S. public is fairly skeptical that the overall impact of increased globalization is good for U.S. economic interests. Nonetheless, education in the future must prepare students to live and work in an increasingly interdependent world because current trends point in that direction.

CHANGES IN TEACHER PREPARATION

Significant changes in society and the world do not mean that most teachers feel prepared to discuss these trends in the classroom. A survey by the National Center for Educational Statistics (1999) found that only 20% of teachers responding felt comfortable developing a multicultural curriculum or working in diverse classrooms. Van Hook (2002) states, "research suggests that many undergraduate programs in teacher education fail to prepare teachers to enter highly diverse classrooms" (p. 256). In light of the growing diversity of students in U.S. schools, why do so many teachers feel unprepared in this area?

● **Greater Multicultural Awareness**   Developing multicultural literacy is not something that can be accomplished in one or two college courses. It is a lifelong endeavor that requires commitment by professional educators to keep learning each year of their careers. One payoff for teachers pursuing multicultural and global literacy is being more highly regarded by students, especially those whose ethnic or cultural backgrounds have often been ignored by schools. The Colombian immigrant student who is introduced to a new teacher in a U.S. school does not often encounter the question, "Are you from Bogota, Cali, Cartagena, Baranquilla, or some other part of the

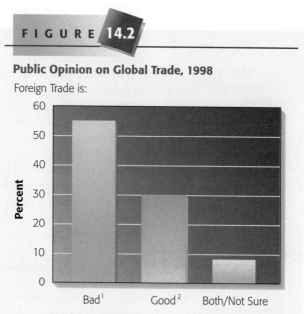

FIGURE 14.2

Public Opinion on Global Trade, 1998

Foreign Trade is:

1. Bad for U.S. economy because cheap imports hurt wages and jobs.
2. Good for U.S. economy; creates foreign demand, U.S. economic growth, and jobs.

Source: WALL STREET JOURNAL. EASTERN EDITION [ONLY STAFF-PRODUCED MATERIALS MAY BE USED] BY CALMES J/BARTLEY, ROBERT L. Copyright 1998 by DOW JONES & CO INC. Reproduced with permission of DOW JONES & CO INC in the format Textbook via Copyright Clearance Center.

As a teacher; you are a leader of the minds of tomorrow and a powerful agent of change. Are you ready to embrace the challenge and responsibility? Are you ready to touch the future?

INTASC

Principle #1

Knowledge of Subject Matter: The teacher understands the central concepts, tools of inquiry, and structures of the subject being taught and can create learning experiences that make these aspects of subject matter meaningful for students.

country?" Imagine how this student would feel if the average teacher showed at least this level of familiarity with an immigrant student's home country? Additionally, having the ability to teach subjects from multicultural perspectives is not only more accurate, but generally tends to improve students' interest in the curriculum.

Why aren't multicultural perspectives routinely incorporated in U.S. schools? One future teacher stated, "If you live in an all-White community, the perceived need for diversity is minimal at best" (Van Hook, 2002, p. 259). Diverse examples in the classroom may not be validated in a particular community. However, this reasoning ignores the high level of mobility of Americans over their lifetimes. Another barrier may be the perceived opposition to multicultural perspectives in the communities schools serve. One study of future teachers found that 63% of the sample felt that parents' biased attitudes and views may prevent diverse topics from being included in the curriculum (Van Hook, 2002). Fears of being criticized by a parent should not be allowed to set the curriculum for an entire class, but they sometimes do. In an increasingly diverse society, failure to include significant elements of diversity throughout the curriculum presents students with an artificial and overly narrow view of knowledge. It is like looking at knowledge through rose-colored glasses. The scenery may look beautiful and soothing, but the viewers realize that this isn't the real world whenever they take off the glasses.

Gay and Howard (2000) point out that 86% of all teachers are European Americans and that African American teachers have declined from a high of 12% in 1970 to around 7% in 1998. Latino (5%), Asian American (1%), and Native American (less than 1%) teachers are still small components of the teaching force (Gay & Howard, 2000). This trend suggests that multicultural competence needs to be incorporated into the preparation of a largely European American and mostly female teaching force. Only 8% of our current teaching force is multiculturally competent. When preservice teachers do not develop a commitment to teaching diverse learners, they often choose to teach only in monocultural school environments (Bradfield-Kreider, 2001).

It is encouraging to note that well-conceived and well-taught university courses in multicultural education can make a significant difference in future teachers' positive attitudes and commitments to diverse learners (Keim, Warring, & Rau, 2001). While working to develop multicultural perspectives, some future teachers pass through a stage of **disequilib-**

rium as they learn to look at the world through the eyes of others and develop concepts to understand new information (Gutierrez-Gomez, 2002). As students gain a stronger multi-cultural knowledge base, they develop more confidence and equilibrium is generally restored. Many future teachers discover their own ethnicity in these courses after beginning the course with a belief that only "other people" had ethnicity, but not them. After developing a sound base of multicultural knowledge, future teachers feel much more confident in cross-cultural contacts and lose most of the fear that they might say something that may label them as insensitive. Figure 14.3 on page 446 shows that when teachers spend more than 8 hours in professional development addressing the needs of English language learners or culturally different students, 38% stated that these activities improved their teaching a great deal.

A study of diversity requirements for teacher preparation in the 50 states and the District of Columbia produced both encouraging and discouraging results. Although many more states have adopted some form of diversity requirement for the licensing of teachers, major inconsistencies existed among states as to what these requirements should be (Miller, Strosnider, & Dooley, 2002). As American schools move forward, educators need to forge more of a consensus regarding diversity requirements for teacher licensing. Multi-cultural education is not a cure-all in teacher preparation, but as Obiakor (2001) suggests, it is "a powerful force for the preparation of future general and special educators" (p. 255). Future teachers being prepared at universities in rural areas need multicultural education as much as those receiving their education in large metropolitan areas.

Teachers feel that the teaching profession is not just about teaching literacy and math-ematical skills, but also about imparting values to students. However, there is a difference of opinion among educators regarding what these values should be. In a study of 79 current teachers and 54 future teachers who were asked what values should be taught in today's schools, respondents identified responsibility (89%), respect (88%), value of cultural diversity (72%), value of religious diversity (53%), and value of people despite their sexual orientation (33%) (Zern, 1997). These findings depict rather clearly that not all aspects of human diversity are equally supported by current or future teachers, but teaching students about cultural diversity and its value is supported by a significant proportion of teachers.

● **Changing Perspectives**   Teachers in the twenty-first century also will need the ability to present curriculum from a global perspective. Very few topics taught in our schools lack a global dimension because most human activities transcend national boundaries. People throughout the world create literature, art, music, science, and mathematics and face social issues and problems. When these topics are taught in U.S. schools, global perspectives are sometimes mentioned, but on the whole, American students do not receive a thoroughly global education. One definition of global education is "an approach that offers the learner a holistic picture of the world" (Kolker, Ustinova, & McEneaney, 1998/1999, p. 77). A key characteristic of teachers who have the ability to provide a holistic global education is that they understand topics from the perspectives of nations other than their own and ask students to consider issues or historical events from the points of view of others. The goal is not to dictate any conclusions to students, but to have them understand that where you are in the world can influence ideas and behavior.

EVOLVING DIMENSIONS OF KNOWLEDGE

Positionality of knowledge suggests that the characteristics of the presenters of knowledge, as well as those of the learners, affect how the same information can be absorbed differently by students. Teachers who have global perspectives attempt to encourage students to be proud of their nation and to also see themselves as part of a larger human family. The two concepts are not seen as opposites. To this end, teachers who foster multicultural and global education understand that students need to develop positive ethnic, national, and global identities. These teachers also understand the difference between natural pride in one's own culture and nation and the assumption that one's culture and nation are superior to all other countries and cultures. McLaren and Fischman (1998) make a bold proposal and argue that teacher education programs need to create teachers who are **agents of social justice**. In an

INTASC

Principle #2

Knowledge of Human Development and Learning: The teacher understands how children learn and develop, and can provide learning opportunities that support their intellectual, social, and personal development.

INTASC

Principle #1

Knowledge of Subject Matter: The teacher understands the central concepts, tools of inquiry, and structures of the subject being taught and can create learning experiences that make these aspects of subject matter meaningful for students.

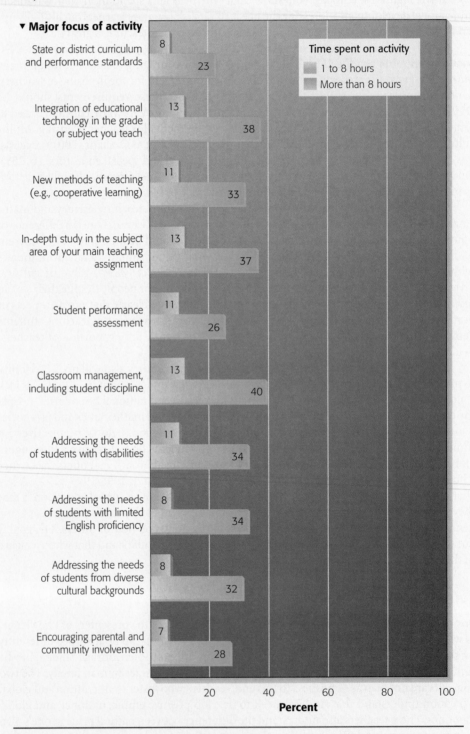

FIGURE 14.3

Improved Teaching through Professional Development

Among full-time public school teachers who participated in professional development activities in the last 12 months, the percentage believing that activities improved their teaching a lot, by major focus of activity and hours spent: 1998.

▼ **Major focus of activity**

Source: U.S. Department of Education, NCES, *Teacher Preparation and Professional Development: 2000* (NCES 2001–088). (Washington, D.C.: NCES, 2001).

The face of American students will continue to change. Your students' appreciation of cultural diversity starts with your being open to global perspectives.

age of globalization teachers need to go beyond the traditional role as presenters of information and exemplify the ethics of caring, compassion, and social justice.

In order to present viable global perspectives to students, you must command sufficient knowledge about places, cultures, and events outside the United States. The tragic events of September 11, 2001, brought a great deal of attention not only to matters of security, but to topics involving the Middle East and the Muslim world. A study about the knowledge and attitudes future teachers had about Islam found the following:

- No respondent was able to identify Indonesia among the three most populous Muslim nations.

- Fewer than 5% of the respondents knew that there were six million Muslims in the United States. One in seven said there were fewer than 20,000.

- About one-third of the respondents said that they had a negative reaction on hearing the term *Islam.*

- Only two respondents said that mainstream Islam was different from the beliefs of Islamic extremists (Mastrilli & Sardo-Brown, 2002).

These findings raise concerns about the abilities of a significant portion of this sample of future teachers to provide fair and enlightened instruction about Islam or nations in the Muslim world. Particularly troubling is the last finding that only two respondents could distinguish between the beliefs of mainstream Islam and those of extremists. Most of these future teachers are likely to see Muslim students as potential threats. How could they be effective teachers and mentors to Muslim students? It is very important for teacher education programs, now and in the future, to ascertain what conceptions teachers are bringing into the profession.

DISTINGUISHING BETWEEN DEEP AND SURFACE CULTURE

To the extent that current or future teachers lack accurate conceptions of culture, geography, or religion, teacher preparation programs have a duty to identify these misconceptions and provide the future teacher with accurate information. Additionally, attitudes that current and future teachers have toward other cultures should be explored. One effective way to do this in university courses or in-service workshops is through simulations. Cross-cultural simulations such as Bafa Bafa, Barnga, Tribal Talk, the Albatross, and the Owl are ways of allowing educators to explore culture through the eyes of another (Delaney-Barmann & Minner, 1996).

Teachers with global perspectives must go beyond teaching that coffee is a leading export of Brazil, Rachmaninoff was a Russian composer, or that Indonesia is the most populous Muslim nation on earth. These are "facts" that happen to pertain to global content. They should be willing to explore global issues in which the United States has a national stake as well as issues in which students have personal stakes. These are often the issues that are more likely to be seen as "controversial" and less likely to be explored in the curriculum. Teachers in the future should also provide students with experiences in the cognitive (knowledge), affective (caring), and participatory (action) domains in their multicultural and global instruction (Diaz, Massialas, & Xanthopoulos, 1999). It is important that American students learn new information about multicultural and global issues, but it is also important that they care enough to act when they believe it is necessary.

Increasing diversity in the United States in the decades ahead and the shrinking of the world into a "global village" make multicultural and global literacy much more than "nice to know" for teachers in the twenty-first century. They are fast becoming professional necessities and current trends will increase their importance in the future.

Who am I? What do I believe?

"The barriers are institutional. People want to protect their programs. They don't want certain populations."

—CAROL, ESOL RESOURCE TEACHER

THINK ABOUT THIS:

As education continues to adjust to meet the needs of our changing society and changing student population, teachers will see their programs evolving as well. Today's teachers need to be more multiculturally and globally competent than ever before. Who will be better prepared to handle these changes, veteran teachers or new teachers? Why?

SHARE and **COMPARE:**

Partner with a classmate and individually identify an event from the last 20 years. Each event must have involved the United States and at least one other nation. Discuss how much each of you knows about the U.S. perspective on each event. How much do you know about the perspective of the other nation(s)? If there is a difference in the knowledge base between the two, how might this affect a class discussion about the events?

SHOULD TEACHERS BE LEADERS AND AGENTS FOR CHANGE?

Traditionally, teachers in the United States have been expected to work as loyal employees in schools and leave the area of decision and policymaking to administrators, school board members, and legislators. This is a very hierarchical notion of education that places individuals vertically in an organization shaped like a pyramid. Teachers have historically occupied the bottom of the educational pyramid—passengers on a plane that someone else always flew. This hierarchical structure is found in many large organizations. Private business has learned that a problem with this structure is that people at the base of the pyramid often feel alienated from the organization's goals, and business has looked for ways to "flatten the pyramid" and give those who provide the goods or services a role in shaping the organization's future. The goal of these reforms is to get away from the notion that some people are paid to work while others are paid to think and decide: all members of the organization have some role in decision making.

EVOLVING LEADERSHIP ROLES FOR TEACHERS

Similar trends have begun in education with the creation of school advisory committees composed of parents, teachers, and administrators and making decisions previously made only by the school principal. This trend is likely to continue and increase in the future as the teaching profession strives for greater professional recognition. Like their counterparts in medicine and law, educators generally want greater control over certain professional matters such as setting standards for their profession and determining violations of professional ethics. This is a logical progression of the teaching profession's efforts over the years to be recognized and compensated in line with other professions. For this trend to continue in the future, teachers must see themselves as educational leaders. It is ironic to note that most universities do not include a single course in educational leadership in teacher preparation programs, although they often have an entire department devoted to this topic. Educational leadership courses are usually reserved for graduate students seeking credentials to become school administrators. What does this say about the university's vision of who school leaders are? The most knowledgeable professional in a school is not necessarily the school's principal. Principals have the most decision-making authority of any single professional in a school, but new models of decision making are structured so that teachers are also expected to share their considerable expertise and participate in decisions. A part of this responsibility is to share effective teaching approaches and new matter information with fellow teachers. This way, professional development is not only continuous but a collective effort by all teachers in a department, grade, or school. Teachers of the future, much more than in the past, need to perceive themselves as educational leaders whether or not they ever work officially as school administrators. While quality school administrators are vital to a school's success, it is interesting to note that when a principal and a teacher in the same school are absent, which one requires a substitute for the day?

GREATER PROFESSIONALISM AND LEADERSHIP

As in all professions, teachers must continue to update their skills in order to keep their professional licenses current. The trend in this area is toward greater, not lesser, professional standards. A few teachers in the United States have received **National Board Certification** in their specialties. However, a board-certified teacher is still much more rare than a board-certified physician. Most teachers have certification only in the state where they teach, and National Board Certification is currently the province of a few "master teachers." It may well be that in the future, National Board Certification will be an expected accomplishment for every teacher who chooses to remain in the profession beyond a few years. When a master's degree and National Board Certification become standard for every teacher with 10 years in the profession, teaching will have made significant strides toward greater professional standing in the eyes of the public. Table 14.1 on page 450 indicates that in a 2002 Harris poll, 70% of respondents said that teachers had "very great prestige" (48%) or "considerable prestige" (22%), which made teaching one of the four most respected professions rated by this poll (Taylor, 2002).

Teaching in the future will likely become more research-based. In schools throughout this nation, teachers converse in the teachers' lounge about students and what works or doesn't work with them and give each other suggestions. However, many of these conversations are anecdotal consisting of what one teacher did to get a student interested in the

TABLE 14.1

Prestige of 22 Professions and Occupations

BASE: ALL ADULTS	VERY GREAT PRESTIGE	CONSIDERABLE PRESTIGE	SOME PRESTIGE	HARDLY ANY PRESTIGE AT ALL	NOT SURE/ REFUSED
	%	%	%	%	%
Doctor	52	32	14	1	1
Scientist	52	29	15	3	2
Fireman	48	32	17	2	1
Teacher	48	22	21	7	1
Military Officer	47	31	18	2	2
Nurse	44	30	20	6	1
Police Officer	40	28	26	5	1
Priest/Minister/Clergyman	32	25	31	10	2
Member of Congress	31	29	29	8	3
Engineer	29	38	27	3	3
Athlete	21	25	37	16	1
Architect	20	35	34	7	3
Business Executive	19	29	38	10	4
Lawyer	17	30	37	15	2
Entertainer	16	25	38	19	2
Union Leader	16	24	34	23	2
Actor	16	21	37	23	3
Banker	15	26	45	13	1
Journalist	14	30	39	14	2
Accountant	10	32	43	14	2
Stockbrocker	10	23	44	21	2
Real Estate Broker/Agent	5	18	45	30	2

Source: H. Taylor, "Scientists, Doctors, Teachers and Military Officers Top the List of Most Prestigious Occupations." *The Harris Poll*® #65: © 2004, Harris Interactive Inc. All rights reserved.

subject compared with another teacher's attempts. Out of these discussions, some good ideas may be exchanged among teachers, but what is often lacking from this discourse is the research that supports successful strategies or tells teachers what is more likely to fail. The teaching profession in the future will have little or no room for educators who do not take professional development seriously and feel that their initial teaching credential should last them an entire professional lifetime. It is also likely that recertification standards will increase for teachers in the future as the profession is expected to do more in an increasingly complex society.

Teachers in the future will need to be better acquainted with existing research as they progress through their teacher preparation programs. Once in the profession, teachers need to keep up with new research by reading professional journals, taking additional university courses, or discussing recent findings with other educators. This is difficult to do when your job description provides little time for these pursuits and when teachers typically have an hour per day for planning and grading assignments for the next day. Teaching, as it is currently configured, is one of the few professions in which practitioners' duties are the same the day they retire as the day they started.

Advancing along the career ladder from a beginning to a master teacher, your responsibilities and opportunities also will change. You will have many opportunities for professional development and advancement.

The future may hold some variation on this theme in which teachers will follow a **career ladder** somewhat similar to what university faculty have today. As teachers become more expert and their abilities are demonstrated by accomplishments such as National Board Certification and graduate degrees, they may spend part of their day teaching students and the other part mentoring new teachers or developing innovative curriculum. Teachers may start their careers as *beginning teachers,* move to being *associate teachers,* and finally become *master teachers.* While there may be more than three categories, or the stages may have different names, a career ladder program would present teachers with continuous avenues of professional development as well as better salaries for those who progress through the system. A master teacher would not have to leave the classroom entirely in order to have different professional responsibilities, because part of a master teacher's job description may be to mentor new teachers or to develop curriculum. Master teachers would teach students part of the day and engage in other professional activities for the rest of the day. This approach is being supported by a number of teachers' unions today and recognizes that teachers have leadership and scholarly abilities they would like to contribute, but they may not want to leave the classroom entirely in order to do this.

ADVOCATING FOR STUDENTS

Another aspect of teacher leadership is serving as advocates for students, especially those whose parents do not understand exactly how school systems function. In many cases, parents do not know the full range of options available to their children in schools. Sometimes administrators inform all parents of the full range of options and sometimes they do not, especially if this creates more work or additional accommodations for the school. When this does not occur, and teachers are aware of all the legal options available to students, teachers who are student advocates inform parents of the full range of options.

Teachers who are leaders and change agents also have the responsibility to discuss all of the effects (good or bad) of educational policy. For example, there is significant evidence that in about two-thirds of states that have implemented high-stakes testing for promotion and high school graduation, dropout rates have increased and high school graduation rates

EDUCATION MATTERS

Career Ladders

While education reform has touched the lives of teachers in many ways, it has not changed the day-to-day life of teachers. In fact, the working world of a teacher has changed little from the beginning of the century. Most teachers work in isolation with traditional pay structures, leaving no job advancement. In the 1980s states responded to the call of "careerlessness" in the profession and made attempts to create new roles within schools for teachers. In the past few years there has been renewed interest in career ladders and alternative compensation systems.

Teacher leadership has been discussed for years, but few districts have institutionalized it as a viable option. It has been tried in the form of "career ladders" that provide career options and new roles for teachers who want to stay in the profession but not in the classroom.

Career ladders can be categorized in two ways: performance-based and job-enlargement. Performance-based ladders allow teachers to receive more money if they progress from novice to expert teacher through a series of developmental practices. Sometimes this is tied to student achievement on tests. Job-enlargement ladders allow teachers to do more work for more pay. Teachers who would normally work after school or in the summer at another job to earn more money for their family would take on these education-related jobs instead. There are benefits to this type of ladder because it keeps interested teachers in the field who may otherwise leave the profession. Career ladders allow teachers to become leaders in their own profession by creating new roles and opportunities in the classroom or beyond the classroom.

The Education Issue: Should teachers have options for career advancement?

How Would Career Ladders Affect Teachers and Students?

These types of programs could keep good teachers in the profession who may be looking for variety in their career. Students could benefit if ladders are tied to performance of teachers. All aspects of the ladder would have to be researched to be sure it met with teacher contracts and guidelines. This idea for the future could affect the profession by making more avenues for teachers to grow and participate professionally.

What's Your Opinion?

1. Do you think teachers should have more options for teacher leadership with increased salaries through career ladders?

2. What can you see as a possible problem with this model?

3. What would have to change about schools to make this work?

Source: "Statewide Teacher Career Ladder," *NASBE Policy Update, 10*(9). Retrieved May 20, 2005, from http://www.nasbe.org/Educational_Issues/New_Information/Policy_Updates/10-09.html

---

have decreased (Amrein & Berliner, 2002). This was certainly not a goal of those who proposed statewide high-stakes testing. However, if this is a result in many states, teachers who are educational leaders have a duty to bring these results to the attention of professional organizations and policymakers. Some changes may be needed, or the notion of high-stakes testing may need to be readdressed, in order to produce lower high school dropout rates and higher graduation rates.

TEACHERS AS ETHICAL ROLE MODELS

Teachers who warn students against cheating, lying, or other forms of dishonesty must serve as **ethical role models** for students and their communities. They cannot engage in these behaviors if they expect to maintain their students' respect. This principle will be as true in the future as it is today. Teachers are held to higher standards by their students than are most other members of their communities. If students learn that other pupils were given grades that they did not earn because of pressure by influential parents, a teacher's credibility suffers instantly. When some teachers voice one opinion in the teachers' lounge and the opposite opinion in front of the principal, they lose legitimacy with their fellow teachers.

Through the Eyes of
Culturally Sensitive Teachers

Advocating for Immigrant Students

Carolyn Dalton was a teacher in an inner-city elementary school in Florida. She had grown up in Great Britain and immigrated to the United States at age 19. She always knew she wanted to teach and pursued her degree in elementary education. Most of the students in her school qualified for free and reduced lunches and many were immigrants from Mexico and Central American nations. Carolyn enjoyed teaching these students and she did something that most teachers didn't do: she lived three blocks from her school. She was both teacher and neighbor to many of her students' families.

After 8 years of teaching at this school, Carolyn and her colleagues got a new principal who made a number of fundamental changes. The major one that affected Carolyn and her students was to abolish separate classes for English language learners. The principal felt that all students should be mainstreamed, period. Carolyn tried to explain to him that if the English language learners were all dispersed, there were not enough ESOL teachers or translators in the school to follow the students and guarantee "understandable instruction." She suggested that these students would have a much harder time understanding, much less doing, their assigned work. However, Carolyn's advice went unheeded.

Carolyn was very discouraged. She knew that academic English took a minimum of around 5 years to acquire and, in the meantime, students needed additional assistance they would not be getting in this new "mainstreamed model." She thought about her students' futures as well as her own. After teaching for 8 years and investing so much of herself in this community, should she continue teaching at this school?

More important, how would her students fare if placed in mainstream classes with minimal support? Carolyn thought long and hard about this dilemma.

She decided that she had invested too much in this school and community to allow one principal to change her career plans. On the matter of the mainstreamed classes, she decided that her principal knew her views and they would simply have to "agree to disagree." She realized that in any other profession or occupation, she could encounter a change in leadership that was headed in the wrong direction because they didn't fully understand all of the variables. Carolyn felt that if the standardized test scores for English language learners dropped after the mainstream model had taken effect, the principal would have to reconsider his idea or have to explain to his superiors why he was sticking to ineffective changes. Besides, she was a teacher for life who would not be easily diverted and there was no substitute for coming to work every morning and hearing an enthusiastic "Miss Dalton! Miss Dalton!"

Points to Ponder

1. Have you ever encountered a decision made by someone in a superior position with which you disagreed? What did you do?

2. Do you think Carolyn Dalton made the right decision regarding her future as a teacher? Why or why not?

3. When you look at the future of the teaching profession, do teachers like Carolyn Dalton help or hurt the profession? Would students and the teaching profession be better served if Carolyn and others like her left the profession to show their displeasure?

A university professor was asked the following by a student preparing to be a teacher: "What do I do if I am ever pressured to change a grade to one that the student didn't earn or to do something else that is fraudulent?" Never do anything or sign anything that your conscience tells you is wrong. If, in the future, the matter is ever investigated, the person who pressured you will forget the conversation and you will often be left alone to defend your action. Teachers occasionally face these and other ethical dilemmas. Those who begin to compromise their ethics, even slightly, find it easier to make deeper compromises in the future. There are many issues for which compromise is appropriate, such as deciding how long to give a student to make up a test. It is difficult to stand your ground if the star athlete has made a poor grade and is ineligible to play in a big game without a better grade. Yet teachers who are leaders recognize the ethics of this situation. Schools have student–athletes, not athlete–students. Arbitrarily changing the grade not only is unethical, but if it should ever be revealed, it could cost the team a victory and you your reputation.

Those who minimize the importance of ethics in education or in human behavior should be reminded that major scandals in business or government (such as, Enron, WorldCom, Watergate, and Abu Ghraib) began as ethical lapses and mushroomed from there. Teachers who want to make education more equitable, or who want to be seen as leaders, realize that their most valuable commodity is their personal and professional reputation. Additionally, students remember your behavior long after they may have forgotten many of the details of your lesson.

'School is a building that has four walls—with tomorrow inside."

—LOIS WALTERS

THINK ABOUT THIS:

After completing this entire book, you should be able to tell now that "school" is indeed so much more than just a building with four walls. Are you ready to take your next step toward touching the future?

SHARE and COMPARE:

As a class or in a small group, explain the similarities between Lois Walters's comment with that of Christa McAuliffe's in the opening chapter. How will *you* affect tomorrow?

FINAL THOUGHTS

By the time you reach this point in the book, many concepts, ideas, and facts have been presented to you about teaching and the teaching profession. You have no doubt realized that themes stressed in this volume include diversity, equity, technology, professionalism, teacher leadership, and ethics. For many readers, this may be the first book in their first college or university course in education. You may have decided to become a teacher before you took this course or read this book, or you may still be undecided. You may like the idea of becoming a teacher, but you may be unsure of facing some of the challenges teachers face.

If we lived in a perfect world, the best among us would become teachers and the rest would divide among all other occupations. There are many things to consider when choosing a path to which you will devote the rest of your life. It is certainly true that in the United States, and in nearly all the world, teaching is not among the most highly paid professions. Yet without teachers, there would be no other professionals. A question to ponder here is, "Who or what defines success?" If you were asked, outside your parents or other family members, who have been the most influential people in your life, the answer would likely be dominated by teachers. What could be a better measure of success than that? A valid standard for success is the number of people in your life that you touch in a positive and profound way. Few professions do this better than teaching.

In planning and writing this book, the three authors have had various conversations regarding the perspective and tone the book should take. We wanted the book to convey to future teachers the joys and rewards of the profession in the hope that readers undecided about teaching would seriously consider joining the profession. We did not want to present a picture of the teaching profession that depicted the field as thoroughly rosy or without challenges. Readers of this book would not believe this depiction and they would naturally compare what they read in this book with their observations in today's schools. Therefore, the authors have attempted to strike a balance between promises and challenges. Only the reader can judge how well this balance was achieved.

In spite of the challenges, the promises of teaching abound now and in the future. This nation will continue to need a high proportion of its best minds in positions where they can promote the intellectual growth of future generations. Nearly every veteran teacher can tell numerous stories of students who have approached them years after they left the classroom with comments like, "You influenced my life in so many significant ways. I didn't realize it then, but I can tell you now!" What motivates people to devote their lives to teaching? One answer is the idealism that we want to leave the world a little bit better than we found it. If this idea appeals to you, you may want to pursue this goal: touch the future, teach!

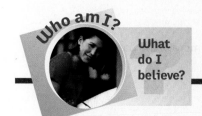

Who am I? What do I believe?

REFLECTIONS

Professional Plan for Adapting to Changes in the Profession

1. Three things I learned from this chapter about my future as a teacher are:

2. Two possible trends that could affect teaching in the future that were not discussed in this chapter are:

   a. _____

   b. _____

3. Two things in this chapter that you would like to learn more about are:

   a. _____

   b. _____

4. I plan to investigate these two areas and learn more about topics in this chapter by:

   _____ Reading some of the book club choices

   _____ Reading sources referenced in the chapter that interest me

   _____ Interviewing beginning and veteran teachers about their opinions of the future of the teaching profession and comparing responses.

   _____ Exploring the websites listed in the Log On section

   _____ Observing several classrooms and taking notes on the specific strategies teachers use that work for them in practice

5. I will include the following in my Touch the Future Portfolio:

_____ Responses to Who Am I? activities

_____ A brief essay on my thoughts about Problems to Possibilities

_____ Responses to the Observation Guide

_____ Other (materials assigned by your instructor):

SUMMARY

What Is Teaching Likely to Look Like in the Future?

- Multicultural and global literacy are likely to become more important for teachers.
- Teachers will need to be leaders in schools and communities.
- Education credentials will need to be even more portable and extensive.
- Accountability is likely to continue to shape teaching and curriculum.
- Technological literacy will be required of teachers and students.
- Parents, students, and community members are likely to participate more in the operation of schools.

What Are Students Likely to Look Like in the Future?

- Most urban school districts will experience a growth in students.
- A greater portion of U.S. students will be students of color.
- American students will continue to have fairly high mobility.
- Overall demands on students' time is likely to increase.

Why Are Multicultural and Global Perspectives Necessary for Future Teachers?

- The minimum education credential will probably increase.
- U.S. schools will need to turn out more graduates who can function well in a global economy.
- Economic interdependence among nations will continue to increase.
- Current research indicates that many undergraduate teacher preparation programs do not adequately prepare teachers to work in diverse classrooms.
- Parental opposition is seen by some teachers as limiting the teaching of diversity issues in the curriculum.
- Teachers believe that the profession should teach values along with content to students.
- Teachers should not dictate conclusions to students but broaden the base of information from which students draw those conclusions.
- Accurate global perspectives are necessary for today's and tomorrow's teachers.
- Teachers need to distinguish between deep and surface culture.

Should Teachers Be Leaders and Agents for Change?

- Today's and tomorrow's teachers are being asked to take on more leadership roles.
- Trends toward greater professionalism such as National Board Certification are likely to continue in the future.
- Professional development will take on greater importance as schools retrain teachers to handle changing circumstances.

- Teacher leaders in the future will take on increasing roles as advocates for students who are not being well served.
- Teachers who want to be leaders must also be ethical role models; otherwise, they may compromise their leadership.

Visit the **Touch the Future . . . Teach!** Companion Website at www.ablongman.com/diaz for additional opportunities.

KEY WORDS

agents of social justice 445	ethical role models 452	portability of education 434
career ladder 451	National Board	positionality of
disequilibrium 444	Certification 449	knowledge 445

CONCEPT REVIEW

1. Identify some trends that are visible today that will affect the future of education in the United States.

2. Explain how increasing diversity in the United States as well as increasing globalization will make it more important for tomorrow's teachers to be multiculturally and globally literate.

3. Identify reasons why equity and achievement are complementary goals in education.

4. Project the role that technology will play in tomorrow's classrooms.

5. Understand how the U.S. student population is changing in numbers and characteristics.

6. Explain how accountability standards and high-stakes testing have affected and will continue to affect the work of schools.

7. Summarize current trends that are shaping changes in teacher preparation.

8. Identify how the teaching profession is moving toward greater professionalism.

9. Explain circumstances that require teachers to be leaders and not just presenters of information to students.

10. Explain how the individual characteristics of the learner can affect attitudes toward new knowledge.

11. Provide examples of roles that teachers play as decision makers.

12. Identify the significance of ethics in the teaching profession and explain why ethics are at the core of what teachers do.

TOUCH THE FUTURE

Read On

Changing American Education: Recapturing the Past or Reinventing the Future?
Katherine M. Borman and Nancy P. Greenman, eds. (New York: State University of New York Press, 1994)
Explores trends in teaching and public education and looks at possibilities for the future.

The Right to Learn: Creating Schools That Work
Linda Darling-Hammond (San Francisco: Jossey-Bass, 1997)
Looks at characteristics of effective schools and discusses how they may be employed in the future.

The Teaching Gap: Best Ideas from the World's Teachers for Improving Education in the Classroom
James Hiebert and James Stigler (New York: Free Press, 1999)
A very practical source that new or veteran teachers may consult to improve classroom practice.

The Courage to Teach: Exploring the Inner Landscape of a Teacher's Life
Parker Palmer (San Francisco: Jossey-Bass, 1997)
An insightful source that explores the motivation that drives teachers and discusses how teachers face daily challenges.

Log On

U.S. Department of Education
www.ed.gov/index.jhtml
> Contains U.S. government publications about maintaining excellence in education; the "Teachers" link includes information about the challenges facing today's teachers, lesson suggestions, and much more; also includes information on student demographics and teacher shortage issues.

Promising Practices: New Ways to Improve Teacher Quality
www.ed.gov/pubs/PromPractice/index.html
> A 1998 online publication by the Department of Education that discusses the nation's goals for achieving and maintaining excellence in the teaching profession.

Free and Appropriate Public Education
www.fape.org
> An organization that works to advocate for students with disabilities and their parents; the site contains links to activist organizations that attempt to reform school practices.

No Child Left Behind
www.ed.gov/nclb
> A U.S. Department of Education site that explains the characteristics and effects of the No Child Left Behind legislation and provides full coverage about the initiative.

TCRecord: The Voice of Scholarship in Education
www.tcrecord.org
> An online publication from the Teacher's College at Columbia University that offers articles about improving teaching and teacher education as well as providing accounts of challenges faced by teachers today and those expected in coming years.

Write On

> *"A teacher affects eternity: he or she can never tell where his or her influence stops."*
> —Henry B. Adams

In your journal, write a brief essay explaining the Adams quote. Discuss in your essay how former teachers affected your life and the choices you have made.

OBSERVATION GUIDE

TEACH: LINKING THEORY TO PRACTICE

Linking
Theory to
Practice

Objective: Interviewing education professionals on the future of the profession
School (use code name): _____ Observer: _____
Meeting: _____ Date: _____
Attendees at Meeting: _____ Time In: _____ Time Out: _____

Directions: Interview at least three professionals in education. One should be a school administrator and the other two should include a beginning teacher (first 3 years) and a veteran teacher (3 or more years). Be sure they understand that the interview will be shared only with your instructor unless they request otherwise. Ask the following questions and record their answers. You may add your own questions to the list if you wish. When you finish the interviews, compare the answers. Are there patterns of similarities in the responses? Are there significant differences in the answers?

1. What has been the major change in the teaching profession since you became an educator?

2. What do you think will be the greatest changes in teaching 20 years from now?

3. What role does professional ethics play in the career of an educator?

4. How do you think increasing diversity in the student population will affect the classroom and/or teacher preparation?

5. To what extent should educators in the United States be aware of what students in other nations are learning and when they are learning it?

6. How well do you think U.S. schools are doing in producing globally literate citizens?

7. What can the United States learn from other nations with regard to education?

8. How would you assess the ability of educators to help shape the lives of students?

Connecting with INTASC: Principle 2

Knowledge of Human Development and Learning: The teacher understands how children learn and develop, and can provide learning opportunities that support their intellectual, social, and personal development.

When speaking with the teachers, find out what efforts they or their school make to meet Principle 2. How will a globalization of society affect how children learn and what they will learn? What does the school do to help teachers understand new information about how children learn? What types of activities does the school offer students to stretch their thinking beyond their local community?

Appendices

Conducting Classroom Observations and Interviews

Included in each chapter of *Touch the Future . . . Teach!* is a section titled "Teach: Linking Theory to Practice." These sections are intended to encourage you to take part in classroom observations and to guide your observations and interviews. By interviewing people involved with education on a day-to-day basis, such as teachers and administrators, and observing procedures in real classroom settings, you can make your learning experience that much more genuine and complete. This appendix offers only a brief introduction to procedures and considerations when observing and interviewing in schools. Your school's field experience office will provide more specific guidelines and suggestions that will be specific to your programs needs. Consult the actual observation activities for more ideas about what to observe.

Conducting field observations and interviews is probably the best way to become familiar with what actually goes on in classrooms. These field experiences allow you to look critically and objectively at what goes on in classrooms. While your own experience in schools as a student may provide you a useful reference point for your studies in education, it is only one perspective. To become a genuine "border crosser" in your work as a teacher, you need to study schools and classrooms in multiple settings—different from those you know best. In addition, you need to apply techniques and insights from the field of educational research. These may include asking certain key questions, being sensitive to cultural variables, and obtaining historical and contextual information that will help you better understand the school or classroom you are interested in learning about. Some of the variables you should explore in your field experiences include the school's mission statement, the school's history, the demographics of the school, and the methods and procedures used to teach and evaluate students.

GETTING STARTED

Where do you begin? First, you need to get yourself placed in a school. Most college and university education departments have a staff member who is assigned to making student placements for field work. Your instructor will likely initiate this process, but you can find out who this person is by going to the department's main office, and then work through them to get your field assignment. In addition, don't be afraid to set up observations on your own. Your school's education department has a formal process for arranging for field work, but feel free to set up observations and interviews of your own in your old elementary, middle, or high school over holiday or semester breaks. When setting up your own classroom observations, always go through the proper channels. Speak with the principal and specific teacher first to make sure the timing works out well for all parties.

BE PROFESSIONAL

When you visit the school to do your observations or interviews, conduct yourself as a professional. Do not overdress, but be as neat as the more carefully groomed teachers. Be discreet about what you see. Your presence is a privilege, not a right. You are a guest in the schools and classrooms you observe. You should not share your observations with friends or make jokes about students or teachers. Discretion is absolutely necessary. You need to be concerned about the rights and feelings of those whom you are observing and interviewing.

BE POLITE

Never force yourself on a setting. If teachers tell you that they are too busy to be interviewed, then find something else to do. Do not insist on conducting an interview.

ESTABLISH GROUND RULES

Sit down with the teacher right away to discuss your role or purpose in the class. Be sure that the teacher to whom you are assigned knows why you are there. Teachers are usually well informed about upcoming observations, but that is not always the case. You may think that you are supposed to be in a certain classroom doing certain things, but the teacher to whom you have been assigned may not have been given much information. If your purpose is to observe, than that is what you should do. If a teacher asks you to start teaching a class, you may need to remind the teacher that you are there to do field research and not to teach. You should not be left in a classroom with students by yourself, nor should you be given papers to grade. After you have been in a setting for a while, you and the teacher may work out an opportunity for you to present a lesson or work with a student for a little bit. Still, the teacher should always be in the room in such instances. This is your first field work, and you have neither the knowledge nor the training to take charge of a classroom yet. Remember, your reason for being there at this point is to observe, interview, and reflect.

RECORD YOUR OBSERVATIONS

Keep a notebook with your observation sheets. Code the information that you collect so that if you lose it, individuals you mention cannot be identified. For example, you do not want a student in a school you are observing to see a comment you may make about a teacher's style or strategies. Use the questions in the observation activities in each chapter to guide your notes.

You also may want to keep a journal for reflections that you consult after each classroom observation or interview that you complete. Use your observation forms to help you review what you saw. Then reflect on the data that you have collected and try to interpret it. Your goal is to construct a clear understanding of what occurs in classroom and school settings. In doing so, you will bring more meaning to your own formal studies in school.

Remember, your primary goal in doing field research is to make meaning of the world. In doing so, you should learn a great deal that is useful not only in life, but also in becoming a better teacher in the process.

Touch the Future Reflective Journal and Portfolio

It is important to think about your own beliefs, opinions, biases, and assumptions throughout this course. As you discuss ideas with your classmates you will discover diverse opinions on a variety of topics. This discussion and reflective thinking is an opportunity for you to clarify what you believe and why you believe it. Social justice and issues of equity are important ones for teachers who believe that all students can learn. How you approach your teaching, how you build a classroom community, and what you bring to the classroom all matter. Maintaining a reflective journal and creating a Touch the Future portfolio are two ways you can document your beliefs and how they relate to the new learning you are exposed to in this text.

DOCUMENTING YOUR INSIGHTS IN A REFLECTIVE JOURNAL

A reflective journal is not a log of your daily activities in which you list what you did and when you did it. It is much more than that. It is a place, like a journal book or folder on your computer, where you can write your questions, dilemmas, suggestions, and insights about what you are reading, observing, or asking teachers in interviews over time.

You will maintain the journal throughout the course, so you can see how you began your thinking in Chapter 1 and where you are at the end of the course in Chapter 14. Sometimes you will write several times in one week because a particular chapter is meaningful to you. Try to write at least once a week so you can track your own development over the course.

An option to personal reflective journaling is to find a partner in the class and write to each other. This dialogue journal approach allows you not only to lay out your thoughts, but also to respond to the insights of one of your classmates. Doing this reflective writing by e-mail is a fast, efficient, and fun way to communicate with a classmate during the course.

GUIDELINES FOR WRITING A PERSONAL REFLECTIVE JOURNAL

- **Step 1: Read** Throughout the chapters you will find various features that will prompt your thoughts. Read them all and select one or more to respond to in your journal. It doesn't matter which ones you choose. All of them relate to key issues that teachers face. If you are writing to a partner you may want to take turns selecting a feature each week. You will note that most of these features have questions embedded in them. Use those questions for your journal prompts. These are the features that can prompt your thoughts and writings:

- *Quotes:*—What did this quote mean to you?

- *Who Am I? What Do I Believe?*—This is a natural for a reflective journal entry. Try it alone or with a partner. Try to do this one for the entire course and then look back at what you wrote for each chapter!

- *Through the Eyes of Culturally Sensitive Teachers*—If this feature calls to you, write about it. Take a page in your journal to write why this story meant something to you.

- *Education MATTERS*—This is a topic that that matters to teachers. Does it matter to you? Why or why not?

- *Building on Educational Foundations*—What do you know about historical, philosophical, or legal foundations? Why do you need to know?

- *Problems to Possibilities*—What do you think and why?

- *Observation Guides*—Bring your journal to any observation or interview! Write your impressions, thoughts, and ideas for future reference.

● **Step 2: Reflect**   Think about the questions asked in the feature or from the observation and make connections to your own beliefs. Do you agree? Disagree? Think this is not important? What other thoughts, judgments, and ideas come up for you as you read, observe, or interview a teacher or student?

● **Step 3: Write**   Carve out some time to write. Make it part of your weekly routine. If you are responding to a feature other than the observation or interview, you can do it as part of your homework for class. If you are in a school, you may want to make some notes and then write your reflection when you have some quiet time to think about what you observed.

You may prefer to just "free write" in your hard-copy journal and let whatever thoughts emerge come out on paper, or you may prefer to scribble some notes and then write your narrative in sentences so you can respond to certain topics. Either way, make sure your voice is on paper. Keep your scribbles in the journal too! You may want them in the future, or you may not have time to respond to all your thoughts in this one entry.

● **Step 4: Reread and Summarize**   Take the time to reread what you wrote. Build this time into your writing time so you have an opportunity to add additional ideas immediately. Also, every few weeks go back and reread what you have written. When you do this, write an entry titled "Summary to Date" so you have a chance to respond to what you have been writing so far. It is fun to look back at what you were thinking at the beginning of the course. At the end write a "Final Reflective Entry" after you have reread all entries.

Remember, you cannot do this incorrectly. There are no right or wrong answers. Select what interests you! Be sure to find out whether grammar, spelling, and writing legibility are part of your course grade before you begin. Is anyone else going to be reading this or is this just for your own personal use? Write on!

CREATING A TOUCH THE FUTURE TEACHER PORTFOLIO

You may use many kinds of portfolio formats while you are in your education program. Courses such as this one may provide a system for documenting what you have learned. You also may be asked to create an electronic portfolio that highlights samples from all of the education courses you have taken. During your student teaching in your senior year you may also be invited to organize your lesson plans and curriculum ideas to share with your university supervisor. Finally, you will most likely want to create a job interview portfolio that showcases all of your learning and accomplishments! This course is an opportunity for you to create a foundational portfolio because you are just at the beginning of your teacher preparation journey.

Education majors often ask this question in a different way: "Do I put items in this portfolio that may not be my best work or should I just show off what I have done well?" A portfolio should showcase your best work unless the professor asks that you include samples from all chapters. Put your best foot forward by keeping responses to chapter questions as well as your reflective journal.

The table of contents will depend on the purpose for your portfolio. Is it for a final grade for the course? Is the professor choosing what will be included or do you get to choose? Do samples from your reflective journal need to be included? Are you doing the portfolio for yourself or for extra credit? The responses to these questions will dictate how you will proceed.

TIPS FOR GETTING STARTED

Decide whether you would like to keep an e-portfolio or a hard copy. You could also start with a hard copy and then transfer it to the computer later. So get started by purchasing a binder with some tabs.

1. *Collect*—Collect samples from your work in this course. These could be journal entries or summaries, completed observation and interview sheets, or responses to any of the features in the text. Keep all samples in one place so you can decide what you want to select for your portfolio.

2. *Select*—Take a few of your samples from the course as you near the end. Remember, a portfolio is a collection—it is not your entire work sample for the course!

3. *Reflect*—Think about why you chose these particular samples. How do they demonstrate your competency?

SAMPLE 1: TABLE OF CONTENTS ORGANIZED BY CHAPTER TOPICS

First Tab: Chapter 1—Title (new tabs for each subsequent chapter)

1. Who Am I? What Do I Believe? responses.

2. First journal entry for course (Chapter 14 would include the Final Reflective Journal summary). Delete if you are not keeping a reflective journal.

3. Response to one or more features.

4. Completed observation and interview sheet with any field notes; you may want to add photos or other artifacts you collected at the school, such as report cards or mission statements.

5. Answers to questions at the end of the chapter (optional).

6. Reflection responses at the end of the chapter.

7. Anything else from the chapter or a final summary of what you learned.

Each chapter could be organized the same way with these kinds of work samples allowing for the final journal entry and the first entry to bookend the chapters.

SAMPLE 2: TABLE OF CONTENTS ORGANIZED BY BOOK THEMES

This system would allow you to collect any information that relates to the following themes highlighted in the text. You would select features, observations, and journal entries that documented your thinking in these areas.

- Tab 1: Professionalism and Standards

- Tab 2: Values and Assumptions

- Tab 3: Multiculturalism and Diversity

- Tab 4: Ethics and Social Justice

- Tab 5: Linking Theory and Practice

- Tab 6: Add a topic of your choice

SHARING YOUR PORTFOLIO

If this is a requirement, you will be sharing your work with your professors and most likely with other classmates. Be sure to proofread and edit your work. If you have elected to do this activity for enrichment or extra credit, congratulations on making a positive professional choice to document your work. Make sure you do share it with your professor and any of the classroom teachers you observed.

Key Contacts

At some point in your work you will need to get information from your state's department of education or from specific professional organizations. State department of education sites are excellent sources for information about certification, grants, and project monies, or to check out a specialized curriculum area (for example, state history). Professional organizations provide information on the latest teaching strategies in the field as well as changes to standards and benchmarks for teaching.

STATE DEPARTMENT OF EDUCATION WEB SITES*

Alabama
www.alsde.edu

Alaska
www.educ.state.ak.us

Arizona
http://ade.state.az.us

Arkansas
http://arkedu.state.ar.us

California
http://goldmine.cde.ca.gov

Colorado
http://cde.state.co.us

Connecticut
www.state.ct.us/sde

Delaware
www.doe.state.de.us

District of Columbia
www.k12.dc.us

Florida
www.firn.edu/doe

Georgia
www.doe.k12.ga.us

Hawaii
http://doe.k12.hi.us

Idaho
www.sde.state.id.us/dept

Illinois
www.isbe.state.il.us

Indiana
www.doe.state.in.us

Iowa
www.state.ia.us/educate

Kansas
www.ksbe.state.ks.us

Kentucky
www.kde.state.ky.us

Louisiana
www.doe.state.la.us

Maine
www.state.me.us/education

Maryland
www.msde.state.md.us

Massachusetts
www.doe.mass.edu

Michigan
www.michigan.gov/mde

Minnesota
http://education.state.mn.us/html/
mde_home.htm

*Source: American Association for Employment in Education.

Mississippi
www.mde.k12.state.ms.us

Missouri
www.dese.state.mo.us

Montana
www.opi.state.mt.us

Nebraska
www.nde.state.ne.us

Nevada
www.doe.nv.gov

New Hampshire
www.ed.state.nh.us

New Jersey
www.state.nj.us/education

New Mexico
http://164.64.166.11/cilt

New York
www.nysed.gov

North Carolina
www.ncpublicschools.org

North Dakota
www.dpi.state.nd.us

Ohio
www.ode.state.oh.us

Oklahoma
www.sde.state.ok.us/home
defaultie.html

Oregon
www.ode.state.or.us

Pennsylvania
www.pde.state.pa.us

Rhode Island
www.ridoe.net

South Carolina
www.myscschools.com

South Dakota
www.state.sd.us/state/deca

Tennessee
www.state.tn.us/education

Texas
www.tea.state.tx.us

Utah
www.usoe.k12.ut.us

Vermont
www.state.vt.us/educ.htm

Virginia
http://pen.k12.va.us

Washington
www.k12.wa.us

West Virginia
www.pen.k12.va.us

Wisconsin
www.dpi.state.wi.us

Wyoming
www.k12.wy.us

State Certification Offices

A teaching certificate or license is valid only in the state for which it is issued. Certification, licensing, and testing requirements are never static. States change requirements constantly. If you are planning to move to another state, you should contact that state's certification/licensing office as the first step. The following websites will guide you. You will also find information at www.nasdtec.org, with links to specific states plus those that participate in the interstate agreement. The U.S. Department of Education website (www.ed.gov) contains many links, including the state sites.

Alabama
www.alsde.edu/html/sections/
section_detail.asp?section=66&

Alaska
www.educ.state.ak.us/
teachercertification

Arizona
www.ade.state.az.us/certification

Arkansas
http://arkedu.state.ar.us/teachers/
index.html

California
www.ctc.ca.gov   or
www.calteach.com

Colorado
www.cde.state.co.us/index_license.htm

Connecticut
www.state.ct.us/sde/dtl/cert/index.htm

Delaware
www.doe.state.de.us

District of Columbia
www.k12.dc.us/dcps/teachdc/
certification.html

Florida
www.firn.edu/doe/edcert/
home0022.htm

Georgia
www.gapsc.com/
TeacherCertification.asp

Hawaii
http://doe.k12.hi.us/

Idaho
www.sde.state.id.us/certification

Illinois
www.isbe.net/teachers.htm/

Indiana
www.state.in.us/psb/

Iowa
www.state.ia.us/boee/

Kansas
www.ksbe.state.ks.us/Welcome.html

Kentucky
www.kyepsb.net/certinfo.html

Louisiana
www.louisianaschools.net/DOE/
lde/tsac/home.html

Maine
http://usm.maine.edu/cehd/etep/
certify.htm

Maryland
http://certification.msde.state.md.us

Massachusetts
www.doe.mass.edu/educators/
e_license.html

Michigan
www.michigan.gov/som/0,1607,7-192-
29939_32383_32505---,00.html

Minnesota
http://education.state.mn.us/
stellent/groups/public/
documents/translatedcontent/
pub_intro_licensure.jsp

Mississippi
www.mde.k12.ms.us/license/index.htm

Missouri
www.dese.state.mo.us/divteachqual/
index.html

Montana
www.opi.state.mt.us/index.html

Nebraska
www.nde.state.ne.us/tcert/tcmain.html

Nevada
www.nde.state.nv.us/licensure/

New Hampshire
www.ed.state.nh.us/

New Jersey
www.state.nj.us/njded/educators/
license/index.html

New Mexico
http://sde.state.nm.us/divisions/
ais/licensure/index.html

New York
www.highered.nysed.gov/tcert/

North Carolina
www.ncpublicschools.org/
employment.html

North Dakota
www.state.nd.us/espb

Ohio
www.ode.state.oh.us/
Teaching-Profession/default.asp

Oklahoma
www.sde.state.ok.us/home/
defaultie.html

Oregon
www.ode.state.or.us/supportservices/
careers.htm
or
www.tspc.state.or.us/
pub.asp?op=0&id=15

Pennsylvania
www.tcs.ed.state.pa.us/

Rhode Island
www.ridoe.net/teacher_cert/
Default.htm

South Carolina
www.scteachers.org/index.cfm

South Dakota
www.state.sd.us/deca/OPA/

Tennessee
www.state.tn.us/education/
lic_home.htm

Texas
www.sbec.state.tx.us/SBECOnline/
certinfo/becometeacher.asp

Utah
www.usoe.k12.ut.us/cert/

Vermont
www.state.vt.us/educ/license/
index.htm

Virginia
www.pen.k12.va.us/VDOE/
newvdoe/teached.html

Washington
www.k12.wa.us/cert/

West Virginia
http://wvde.state.wv.us/certification

Wisconsin
www.dpi.state.wi.us/dpi/dlsis/
tel/index.html

Wyoming
www.k12.wy.us/ptsb/

**United States Department of Defense
Dependents Schools**
www.odedodea.edu/pers

PROFESSIONAL ASSOCIATIONS AND ORGANIZATIONS

The following professional organizations can offer ongoing information about changes in your field, opportunities for professional development, changes in standards and professional benchmarks, and much more.

Professional Teachers' Associations

American Federation of Teachers (AFT)
www.aft.org

Association for Supervision and Curriculum Development (ASCD)
www.ascd.org

National Education Association (NEA)
www.nea.org

Administrative

American Association of School Administrators (AASA)
www.aasa.org

Council of Chief State School Officers
www.ccsso.org

National Association of Elementary School Principals (NAESP)
www.naesp.org

National Association of Secondary School Principals (NASSP)
www.nassp.org

National Board for Professional Teaching Standards (NBPTS)
www.nbpts.org

National Catholic Educational Association (NCEA)
www.ncea.org

National Parent Teacher Association (PTA)
www.pta.org

National School Boards Association (NSBA)
www.nsba.org

Higher Education

American Association for Higher Education
www.aahe.org

American Association of University Women (AAUW)
www.aauw.org

American Educational Research Association (AERA)
www.aera.net

American Library Association (ALA)
www.ala.org

National Association for the Education of Young Children (NAEYC)
www.naeyc.org

Disciplines

American Alliance for Health, Physical Education, Recreation, and Dance (AAHPERD)
www.aahperd.org

American Association for Health Education (AAHE)
www.aahperd.org/aahe

American Council on the Teaching of Foreign Languages
www.actfl.org

Computer-Using Educators (CUE)
www.cue.org

Consortium for School Networking (CoSN)
www.cosn.org

Council for Exceptional Children (CEC)
www.cec.sped.org

International Reading Association (IRA)
www.reading.org

International Society for Technology in Education (ISTE)
www.iste.org

National Art Education Association
www.naea-reston.org

National Association for Gifted Children (NAGC)
www.nagc.org

National Association for Music Education
www.menc.org

National Association for Sport and Physical Education (NASPE)
www.aahperd.org/naspe

National Council for the Social Studies (NCSS)
www.ncss.org

National Association of Biology Teachers
www.nabt.org

National Council of Teachers of English (NCTE)
www.ncte.org

National Council of Teachers of Mathematics (NCTM)
www.nctm.org

National Science Teachers Association (NSTA)
www.nsta.org

GLOSSARY

acceptable use policy (AUP) A school policy that defines precisely how computers may or may not be used in the schools.

adaptive technology Also called *assistive technology*. It augments a student's ability to perform classroom tasks required of all students, in much the way glasses help some of us to read.

adequate yearly progress (AYP) A proficiency level mandated by No Child Left Behind that indicates that children are learning at an acceptable level and pace.

adoption state A state in which textbook approval and use in classrooms is overseen by the state department of education.

agents of social justice Teachers who go beyond the traditional role as presenters of information and exemplify the ethics of caring, compassion, and social justice.

American Federation of Teachers Second-best-known national professional organization for teachers.

artifact A document that demonstrates or shows evidence of a skill or competency.

assess To evaluate students' progress and then use that information to set new goals for learning.

assistive technology See *adaptive technology*

authentic assessments Less concrete, more subjective measures of students' knowledge that require students to apply knowledge in a variety of ways. Unlike tests and quizzes, which are graded based on the number of correct responses, authentic assessments are graded on a number of other factors such as effort, execution, creativity, and the ability to accurately convey knowledge of a subject area.

back planning Creating a long-range plan that indicates where a teacher wants to be at the end of the year, and then working backwards to determine what needs to be done to meet the end goal.

basal textbook program A series of textbooks that provide basic grade-appropriate information in various K–8 subject areas. Because all the materials are from the same series, the content and strategies build off each other from one year to the next.

Basic Interpersonal Communication Skills (BICS) A level of English language development that allows students to communicate with their peers and teachers.

behaviorism A movement in psychology that emphasizes that human behavior is not so much dependent upon mental states, but is based more on the response of a subject to external stimuli.

behavior management The skills teachers use to maintain order in the classroom and deal with behavioral problems in such a way that students are able to remain focused on learning.

bilingual education An approach to instruction in which non-English-speaking students are given intensive English instruction, with their other subjects taught in the native language. In many programs English language instruction is added to the subject areas as students' English abilities progress.

Bloom's Taxonomy An approach that identifies six levels of thinking and that promotes the use of specific words and actions to encourage certain student behaviors and to develop students' ability to think critically.

border crosser A teacher who helps students who are unfamiliar with school culture negotiate the expectations and demands of school in ways they can accept.

brain-based learning theory A theory of learning based on the belief that traditional schooling and lesson plans often inhibit learning by discouraging the brain's natural process because of the way the learning is structured and delivered.

Brown v. Board of Education of Topeka The 1954 Supreme Court decision that overturned *Plessy* v. *Ferguson* by arguing that students at all levels of the education system must have equal access to the opportunity to learn, and that racial differences cannot be used as a means of classifying or discriminating against any group of individuals in the society.

building-based support team (BBST) A special problem-solving team made up of parents, teachers, and administrators that reviews referral requests for problem students and analyzes the options for classroom teachers.

burnout As defined by Gary Dworkin, "an extreme form of role-specific alienation characterized by a sense that one's work is meaningless and that one is powerless to effect changes which would make the work more meaningful."

career-change teacher An adult who leaves another career to become a teacher.

career ladder A formal structure of professional advancement and leadership opportunities available to teachers as they become more expert and accomplished. For example, a teacher might start a career as a *beginning teacher,* move to *associate teacher,* and finally become a *master teacher.*

caring teacher   A teacher who is concerned with the transfer of knowledge, but who believes the needs of students are most important.

certification   Obtaining a license from a state department of education indicating completion of requirements for teaching in the public school system.

charter school   A sectarian public school financed through public funding that operates independently from many of the regulations of more traditional public schools. Under a charter, an independent group contracts with a public school system to achieve certain goals and then is granted a contract to achieve those goals within a specified time.

classroom climate   The tone of the classroom and a teacher's effect on students.

classroom management   An umbrella term that refers to how teachers arrange their classrooms for learning, how they interact with their students and encourage their students to interact with each other, how they handle student misbehavior, how they establish and enforce rules, and how they manage their time.

code of ethic   A statement of principles that serve as helpful guidelines for teachers to apply to daily situations.

cognitive academic language proficiency (CALP)   A level of English language development that allows students to go beyond communicating with peers and teachers to understanding textbooks, essays, or standardized tests.

collaborating   Working with other teachers cooperatively to create a positive learning environment or to address issues that may threaten the environment.

collective bargaining   Negotiations between labor groups and management. In education, teachers are represented in negotiations with a district school board and the final agreement reached applies to everyone in the group.

common school   A school that provides mass universal public education at the elementary level—a "common schooling"—to all people. An embodiment of Jefferson's idea of a universal education system for citizens.

community school   A school that provides more than just education services; it also reaches out to help parents and their families with a number of other services such as health, employment, and legal assistance.

compensatory funding   Funding provided, usually from the federal government, as part of an effort to overcome past social injustices or inequity. For example, schools with large numbers of minority students in poor inner-city areas often receive funding to compensate them for past social injustices.

conflict theory model   A sociological model of schooling that argues that schools reproduce and maintain the existing class and social power structures in a society, and that they reflect the competition between various groups for power and status.

constructivism   An approach that encourages students to actively construct their learning, thereby understanding the world by inventing or constructing it.

contract   An official employment document signed by the prospective teacher and the school district that outlines the terms of agreement, including salary, benefits, and any extra duties.

core knowledge   Knowledge that is essential.

corrective discipline   Correcting students' behavior after all other attempts at discipline have been exhausted.

co-teaching   Sharing instructional responsibilities with another teacher, thereby capitalizing on each other's strengths.

cultural additive stage   Placing content or information about minority group achievements in separate courses or units rather than fully integrating such information into the mainstream curriculum.

cultural capital   The idea that teaching certain knowledge or information to its students is an investment for a society.

culturally relevant classroom   A classroom that becomes a place for learning because of its caring and inclusive practices for all students.

curriculum   The regular or a particular course of study in a school.

curriculum framework   A statewide content standard that must be adhered to at a particular grade level.

deficit model   A perspective that focuses on what students and their families lack rather than what they have.

democratic classroom   A classroom that encourages students to learn how their own actions impact the group and that is organized in such a way that facilitates a community of learners that work together, rather than one in which teachers exert power and control.

developmental continuum   A pattern of professional development involving three life-cycle phases: novice, apprentice, and professional.

differentiated instruction   An instruction method that encourages the use of multiple instructional options in order to meet the needs of each student and adapt as necessary to individual learning styles.

direct instruction   A teacher-centered approach to conveying information to students. This type of instruction is most successful when introducing new topics or skills at beginning levels of thinking, and it is most often delivered to the whole class (although it can be delivered one-on-one).

discipline   The action required by teachers or school administrators toward individual students or groups of students who disrupt the educational process or who do not adhere to pre-established rules.

discipline plan   A plan that lists rules, rewards, and consequences for disruptive behavior. These rules are clearly stated to the students and are consistent with the school's mission or guiding goals.

disequilibrium A state of uneasiness with unfamiliar perspectives and conditions. Once confidence with conditions and a knowledge base are established, equilibrium is restored.

disposition A person's prevailing moods, which are informed by his or her values, commitments, and professional ethics—and which, in turn, influence the treatment of students, families, colleagues, and communities.

distance learning Coursework that can be taken either through the mail or over the Internet; teachers learn new information at their computers in the comfort of their own school or home.

duty Extra responsibilities outside of their own classrooms assigned to teachers by the school. These duties include playground monitoring, cafeteria duty, duty outside the bathroom, or study hall.

education reform Efforts, often political in nature, to change the current education system in order to improve the quality of education.

educentric perspective An "expert" view of education that excludes parents and community members as shapers of school policy and relies solely on information from education experts.

effective teacher A teacher who reaches students and makes a difference in their lives.

electronic portfolio Electronic documentation of in-class experiences and projects.

English for Speakers of Other Languages (ESOL) A program in which the use of complex English is minimized and students are brought along slowly in the new language.

English immersion An approach to instruction in which English language learners are taught English as quickly as possible with little or no regard for their native language literacy. A sink-or-swim approach.

English language learner (ELL) A students whose first language is not English.

equal treatment The subjection of all students to the same process or treatment.

equitable treatment Instruction and support that meet the needs of all students; instruction is adapted as necessary for individual needs. Equitable treatment forces educators to focus on results and to evaluate teaching methods in light of these results.

essentialism A philosophical model first introduced by William Bagley that espouses that the purpose of education is to learn certain basic or "essential" knowledge provided by disciplines such as literature, math, science, and history.

establishment clause A section of the Constitution that guarantees all citizens the right to follow their personal religious faith.

ethical role model A teacher who engages in ethical behaviors as a model to students and ultimately maintains the students' respect as a result.

ethnicity A common national origin, set of customs, and/or language that historically connects a group of people.

existentialism A model of schooling that maintains that the student knows from within what is important for him or her to pursue in terms of education.

extrinsic reward An external, tangible reward such as a salary or bonus that attracts people to or keeps them in teaching.

family household A social unit of two or more people related by birth, marriage, or adoption who live together in a household.

formal assessment A systematic approach to evaluating student learning that results in the assignment of a grade to the student's work.

formal curriculum The formal course of study outlined by instructional leaders and state education leaders as necessary for appropriate educational advancement.

formal school culture Public documents that list school policies, codes, formal communications, contracts, curriculum guidelines, and other information that outlines how the school functions.

foundations of education A broadly conceived field of educational study that derives its character and methods from a number of academic disciplines, combinations of disciplines, and area studies, including: history, philosophy, sociology, anthropology, religion, political science, economics, psychology, cultural studies, gender studies, comparative and international education, educational studies, and educational policy studies.

free and appropriate public education (FAPE) A provision first identified under the All Handicapped Children Act and later reauthorized under the Individuals with Disabilities Education Act (IDEA) requiring services designed to meet, at no cost to students, the educational needs of students with disabilities as adequately as it meets the needs of nondisabled students within the jurisdiction of a school district.

full inclusion school A school that includes students with severe disabilities in mainstream classrooms with the assistance of special teacher's aides who are assigned to work with them in the classroom.

full practicum Also called *student teaching,* these full-immersion experiences place preservice teachers in a classroom five days a week for a full semester or even an entire school year. Student teachers often take full control of the classroom after a period of time working alongside the supervising teacher.

full-service school A school where parents can access a wide range of social and health services without leaving the school campus.

functionalist model A sociological model of schooling that recognizes schools as an essential element in the social system; it emphasizes the function of socializing students to be part of the social, economic, and political institutions of a culture.

gender   Classification of an individual's sex; may also be used to describe the socially inscribed characteristics of women and men.

generational poverty   Poverty that is systemic, lasting two generations or longer.

gifted and talented   Students who are advanced academically and who require additional work in order to remain interested and motivated.

Great School Legend   The idea of education as the great equalizer in American culture.

guided teaching   A balanced approach that uses both teacher-centered and student-centered approaches to learning. This approach is sometimes referred to as the *eclectic* or *integrated* approach. In guided instruction, teachers often end the class by directing students to summarize what they have learned. This brief period allows teachers to revisit the objectives stated at the beginning of the lesson.

hidden curriculum   Curriculum that promotes cultural mores and values that students must master in order to move satisfactorily through the school. Unintended outcomes of the schooling that take place in classrooms beyond the teaching of official subject matter, outside of the course materials and the scheduled lesson content.

high-stakes testing   A type of testing whose results can determine a student's advancement or a school's accreditation. Penalties may include students not passing to the next grade; students receiving a certificate of completion instead of a high school diploma; or a school being placed on probation, losing funds, or possibly losing students to other schools and being closed.

household   A living arrangement in which people live together in one housing unit.

individualized education plan (IEP)   A specialized instructional plan that outlines the support the student needs to be successful in school. An IEP lists the student's goals and objectives for the school year.

induction program   A district program designed to retain highly qualified, effective teachers in their classrooms.

informal assessment   Ongoing, day-to-day assessment of student progress that may be administered in the form of homework assignments, periodic observations of student participation in the classroom, or small, informal meetings between teachers and individual students.

informal curriculum   Informal instruction involving social matters, such as social behaviors and gender roles.

informal school culture   Subtle, unspoken rules of conduct known only to school insiders and shared only with individuals of their choosing.

inquiry   A systematic process of data collection used to answer specific questions, such as those needed to resolve classroom or behavior management problems.

in-service education   Also called *professional development.* The ongoing process of applying and learning new skills and knowledge while teaching.

institutional sexism   A pattern of behavior wherein individuals' interactions with or expectations of males and females are influenced by commonly held misconceptions about socially appropriate male and female behaviors.

instructional technology   "New" media used in the classroom to advance learning.

International Society for Technology in Education (ISTE)   A professional organization for teachers who use computers in their day-to-day work in the classroom.

interpretivist model   A sociological model of schooling that argues that we must understand schools in the context of the communities and cultures in which they are located, constantly analyzing, revising, and reinterpreting what we see based on our position or location in the culture.

interstate agreement   A document of agreement between various states that allows reciprocity and licensure transfer.

Interstate New Teacher Assessment and Support Consortium (INTASC)   A consortium of state education agencies and national educational organizations dedicated to the reform of the preparation, licensing, and professional development of teachers.

intrinsic reward   An internal, intangible reason that keeps an individual in teaching.

involuntary minority group   A group of people who were initially brought into the United States against their will.

laboratory school   A school run by a college or university that serves as a demonstration school by modeling the best teaching practices, testing new strategies, and offering the college or university age-appropriate subjects and environments in which to test new theories and observe children and their development.

Latinegro   A Latino of African ancestry.

Lau v. Nichols   A landmark Supreme Court decision in 1974 that, while not mandating bilingual education, required understandable instruction for limited or non-English-speaking students.

least restrictive environment   An educational setting in which a child with disabilities can receive an appropriate education designed to meet his or her individual needs alongside nondisabled peers.

lesson plan   A written plan of each lesson, including the rationale for using certain teaching strategies and learning theories, that also notes any special considerations that may need to be taken into account for certain students.

life adjustment education   A post–World War II curriculum developed to provide the skills necessary to become useful members of society, emphasizing citizenship, family life, health and hygiene, and leisure.

lifelong learner An educator who learns and grows alongside students, thereby adapting to the ongoing changes in the field.

limited English proficiency (LEP) learner In an academic setting, a student whose native language is a language other than English or who comes from an environment where a language other than English is dominant; this heritage affects the individual's ability to successfully achieve in classrooms where the language of instruction is English.

mainstreaming The practice of integrating students with special needs (both physically and mentally challenged, as well as gifted and talented) into "normal" educational settings.

mentee A new teacher being mentored; mentoring may include observation visits as well as time devoted to analyzing student work and team teaching.

mentor An experienced colleague whose job is to provide support for new teachers easing into the daily routines of the school and community, including familiarization with district curriculum, providing guidance on school and district policies, and serving as a sounding board for ideas and concerns.

merit pay A controversial practice of paying teachers bonuses for reaching pre-established goals.

mission statement A relatively short written document that states in clear and succinct terms the fundamental values and beliefs of the school.

Montessori method A teaching technique created by Italian physician Maria Montessori that utilizes and encourages hands-on learning materials.

National Board for Professional Teaching (NBPT) A professional organization that offers special licensure for experienced teachers. This national license is an intensive reflective program that can increase the status of their district and result in future leadership roles in the school or the community.

National Council for the Accreditation of Teacher Education (NCATE) A national accreditation organization designed to ensure that teacher education programs follow established and agreed-upon criteria for preparing future teachers adequately. See also *TEAC*.

National Defense Education Act A 1958 Congressional initiative to improve the academic quality of schools, provide vocational training, and build new classrooms in response to a perceived inferiority to Soviet scientific and technological development.

National Education Association The largest national professional organization for teachers.

neighborhood school A school controlled by local leaders whose student population is determined by geography or proximity to the school, rather than by racial, economic, or social quotas.

New Teacher Center (NTC) A hands-on induction program at the University of California at Santa Cruz that enables university faculty to work with teachers and mentors directly to provide training and professional development.

No Child Left Behind Act 2001 legislation that ensures that all children have a fair, equal, and significant opportunity to obtain a high-quality education and attain a minimum proficiency on challenging state academic achievement standards and state academic assessments.

normal school A school designed for the sole purpose of training teachers.

null curriculum The lessons that are taught as a result of *not* teaching something; hidden messages.

operant conditioning A form of behavioral training based on the association between a behavior and a consequence, such as a reward or a punishment.

opportunity to learn A powerful predictor of student achievement based on a school's access to resources that can improve educational opportunities.

oppositional identity A sociological term for the behavior of a minority group that adopts a strategy of "racelessness" by taking on the cultures and customary behaviors of the mainstream group in an effort to gain acceptance.

orthodoxy The degree to which an individual is a strict or literal believer in a faith.

pedagogy The science of teaching.

peer coaching An arrangement that allows two teachers to work together, sometimes observing each other's classroom, and exchanging feedback.

perennialism A philosophical model based on the belief in "perennial" wisdom or knowledge that has been accumulated over the ages and is found in great works of literature and art, as well religious texts such as the Koran and the Bible.

permeable family The postmodern family that reflects contemporary assumptions that are global and ever-changing. The permeable family may include single parents, two working parents, or blended, remarried, and adoptive parents.

philosophy of education A personal credo that identifies an individual's beliefs about education and, more specifically, about the act of teaching.

plagiarism The unacceptable use of materials written and published by someone else without proper citation of original author or permission to use the material.

Plessy v. Ferguson: The 1896 Supreme Court decision that established a rationale for separate but equal treatment of the Black and White races in the United States.

portability of education The transfer of educational training of students to other states, regions, or nations.

portfolio A collection of students' work in any content area that exemplifies and documents their learning over time.

positionality of knowledge A dimension of knowledge that suggests that the characteristics of the presenters of knowledge, as well as those of the learners, affect how the same information can be absorbed differently by students.

pragmatism An educational approach based on the teachings of John Dewey, who believed that education should be grounded in the real world and the actual experiences of the child.

the Praxis Series: Professional Assessments for Beginning Teachers A series of tests used by a large number of states to examine teachers' knowledge of subject matter and preparedness.

prepracticum Preservice opportunities to visit classrooms and observe, interview, and practice strategies students are learning in order to increase their level of confidence. Visits may be once a week, once a month, or more frequently.

preventive discipline Discipline that promotes positive behaviors.

principal A school official who oversees all matters involving his or her specific school, while staying within the guiding principles of the entire district.

private school A secondary or elementary school run and supported by private individuals or a corporation rather than by a government or public agency.

professional development The process of advancing knowledge and enhancing professional practices through continuing education efforts such as district workshops and coursework.

professional development school (PDS) model A program in which theory and practice are integrated by having experienced K–12 classroom teachers work closely with college and university professors to help train future teachers.

professional ethics Values and beliefs that influence professional decisions, behavior, and practices. Teachers are expected to reflect honesty, trust, confidentiality, fairness, responsibility, and respect for others in their decision-making.

professional portfolio Also called a *teacher portfolio.* Samples of a teacher's work that represent the skills and dispositions developed during teacher preparation.

progressivism A philosophical model that draws on the idea that the child is the center of the educational process, and that progressive education has a strong practical or pragmatic orientation.

Public Law 94-142 The 1975 law, also known as the Education for All Handicapped Children Act, that established that students with special needs must be educated in the "least restrictive" environment possible.

pull-out program A program that pulls students with special needs out of the regular classroom setting to learn and practice skills one on one with a special education teacher.

race People who belong to the same genetic stock. A socially constructed phenomenon that has often been used as a means to justify economic, social, political, psychological, religious, ideological, and legal systems of inequality.

reading recovery program A program for struggling readers that provides direct instruction to students in separate study rooms.

recertification Renewal of a license periodically as determined by the state education office for the purpose of ensuring that all teachers are up to date on current teaching strategies and content.

reciprocity Agreement between states that allows a teacher educated in one state to teach in another state without having to complete student teaching or take additional courses in the new state. Reciprocity does not imply automatic exemption from any state licensing tests.

reflective practitioner A teacher who actively thinks about instruction and the experience of the learners as a way of evaluating his or her own practices and improving teaching.

resiliency The ability to bounce back from adversity and adapt successfully.

resiliency mentor A teacher who understands the home lives of students and incorporates that information into instruction, as well as helping students adapt to the overall school environment.

resistance theory Giroux's idea that many lower-class students behave badly in school as an expression of healthy resistance rather than passively accepting rules that ultimately limit their chances to succeed.

riffing The practice of dismissing tenured teachers, based on seniority, during periods of financial crisis.

rubric A scoring guide that clearly defines the criteria for grading performance. It answers the question, "Why did you give me that grade?" Rubrics let the students know what the expectations are for successful completion of a task.

scheme A form of mental organization used to adapt to one's environment. Jean Piaget argued that human beings adapt to their environment by replacing their reflexes with constructed schemes of the world.

school board A body of school officials that oversees major decision-making throughout the school district and establishes policies and rules for the entire school.

school culture The atmosphere in the school created by interactions among and between teachers, students, and other school personnel. The set of norms, values and beliefs, rituals and ceremonies, symbols and stories that make up the "persona" of the school.

scope and sequence The range of skills and knowledge that are taught at particular grade levels.

silenced dialogue The cessation of discussion that occurs when talks with those in the "culture of power" prove fruitless.

situational poverty Poverty that is temporary, caused by circumstances such as divorce, death, or illness.

social capital The social networks and interactions of people within a community that promote involvement, commitment, and trust.

social efficiency movement A social movement whose believers tried to increase industrial productivity through scientific management. Educators attempted to apply its principles to increase the effectiveness of schools.

social reconstructionism A model of education, articulated in the work of George Counts, that purports that schools serve to create a more just social and political order by examining and testing ideas critically.

socioeconomic status An individual's or group's position within a social structure based on a combination of variables, including occupation, education, and economic success.

special needs legislation Government mandates that provide funding for programs that offer additional support to students who need remediation or special projects in order to succeed in the classroom.

standardized tests Tests that incorporate standard methods of developing items, administering the test, scoring it, and reporting the scores.

student-centered community A community whose focus is on offering students opportunities to experiment and investigate and thereby hone critical thinking skills, demonstrate responsibility, learn to work cooperatively with others, and become independent thinkers.

student contract A document that outlines the terms of an agreement a student reaches with the teacher, often for the purpose of modifying behavior.

student referral process A formal process for obtaining the individual support a student needs. Includes writing a report providing specific details about the situation that warranted initiating the referral; a dated log that clearly notes the date, time, and location of incidents as they arise; and meeting with other school personnel and parents to chart a course of action.

style delineator approach Anthony Gregorc's approach that breaks learning styles into four qualities: two perceptual categories: (1) one that focuses on fact-based, physical information (concrete) and (2) the other that focuses on logical, deductive reasoning (abstract); and two styles for ordering information: (3) an organized sequence (sequential) and (4) a disorganized sequence (random).

superintendent A school official whose primary job is to oversee all aspects of the entire school district, much as a CEO would for a business.

supportive discipline Assistance provided by teachers to help students channel their own behaviors productively and gain control through agreed-upon signals.

teacher certificate A license that indicates a teacher candidate has met the requirements and skills necessary to qualify to teach in the state.

Teacher Education Accreditation Council (TEAC) An organization similar to NCATE that is dedicated to improving academic degree programs for professional educators pre-K through grade 12.

teacher leadership Advanced professional development opportunities that enable experienced teachers to take roles of leadership among their peers and to practice using inquiry to improve teaching and problem-solving strategies.

teacher portfolio Samples of a teacher's work that represent the skills and dispositions developed during teacher preparation. See *professional portfolio.*

teacher-proof curriculum A system in which the curriculum is managed at the upper levels of the administrative system and delivered, according to s pecific administrative instructions, by the teacher in the classroom, with no personal interjection.

teaching as a vocation The concept that teaching is a calling—something people are drawn to or compelled to do.

teaching license Evidence that a person has completed the teaching requirements of a state.

Telecommunications Act of 1996 Ruling that requires schools and libraries to have access to state-of-the-art services and technologies at discounted rates.

tenure A policy that protects teachers from arbitrary actions by school officials after serving a three- to five-year probationary period of employment.

Theory of Multiple Intelligences Howard Gardner's theory that states that each person possesses, not one, but eight intelligences that incorporate talents and skills beyond math and verbal skills.

tool function of computers Students use the computer as a tool to type a paper or create a spreadsheet, or to access the Internet to research.

tracking Guiding students' course selection based on various career paths, such as college preparatory or vocational/technical curriculum.

tutee function of computers Use of a computer to do particular tasks, programmed by student.

tutor function of computers Use of the computer to drill students in ways that are typical of rote memorization and learning exercises.

two-way immersion (TWI) program A dual-language program that offers instruction in English and a foreign language to a student population composed of native English speakers as well as English-as-a-second-language learners.

type I application of computers Use of the computer to complete a task more efficiently or effectively than it has been done before.

type II applications of computers A totally new use of the computer; to use the computer to expand a lesson in a way unique to the technology, such as with simulation programs.

unit plan Mapping out content instruction based on thematic units.

Vocational Rehabilitation Act of 1973 Provides a rationale for the equitable treatment of people with special needs in all areas involving support from the federal government.

voluntary minority group A group of immigrants who moved to the United States willingly.

voucher An alternative funding program that provides funds to parents, allowing them to purchase education for their children on the open market. Vouchers can be used toward the cost of tuition at private schools and even schools that are church affiliated.

White flight The pattern of movement of Whites to the suburbs in response to efforts to integrate urban neighborhoods.

White privilege Institutional advantages realized by Whites in the United States because their race is generally recognized as the national identity of Americans.

with-it-ness Teachers' awareness of students' behavior and work performance in the classroom.

REFERENCES

Adelman, C. (1998). *Answers in the toolbox.* Washington, DC: U.S. Department of Education.

Agosto, R. (1999). Community schools in New York City: The Board of Education and the Children's Aid Society. *NASSP Bulletin, 83*(611), 57–63.

Allen, L. (2001). From plaques to practice: How schools can breathe life into their guiding beliefs. *Phi Delta Kappan,* 289–293.

Allen, N., Christal, M., & Perrot, D. (1999). Native American schools move into the new millennium. *Educational Leadership, 56*(7), 71–74.

Alvarado, A. (1998). Professional development *is* the job. *American Educator, 22*(4), 18–23.

American Federation of Teachers. (2004). Teacher salaries remain stagnant but health insurance costs soar. Retrieved May 3, 2005, from http://www.aft.org/presscenter/releases/2004/071504.htm

Amrein, A. L., & Berliner, D. C. (2002). *An analysis of some unintended and negative consequences of high-stakes testing.* Tempe, AZ: Education Policy Studies Laboratory, Education Policy Research Unit.

Andrew, J., & Robottom, I. (2001). Science and ethics: Some issues for education. *Science Education, 85*(6), 769–780.

Anti-Defamation League. (2001). *Religion in public schools: Guidelines for a growing and changing phenomenon.* New York: Author.

Anyon, J. (1981). Social class and school knowledge. *Curriculum Inquiry, 11*(1), 3–42.

Apple, M. (1989). Regulating the text: The socio-historical roots of state control. *Educational Policy, 3*(2), 107–123.

Apple, M. W. (1986). *Teachers and texts: a political economy of class and gender relations in education.* New York: Routledge & Kegan Paul.

Apple, M. W. (1993). *Official knowledge: Democratic education in a conservative age.* New York: Routledge.

Apple, M. W. (2001). *Educating the "right" way: Markets, standards, God, and inequality.* New York: Routledge Falmer.

Apple, M. W., & Christian-Smith, L. K. (1991). *The politics of the textbook.* New York, Routledge.

Associated Press (2005). Press Release from the Washington, DC: Department of Education.

Attewell, P. (2000). Mirage of meritocracy. *American Prospect, 11*(16), 12–14.

Baldwin, J. (1998). If Black English isn't a language, then tell me, what is? In T. Perry & L. Delpit (Eds.), *The real Ebonics debate: Power, language, and the education of African-American children* (pp. 67–70). Boston: Beacon Press.

Barth, R. S. (1990). *Improving schools from within.* San Francisco: Jossey-Bass.

Barth, R. S. (2001). *Learning by heart.* San Francisco: Jossey-Bass.

Bassey, M. O. (2003). Foundational studies in teacher education. In G. Noblitt & B. Hatt-Echevererria (Eds.), *The future of educational studies.* New York: Peter Lang.

Bauch, P. A. (2001). School-community partnerships in rural schools: Leadership, renewal, and a sense of place. *Peabody Journal of Education, 76*(2), 204–221.

Bauer, E. B. (1999). The promise of alternative literacy assessments in the classroom: A review of empirical studies. *Reading research and instruction, 38*(2), 153–168.

Bemis, D. (1999). *Effects of mentoring on new teacher retention rates in selected suburban schools.* Unpublished doctoral dissertation, Boston College, Chestnut Hills, MA.

Benjamin, S., & Sanchez, S. (1996). *Should I go to the teacher? Developing a cooperative relationship with your child's school community.* Portsmouth, NH: Heinemann.

Berliner, D. (1985, April). *Effective and ineffective session opening: Teacher activity and task structures.* Paper presented at the American Educational Research Association meeting, Chicago, IL.

Berliner, D. C., & Biddle, B. J. (1995). *The manufactured crisis: Myths, fraud and the attack on America's public schools.* Reading, MA: Addison-Wesley.

Bethpage Union Free School District (n.d.). K–5 social studies. Retrieved May 6, 2005, from http://www.bethpagecommunity.com/Schools/socialst/k5/k5.htm

Bloom, B. (1956). *Taxonomy of educational objectives: The classification of educational goals.* United Kingdom: Longman Group.

Bloom, R. B. (1976). Morally speaking, who are today's teachers? *Phi Delta Kappan* (May), 624–625.

Bluestein, J. (1995). *Mentors, masters, and Mrs. MacGregor.* Deerfield Beach, FL: Health Communications.

Bobbitt, J. F. (1918). *The curriculum.* Boston, New York: Houghton Mifflin.

Bosch, K., & Kersey, K. (2000). *The first-year teacher: Teaching with confidence (K–8).* Washington, DC: NEA Professional Library.

Boston Public Schools. (1998, March 9). *High school restructuring.* Boston: Author.

Bowers, C. A. (1988). *The cultural dimensions of educational computing.* New York: Teachers College Press.

Bowers, C. A. (1995). *Educating for an ecologically sustainable culture: Rethinking moral education, creativity, intelligence, and other modern orthodoxies.* New York: State University of New York Press.

Bowers, C. A. (2000). *Let them eat data: How computers affect education, cultural diversity, and the prospects of ecological sustainability.* Athens: University of Georgia Press.

Bowman, R. F. (1996, Summer). Revisiting tomorrow's classrooms. *The Educational Forum, 60,* 304–307.

Boyle, M. (2001). Analysis of student work gives Bernadette direction. *New Teacher Center Reflections, IV*(2), 1–12.

Bradfield-Kreider, P. (2001). Personal transformations from the inside out: Nurturing monocultural teachers' growth toward multicultural competence. *Multicultural Education, 8*(4), 31–34.

Brantlinger, E. (1995). Social class in schools: Students' perspectives. *Research Bulletin, 14* (March).

Breaux, A. (2003). *101 answers for new teachers and their mentors: Effective teaching tips for daily classroom use.* Larchmont, NY: Eye on Education.

Broidy, S., & Jones, S. P. (1998). Sources of professional ethics. *Educational Studies, 29*(1), 3–13.

Bromfield, M., Deane, H., & Burnett, E. (2003). *From surviving to thriving: A guide to beginning teachers.* Brookline, MA: Brookline Books.

Bryk, A. S., & Schneider, B. (2002). *Trust in schools: A core resource for improvement.* New York: Russell Sage.

Buntin, J. (2002). Special ed's dark secret. *Governing, 16*(1), 44–46.

Burke, S., & White, G. (2001). The influence of district characteristics on intra-district resource allocations. *Journal of Educational Finance, 26*(3), 258–266.

Buttery, T. J., & Anderson, P. J. (1999). Community, school, and parent dynamics: A synthesis of literature and activities. *Teacher Education Quarterly, 26*(4), 111–122.

Button, W. H., & Provenzo, E. F., Jr. (1989). *History of education and culture in America.* Upper Saddle River, NJ: Prentice Hall.

Campbell, E. (1997). Connecting the ethics of teaching and moral education. *Journal of Teacher Education, 48*(4), 255–263.

Casanova, P. G. (2000). The future of education and the future of work. *NACLA Report on the Americas, 33*(4), 38–41.

Casper, L. M., & Fields, J. (2000). *America's families and living arrangements: Population characteristics.* Washington, DC: U.S. Census Bureau.

Center for Education Reform, (2002). Data retrieved April 20, 2005, from http://www.edreform.com/pubs/chglance.htm

Center for Media Education. (2002). Children & television: Frequently asked questions. Retrieved June 11, 2002, from http://www.cme.org/children/kids_tv/c_and_t.html

Chang, F. Y. (1994). *School teachers' moral reasoning.* In J. R. Rest & D. Narváez (Eds.), *Moral development in the professions: Psychology and applied ethics.* Hillsdale, NJ: Lawrence Erlbaum.

Charles, C. M. (1999). *Building classroom discipline.* New York: Longman.

Chase, C., & Chase, J. (1993). *Tips from the trenches: America's best teachers describe effective classroom methods.* Lancaster, PA: Technomic.

Chrispeels, J. H. (2002). Effective schools—The California Center for Effective Schools: The Oxnard School District Partnership. *Phi Delta Kappan, 83*(5), 382.

Christian, D., Howard, E. R., & Loeb, M. (2000). Bilingualism for all: Two-way immersion education in the United States. *Theory into Practice, 29*(4), 258–266.

Clark, R. (2003). *The essential 55.* New York: Hyperion.

Clewell, B. C., Puma, M., & McKay, S. A. (2001). *Does it matter if my teacher looks like me? The impact of teacher race and ethnicity on student academic achievement.* New York: Ford Foundation.

Colbert, J. A., & Wolff, D. E. (1992). Surviving in urban schools: A collaborative model for beginning teacher support program. *Journal of Teacher Education, 43,* 193–199.

Coley, R. (2001). *Differences in the gender gap: Comparisons across racial/ethnic groups in education and work.* Princeton, NJ: Education Testing Service, Policy Information Center. Retrieved May 3, 2005, from http://www.ets.org/research/pic/gender.pdf

Collier, V., & Thomas, W. (2004). The astounding effectiveness of dual language programs for all. *NABE Journal of Research and Practice, 2*(1), 1–20.

Collison, M. N. K. (1999). For Hispanics, demographic imperative drives educational mandate. *Black Issues in Higher Education, 16*(17), 56.

Connors, N. (2000). *If you don't feed the teachers they eat the students.* Nashville, TN: Incentive.

Conroy, P. (1972). *The water is wide.* Boston: Houghton Mifflin.

Constantino, P., & De Lorenzo, M. (2002). *Developing a professional teacher portfolio.* Boston: Allyn & Bacon.

Cook-Gumperz, J., & Szymanski, M. (2001). Classroom "families": Cooperating or competing—girls' and boys' interactional styles in a bilingual classroom. *Research on Language and Social Interaction, 34,* 107–130.

Coontz, S. (1992). *The way we never were: American families and the nostalgia trap.* New York: Basic Books.

Council of Learned Societies in Education. (1996). *Standards for academic and professional instruction in foundations of education, educational studies, and educational policy studies* (2nd ed.). San Francisco: Caddo Gap.

Council of Learned Societies in Education. (1996). *Standards for academic and professional instruction in foundations of education, educational studies, and educational policy studies* (2nd ed.). San Francisco: Caddo Gap.

Cremin, L. A., ed. (1957a). *Horace Mann, the republic and the school: The education of free men.* New York: Columbia University Teachers College.

Cremin, L. (1957b). *The republic and the school; The education of free men.* New York: Teachers College Press.

Cruz-Janzen, M. I. (2000). Interracial children face many difficulties. In B. J. Grapes (Ed.), *Interracial relationships.* San Diego, CA: Greenhaven Press.

Cuban, L. (1986). *Teachers and machines: The classroom use of technology since 1920.* New York: Teachers College Press.

Cuban, L., & Shipps, D. (2000). *Reconstructing the common good in education: Coping with intractable dilemmas.* Stanford, CA: Stanford University Press.

Cummins, J. (1984). *Bilingualism and special education: Issues in assessment and pedagogy.* San Diego, CA: College Hill Press.

Cummins, J. (2000). Beyond adversarial discourse: Searching for common ground in the education of bilingual students. In C. J. Ovando & P. McLaren (Eds.), *The politics of multiculturalism and bilingual education: Students and teachers caught in the cross fire.* New York: McGraw-Hill Higher Education.

Danielson, C. (1996). *Enhancing professional practice: A framework for teaching.* Alexandria, VA: Association for Supervision and Curriculum Development.

Darling-Hammond, L. E. D. (1996). *What matters most: Teaching for America's future.* New York: National Commission on Teaching & America's Future.

Darling-Hammond, L., & Youngs, P. (2002). Defining "highly qualified teachers": What does "scientifically-based research" actually tell us? *Educational Researcher, 31*(9), 13–25.

David, J. L., & Shields, P. M. (2001). *When theory hits reality: Standards-based reform in urban districts, final narrative report.* Menlo Park, CA: SRI International.

Davis, B. D., & Miller, T. R. (1996). Job preparation for the 21st century: A group project learning model to teach basic workplace skills. *Journal of Education for Business, 72* (November/December), 69–73.

Dayton, J. (1998). An examination of judicial treatment of rural schools in public school funding equity litigation. *Journal of Educational Finance, 24*(2), 179–205.

Deal, T. E., & Peterson, K. D. (1999). *Shaping school culture: The heart of leadership.* San Francisco: Jossey-Bass.

DeBruyn, R. (2001). Practical strategies to motivate procrastinating students. *The master teacher, 34*(15), 1–6.

Dede, C. (2002). Of journalists and geneticists: Tough times for good work. Harvard Graduate School of Education. Unpublished thesis.

Dee, T. S. (2000). *Teachers, race, and student achievement in a randomized experiment.* Cambridge, MA: National Bureau of Economic Research.

Deering, T. E. (1998). The ethical perspective of British and American preservice teachers. *Educational Research, 40*(3), 353–358.

Delaney-Barmann, G., & Minner, S. (1996, Summer). Cross-cultural workshops and simulations for teachers. *The Teacher Educator, 32,* 37–47.

Delpit, L. (1995). *Other people's children: Cultural conflict in the classroom.* New York: New Press.

DeNavas-Walt, C., & Cleveland, R. (2002). *Current population reports, P60-218, Money Income in the United States: 2001.* Washington, DC: U.S. Government Printing Office.

Dewey, J. (1897, January 16). My pedagogic creed. *School Journal, 54*(3), 77–80.

Dewey, J. (1907). The school and social progress. In J. Dewey, *The School and Society* (pp. 19–44). Chicago: University of Chicago Press.

Dewey, J. (1976). *The middle works* (J. A. Boydston, Ed.). Carbondale: University Press. (Original work published 1938)

Dewey, J. (1980). *School and society.* Carbondale: Southern Illinois University Press.

Diaz, C. F., Massialas, B. G., & Xanthopoulos, J. A. (1999). *Global perspectives for educators.* Boston: Allyn & Bacon.

Diessner, R. (1991). *Teacher education for democratic classrooms: Moral reasoning and ideology critique.* Seminar presented at the annual conference of the Association for Moral Education, Athens, GA.

Dixon, R. G. D. (1994). Future schools and how to get there from here. *Phi Delta Kappan, 75,* 360–365.

Dreikurs, R., & Stolz, V. (1964). *Children: The challenge.* New York: Hawthorn Books.

Dryfoos, J. G. (1996, April). Full-service schools. *Educational Leadership, 53,* 18–23.

Dudley-Marling, C. (1993). Living and learning in a community of learners. In J. Andrews & J. Lupart (Eds.), *The inclusive classroom: Educating exceptional children.* (pp. 589–611). New York: Holt, Rinehart.

Dunlap, C. Z., & Alva, S. A. (1999). Redefining school and community relations: Teachers' perceptions of parents as participants and stakeholders. *Education Quarterly, 26*(4), 123–133.

Dworkin, G. (2002). Teacher burnout. In D. L. Levinson, P. W. Cookson, Jr., & A. R. Sadovnik (Eds.), *An encyclopedia of education and sociology* (pp. 659–664). New York: Routledge.

Easton, L. (2002). Lessons from learners; For this alternative school, listening is the best reform strategy. *Education Week, (24),* 33–36.

Edelmann, T. B. (1997, October/November). Schools and neighborhoods: Stabilizing partners. *Momentum 28,* 54–56.

Educational Testing Service. (2004). The Praxis Series: Advancing professional excellence. Available online at http://www.ets.org

Edwards, P. A., Pleasants, H. M., & Franklin, S. (1999). *A path to follow: Learning to listen to parents.* Portsmouth, NH: Heinemann.

Eisenman, R. (2001). Demographic profiling. *Policy Evaluation, 7*(2), 4–11.

Eisenstein, E. (1983). *The printing revolution in early modern europe.* New York: Cambridge University Press.

Eisler, R. (2000). The partnership school of the future. *Tikkun, 15*(1), 62–63.

Eisner, E. (2001, January). What does it mean to say a school is doing well? *Phi Delta Kappan, 82*(5), 367–372.

Eisner, E. W. (1985). *The educational imagination: On the design and evaluation of school programs* (2nd ed.). New York: Macmillan.

Elkind, D. (1993, April/May). Whatever happened to childhood? *Momentum, 24*(2), 18–19.

Elkind, D. (1995, Spring). The young child in the postmodern world. *Dimensions of Early Childhood, 23*(5), 6–9, 39.

Elmore, R. (2002, November). The price of accountability: Want to improve schools? Invest in people who work in them. *Results, 1*, 6.

Epstein, J. L., & Sanders, M.G. (1998). What we learn from international studies of school–family–community partnerships. *Childhood Education, 74*(6), 392–394.

Evertson, C., Emmer, E. T., & Worsham, M. E. (2000). *Classroom management: For elementary teachers* (5th ed.). Boston: Allyn & Bacon.

Ewing, N. J. (2001). Teacher education: Ethics, power, and privilege. *Teacher Education and Special Education, 24*(1), 13–24.

Farkas, S., Johnson J., & Foleno, T. (2000). *A sense of calling: Who teaches and why.* New York: Public Agenda.

Feiman-Nemser, S. (2001a). From preparation to practice: Designing a continuum to strengthen and sustain teaching. *Teachers College Record, 103*(6), 2–11.

Feiman-Nemser, S. (2001b). Helping novice learners to teach: Lessons from an exemplary support teacher. *Journal of Teacher Education, 52*(1), 17–30.

Ferguson, R. (1998). Can schools narrow the black-white test score gap? In C. Jencks & M. Phillips (Eds.), *The black-white test score gap* (pp. 318–374). Washington, DC: Brookings Institute.

Ferrandino, V. (2000). Our children—our schools—our future. *Principal, 80*(1), 72.

Finn, J. D. (1998). Parental engagement that makes a difference. *Educational Leadership, 55*(8), 20–24.

Fischer, L., Schimmel, D., & Kelly, C. (1999). *Teachers and the law.* New York: Longman.

Flecca, S. (2002). *The impact of MCAS on fourth graders.* Unpublished student research. Boston: Boston College.

Frazier, H. (1997, February 6). Derailing student tracking. *Black Issues in Higher Education, 13*, 12–13.

Freeman, N. K. (1998). Morals and character: The foundations of ethics and professionalism. *The Educational Forum, 63*(1), 30–36.

Freeman, N. K. (2000). Professional ethics: A cornerstone of teachers' preservice curriculum. *Action in Teacher Education, 22*(3), 12–18.

Freire, P. (1995). *Pedagogy of hope.* New York: Continuum.

Freitas, D. J. (1999). A professional code of ethics for teacher educators: A proposal to stimulate discussion and debate. *Action in Teacher Education, 20*(4), 96–99.

Friedman, A. (2003, May). *Inquiry presentations.* Paper presented at "Celebrating Our Community of Learners, Boston College, Boston, MA.

Fuery, C. (2001). *Still teaching after all these years.* Captiva, FL: Sanibel SandDollar.

Gallagher, J., Harradine, C. C., & Coleman, M. R. (1997). Challenge or boredom? Gifted students' views on their schooling. *Roeper Review, 19*(3), 132–136.

Gándara, P. (1995). *Over the ivy walls: The educational mobility of low-income Chicanos.* Albany: State University of New York Press.

Gardner, H. (1993). *Frames of the mind: The theory of multiple intelligences.* Philadelphia: Basic Books.

Gay, G., & Howard, T. C. (2000). Multicultural teacher education for the 21st century. *The Teacher Educator, 36*(1), 1–16.

Gay, Lesbian, and Straight Education Network. (2005). A Message from the founder and executive director: One decade ago. . . . New York: Author. Retrieved May 3, 2005, from http://www.glsen.org/cgi-bin/iowa/all/about/index.html

Gerald, D., & Hussar, W. (2003). Projections of education statistics to 2013. *Education Statistics Quarterly, 5*(4), 125–134.

Gerwitz, C. (2002). "Trusting" school community linked to student gains. *Education Week.* Betheseda, MD: 22.

Gillingham, M. G., & Topper, A. (1999). Technology in teacher preparation: Preparing teachers for the future. *Journal of Technology and Teacher Education, 7*(4), 303–321.

Gimbel, P. (2003). *Solutions for promoting principal-teacher trust.* Lanham, MD: Scarecrow Press.

Giroux, H. (1981). *Ideology, culture, and the process of schooling.* Philadelphia: Temple University Press.

Giroux, H. (1988). *Teachers as intellectuals: Toward a critical pedagogy of learning.* Granby, MA: Bergin & Garvey.

Giroux, H. (1992). *Border crossings: Cultural workers and the politics of education.* New York: Routledge.

Giroux, H. (1996). *Pedagogy of hope.* Boulder, CO: Westview Press.

Goddard, J. (2005, January 5). In Florida, a bid to expand the teacher pool. *Christian Science Monitor.* Available online at http://www.csmonitor.com.

Gold, V., & Chamberlin, L. Ways to reduce student behavior problems. *American Secondary Education, 24*(4), 30–31.

Grant, G., & Murray, C. E. (1999). *Teaching in America: The slow revolution.* Cambridge, MA: Harvard University Press.

Grasha, A. F. (1994). A matter of style: The teacher as expert, formal authority, personal model facilitator, and delegator. *College Teaching, 42*, 142–149.

Greenberg, R. (1999/2000). Substance abuse in families: Educational issues. *Childhood Education, 76*(2), 66–69.

Greer, C. (1972). *The great school legend: A revisionist interpretation of American public education.* New York: Basic Books.

Gutek, G. (2004). *Philosophical and Ideological Voices in Education.* Boston: Allyn and Bacon.

Gutierrez-Gomez, C. (2002). Multicultural teacher preparation: Establishing safe environments for discussion of diversity issues. *Multicultural Education, 10*(1), 31–39.

Haberman, M. (1996). The pedagogy of poverty versus good teaching. In N. Press (Ed.), *City kids, city teachers.* New York: Kappa Delta Pi.

Haberman, M. (2002, October 1). Who is and isn't qualified to teach? *The Washington Post,* p. A11.

Hansen, D. (1995). *The call to teach.* New York: Teachers College Press.

Harmon, A. (2004, August 26). Internet gives teenage bullies weapons to wound from afar. *The New York Times,* pp. 1A, 21A.

Hawkes, B. (1995). First year teaching strategies: A collection of student views. Retrieved May 20, 2005, from http://aci.mta.ca/MtATeach/FirstYear.html

Haynes, C. (1999). *A teacher's guide to religion in the public schools.* Nashville, TN: First Amendment Center.

Hehir, T. (2002). Let's stop devaluing disabilities. *Principal, 82*(2), 32–36.

Henshaw, S. K. (2003). *U.S. teenage pregnancy statistics with comparative statistics for women aged 20–24.* New York: Alan Guttmacher Institute.

Hobson, D. (1996). Beginning with self: Using autobiography and journal writing in teacher research. In G. Burnaford, J. Fischer, & D. Hobson (Eds.), *Teachers doing research: Practical possibilities* (pp. 263–287). Mahwah, NJ: Lawrence Erlbaum.

Hodgkinson, H. (1998). Demographics of diversity for the 21st century. *Education Digest, 64*(2), 4–7.

Hodgkinson, H. L. (2000). High school demographics demand change. *The Education Digest, 66*(1), 10–14.

Hodgkinson, H. L. (2000/2001). Educational demographics: What teachers should know. *Educational Leadership, 58*(4), 6–11.

Howard, G. R. (1999). *We can't teach what we don't know: White teachers, multiracial schools.* New York: Teachers College Press.

Hulsebosch, P., & Logan, L. (1998). Breaking it up or breaking it down: Inner-city parents as co-constructors of school improvement. *Education Horizons, 77*(1), 30–36.

Hussar, W. J. (1999). *Predicting the need for newly hired teachers in the United States to 2008–09.* Washington, DC: U.S. Department of Education, National Center for Education Statistics.

Intrator, S. (2002). *Stories of the courage to teach: Honoring the teacher's heart.* San Francisco: Jossey-Bass.

Ivanhoe School. (2000). Ivanhoe curriculum committee. Retrieved May 6, 2005, from http://www.lausd.k12.ca.us/Ivanhoe_EL/Committees/Curriculum/

Jackson, C. H. (1996, November). The community: A school's best resource. *Principal, 76,* 22–23.

Jackson, P. W. (1968). *Life in classrooms.* New York: Holt, Reinhart, & Winston.

Johnson, B. (1993). Community and contest: "Midwestern men and women creating their worlds in conversational storytelling." In D. Tannen (Ed.), *Gender and conversational interaction* (pp. 62–80). New York: Oxford University Press.

Johnson, S. (1990). *Teachers at work: Achieving success in our schools.* New York: Basic Books.

Johnson, S. M., & Kardos, S. M. (2002). Keeping new teachers in mind. *Educational Leadership, 59*(6), 12–16.

Jones, J. M. (n.d.). *The standards movement—Past and present.* Retrieved May 6, 2005, from http://my.execpc.com/~presswis/stndmvt.html

Kahlenberg, R. (1999, March 31). Economic school desegregation. *Education Week.* Retrieved May 3, 2005, from http://www.edweek.org/ew/ew

Keim, J., Warring, D. F., & Rau, R. (2001). Impact of multicultural training on school psychology and education students. *Journal of Instructional Psychology, 26*(4), 249–252.

Kelly, K. (2000). New Independence for Special Needs Students. In D. T. Gordon (Ed.), *The digital classroom: How technology is changing the way we teach and learn* (pp. 336–350). Cambridge, MA: Harvard Education Letter.

Kennard, W. R. (2000, January 14). E-rate: A success story. Speech presented to the Educational Technology Leadership Conference—2000 Council of Chief State School Officers, Washington, D.C. Retrieved May 20, 2005, from http://www.fcc.gov/Speeches/Kennard/2000/spwek002.html

Kidd, G. J. (1996). Using the Internet as a school. *The Educational Forum, 60,* 256–258.

Kloosterman, V. I. (2003). *Latino students in American schools.* Westport, CT: Praeger.

Kohn, A. (1998). *Beyond discipline: From compliance to community.* Alexandria, VA: Association for Supervision and Curriculum Development.

Kolker, J. M., Ustinova, H. S., & McEneaney, J. E. (1998/1999). School-university partnerships for global education: Toward a model for educational reform. *International Journal of Social Education, 13*(2), 77–88.

Kosmin, B., Mayer, E., & Keysar, A. (2001). *American religious identification survey.* New York: Graduate Center of the City University of New York.

Kottkamp, R. B., Provenzo, E. F., Jr., & M. M. Cohn (1986). Stability and change in profession: Two decades of teacher attitudes, 1964–1984. *Phi Delta Kappan 67*(8), 559–567.

Kounin, J. (1970). *Discipline and group management in classrooms.* New York: Holt, Rinehart & Winston.

Kozol, J. (2000). Foreword. In D. Meier, *Will standards save public education?* Boston: Beacon Press.

Kramer, S. N. (1989). *History begins at Sumer: Thirty-nine firsts in man's recorded history.* Philadelphia: University of Pennsylvania Press.

Labaree, D. (1994). An Unlovely Legacy. *Phi Delta Kappan, 75*(8), 592.

Ladson-Billings, G. (1994). *The Dreamkeepers: Successful teachers of African American children.* San Francisco: Jossey-Bass.

Larrivee, B. (1999). *Authentic classroom management: Creating a community of learners.* Boston: Allyn & Bacon.

Lass, A. H., & Tasman, N. L. (Eds.). (1980). *Going to school: An anthology of prose about teachers and students.* New York: New American Library.

Lawrence-Lightfoot, S. (2002, October). *The centrality of respect*. Paper presented at the 3rd Annual Lynch School Symposium on Educational Excellence and Equity, Boston College: Lynch School of Education, Boston, MA.

Lawrence-Lightfoot, S. (2003). *The essential conversation: What parents and teachers can learn from each other*. New York: Random House.

Lewis, A. (2001). Toward a nation of "equal kids." *Phi Delta Kappan, 83*(9), 647–648.

Lewis, A. C. (2002). Washington Commentary—The will to leave no child behind? *Phi Delta Kappan, 83*(5), 343.

Li, D., & Nes, S. L. (2001). Using paired reading to help ESL students become fluent and accurate readers. *Reading Improvement, 38*(2), 50–61

Library of Congress. (2005). Dorothea Lange's "Migrant Mother": Photographs in the Farm Security Administration Collection: An overview. Retrieved June 4, 2005 from http://www.loc.gov/rr/Print/list/128_migm.htm

Lieberman, A. (1998). *Building a professional culture in schools*. New York: Teachers College Press.

Lord, M. (1998, March 2). Preparing managers for the 21st century. *U.S. News & World Report, 124*, 72.

Ludlow, B. L., & Duff, M. C. (1998). Distance education and tomorrow's schools. *Phi Delta Kappa Fastbacks* (439), 7–55.

Luekens, M., Lyter, D., & Fox, E. (2004). *Teacher attrition and mobility: Results from the teacher follow-up survey 2000–01* (NCES 2004-301). Washington, D.C: U.S. Government Printing Office.

Lutz, F. (1995). Race, class, and the American schools. *Catalyst for Change, 24*, 5–8.

Mabie, G. E. (1996). Addressing the needs of tomorrow's learners. *The Educational Forum, 60*, 300–303.

Maddux, C. D. (1986). Issues and concerns in special education microcomputing. *Computers in the Schools, 3*(2–4), 3.

Maheady, L., Harper, G. F., & Mallette, B. (2001). Peer-mediated instruction and interventions and students with mild disabilities. *Remedial and Special Education, 22*(1), 4–14.

Mallery, J. L., & Mallery, J. G. (1999). The American legacy of ability grouping: Tracking reconsidered. *Multicultural Education, 7*(1), 13–15.

Malveaux, J. (2000). If children are the future, invest in them today. *Black Issues in Higher Education, 17*(16), 45.

Massachusetts Coalition. (2002). Panel presentation: New teachers sharing expectations at the Title II Conference, Sturbridge, Massachusetts.

Master Teacher. (2002). You can handle them all: A reference for handling over 117 misbehaviors at school and home. Retrieved May 20, 2005, from http://www.disciplinehelp.com

Mastrilli, T., & Sardo-Brown, D. (2002). Pre-service teachers' knowledge about Islam: A snapshot post September 11, 2001. *Journal of Instructional Psychology, 29*(3), 156–161.

Mathews, J. (2003, October 1). Not quite piling on the homework. *The Washington Post*, p. A01.

Maushak, N. J., Kelley, P., & Blodgett, T. (2001). Preparing teachers for the inclusive classroom: A preliminary study of attitudes and knowledge of assistive technology. *Journal of Technology and Teacher Education, 9*(3), 419–431.

McAdoo, M. (2000). The Real Digital Divide: Quality Not Quantity. In D. T. Gordon (Ed.), *The digital classroom: How technology is changing the way we teach and learn* (pp. 143–153). Cambridge: MA: Harvard Education Letter.

McCaffrey, A. (1970). *The ship who sang*. New York: Ballantine Books.

McIntosh, P. (1990). White privilege: Unpacking the invisible knapsack. *Independent School, 49*(2), 31–36.

McLaren, P. (1998). *Life in schools: An introduction to critical pedagogy in the foundations of education* (3rd ed.). New York: Longman.

McLaren, P., & Fischman, G. (1998, Fall). Reclaiming hope: Teacher education and social justice in the age of globalization. *Teacher Education Quarterly, 25*(4), 125–133.

Meier, D. (1995). *The power of their ideas: Lessons for America from a small school in Harlem*. Boston: Beacon Press.

Metzger, M. (2002). Learning to discipline. *Phi Delta Kappan*. Retrieved May 20, 2005, from http://www.pdkintl.org/kappan/k0209met.htm

Miami–Dade County Public Schools. (2004). Data available online at http://www.dade.k12.fl.us

Miller, M., Strosnider, R., & Dooley, E. (2002). States' diversity requirements for teachers. *Teacher Education and Special Education, 25*(1), 32–40.

MIT Epistemology and Learning Group. (2002). LEGO/LOGO. Retrieved June 10, 2002, from http://el.www.media.mit.edu/groups/el/projects/legologo/

Mittelstadt, J. (1997). Educating "our girls" and "welfare mothers": Discussions of education policy for pregnant and parenting adolescents in federal hearings, 1975–1995. *Journal of Family History, 22*, 326–353.

Moir, E. (2003a). Listening to the voices of new teachers. *New Teacher Center Reflections, 6*(1), 1–3.

Moir, E. (2003b). *Maximum mentoring: An action guide for teacher trainers and cooperating teachers*. Thousand Oaks, CA: Corwin Press.

Moir, E. (2003c). Quality mentoring for quality teaching. *The New Teacher Center Reflections, 4*(1), 1.

Mora, M. T. (2000). English-language assistance programs, English-skill acquisitions, and the academic progress of high school language minority students. *Policy Studies Journal, 28*(4), 721–738.

Moran, C., Stobbe, J., Baron, W., Miller, J., & Moir, E. (2000). *Keys to the classroom: A teacher's guide to the first month of school*. Thousand Oaks, CA: Corwin Press.

Moravec, J. (1988). *Mind children: The future of robot and human intelligence*. Cambridge, MA: Harvard University Press.

Morgan, A. D., Matranga, M., & Peltier, G. L. (1998). What issues will confront public education in the years 2000 and 2020? Predictions of chief state school officers. *The Clearing House, 71*(6), 339–341.

Morris, J. E. (2002). A "community bonded school" for African American students, families, and a community. *Phi Delta Kappan, 84*(3), 230–234.

National Center for Educational Statistics (1999). *Teacher quality: A report on the preparation and qualifications of public school teachers.* Washington, DC: Author.

National Center for Educational Statistics. (2002a). *Current expenditures for public elementary and secondary education, by state, for grades pre-kindergarten through 12: Fiscal years 1998 to 2002 (school years 1997–98 to 2001–02).* Available online at http://nces.ed.gov/quicktables

National Center for Educational Statistics. (2002b). *Digest of education statisitics, 2002* (Chapter 7. Learning Resources and Technology). Retrieved May 20, 2005, from http://nces.ed.gov/programs/digest/d02/lt4.asp#c7

National Center for Educational Statistics. (2004c). *Overview of public elementary and secondary schools and school districts: School year 1999–2000.* Retrieved April 20, 2005, from http://nces.ed.gov/pubs2001/overview/index.asp

National Center for Education Statistics. (2002d). *Projections of education statistics to 2012.* Washington, DC: U.S. Department of Education.

National Council for the Accreditation of Teacher Education. (1997). *Technology and the new professional teacher: Preparing for the 21st century classroom.* Washington, DC: Author.

National Council for the Accreditation of Teacher Education. (2000). *NCATE standards.* Washington, DC: Author. Retrieved May 20, 2005, from http://www.ncate.org/documents/unit_stnds_2002.pdf

National Council for the Accreditation of Teacher Education. (2001). *Professional standards for the accreditation of schools, colleges, and departments of education.* Washington, DC: Author.

National Education Association. (1990–1991). *Status of the American public school teacher.* Washington, DC: Author.

National Education Association. (2004a). Attracting and keeping quality teachers. Retrieved September 28, 2004, from www.nea.org/teachershortage

National Education Association. (2004b). NEA Study: Stagnant resources jeopardize public schools," Retrieved May 26, 2004 from http://www.nea.org/newsreleases/2004/nr040526.html

NEA Today (2002–2005). Retrieved from http://www.nea.org/neatoday.

Nelsen, J., Escobar, L., Ortolano, K., Duffy, R., & Owen-Sohocki, D. (2001). *Positive discipline: A Teacher's A–Z Guide.* New York: Random House.

New York: 41 percent increase in tuition proposed. (2003, January 18). *South Florida Sun-Sentinel,* p. 3A.

Nieto, S. (2001). *We speak in many tongues: Language diversity and multicultural education for the 21st century.* New York: Longman.

Nieto, S. (2003a). Profoundly multicultural questions. *Educational Leadership, 60*(4), 8–10.

Nieto, S. (2003b). *What keeps teachers going?* New York: Teachers College Press.

Nieto, S. N. (2002/2003). Profoundly multicultural questions. *Educational Leadership, 60*(4), 6–10.

Noddings, N. (1984). *Caring: A feminine approach to ethics and moral education.* Berkeley: University of California Press.

Noddings, N. (1988). An ethic of caring and its implications for instructional arrangements. *American Journal of Education, 96*(2), 215–230.

Noddings, N. (1990). Ethics from the standpoint of women. In D. L. Rhode (Ed.), *Theoretical perspectives on sexual difference* (pp. 160–173). New Haven, CT: Yale University Press.

Nowell, A. (1998). Trends in gender differences in academic achievement from 1960 to 1994: An analysis of differences in mean, variance, and extreme scores. *Sex Roles: A Journal of Research* (July), 1–15.

Oakes, J. (1995, Summer). Two cities' tracking and within-school segregation. *Teachers College Record, 96,* 681–690.

Oakes, J., & Lipton, M. (1992). Detracking schools: Early lessons from the field. *Phi Delta Kappan, 73*(6), 448–454.

Obiakor, F. E. (2001). Multicultural education: Powerful tool for preparing future general and special educators. *Teacher Education and Special Education, 24*(3), 241–255.

Office of Technology Assessment, Congress of the United States. (1995). *Teachers & technology: Making the connection* (Report No. OTA-HER-616). Washington, D.C.: U.S. Government Printing Office.

Ogawa, R. T. (1998). Organizing parent-teacher relations around the work of teaching. *Peabody Journal of Education, 73*(1), 6–14.

Ogbu, J. U. (1995). Understanding cultural diversity and learning. In J. A. Banks & C. A. McGee Banks (Eds.), *Handbook of research on multicultural education.* New York: Macmillan.

Okpala, C. O. (2002). Educational resources, student demographics, and achievement scores. *Journal of Educational Finance, 27*(3), 885–907.

Okpala, C., Smith, F., & Jones, E. (2000). A clear link between school and teacher characteristics, student demographics, and student achievement. *Education 120*(3), 487–494.

Ooka Pang, V. (1995). Asian Pacific American students: A diverse and complex population. In J. A. Banks & C. A. McGee Banks (Eds.), *Handbook of research on multicultural education.* New York: Macmillan.

Osterling, J. P., Violand-Sánchez, E., & von Vacano, M. (1999). Latino families learning together. *Educational Leadership, 57*(2), 64–68.

Oswald, D. P., Coutinho, M. J., & Best, A. M. (1999). Ethnic representation in special education: The influence of school-related economic and demographic variables. *Journal of Special Education, 32*(4), 194–206.

Oxford english dictionary. (1989). New York: Oxford University Press. Available online at http://www.oed.com

Papert, S. (1993). *The children's machine: Rethinking schools in the age of the computer.* New York: Free Press.

Parenti, J. G. (2001). *First year urban teacher: Practical classroom management techniques.* Philadelphia: Teacher for Hire.

Payne, R. K. (2001). *A framework for understanding poverty.* Highland, TX: AHA! Process.

Pelletier, C. (2002). *Techniques and strategies for coaching student teachers* (2nd ed.). Boston: Allyn & Bacon.

Pelletier, C. (2004). *Strategies for successful teaching: A comprehensive guide.* Boston: Allyn & Bacon.

Pepper, K., & Rowland, S. T. (2000). Teachers for the 21st century. *The Delta Kappa Gamma Bulletin, 66*(2), 45–49.

Perrone, V. (1991). *A letter to teachers.* San Francisco: Jossey-Bass.

Pickering v. Board of Education, 391 U.S. 563 (1968).

Pierce v. Society of the Sisters of the Holy Names of Jesus and Mary, 268 U.S. 510, 45 S. Ct. 571 (1925).

Planned Parenthood of Connecticut. (1998). Just the facts on gay, lesbian and bisexual youth in schools. Retrieved May 3, 2005, from http://www.ppct.org/facts/research/lgbt_youth.shtml

Popham, W. (1999). *Classroom assessment; What teachers need to know.* Boston: Allyn and Bacon.

Porath, M. (1996, September). Affective and motivational considerations in the assessment of gifted learners. *Roeper Review, 19,* 13–17.

Portner, H. (2002). *Being mentored: A guide for protégés.* Thousand Oaks, CA: Corwin Press.

Postman, N. (1982). *The disappearance of childhood.* New York: Delacorte.

Postman, N. (1984). *Amusing ourselves to death.* New York: Viking.

Power, B., & Hubbard, R. (1996). *Oops: What we learn when our teaching fails.* York, ME: Stenhouse.

President's Advisory Commission on Educational Excellence for Hispanic Americans. (2003). *From risk to opportunity: Fulfilling the educational needs of Hispanic Americans in the 21st century.* Washington, DC: Author.

President's Advisory Commission on Educational Excellence for Hispanic Americans. (2003). *From risk to opportunity: Fulfilling the educational needs of Hispanic Americans in the 21st century.* Washington, DC: Author.

Provenzo, E. F. (2000). Educational technologies. In D. Gabbard (Ed.), *Knowledge and power in the global economy: Politics and rhetoric of school reform* (pp. 297–302). Mahwah, N.J.: Lawrence Erlbaum.

Provenzo, E. F., Jr. (2002). *Teaching, learning, and schooling: A 21st century perspective.* Boston: Allyn & Bacon.

Provenzo, E. F., and Brett, A. (1995). *Adaptive technology for special human needs.* Albany: State University of New York Press.

Provenzo, E. F., and Brett, A. (2000). *The complete block book.* Syracuse, NY: Syracuse University Press.

Records of the governor and Company of the Massachusetts Bay. (1853). Vol. 2 (p. 203). Boston: W. White.

Rich, D. (1998). Reaching the family: How teachers build the policy bridge. *Educational Horizons, 76*(2), 77–80.

Riggins, J., & Erikson, H. (2002). Should teachers have students correct each other's papers? *NEAToday.* National Education Association.

Riley, R. W. (1997). U.S. education: Challenges ahead. *Forum for Applied Research and Public Policy, 12,* 57–61.

Rist, R. (2000). Student social class and teacher expectations: The self-fulfilling prophecy in ghetto education. *Harvard Educational Review, 70*(3), 257–301.

Robinson-Zañartu, C., & Majel-Dixon, J. (1996, Fall). Parent voices: American Indian relationships with schools. *Journal of American Indian Education, 36,* 33–54.

Rockwell, S. (1995). *Back off, cool down, try again: Teaching students how to control aggressive behavior:* Arlington, VA: Council for Exceptional Children.

Rose, L., & Gallup, A. (2003). The 35th annual Phi Delta Kappa/Gallup Poll of the public's attitudes toward the public schools. *Phi Delta Kappan, 85*(1), 41–56.

Rowand, C. (2000, April). Teacher use of computers and the Internet in public schools. *Stats in Brief.* Retrieved June 10, 2002, from http://nces.ed.gov/pubs2000/2000090.pdf

Sadker, M., & Sadker, D. (1995). *Failing at fairness: How our schools cheat girls.* New York: Scribner.

Sadker, M., Sadker, D., & Long, L. (1997). Gender and educational equity. In J. A. Banks & C. M. Banks (Eds.), *Multicultural education: Issues and perspectives* (3rd ed., 139–142). Boston: Allyn & Bacon.

Salend, S. J., Duhaney, L. M., & Montgomery, W. (2002). A comprehensive approach to identifying and addressing issues of disproportionate representation. *Remedial and Special Education, 23*(5), 289–299.

Saltman, K. (2000). *Collateral damage: corporatizing public schools—a threat to democracy.* Lanham, MD: Rowman & Littlefield.

Saphier, J., & Gower, R. (1997). *The skillful teacher: Building your teaching skills* (5th ed.). Carlisle, MA: Research for Better Teaching.

Saphier, J., & Haley, M. A. (1993a). *Activators: Activity structures that engage students' thinking before instruction.* Acton, MA: Research for Better Teaching.

Saphier, J., & Haley, M. A. (1993b). *Summarizers: Activity structures to support integration and retention of new learning.* Acton, MA: Research for Better Teaching.

Schön, D. (1983). *The reflective practitioner: How professionals think in action.* London: Temple Smith.

Schoorman, D. (2001). Addressing the academic needs of immigrant students. In C. Diaz (Ed.), *Multicultural education in the 21st century* (pp. 85–108). New York: Longman.

Schoorman, D., & Jean-Jacques, V. (2003). Facilitating the adaptation of recent immigrant students: The need for complex, community-wide efforts. Paper presented at the annual conference of the American Educational Research Association, Chicago, IL, April 24, 2003.

Schwartz, W. (1998, November). The schooling of multiracial students. ERIC Clearinghouse on Urban Education, no. 138. (ERIC Document Reproduction Service No. EDO-UD-98-8).

Secada, W. G. (2002). *Review of research in education.* Washington, DC: American Educational Research Association.

Senge, P. (2000). *Schools that learn: A fifth discipline fieldbook for educators, parents, and everyone who cares about education.* New York: Random House.

Sergiovanni, T. J., & Starratt, R. J. (2002). *Supervision: A redefinition* (7th ed.). New York: McGraw-Hill.

Shagoury Hubbard, R., & Miller, B. (2003). *The art of classroom inquiry: A handbook for teacher researchers.* Portsmouth, NH: Heinemann.

Shen, J. (1997). The evolution of violence in schools. *Educational Leadership, 55,* 18–20.

Shen, J. (2003). Have minority students had a fair share of quality teachers? Results from a longitudinal study. *Poverty & Race, 12*(4).

Shepard, R. G., Trimberger, A. K., & McClintock, P.J. (1999). Empowering the family-school partnerships: An integrated hierarchial model. *Contemporary Education, 70*(3), 33–37.

Short, D. J., & Boyson, B. A. (2000). Newcomer programs for linguistically diverse students. *NASSP Bulletin, 84*(619), 34–42.

Simkins, M. B. (1996, October). Ten ways to bring the community into your school. *Thrust for Educational Leadership, 26,* 22–24.

Sleeter, C. (2000). Multicultural education, social positionality, and whiteness. In E. M. Duarte and S. Smith (Eds.). *Foundational perspectives in multicultural education.* New York: Longman.

Smith, M. K. (2001). *Social capital.* In *The Encyclopedia of Informal Education.* Retrieved April 20, 2005, from http://www.infed.org/biblio/social_capital.htm

Smith-Maddox, R. (1999). The social networks and resources of African American eighth graders: Evidence from the National Education Longitudinal Study of 1988. *Adolescence, 34*(133), 169–183.

Soller, J. (2003). Reoccurring questions about giftedness and the connections to myths and realities. *Gifted and Talented, 7*(2), 42–48.

Soto, L. L. (1997). *Language, culture, and power: Bilingual families and the struggle for quality education.* Albany: State University of New York Press.

Spring, J. (2004). *American education* (11th ed.). Boston: McGraw-Hill.

Stachowski, L. L., & Mahan, J. M. (1998). Cross-cultural field placements: Student teachers learning from schools and communitites. *Theory into Practice, 37*(2), 155–162.

Starr, L. (2002). Peer grading vs. privacy: The Supreme Court rules, *Education World,* Feburary 26, 2002

Steffy, B. E., Wolfe, M. P., Pasch, S. H., & Enz, B. J. (Eds.). (2000). *Life cycle of a career teacher.* Thousand Oaks, CA: Corwin Press.

Stiggins, R. (2002). Assessment for learning: A vision for the future. *Education Week, 10,* 16.

Tannen, D. (1994). *You just don't understand women and men in conversation.* New York: Ballantine Books.

Tatum, B. (1997). *Why are all the Black kids sitting together in the cafeteria?* New York: Basic Books.

Taylor, B. O. (2002). Effective schools—The effective schools process: Alive and well. *Phi Delta Kappan, 83*(5), 375.

Taylor, H. (2002). Scientists, doctors, teachers and military officers top the list of most prestigious occupations. Harris Poll #54. Rochester, NY: Harris Interactive.

Taylor, R. (ed.). (1980). *The computer in the school: Tutor, tool, tutee.* New York: Teachers College Press.

Tetreault, M. (1997). Gender-balanced curriculum. In J. A. Banks & C. M. Banks (Eds.), *Multicultural education: Issues and perspectives* (3rd ed., pp. 158–163). Boston: Allyn & Bacon.

Tom, A. R. (1984). *Teaching as a moral craft.* New York: Longman.

Tomlinson, C. (1999). *The differentiated classroom: Responding to the needs of all learners.* Alexandria, VA: Association for Supervision and Curriculum Development.

Tomlinson, C. (2001). *How to differentiate instruction in mixed-ability classrooms* (2nd ed.). Alexandria, VA: Association for Supervision and Curriculum Development.

Tye, B. B., & O'Brien, L. (2002). Why are experienced teachers leaving the profession? *Phi Delta Kappan, 84*(1), 24–32.

U.S. Census Bureau. (1999). *Statistical abstract of the United States.* Washington, DC: U.S. Government Printing Office.

U.S. Census Bureau. (2000a). *Building strong families: Insights from research from the U.S. Census Bureau.* Washington, DC: U.S. Department of Commerce.

U.S. Census Bureau. (2000b). *Statistical Abstracts of the United States 2000.* Washington, DC: U.S. Government Printing Office.

U.S. Census Bureau. (2003a, June). *Children's living arrangements and characteristics: March 2002.* Washington, DC: U.S. Department of Commerice.

U.S. Census Bureau. (2003b). *Statistical abstract of the United States.* Washington, DC: U.S. Government Printing Office.

U.S. Charter Schools. (2004). Data available online at http://www.uscharterschools.org/pub/uscs_docs/ home.htm

U.S. Department of Commerce. (2000). Americans in the information age falling through the net. Retrieved June

10, 2002, from http://www.ntia.doc.gov/ntiahome/digitaldivide/

U.S. Department of Education. (1998). *Promising practices: New ways to improve teacher quality.* Washington, DC: U.S. Government Printing Office.

U.S. Department of Education. (n.d.). No child left behind. Retrieved May 6, 2005, from http://www.ed.gov/nclb/overview/intro/index.html

U.S. Department of Education, National Center for Education Statistics. (1997). *The condition of education.* Washington, DC: Author.

U.S. Department of Education, National Center for Education Statistics. (1999). Fast Response Survey System, "Survey on Public School Teachers' Use of Computers and the Internet," FR SS 70.

U.S. Department of Education, National Center for Education Statistics. (2001). Chapter 7: Learning resources and technology. *Digest of Education Statistics, 2001.* Retrieved May 20, 2005, from http://nces.ed.gov/programs/digest/d01/lt7.asp

U.S. Department of Education, National Center for Education Statistics. (2002). *The condition of education 2002* (NCES 2002-025). Washington, DC: U.S. Government Printing Office.

U.S. Department of Education, National Center for Education Statistics. (2003a). *The condition of education.* Washington, DC: Author.

U.S. Department of Education, National Center for Education Statistics. (2003b). *Digest of education statistics, 2002* (NCES 2003-060). Washington, DC: U.S. Government Printing Office.

U.S. Department of Education, National Center for Education Statistics. (2004). *The condition of education 2004: Elementary and secondary education: Past and projected elementary school enrollments.* Washington, DC: U.S. Government Printing Office.

Van Hook, C. W. (2002). Preservice teachers perceived barriers to the implementation of a multicultural curriculum. *Journal of instructional psychology, 29*(4), 254–264.

Van Horn, R. W. (1997, June). Virtual K–12 schools: Is the future here already? *Phi Delta Kappan, 78,* 807–808.

Viadero, D. (2000, March 22). Students in dire need of good teachers often get the least qualified or experienced. *Education Week.* Retrieved May 3, 2005, from http://www.edweek.org/ew/ew

Viadero, D. (2001, September 19). Teachers' race linked to students' scores. *Education Week.* Retrieved May 3, 2005, from http://www.edweek.org/ew/ew

Villani, S. (2002). *Mentoring programs for new teachers: Models of induction and support.* Thousand Oaks, CA: Corwin Press.

Virginia Department of Education, Division of Technology. (n.d.). *Acceptable use Policies: A handbook.* Retrieved November 2, 2003, from http://www.pen.k12.va.us/go/VDOE/Technology/AUP/home.shtml#intro

Vollmer, J. R. (2001). Community permission: The prerequisite for change. *School Administrator, 58*(7), 28–31.

Wagner, C. (2002). School culture audit. *Journal of Staff Development, 23*(3), 46–47.

Walker, J. D., & Hackmann, D. G. (1999). Full-service schools: Forming alliances to meet the needs of students and families. *NASSP Bulletin, 83*(611), 28–37.

White, L. J. (1998, January/February). National PTA standards for parent/family involvement programs. *High School Magazine, 5,* 8–12.

Winch, J., & Gingell, J. (1999). *Key concepts in the philosophy of education.* New York: Routledge.

Winn, M. (1983). *Children without childhood.* New York: Pantheon Books.

Wolf, K. (1996). Developing an effective teaching portfolio. *Educational Leadership, 53*(6), 34–37.

Wolfgang, C. H. (2004). *Solving discipline problems: Methods and models for today's teachers* (6th ed.). Hoboken, NJ: Wiley.

Wong, H. K., & Wong, R. T. (1991). *The first days of school: How to be an effective teacher.* Sunnyvale, CA: Harry K. Wong.

Woolfolk, A. (2004). *Educational Psychology,* 9th edition. Boston: Allyn and Bacon.

Zehr, M. (2001, August 8). Schools grew more segregated in 1990s, report says. *Education Week.* Retrieved May 3, 2005, from http://www.edweek.org/ew/ew

Zentella, A. C. (1997). *Growing up bilingual: Puerto Rican children in New York.* Malden, MA: Blackwell.

Zern, D. S. (1997). The attitudes of present and future teachers to the teaching of values (in general) and of certain values (in particular). *Journal of Genetic Psychology, 158,* 505–507.

NAME INDEX

SUBJECT INDEX

PHOTO CREDITS